Child Abuse,
Child Exploitation, and
Criminal Justice Responses

THEORY AND PRACTICE IN CRIMINAL JUSTICE SERIES

Series Editor

Kimberly A. McCabe, University of Lynchburg, mccabe@lynchburg.edu

Theory and Practice in Criminal Justice provides professors with textbooks that cover popular criminal justice topics. This series of textbooks are comprehensible to students, while also having direct coverage and case examples. Each textbook in the series includes both core textbooks and supplemental textbooks, with complementing formats to allow instructors to utilize them together for the same course. Finally, the authorship of this series incorporates an academic and practitioner perspective that brings scholarship and real-life experiences to the student for a better preparation in the classroom and to the field.

Books in the Series

Acts of Violence in the School Setting: National and International Responses, By Kimberly A. McCabe—With Brianna Egan and Toy D. Eagle

Child Abuse, Child Exploitation, and Criminal Justice Responses, By Daniel G. Murphy and April G. Rasmussen

Sex Crimes and Offenders: Exploring Questions of Character and Culture, By Mary Clifford and Alison Feigh

Child Abuse, Child Exploitation, and Criminal Justice Responses

◆ ◆ ◆

Daniel G. Murphy

University of Lynchburg

April G. Rasmussen

Central Virginia Community College and University of Lynchburg

ROWMAN & LITTLEFIELD
Lanham • Boulder • New York • London

Executive Editor: Kathryn Knigge
Editorial Assistant: Charlotte Gosnell
Executive Marketing Manager: Johnathan Raeder
Interior Designer: Text A by Ilze Lemesis

Credits and acknowledgments for material borrowed from other sources, and reproduced with permission, appear on the appropriate page within the text.

Published by Rowman & Littlefield
An imprint of The Rowman & Littlefield Publishing Group, Inc.
4501 Forbes Boulevard, Suite 200, Lanham, Maryland 20706
www.rowman.com

6 Tinworth Street, London SE11 5AL, United Kingdom

British Library Cataloguing in Publication Information Available

Library of Congress Cataloging-in-Publication Data Available

Library of Congress Control Number: 2019954317

ISBN: 978-1-5381-2225-9 (cloth: alk. paper)
ISBN: 978-1-5381-2226-6 (pbk.: alk. paper)
ISBN: 978-1-5381-2227-3 (electronic)

∞™ The paper used in this publication meets the minimum requirements of American National Standard for Information Sciences—Permanence of Paper for Printed Library Materials, ANSI/NISO Z39.48-1992.

Contents

◆ ◆ ◆

Preface

THERE ARE FEW THINGS IN OUR SOCIETY that provoke such raw emotions as that of child abuse. Most people, justifiably so, are outraged when they hear of allegations of abuse, and their anger is intensified as they learn of what seems to be an inappropriate criminal justice response. However, the debate on child abuse usually happens though visceral emotions rather than facts. Taking emotions out of a child abuse debate is much easier said than done, but it is of utmost importance to identify the facts. When the reader has a better understanding of the scope of child abuse, they can become more objective but still maintain their passion about ways to protect this vulnerable and targeted population.

This book has given the authors a great opportunity to share knowledge relating to child abuse, but it is also important to acknowledge how much we have learned while furthering our research on such a complex but worthy topic. Our collaboration will acknowledge the subjectivity of child abuse and the unique challenges of investigating these offenses while ultimately bringing the perpetrators to justice. We will present research from various perspectives of child abuse, including both national and international issues and how abuse is addressed within special jurisdictions. We hope the reader will appreciate the uniqueness of this material as both authors will be contributing facts based not only through scholarly research, but through their own practical experience working in field, thus providing much personal insight. Throughout the book the reader will review case studies that are legitimate examples of instances we have either personally investigated or aided in the investigation. Cases with names given have had those names changed for the purpose of protecting the identity of the victims.

We will also be providing additional personal insight from various other practitioners working to protect children. Although the book will address what appears to be insurmountable aspects of child abuse, our background in criminal investigations and medical forensics will demonstrate how these two areas of expertise can collaborate to achieve the objective of working as a team to facilitate safeguarding children.

We have much to be thankful for, especially having the opportunity to write this book. This monumental task could not have been accomplished without the help and support of our families. Their patience and notably their inspiration have made this task achievable. We would be amiss if we did not mention Brian Orrock, criminology major at the University of Lynchburg, who was a tremendous help as he assisted in the verification of so many academic resources. Also a special thanks to Dr. Kimberly McCabe of the University of Lynchburg, who recommended us for this monumental but rewarding venture.

Foreword

◆ ◆ ◆

CHILD ABUSE, CHILD EXPLOITATION, and the *Criminal Justice Response,* written by Daniel Murphy and April Rasmussen, is a fantastic addition to the textbooks that focus on child abuse. This textbook, based in a practical criminal justice perspective of victim's rights and offender motivations, provides a fresh and informative approach to explaining the victimization of children.

Both Murphy and Rasmussen have practitioner and academician experience, and this is obvious to the reader. Murphy's work as an investigator in cases of child abuse and Rasmussen's work as a forensic nurse help to provide real-world discussions and explanations. The strengths of the textbook are demonstrated in every chapter from the case files of child physical and sexual abuse victims to the discussions on false allegations, medical mimickers, and criminal justice responses.

Within this textbook, domestic violence, school violence, and human trafficking are explored as related to child abuse through both a national and international lens. In addition, special populations and jurisdictions, normally not included in the research on child abuse, provide readers additional information on the victimization of children.

This textbook is recommended to anyone wishing to further their understanding of child abuse and neglect. From the perspective of a professor who teaches courses on child abuse, this book would be an excellent required text. In addition, this book is applicable to courses on victimology and juvenile delinquency. Individuals, seeking a textbook to discuss child abuse within criminal justice coursework, would benefit from the selection of *Child Abuse, Child Exploitation, and the Criminal Justice Response* for the betterment of their students.

1

Overview of Child Abuse

◆ ◆ ◆

CHILD ABUSE DEFINED

BEFORE YOU CAN RESPOND to an allegation of child abuse, you must be able to identify it. To help in recognizing child maltreatment, there needs to be some type of criteria to meet the standard of abuse. The Child Abuse Prevention and Treatment Act (CAPTA) defines child abuse as "Any recent act or failure to act on the part of a parent or caretaker, which results in death, serious physical or emotional harm, sexual abuse, or exploitation, or an act or failure to act which presents an imminent risk or harm."[1] Although this definition can be used as a guideline, research will clearly show how subjective the term child abuse can be. Defining child maltreatment can also vary among state statutes.[2] Child abuse is broken down into four main categories: (1) physical, (2) psychological/emotional, (3) sexual, and (4) neglect. Each category of abuse is subjective as people are influenced by their own personal belief as to what constitutes abuse. Not only are there varying opinions of what amounts to child abuse, there are several perspectives on what defines a child.

CHILD DEFINED

Eighteen years of age seems to be the universal dividing line between childhood and adulthood.[3] Nevertheless, how the criminal justice system identifies a child depends on what interaction the young person is involved in as the legal status of a child can vary between a perpetrator and a victim. The classification of a child can also vary from state to state. For instance, person who is sixteen in one state can be charged as an adult, but that same sixteen-year-old can be charged as a juvenile in a different state despite committing the same criminal act. Additionally, a "child" can obtain a driver's license before the age of eighteen, but will face adult consequences for violation of a motor vehicle law. "A child," depending on the state, can be certified as an adult based on age and the criminal act.

The varying concepts as to what defines a child are not solely based on criminal responsibility, but are also based on the circumstances surrounding the young person's victimization. The age of consent laws have clouded what is considered sexual abuse as the laws vary from state to state. For example, there may not be any criminal charge against someone who engages in sexual intercourse with a person under the age of eighteen in one state, but that same individual could be charged with statutory rape if they engaged sexual intercourse with that same young person in another state. Contrary to sexual abuse, physical abuse appears more absolute when defining what constitutes a child. For instance, if a parent strikes their eighteen-year-old child as a form of discipline, that parent may be charged with assault; however, this same parent may be protected from any criminal action (under the concept of corporal punishment) if they strike their seventeen-year-old child for the same reason. Finally, the issue of neglect can also be subjective when defining a child. A parent could be charged with educational neglect for not providing their child with a proper education. However, there are laws that don't require a child to compulsory school attendance once they reach the age of sixteen. Despite this, the parent could still be charged with supervisory or physical neglect for that same child if they were not being properly cared for. This subjectivity in defining a child and what constitutes abuse has put in question the accuracy of child abuse statistics.

STATISTICS ON ABUSE

Although there are several resources available to obtain quantitative data on child abuse, their reliability for accuracy is debatable. Statistics on child abuse are difficult to interpret and compare as there is little consistency as to how the data are collected.[4] Additionally, there are several cases of child abuse that involve poly-victimization.[5] This refers to children who are subjected to more than one type of abuse, but not all the various incidents of abuse are reported and calculated. In some circumstances, a child's victimization is never identified. This failure to identify victimization is referred to as the dark figure of crime.[6] Children may not disclose their victimization for a variety of reasons including the manipulation or fear of the abuser. Additionally, the emotional toll that some children face from their abuser prevents them from disclosing well into their adulthood, whereas some victims of abuse may never disclose. For the children that are willing to disclose their abuse, there are several agencies that collect data on victimization. "The Child Abuse Prevention, Adoption, and Family Services Act of 1988 mandated that The Department of Health and Human Services (HHS) establish a national data collection program on child maltreatment. In 1990 the National Child Abuse and Neglect Data System (NCANDS) began operating."[7]

Child Protective Services

Child Protective Services (CPS) throughout the country submits their data to NCANDS, which is published annually. CPS is the primary data system for collecting quantitative information on child abuse. Anyone who suspects child abuse can contact their local CPS agency, who then forwards all the data to NCANDS. CPS separates their data into those that are "screened in," which are referred to as reports, and calls that are "screened out" that will not generate an investigation. The following charts from the Department of Health and Human Services display the rate of cases that are screened in and the ages and ethnic backgrounds of victims who have been identified.

Law Enforcement

Another source for collecting quantitative data on child abuse is law enforcement, although it is a poor indicator on the actual amount of abuse. Local law enforcement records all reported crimes, including crimes against children, and forwards the data to the Federal Bureau of Investigation (FBI), who publishes these data through the Uniform Crime Report (UCR) on an annual basis. When law enforcement receives a child abuse complaint, they will forward the information to the FBI and CPS. In contrast, CPS may only notify law enforcement if the reported abuse is criminal in nature or if there is an immediate concern for someone's safety. If CPS does report allegations of abuse to law enforcement that does not reach the level of a criminal act, this information will not be forwarded to the FBI as it does not meet the criteria for the UCR. In contrast, CPS will investigate criminal and non-criminal allegations of abuse, thus being the more accurate resource on child abuse data.

Victimization Surveys

The National Crime Victimization Survey (NCVS) is a nationwide sample of citizens regarding victimization and is considered by some the gold standard for measuring crime. Data are collected by the U.S. Bureau of Census in cooperation with the Bureau of Justice Statistics. The NCVS collects detailed information on certain types of crimes including rape, but only interviews household members over the age of twelve.[8] This kind of data collection is significantly flawed as the majority of child abuse victims are under the age of twelve. Finally, unlike reports to CPS and law enforcement, the legitimacy of the child abuse disclosures reported in these surveys is not investigated to ensure validity.

Other Surveys

There have been other surveys used in the past to measure child maltreatment such as the Developmental Victimization Survey (2003 and 2004), questioning a child, or their parent proxy if the child is between the ages of two to seventeen, as to how much violence they were exposed to, or if they were a victim of violence. In 1994 and 1995, the Add Health Study sampled adolescents in the seventh through twelfth grade, asking if they were ever victims of child abuse.[9] In 2007 and 2008, the National Survey of Children's Exposure to Violence (NatSCEV) was also utilized to survey the level of violence that children were exposed to. The survey included children up to the age of seventeen and interviewed children under the age of ten by proxy by those who were familiar with the child.[10]

Table 1.1 Screened-in and Screened-out Referrals, 2017[1]

State	Screened-in Referrals (Reports)	Screened-out Referrals	Total Referrals	Screened-in Referrals (Reports), Percent	Screened-out Referrals, Percent	Total Referrals Rate per 1,000 Children
Alabama	27,677	470	28,147	98.3	1.7	25.7
Alaska	9,372	9,167	18,539	50.6	49.4	100.2
Arizona	47,108	29,035	76,143	61.9	38.1	46.6
Arkansas	36,095	20,888	56,983	63.3	36.7	80.8
California	233,701	166,486	400,187	58.4	41.6	44.2
Colorado	34,316	60,823	95,139	36.1	63.9	75.4
Connecticut	20,021	21,340	41,361	48.4	51.6	55.6
Delaware	6,484	13,067	19,551	33.2	66.8	95.6
District of Columbia	7,318	7,290	14,608	50.1	49.9	117.3
Florida	173,138	63,527	236,665	73.2	26.8	56.3
Georgia	88,923	33,829	122,752	72.4	27.6	48.8
Hawaii	1,871	2,576	4,447	42.1	57.99	14.5
Idaho	8,568	12,380	20,948	40.9	59.1	47.2
Illinois	74,353	—	74,353	—	—	—
Indiana	126,719	42,200	168,919	75.0	25.0	107.4
Iowa	30,853	21,103	51,956	59.4	40.6	71.0
Kansas	23,705	15,674	39,379	60.2	39.8	55.3
Kentucky	56,240	54,292	110,532	50.9	49.1	109.4
Louisiana	19,851	24,942	44,793	44.3	55.7	40.4
Maine	8,016	7,899	15,915	50.4	49.6	63.0
Maryland	22,037	31,240	53,277	41.4	58.6	39.5
Massachusetts	45,086	37,742	82,828	54.4	45.6	60.5
Michigan	89,736	60,022	149,758	59.9	40.1	68.8
Minnesota	32,477	58,243	90,720	35.8	64.2	69.9
Mississippi	27,775	5,492	33,267	83.5	16.5	46.6

State					
Missouri	65,096	20,526	85,622	76.0	24.0	61.9
Montana	9,843	7,779	17,622	55.9	44.1	77.0
Nebraska	13,199	22,226	35,425	37.3	62.7	74.5
Nevada	15,373	20,831	36,204	42.5	57.5	52.8
New Hampshire	9,578	5,375	14,953	64.1	35.9	57.8
New Jersey	57,026	–	57,026	–	–	–
New Mexico	21,691	17,475	39,166	55.4	44.6	80.2
New York	165,477	–	165,477	–	–	–
North Carolina	67,550	–	67,550	–	–	–
North Dakota	3,982	–	3,982	–	–	–
Ohio	83,750	98,826	182,576	45.9	54.1	70.1
Oklahoma	35,553	42,527	78,080	45.5	54.5	81.4
Oregon	35,708	36,213	71,921	49.6	50.4	82.3
Pennsylvania	46,208	–	46,208	–	–	–
Puerto Rico	10,613	–	10,613	–	–	–
Rhode Island	5,817	7,533	13,350	43.6	56.4	64.4
South Carolina	36,744	9,318	46,062	79.8	20.2	41.7
South Dakota	2,492	13,445	15,937	15.6	84.4	74.2
Tennessee	74,497	55,610	130,107	57.3	42.7	86.3
Texas	198,083	56,954	255,037	77.7	22.3	24.6
Utah	20,736	18,486	39,222	52.9	47.1	42.3
Vermont	4,320	15,436	19,756	21.9	78.1	169.1
Virginia	32,754	43,993	76,747	42.7	57.3	41.1
Washington	36,023	59,580	95,603	37.7	62.3	58.1
West Virginia	26,219	13,518	39,737	66.0	34.0	107.5
Wisconsin	27,140	51,428	78,568	34.5	65.5	61.3

1 U.S. Department of Health & Human Services, Administration for Children and Families, Administration on Children, Youth and Families, Children's Bureau. (2019). Child Maltreatment 2017. Available from https://www.acf.hhs.gov/cb/research-data-technology/ statistics-research/child-maltreatment.

Table 1.2 Victims by Race and Ethnicity, 2017[1]

State	African American	American Indian or Alaska Native	Asian	Hispanic	Multiple Race	Pacific Islander	White	Unknown	Total
Alabama	2,887	8	14	488	356	4	6,976	114	10,847
Alaska	72	1,409	25	105	374	50	545	203	2,783
Arizona	855	400	26	3,764	409	13	3,469	973	9,909
Arkansas	1,633	14	10	572	725	44	6,264	72	9,334
California	8,745	595	1,454	36,063	1,436	197	13,201	3,921	65,342
Colorado	1,049	72	79	4,270	475	27	5,473	133	11,578
Connecticut	1,970	12	50	2,682	468	8	2,982	270	8,442
Delaware	693	4	8	191	56	3	585	2	1,542
District of Columbia	—	—	—	—	—	—	—	—	—
Florida	11,745	43	124	7,001	1,952	19	17,525	1,694	40,103
Georgia	3,692	6	47	644	593	2	5,353	150	10,487
Hawaii	17	—	131	32	520	309	233	38	1,280
Idaho	11	33	—	204	18	2	1,430	134	1,832
Illinois	9,340	20	229	4,840	688	12	13,426	196	28,751
Indiana	4,814	13	40	2,503	2,109	17	19,670	32	29,198
Iowa	1,400	113	73	970	395	25	7,499	168	10,643
Kansas	421	30	29	553	271	5	2,810	34	4,153
Kentucky	2,010	10	41	888	1,117	7	17,481	856	22,410
Louisiana	4,464	15	16	324	267	8	5,005	257	10,356
Maine	65	17	3	214	111	1	2,176	888	3,475
Maryland	3,292	7	43	603	171	7	2,320	1,136	7,578
Massachusetts	3,301	31	332	7,713	1,267	6	9,343	3,099	25,092
Michigan	10,441	138	98	2,769	3,544	15	20,540	519	38,064
Minnesota	1,926	798	236	1,049	1,189	3	3,269	239	8,709
Mississippi	4,016	10	14	237	176	7	5,590	379	10,429
Missouri	761	7	15	275	78	8	3,149	292	4,585
Montana	45	519	6	209	210	5	2,305	235	3,534

Nebraska	414	210	31	611	228	3	1,603	146	3,246
Nevada	1,114	30	41	1,150	298	46	1,678	502	4,859
New Hampshire	25	1	5	75	43	4	879	116	1,148
New Jersey	2,060	1	70	1,996	192	11	2,213	155	6,698
New Mexico	233	739	3	5,259	117	4	1,845	377	8,577
New York	19,557	254	1,544	18,251	2,697	32	21,130	7,761	71,226
North Carolina	2,140	202	27	865	372	7	3,663	116	7,392
North Dakota	111	404	—	1339	152	4	1,070	101	1,981
Ohio	6,127	4	55	1,388	2,211	10	14,694	408	24,867
Oklahoma	1,290	1,080	35	2,527	3,913	9	5,603	—	14,457
Oregon	428	306	77	1,482	421	52	6,742	1,562	11,070
Pennsylvania	1,036	1	23	523	309	2	2,656	75	4,625
Puerto Rico	—	—	—	—	—	—	—	—	—
Rhode Island	346	13	15	829	261	—	1,439	192	3,095
South Carolina	6,538	15	52	762	530	9	8,382	783	17,071
South Dakota	46	537	9	121	184	—	415	27	1,339
Tennessee	—	—	—	—	—	—	—	—	—
Texas	11,652	63	307	27,297	2,114	45	18,499	1,529	61,506
Utah	271	205	73	2,048	195	177	6,898	80	9,947
Vermont	13	—	4	6	4	—	784	67	878
Virginia	1,565	3	37	659	431	11	3,328	243	6,277
Washington	324	214	62	835	522	41	2,148	240	4,386
West Virginia	186	—	3	51	399	1	5,825	31	6,496
Wisconsin	1,058	236	68	552	230	1	2,678	79	4,902
Wyoming	24	23	1	142	8	—	713	39	950
National	**135,953**	**8,865**	**5,864**	**146,731**	**34,806**	**1,273**	**293,504**	**30,663**	**657,479**
Reporting States	**49**	**49**	**49**	**49**	**49**	**49**	**49**	**49**	**49**

Note: Not all states comply with submitting data as the program is voluntary.
U.S. Department of Health & Human Services, Administration for Children and Families, Administration on Children, Youth and Families, Children's Bureau. (2019). Child Maltreatment 2017. Available from https://www.acf.hhs.gov/cb/research-data-technology/statistics-research/child-maltreatment.

Analyzing data on child maltreatment from numerous resources can be beneficial as more abuse may come to light, but the varying ways to measure abuse can be confusing to those researchers who are looking for consistent quantitative data. Despite the act of collecting data for such offenses being something that has evolved with time, researchers acknowledge and report that child maltreatment has existed throughout history.

HISTORY OF CHILD ABUSE

Child maltreatment has existed throughout human history; however, what we consider child abuse today may not have been viewed as abuse in earlier times. The following time periods and locations around the world provide a brief overview of some of the history relating to the treatment of children.

Antiquity

In ancient Egypt, half-brothers and half-sisters were expected to engage in sexual activity with each other in preparation for marriage, and sibling incest among royalty was considered reasonable. Children would commonly marry between the ages of thirteen to fifteen. To help prepare children for sexual activity, nurses and wet nurses would play with the male genitalia in their mouths to help little boys have stronger erections.[11] Although not specifically dating back to the antiquity period, it has been a long-standing custom for mothers within the Arab/Muslim world to stroke baby boys' genitals to soothe them and reinforce a sexual and emotional connection.[12] In Greece during the period of antiquity, men considered women inferior and sex was rarely engaged in as it was usually used for the purpose of providing offspring. Boys would routinely perform fellatio on men and ingest their semen as a ritual into manhood.[13] Rome had emperors such as Tiberius who would train little boys referred to as "minnows" to chase after him while he would be swimming and have the boys get between his legs to lick and nibble at him.[14] Sexual abuse was not the only form of child maltreatment during this period. Children, who threatened the family economics by their mere existence, were exposed to the elements and left to die. In Greece, a child was considered the property of their father.[15] Most Greek cities allowed the father the right to kill his child at birth or to sell his children to slave dealers. Spartan law decreed that Spartan infants were required to be examined by the older men of the community to value their worth. A child that was considered weak or deformed would be thrown into a deep cavern at the foot of Mount Taygetus.[16] Having a healthy, strong child was imperative as a Spartan boy was trained for war by living off the land and was encouraged to steal for food if starving, but would be flogged if caught.[17] Ancient history revealed that infanticide was practiced in many societies which today refers to the killing of an infant, although during ancient times infanticide referred to killing children up to around the age of seven.[18] Pliny the Elder, a Roman author, wrote that men tried to improve their virility by consuming the leg marrow and brain of an infant and used part of the body as a love potion.[19] Rome itself displayed a history of showing no consideration for infants, especially for those who were disabled, as malformed newborns were not regarded as human and were usually killed shortly after birth.[20] Around this same period, some parents killed their children just to remove the anxiety of having to take care of them.[21] In some areas of the world killing a child was based on gender. For example in China, baby girls were murdered at a high rate since they did not have the same rights and were not valued as much as boys.[22] Infanticide was common and practiced for many reasons including controlling and regulating the population so that resources could be reserved for the strongest valued members of society.[23]

Middle Ages

The Middle Ages did not have the same level of abuse as that of the antiquity period, but it still wasn't without controversy as to the care of children. During the Middles Ages, laws forbidding infanticide were passed, although it wasn't clear that these laws were enforced. Infanticide was more common during the famine years, but decreased post plague years. Overall, evidence does not support sweeping claims of child brutality with child-rearing practices during the Middle Ages.[24] Nonetheless, child abuse still existed. Cases of infanticide during this time period included mothers deliberately suffocating their offspring or abandoning them in the streets. In other instances, destitute parents abandoned their unwanted children by bringing them to monasteries to be raised by monks.[25] Although the Middle Ages were still susceptible to abuse, it was not accepted by society and frowned upon by religious leaders. However, the murder of children as satanic sacrifices was considered a hidden crime even though these acts were still orchestrated through the minds of satanic sadists. One of the most statistical perversions on record is that of Countess Elizabeth Bathony of Hungary, who murdered over six hundred children after sexually molesting them and used their blood as body lotion.[26]

Victorian England

The Central Criminal Court at Old Bailey in London, England, is a symbol of justice that is exemplified through an inscription above the main entrance to the present court which states "Defend the Children of the Poor and Punish the Wrong-Doer"; this is a reflection of the ideals of that time period.[27] Despite this, the treatment of children during this era did not reflect the values suggested in the inscription as sexual abuse of children through incest and prostitution was commonplace and the laws on the age of consent were in dispute. A girl at twelve years of age was considered a mature sexual agent in 1870; however, the statutory age for consent for girls in 1875 was raised from twelve to thirteen, and then increased again to sixteen in 1885. Nevertheless, incest was not ruled a criminal offense until 1908. At that time there were legislators who didn't support the idea of raising the age of consent as it would increase the possibility of blackmailing by girls who would dress up to make themselves look older.[28] The focus of sexual abuse during this period was gender specific as child-saving agencies spoke almost exclusively of concern for young girls. Sexually abused girls were seen as a "polluting influence" to other children, and their loss of innocence made them misfits that needed retraining or reforming in a special institution.[29]

Colonial America

The level of abuse and neglect is impossible to measure during this era, but the laws in and of themselves speak loudly on the treatment of children. For instance, in 1681 any child over sixteen years of age who cursed or struck their natural parents was subject to the death penalty, although they could provide a defense if they could show that their parents provoked them with extreme or cruel correction. Children aged sixteen years or older could also be executed for arson; being a rebellious or stubborn son and denying the scriptures could result in a child's death. In Salem, Massachusetts, courts gave a master the right to discipline a servant but ruled in the case of Phillip Fowler that this master had gone too far by hanging a boy by his heels as butchers do for slaughter.[30] Colonial America also had a different concept of sexual abuse when compared to today's standards. Some states chose ten as the age of consent, whereas others chose twelve. In Delaware, the age of consent was seven.[31] In addition to the controversy of sexual abuse through the age of consent, there were also acts of discipline that today could be considered physical abuse and neglect when compared to that of the colonial period. Whipping a child was not considered physical abuse as the concept of "Spare the Rod and Spoil the Child" was the philosophy that was referenced and condoned through various scriptural passages. Child neglect during the colonial period included failing to provide values relating to religion, labor, and family order. In all New England colonial courts, only the natural father could be charged with child abuse.[32] As we review the abuse and laws relating to child maltreatment within the colonial era, the actions, although they may seem deplorable, may come across as less appalling in comparison to the treatment of African American children.

Slavery

There certainly are some aspects of American history that can only be recorded as shameful. The concept of owning another human being is inconceivable to Americans today, but the slavery of African Americans is nevertheless part of American history. Although there are conflicting accounts of the first Negro slaves in America, it was recorded that in the summer of 1619, a ship named the White Lion arrived at Point Comfort with twenty Negroes. This acquisition was the result of a coordinated attack on foreign shipping, and the victors divided the spoils. The gains in one particular case were African slaves from a Portuguese slave ship.[33] From the colonist's perspective, these slaves were needed to help maintain the large plantations that were being formed in America. Before we discuss the abuse of African children among the plantations, it is important to note the atrocities they experienced through their journey to America. Children were an attractive commodity as they were easier to seize and required less space on the ships. Although young boys and girls were allowed to walk about the deck unfettered, some children were exposed to sexual exploitation on the ship while their parents could do nothing but witness the assault. Children were so consumed with anxiety during these trips that some completed suicide, and jumping overboard was a common form of resistance to their captivity.[34] The exact number of Africans who died in transport is unknown, but it is estimated that around eleven million children and adults disembarked into America.[35] Upon arrival, the abuse of children continued as it was common practice that the children were separated from their parents. This was emotionally devastating to the children as they were forced to leave their loved ones behind. This usually occurred when slave owners would sell their slaves in public or private markets.[36] This was not done out of spite, but more as a business transaction or a gesture from one slave owner to another as some slaves were given as gifts to newly married couples or in the event of the birth of a baby.[37] Children born to men and women owned by different people became the property of the mother's owner.[38] To strengthen the numbers of slaves, owners would breed both women and children to increase the slave population. Some children never knew their mothers as they were sold immediately after birth, whereas others stayed with their mother and eventually became part of the slave owner's workforce.[39] When children were able to stay with their parents, the parents had limited authority over their own children. In fact, in some cases, the slave owner would name the child, while other owners would decide what clothing they would have.[40]

House of Refuge Movement (1800s)

The House of Refuge Movement represented a new approach by reformers to deal with problem children as these institutions were being used in lieu of families, churches, and informal community controls. The concept of the movement according to reformers, who were mostly men from established families, was to oversee the morality and protect their way of life from the threat posed by the poor. Reformers believed that having separate institutions for the youth would shield them from the corrupting influences of adult institutions.[41] In 1825, New York State passed a law permitting the incarceration of neglected and dependent children. Children were placed in a house of refuge to intervene in neglectful home environments and placed them in a controlled environment along with juvenile delinquents.[42] The house of refuge also served as an alternative for the incarceration for delinquent youth. The New York House of Refuge was part of a larger educational reform as a method to fight poverty and crime.[43] By the mid-1800s, the house of refuge was declared a great success. However, this enthusiasm did not last long. By 1850, the house of refuge was considered a failure as these facilities were like prisons.[44] During this movement, corporal punishment was widely used to keep children orderly and productive, and it was not considered child abuse.[45] However, children were facing deplorable conditions with overcrowding and abuse by staff. The concept of the house of refuge during this period completely conflicts with addressing child maltreatment today as the focus then was removing children from a poor environment instead of adjudicating or punishing abusive parents.

The Progressive Era

Between 1870 and 1900, the U.S. Census reported that children aged ten to fourteen who were working for wages increased by 22 percent.[46] The progressive era campaigned against the abuse of child labor, which was a response to the negative effects of industrialization and the need for inexpensive labor. Hundreds of thousands of children worked in textile mills, coal mines, sweatshops, farms, and ranches throughout America. The progressive movement fought against child labor, although agricultural labor was generally ignored.[47] Although child labor was a primary focus with reformers, progressive activists also focused on juvenile justice, playgrounds, and pensions for widowed mothers, health care, and housing.[48] Nevertheless, reformers' view on child welfare was controversial. Reformers during this period believed that some children who had families were still considered homeless and actual orphans who had broken no laws might be so degraded that they would be considered a danger to society and needed rescuing. The reformers thus expanded the definition of dependency to include such conduct as visiting pool halls on a regular basis or using liquor or drugs. Progressives who worked with the juvenile courts blurred the lines between dependent, neglected, and delinquent children.[49] The era of socialized juvenile justice was established. The primary focus of authorities now was to treat and rehabilitate the juvenile rather than punish the child for any misconduct.[50] However, the progressive era was controversial with the overreaching by some reformers who thought they were acting in the best interest of the children and society. In 1899, Illinois Cook County created the first juvenile court for the treatment and control of dependent, neglected, and delinquent children.[51]

CONCLUSION

The History of Child Abuse produces numerous examples of child maltreatment that would not be acceptable under today's standards of childcare. However, the standards that we rely on today to identify abuse are subjective. There are individual opinions as well as statutory differences within our current society that have varying declarations as to what is considered child abuse. In fact, our criminal justice system is not even unified as to what delineates a child. Due to the subjectivity of identifying what constitutes child maltreatment, the actual measurement of child abuse can be skewed. The flaws identified within each measuring system further put into question the accuracy of child abuse statistics.

PURPOSE OF THE BOOK

The purpose of this book is to evaluate child abuse by recognizing how significant the problem is through the subjectivity of identifying and defining what constitutes child maltreatment. We will explore the four main categories of child abuse (physical, sexual, emotional, and neglect) and explain how each type of abuse occurs, who is most likely to perpetrate these offenses, and specify the most likely victim under each category. Also, the reader will see child abuse from an international perspective and will address areas of the world that are more prone to certain aspects of abuse. Additionally, we will explain how to identify each category of abuse through both physical and behavioral indicators, and address the short- and long-term consequences of each type of victimization. The book was also designed to address areas of abuse where to date the research has been limited. Specifically, this book will address child abuse from the earliest stages of fetal abuse to the final stage of child fatalities. In addition the reader will learn of the abuse that takes place through family domestic violence, dating violence, and the specific abuse that occurs within a school setting. This material is written with the intention of being distinctive as the reader will also have the opportunity to review a comprehensive analysis of why and how false allegations occur. Finally, this textbook will cover child abuse relating to specific jurisdictions such as the military, Native Americans, and those who live in the shadow of illegal immigration. In summary, this book is designed to prepare individuals who are considering working in the field of child protection or for anyone who desires to learn more about abuse so they can properly advocate for children.

REVIEW QUESTIONS

1. Why is it so difficult to accurately measure child abuse?

2. How do law enforcement and CPS differ in collecting child abuse data?

3. What are the four categories of abuse?

4. Why were children placed in the house of refuge?

5. What were the goals of the reformers during the progressive era?

KEYWORDS

Antiquity: ancient history prior to the Middle Ages
Reformer: a person devoted to bringing about change
Middle Ages: a period of time between antiquity and modern times
House of refuge: an institution used to protect the homeless or destitute
Age of consent: the age a person can legally give consent to sexual intercourse or marriage
Child Protective Services
Victimization surveys
CAPTA: Child Abuse Prevention and Treatment Act, which provides federal funding to states in support of preventing, assessing, investigating, prosecuting, and treating child abuse
Progressive era

NOTES

1. Brett Drake and Melissa Jonson-Reid, "Defining and Estimating Child Maltreatment," in J. Bart Klika and Jon R. Conte (eds.), *The APSAC Handbook on Child Maltreatment*, fourth edition (Thousand Oaks, CA: Sage, 2018), 15.

2. Drake and Jonson-Reid, "Defining and Estimating Child Maltreatment," 16.

3. Drake and Jonson-Reid, "Defining and Estimating Child Maltreatment," 15; Parminder Singh Bhuller, *Corporal Punishment in Schools* (New Delhi: Laxmi Enterprises, 2014), 22.

4. Stephen Meyer, *Child Abuse and Domestic Violence: Information Plus* (Farmington Hills, MI: Cengage, 2017), 21.

5. Cindy L. Miller-Perrin, Robin D. Perrin, and Claire M. Renzetti, *Violence and Maltreatment in Intimate Relationships* (Thousand Oaks, CA: SAGE, 2018), 7.

6. Elizabeth Quinn and Sara Brightman, *Crime Victimization: A Comprehensive Overview* (Durham, NC: Carolina Academic Press, 2015), 26; Anthony Walsh and Cody Jorgensen, *Criminology: The Essentials*, third edition (Thousand Oaks, CA: SAGE, 2018), 41.

7. Meyer, *Child Abuse and Domestic Violence: Information Plus*, 21.

8. Harvey Wallace and Cliff Roberson, *Victimology: Legal, Psychological, and Social Perspectives*, fourth edition (Upper Saddle River, NJ: Pearson, 2015), 55.

9. Drake and Jonson- Reid, "Defining and Estimating Child Maltreatment," 27–29.

10. National Survey of Children's Exposure to Violence. http://www.unh.edu/ccrc/projects/natscev.html.

11. Sander J. Breiner, *Slaughter of the Innocents: Child Abuse Through the Ages and Today* (New York, NY: Plenum Press, 1990), 24.

12. Nancy H. Korbin, *The Banality of Suicide Terrorism: The Naked Truth About the Psychology of Islamic Suicide Bombing* (Washington DC: Potomac Books Inc, 2010), 16.

13. George Rousseau, *Children and Sexuality: From the Greek to the Great War* (London: Palgrave Macmillan, 2007), 16.

14. R.E.L. Masters and Eduard Lea, *Sex Crimes in History: Evolving Concepts of Sadism, Lust-Murder, and Necrophilia from Ancient to Modern Times* (New York, NY: The Julian Press, 1963), 35.

15. Mason P. Thomas, "Child Abuse and Neglect Part 1: Historical Overview, Legal Matrix, and Social Perspectives," *North Carolina Law Review* 50, no. 2 (1972): 295.

16. Christine Alder and Ken Polk, *Child Victims of Homicide* (New York, NY: Cambridge University Press, 2001), 33.

17. Breiner, *Slaughter of the Innocents: Child Abuse Through the Ages and Today*, 50–52.

18. Monica L. McCoy and Stephanie M. Keen, *Child Abuse and Neglect*, second edition (New York, NY: Psychology Press, 2014), 4.

19. Breiner, *Slaughter of the Innocents: Child Abuse Through the Ages and Today*, 117.

20. M. Obladen, "Right to Sin: Laws on Infanticide in Antiquity," *Neonatology* 109, no. 2 (2016): 56–61.

21. Clifford K. Dorne, *Child Maltreatment: A Primer in History, Public Policy and Research*, second edition (Albany, NY: Harrow and Heston Publishers, 1997), 17.

22. Dorne, *Child Maltreatment: A Primer in History, Public Policy and Research*, 16.

23. Cynthia Crosson-Tower, *Understanding Child Abuse and Neglect*, eighth edition (Boston, MA: Pearson, 2010), 1.

24. Jerome Kroll and Bernard Bachrach, "Child Psychiatry Perspective: Child Care and Child Abuse in Early Medieval Europe," *Journal of the American Academy of Child Psychiatry* 25, no. 4 (1986): 563; Monica L. McCoy and Stephanie M. Keen, *Child Abuse and Neglect*, 4.

25. Preston Elrod and R. Scott Ryder, *Juvenile Justice: A Historical, and Legal Perspective* (Sudbury, MA: Jones and Bartlett, 2005), 95.

26. Obi N.I. Ebbie, "Definition and Historical Antecedents of Criminal Abuse of Women and Children," in Obi N.I. Ebbe and Dilip K. Das (eds.), *Criminal Abuse of Women and Children: An International Perspective* (Boca Raton, FL: CRC Press Taylor & Francis Group, 2010), 13–14.

27. Louise A. Jackson, *Child Sexual Abuse in Victorian England* (New York, NY: Routledge, 2000), 1.

28. Jackson, *Child Sexual Abuse in Victorian England*, 12–16.

29. Jackson, *Child Sexual Abuse in Victorian England*, 3–4.

30. LeRoy Ashby, *Endangered Children: Dependency, Neglect, and Abuse in American History* (New York, NY: Twayne Publishers, 1997), 12; Preston Elrod and R. Scott Ryder, *Juvenile Justice: A Social, Historical, and Legal Perspective*, 102.

31. Michael Castleman, "Age of Consent: How Old is Old Enough for Sex?" *Psychology Today* (Feb. 1, 2017); David A. Price, *Love & Hate in Jamestown: John Smith, Pocahontas, and The Start of a New Nation* (New York, NY: Vintage Books, 2003), 160.

32. Ashby, *Endangered Children: Dependency, Neglect, and Abuse in American History*, 12–13; McCoy and Keen, *Child Abuse and Neglect*, 5.

33. Price, *Love & Hate in Jamestown: John Smith, Pocahontas, and the Start of a New Nation*, 194–95.

34. Wilma King, *Stolen Childhood: Slave Youth in Nineteenth-Century America*, second edition (Bloomington, IN: Indiana University Press, 2011), 2–17.

35. Lisa A. Lindsay, *Captives as Commodities: The Transatlantic Slave Trade* (Upper Saddle River, NJ: Pearson Prentice Hall, 2008), 7.

36. King, *Stolen Childhood: Slave Youth in Nineteenth-Century America*, 232.

37. King, *Stolen Childhood: Slave Youth in Nineteenth-Century America*, 235.

38. King, *Stolen Childhood: Slave Youth in Nineteenth-Century America*, 41.

39. Pamela D. Bridgewater, "Un/Re/Dis Covering Slave Breeding in Thirteenth Amendment Jurisprudence," *Washington and Lee Journal of Child Rights and Social Justice* 7, no. 1 (2001): 21–22, https://scholarlycommons.law.wlu.edu/cgi/viewcontent.cgi?referer=https://www.google.com/&httpsredir=1&article=1099&context=crsj.

40. King, *Stolen Childhood: Slave Youth in Nineteenth-Century America*, 50–64.

41. Elrod and Ryder, *Juvenile Justice: A Social, Historical, and Legal Perspective*, 105.

42. Dorne, *Child Maltreatment: A Primer in History, Public Policy and Research*, 19.

43. Josie Madison, "Coercion, If Coercion Be Necessary: The Educational Function of the New York House of Refuge, 1824-1874," *American Educational History Journal* 39, no. 1-2 (2012): 401–02.

44. Steven M. Cox, Jennifer M. Allen, Robert D. Hanser, and John J. Conrad, *Juvenile Justice: A Guide to Theory, Policy, and Practice* (Thousand Oaks, CA: SAGE, 2018), 6.

45. Dorne, *Child Maltreatment: A Primer in History, Public Policy and Research*, 22.

46. James Marten, *Childhood and Child Welfare in the Progressive Era: A Brief History with Documents* (Boston, MA: Bedford/St Matins, 2005), 8.

47. Marten, *Childhood and Child Welfare in the Progressive Era: A Brief History with Documents*, 63.

48. Marten, *Childhood and Child Welfare in the Progressive Era: A Brief History with Documents*, 3.

49. Ashby, *Endangered Children: Dependency, Neglect, and Abuse in American History*, 81–82.

50. Cox et al., *Juvenile Justice: A Guide to Theory, Policy, and Practice*, 7.

51. Ashby, *Endangered Children: Dependency, Neglect, and Abuse in American History*, 81.

2

Child Physical Abuse

◆ ◆ ◆

CHILD PHYSICAL ABUSE IS A GLOBAL problem that has long-term consequences to the abused. Child abuse is defined by the Federal Child Abuse Prevention and Treatment Act as "any recent act or failure to act on the part of a
parent or caregiver which results in death, serious physical or emotional harm,
sexual abuse or exploitation" or "an act or failure to act which presents an
imminent risk of serious harm."[1] The most recent statistic from 2015 indicates
that in the United States, 1,670 children died from abuse. On average, about
seven hundred thousand children are abused each year. Child Protective Services
are involved with about 3.4 million children annually.[2] Of the child fatalities,
most were under the age of four years old.

The World Health Organization has identified risk factors for children that
may increase the likelihood of child maltreatment. These include:

- Being under four years old or an adolescent
- Being an unwanted child, or failing to meet parental expectations
- Special needs (physical or mental impairments).

Risk factors of the parent are:

- Difficulty bonding with newborn
- Being maltreated as a child
- Unrealistic expectations of normal growth and development of a child
- Alcohol and substance abuse
- Being involved in criminal activity
- Financial difficulties.

Characteristics of the family include:

- Physical, developmental, or mental health problems of a family member
- Violence in the home
- Isolation from family and social support.

Community and societal factors that may contribute to the risk of child maltreatment are:

- Gender and social inequality
- Lack of adequate housing or services to support families in need
- High levels of unemployment and poverty
- Access to alcohol and drugs
- Social and cultural norms that promote and accept violence toward others, support corporal punishment, or support rigid gender roles
- Social, economic, health, and education policies that lead to poor living conditions.[3]

Most children are active with little fear of outcomes resulting in injury. Statistically, males have a slightly higher rate of being physically abused than females. Infants and toddlers are at a higher risk of fatal and severe physical abuse.[4] The challenge is to be able to identify accidental injuries from non-accidental injuries. Medical providers, law enforcement, and child protective services all need to be able to recognize what is normal, what might be normal, and what injuries do not match. The story is important: the story from the caretaker, the story from the child, the story from the emergency medical responders that responded to the scene, the story from the doctors and the nurses once the child begins to receive medical treatment, and finally, the story to the investigative agencies. When the story is not true, it can be difficult to keep all of the details in order from one person to the other. The professionals that interact with this child need to communicate and compare those stories, identify the injuries, and determine if the story matches the injury. Once all the information can be compiled, it can help determine accidental versus non-accidental injuries.

CORPORAL PUNISHMENT

Making determination of what is physical abuse even more complicated, corporal punishment also is a key element. Corporal punishment is defined as physical punishment to a child in response to a perceived misbehavior.[5] In the United States, corporal punishment is legal, and in my experience, I have seen judges in court rule that corporal punishment is acceptable.

In the United States, it is acceptable to spank or hit with an object (such as a belt) as long as significant marks are not left behind. Some investigating agencies use a twenty-four-hour rule, meaning if there are no significant marks within twenty-four hours then the punishment was not considered abusive. Many experts and advocates support the use of corporal punishment, but research also supports that unintended consequences can occur. Advocates against corporal punishment suggest that children that are spanked will be more aggressive and will have delinquent and antisocial behavior, and it will have a negative impact between the parent-child relationship. These advocates also promote that these behaviors carry into adulthood. Describing behaviors such as aggression, antisocial behavior, increase in criminal activity, mental health issues, and becoming physically abusive to their own child. Right or wrong, corporal punishment is legal, but a fine line does exist between discipline and abuse.

TYPES OF INJURIES

This chapter is going to break down types of injuries received during abuse and what treatment is recommended.

Skin Injuries

Skin is the largest organ of the body consisting primarily of two layers: the epidermis and the dermis. The epidermis is the outer layer of skin that acts as a barrier. The primary roles of the epidermis are to prevent evaporative fluid loss and to protect the body from penetration of substances.[6] The epidermis is composed of keratinocytes. Keratinocytes are basal cells that form keratin. Keratin is a fibrous structural protein that is in the material that makes up hair and the outer layer of human skin. Also within the epidermis are melanocytes. Melanocytes are cells that provide pigmentation to the skin.

STRUCTURE OF THE SKIN

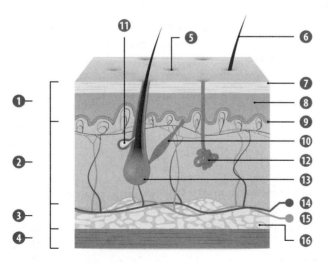

1. Epidermis
2. Dermis
3. Hypodermis
4. Muscle
5. Pores
6. Hair shaft
7. Stratum corneum
8. Squamous cells
9. Basal cells
10. Arrector pili muscle
11. Sebaceous (oil) gland
12. Sweat pore
13. Hair follicle
14. Artery
15. Vein
16. Adipose tissue

Skin Layers Diagram
© iStock / Getty Images Plus / Paladjai

The dermis lies just below the epidermis and covers the subcutaneous fat layer. The dermis nourishes the epidermis and provides the structural integrity of the skin. The dermis consists of collagen, elastin fibers, blood vessels, and nerves. Collagen is what is responsible for maintaining the structure of the skin. Elastin helps provide flexibility of the skin and the ability for the skin to return to its normal state.[7]

Below the dermis is the subcutaneous fat layer. This layer will deform easily and consists of lobules and adipocytes. Capillaries are abundant in this layer and when damaged, blood will leak into the perivascular tissue. When bruises are noted to the skin, bleeding has typically occurred within this layer.[8]

Skin injuries such as bruises and abrasions are common in accidental trauma. Skin injuries are also a common finding in children that are physically abused. Careful evaluation to determine if the injury is accidental or non-accidental can be challenging and requires careful evaluation.

Bruising of the skin is from blunt force trauma that disrupts the underlying blood vessels and causes leaking and collection of blood in the dermal layers of the skin.[9] When damage to the capillaries occurs, it results in hemoglobin and blood cell breakdown, causing the bruise to develop multiple colors that can range from blue, purple, red, black, green, brown, and yellow. When evaluating children that are abused, it would be convenient to say that the color of bruise represents a time frame in which the injury occurred; however, there is no research to back up aging bruises. The best guess on aging a bruise is if the bruise has any yellow, it is likely to be older than eighteen hours. Bruises that occur at the same time can be different in color. Red bruising can be present in the bruise regardless of how old the bruise is. The amount of force applied, the area of the body injured, and the pigmentation of the skin are all factors in how the bruise will emerge. Bony surfaces with a thin layer of skin such as the periorbital area will bruise easier than an area that does not overlie a bony surface, like the abdomen.

When evaluating children, it is important to get the history of the incident, medical history of the child, and a family history. Evaluate if there is a bleeding disorder in the family history. Consider the age of the child and the location of the injuries. Accidental injuries to a child are typically found over bony prominences to the front of the child. Common accidental areas of injury are:

1. Forehead
2. Chin
3. Elbows
4. Shins.

Consider the age of the child with these injuries. Is the child mobile? A child that is not mobile should not have bruising. If a non-mobile child presents with bruising, a thorough medical assessment is necessary.

If injuries in children are in the location of the red triangle, it should be red flag for non-accidental trauma.

Uncommon areas of injury in children are:

1. Face (other than the forehead and chin)
2. Abdomen
3. Hips
4. Back
5. Buttocks
6. Upper arms
7. Forearms
8. Posterior legs
9. Hands
10. Feet
11. Ears
12. Genitalia (without a history of a straddle injury).

Bruising that is a red flag for abuse will occur in the torso, ear, and neck region (TEN) in children up to four years of age or in any location in an infant under four months. The acronym to remember this is TEN-4. This model was found to have a 97 percent accuracy and a specificity of 84 percent for predicting abuse.[10]

Labbé and Caouette conducted a study involving 1,467 children from the ages of zero to seventeen. These children were being seen for reasons other than trauma for a total of 2,040 visits. The examiners followed these children over a period of one year. What was found is that the majority of the children nine months and older had at least one recent skin injury (skin injury was typically a bruise, but also may include abrasions). A total of 17 percent of these children had at least five skin injuries, 4 percent had ten or more, less than 1 percent had fifteen or more, and less than 0.2 percent had twenty or more. The typical site for these injuries was the lower leg. During the summer months, it was noticed that there was an increase in skin injuries. This study concluded that skin injuries were noted to be rare in children younger than nine months old and it is rare to find more than fifteen injuries in any child.[11]

When documenting bruises and other skin injuries in children, it is important to note the location, color, size, and pattern of the injury. Remember to document the history and complete a thorough head-to-toe assessment despite the history to examine areas where skin injuries are not immediately obvious. For all children, you should undress to assess for every complaint in which the child is receiving medical treatment.

CASE STUDY #1

A six-year-old female presents with bruises to the face, abdomen, and back. Her mother states that the child bruises easily and is being treated at another facility for this. On head-to-toe assessment, it is noted that the child has bruises in areas that are uncommon to bruise in children but zero bruises in areas that are commonly injured. What are your thoughts?

Patterned Injuries

When assessing skin injuries, another red flag is injuries that are indicative of a pattern. The pattern can be in the shape of the impacting object or the shape of something that is between the skin and the object. The pattern may follow the contour of the body, indicating a flexible object was used (i.e., belt) or it may appear only on the portion of the body that was stuck if a rigid item was used (i.e., spoon). The hand is a common object used to impact a child and can leave a distinctive pattern of injury as the capillaries break between the fingers and blood is pushed away from the point of impact,[12] which is referred to as sparing.

Table 2.1   Red Flags for Child Abuse

Bruising in a child younger than nine months of age OR a child that is NOT cruising
Bruising to soft tissue; away from bony prominences
Bruising to the TEN region, upper arms, hands, and feet
Multiple bruises in clusters
Bruises that are uniform in shape
Bruises that are indicative of a pattern or a ligature

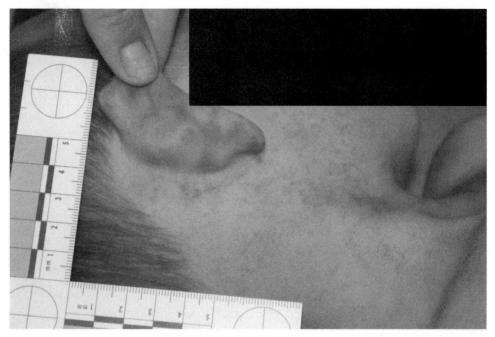

4-year-old male whose father strangled him and pinched his penis to punish for getting a "red" card in school. Note: without a thorough assessment, bruising behind the ear and the penis would easily be missed. Petechiae noted to right side of the face and right lateral neck from being strangled by his father.

16-year-old female assaulted by mom and mom's boyfriend. Slap marks to the chest.

Table 2.2   Pattern of Injury

Slap marks	Typically creates two or three parallel/linear marks with sparing in between the marks (may leave full handprint).
Closed fist punch	Round bruises that correspond with the knuckles of the hand.
Grip/grab marks	Relatively round marks that correspond with fingertips and/or thumb.
Belt/electrical cord	Loop marks or parallel lines of bruising or petechiae with central sparing. These marks will follow the contour of the body. May also have circular marks from the holes in the belt or square or patterned marks from the buckle (need a good description of the belt).
Other household objects	Patterns can be in any shape of the object used (i.e., spoon, flyswatter, spatula, etc.).
Human bite	Ovoid pattern injury. May have bruising and abrasions. May have teeth imprints.
Strangulation	Bruises and abrasions to the neck. The description of the type of strangulation is important in determining types of injury suspected and location of injury (one hand, two hand, chokehold). Petechiae may be present at or above the level of compression, including eyes and mouth. Subconjunctival hemorrhages may be noted.
Binding/ligature	Marks around the wrists, ankles, neck, or mouth.
Hair pulling	Traumatic alopecia; may have petechiae, bruising, swelling on underlying scalp. Reports of tenderness to the site.

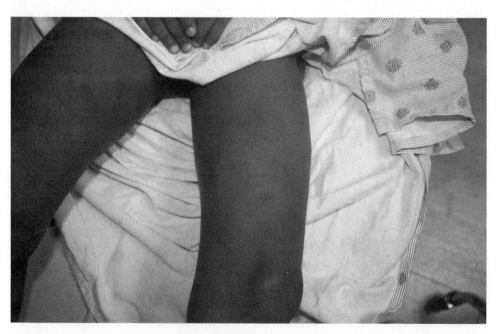

A 4-year-old female that was beaten with a belt by her father. These are looped patterned injuries that follow the contour of the body.

Bite Marks

Bite marks to children are strong indicators of abuse. Bite marks can be located anywhere on the body. The appearance of the bite mark will depend on the angle of the teeth, the body part that is bitten, the amount of force applied, and the amount of movement between the biter and the person being bit.

The most common shape of a human bite is an ovoid shape. There are three distinct features of human bites:

1. Bite mark: ovoid pattern injury. Tooth imprints may be present. Size and shape are important. Adult bite marks can be differentiated from a child's bite based on distance between the maxillary canines. The normal maxillary canine in adults is 2.5 to 4.0 centimeters. If the intercanine distance is less than 2.5 centimeters, a child probably caused the bite; greater than 3.0 centimeters, the bite was most likely by an adult.[13]
2. Suck mark is caused by pulling of the skin into the mouth, creating negative pressure.
3. Thrust mark is caused by the tongue pushing against the skin, which is trapped behind the teeth.[14]

Human bite marks should be differentiated from animal bite marks. When evaluating a bite be aware that human bite marks normally do not tear flesh,

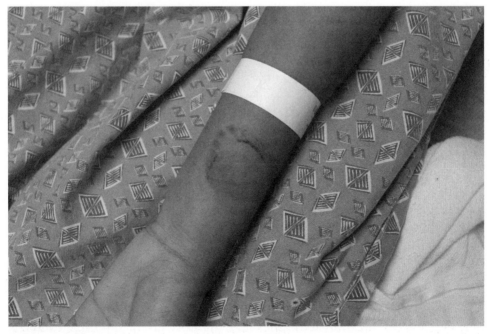

Adult bite mark
- ovoid pattern with tooth impression
- suck mark
- thrust mark

whereas animal bite marks do. Animal bite marks tend to have a puncture appearance versus the ovoid pattern appearance.

Subgaleal Hematomas

This is a potentially life-threatening extracranial hematoma that occurs in neonates after prolonged exposure to instrumental deliveries. It is rare to have incidents of subgaleal hematomas (SGHs) after the neonate period. There are instances, however, of forces being applied to the scalp such as hair pulling that will cause the veins in the subgaleal space to rupture. The vast majority of SGHs are self-limiting and will reabsorb. If symptoms continue to progress, the SGH may need to be aspirated.

Signs and symptoms of SGH are scalp swelling across the suture lines and complaints of headaches, vomiting, drowsiness, and amnesia. Diagnostically, a computed tomography scan of the head should be completed.[15]

Oral Injuries

A common area of injury in child abuse cases is the head, face, and neck. Intraoral injuries, however, can be easily missed. Unless the provider looks inside the oral cavity, subtle and not so subtle injuries can be overlooked. Injuries can occur to the lips, teeth, gingiva, tongue, hard and soft palate, jaw, and the frenulum. Even if the provider does a proper assessment, a delay in treatment can allow for the healing of these injuries. The mucosa to the mouth heals very quickly: Imagine burning your mouth on something hot. It hurts the first day and maybe some the second day; by the third day, it is no longer even a thought. The concept is the same for abusive injuries sustained by children—they heal quickly.

Oral injuries can occur by accident in children that are mobile. Non-ambulatory children should not have oral injuries without a plausible story. Infants that have not gotten teeth will not cause lacerations and bruising to their mouths. This chapter is on physical abuse, but an important consideration as well is sexual abuse to the oral cavity.

Intraoral injuries are the second most common cause of sentinel injuries after bruising. The most common area of injury is lacerations and bruising to the mouth. Fractured teeth, bruising and/or petechiae to the hard and soft palate, fracture to the jaw, and tongue lacerations are some additional injuries that may be noted.

The frenulum is a small fold or ridge of tissue that is found beneath the upper and lower lip and the tongue. Lingual and labial frenula tears as well as sublingual hematomas are typically caused by a direct blow to the mouth, forced feedings, or an object forced into the mouth of the child. In the past, frenulum tears were pathognomonic for abuse; further research now supports that these injuries can come from other trauma. Again, when evaluating for child abuse, take into account the mobility of the child, the story given, and if the child has teeth. If the child is non-ambulatory, frenulum tears are highly suspicious for abuse.

Burns

Burns are the third leading cause of death in children, behind motor vehicle accidents and drownings. According to the World Health Organization, more than three hundred thousand people die each year from burn injuries; a third of that population is younger than the age of twenty. The highest incidence of child fatalities with burns are children younger than the age of five with the greatest prevalence at the age of one.[16] Burns in children account for the greatest length of stay in hospital admissions. During the toddler stage, children become more exploratory with no regard for danger, causing them to be at higher risk for unintentional injuries. Adolescents, especially males, exhibit more risk-taking behavior, without regard for the danger. I had a fourteen-year-old male, who was out of school and whose parents were at work, decide to set his clothes on fire to make a video. He could not put the fire out and ended up with deep partial thickness burns to his legs.

In evaluating children that present with burns, it was noted that children that sustain unintentional burns before their third birthday are five times more likely to be maltreated.[17]

Risk factors associated with burns include:

1. Males
2. Low socioeconomic status
3. Low educational level of the caretaker
4. Home crowding.

The incidence of burns is greatest when it is cold outside. The most frequent area in the household for a burn to occur is in the kitchen during food preparation or during mealtime. The most common type of burn sustained by children are scald burns.

Red flags to consider when evaluating for intentional burns include:

1. Already known to the Department of Social Service
2. History of intimate partner violence in the home
3. Blaming another sibling
4. Preceding trigger to the abuse (i.e., soiling themselves)
5. Other unexplained injuries
6. Previous burn
7. Inadequate supervision.

⚑ Historically, burns were classified as first-degree to fourth-degree burns. This classification system is antiquated. In a burn injury, some cells die because of traumatic or ischemic necrosis. There is a disruption in the collagen cross-link into the connective tissue. This results in abnormal osmotic and hydrostatic pressure gradients in which the intravascular fluid is forced into the interstitial spaces.[18] Tissue damage is the outcome, which is why the newer burn classification is based on the burn wound depth.

Superficial Burns

These affect the epidermis layer of the skin. They are usually caused by ultraviolet radiation from the sun (sunburn). The epidermis does not contain a blood supply; however, this area will still become red due to the irritation of the vascular plexus. No blisters are present in a superficial burn, and the surface of the burn is dry.[19]

Superficial Partial Thickness Burns

This type of burn extends through the epidermis, downward into the papillary (superficial) layer of the dermis. The dermis becomes inflamed, causing redness to the area. When you apply pressure to the reddened area, the area blanches and then will have a quick capillary refill response.

Superficial partial-thickness burns will have thin-walled, fluid-filled blisters that will develop rapidly after the burn takes place. Once the blisters burst, the nerve endings become exposed, which activates the pain receptors. This wound will be sensitive to light touch and temperature, which will cause pain. The epidermis is breached in this type of burn, allowing body fluid to leak onto the wound surface.[20]

Deep Partial Thickness Burns

This type of burn extends deeper into the dermis layer and presents as a mixed red or waxy white tissue. This burn will continue to blanch when pressure is

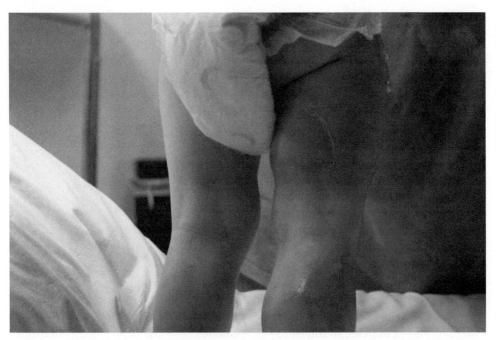

Note the thin walled, fluid-filled blisters. You can also see the moist pink tissue to the left shoulder where a fluid filled blister has burst.

applied but will have delayed or absent capillary refill response. Blisters are usually absent; the exposed surface will still be moist. Edema (swelling) will be noted but pain sensation is altered.[21]

Full Thickness and Subdermal Burns

Full thickness burns extend all the way through the epidermal and dermis layers into the subcutaneous tissue. A subdermal burn will damage muscle and bone. The fluid and protein will shift from the capillaries to the interstitial space, causing the area to become edematous. An immediate immunologic response will follow, potentiating the risk of sepsis.[22]

When evaluating the children that present with burns, it must be determined the amount of body surface area that is burned. This will help guide the provider to a decision tree on treatment of the burn. The Lund and Browder chart is best used with young children to accommodate for the body proportions. The Wallace rule of nines can be used for older children.

The types of burns that will be covered is based on the source that caused the damage to the skin.

1. Thermal burns (scald, contact, flame, or radiation injury)
2. Chemical
3. Electrical
4. Friction or abrasion
5. Ultraviolet radiation

Thermal Burns

Thermal burns are the most common type of burn that are seen with children. The most common thermal burn is a scald burn.

Scald

A scald burn occurs when skin is exposed to a hot liquid or steam. Scald burns can be further broken down to include immersion burns, flowing water scald burns, splash/splatter burns, and contact burns. The majority of all scald burns are accidental and occur when a hot liquid is spilled onto a child. This will typically occur in the home environment, usually in the kitchen. Children will pick up a hot cup and pour it onto themselves; reach up to the stovetop and grab a pan handle, causing the contents to fall on them; or cook a noodle container and get it out of the microwave, find it too hot to grab, and spill the contents onto themselves. Tap water is the most common liquid to cause scald injuries in children. The average age of children to present with scald injuries is from zero to four years old.[23] If a child under the age of five presents with a scald injury, it needs to be worked up as possible non-accidental burn. Unintentional burns tend to be to the anterior surface of the child; if the burn is posterior, suspicion should be raised. These situations can happen quickly; the role of the provider is to assess, treat, and determine if the history matches the burn.

Immersion Burns

Immersion burns occur when a child's body or limb essentially is dipped into a hot liquid. This can be accidental or non-accidental. Accidental immersion burns can occur when a hot beverage is in reach of the child and the child puts his hand in the cup or a child falls into a hot liquid source. What would occur next is the child will immediately withdraw the part that is immersed (if the child is able) and probably cry, alerting the caregiver to the injury. With accidental immersions, the duration of time exposed to the hot liquid is short; therefore, you would expect to have indistinct borders with or without a spill/splash pattern. The depth of the injury is going to be variable. The history of the event provided by the caregivers will match the burn pattern.

Intentional immersion burns can have unique patterns. Uniform burn depth may be circumferential and could be to a single extremity, bilateral extremities, to the trunk, or to the buttocks. The child, in an attempt to withdraw from the hot substance due to pain, will typically pull the legs or arms back causing flexion sparing. Immersion burns many times have distinct linear areas of demarcation between the burned tissue and the uninjured tissue. Some areas of the skin may not have burns, which is called sparing. The area may not be burned because the child was being held in such a way that part of the body was spared; in cases of immersion into hot water into the bathtub, for example, the cool porcelain of the tub will spare the portion of the buttock in direct contact with the tub.

Flowing Water Scalds

This particular type of burn is an accidental burn in which the child turns the tap water on themselves. The hot water from the tap (dependent on the hot water setting in the home) can burn the child.

CASE STUDY #2

Mom usually gives the children a bath. The mother had to run to the store and left her boyfriend to give the one-year-old and two-year-old children a bath. Mom normally turns the hot water off at the water line but did not on this day; boyfriend did not know that she did this. Boyfriend was in the kitchen cooking dinner when the two-year-old came into the kitchen. A few minutes later, boyfriend went to check on the one-year-old and the child was face down in the tub. The child had anterior and posterior scald wounds. What happened was when the older child got out of the tub, the child accidentally turned on the hot water faucet. The one-year-old had direct impact from the hot water, went into shock, and fell into the tub of hot water.

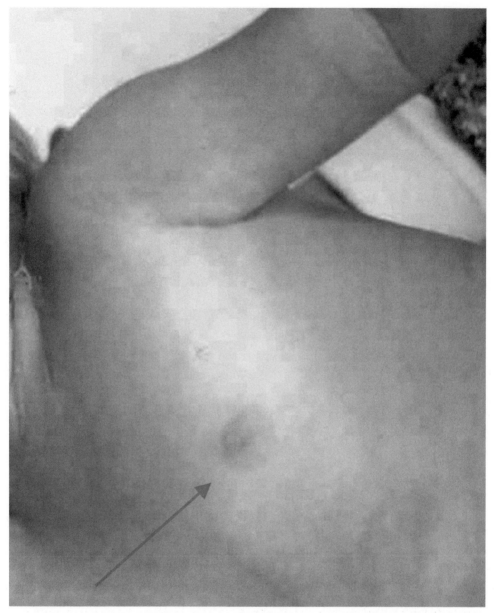

A 6-month-old female brought in with complaints of her 4-year-old brother throwing a hot cup of water on her. Note the sparing that lines up with the left arm. This appears to be an immersion burn, where the portion over the chest and abdomen was spared from the arm being held over that area.

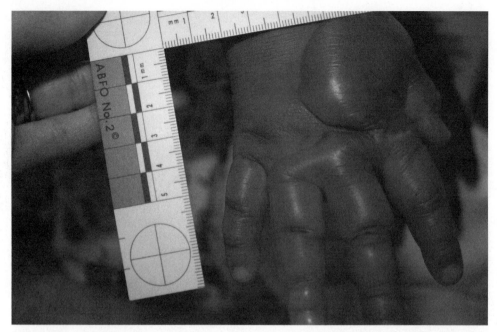

4-year-old girl was punished by mother; forced to place both hands in hot water in the sink.

Critical thinking:

1. Was this accidental or non-accidental?
2. Is there an issue of neglect? If so, what?

Spill/Splatter Burns

Spill/splatter burns are a common scald-type burn seen accidentally in children. Scald burns are also the most common burn in non-accidental trauma.[24] When you think about the burn pattern to expect, imagine a child pulling a hot liquid from above. The immediate area of impact of the liquid will have the greatest depth of burn. As the liquid continues to run down the body, the liquid is cooling, causing the burn to be less severe. Patterns seen with spills are typically burns to the upper limbs, neck, head, and upper trunk. You would expect this burn to be to the anterior surface, and 80 percent of the time, the burn is asymmetric.[25] When evaluating the pattern of injury, it is important to note what the child was wearing at the time of the burn. Multiple layers of clothing will decrease the amount of burn, versus just wearing a diaper with no barrier between the hot substance and the body. Note any other injuries on the child. Note if there are burns to the hand or if the story is the child picked up a hot object causing the child to spill the hot liquid.

For a hot liquid to cause a thermal burn to a child, the temperature has to be at least 140 degrees Fahrenheit. The average hot beverage is 160 to 180 degrees Fahrenheit. Exposure to a child of 140 degrees Fahrenheit for five seconds is enough to cause a full thickness burn.[26]

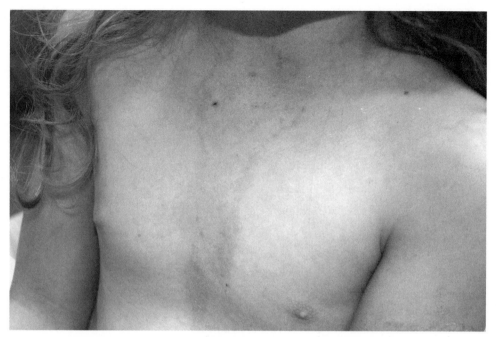

6-year-old female abandoned by her mother. It was reported to the hospital that the child has a sunburn. Note the initial area of contact to the chest and how it runs down her chest.

Contact Burns

Contact burns are the second most common type of thermal injury. Contact burns are thermal injury to the skin secondary to prolonged contact with a hot solid or smoldering source. Objects used can range from items like irons, cigarettes, lighters, oven doors, hair straighteners, etc. Abusive contact burns typically will produce a branding type injury due to the hot object being held against the skin. Contact burns tend to have distinct margins and patterns from the object used. The burns may be in clusters, typically seen with cigarette burns, and in areas covered by clothing.[27]

When providing care for patients with what appears to be contact burns, get a good history from the child and the caregiver separately. Photograph the injury if able and measure the area of the burn. This is especially important when the investigators are going back to the scene to try to identify the object used. With photographs and measurements of the burn, the investigators can help correlate the object to the wound.

Cigarette burns can occur from children accidentally brushing up against a lit cigarette. This does not cause a full thickness burn, and the child will pull away quickly from the heat source. These burns tend to be on an area not covered by clothing. Abusive cigarette burns tend to be hidden under clothing and cause a deep partial to full thickness burn. A typical cigarette burn is five to ten millimeters in circumference with sharply devinded margins. A cigarette burn

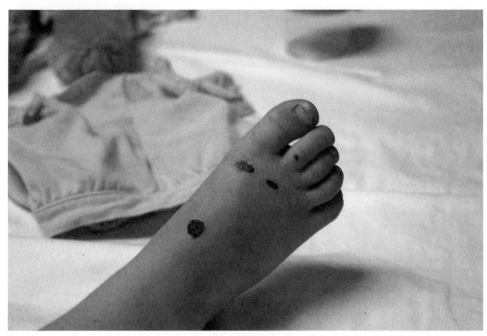

Report of a 4-year-old female that had stepped on a cigarette causing a burn. This is why initial histories are so important. The story has not been thought through, and definitely not likely that this injury was accidental.

has a more crater-like appearance than normal burns. If untreated, scarring will likely result in the area.

Flame Burns

Flame burns in the pediatric population most commonly occur during house fires. Residential fires are a leading cause of death in the pediatric population. Flame burns can also be caused by an abusive act such as holding a flame to the child's body, causing a burn, or igniting the clothing worn by the child.

Chemical Burns

Chemical burns are a less common form of pediatric burns, ranging from 2 to 10 percent, depending on the source. Chemical burns result from a corrosive agent coming in contact with the skin. The most common agents are acid and/or alkali base. With chemical burns, the tissue damage will occur until the corrosive agent is properly removed. Pain may not occur immediately, but as the tissue is damaged, pain will develop.

Acid exposure releases hydrogen ions and produces coagulation necrosis, resulting in eschar formation limiting the depth of the burn, with the exception of hydrofluoric acid which has a similar reaction as alkali products. Alkali substances joins with protons and lipids to form soluble complexes that allow

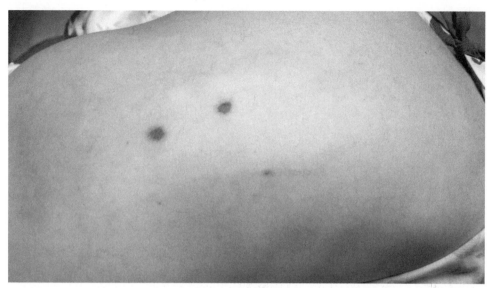

5-year-old with cigarette burns to the back. Note the crater-like appearance of the burn.

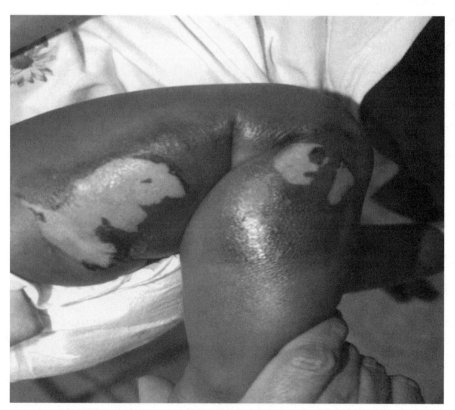

14-month-old child with unknown trauma. Presents with a contact burn. When investigators went to the scene, an iron was collected that matched the exact size of the contact burn on the child.

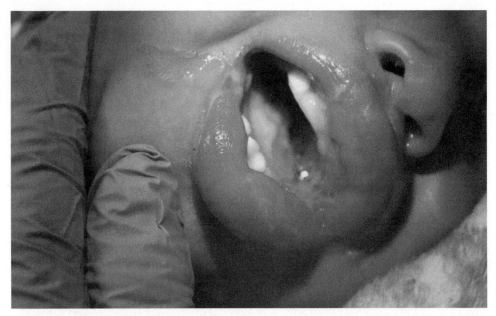

18-month-old female that was reported to have bit an electrical cord. This story was disproved and the investigative team was suspicious that a chemical had been poured in the mouth. By the time the investigators got to the house, no household chemical agents could be found

Table 2.3

Acid	Industrial Use	Domestic Use
Hydrofluoric acid	Glass etching, microchip manufacturing, germicides, dye, fireproofing material	Rust remover, chrome wheel cleaner
Carbolic acid	Synthetic manufacturing	Chemical peels, pharmaceuticals
Sulfuric and hydrochloric acid	Refining and manufacturing reagent	Drain decloggers, toilet bowl cleaners
Nitric acid	Iron/steel casting, electroplating, fertilizer manufacturing and engraving	Engraving, dishwasher detergent
Acetic acid	Solvent	Hair wave neutralizer
Formic acid	Acrylate glue manufacturing, tanning	Tanning, glue
Oxalic acid	Leather tanning, blueprint paper	Leather tanning, blueprint paper
Alkali	**Industrial Use**	**Domestic Use**
Bleach	Disinfectant	Cleaning
Anhydrous ammonia	Fertilizer	Fertilizer
Cement (calcium oxide)	Construction	Construction
Lye (sodium hydroxide)	Manufacturing soaps, petroleum, paper and metal processing	Drain and oven cleaners, paint remover
Lime	Agriculture, cement	Agriculture, cement

Adapted from Aaron Monseau, Z. Reed, K. Langley, and C. Onk, "Sunburn, Thermal and Chemical Injuries to the Skin," *Primary Care: Clinics in Office Practice* 42 (2015): 591–605.

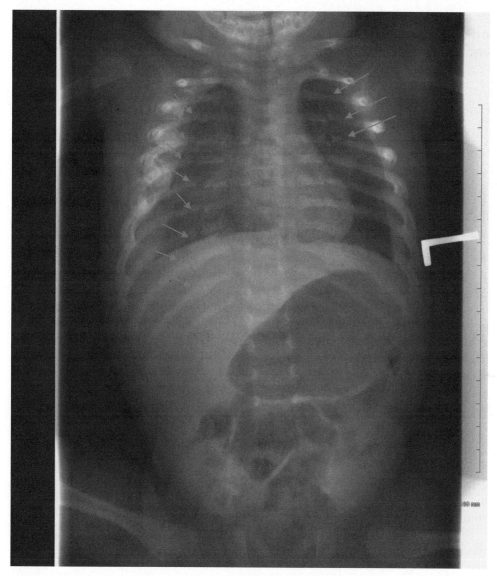

Remember when evaluating injuries, that the angle of the object used can greatly change the look of the injury.

deeper penetration of the substances into the skin. You will see more extensive burns from alkali substances.[28]

Electrical Burns

Electrical burns account for only 2 to 3 percent of burns in children. Most of the electrical burns that are treated in the hospital are from a household accident. The most common forms of unintentional electrical burns are from children touching an exposed electrical cord or from biting the cord. On rare occasions an electrical burn may come from inserting an object into an outlet. While this type of burn is rare and not typically an abusive-type burn, consideration should be given to caregiver neglect in regard to lack of supervision.

Other Burns

Friction Burns

These burns occur when something is dragged or pulled across the skin such as a rope or carpet. Typically, this type of burn will affect the bony prominences.

Microwave Burns

There are a few case-specific examples in which children were placed in the microwave and sustained full thickness burns. Microwave burns are a radiation-type burn that is thermal in nature to the living tissue and produces severe burns to the skin.

Frostbite

Frostbite is another form of a thermal injury to the tissue. Frostbite occurs when tissue is exposed to temperatures that are less than the freezing point of intact skin. The severity of frostbite is determined by the duration of the exposure, temperature gradient at the surface of the skin, wind chill, and clothing that is worn. The most common areas to become frostbit are fingers, toes, ears, and the nose. The longer the exposure to the freezing temperatures, the greater the damage to the tissue.[29]

Ultraviolet Radiation

The most common type of burn in this category is a sunburn. This type of burn is from prolonged exposure to the sun without proper sunscreen or shade. This burn is typically unintentional but can be intentional. Sunburn especially on younger children could be viewed as a form of neglect.

Medical Perspective

Throughout the chapter, burns are discussed as being a common accidental form of injury. While it is most often accidental, when it is not, many times the burn is a sentinel event for abuse. Most of the time children that are suffering an abusive type of burn will have additional injuries on them, such as bruises or fractures. A child that presents with burns to the feet, buttocks, back, and perineum area at high risk of suffering from non-accidental trauma.

When obtaining a history of the event, some questions to consider are the following:

1. What was happening just before the burn occurred?
2. What is the location where the burn took place? (at home, in the kitchen)
3. Describe what happened when the child was burned.

4. What clothing was the child wearing?
5. What is the burn source?
6. How long was the exposure and what temperature?
7. What first aid was rendered?
8. What was the initial appearance of the burn?
9. Severity of the burn? (body surface area and depth)
10. What was the time of injury? What is the time in which medical care was sought?
11. Does the caregiver also have burns?

When assessing these children, begin with the airway, breathing, circulation (ABCs); assess the extent of the burn; and then complete a head-to-toe assessment.

Remember a burned child aged two and under still should have a skeletal survey completed, as any other child with concerning injuries.

Skeletal Injuries

The second most common injury to children in non-accidental trauma is fractures. Just like skin injuries, fractures are also a common accidental injury. As medical providers and investigating agencies the first priority is treatment of the injury but as that occurs it is necessary to know the manner in which the injury occurred. It is difficult to be able to determine at times if the injury is accidental or non-accidental; about 20 percent of children that receive medical treatment for abusive fractures are not identified and are sent back to the dangerous environment.

The chief complaint for fractures from abuse is not *hey, I just threw my child across the room, and now he is not moving his leg.* The fact is, children that present with fractures from abuse are normally infants and toddlers, so a history cannot be obtained from them. The caregiver's most frequent stories are that the child is not moving their arm or leg, or they have been crying more than normal. To make it even more complicated, many times infants do not have bruising at the fracture site to alert the medical providers of an injury. A careful history and physical assessment are necessary.

When evaluating the fracture, a full description of how the incident occurred is helpful while considering the growth and developmental level of the child. Compare it all to the type of fracture that is diagnosed. In determining if the story makes sense, ask these questions for each child with a fracture, so it is standardized and the provider can remain objective.

- Who: Who was with the child at the time the event occurred? Who was caring for the child? What other adults were present? What other children were present? What are the ages of the other adults and children? Who is giving the history to the medical provider? Is that the same person that was present when the event occurred? Is that person able to answer additional questions about the event? (If a lie has been developed, it is difficult for the historian and other adults present to keep the story from changing.)

- What: What happened or what did you notice? What did the child fall from? What type of surface did the child fall onto? What position was the child in when you found them?
- When: When did the event happen? When did you notice something was abnormal? This allows the provider to note if there has been a delay in care. This is especially important with dislocated fractures that may have negative consequences in the healing of the injury with a delay of care.
- Where: Where did the event take place? Please note if the location changes as the story is repeated.
- How: How did the child act directly after the event took place? What did the child do? (Is the story that the child fell off the bed and walked to the kitchen when the child has a displaced femur fracture? This would not be possible.)
- Why did you seek medical care? In accidental trauma, the obvious answer would be concern for the child. Many times, in non-accidental trauma, the caregiver involves another adult and that person insists that the child receive medical care: *I called my aunt, who is a nurse . . . she came over to the house and said you need to take that baby to the hospital.*

The story is documented, so what type of fracture is present?

1. What bone is involved?
2. What type of fracture? (greenstick, spiral, etc.)
3. Is the fracture displaced?
4. Is the fracture acute or healing?
5. Are there other fractures that do not coincide with the event reported?

Research supports that abusive fractures will typically occur in infants and toddlers. In children younger than one year old the most common fractures noted are skull fractures and extremity fractures. Of the extremity fractures, femurs are the most common area of injury and humerus fractures are the second most common. In this same age group 17 percent of infants with skull fractures were from abuse; 30 percent of femur fractures in infants were from abuse; and 43 percent of humerus fractures in infants were from abuse.[30]

It is important to know the dynamics of fracture types to be able to determine if the fracture is consistent with the story being given. Some common childhood fracture types are listed in the following:

1. Buckle fracture (Torus): Bone deforms but does not crack. It is a stable injury but is painful. Common injury found in children.
2. Comminuted fracture: The bone is fractured into multiple pieces.
3. Greenstick fracture: A bone fractures on one side but not all the way through the bone because the bone can bend. (Think of a forsythia

branch and how it can bend without breaking.) This is a common type of fracture in children.

4. Nursemaid elbow: When two of the three bones forming the elbow joint are disrupted. This is a common injury in preschool children.
5. Oblique fracture: A fracture that is diagonal to the long axis of the bone.
6. Spiral fracture: A fracture in which at least one part of the bone has been twisted.
7. Transverse fracture: A bone breaks at a right angle to the long axis of the bone.

Accidental injuries can cause fractures to the same bones as non-accidental injuries. There are some bones, however, that are considered highly suspicious for abuse as they are more difficult to injure from an accidental mechanism. Red flag fractures for abuse include:

- Metaphyseal fractures
- Rib fractures
- Scapular fractures
- Sternal fractures
- Pelvis fractures.

Interpretation of the x-rays can be a challenge, especially in young children. Factors that can mimic fractures include the following:

1. Accessory ossicles are normal skeletal variants of the foot and ankle. Accessory ossicles are typically asymptomatic but can become painful with fractures and dislocations. Accessory ossicles can simulate a fracture and cause a decrease in range of motion, which can be confusing and cause a false interpretation of a fracture on x-ray.[31] These can be distinguished from a fracture from the smooth, well-corticated (hard outer layer) of the bone.[32]
2. Growth plates (physis) or unfused apophyses in children have an irregular appearance that can mimic fractures.
3. Nutrient artery foramen are present on one side of the bone. The nutrient artery is located in a tunnel within the cortex of long bones. The nutrient arteries contribute to the blood supply of the bone. The foramen will run in an angle that can mimic an oblique fracture.

Physical abuse should be considered as a differential diagnosis for children with fractures in the following situations:

1. Fractures in non-ambulatory infants (especially without a clear description of the trauma that caused the injury and/or the child does not have a medical condition that predisposes them to fragile bones)
2. Children with multiple fractures
3. Children with multiple fractures in multiple stages of healing

4. Infants and children with rib fractures
5. Infants and children with humerus or femur fractures
6. Infants and children with unusual fractures such as scapula, classic metaphyseal lesions of the long bones, vertebrae, and sternum
7. History of the trauma does not explain the fracture type.[33]

Skull Fractures

Skull fractures are the most common type of fracture in children younger than two years old, with 30 percent of these fractures being attributed to abuse.[34] Fractures can be accidental from a short fall or non-accidental. Short falls typically attributed to linear skull fractures in infants/toddlers are from a distance of about three to six feet. Types of falls reported are typically from incidents with highchairs, changing tables, shopping carts, and countertops. A linear fracture to the parietal scalp is the most common skull fracture for both accidental and non-accidental injuries. Skull fractures that are complex or bilateral should cause an increase in suspicion for non-accidental trauma.

Skull fracture terminology is as follows:

- Linear: Thin break in the skull that does not cause the bone to move. Most common type of skull fracture. Also can be called simple or single.
- Diastatic: A fracture that occurs along the suture line of the skull. Typically seen in children younger than three years old.
- Depressed: Fracture to the skull in which the broken bone is displaced inward.
- Basilar: Fracture at the base of the skull.
- Stellate: Fracture to the skull that results in multiple linear fractures radiating from the impact site.
- Simple: Linear parietal fracture
- Complex: All other skull fractures that include multiple, depressed, basilar, stellate, compound, and comminuted fractures.

When the injury is from abuse, many times a traumatic story is not given. The child will typically present with head swelling or vomiting. Once a fracture is identified, the caregiver may develop a story at that time. It is important to understand if the story is consistent with the injury. The cause of most simple fractures in children is from a fall; however, the most common story from a caregiver due to non-accidental trauma is also that of a fall.

Neck Injury and Spinal Cord Fractures

Spinal cord trauma from non-accidental methods is still in the baby stages of research and has been considered an uncommon injury in child abuse. In the past, spinal cord injuries in children are more often attributed to accidents such as motor vehicle or car versus pedestrian situations. Research suggests that only 2 to 3 percent of fractures to children are to the spine, with the most common spinal cord injury being related to the cervical spine. The incidence of cervical spine injuries is more common in children younger than five years old or over the age of ten.[35]

Children with inflicted trauma to the spinal cord typically will present as a multi-system trauma with complaints from respiratory distress and/or decreased level of consciousness, making it difficult to recognize that the spinous process may by injured. Younger children will present with injuries more likely to the upper spine and have a higher risk of death than the older children. As research is developing, it is becoming more apparent that inflicted trauma is a more common cause of cervical spine and/or spinal cord injuries than what was originally reported.[36] The injuries suffered are more likely injuries related to the ligaments which will not be identified in the radiological imaging. Studies suggest that 1 percent of the children that suffer abusive head trauma will have a co-existing trauma to the spinal cord. It is estimated that between 1 and 3 percent of abusive fractures are to the vertebrae.[37]

Textbox 2.1.   Imaging Considerations for Spinal Cord Injuries

1.   Complete skeletal survey
2.   Dedicated spine films (if injury is detected)
3.   Computed tomography scan
4.   Magnetic resonance imaging of entire spine

In order to understand the unique injuries to the spinal cord of a child, it is important to understand the anatomy of the neck and spinal cord and compare the anatomy of a child to that of an adult. The spinal column of the neck consists of seven vertebrae. The vertebrae have a cylindrical body that surrounds a canal in which the spinal cord lies. The fulcrum of cervical flexion in an infant is at the level of C2-3, compared to that of children older than twelve years through adulthood, which is at the level of C5-6.[38]

The infant spine is more elastic than an adult spine. The makeup of the infant spine is more cartilage and ligaments, which creates greater flexibility to the spinal column but not to the spinal cord itself. The facet joints of the spine are more horizontal, which allows for greater motion between the vertebrae.[39] This flexibility decreases the possibility of a cervical fracture with hyperflexion or extension of the spinal column; however, the spinal cord is unable to stretch with the spinal column, causing injury. This injury is not visible by radiographic imaging in patients up to eight years old, which is referred to as SCIWORA (spinal cord injury without radiographic abnormality).[40] Additional injuries that can be noted are spinal cord swelling, contusions, lacerations, and axonal injuries to the cervical spine. The infant is at greater risk for these types of injury due to the anatomical nature of infants with the larger head and low muscle tone of the neck.

Additional neurological signs and symptoms that a child may present with include:

1. Coma
2. Seizures
3. Lethargy
4. Neck rigidity
5. Limp, hypotonic extremities
6. Leg pain on flexion.

Fractures to the thoracolumbar spinal column in non-accidental trauma is less common in young children. The most common complaint on presentation to the emergency department is lethargy or difficulty with crawling or walking. Additionally, on assessment, the child may have tenderness at the point of injury and ecchymosis. With thoracolumbar fractures, the pediatric population has a greater propensity to recover without neurologic deficits than the adult population.

When children present with spinal column injuries, it is typically in conjunction with other injuries as well. A detailed neurological assessment is important.

Rib Fractures

Rib fractures in children younger than three years old are rare to occur accidentally and are more likely from non-accidental trauma. In older children, rib fractures may be seen with a history of trauma such as a motor vehicle collision or car versus pedestrian accident.

Children present with various complaints such as difficulty breathing, fussiness, altered mental status, or not acting right. A head-to-toe assessment is performed and imaging is completed such as a chest x-ray or skeletal survey, which is how the rib fractures are typically identified. Most of the time, when young children have rib fractures, trauma is not in the initial complaint. No story of trauma may be given. The caregiver may want to convince the medical professional that the rib fracture may have occurred through the birthing process or from a history of cardiopulmonary resuscitation being performed. Multiple studies have been completed on birth trauma causing rib fractures and found that rib fractures due to birth trauma are very rare; it is helpful to obtain medical records regarding the birth in an effort to identify if complications had occurred.[41]

Maguire et al. completed a study of 923 infants in which cardiopulmonary resuscitation had been performed; of all of these cases only three of these children sustained rib fractures.[42] Multiple research studies have been able to dispel these excuses. Infants do not fracture easily; without having some type of bone disease to make the bones more fragile, the likely cause for the rib fractures is in fact non-accidental trauma.

The placement of the rib fracture is also important, especially if a story is given describing the trauma. Rib fractures that occur in the posterior or lateral positions require an anterior-posterior compression force. Circumferential compression causes a levered force applied to the rib and vertebral body. Rib fractures related to child abuse are often posterior rib fractures and bilateral. When a young child presents with posterior rib fractures, additional injuries need to be considered such as abusive head trauma. It is important to note that acute rib fractures may be difficult to view upon initial presentation. Consideration should be given to repeat a chest x-ray in one to two weeks to assess for callus formation to the ribs to confirm rib fractures.

Scapular Fractures

Scapular fractures are rare and when seen they are associated with significant trauma such as motor vehicle collisions. Therefore, scapular injuries in children are rare, and there is little supporting research regarding these fractures. Reasons given by Kaczor and Pierce regarding the rare incidence of scapular fractures are due to the protective nature of the surrounding anatomy, including the ribs and soft tissue. The second reason is that that scapula is a more mobile-type bone, therefore decreasing the likelihood of a fracture.[43] Thompson et al. report that scapular fractures are from a blunt force. Those that do sustain scapular fractures also average 3.9 additional major injuries. With the additional trauma that presents along with scapular fractures, it is not unusual to have a delay in the diagnosis of this fracture.[44]

Extremity Fractures

Fractures to the upper extremities compound the majority of fractures in children. Most of the time, these fractures are from accidental causes such as falls or motor vehicle collisions, but they can also be caused by non-accidental trauma. Humeral and femur fractures are the second most common fracture site caused by abuse.[45]

Upper Extremity Fractures

Humeral fractures are the most common extremity fracture in a child with the trauma history of a fall. The humerus is also the most common bone injured in children from abuse. These types of fractures are more commonly seen in children aged six to thirteen. In multiple studies, however, it has been noted that the presence of humeral fractures in children younger than two is a red flag for abuse.[46]

Supracondylar fractures are a form of humeral/elbow fracture common to children four and older. The mechanism of injury for this type of fracture is from falling onto an outstretched arm. The outstretched arm tends to be the non-dominant arm of the child. This type of fracture is commonly seen with a history of playing on the playground and falling off an object like monkey bars.

Nursemaid's elbow: The annular ligament is what secures the radial head to the ulna. In children younger than five years old, this ligament is only loosely attached to the radius. With extension of the arm and forced pronation of the elbow, the annular ligament will slip over the radial head causing it to be entrapped within the radiocapitellar joint. This is a common injury seen in young children and is typically an accidental injury. The common mechanism is lifting a child by the wrist.[47]

The child will complain of pain and will not want to move the arm. With a history given to coincide with the mechanism of injury and the physical symptoms to support this injury, a radiograph is not necessary. Two common maneuvers are used to reduce the nursemaid's elbow. The first is supination with flexion and the second is supination with extension.[48] When the ligament has been successfully reduced, the child should have immediate relief and return to baseline.

Radius/ulnar fractures: Radial and ulnar fractures are common childhood fractures. The fractures to the lower arm generally are obtained from an outstretched arm during a fall. These fractures can also occur from some form of blunt force trauma. I have seen many children that have climbed on a dresser using the drawers as steps; the dresser will have an object such as a television and become off center, falling on the child and causing a transverse fracture to the lower arm. A child that is hit with an object on the arm can also cause a transverse fracture (also known as a nightstick injury) that is from abuse. It is difficult to try to differentiate between the history and the injury sometimes to determine accidental versus non-accidental.

Forearm fractures are, however, uncommon in young children and rare in infants because they do not have the ability to offset the loading conditions that are required to fracture the arm.

Hand fractures are considered an uncommon finding in children, especially young children from infancy to about two. It is suggested, however, that these fractures may be more common than realized and are highly suspicious for abuse in the younger population. The fractures can be easily missed from poor quality x-rays or lack of obtaining x-rays of the hands.[49] As a child gets older, hand fractures may be more prevalent in household accidents and sports-related injuries.

Some research supports removing hand x-rays from the skeletal survey to decrease radiation exposure. Lindberg et al. reviewed 2,049 skeletal surveys and recognized that hand, foot, pelvis, and spinal injuries are not as uncommon as originally thought. As these areas are relatively specific to abuse injuries, it is suggested that when evaluating children for abuse, x-rays are completed on the hands as part of the skeletal survey.[50]

Lower Extremity Fractures

Femur Fractures

The femur is the thigh bone in the leg and considered the largest bone in the body. This fracture is one of the most frequent seen in pediatric admissions. The exact amount of force necessary to fracture the femur is not known; in children both high and low velocity can cause the fracture. However, it would be considered rare for a non-ambulatory infant to have a femur fracture without a good history. As the child becomes an adolescent, and the bone has fully formed, high-velocity trauma is necessary to cause a fracture. High-velocity trauma is considered motor vehicle accidents, car versus pedestrian accidents, falls, and child abuse.

Researchers are trying to differentiate abusive femur fractures versus non-abusive fractures. Several years ago, when I (A. Rasmussen) began practicing, it was believed that a spiral femur fracture in a young child was always abuse. Now it is understood that with the right twisting motion, a child may accidentally fracture the femur. In the case of a young child, the velocity does not have to be that high. Once believed to be classic abuse, this has been disproven.

Example 1: A three-year-old girl was twirling and playing on the living room floor. The floor had just been mopped. The girl jumped from the couch and landed on the wet floor as she was twirling, causing her to twist and fall, fracturing her femur.

Example 2: A four-year-old male was running outside playing football with his older cousins. As the child was running, he stepped in a hole. His body continued to go forward, but his leg stayed in the hole causing his leg to twist and the child to fall.

Both are plausible stories as to how this injury could occur.

When evaluating children with femur fractures, you always have to go back to the basics. Is the child ambulatory? If not, it is a high risk for abuse. What is the history given with the injury? Does the fracture type fit the history? What stage of growth and development is the child? Does the child have the physical ability to carry out the act that matches the story? Are there any medical conditions that can explain how the fracture could have occurred? These observations and a thorough history are the best and really only way to determine a suspicion of abuse. When analyzing the data, remember that a delay in suspicion or delay in report equals a delay in a multi-disciplinary process to come together and protect the child, causing a potential for greater harm to the child.

Tibia/Fibula Fractures

The lower leg, including the tibia and the fibula, are the third most common pediatric long bone fractures. Like the femur fracture, even though these bones are a common injury, it would be considered as a highly suspicious type of injury for children that are non-ambulatory. By the age range of nine months to around three years old, it is common for a child to have a toddler's fracture with little to no history of trauma.

In 1964, Dunbar described a toddler's fracture as an oblique, nondisplaced fracture of the distal one-third of the tibia; now the proximal and mid tibia are also included.[51] The most common complaint for this type of fracture is the caregiver noticed the child was not using the leg. Like all the other fractures, while a toddler's fracture is a common accidental injury, it can also be caused from an abusive act such as grabbing, yanking, or twisting the lower leg.

Foot Fractures

Injuries to the feet are uncommon in children. Fractures that do occur typically occur in the older children. The metatarsal is the most likely area to be injured. Without a good history, a child with a fracture to the foot is highly suspicious for abuse.

As with hands, some research supports removing foot x-rays from the skeletal survey to decrease radiation exposure. In their review of 2,049 skeletal surveys, Lindberg et al. found that hand, feet, pelvis, and spinal injuries are not as uncommon as originally thought. Because these areas are relatively specific to abuse injuries, it is suggested that, when evaluating children for abuse, x-rays are completed on the feet as part of the skeletal survey.[52]

Classic Metaphyseal Lesions

The classic metaphyseal lesion (CML-)type injury is highly specific for infant abuse and the most common fracture type found in fatal abuse cases. CML fracture "involves disruption of the primary spongiosa and calcified cartilage core at the metaphysis of long bones, the site where maximum bone growth and turnover is occurring."[53] CMLs may occur along the ends of any long bone of the extremities; the distal tibia is the most common site, followed by the proximal tibia and the distal femur.[54]

This injury is consistent with the flailing of the limbs back and forth, causing a disc-shaped fragment to the bone. This fracture is identified on x-ray as a corner fracture or a bucket handle fracture. As classic a sign as this injury is for abuse, it is also a more difficult fracture to interpret by x-ray and can be missed. This fracture is highly associated with abusive head trauma.

Standard of Care

When a child presents with an injury, it is appropriate to get an x-ray of an isolated complaint. If the child is younger than the age of two and has a fracture and there is a suspicion of abuse, it is recommended by the American Academy of Pediatrics to obtain a skeletal survey of that child.[55] If a child is older than the age of two, it should be up to the clinical judgment of the provider.

Abusive Head Trauma

Head trauma is the leading cause of child physical abuse fatalities; the children that do survive often have neurological deficits. The Centers for Disease Control and Prevention defines pediatric abusive head trauma as an injury to the skull or intracranial contents of an infant or young child (younger than the age of five) due to inflicted blunt force impact and/or shaking.[56] The description of abusive head trauma has replaced the term shaken baby syndrome, therefore allowing a more global view of the injuries a child could sustain. Crying is believed to be a trigger for this injury. Children younger than one year old are the highest risk group. This is a lifetime injury of a surviving child that not only affects the child, but the people around them.

Head trauma in infants and toddlers can be difficult to diagnose. Children can present with vague symptoms such as vomiting, irritability, and lethargy—symptoms most children present with when they have a virus. When the caregiver does not give a history of trauma, the provider would not suspect abusive head trauma. With the radiation concerns of performing x-rays or computed tomography scans, these children would not warrant exposure. They are diagnosed with a generic diagnosis such as a virus and sent home, perhaps with the abuser. Population studies suggest that twenty-five to thirty children out of one hundred thousand under the age of one suffer from abusive head trauma. This number can only be viewed as skewed and greatly underrepresented due to underdiagnosis or missed diagnosis of these children.[57]

Mechanism of Injury

1. Impulsive loading, which is nonimpact forces that are generated by acceleration and deceleration of the cranial vault. Impulse loading causes shearing forces to the brain and meninges.
2. Impact loading is the direct application of force to the head. Impact loading corresponds with injuries such as skull fractures and parenchymal contusions with associated focal extra-axial and subperiosteal hemorrhages.[58]

CASE STUDY #3

A three-month-old boy was home alone with his mother's boyfriend. The boyfriend was playing video games and the little boy began to cry. The boyfriend was angry that the child interrupted his video game and shook the boy (impulsive loading) and threw him up against the wall (impact loading), causing multiple bleeds to his brain. When asked if the child had done anything different that day, the boyfriend stated yes, he pooped when he does not normally poop.

Red flags with history:

1. Inconsistent history is given; story is changing and/or evolving.
2. The history does not match the severity of the injury.
3. The history does not match the growth and development level of the child.

The head in an infant is not fully matured. It is an unmyelinated baby brain, the skull is more flexible with larger fontanels, the sutures are more pliable, and they have weak neck muscles that are unable to support the head; this sets the infant up to a poorer outcome after being shaken. The most common injury seen with abusive head trauma is subdural hematomas; however, the pediatric brain can have subdural hematomas from accidental trauma, so it is not pathognomonic for abuse. Subdural hematomas in conjunction with retinal hemorrhages does increase the suspicion for abuse. Other injuries that may be noted with abusive head trauma are posterior/lateral rib fractures, spinal cord injury from hyperextension and flexion, and CML injuries.

Traumatic Brain Injuries

Cortical contusion is an impact injury to the cerebral cortex. This injury often will extend deeper into the adjacent subcortical white matter. The implication for this injury is due to trauma; it would be expected to see additional signs of injury such as a skull fracture or contusions. Impact injuries that will cause cortical injuries in the adult or older child will likely cause an axonal injury in the immature brain.[59] It would be unusual to see cortical contusions in an infant.

Brain swelling (edema) occurs more often in children than adults. Research suggests that as many as 65 percent of children with abusive head trauma have signs of brain swelling. "Cerebral autoregulation is impaired in these severely injured children and this may lead to hyperemic brain swelling and intracranial hypertension."[60] Brain swelling can cause additional complications to the primary injury. As the brain swells, intercranial pressures rise, which impairs cerebral perfusion. With poor cerebral perfusion, the brain can become ischemic (lack of oxygen to the brain). As the secondary factors worsen, the brain may herniate into the brain stem, causing death.

Subdural hematoma is considered the cardinal cranial injury in abusive head trauma. While this injury is common, it also can be present for accidental injuries as well. When evaluating a child for potential abuse, other factors, such as retinal hemorrhages, corner fractures, rib fractures, head-to-toe assessment with documentation of any trauma, statements made from the caregivers, and the child's growth and development stage, need to be reviewed.

The subdural area is between the dura and the arachnoid space. The subdural space sits under the skull outside of the brain. Subdural hematoma is the rupture of one or more of the bridging veins that runs from the cerebral cortex to the venous sinus. As the blood accumulates, pressure is placed on the brain. The mechanism is extreme angulation with acceleration and deceleration forces, with or without impaction. Subdural hematomas can develop from shaking as well as from a motor vehicle accident. It is unlikely that a short fall will cause this severe of an injury. Research conducted to determine the likelihood of a subdural hematoma in an accidental injury versus a non-accidental injury shows that only 7 percent of accidental head injuries resulted in a subdural hematoma; 80 percent of that population was from a motor vehicle collision. In contrast, 69 percent of children with inflicted head injuries were diagnosed with subdural hematoma.[61]

Subarachnoid hemorrhage: The subarachnoid space is the fluid-filled space below the arachnoid membrane and the pia mater. Blood vessels run through this space and are subject to the tearing of the cortical veins. Subarachnoid hemorrhages many times occur in conjunction with subdural hematomas.

Epidural hematoma: The epidural space is located between the dura mater and the vertebral wall. Epidural hematoma is the accumulation of blood between the skull and the stripped dura membrane. Epidural hematomas are usually from an arterial bleed, unlike the subdural hematoma which is venous. Epidural hematomas are a less common injury with abusive head trauma than subdural hematomas and subarachnoid hemorrhages.

The cause of an epidural hematoma is a linear impact to the calvarium that directly lacerates a vessel or the dura. A skull fracture is usually associated with this type of injury. In infants, a parietal epidural hematoma from a laceration to the middle meningeal artery can expand rapidly. A venous epidural hematoma from the laceration of the superior sagittal or transverse dural sinus does not expand as rapidly and will typically tamponade itself.[62]

Associated Injuries

Retinal hemorrhages are often found in infants that suffer abusive head trauma. While retinal hemorrhages are strongly associated with abusive trauma, other factors can cause them, so they cannot be exclusively associated with abusive head trauma. In examining the retinas of fatal abusive head trauma cases, 85 to 100 percent had retinal hemorrhages.[63]

Anatomy of the eye:

1. Sclera is the outermost component of the eyeball. This is a firm layer of connective tissue that attaches to the extraocular muscles. This is the white part of the eye that you can see.
2. Choroid (uveal tract). This is the next layer going into the eye. This layer is highly vascularized and supplies blood to the outer retinal layers. This layer also regulates the temperature of the eyeball.
3. Retina. This is the innermost layer of the eye. The vitreous humor is located within this area and stabilizes the retina from detachment. The retina itself has ten additional layers.[64]

Types of retinal hemorrhages:

1. Preretinal: lies on the retina
2. Intraretinal: lies within the layers of the retina
3. Subretinal: lies under the neurosensory retina.

With the high association between retinal hemorrhages and abusive head trauma, an ophthalmological consult should be done within the first twenty-four hours of presentation, but no later than seventy-two hours. Retinal hemorrhages can heal quickly—some within days, some may take one or two weeks. Therefore, the sooner an ophthalmologist can document these injuries, the better.

Hansen et al. examined the difference in the appearance of retinal hemorrhages from accidental trauma, medical illnesses, and abusive head trauma. In non-abusive cases of retinal hemorrhages, there is usually only one hemorrhage at one layer of the retina. What was identified is that two-thirds of infants with abusive head trauma have severe retinal hemorrhages that were bilateral, in multiple layers of the retina, and too numerous to count.[65]

Differential diagnosis for retinal hemorrhages:

1. Birth trauma: Most common cause of retinal hemorrhage. Typically will resolve within a few weeks.

2. Coagulation disorders.
3. Sepsis.
4. Increased intracranial pressure.
5. Accidental head injury: A total of 3 to 5 percent of these children have retinal hemorrhages associated with a blunt impact such as a fall. Retinal hemorrhages are usually few in number and unilateral.
6. Meningitis.
7. Leukemia.
8. Vasculitis.

Most of the differential diagnoses can be ruled in or out with a good history and medical evaluation that includes bloodwork.

Rib fractures: Refer to section on rib fractures.

CMLs: Refer to section on CMLs.

Thoracic Injuries

Most thoracic injuries in children are due to blows or a crush injury. Abusive injuries involving the heart are rare. Pulmonary injuries that include contusions, lacerations resulting in a pneumothorax, hemorrhagic effusions or pneumomediastinum, and pulmonary edema have been documented in children with head trauma or suffocation.[66] Rib fractures are strongly associated with abuse but are usually found incidentally when evaluating the child for other injuries. Rib fractures from abuse occur most often from squeezing the chest, as seen in abusive head trauma. Rib fractures can be multiple and unilateral or bilateral. These fractures are difficult to interpret when they are acute. If suspicion is high for rib fractures, the child should be scheduled for a repeat x-ray in two to three weeks, at that time callus formation will have developed and allow for a more accurate interpretation of findings for rib fractures.

Abdominal Injuries

Abdominal injuries are the second cause of death behind head injuries, with motor vehicle collisions being the most common cause in children older than two. Abuse is the most common cause of death in children under the age of two. Diagnosis can be difficult and easily missed in these children. The history of the presenting complaint is not usually an accurate history of the trauma. A total of 80 percent of the children that present with abdominal trauma do not have any type of external injuries noted. If you think about bruising, a bony prominence is needed—the bony prominence for the abdomen is the spinal column. An excellent physical exam is warranted, noting any distention and rigidity in the abdomen. In cases in which abuse is suspected, the provider should draw preliminary labs to assess for potential abdominal trauma.

Children have less musculature to the abdomen and thinner abdominal walls. The diaphragm sits more horizontally than it does in adults. The liver and spleen are situated more anteriorly than in adults and not protected by the ribcage. The ribs are more pliable and compressive and can cause injury to the solid organs beneath them. All abdominal contents are subject to injury in abusive trauma. Liver and small bowel are the most frequently injured organs. Morbidity and mortality are greater in children admitted for abusive abdominal injuries than for children that present from accidental trauma due to a delay in treatment or misdiagnosis.

Liver trauma: The liver is the most common solid organ injured in inflicted abdominal trauma. The left lobe is the most common area of injury in abusive trauma because the mechanism (hit or punch) is more centrally located, versus a more lateral mechanism in accidental traumas. Liver injuries range from small lacerations, contusions, subcapsular hematomas, and large lacerations. These injuries are graded by severity from Grade 1 to Grade VI, with Grade VI being the most severe. Most injuries are treated non-operatively.

Pancreas trauma: The pancreas is not frequently injured in inflicted abdominal trauma due to bowel overlay. When the pancreas is injured, it is typically associated with hepatic injuries and/or duodenal injuries. Lacerations of the pancreas can be complicated by pseudocyst formations.[67] Pseudocysts can develop from inflammation caused by trauma and can be problematic if they rupture.

Adrenal hemorrhage: The adrenal gland is protected in the abdominal cavity and is rarely injured. Direct blunt trauma can damage the adrenal gland causing hemorrhaging. This finding is not a primary complaint and is found during diagnostic testing as an incidental injury.

Splenic trauma: The spleen is also protected in the abdominal cavity and is not seen as commonly in inflicted trauma. Splenic injuries are more common with a history given of a fall. The spleen is graded on severity from Grade I to Grade V, with Grade V being the most severe. Typically, this will be treated non-operatively.

Hollow viscus trauma: Hollow viscus injuries are more commonly seen with inflicted abdominal trauma than in accidental trauma. The duodenum and proximal jejunum are the most frequently injured due to the location near the spinal column. Types of injuries that are noted range from hematomas to perforations and transections.[68]

PROVIDER ROLE

Step 1: History

- Interview parent/caregivers separately.
- Allow the parent/caregiver to provide a history without interruption when able.
- Document the history in quotations.
- Ask additional questions:
  - Where did the event occur?
  - When did the event take place? (time and date)
  - Who was present at the time of the injury? Is that person present at the hospital?
  - What treatment has been rendered prior to medical treatment?

- o Why did you bring the child to the hospital? (especially if there is a time delay)
- o Tell me about the day, prior to this event.
- o What are the child's normal feeding times? How much does the child normally eat?
- o When was the last normal feeding?
- o When was the last time the child was acting completely normal?
- o Did mom have a normal or complicated pregnancy?
- o Was the child born on time, premature, or late?
- Questions to consider medically:
  - o Is the child's development level consistent with the history given?
  - o Is the history given consistent with the injuries sustained?

Step 2: Perform a complete examination with the child fully unclothed. YOU MUST UNDRESS TO ASSESS.

- Document the overall appearance of the child.
- Document all external findings (bruises, lacerations, burns, etc.).
- Document any intraoral lesions; assess the frenulum.
- Assess for subconjunctival hemorrhages.
- Photograph the findings (best done if you have forensic nurses at your facility).
  - o If no forensic nurses, check policy on photographing patients.
  - o Request law enforcement to photograph.

Step 3: Diagnostic workup

- **Labs**
  - o Complete blood count
  - o Basic metabolic profile
  - o Coagulation studies
  - o Hepatic and pancreatic enzymes
  - o Uric acid
  - o Urine drug screen (consider, based on child's presentation)
  - o Alcohol level (consider, based on child's presentation)
- **X-rays and computed tomography scans**
  - o Skeletal survey
    - □ On all children of suspected abuse younger than two years old
    - □ Clinical judgment on children older than two years old
  - o Computed tomography/magnetic resonance imaging of head
  - o Computed tomography of abdomen with contrast enhancement (if abdominal injuries are suspected)

Step 4: Manage acute medical problems

Step 5: Notify child protective services, as mandated in your state. Notification of law enforcement is also mandated in some states. Know your state guidelines.

Step 6: Hospitalize the child if needed

- Hospitalize for further medical workup and treatment.
- Hospitalize for safety purposes, until proper, safe placement of the child can be established by child protective services.

Step 7: Consults

- Forensic nurse examiners (if not already consulted)
- Surgeon (if not already consulted)
- Ophthalmology
- Other

CONCLUSION

Determining child physical abuse can be difficult. It is hard to distinguish between accidental versus non-accidental injuries. Perhaps you can't. Provider might be worried of the ethical implications of accusing someone of abuse that may be innocent. As medical providers, the providers are not the accusers. The providers look, listen, and assess. Providers use clinical judgment to compare what we are seeing to what we are hearing. Most of the children are not able to speak up for themselves. They are either non-verbal or just too scared. Providers have to be confident in saying what is normal and what is not for that child. I heard a wise emergency room doctor say in a lecture that we all have our own graveyards of patients that we have seen. I have my graveyard for sure. When I look back, I have to wonder, did I do all that I could do to save that child? If I answer yes, then great; if I am not sure, then I have work to do. Providers have to be confident in speaking up for those that can't speak up for themselves.

REVIEW QUESTIONS

1. Discuss how to address the question of dating bruises in child abuse cases.

2. Explain the anatomic structure of the infant and toddler that causes them to be more prone to head injury.

3. Discuss the difficulties in identifying head, thoracic, and abdominal injuries in children.

4. Discuss normal areas of injury in a child and why. What signs of "normal injury" would cause suspicion for non-accidental trauma?

KEYWORDS

Corporal punishment: Physical punishment that involves hitting, flogging, etc.

Epidermis: The outer layer of the skin.

Dermis: Layer of tissue that lies just below the epidermis and covers the subcutaneous fat layer.

Bruise: Injury that is transmitted through unbroken skin causing a rupture of small blood vessels. The blood escapes into the tissue and causes discoloration to the skin.

Petechiae: Small pinpoint, round spots that are due to rupturing of blood vessels. Petechial bruising is usually less than three millimeters in size.

Patterned injury: Distinct pattern of injury that reproduces the characteristics of an object that was used to cause the injury.

Contact injury: Thermal injury to the skin secondary to prolonged contact from a hot solid or smoldering source.

NOTES

1. Cindy W. Cristian, "The Evaluation of Suspected Child Physical Abuse," American *Academy of Pediatrics* 135, no. 5 (2015): 1337–54.

2. National Children's Alliance. Accessed September 2018. Available from http://www.nationalchildrensalliance.org/media-room/nca-digital-media-kit/national-statistics-on-child-abuse/.

3. World Health Organization. Accessed September 2018. Available from http://www.who.int/news-room/fact-sheets/detail/chcild-maltreatment.

4. National Children's Alliance. Accessed September 2018. Available from http://www.nationalchildrensalliance.org/media-room/nca-digital-media-kit/national-statistics-on-child-abuse/.

5. Adam J. Zolotor, "Corporal Punishment," *Pediatric Clinics of North America* (2014): 971–78.

6. F.M. Hendriks, D. Brokken, C.W.J. Oomens, D.L. Bader, and F.P.T. Baaijens, "The Relative Contributions of Different Skin Layers to the Mechanical Behavior of Human Skin in Vivo Using Suction Experiments," *Medical Engineering & Physics* 28 (2006): 259–66.

7. Tara L. Harris and Emalee G. Flaherty, "Bruises and Skin Lesions," in Carole Jenny (ed.), *Child Abuse and Neglect Diagnosis, Treatment, and Evidence* (St. Louis: Elsevier Saunders, 2011), 239–51.

8. Hendriks, Brokken, Oomens, Bader, and Baaijens, "The Relative Contributions of Different Skin Layers to the Mechanical Behavior of Human Skin in Vivo Using Suction Experiments."

9. Tomika Harris, "Bruises in Children: Normal or Child Abuse?" *Journal of Pediatric Health Care* 24, no. 4 (2010): 216–21.

10. D. Chapple, "More Than Just a Bruise: Recognizing Child Physical Abuse," *BC Medical Journal* 57, no. 5 (2015): 288–92.

11. Jean Labbé and Georges Caouette, "Recent Skin Injuries in Normal Children" *Pediatrics* 108, no. 2 (2001): 271–76.

12. Hendriks, Brokken, Oomens, Bader, and Baaijens, "The Relative Contributions of Different Skin Layers to the Mechanical Behavior of Human Skin in Vivo Using Suction Experiments."

13. Hendriks, Brokken, Oomens, Bader, and Baaijens, "The Relative Contributions of Different Skin Layers to the Mechanical Behavior of Human Skin in Vivo Using Suction Experiments."

14. James A. Monteleone and Michael Graham, "Identifying, Interpreting, and Reporting Injuries," in Elaine Steinborn (ed.), *Quick-Reference Child Abuse for Healthcare Professionals, Social Services, and Law Enforcement* (St. Louis, MO: G.W. Medical Publishing, Inc., 1998), 144.

15. Sumit Bansal, R. Sahu, and A. Patnaik, "Adult-Onset Subgaleal Hematoma Caused by Hair Pulling: A Rare Occurrence," *Indian Journal of Neurotrauma* 14 (2017): 107–08.

16. World Health Organization. Accessed September 2018. Available from http://www.who.int/news-room/fact-sheets/detail/chcild-maltreatment.

17. Sabine Maguire, C. Okolie, and A. Kemp, "Burns as a Consequence of Child Maltreatment," *Pediatrics & Child Health* 24, no. 12 (2014): 557–61.

18. R. Michael Johnson and R. Richard, "Partial-Thickness Burns: Identification and Management," *Advances in Skin & Wound Care* 16, no. 4 (2003): 178–89.

19. Maguire, Okolie, and Kemp, "Burns as a Consequence of Child Maltreatment."

20. Johnson and Richard, "Partial-Thickness Burns: Identification and Management."

21. Johnson and Richard, "Partial-Thickness Burns: Identification and Management."

22. Johnson and Richard, "Partial-Thickness Burns: Identification and Management."

23. Johnson and Richard, "Partial-Thickness Burns: Identification and Management."

24. Johnson and Richard, "Partial-Thickness Burns: Identification and Management."

25. Johnson and Richard, "Partial-Thickness Burns: Identification and Management."

26. Johnson and Richard, "Partial-Thickness Burns: Identification and Management."

27. Maguire, Okolie, and Kemp, "Burns as a Consequence of Child Maltreatment."

28. Aaron Monseau, Z. Reed, K. Langley, and C. Onk, "Sunburn, Thermal and Chemical Injuries to the Skin," *Primary Care: Clinics in Office Practice* 42 (2015): 591–605.

29. Monseau, Reed, Langley, and Onk, "Sunburn, Thermal and Chemical Injuries to the Skin."

30. Mary C. Pierce, K. Kaczor, D. Lohr, K. Richter, and S.P. Starling, "A Practical Guide to Differentiating Abusive from Accidental Fractures: An Injury Plausibility Approach," *Clinical Pediatric Emergency* 13, no. 3 (2012): 166–77.

31. Niger Keles-Celik, O. Kose, R. Sekerci, G. Aytec, A. Turan, and F. Guler, "Accessory Ossicles of the Foot and Ankle: Disorders and a Review of Literature," *Cureus* 9, no. 11 (2017): 1–18.

32. David T. Schwartz and E. Reisdorff, "Fundamentals of Skeletal Radiology," in John J. Dolan, Susan R. Noujaim, and Peter J. Boyle (eds.), *Emergency Radiology* (New York: McGraw-Hill Companies, 2000), 11–25.

33. Cristian, "The Evaluation of Suspected Child Physical Abuse."

34. Maguire, Okolie, and Kemp, "Burns as a Consequence of Child Maltreatment."

35. James P. Sieradzki and John F. Sarwark, "Thoracolumbar Fracture-Dislocation in Child Abuse: Case Report, Closed Reduction Technique and Review of Literature," *Pediatric Neurosurgery* 44 (2008): 253–57.

36. Joanne Baerg, A. Thirumoorthi, R. Hazboun, R. Vannix, P. Krafft, and A. Zouros, "Cervical Spine Injuries in Young Children: Pattern and Outcomes in Accidental versus Inflicted Trauma," *Journal of Surgical Research* 219 (2017): 366–73.

37. A.M. Kemp, A. Joshi, M. Mann, V. Tempest, A. Liu, S. Holden, and S. Maguire, "What are the Clinical and Radiological Characteristics of Spinal Injuries from Physical Abuse: A Systematic Review," *Archives of Disease in Childhood* 95 (2010): 355–60.

38. Pierce, Kaczor, Lohr, Richter, and Starling, "A Practical Guide to Differentiating Abusive from Accidental Fractures."

39. Stephen C. Boos and K. Feldman, "Neck and Spinal Cord Injuries in Child Abuse," in Carole Jenny (ed.), *Child Abuse and Neglect Diagnosis, Treatment, and Evidence* (St. Louis: Elsevier Saunders, 2011), 392–401.

40. Johnson and Richard, "Partial-Thickness Burns: Identification and Management"; Pierce, Kaczor, Lohr, Richter, and Starling, "A Practical Guide to Differentiating Abusive from Accidental Fractures."

41. Kim Kaczor and Mary Clyde Pierce, "Abusive Fractures," in Carole Jenny (ed.), *Child Abuse and Neglect Diagnosis, Treatment, and Evidence* (St. Louis: Elsevier Saunders, 2011), 275–316.

42. Sabine Maguire, M. Mann, N. John, B. Ellaway, J. Sibert, and A. Kemp, "Does Cardiopulmonary Resuscitation Cause Rib Fractures in Children? A Systemic Review," *Journal of Child Abuse & Neglect* 30 (2006): 739–51.

43. Kim Kaczor and M. Pierce, "Abusive Fractures," in Carole Jenny (ed.), *Child Abuse and Neglect Diagnosis, Treatment, and Evidence* (St. Louis: Elsevier Saunders, 2011), 275–95.

44. D.A. Thompson, T. Flynn, P. Miller, and R. Fischer, "The Significance of Scapular Fracture," *Journal of Trauma Surgery* 10 (1985): 974–77.

45. Norell Rosado, E. Ryznar, and E. Flaherty, "Understanding Humerus Fractures in Young Children: Abuse or Not Abuse?" *Journal of Child Abuse & Neglect* 73 (2017): 1–7.

46. Rosado, Ryznar, and Flaherty, "Understanding Humerus Fractures in Young Children"; David M. Chuirazzi and R. Riviello, "The Elbow and Distal Humerus," in John J. Dolan, Susan R. Noujaim, and Peter J. Boyle (eds.), *Emergency Radiology* (New York: McGraw-Hill Companies, 2000), 77–100.

47. Chuirazzi and Riviello, "The Elbow and Distal Humerus."

48. Chuirazzi and Riviello, "The Elbow and Distal Humerus."

49. Paul Kleinman, N. Morris, J. Makris, R. Moles, and P. Kleinman, "Yield of Radiographic Skeletal Surveys for Detection of Hand, Foot, and Spine Fractures in Suspected Child Abuse," *American Journal of Roentgenology* 200 (2013): 641–44.

50. Daniel M. Lindberg, N. Harper, A. Laskey, and R. Berger, "Prevalence of Abusive Fractures of the Hands, Feet, Spine, or Pelvis on Skeletal Survey: Perhaps 'Uncommon' is More Common Than Suggested," *Pediatric Emergency Care* 29, no. 1 (2013): 26–29.

51. Abigail M. Schuh, K. Whitlock, and E. Klein, "Management of Toddler's Fractures in the Pediatric Emergency Department," *Pediatric Emergency Care* 32, no. 7 (2016): 452–54.

52. Lindberg, Harper, Laskey, and Berger, "Prevalence of Abusive Fractures of the Hands, Feet, Spine, or Pelvis on Skeletal Survey."

53. Kaczor and Pierce, "Abusive Fractures."

54. Andy Tsai, P. Johnston, J. Perez-Rossello, M. Breen, and P. Kleinman, "The Distal Tibial Classic Metaphyseal Lesion: Medial versus Lateral Cortical Injury," *Pediatric Radiology* 48 (2018): 973–78.

55. Cristian, "The Evaluation of Suspected Child Physical Abuse."

56. Jennifer Hansen, E. Killough, M. Moffatt, and J. Knaff, "Retinal Hemorrhages: Abusive Head Trauma or Not?" *Pediatric Emergency Care* 34, no. 9 (2018): 665–70.

57. Jason N. Wright, "CNS Injuries in Abusive Head Trauma," *American Journal of Roentgenology* 205, no. 5 (2017): 991–1001.

58. Hansen, Killough, Moffatt, and Knaff, "Retinal Hemorrhages: Abusive Head Trauma or Not?"

59. Glenn A. Tung, "Imaging of Abusive Head Trauma," in Carole Jenny (ed.), *Child Abuse and Neglect Diagnosis, Treatment, and Evidence* (St. Louis: Elsevier Saunders, 2011), 373–91.

60. Tung, "Imaging of Abusive Head Trauma," 378.

61. Tung, "Imaging of Abusive Head Trauma."

62. Tung, "Imaging of Abusive Head Trauma."

63. Hansen, Killough, Moffatt, and Knaff, "Retinal Hemorrhages: Abusive Head Trauma or Not?"

64. Hansen, Killough, Moffatt, and Knaff, "Retinal Hemorrhages: Abusive Head Trauma or Not?"

65. Hansen, Killough, Moffatt, and Knaff, "Retinal Hemorrhages: Abusive Head Trauma or Not?"

66. Cristian, "The Evaluation of Suspected Child Physical Abuse."

67. Sandra M. Herr, "Abdominal and Chest Injuries in Abused Children," in Carole Jenny (ed.), *Child Abuse and Neglect Diagnosis, Treatment, and Evidence* (St. Louis: Elsevier Saunders, 2011), 326–31.

68. Herr, "Abdominal and Chest Injuries in Abused Children."

3

Sexual Abuse

◆ ◆ ◆

THE MERRIAM-WEBSTER DICTIONARY defines innocence as "Freedom from guilt or sin through being unacquainted with evil."[1] The idea of someone having sex with a child is often thought of as pure evil, which in turn generates significant anger in our society. We demonize anyone who tries to take away the innocence of a child and label them publicly as a sex offender. Although there is justifiable outrage when we hear that a child has been sexually abused, we as a society send a different message as to what is considered the innocence of a child and what constitutes sexual abuse. The customary definition of sexual abuse is fluctuating not only through the implementation of new laws; in addition, we have changing perceptions of a what constitutes a child as we continue lowering what is consider the age of innocence.[2]

THE CULTURE OF SEXUALIZING CHILDREN

James Kincaid, the author of *Erotic Innocence*, argues that our culture enthusiastically sexualizes a child while denying that we are doing any such thing. He argues that we have become so engaged with childhood eroticism (molestation, incest, abduction, pornography) that we have come to take for granted the allure of children.[3] These statements are obviously disturbing and may be offensive to some, but is there any validity to his argument? Do we unwittingly or even wittingly sexualize our children by making them appear older or display them in a way that entices one's sexual desire? For example, a great deal of controversy was created when child actress Brooke Shields appeared in a television commercial promoting Calvin Klein jeans. At age fifteen, Brooke Shields famously said these sexually suggestive words: "Do you know what comes between me and my Calvins? Nothing."[4]

Does our culture contribute to sexual abuse by parents or organizations sexualizing our children? If so, how significant is this problem? Has sexual abuse become such a substantial issue due to our inability or unwillingness to preserve the innocence of our young ones? Forces such as religion, parental authority, and tradition no longer have as much legitimacy in enforcing sexual norms as they may have had in the past. The result has been that many people are confused about sexual norms as they consider what is permissible and what type of sexual behavior would be considered taboo.[5] Another example of how we are sexualizing our children is through the continual expansion of our "age of consent" laws, which define at which age it is socially acceptable to engage in sex. These issues not only cloud the definition of innocence, but additionally blur the lines as to what society views as child sexual abuse.

AGE OF CONSENT

The "age of consent" laws determine whether a person can legally engage in sexual activity based on their age. If their age is aligned within the statutory requirements, participating in sexual activity would not be considered sexual abuse. The merits of using such laws in defining sexual abuse are questionable as the difference in age by merely a twenty-four-hour period (one day) can separate a sexual abusive act from that of an acceptable one. These sexual encounters can sometimes fall under the "Romeo and Juliet Laws." The term "age of consent" obviously implies that a person has reached an age capable of giving consent. The question that is controversial is whether a child is capable of giving consent. For consent to occur, two conditions must prevail: (1) a person must know what they are consenting to, and (2) that person must have true freedom to say yes or no. Children may know that the physical sensations feel pleasurable and on that basis may make the choice to engage in sex.[6] Some children, however, may feel pressured to engage in sex with an adult or older adolescent and due to their age feel incapable of denying the requests of the older figure. It has also been argued that girls may often consent to sex to feel like they are loved and feel closer to someone or to increase their popularity, but generally it is not the result of their own sexual desire.[7] Other youngsters may be unaware of the repercussions that are associated with engaging in sex (sexually transmitted diseases, pregnancy, etc.). Opposing views would argue that not all adults have full knowledge of consequences when entering into a sexual relationship and that full consent may not be present in all adult-adult encounters. Others argue that children should have the right to express themselves sexually and choose who they desire for sexual partners.[8] There is additionally a debate as to the appropriate age that a child can give consent. As the age of consent is as low as thirteen in some states, legislators who created these consent laws either personally believe that it's acceptable for children to engage in sex or are simply representing what their constituency desires. The debate as to whether children can legally engage in sex is not an issue exclusive to the United States. The International Planned Parenthood Federation has released a report titled *Exclaim! Young People's Guide to "Sexual Rights: An IPPF Declaration."* Although they continuously use the term "young people" instead of children, this organization makes statements of how "young people" should have the same rights as adults. The International Planned

Parenthood Federation believes that "young people" have the right to be sexually gratified, stating "Young people are sexual beings." They have sexual needs, desires, fantasies, and dreams. It is important for all young people around the world to be able to explore, experience, and express their sexualities in healthy, positive, pleasurable, and safe ways. This can only happen when young people's sexual rights are guaranteed.[9] The question that arises is whether these laws were created to help distinguish sexual abuse from that of a consenting act or were they were constructed as a "safety net" to protect those who are sexually attracted to children since those who engage in sex that are within the legal realm of consent laws will not be categorized as sexual abuse victims.

DEFINING SEXUAL ABUSE

There have been numerous definitions of sexual abuse arising from researchers and professionals working from varying academic perspectives. Some researchers define sexual abuse when the offender is a legal adult, whereas others may include older adolescents, which contributes to the age of consent debate. Other researchers may find distinction in the term depending on whether there was sexual contact. Child sexual abuse can be broadly defined as

> any sexual activity undertaken by an older or more powerful person deliberately involving a child under the age of 18, with or without a child's knowledge, apparent consent/assent, for the purpose of sexual gratification contact such as touching (with or without permission) of a child's genitals, anus, or breasts, and/or having a child touch the sexual parts of a person's body. It also includes non-contact sexual behavior such as exhibitionism, voyeurism, involving children in the making or watching of pornography, and propositioning or harassing a child in a sexual manner.[10]

DEFINING RAPE

Rape has consistently been classified as a crime of violence. This certainly can be true when describing sexual assaults involving adult victims, but this classification is a little more ambiguous when you're describing sexual assaults involving children. Although there are some sexual assaults involving violence with children (especially with strangers), the vast majority of sexual assaults involving children are committed through manipulation. A common theme, however, in both adult and child victims is that the offender is controlling their victim whether there is violence employed or not. In 2013, the Federal Bureau of Investigation revised their definition of rape so that it no longer required the term *force* to meet its criteria for rape. The new definition states rape is penetration, no matter how slight, of the vagina or anus with any body part or object, or oral penetration by a sex organ of another person, without the consent of the victim. The Federal Bureau of Investigation defines statutory rape as there is no force used but the victim is under the age of consent.[11]

MEASURING SEXUAL ABUSE

Measuring the actual amount of sexual abuse is a daunting task, as previously discussed in chapter 1, as many victims may never disclose the abuse that they suffered as a child. Additionally, the varying interpretations of statutory rape through age of consent laws skew the actual rate of sexual abuse. For cases that are reported to the Department of Health and Human Services, sexual abuse typically accounts for around 10 percent of all child maltreatment complaints (see table 3.1). The reporting of sexual abuse can come in various formats, as discussed previously in our definition of sexual abuse.

TYPES OF ABUSE

There are several ways that someone may sexually abuse a child. As stated previously, sexual abuse can be categorized as both contact and non-contact encounters. Contact encounters can include how one touches the child or how the child touches the offender. It should be noted that in many cases, non-contact sexual abuse can lead to sexual contact.

Examples of contact sexual abuse include:

- Penile penetration of the vagina
- Penile penetration of the anus
- Digital penetration of the vagina or anus
- Fellatio
- Cunnilingus
- Dry humping
- Touching the genitalia of a child for sexual gratification
- Touching the breasts of a child for sexual gratification.

Examples of non-contact sexual abuse include:

- Voyeurism
- Sexting
- Indecent exposure
- Masturbating in front of the child
- Mutual masturbation
- Watching a child undress
- Asking child to engage in sexual activity
- Talking to a child in a sexual manner
- Taking sexually explicit pictures of a child
- Having child look at sexually explicit material
- Soliciting a child for sex.

CASE STUDY #1 (NON-CONTACT TO SEXUAL CONTACT)

Angela, age eleven, reported to the police that her uncle has repeatedly fondled her breasts, and on one occasion he placed his hands down her pants and touched her vagina. She also stated that she caught her uncle previously watching her urinate (voyeurism) from a peep hole that was created in her bathroom. An examination of the bathroom revealed a small hole discreetly located high on the wall across from the toilet where the angle allowed the offender to view the genitalia of anyone who sat on the toilet to urinate. The offender was charged with sexual assault and invasion of privacy. The defendant was convicted and sentenced to three to five years in prison.

Intrafamilial Sexual Abuse

Intrafamilial sexual abuse refers to sexual abuse of a child by a family member who is related by blood or affinity. The term incest is commonly used when describing intrafamilial abuse. Incest traces back as far back as Biblical times where it is recorded in Genesis 19 that Lot had sexual intercourse with both of his adult daughters. Incest continues to occur today. Mental health workers once thought incest was extremely rare and was confined to extremely degenerate families, but their outlook has changed; many social workers and clinicians feel it is happening at epidemic proportions. Father-daughter incest is still considered the most common form of intrafamilial abuse today.[12] During this form of incest, the child perceives this sexual encounter as a way to become closer to their parent, only to later discover that this was abuse and realizes this relationship was inappropriate. Unfortunately, this realization creates a feeling of guilt and shame as they feel that they are somewhat responsible. In some instances, the mother is knowledgeable of the abuse but yet blames the daughter.[13] Brother and sister sexual relations may be the most common form of incest; however, it is less likely to be in the public light. Other forms of incest include, but are not limited to, grandparent-grandchild, uncle-niece, and mother-son.[14] Past research has demonstrated that females are more likely to be victims of intrafamilial abuse. Additionally, younger children are more likely to be victims of intrafamilial abuse, whereas older children are more likely to be victims of extrafamilial abuse.[15]

Extrafamilial Sexual Abuse

Extrafamilial abuse refers to persons outside the family such as strangers, teachers, coaches, neighbors, etc. In general, research shows that extrafamilial abuse is more common than familial abuse, although there is only a slight difference in the rate of abuse.[16] There are several types of sex offenders who can be categorized under extrafamilial abuse as anyone outside of the family setting is capable of harming a child. This can include, but not limited to, neighbors, friends of the family, or acquaintances of the child. However, there is a significant population of sexual predators who are categorized as extrafamilial abusers through their employment. This type of abuse is referred to as institutional sexual abuse.

Institutional Sexual Abuse

Institutional sexual abuse can be defined as instances in which those working on behalf of an organization use their authority and power in order to victimize others.[17] Many of these abusers are misusing their authority or are manipulating moral standards by gaining the child's trust.[18] Those perpetrators who sexually victimize children may choose a profession that allows easy access to children such as clergy, teachers, medical personnel, scout leaders, coaches, or even a live-in nanny. There are significant high-profile cases in which a sexual predator is discovered within the context of institutional sexual abuse, and the organization was cognizant of the abuse, thus failing to protect the children in their care. For example, the continuous controversy of the Catholic Church: the Church had knowledge of priests sexually abusing children and transferred the offenders to a different jurisdiction instead of reporting the abuse to the proper authorities. Historically, clergy members have targeted and victimized children from broken homes or who those who may appear vulnerable. In one study of Catholic priests and deacons in the United States who abused minors between the years of 1950 and 2002, it was discovered that the most common complaint was the touching over the victim's clothing or the priest's clothing.[19] The allegations continued in 2018 against the Catholic Church. Pennsylvania reported that over one thousand children have been abused over the last seventy years.[20] Another high-profile case involving an institutional sexual predator that garnered significant media coverage and outrage was the case of Larry Nassar, the doctor accused of sexually assaulting hundreds of girls who participated in the sport of gymnastics over the years. Allegations include, but are not limited to, digital penetration of the vagina and anus. Larry Nassar was finally charged in 2016 for criminal sexual assault and for possession of child pornography, although the allegations of sexual misconduct go all the way back to 1998 when a complaint was filed with Michigan State University.[21] It has been reported that adolescent caretakers commit the most serious abuse, which means that a child's normal babysitter is the most likely type of caretaker to sexually abuse a child.[22] Finally, when a teacher uses their authority to abuse a child, this is likewise considered a form of institutional abuse.

Table 3.1 Maltreatment Types of Victims, 2016[1]

State	Medical Neglect, Percent	Neglect, Percent	Other, Percent	Physical Abuse, Percent	Psychological Maltreatment, Percent	Sexual Abuse, Percent	Unknown, Percent	Total Maltreatment Types, Percent
Alabama	0.8	40.4	—	53.2	0.3	15.3	—	110.1
Alaska	2.3	76.6	—	12.0	31.6	5.8	—	128.3
Arizona	—	92.7	—	8.3	0.1	3.5	—	104.6
Arkansas	13.5	56.3	0.0	20.9	1.2	20.4	—	112.5
California	0.2	86.1	0.4	8.6	11.7	5.3	—	112.4
Colorado	1.6	80.5	—	11.5	2.8	9.5	0.3	106.3
Connecticut	3.0	84.9	0.1	6.7	29.6	4.7	—	128.9
Delaware	1.5	28.7	13.1	19.2	38.5	9.0	—	110.0
District of Columbia	—	85.4	0.1	19.2	—	5.3	—	110.0
Florida	2.5	56.2	46.1	8.7	1.2	6.2	—	121.0
Georgia	2.3	75.9	—	10.3	20.5	4.0	—	113.0
Hawaii	1.0	14.3	87.7	10.3	0.8	5.0	—	119.0
Idaho	0.3	79.2	0.8	21.1	—	3.7	—	105.1
Illinois	2.1	69.6	0.0	22.3	0.1	15.0	—	109.1
Indiana	—	89.1	0.0	7.2	—	9.1	—	105.5
Iowa	1.0	82.5	0.4	13.9	0.7	6.7	—	105.1
Kansas	2.5	16.5	28.5	22.1	14.4	26.9	—	110.9
Kentucky	2.3	93.4	—	7.8	0.2	3.9	—	107.7
Louisiana	—	85.8	—	15.0	0.4	5.3	0.0	106.6
Maine	—	63.3	—	30.9	33.5	8.1	—	135.7
Maryland	—	59.9	—	22.8	0.2	24.3	—	107.2
Massachusetts	—	94.9	0.1	8.9	0.1	2.4	—	106.3
Michigan	2.1	80.6	0.0	23.5	0.4	3.0	—	109.7
Minnesota	0.9	62.6	—	32.0	0.9	16.2	—	112.6
Mississippi	3.8	76.8	0.3	15.0	13.2	9.9	—	118.8
Missouri	3.7	62.4	—	30.5	10.6	24.2	—	131.3
Montana	0.1	96.5	0.2	4.1	1.9	3.1	—	105.9

(continued)

Table 3.1 *(continued)*

State	Medical Neglect, Percent	Neglect, Percent	Other, Percent	Physical Abuse, Percent	Psychological Maltreatment, Percent	Sexual Abuse, Percent	Unknown, Percent	Total Maltreatment Types, Percent
Nebraska	—	86.0	—	12.0	1.0	6.4	—	105.3
Nevada	1.8	80.3	—	26.2	0.5	5.5	—	114.4
New Hampshire	2.7	86.2	—	8.4	1.5	8.7	—	107.5
New Jersey	1.9	79.7	—	13.5	0.6	10.0	—	105.6
New Mexico	3.7	81.4	—	12.4	23.5	2.6	—	123.6
New York	5.9	95.4	27.8	9.6	0.7	3.2	—	142.6
North Carolina	0.4	52.9	1.2	25.1	1.1	19.3	0.9	101.0
North Dakota	2.3	76.5	—	9.8	32.2	2.9	—	123.7
Ohio	1.8	44.3	—	45.3	3.4	19.0	—	114.0
Oklahoma	1.4	79.1	—	14.6	25.4	4.5	—	125.1
Oregon	1.3	53.0	48.7	10.7	2.1	8.9	—	124.6
Pennsylvania	4.6	5.9	1.4	42.0	1.6	48.0	—	103.6
Puerto Rico	—	—	—	—	—	—	—	—
Rhode Island	1.7	54.5	2.2	14.3	38.0	4.4	—	115.0
South Carolina	2.1	59.7	0.7	52.9	0.8	4.4	—	120.6
South Dakota	—	89.6	—	11.2	2.2	4.5	—	107.6
Tennessee	1.5	26.2	—	60.7	2.8	27.4	—	118.6
Texas	2.1	82.4	0.0	14.5	0.6	9.9	—	109.5
Utah	0.4	28.7	1.7	45.4	29.7	17.4	0.0	123.1
Vermont	1.3	1.5	—	53.0	0.1	46.1	—	102.1
Virginia	2.7	63.4	0.1	31.0	1.3	11.7	—	110.2
Washington	—	77.9	—	21.7	—	10.0	—	109.7
West Virginia	6.0	42.7	0.0	77.9	62.8	4.3	—	193.7
Wisconsin	—	67.1	—	17.4	0.5	20.8	—	105.7
Wyoming	0.3	74.7	0.9	3.1	23.2	8.0	—	110.2
National	**2.1**	**74.8**	**6.9**	**18.2**	**5.6**	**8.5**	**0.0**	**116.2**

1 U.S. Department of Health & Human Services, Administration for Children and Families, Administration on Children, Youth and Families, Children's Bureau. (2018). Child maltreatment 2016. Available from https://www.acf.hhs.gov/cb/research-data-technology/statistics-research/child-maltreatment.

THE ATTRACTION TO CHILDREN

It would be naïve not to accept the fact that there is a segment of the population that is sexually attracted to children. As disturbing as this realization may be, we are somewhat fortunate that not all potential perpetrators act on their desires. However, when someone acts on those urges, they are committing a crime where they can properly be classified as a sex offender or child molester. There is certainly a justified fear that someone may sexually abuse a child, but the media gives a false sense of reality when they suggest that strangers are those who predominately place children at risk when in reality most victims of sexual abuse are violated by someone known to them, with some estimates as high as 95 percent of sexual abuse cases.[23] However, the term stranger danger has more validity through online victimization where victimization rates by strangers is reported in more than half of the victimization cases.[24] Child molesters usually are no less intelligent than the average person, and they usually don't have an extensive criminal record; few would be considered legally insane.[25] For someone to sexually abuse a child, the potential offender must meet four preconditions. There are different classifications for perpetrators who are sexually attracted to children as their preference may be based on age or physical appearance.

- **Precondition 1: motivation to sexually abuse.** There are three subcategories for this motivation:
    1. Emotional congruence, relating sexually to a child, which satisfies an important emotional need
    2. Sexual arousal in that the child is a potential source for sexual gratification
    3. Blockage in those alternative sources for sexual gratification is not available.

    These three components are not themselves preconditions as each one is not required for the sexual abuse to occur.
- **Precondition 2: overcoming internal inhibitors.** A potential offender must overcome their internal inhibitions against acting on their desires. Disinhibition, which makes someone less inhibited, is not in itself a source of motivation, but the very reason the motivation is unleashed. Many people who have a strong sexual interest in children will not act on their desires because of their internal inhibition.
- **Precondition 3: overcoming external inhibitors.** This precondition concerns the environment surrounding the offender and the child. The external influences can be the supervision of the child from other persons or the offender themselves. Parents, neighbors, siblings, teachers, or anyone else who interacts closely with a child and are familiar with their activities may inhibit abuse. External inhibitors can simply be the absence of any opportunity to be alone with a child.
- **Precondition 4: overcoming the resistance of the child.** Children have the capacity to avoid or resist abuse. Children can simply say no to any "sexual games" the perpetrator wants to initiate or the child may in some

circumstances fight back or run away. This is difficult for many children as they are young, naïve, or have a special relationship with the offender.[26]

PEDOPHILIA

Pedophilia is defined as the ongoing sexual attraction to prepubertal children. In the new *Diagnostic and Statistical Manual of Mental Disorders*, which is used by health care professionals throughout the United States, pedophilia is categorized as the sexual preference of prepubescent children and a disorder in the case of additional factors. "These factors include experiencing significant distress and impairment by fantasies and urges, or the acting out on behavioral level, including child pornography consumption and/or committing hands-on child sexual abuse offenses."[27] P.E. Dietz (1983) classifies pedophiles under two main categories (situational and preferential).[28]

Situational Pedophile

Situational pedophiles are categorized under four subtypes.

1. **Regressed:** When these offenders molest, they often turn to a victim as a substitute for the preferred adult companion. They may use force, promises, and other types of coercion in order to engage in sex with children. Among incest offenders, the regressed pedophile would be considered the most common.
2. **Morally indiscriminate:** This offender is considered a user and an abuser of all sexual encounters which include children who are vulnerable and available. These offenders may have an antisocial personality disorder. The majority of their victims are strangers.
3. **Inadequate:** They are sexually involved with children out of insecurity and curiosity. Due to their lack of impulse control, they can become angry and can potentially hurt the child.
4. **Indiscriminate:** They are often referred to by law enforcement as "try-sexual," meaning that they will try anything. They are more likely to have multiple victims.

Preferential Pedophile

The preferential pedophile has a preference for children and is categorized under three subtypes.

1. **Seductive:** Also known as fixated, this predator will seduce and court their victims. They are the master of manipulation. Over time, they gradually lower the child's inhibitions. If threats or violence are used, it is likely used as a tactic to avoid detection or prevent the child from disclosing their abuse. These offenders can abuse children for a significant length in time. These types of offenders are known to abuse multiple children simultaneously.

2. **Sadistic:** This offender often stalks and uses force to obtain compliance and inflicts pain to become sexually gratified. These types of offenders are considered rare.

3. **Introverted:** This subtype prefers children but lacks social and interpersonal skills to seduce them. They have little or no communication with their victims. These offenders are more likely to be found in playgrounds or other areas where children may gather.[29]

Infantophilia

A new subcategory of pedophilia includes infantophilia, which is classified as the sexual attraction to victims who are younger than five years of age. Perpetrators of sexual abuse toward infants or toddlers were opportunistic family members, babysitters, or day care workers.[30] The victims of this category are especially vulnerable as they have limited or no ability to communicate their abuse.

Hebephilia

This refers to the sexual interest in pubescent children who are showing the early signs of sexual development. The sexual offending usually involves children eleven to fourteen years of age; however, some children become pubescent at an earlier age.[31] With hebephilia, the focus of the interest is of some secondary sex characteristic development, whereas older adolescents may appear to be sexually mature, similar to adults, even if they are under the local legal age of consent for sexual activity.[32] Vulnerable children in this category include children who are just entering the age of babysitting and children engaged in extracurricular activities in middle school.

Ephebophilia

This refers to the sexual attraction to older adolescents. The controversy surrounding this attraction is that in some cases, this is not considered a deviant act as the age of consent laws allow adults to have sex with older teens. However, this same sexual encounter may be considered illegal, if not immoral, when the adult is in a position of authority such as a high school teacher and their students.

FEMALE SEX OFFENDER

There is certainly an accurate perception with supportive scholarly research to support the argument that both women and female children are the most likely victims of sexual assault. Empirical research will also prove that men and juvenile boys are the primary offenders of sexual assault. However, although men commit more sexual offenses compared to women, the amount of female sex offenders is worthy of further study. In fact, scholarly research on female offenders has increased significantly, although scholarly attention to female perpetrators remains relatively low compared to the same attention given to male offenders.[33] It is imperative that professionals recognize that sexual abuse by female perpetrators exists and that it is not as rare as once thought.[34] For instance, a mother can mask sexually inappropriate contact through the guise of bathing or dressing or undressing the victim.[35] One of the first typologies of female offenders was introduced in 1989, defining female sex offenders under three categories.

- **Teacher/lover offender:** This type of offender believes she has no malice toward children as she falls in love with an adolescent male who becomes her sexual partner. She sees him as her equal and would not have sexual relations with him unless it was a positive interaction that the boy desires. She believes the sexual favors are an act of kindness as sex is so important to adolescent males, and that adolescent males are ready and willing to engage in sex at every opportunity. Some women in this category were so brutalized by men that they turn to an adolescent male, and when they fall in love, they revert to adolescent feelings and behaviors while hoping the boy will fall in love with them.
- **The intergenerational predisposed offender:** In this category, the female offender has a history of sexual abuse victimization. These offenders also have psychological problems with deviant sexual fantasies.
- **Male-coerced offender:** This refers to a female who commits sexual abuse in conjunction with a male offender; the female offender is often in a romantic relationship with their co-offender.[36]

CASE STUDY #2 (NEIGHBOR ABUSE)

Jenny, twelve years of age, reported that her adult neighbors (Jason and Jeannine) performed cunnilingus on her while she was at their residence. She stated that these neighbors would take turns while the other watched. Jenny stated that this only happened once as she never returned to that house. Both Jason and Jeanine were charged with aggravated sexual assault on a child. Jason, who had been charged twice before in different states only to have the charges dropped, was unwilling to speak with the police. Jeannine, through an agreement with the prosecutors, agreed to testify against her husband in exchange for a deal that guaranteed her no jail time. Jeannine admitted to her involvement and stated that she only went along with the act as she was afraid of her husband. Jeannine further went on to acknowledge that the victims in the cases of her husband's previous arrests had dropped the charges in fear of the perpetrator. Jason was subsequently sentenced to three years in prison.

JUVENILE OFFENDERS

There may be a misperception as to who commits sexual abuse against children, as many may believe that sex offenses are committed only by "dirty old men." In reality, juveniles are both victims and perpetrators of sexual assault. One of the first noted typologies addressing juvenile sex offenders was by Michael O'Brien and Walter Bera, who classified juvenile sex offenders through seven separate categories.

- **The naïve experimenter** is usually young and has little history of acting out. They have adequate social skills and peer relationships. They appear to be sexually naïve and engage in sexual abuse if the opportunity is available. Their primary motivation is to explore or experiment as they are experiencing new sexual feelings.
- **The undersocialized child exploiter:** They have no close relationships and only a few school acquaintances. They could be considered a loner as they spend most of their time at home. They can be well liked by their parents and do well in school. While playing with younger children, they would become involved sexually requiring oral genital contact and fondling. They have few friends their own age and are considered undersocialized. They are often close to their mother but may be distant from their father. Their motivation for abuse is typically to achieve intimacy, self-importance, self-esteem, or autonomy.
- **The pseudo-socialized child exploiter:** This offender is usually an older adolescent with good social skills. They are considered comfortable but not intimate in peer settings. They may have been a victim of child abuse. They are often gifted and intellectual. This offender is highly rationalized as they show no remorse or guilt. They consider the abuse as mutual, intimate, and noncoercive.
- **The sexual aggressive:** This juvenile may have a history of psychological issues or a history with substance abuse. Their sexual abuse can be single and unpredictable, and they may commit bizarre or ritualistic acts against children, peers, and/or adults.
- **The sexually compulsive:** The family of a sexually compulsive offender is usually seen as rigidly enmeshed. The parents are usually emotionally repressed and have difficulty expressing intimacy. The juvenile offender is unable to express negative emotions in any straightforward manner. Their offenses are usually non-contact such as peeping through windows, obscene phone calls, exhibitionism, or fetishes like stealing girls' undergarments.
- **The disturbed impulsive:** These juveniles may have a history of psychological problems or a long history of substance abuse. The offense may reflect a malfunction of normal inhibitory mechanisms due to some type of thought disorder or the result of chemical abuse. This category is complex and individually determined.
- **The group-influenced:** This offender is usually a younger teen who is not likely to have prior involvement with the criminal justice system. The abuse occurs in a group setting where the perpetrator usually knows their victim. The offender defers their responsibility to the victim or to the other members of the group. Their motivation for sexual abuse can be attributed to peer pressure or being a follower, and attempting to gain peer attention or approval.[37]

As perpetrators, juvenile sex offenders were somewhat more likely to victimize acquaintances (63 percent versus 55 percent). Victims of juvenile sex offenders are overwhelmingly female, although slightly less than adult-perpetrated sex offenses. Additionally, juvenile sex offenders target male victims at a higher rate than adult male perpetrators and are more likely to commit sodomy and molestation compared to adults (61.9 percent versus 48.6 percent).[38] Juveniles are also less likely, compared to adults, to sexually offend a minor in their home but are more likely to sexually victimize a child in school.[39] Juvenile offender cases can be difficult to investigate, especially if the victim is the sibling of the offender. The sibling who sexually abuses a young sibling is usually the older brother with the average age of sexual abuse occurring when the offender is fifteen years of age.[40] Juvenile sex offenders tend to experience a great deal of family dysfunction, lack of attachment, physical abuse/neglect, and substance abuse.[41]

The most basic typologies for classifying juvenile sex offenders are dichotomous and relate to age as they are distinguished between adolescent or a preadolescent offender who abuses children or peers/adults. Those who abuse children are often siblings or other relatives. These offenders rely on opportunity, trickery, bribes, or threats, and commonly suffer from low self-esteem.[42] One of the most significant challenges during an investigation among sibling sexual abuse is the lack of cooperation from the perpetrator's parents: although they are upset about the abuse that took place, they are reluctant to cooperate with investigators as they don't want the perpetrating child to face any legal repercussions.

CASE STUDY #3 (PARENTS HINDERING INVESTIGATION)

Courtney, fourteen years of age, disclosed to her parents that her older brother, aged sixteen, had been repeatedly sexually assaulting her for years. When the parents learned of this abuse, they placed Courtney in a secure mental health facility for treatment as she was experiencing significant mental trauma from her repeated abuse. The mental health clinicians, who are mandated reporters, filed an official report based on the disclosure of sexual abuse. The police and social services responded to the facility to conduct an investigation. Upon their arrival, an administrator for the facility told the investigators that that couldn't see Courtney, because her parents did not want her talking to the authorities. The investigators explained to the administrator that they were required by law to investigate the allegation of abuse. The police and social service workers were still denied access to the facility and were forced to get an emergency court order to either forcefully remove the child if necessary or gain access to the child to check on their welfare. The mental health facility reluctantly allowed the investigators to see Courtney after receiving the court order. During the interview of Courtney, she admitted that she was indeed sexually abused, but was not willing to give any details since she did not want her brother to get in trouble and divulged that her parents didn't want her to talk to us. An attempt was made to interview the older brother, but this effort was thwarted. Based on the lack of cooperation from the entire family, there was insufficient evidence to continue an investigation.

WHO ARE THE VICTIMS?

It is difficult to measure the rate of victimization based on a child's disclosure as children may be reluctant to disclose their abuse, thus hiding their childhood victimization. Researchers may have to rely on adults disclosing their childhood victimization to get a clearer picture on the level of abuse. Victims of sexual abuse may also have particular characteristics that could lend them more vulnerable to abuse, whether it's their physical characteristics or their unique vulnerability. Data supporting these variables can be challenging as victims of sexual abuse may not disclose their abuse, making a quantitative analysis of frequency less dependable. However, the sex offender may look for that child who doesn't have as many external inhibitors such as lack of parental supervision, thus making them an easier target.

Despite all this, there are still data available that reflect the rate of sexual abuse based on child sexual abuse complaints. In 2016, the Department of Health and Human Services reported that there were 44,468 complaints filed for sexual abuse of a child, which comprises 6.6 percent of all child abuse complaints that year.[43] The National Incidence Study of Child Abuse and Neglect, through its data collection between 2005 and 2006, was more specific in identifying child sexual abuse victims. The incidence rates for sexual abuse were three per one thousand for girls and 0.06 per one thousand for boys.[44] The most common age for sexual abuse to occur is when the child is between eight and twelve.[45] The gender of the victim is a significant factor when addressing sexual abuse. Although the majority of sexual abuse victims are females, male victims face unique challenges. Male victims, when faced with the inescapable need to disclose an event, may overtly minimize the impact fearing allegations of homosexuality and the socialization of being macho. Older males are more likely to withhold their abuse as they are aware of the social cost of making their victimization public.[46] Other challenges male victims face are the guilt associated with arousal. A boy having an erection or even an orgasm may feel ashamed, preventing them from disclosing their victimization. When abuse does happen with boys, it is usually at a younger age when compared to that of girls, and the abuse of boys occurs for shorter periods of time and is more likely to have taken place outside the family.[47] Although victims come from all demographics, there are some specific characteristics where the victim is sexually abused by a juvenile offender. Juvenile sex offenders are much more likely than adults to target a child as their victim. Some of the factors involving victims of juvenile perpetrators include:

- When juvenile sex offenders are themselves six to nine years old, the mean age of their victim is between five and seven.
- When juvenile sex offenders are age fifteen to seventeen, the mean age of their victims is between eleven and thirteen.
- When victims are younger than age twelve, there is a marked peak for offending by thirteen- to fourteen-year-olds, and then a dramatic decline in the targeting of these young victims by youth fifteen years of age and older.
- Youth age fifteen and older primarily target postpubescent victims.[48]

ABUSE VICTIMS BECOME ABUSE PERPETRATORS?

There is a significant misperception as to the likelihood of an abused child later becoming a child perpetrator. Many sex offenders may report that they were victims of sexual abuse; however, there is no evidence to show such a correlation. A sex offender's claim of being a sexual abuse victim may be a ploy to elicit sympathy from a judge or jury during their sentencing hearing.[49] In a study of 843 subjects attending a specialist's forensic psychotherapy center, consisting of 747 males and ninety-six females to determine if there was a victimization perpetrator correlation, the overall rate of perpetrators who reported sexual victimization was 35 percent. Of the ninety-six females, 43 percent had been victims of sexual abuse, but only one became a perpetrator. A higher percentage of male perpetrators were sexual abuse victims, especially if they were abused as a child by a female relative. The conclusion of this study reported that the victim-to-victimizer cycle was in the minority for male perpetrators and virtually non-existent for female victims studied.[50] Other research, through multiple studies, has also concluded that sexually abused boys are more likely to become perpetrators, whereas sexually abused girls becoming perpetrators is almost non-existent.[51]

HOW DOES ABUSE OCCUR?

The first obstacle that prevents a perpetrator from abusing is denying access to a child. Unfortunately, this obstacle is easily overcome, especially if the abuser is a family member. It may be virtually impossible for a child to avoid a perpetrator who resides in the same household. Outside the household, as stated in the discussion of institutional abuse, are the offenders who join an organization for the purpose of accessing children. Many of these offenders can appear trustworthy and charismatic, and use these traits to groom the caretaker.

Grooming the caretaker happens by perpetrators who condition parents or other guardians to gain their trust with their children, thus allowing the perpetrator access to the child. Note that the process of grooming the caretaker is not necessary when soliciting a child online as there is no need to gain the trust of a parent in this scenario.

Grooming a child refers to gaining the trust of a child and forming a relationship that can be used to sexually abuse the child. Once a child has been targeted, the perpetrator will groom the child similar to what is seen in an adult courtship.[52] The perpetrator tries to form a friendship with the child, which can lead to trust and lowering the child's inhibition. Part of the process of lowering the inhibition is touching the child in a non-sexual manner such as tickling or hugs, or touching the child accidently which may appear to have been done innocently.[53] These tactics desensitize the child both physically and psychologically. The gradual progression toward sexual contact can include looking at dirty pictures or mutual masturbation. When contact is made, the victim may feel that the sexual contact was partially their idea, which helps with the continued grooming process maintaining control over the child by ensuring the abuse is kept secret. Some of the other tactics by family members and/or other perpetrators in the community to ensure the child keeps silent can be, but are not limited to, threats such as:

- "I'll kill your dog if you tell."
- "I'll take away all your toys."
- "Daddy will go to jail if you tell."
- "Mommy won't love you anymore."
- Male victims may be told "Everyone will think you're gay."
- "Nobody will believe you."
- "You can be arrested for having sex under age."

WHEN A CHILD DISCLOSES ABUSE

Some children may never disclose their abuse and keep their victimization a secret throughout their lifetime. When a child, due to courage or any other factor, does disclose abuse, it is rarely revealed directly to law enforcement or a social service agency. Some may reveal their victimization during an unrelated counseling session, whereas others may report to a school official, a friend, or a non-offending family member. Still other victims may disclose after being confronted by caretakers or other concerned observers who may observe evidence of sexual abuse victimization through either physical or behavioral indicators. In these cases, it is important for the investigator or caretaker to understand the sensitivity involved in disclosure as some victims may be extremely reluctant to disclose what has happened to them even if it appears obvious to the observer that the abuse has occurred. It is quite rare for a child to report their victimization directly to social services and law enforcement. The agencies that are trained to respond to these disclosures rely on secondhand accounts because the child may tell a responsible adult who then contacts the appropriate authorities. How the "responsible" adult reacts to the child's disclosure can be detrimental to the investigative agencies.

FAMILY REACTION TO DISCLOSURE

Depending who the child discloses to, the reaction may vary. In most circumstances, someone outside the family is likely to be very supportive to the child, but family members, depending on who is being accused, can vary in their reactions. When a child discloses that a family member has been abusing them, the non-offending parent or other family members may respond in disbelief. Once a disclosure is made, the child or the perpetrator will be forced to leave the residence until the investigation is complete. In cases where other members of the family may believe the child, those members may still become extremely emotional, creating a stressful environment, especially when the person accused of abuse lives in the same household as the child alleging abuse. In cases where the child is not believed, there is a higher probability that the child will be removed from the home as social services may discover that the non-offending parent is unwilling to protect their child due to their unbelief.

RETRACTION

The reaction of family members to the disclosure of abuse can lead a child to retract their claim of maltreatment even though even though the abuse actually occurred. Children can face different forms of hostilities as family members become angry with the child as they believe the child caused the family disruption and hardship because of what they believe to be a false allegation. Even when the child is believed, tensions can remain high in a household, as in many cases the primary wage earner may be the one accused, and they are either in jail awaiting trial, lost their job, or been forced out of their home due to the allegation. The household is now facing the possibility of financial turmoil and in some cases the family may be forced to leave their residence. Additionally, children although believed can be persuaded to change their account of what happened on the misguided assumption that the offender has learned their lesson and the abuse will no longer occur. Furthermore, some children may feel that although they did not like the abuse they were experiencing, that at least there wasn't so much tension in the family household and that nobody was mad at them. For this, and for many other reasons, children may recant their disclosure as a way to bring the family back together again; the child is willing to tolerate the possibility of more abuse as a lesser of two evils. It is important for investigators and attorneys who are prosecuting the case to not automatically dismiss the allegation as the child and their family may just need additional support to get through this difficult moment in their lives.

CASE STUDY #4 (RECANTING HER STORY)

Dianne, twelve years of age, reports to her guidance counselor that her biological father had been having sexual intercourse with her when her mother was not home. This was reported to the police, resulting in a search warrant of the child's bedroom; during the search, the bedsheets and a tube of KY Jelly found next to her bed were confiscated. While the search was being conducted, the father remained silent while the mother of Dianne yelled at her husband for the abuse. Dianne was placed in foster care while the investigation ensued. Approximately one month later, the prosecutor for this case notified law enforcement that Dianne had recanted her disclosure and they were going to drop the charges against Dianne's father. Law enforcement conducted a second interview and questioned Dianne about the abuse. Dianne was very upset indicating how much stress was in the household since her father was ordered out of the house allowing Dianne to return home. Dianne further elaborated and told law enforcement that both her brother and mother were upset with her although they believed the allegation. When Dianne was questioned again about the validity of her allegation she stated that the sexual abuse did indeed occur, but she didn't want everyone upset with her. She did however agree to testify against her father for the sexual abuse. On the day of the trial, Dianne sat outside the courtroom beside her mother and paternal grandmother. The victim advocate came out of the courtroom to tell Dianne it was time for her to testify. As Dianne started walking toward the courtroom, her grandmother said, "You will go to Hell for lying about your father." Dianne's father was subsequently convicted of sexual assault.

SEXUAL ABUSE AND TECHNOLOGY

Although technology has improved the lives of children and adults alike in many facets of modern life, it has also incorporated vulnerabilities for victims in a variety of modalities. In today's world of technology, child maltreatment may be difficult to detect as the perpetrator may be a chat room partner that the child has met online.[54] The technology of the internet has made it easier for people to locate and interact with other individuals who share their desires. Cybersex is common in Western nations where individuals use explicit dialogue and role playing in various chatrooms.[55]

Soliciting a Child Online

Cybersex may be considered deviant or even dangerous when adults express their fantasies toward children; it can also be illegal if these fantasies turn into reality as they use the internet to solicit a child into having sex in order to fulfill their fantasies. Although minors are more likely to be victimized in the real world versus those who are abused online,[56] there still remains a significant danger with online sexual offender behaviors, especially if the online victimization can lead to real world victimization. In one study of 2,051 adolescents (aged ten to seventeen), 6 percent of the respondents claimed victimization during their lifetime. For those youth that reported victimization during the last year, almost all of them (96 percent), reported offline victimization during that same time period.[57] The process of grooming a child online is easier compared to that of offline grooming as the perpetrator not only can avoid the child's caretaker, but they can disguise their identity by creating false online profiles,[58] making it easier to lower a child's inhibition. The potential victim may believe they are corresponding with one of their peers rather than an adult. For instance, an adult male perpetrator can pretend to be a female adolescent online by using a factitious screen name, a stolen photo, and falsified biographies complete with local schools and activities with which the targeted child may be familiar.[59] This deception can create a false sense of security for the victim that may lead to an offline encounter.

Sexting

This refers to the sending of sexually explicit messages or photos through an electronic device, primarily done by mobile phones. A significant amount of child pornography originates from adolescents giving what they believe is a private message or photo to someone they are willing to communicate with. The controversy with child pornography being distributed among adolescents is whether those involved should be treated as sexual deviants and face penalties under child pornography statutes or be considered children sharing private photos among themselves. Unfortunately, many of these photos that are meant to be private are released electronically for virtually anyone to see, thus these "private" photos are then used by adults for sexual gratification. There is a debate as to what constitutes child pornography in relation to sexting. Should a photo sent while sexting be deemed child pornography based on its contents or on who is viewing it? In one study that was designed to identify user awareness regarding of the laws regarding sexting, a survey of 120 participants (51.7 percent being male) aged eighteen to thirty were asked, upon receiving different scenarios of sexting, what was considered illegal activity. The results of this study indicated that regardless of sex or age, participants were aware of what was considered either lawful or unlawful. However, the male participants were more likely than the females to recognized sexting as illegal if the activity involved children receiving pornography.[60]

CHILD PORNOGRAPHY

This refers to the possession, trade, advertising, and production of images that depict the sexual abuse of children. It is almost exclusively online now where sexual deviants can hide and transfer photos of a child under the secrecy of the web, chat rooms, and file sharing systems. Once these pictures are released electronically, it is impossible to retrieve them and the victims of child pornography will continue to suffer from the distribution of these exploitive and victimizing pictures and videos. The children may also be subjected to additional victimization knowing that these images are traded among other offenders who receive sexual gratification while viewing the images. The problem of child pornography is enhanced as advances in computer memory storage, the speed of downloading and uploading, and the growth in file sharing technologies make it easier to possess and distribute large volumes of child sex abuse images.[61]

Manufacturing of Child Pornography

This conjures up images of production factories with assembly lines with some elaborate distribution center that employs, uses, persuades, induces, or coerces a child for the purpose of producing a visual depiction of sexually explicit conduct. In reality, the manufacture of child pornography can be achieved by anyone with a digital camera who takes a picture of a child displaying genitalia in a lewd or lascivious way.[62]

Historically, child pornography laws were first addressed and regulated through obscenity laws as defined under *Miller v. California* (1973) to determine if the average person would consider material obscene. The standards for child pornography were considered qualitatively different than adult pornography and therefore different standards should be addressed as in *New York v. Feber*, which ruled that the distribution of child pornography should be prohibited even if the material does not meet the obscenity standards set forth in the Miller case. In an effort to provide even further protection toward children, look to *The United States v. Dost* (1986). The Dost case created a six-prong test to determine whether material was considered child pornography, although the material did not have to meet all six categories to be deemed child pornography.

1. Whether the genitals or pubic area are the focal point of the image
2. Whether the setting of the image is sexually suggestive

3. Whether the child is depicted in an unnatural pose or inappropriate attire considering their age
4. Whether the child is partially or fully clothed or nude
5. Whether the image suggests sexual coyness or willingness to engage in sexual activity
6. Whether the image is intended or designed to elicit a sexual response in the viewer.

However, in the case of *Ashcroft v. Free Speech Coalition* (2002), the U.S. Supreme Court made a controversial ruling stating that digital images (computerized generated pictures) of child pornography, no matter how disturbing, were not considered child pornography in that there was no actual harm to children.[63] Another form of child pornography is created through sexting.

CHILD PROSTITUTION

It is difficult to measure the amount of childhood prostitution in the United States as the activity is clandestine in nature. Children who enter a life of prostitution, often at a young age, constitute a population that is virtually invisible. Childhood prostitution only comes into light when it comes to the attention of the child welfare system or law enforcement. Although it is difficult to measure, we understand that a great deal of child prostitution comes from children who have run away from home and are surviving on the streets in exchange for sexual services. Children may initiate the sexual encounter themselves or find themselves under the control of an exploiting adult who receives money or drugs from clients in exchange for having sex with the children the exploiter controls.[64] The majority of adult female sex workers entered prostitution as a child in an attempt to regain control of their lives and their sexuality. In the United States, at least 70 percent of women involved in prostitution entered this commercial sex industry before reaching eighteen years of age.[65] Other girls entered prostitution as they have perceived their sexuality as a way to garner power over men and obtain financial awards. Many girls who have entered prostitution enter an environment of violence and in some cases an environment of violence was the initial reason for leaving their homes.[66] In other cases, drug-dependent parents may prostitute their children in order to feed their own drug dependency. Although estimates of the amount of childhood prostitution may be crude at best, the problem is still considered substantial, especially when there are networks that traffic children for sex.

HUMAN TRAFFICKING IN THE UNITED STATES

The United States defines human trafficking as:

- Sex trafficking in which a commercial sex act is induced by force, fraud, or coercion, or in which the person induced to perform such act has not attained eighteen years of age;
- The recruitment, harboring, transportation, provision or obtaining of a person for labor or services, through the use of force, fraud, or coercion

for the purpose of subjection to involuntary servitude, peonage, debt bondage, or slavery.[67]

There may be a misperception that human trafficking is not a significant problem in the United States compared to other nations. Unfortunately, human trafficking is a momentous problem in the United States where children are either imported in or are U.S. citizens. In fact, American-born citizens make up the largest percentage of sex trafficked children in the United States.[68] The U.S. Department of Justice reports that the age females begin prostitution in the United States is between twelve and fourteen years. The Federal Bureau of Investigation further explains boys and transgender youth start engaging in prostitution between the ages of eleven to thirteen years on average.[69] According to the Polaris (an organization serving victims and survivors of human trafficking) report in 2014, there were 1,607 cases of children being trafficked, with 84 percent of these children being used for sex, with an additional 3 percent being trafficked for both sex and labor. A breakdown shows that 1,393 were female, 231 were male, and ten were identified as transgender. The top five nations that were discovered as trafficking humans were:

1. United States
2. Mexico
3. China
4. Guatemala
5. Russia.[70]

Although there is a significant number of children brought in from other countries through false pretenses such as employment or educational opportunities, others may be imported through force (abduction). Victims tend to be recruited primarily from Mexico and East Asia. Typically the countries from where these victims originate tend to have unstable political climates and are economically disadvantaged.[71] A child who is an American citizen may be trafficked for some of the same reasons as citizens of other countries, such as false pretenses (modeling careers, other employment opportunities, etc.); however, there are certain risk factors for American children who do become targets. For instance, although victims of trafficking in the United States are disproportionately female as with other countries, it should be noted that there is evidence that suggests that LQBTQ youth may be five times more likely than heterosexual youth of the same age to be victims of trafficking as they have an increased chance of having feelings of rejection and alienation that are often experienced by this segment of our population.[72] Although runaway children are at an increased risk of being trafficked, throwaway children are at an even greater risk as they are not reported missing and therefore no one is looking for them. According to the UN Children's Fund, one in three young people are solicited for sex within forty-eight hours of running away or being homeless.[73] Other risk factors include drug dependency, mental illness, emotional distress, childhood sexual abuse, and lack of social support.[74] In response to the problem of child sex trafficking, the Child Exploitation and Obscenity Section of the U.S. Department of Justice was created. This section was established in 1987 to protect the welfare of American children by enforcing federal statutes relating to the exploitation of children including sex trafficking.[75] By the mid-1990s the U.S. government recognized the need to have laws that specifically address the crime of human trafficking. Congressman Chris Smith of New Jersey authored the original Trafficking Victims Act, which was signed into law by President Clinton in 2000.[76] The Trafficking Victims Protection Act of 2000 provides a two-tiered definition of trafficking, which includes several forms of trafficking in persons and sex trafficking, which transformed 18 USC 1591 and 18 U.S.C. 2421-2423 (the law) into four primary statutes. These statutes criminalize prostituting minors in interstate commerce and ensure that when foreign nationals are identified as trafficking victims they are able to receive benefits and services to the same extent as a refugee following certification/eligibility requirements set forth by the Department of Health and Human Services.[77]

SEX RINGS

Although the U.S. government has taken great strides in combatting human trafficking, the problem still exists as some victims can be trafficked through the sexual exploitation of a parent or an older boyfriend, whereas others can be victimized through extensive criminal networks that form sex rings where children can be transported across state lines for the purpose of sexual exploitation. The ability to access children through various jurisdictions is a rather new phenomenon, although sex rings have been in existence throughout history. The introduction of the internet created an ease in forming both national and international networks. Sexual offenders can now readily communicate and can conspire through relatively secret tactics to exploit children throughout the country.[78] To elaborate on the enormity of this powerful enterprise, between January 25 to 27, 2018, law enforcement in the United States arrested more than five hundred suspects and rescued forty-five adults and eleven girls from a sex trafficking ring in California.[79] The venue for these operations can include, but are not limited to, hotels, truck stops, street corners, escort services, spas, online solicitation, or any place of residence. One of the more infamous sex rings that was known for its attraction to boys was NAMBLA.

NAMBLA

The North American Man/Boy Love Association, or NAMBLA, was established in 1978 where members would pay a thirty-five-dollar annual membership. NAMBLA's goal is to end the oppression of men and boys in mutually consensual relationships. These offenders would fall in to the category of an ideological offender, where they believe that having sex with boys will actually benefit the child.[80] The organization believes that ageism is the problem that causes people to oppose these types of relationships where boys are not given the rights to make decisions about their bodies. The organization does not promote violating the law but wants society not to stigmatize the relationship between a man and a boy. In addition to advocating for consensual relationships, NAMBLA appears to advocate for youths in other areas as well, as they condemn the use of corporal punishment for children. It is clear, however, that NAMBLA's main goal is to legitimize behavior that is illegal in an attempt to change the popular perspective that these relationships are harmful to children.[81] NAMBLA believes in the liberation of children from the repressive bonds of society by allowing them to explore their sexuality, believing they should have the same rights as mainstream society.[82] From a legal perspective, NAMBLA is careful about protecting the organizatio and its members as they caution members about what they write whether real or imaginary. In its prison program, members can write to inmates convicted of sexual assault but are informed that the mail can be read and that it might be considered contraband.[83] NAMBLA still exists today, but only as a small entity compared to its most prevalent days. Concerted efforts by law enforcement have significantly impacted the strength of this organization. Additionally civil litigation has been filed against the organization as recently as 2018 by the parents of ten-year-old Jeffrey Curley for his rape and murder in 1997. The American Civil Liberties Union is defending NAMBLA in this as a wrongful death lawsuit, which accuses NAMBLA of inciting two men (Charles Jaynes and Salvatore Sicari) in the murder of Jeffrey Curley. It was reported that Jaynes was reviewing the NAMBLA website shortly before Jeffrey's murder. Jaynes and Sicari were sentenced to life in prison for Jeffrey's murder as prosecutors described how Jaynes and Sicari, on October 1, 1997, lured Jeffrey Curley into a vehicle with the promise of fifty dollars and a new bicycle. When Jeffrey resisted their sexual advances, the men suffocated and killed Jeffrey and then molested him after his death, eventually stuffing him in a container of concrete and dropping him in a river.[84]

BEHAVIORAL INDICATORS

Behavioral indicators can be an invaluable tool in identifying and corroborating sexual abuse. Although not all sexual abuse behavioral indicators are the result of victimization, they are, as the word implies, indicators that should create further inquiry. Behavioral indicators can at times be obvious signs of sexual abuse such as watching a child act out in a sexual manner where the immediate response would be, "Where did they learn that behavior?" Other behavioral indicators may be a great deal more subtle. For instance, parents of an abused child may see their child being disruptive or acting out in a way that generates concern. Other parents may take their child to drug counseling, which may be the result of a court order in response to drug possession. The parent may pursue counseling for their child in hopes of changing their behavior not realizing that the causation of this behavior is sexual abuse. The trained investigator can use behavioral indicators to validate the truthfulness of the child's disclosure. If the allegation is fellatio where the child was forced to place their mouth on the offender's penis, then a possible indicator would be that the child had recently displayed an obsession with constantly brushing their teeth. Behavioral indicators can also be used to support the timeline of the abuse. For instance, if the child states that the abuse started nine months ago and family members describe how their child started acting differently in the last nine months, that can be used to corroborate the timeline of the victimization. There are several behavioral indicators of sexual abuse; these can include, but are not limited to:

- Aggression
- Overly compliant or passive behavior
- Depression
- Unreasonable fear (being alone with someone)
- Sleep disturbances
- Change in academic performance
- Acting out sexually with other children
- Change in appearance (some children may dress more seductively while others may try to make themselves look less appealing)
- Change in hygiene (brushing teeth excessively, constant showering, or failing to keep clean)
- Running away
- Drug abuse
- Self-mutilation
- Suicide attempts
- Animal abuse
- Bedwetting.

PHYSICAL INDICATORS

In evaluating children victims of sexual abuse allegations, the provider first must understand what a normal examination consists of, the varying types of hymens, and dispel myths regarding the hymen. All sexual assault examinations should consist of an introduction, a health history, head-to-toe examination, referrals, discharge instructions, and follow-up examination discussion if necessary.

The medical history is necessary to obtain on all children. Medical history should include chronic illnesses, recent illness, medications, allergies, and any recent trauma. Height, weight, and vital signs need to be recorded in the electronic record. The provider needs a description of the concerns and any symptoms that are present such as pain or bleeding. While obtaining a history, it is important to note any urinary symptoms, history of constipation, and/or history of diarrhea. The child should be referred to a program that has a sexual assault nurse examiner (SANE) or a forensic nurse examiner (FNE), if available in that region.

The SANE (or FNE) that is trained to evaluate prepubescent children with allegations of sexual assault is the ideal referral for the patient. The SANE can address the medical and psychological needs of the child while preserving and collecting evidence. Children that have been sexually assaulted should be seen within 120 hours of the assault. Prepubescent children should be referred up to one year post sexual assault incident. The rationale in most pediatric examinations, acute or chronic, is that the child will have a normal examination based on the type of assault, the time that has elapsed, and the healing that may have occurred. The SANE exam does not just identify acute injuries. Research that addresses pediatric examinations by a SANE or FNE confirms the benefits of the exam. The SANE (FNE) does not force examinations on the child and, if done correctly, should not cause additional trauma to the child. The SANE (FNE) is able to reassure the child that they are okay, that they are not damaged, that they are not in trouble, and no one can look at them and tell that something has happened. The International Association of Forensic Nursing has written a position paper regarding the care of prepubescent pediatric sexual abuse patients and recognize in this paper that child sexual abuse patients are at greater risk for a number of adverse psychological and somatic problems that may extend into adulthood.[85] This crime against the child does not go away when the "external" wounds heal. The sooner the child has someone who can address the physical and emotional needs as found in SANE examinations, the better the outcome, and the ability to cope with the long-term effects.

CASE STUDY #5

A fifteen-year-old female presents to the hospital with her mother. The triage nurse pages the forensic nurse and states that the child and the mother are arguing with each other. An allegation had been made that the fifteen-year-old girl had been having sex with the thirty-year-old neighbor; she was spotted coming out of his trailer. After speaking with the mother, she had just been told that the neighbor had been sexually abusing the child, and the mother wanted the child evaluated. The forensic nurse spoke with the child, who gave a clear disclosure of the sexual abuse that had been happening over the past year. The child was cooperative and agreed to talk with the forensic nurse. When discussing the next step, the head-to-toe assessment, and the genital examination, the child began to cry and state that she was not going to have the examination, that "no one could look at her down there." At this point, the forensic nurse questioned her as to why, and she would only say that she did not want an exam. After talking further about her situation, the child disclosed that this neighbor had told her that she looked weird and her genitalia was like that of a monster and no one would ever want her. The child was terrified at having a medical professional confirm what this monster had told her. After a great deal of talking and reassurance of the child, she agreed to have the examination completed, and her exam was completely normal. When I told her this, she began crying saying, "No, he said I looked like a monster down there and something is wrong with me." This child had been carrying this with her, afraid to tell anyone. The entire time, this was a tactic by this offender to keep her quiet. Having an expert in the field confirm that the anatomy was normal and no one would be able to tell what had been happening to her was one of the first steps to her healing process.

In order to understand what is considered normal during an evaluation, it is important to be familiar with the anatomy.

Female Anatomy

- Mons pubis: Rounded, fleshy area that sits over the pelvic bone. It is created by an underlying fatty pad. This is the area where you see pubic hair grow.
- Clitoris: Erectile tissue below the mons pubis and above the urinary meatus. Covered by the clitoral hood (prepuce).
- Urethral meatus: The opening of the urethra that allows urine to exit the body. Located just below the clitoris.
- Labia majora: Outer lips of the vagina.
- Labia minora: Inner lips of the vagina.
- Vestibule: Almond-like space between the lines of attachment of the labia minora. There are four structures that open into the vestibule: urethral meatus, vaginal orifice, and two Bartholin glands.
- Hymen: Membranous collar that surrounds the vaginal opening. Separates the external genitalia from the vagina. Many myths surround the

Anatomy of Human Vagina

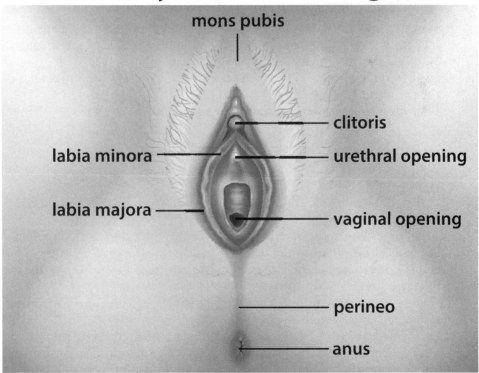

Female Anatomy
© iStock / Getty Images Plus / Pavlo Vanzhula

hymen, which will be discussed a little later in this chapter. Hymens come in a variety of shapes and sizes.

- Fossa navicularis: Concave area that sits just below the hymen, but above the posterior fourchette.
- Posterior fourchette (commissure): Band or fold of mucous membranes that connects the posterior ends of the labia minora. This is the most frequent arear of injury in consensual and non-consensual intercourse. Injuries to this area are commonly referred to as a "mounting injury."
- Perineum: Lies between the posterior fourchette and the anus in females.
- Vagina: Tubular structure with vaginal rugae. Extends from the hymen to the cervix. Rugae assist with the ability of the vagina to distend.
- Cervix: Neck of the uterus. Rounded surface that protrudes into the vagina.

Male Anatomy

- Mons pubis: Rounded, fleshy area that sits over the pelvic bone. It is created by an underlying fatty pad. This is the area where you see pubic hair grow.
- Penile shaft: Composed of erectile tissue. The urethra passes through this tissue.
- Glans penis: Cap-shaped tissue at the end of the penis. Glans is either circumcised or uncircumcised.
- Corona: A rounded, projecting border around the base of the glans.
- Urethral meatus: External opening from the bladder, located at the glans.
- Scrotum: External pouch or sac; contains the testicles.
- Median raphe: Ridge or furrow that marks the union of the two sides of the perineum.
- Perineum: Lies between the scrotum and the anus.

Anus

- Buttock: Two rounded areas that come together to form the posterior trunk.
- Perianal folds: Wrinkles or folds that extend from the anus. Created by contractions of the external anal sphincter.
- Anal verge: Tissue that overlies the division of the external anal sphincter at the most distal portion of the anal canal.
- Anus: Lower opening of the digestive tract; provides an opening for the release of feces.
- Anal skin tag: Protrusion of anal verge tissue that interrupts the normal symmetry of the perianal skin folds.
- Pectinate/dentate line: The saw-toothed line of demarcation between the distal portion of the anal value and the pectin. Smooth zone of stratified epithelium that extends to the anal verge.

Figure diagram of anatomical structure of male genital organs

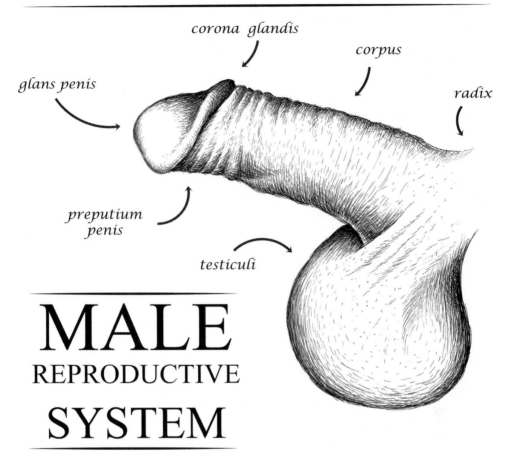

corona glandis

corpus

glans penis

radix

preputium
penis

testiculi

MALE
REPRODUCTIVE
SYSTEM

Male Anatomy
© iStock / Getty Images Plus / Pavlo Vanzhula

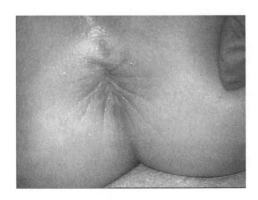

Normal anal examination

Evaluating children over a period of time, it is clear that the sequence of events toward sexual maturation is predictable. In the mid-1900s, James Tanner, a British pediatrician, noted the growth pattern of children over the years and developed a Tanner scale (stages). The Tanner scale, or Tanner stages, identify whether a patient should be treated physically as a child, adolescent, or an adult. Five Tanner stages were listed for females based on breast and pubic hair growth. Five Tanner stages were also identified in males based on pubic hair and penile development. The caveat to the Tanner stages is many adolescents and adults shave their pubic hair, making it difficult to stage.

The Tanner stages for females are as follows:

Stage 1: Prepubertal with no breast development and no pubic hair growth
Stage 2: Breasts bud and areola enlarges; sparse growth of long, slightly pigmented hair (straight or curled) along the labia majora
Stage 3: Further enlargement of breast and areola; darker, coarser, and more curled hair spreading sparsely over the mons pubis
Stage 4: Areola and papilla form a secondary mound above the level of the breast; adult pubic hair covering small area of the mons pubis
Stage 5: Mature state; areola recesses and only papilla projects; adult pubic hair in full quantity with horizontal (feminine) distribution and spread to medial surface of the thighs.[86]

The Tanner stages for males are as follows:

Stage 1: Prepubertal with no hair
Stage 2: Scrotum and testes enlarge; scrotum skin reddens and changes in texture; sparse growth of long, slightly pigmented hair (straight or curled) at the base of the penis
Stage 3: Penis lengthens; further growth of testes; more curled hair spreading sparsely over the mons pubis
Stage 4: Penis grows in breadth; glans develops; testes and scrotum grow larger; scrotum skin darkens; adult pubic hair covering small area of the mons pubis
Stage 5: Adult genitalia; adult pubic hair in full quantity with spread to medial surface of the thighs.[87]

It is important to assess the Tanner stage of the breast separate from Tanner stage of the genitalia. It is possible to develop at different stages.

As a child matures, as noted with the Tanner stages, the body is undergoing changes. The change that is focused on so often is the hymen. The hymen has many misunderstandings around it as well as many myths. The next section is going to identify the normal development of the hymen, identify the normal types of hymen that are seen upon examination, and dispel some myths related to the hymen.

The effects of estrogen are first noted at the birth of a female child; maternal estrogen crosses the placenta during gestation. The hymen of a newborn girl appears thickened and pale, and the child may have some white discharge.

The maternal estrogen gradually leaves the infant body over a period of a few months, but can take as long as two to three years. Once the estrogen is eliminated, the hymen becomes thin and less redundant with sharp-defined edges. At this time, the hymen is highly sensitive to touch, the slightest touch will cause pain. During this period is when caretakers all of a sudden notice a "large vaginal opening" and panic that the child must have been sexually abused. The fact is that the hymen typically does not cover the vaginal opening; it surrounds the vaginal opening. When the hymen is no longer estrogenized, the vaginal opening can be seen. The hymen takes on multiple forms, which is normal, as follows:

- **Annular hymen:** The hymenal tissue extends completely around the vaginal orifice.
- **Crescentic hymen:** The hymenal tissue attaches at approximately the 11 o'clock and the 1 o'clock position, with no tissue between the attachments.
- **Cribriform hymen:** The hymen has multiple small openings.
- **Imperforate hymen:** The hymenal membrane has no openings.
- **Septate hymen:** The hymen with two or more openings. Bands of tissue bisect the opening.
- **Fimbriated hymen:** The hymen with multiple projections and indentations along the edge, creating a ruffled-like appearance.
- **Redundant hymen:** Hymenal tissue tends to fold back upon itself or protrude. Redundant hymen is estrogenized.

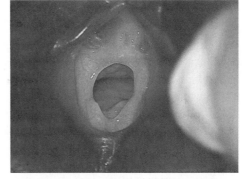

Annular Hymen

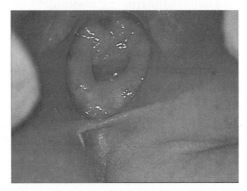

Crescentic Hymen

The redundant hymen is the type of hymen seen most commonly in adolescents and adults. It is difficult to fully appreciate the edges of a redundant hymen to determine if injuries have occurred. Other techniques can be utilized so that the hymenal edges can be fully appreciated. One technique is using a catheter. The catheter is inserted just past the balloon. Using five to ten milliliters of sterile water, fill the balloon. Once the balloon is inflated, gently tug back on the catheter so all edges of the hymen can be viewed. Photograph the hymen. Deflate the balloon before removing from the vaginal opening.

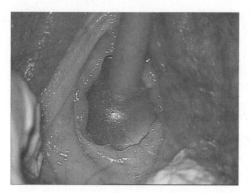

Redundant hymen using catheter to better visualize the hymenal edges

If the patient does not tolerate the catheter, a cotton-tipped swab can be used. Place the swab just inside the vaginal opening and gently pull back on the hymenal edges so that the hymen can be fully viewed.

Note, neither the catheter nor the cotton-tipped swab techniques are to be used on prepubescent children!

Common normal findings during examination include **vestibular bands,** which are small bands of tissue lateral to the urethral orifice that connect the periurethral tissues to the anterolateral walls of the vestibule (urethral support ligaments), or bands of tissue lateral to the hymen that connect to the vestibular wall.[88]

When completing an examination, if the examiner is not careful, they can cause injury on the child themselves. The examiner should be aware of the preferred positions of examination and how to separate and apply traction to the labia on examination.

Frog leg position: The most preferred position to examine a prepubescent child is the frog leg position. In the frog leg position, you ask the child to lie on their back and put the bottoms of their feet together.

Knee chest position: Ask the child to lie on their stomach. Have the child place their head and chest on the bed and put their buttocks up, while they

Redundant hymen using a cotton tipped applicator to better visualize hymenal borders

are on their knees. (I usually will lighten it up by telling children that this is how a lot of babies like to sleep.)

Caregiver's lap: Sometimes, it does not matter how good a rapport you have built with the child, when it comes to the exam, they do not want to get in frog leg or knee chest positions. It is good to try and think outside of the box and find out what will make the child comfortable. Caregiver's lap is a position where the child may be more willing to allow the examination. You explain to the caregiver that they will need to straddle the stretcher and place the child in their lap, moving the buttocks forward on the stretcher so an exam can take place.

Once the child is positioned, the examiner will need to separate the labia to visualize the hymenal opening. While the child is in frog leg, knee chest, or the caregiver's lap, the examiner will place a hand on each side of the labia majora and gently pull the labia apart to provide a gross view of the genitalia.

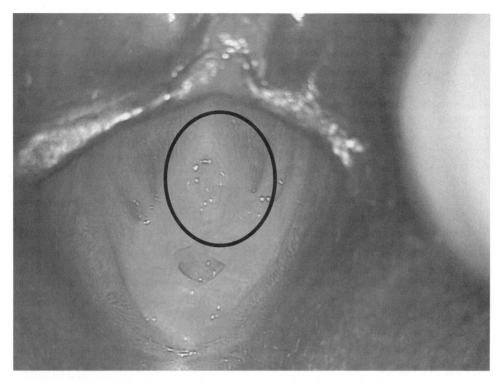

Peri-hymenal bands

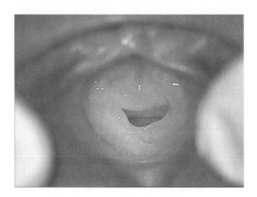

A pre-pubescent crescentic hymen in frog leg position

A pre-pubescent crescentic hymen in the knee chest position

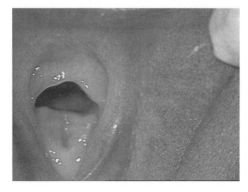

After you have separated the labia, gently pinch the labia majora and pull the labia majora outward and downward. This technique of labial traction enhances the visualization of the hymen and will allow the hymen the ability to open so that the hymenal edges can be seen.

The Hymen

The hymen was named after the Greek God of marriage, Hymenaes.[89] The hymen remains a topic of conversation and a very misunderstood tissue for medical professionals, patients, and caregivers alike. Multiple myths evolve around the hymen. The most common one is that the hymen covers the vaginal opening and has to be popped like a cherry when you lose your virginity. This is so far off base and has caused so much confusion and heartache. Michelle Ditton and Laurie Gray have written a book that addressed debunking myths in sexual assault cases. This next section is going to include some hymenal myths.

1. **The hymen is broken and will bleed the first time penetration occurs.** As has been discussed earlier in the chapter, when a girl reaches puberty, the hymen becomes redundant and elastic and is able to stretch. The hymen also is the tissue that surrounds the vaginal opening, *not* tissue that covers the vaginal opening. Yes, the first time penetration occurs, the girl may bleed, but she may not. The second time penetration occurs, the girl may bleed, but she may not. The fiftieth time penetration occurs, the girl may bleed, but she may not. Bleeding depends on if an injury has occurred from the penetration. Injuries can occur in consensual and non-consensual intercourse. Injuries can occur from the type of penetration (penis, finger, or object), the position the person was in during penetration, the angle of penetration, amount of lubrication present, and the amount of time that penetration lasted. Multiple factors can cause the hymen to bleed; first-time penetration is not one of them.

   Think of the hymen as like a scrunchie that is placed in hair to make a ponytail. The scrunchie goes around the hair, like the hymen goes around the vaginal opening. The scrunchie stretches but does not break as more hair is pulled through the opening; the hymen will usually stretch and not break to accommodate penetration.

2. **Girls can be born without a hymen.** This statement is a myth. In fact, the hymen is part of the vaginal birth canal. In the third month of gestation, the precursor of the uterus and proximal vagina, the uterovaginal primordium, comes in contact with the more anterior urogenital sinus. These structures fuse to form the vaginal lumen. The end point of the vaginal lumen does not canalize and remains separated from the urogenital sinus forming a mucosal barrier. This mucosal barrier is the hymen. The hymen is made up of collagenous connective tissue and squamous epithelium.[90] All girls are born with a hymen.

3. **If I use a tampon, I will lose my virginity.** The technical definition of virginity according to Merriam-Webster is "the state of never having sexual

intercourse." To take it a step further, virginity is a state of mind, so I truly believe that a person is a virgin until that person consents to sexual intercourse. The rapist or the molester does not have the right to take that away from anyone. So, to go back to the tampon: A tampon is an object used as an instrument during the menstrual cycle. It is inserted vaginally, but not used as sexual intercourse. The hymen is a ring around the vaginal opening that the tampon passes through. Since the hymen is elastic and can stretch, the hymen will accommodate tampons with a relatively low chance of injury.

When reviewing websites for tampon brands, the companies address this very issue.

The frequently asked questions on the Playtex website include:

Q: *Will using a tampon cause me to lose my virginity?*

A: *No. You don't have to worry about losing your virginity when using a tampon. You will remain a virgin until you have sexual intercourse.*[91]

Tampons have no effect on virginity.

4. **Masturbation can injure the hymen.** Masturbation is for pleasure. Girls that masturbate do so through stimulation of the clitoris. Boys that masturbate stimulate the penis. Masturbation would not be done if it was painful. The clitoris is toward the upper portion of the female anatomy and does not lie within the labia majora and labia minora like the hymen does. Masturbation is not likely to cause injury; however, anything is possible. If the story was masturbation with a hymenal injury, suspicion would be warranted until proven otherwise.

5. **A properly trained doctor or an FNE will be able to identify if a girl has been vaginally penetrated.** Imagine a teenager being brought into the hospital by her parents, stating that they want a virginity check of their daughter. Even worse, law enforcement waiting to hear if the hymen was intact before deciding to investigate a reported rape. One of my (A. Rasmussen) biggest pet peeves in the world of forensics is to be asked: if her hymen is intact, that means she has never had sex, right? Absolutely wrong!

To confirm what has been said multiple times in this chapter, the hymen is a ring-like collar that surrounds the vaginal opening. As a child becomes an adolescent, the hymen will become estrogenized and more elastic with the ability to stretch. The hymen is made to accommodate objects to include tampons, speculums, a penis, and yes, even a baby. The hymen may accommodate without any signs of injury, yet penetration did occur. They hymen may have had a tear, but the hymenal tissue is like that of the mucosal tissue in your mouth. Think of when the mouth is burned on something hot, it hurts for a day, and by the second day it is just a thought, and most likely completely healed. The hymen, if injured, will also heal quickly and may heal will no definite signs of trauma.

It does not matter how trained the examiner or doctor is, it is impossible to just visualize a hymen and say yes or no the hymen has been penetrated. The examiner should not use the word intact, which can be confusing. The examiner can state that there are no injuries noted at this time. There may not be injuries because:

- No penetration has occurred.
- Penetration that may have occurred did not cause injury.
- If injuries were present at the time of the event, the injuries have had sufficient time to heal without leaving any signs of trauma.

It is always good practice to reiterate to the caregivers or to law enforcement that not having any acute finding does not mean that nothing has happened. It is important to listen to what the child is saying and to conduct a full investigation. If trauma is noted by the examiner, then the trauma should be described. To document genital injuries, the clock format should be utilized. When testifying to the jury, I explain this by saying, imagine 12 o'clock is toward your belly button (umbilicus) and 6 o'clock is toward your anus. At that point the description of the anatomy (as described earlier in the chapter) can be reviewed, with identification of the injuries. For example, a tear was noted to the hymen at the 9 o'clock position. The hymen is separated into halves. The anterior rim of the hymen is from 9 o'clock to 3 o'clock. The posterior rim of the hymen is from 3 o'clock to 9 o'clock. It is more common to acquire injuries to the posterior rim of the hymen.

When describing the findings, the most common acroynm to use is TEARS:

- *Tears*
- *Ecchymosis*
- *Abrasions*
- *Redness*
- *Swelling*

When should a child or adolescent be scheduled for an examination?
An emergency evaluation should be scheduled when there are:

- Medical, psychological, or safety concerns such as acute pain or bleeding, suicidal ideation, or suspected human trafficking
- Alleged assault that may have occurred in the past 120 hours (time may be different based on the state guidelines)
- Need for emergency contraception
- Need for postexposure prophylaxis for sexually transmitted infections.

An urgent evaluation should be scheduled when there is:

- Suspected or reported sexual contact within the previous two weeks, without emergency medical, psychological, or safety needs identified.

A non-urgent evaluation should be scheduled when there are:

- Discolsure of abuse by child (suspected abuse more than two weeks prior)
- Sexualized behaviors
- Sexual abuse suspected by a professional member of the multi-disciplinary team
- Family concern for sexual abuse
- Abuse has happened within the past year for prepubertal child.

The expectation when completing examinations for sexual assault allegations is that the examination will be normal. It is critical to recognize normal examinations, medical abnormalities, and abnormal examinations. If the suspicion is that the child is presenting with an abnormal examination, the child should return in two weeks for follow up to see if what may have initially appeared as an injury has healed or if it has remained the same.

The next few photographs are examinations that were not considered normal examinations.

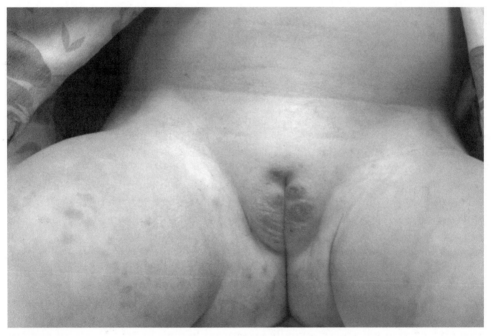

A 2-year-old female that presents with ulcerations to her labia majora. When gathering a history from the caregiver, no concerns were raised of sexual abuse. Caregiver states that the child is recovering from an outbreak of chicken pox.

LONG-TERM EFFECTS

The long-term effects of sexual abuse can vary with each victim as the level of childhood resilience can continue into adulthood with limited consequences. However, some adults who are victimized as children are severely traumatized, and they are unwilling or unable to discuss their childhood trauma, preventing

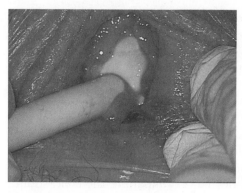 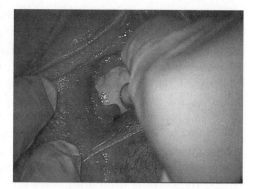

The next two photographs are of the same victim. This is a 17-year-old female that was raped by her best friend. This child has a redundant hymen in which a catheter was used to assess the hymenal edges. Findings:

- Labia Minora
- Red discharge at 3:00
- Circumferential redness
- Blue bruise from 3:00-5:00
- Hymen
- Red substance noted
- Acute transection noted from 3:00-6:00
- Deep notch at 9:00

researchers from accurately measuring the long-term effects of childhood sexual abuse. Age can be another factor relating to long-term effects as younger children may not remember the abuse; therefore, they may not suffer psychological repercussions. Additionally, the length and/or frequency of the abuse may be a contributing factor for long-term repercussions. Furthermore, the specific perpetrator can be a substantial factor as to any long-term effects. For instance, sexual abuse by the child's biological father may be more detrimental to the child when compared to a distant relative, as the trusting bond between a parent and child is broken. Researchers have attempted to evaluate the long-term effects of childhood sexual abuse in adults and compare it with adults who have not experienced victimization. In one study with a population of 9,367 participants, 54 percent women and 46 percent men, evaluating long-term effects of abuse, it was discovered that both male and female victims suffered long-term consequences through their victimization of abuse. This study found that both men and women who were sexually victimized had an increased risk of alcohol and drug abuse, suicide attempts, marrying an alcoholic, and facing marital and family problems. Furthermore, the study showed that adults who experience intercourse through their childhood victimization had an elevated risk of mental health, behavioral, and social problems in adulthood. Although sexual abuse affected both genders, other research on long-term effects has been gender specific.[92] For instance, there have been a great number of studies suggesting women who are victims of childhood sexual abuse also become victims later in life. In one gender-specific study, there was evidence to support this theory, although this study revealed that women who were sexually victimized before the age of thirteen were at greater risk of being sexually victimized later in life. The statistical data in such studies may be the direct result of adult victims who were candid enough to discuss both victimizations.

A suggested point of evidence that supports the connection between childhood victimization and adult victimization is that childhood sexual victimization may force children to leave their homes at an earlier age as they wish to avoid further abuse. These young people may marry early and become dependent on their spouse, making them vulnerable to both physical and sexual abuse. Others may not marry immediately but run away from home, making them more vulnerable to rape. There are still others that may be more likely to be victimized in their adulthood as they have low self-esteem, making them easier targets for sexually exploitive men.[93] Sexual dysfunction can also be the result of child sexual abuse as some victims often avoid sexual intimacy and avoid any relationship that they feel may lead to sex. Conversely, some victims may become sexually promiscuous, although that may not have any attachment to their sexual partner.[94]

Finally, childhood victimization can lead to adult criminal activity. Research has shown that both men and women who are incarcerated have had a history of sexual abuse, especially for the females who are incarcerated.[95] Some recent figures show that 44 percent of incarcerated women had either been physically or sexually abused as a child, and approximately half of them had used alcohol or drugs when they were arrested.[96]

INTRAINDIVIDUAL THEORIES

The concept that sexual abuse of a child can be attributed to some type of biological or psychological theory is disturbing. There could be an argument that the perpetrator cannot help their behavior and therefore the criminal justice response to sex offenders would be treatment instead of punishment. Our criminal justice system today still views sexual offenses as crimes, although some type of therapy is commonly implemented in conjunction with criminal justice sanctions. One of the arguments to support the concept that sex offenders cannot control their behavior is the fact that society keeps a public registry of sex offenders as there is a concern that they will reoffend, and this is not done for other crimes. Additionally, sex offenders who complete their criminal sentence can be held through civil sanctions on the belief that they are a continued threat to society. There has been genetic research of pedophilia, but the etiology of pedophilia is still largely unknown. This disorder is thought to be caused by an undetermined distribution of psychological, sociological, or biological factors. Although there is very little genetic research in this area, there have still been several studies that have begun to explore and implicate potential contributing genetic influences on sexual behavior.[97] Psychological explanations such as the psychoanalysis where Sigmund Freud focused on mental disorders arising from the conflict between society and the instinctive needs of the individual can be debated as an explanation for such deviant behavior. Freud argued that the individual personality consisted of three parts: the id, which consists of instinctual desires; the ego, the rational part of your personality; and the super ego, which represents the internalization of society's moral code.[98] Using Freud's analysis, one can argue that this concept separates the attraction toward children from those who act out on their attraction. Although an individual may be drawn to a child, their super ego identifies the taboo associated with child abuse, hindering their ability to act on their desires. In contrast, if the id is the primary motivating factor, the offender will act on their desires. This theory is consistent with the research presented by David Finkelhor. Finkelhor's first two preconditions, as discussed earlier in this chapter, have to be met before someone will actually sexually abuse a child as the potential offender must deal with their own internal inhibitors. Although most jurisdictions throughout the world treat sex offenses against children as criminal offenses instead of an illness, the government of Greece took a controversial stance by identifying pedophilia as a disability with the potential for financial compensation. The Greece National Confederation of Disabled People called the action incomprehensible.[99]

CASE STUDY #6 (JAIL THEN RAPE)

A twenty-eight-year-old man was serving time for sodomy of a boy under the age of thirteen and was released from custody. He was invited over to a friend's house the very next day. While over at his friend's house, he sodomized another boy under the age of thirteen. This man was unable to go twenty-four hours from his release before raping another child.

SOCIOLOGICAL THEORIES

The argument that sexual abuse is learned behavior is controversial as studies have shown the majority of male victims of sexual abuse did not become sexual abuse perpetrators, and female victims who become perpetrators are almost nonexistent. However, there still have been studies that reveal that some offenders abuse children through what they learned as a child. Some notable sociological theories that form a correlation between sexual abuse and what is learned include but are not limited to the following.

Attachment theory describes how infants mimic emotional and behavioral characteristics of their primary caretaker. Depending on how this attachment develops, the infant can be at a higher risk of social dysfunction where this deficit in intimacy can lead a person to be a sex offender in order to address those needs.[100] One of the most comprehensive models describing attachment to sex offenders and their victims is from Tony Ward, who provides an in-depth analysis of attachment style and intimacy deficits. He defines this association as the following:

> **In the anxious/ambivalent attachment style,** the individual has a negative view of themselves but a positive view of others, which leads them to seek approval from others. They desire intimacy but fear relationships. If this type of attach-

ment style manifests as a sexual offence, they will seek a victim whom they can control and who "looks up" to them. Hence, the victim of this offender type will often be a child who is known to the offender, and the offending will require minimal use of coercion or force. The offender is likely to groom their prospective victim and attempt to form a relationship with them.

In the first type of avoidant attachment style, the individual has a negative view of themselves and also a negative view of others, seeing them as untrustworthy. They may seek a sexual relationship but avoid intimacy, and lack the social skills to form a healthy adult romantic relationship even if they desire one. This will result in the person seeking impersonal sexual contact, and some will resort to coercion if necessary. Their victims may be adults or children, and they are less concerned with a specific gender.

In the second type of avoidant attachment style, the individual has a positive view of themselves and a negative view of others, blaming others for any problems in their lives. They are hostile and do not desire close relationships. This type of offender is the most aggressive and will use force against adults and children. The use of force is a way of expressing aggression and not simply instrumental to committing the act.[101]

The routine activities theory is another notable sociological theory relating to sexual abuse that addresses three elements needed for victimization:

1. Motivated offender
2. Attractive target
3. Lack of guardianship.

Children have limited autonomy when selecting their environment. When children are at home, the motivated offender can be the parents, siblings, or any person who has access to a child in the privacy of their home. Additionally, children don't choose their school or neighborhood they live in, thus leaving them vulnerable to any predator that can access them. As children age and gain more control over their environment, the potential for victimization decreases. In addition to the child's environment, dependency on a caretaker places the child at greater risk to become a target for abuse. As children become naturally more independent as they increase in age, the rate of their victimization decreases.[102]

CONCLUSION

The sexual abuse of a child can generate significant anger, but there is also a debate as to what is considered sexual abuse. As a society we condemn sexual abuse but tend to tolerate the sexualization of children, which is controversial not only from a moral perspective but from a legal perspective as we allow children to engage in sexual activity through the "age of consent" laws. However, the concept of sexual abuse is not tolerated as there are laws that address the abuse of children. Sexual abuse involves both contact and non-contact offenses. This type of abuse is also classified from the relationship of the offender and the child. The two general categories are extrafamilial, which refers to abuse outside of the family, and intrafamilial abuse (incest), which refers to abuse within the family. There are specific categories for perpetrators that abuse children based on the type of attraction they have. Pedophilia refers to the sexual attractions of prepubescent children; hebephilia refers to the sexual attraction of early pubescent children; ephebophilia refers to the attraction of older adolescents. A fairly recent category of sexual attraction has been established called infantophilia, which refers to the attraction to children five years of age and younger. In addition to the classification of attractions are the categories of sexual predators. Although men commit the vast majority of sex offenses against children, women offenders, despite being much rarer, can abuse children. When women sexually abuse a child, they usually fall under one of three categories: predisposed, teacher/lover, and male-coerced. It should also be noted that juvenile offenders commit a significant amount of the sexual abuse against other children, including their siblings. Institutional abuse is when sexual offenders use their employment in a position of authority to abuse children. It should also be noted that a significant amount of sexual abuse occurs through technology where children can be solicited to engage in sex via the internet or have sexually explicit language or photos sent to them via mobile phones. Child pornography is a worldwide problem, and the disbursement of these photos is easily hidden through the secrecy of the internet. Victims of sexual abuse can be any age. Research has found that children between the ages of eight to twelve are the most commonly victimized. Although children can eventually become perpetrators, research has indicated that most male victims do not become perpetrators and female victims almost never become perpetrators. Some sexual abuse can be committed through human trafficking networks where sex rings victimize countless children. Although sexual abuse can be identified through a child's disclosure, child advocates may have to rely on behavioral and physical indicators to identify victims of sexual abuse. In an attempt to help identify how abuse occurs, it is important to identify sexual causation. Research has shown that sexual abuse causation can be attributed to both intraindividual theories and sociological theories.

REVIEW QUESTIONS

1. Why is child pornography so easily distributed?

2. How do the "age of consent" laws sexualize children?

3. Why is sexual trafficking of children so prevalent in the United States?

4. How can behavioral indicators be used to establish a time frame of sexual abuse?

5. Why would a sexual abuse victim recant their disclosure?

KEYWORDS

Human trafficking: The recruitment, harboring, transportation, provision, or obtaining of a person for labor or services, through the use of force, fraud, or coercion for the purpose of subjection to involuntary servitude, peonage, debt bondage, or slavery

NAMBLA: North American Man/Boy Love Association

Child pornography: The possession, trade, advertising, and production of images that depict the sexual abuse of children

Sexting: The sending of sexually explicit messages or photos through an electronic device

Ephebophilia: The sexual attraction to older adolescents

Hebephilia: The sexual interest in pubescent children who are showing the early signs of sexual development

Infantophilia: A new subcategory of pedophilia, the sexual attraction to victims who are younger than five years of age

Pedophilia: The ongoing sexual attraction to prepubertal children

Institutional sexual abuse: Instances in which those working on behalf of an organization use the authority and power given to them in order to victimize others

Extrafamilial sexual abuse: Sexual abuse by persons outside the family such as strangers, teachers, coaches, neighbors, etc.

Intrafamilial sexual abuse: Sexual abuse of a child by a family member who is related by blood or affinity

Age of consent: Laws are based on whether children can legally engage in sexual activity and if their ages fall within the statutory requirements

NOTES

1. Merriam-Webster, "Innocence." Retrieved 8/22/19. https://www.merriam-webster.com/dictionary/innocence.

2. James R. Kincaid, *Erotic Innocence: The Culture of Child Molesting* (Durham, NC: Duke University Press, 1998), 54.

3. Kincaid, *Erotic Innocence: The Culture of Child Molesting*, 13.

4. Isabel Wilkenson, "The Story Behind Brooke Shields Famous Calvin Klein Jeans," *New York Times* (December 2, 2015).

5. David Finkelhor, *Child Sexual Abuse: New Theory & Research* (New York, NY: Free Press, 1984), 8.

6. Finkelhor, *Child Sexual Abuse: New Theory & Research*, 17.

7. Michelle Oberman, "Turning Girls into Women: Re-Evaluating Modern Statutory Rape Law," *The Journal of Criminal Law and Criminology* 85, no. 1 (1994): 19.c

8. Finkelhor, *Child Sexual Abuse: New Theory & Research*, 19.

9. J.L. Cook, *As You Were: Child Sex Abuse in the Military* (Rib Lake, WI: Ice Age Press, 2016), 35–36; International Planned Parenthood Federation, *Exclaim! Young People's Guide to "Sexual Rights: An IPPF Declaration"* (London: International Planned Parenthood Federation, 2011), 39.

10. Jon R. Conte and Viola Vaughan-Eden, "Child Sexual Abuse," in J. Bart Klika and Jon R. Conte (eds.), *The APSAC Handbook on Child Maltreatment*, fourth edition (Los Angeles, CA: Sage, 2018), 95–96.

11. Federal Bureau of Investigation, accessed January 31, 2019. Available from https://ucr.fbi.gov/crime-in-the-u.s/2013/crime-in-the-u.s.-2013/violent-crime/rape.

12. David Finkelhor, *Sexually Victimized Children* (New York, NY: The Free Press, 2010), 88–89.

13. G.K. Moffatt, *Wounded Innocents and Fallen Angels: Child Abuse and Child Aggression* (Westport, CT: Praeger, 2003), 239.

14. Finkelhor, *Sexually Victimized Children*, 88–89; Ali Yildirim, Erdal Ozer, Hassan Bozkurt, Sait Ozsoy, Ozgur Enginyurt, Durmus Evcuman, Riza Yilmaz, and Yunus Emre Kuyucu, "Evaluation of Social and Demographic Characteristics in a University Hospital in Turkey," *Medical Science Monitor: International Medical Journal of Experimental and Clinical Research* 20 (2014): 694.

15. Angela G. Rabin, "Child Sexual Abuse," in Francis P. Reddington and Betsy Wright Kreisel (eds.), *Sexual Assault: The Victims, the Perpetrators, and the Criminal Justice System*, third edition (Durham, NC: Carolina Press, 2017), 241; David G. Fischer and Wendy L. McDonald, "Characteristics of Intrafamilial and Extrafamilial Child Sexual Abuse," *Child Abuse and Neglect* 22, no. 9 (1998): 916–17.

16. Fischer and McDonald, "Characteristics of Intrafamilial and Extrafamilial Child Sexual Abuse," 915.

17. Jason Spraitz, "Institutional Sexual Abuse," in Carly M. Hilinski-Rosick and Daniel R. Lee (eds)., *Contemporary Issues in Victimology: Identifying Patterns and Trends* (Lanham, MD: Rowman & Littlefield, 2018), 225.

18. David Finkelhor, "The Trauma of Child Sexual Abuse: Two Models," *Journal of Interpersonal Violence* 2, no. 4 (1987): 352.

19. John Jay College of Criminal Justice, *The Nature and Scope of Sexual Abuse of Minors by Catholic Priests and Deacons in the United States 1950-2002*, 55. Accessed September 18, 2018. Available from http://www.usccb.org/issues-and-action/child-and-youth-protection/upload/The-Nature-and-Scope-of-Sexual-Abuse-of-Minors-by-Catholic-Priests-and-Deacons-in-the-United-States-1950-2002.pdf.

20. Laurie Goodstein and Shawn Otterman, "Catholic Priests Abused 1,000 Children in Pennsylvania, Report Says," *New York Times*, August 14, 2018. Accessed September 18, 2018. Available from https://www.nytimes.com/2018/08/14/us/catholic-church-sex-abuse-pennsylvania.html.

21. Jen Kirby, "The Sex Abuse Scandal Surrounding USA Gymnastic Team Doctor Larry Nassar, Explained," *Vox*, May 16, 2018. Accessed September 11, 2018. Available from https://www.vox.com/identities/2018/1/19/16897722/sexual-abuse-usa-gymnastics-larry-nassar-explained.

22. Lawrence Miller, "Sexual Offenses Against Children: Patterns and Motive," *Aggression and Violent Behavior* 18, no. 5 (2013): 511.

23. Deborah L. Laufersweiler-Dwyer and Gregg Dwyer, "Sex Offenders and Child Molesters," in Francis P. Reddington and Betsy Wright Kreisel (eds.), *Sexual Assault: The Victims, the Perpetrators, and the Criminal Justice System*, third edition (Durham, NC: Carolina Press, 2017), 318; P.E. Dietz, "Sex Offenses: Behavioral Aspects," in S.H. Kadish (ed.), *Encyclopedia of Crime and Justice* (New York, NY: Free Press, 1983), 1485–93.

24. Megan Stubbs-Richardson and David C. May, "Predictors of Adolescent Online Sexual Behaviors," in Elizabeth C. Dretsch and Robert Moore (eds.), *Sexual Deviance Online: Research and Readings* (Durham, NC: Carolina Academic Press, 2014), 88.

25. S. Maddan and L. Pazzani, *Sex Offenders: Crimes and Processing in the Criminal Justice System* (New York, NY: Wolters Kluwer, 2017), 96.

26. Finkelhor, *Child Sexual Abuse: New Theory & Research*, 54–60.

27. Gilian Tenbergen, Matthias, Helge Frieling, Jorge Ponseti, Martin Walter, Henrik Walter, Klaus M. Beier, Boris Schiffer, and Tillmann H.C. Kruger, "The Neurobiology and Psy-

chology of Pedophilia: Recent Advances and Challenges," *Frontiers in Human Neuroscience* 9, no. 344 (2015): 2.

28. Dietz, "Sex Offenses: Behavioral Aspects," 1485–93.

29. Laufersweiler-Dwyer and Dwyer, "Sex Offenders and Child Molesters," 313–14; Dietz, "Sex Offenses: Behavioral Aspects," 1485–93; Michael Davis, "Differentiating Child Sexual Abusers," *InPsych*, accessed August 28, 2018. Available from https://www.psychology.org.au/inpsych/2013/october/davis.

30. David M. Greenberg, John Bradford, and Susan Curry, "Infantophilia—A New Subcategory of Pedophilia? A Preliminary Study," *The Bulletin of the American Academy of Psychiatry and the Law* 23, no. 1 (1995): 63; D.H. Schetky, "The Sexual Abuse of Infants and Toddlers," in A. Tasman and S.M. Goldfinger (eds.), *Review of Psychiatry*, volume 10 (Washington, DC: American Psychiatric Press, 1991), 308–19.

31. Skye Stephens, Michael C. Seto, Alasdair M. Goodwill, and James M. Cantor, "Age Diversity Among Victims of Hebephilic Sexual Offenders," *SAGE* 30, no. 3 (2018): 322–24.

32. Skye Stephens, Michael C. Seto, Alasdair M. Goodwill, and James M. Cantor, "Evidence of Construct Validity in the Assessment of Hebephilia," *Archives of Sex Behavior* 46, no. 1 (2017): 301.

33. Brenda L. Russell, *Perceptions of Female Offenders: How Stereotypes and Social Norms Affect Criminal Justice Response* (Reading, PA: Springer, 2013), 1–2.

34. Jacqui Saradjian, "Understanding the Prevelance of Female-Perpetrated Sexual Abuse and the Impact of That Abuse on Victims," in Theresa A. Gannon and Franca Cortoni (eds.), *Female Sexual Offenders: Theory, Assessment and Treatment* (Chichester, UK: Wiley Blackwell, 2010), 29.

35. Frank G. Bolton, Larry A. Morris, and Ann E. MacEachron, *Males at Risk: The Other Side of Child Sexual Abuse* (Newbury Park, CA: Sage, 1989), 53.

36. Jane Kinder Matthews, Ruth Matthews, and Kathleen Speltz, "Female Sexual Offender: A Typology," in Michael Quinn Patton (ed.), *Family Sexual Abuse: Frontline Research and Evaluation* (Newbury Park, CA: Sage, 1991), 209; Christina Mancini, *Sex Crime Offenders & Society* (Durham, NC: North Carolina Press, 2014), 20.

37. Matthew O'Brien and Walter Bera, "Adolescent Sexual Offenders: A Descriptive Typology," *Preventing Sexual Abuse* 4, no. 3 (1986):3–4.

38. Mancini, *Sex Crime Offenders & Society*, 108.

39. Evan M. Daly, *Child Abuse: What You Need to Know* (Miami, FL: Parker Publishing, 2017), 86.

40. Tammara Hillard, "Childhood Sexual Abuse," paper presented at the 33rd International Symposium on Child Abuse, Huntsville, Alabama, March 27–30, 2017.

41. K.J. Terry, *Sexual Offenses and Offenders: Theory, Practice, and Policy*, second edition (Belmont, CA: Wadsworth, 2013), 127.

42. Gina Robertiello and Karen J. Terry, "Can We Profile Sex Offenders? A Review of Sex Offender Typologies," *Aggression and Violent Behavior* 12, no. 5 (2007): 515.

43. U.S. Department of Health and Human Services, *Child Maltreatment 2016* (Washington, DC: U.S. Department of Health and Human Services, 2006), 45.

44. Stephen Meyer, *Child Abuse and Domestic Violence: Information Plus* (Farmington Hills, MI: Cengage, 2017), 67.

45. Finkelhor, *Child Sexual Abuse: New Theory & Research*, 23.

46. Bolton, Morris, and MacEachron, *Males at Risk: The Other Side of Child Sexual Abuse*, 43.

47. Cynthia Crosson-Tower, *Understanding Child Abuse and Neglect*, eighth edition (Boston, MA: Pearson, 2010), 135.

48. Daley, *Child Abuse: What You Need to Know*, 87.

49. Daley, *Child Abuse: What You Need to Know*, 84.

50. M. Glasser, I. Kolvis, D. Campbell, and A. Glasser, "Cycle of Child Sexual Abuse: Links Between Being a Victim and Becoming a Perpetrator," *The British Journal of Psychiatry* 179, no. 6 (2018): 482–94; Mancini, *Sex Crime, Offenders & Society*, 109.

51. Malory Plummer and Annie Cossins, "The Cycle of Abuse: When Victims Become Offenders," *Trauma, Violence & Abuse* 19, no. 3 (2018): 300.

52. Monica L. McCoy and Stephanie M. Keen, *Child Abuse and Neglect*, second edition (New York, NY: Psychology Press, 2014), 160.

53. Georgia M. Winters and Elizabeth L. Jeglic, "Stages of Sexual Grooming: Recognizing Potentially Predatory Behavior of Child Molesters," *Deviant Behavior* 38, no. 6 (2016): 724–33.

54. Kimberly A. McCabe and Daniel G. Murphy, *Child Abuse: Today's Issues* (Boca Raton, FL: CRC Press, 2016), 131–33.

55. Craig J. Forsyth and James F Quinn, "A Swell of the Nasty: The New Wave of Sexual Behavior in the Back Places of the Internet," in Elizabeth C. Dretsch and Robert Moore (eds.), *Sexaul Deviance Online: Research and Readings* (Durham, NC: North Academic Press, 2014), 16–17.

56. Ursula Lande, "Child Pornography and Child Sexual Abuse," in Elizabeth C. Dretsch and Robert Moore (eds.), *Sexual Deviance Online: Research and Readings* (Durham, NC: Carolina Academic Press, 2014), 39.

57. Kimberly J. Mitchell, David Finkelhor, Janis Wolak, Michele L. Ybarra, and Heather Turner, "Youth Internet Victimization in a Broader Victimization Context," *Journal of Adolescent Health* 48, no. 2 (2011): 128.

58. Linda Trischitta, "New Technology Makes It Easier to Distribute Child Pornography," in Stefan Kiesbye (ed.), *Child Pornography: At Issue* (Farmington Hills, MI: Cengage, 2013), 50.

59. Trischitta, "New Technology Makes It Easier to Distribute Child Pornography," 51.

60. Kimberly A. McCabe and Olivia C. Johnston, "Perceptions on the Legality of Sexting: A Report," *Social Science Computer Review* 32, no. 6 (2014): 766–68.

61. U.S. Department of Justice, "Child Pornography Presents a Real and Growing Threat to Children," in Stefan Kiesbye (ed.), *Child Pornography: At Issue* (Farmington Hills, MI: Cengage, 2013), 12–13.

62. Virginia M. Kendall and T. Markus Funk, *Child Exploitation and Trafficking: Examining the Challenges and U.S. Responses* (Lanham, MD: Rowman & Littlefield, 2012), 22.

63. Ursula Lande, "Child Pornography and Child Sexual Abuse," 42–44.

64. Ann Wolbert Burgess, Chery Regehr, and Albert R. Roberts, *Victimology: Theories and Applications*, second edition (Burlington, MA: Jones & Bartlett Learning, 2013), 248.

65. John Wall, *Children's Rights: Today's Global Challenge* (Lanham, MD: Rowman & Littlefield, 2017), 101.

66. Stacey L. Mallicoat, *Women and Crime*, second edition (Thousand Oaks, CA: Sage, 2015), 320–22.

67. Office of Justice Programs: National Institute of Justice, "Human Trafficking," accessed October 4, 2018. Available from https://www.nij.gov/topics/crime/human-trafficking/pages/welcome.aspx.

68. Nita Belles, *In Our Backyard: Human Trafficking and What Can We Can Do To Stop It* (Grand Rapids, MI: Baker Books, 2015), 133.

69. Robert J. Meadows, *Understanding Violence & Victimization*, seventh edition (New York, NY: Pearson, 2019), 192.

70. Polaris, "Child Trafficking and the Child Welfare." Accessed October 4, 2018. Available from https://polarisproject.org/sites/default/files/Child%20Welfare%20Fact%20Sheet.pdf.

71. Neha A. Deshpande and Nawal M. Nur, "Sex Trafficking of Women and Girls," *Reviews in Obstetrics & Gynecology* 6, no. 1 (2013): 25; David R. Hodge, "Sexual Trafficking in the

United States: A Domestic Problem with Transnational Dimensions," *Social Work* 53, no. 2 (2008): 145–46.

72. U.S. Department of Health and Human Services Administration for Children, Youth, and Families, *Guidance to States and Services on Addressing Human Trafficking of Children and Youth in the United States*, 5, accessed October 4, 2018. Available from www.acf.hhs.gov.

73. UN Children's Fund, "End Trafficking," accessed October 17, 2018. Available from https://www.unicefusa.org/sites/default/files/assets/pdf/EndTrafficking_OnePager_FINAL.pdf.

74. National Center on Safe Supportive Learning Environments, "Risk Factors and Indicators." Available from https://safesupportivelearning.ed.gov/human-trafficking-americas-schools/risk-factors-and-indicators.

75. Cindy L. Miller-Perrin and Robin D. Perrin, *Child Maltreatment: An Introduction* (Thousand Oaks, CA: Sage, 2013), 118.

76. Nita Belles, *In Our Backyard*, 36; Kimberly A. McCabe, *The Trafficking of Persons: National and International Responses* (New York, NY: Peter Lang Publishing, 2008), 17.

77. Virginia M. Kendall and T. Markus Funk, *Child Exploitation and Trafficking: Examining the Global Challenges and U.S. Responses* (New York, NY: Rowman & Littlefield, 2012), 108.

78. Crosson-Tower, *Understanding Child Abuse and Neglect*, 195.

79. Jovana Lara, "Human-Trafficking Crackdown; 510 Arrested, 56 Rescued in California," *ABC News*, January 30, 2018, accessed October 1, 2018. Available from https://abc-7news.com/hundreds-arrested-in-human-trafficking-crackdown-in-california/3008362/.

80. Bolton, Morris, and MacEachron, *Males at Risk: The Other Side of Child Sexual Abuse*, 50.

81. S. Maddam and L. Pazzani, *Sex Offenders: Crimes and Processing in the Criminal Justice System* (New York, NY: Wolters Kluwer, 2017), 106.

82. Mary DeYoung, "The World According to NAMBLA: Accounting for Deviance," *A Journal of Sociology and Social Welfare* 16, no. 1 (1989): 120.

83. Maddam and Pazzani, *Sex Offenders*, 106.

84. Bryan Robinson, "ACLU Represent Man-Boy Love Group," *ABC News*, August 31, 2018.

85. International Association of Forensic Nursing. Available from https://www.forensic-nurses.org/default.aspx.

86. Michelle Ditton and Laurie A. Gray, "Female Anatomy," in *The ABC's of Sexual Assault: Anatomy, "Bunk" and the Courtroom of Sexual Assault* (Fort Wayne, IN: Socratic Parenting LLC, 2015), 29–37.

87. Michelle Ditton and Laurie A. Gray, "Male Anatomy," in *The ABC's of Sexual Assault: Anatomy, "Bunk" and the Courtroom of Sexual Assault* (Fort Wayne, IN: Socratic Parenting LLC, 2015), 38–42.

88. Rich Kaplan, Joyce Adams, Suzanne Starling, and Angelo Giardino, *Basic Anatomy of the Genitalia and Anus. Medical Response to Child Sexual Abuse A Resource for Professionals Working with Children and Families* (St. Louis, MO: STM Learning, Inc, 2011), 10.

89. Sara T. Stewart, "Hymenal Characteristics in Girls With and Without a History of Sexual Abuse," *Journal of Child Sexual Abuse* 20 (2011): 521–36.

90. Stewart, "Hymenal Characteristics in Girls With and Without a History of Sexual Abuse."

91. Playtex, accessed March 8, 2019. Available from http://www.playtexplayon.com/tampon-faq/tampon-myths.

92. Shanta R. Dube, Robert F. Anda, Charles L. Whitfield, David W. Brown, Vincent J. Felitti, Maxia Dong, and Wayne H. Giles, "Long-Term Consequences of Childhood Sexual Abuse by Gender of Victim," *American Journal of Preventative Medicine* 28, no. 5 (2005): 434.

93. Finkelhor, *Child Sexual Abuse: New Theory & Research*, 193–94.

94. Crosson-Tower, *Understanding Child Abuse and Neglect*, 372; McCabe and Murphy, *Child Abuse: Today's Issues*, 52.

95. Frank Schmalleger, *Criminal Justice: A Brief Introduction*, twelfth edition (Boston, MA: Pearson, 2018), 384; Caroline Wolf Harlow. "Prior Abuse Reported by Inmates and Probationers," U.S. Department of Justice, April 1999, accessed October 8, 2018. Available from http://www.iapsonline.com/sites/default/files/Prior%20Abuse%20Reported%20by%20Inmates%20and%20Probationers.pdf; Meadows, *Understanding Violence & Victimization*, 74.

96. Roslyn Muraskin, *Women and Justice: It's a Crime*, fifth edition (Boston, MA: Pearson, 2012), 339.

97. Collen M. Berryessa, "Potential Implications of Research on Genetic or Heritable Contributing to Pedophilia for the Objective of Criminal Law," *Recent Advances in DNA & Gene Sequences* 8, no. 2 (2014): 66.

98. Steven E. Barkan, *Criminology: A Sociological Understanding* (Boston, MA: Pearson, 2015), 119.

99. David Bohon, "Greece Recognizes Pedophilia as a Disability," *New American*, January 13, 2012.

100. Debbie Kyle, "Examining Sexual Offences through a Sociological Lens: A Socio-cultural Explorations of Casual and Desistance Theories," *European Journal of Probation* 8, no. 3 (2016): 172–73.

101. Tony Ward, Stephen Hudson, William L. Marshall, and Richard Siegert, "Attachment Style and Intimacy Deficits in Sexual Offenders: A Theoretical Framework," *Journal of Research and Treatment* 7, no. 4 (1995): 326; Kyle, "Examining Sexual Offences through a Sociological Lens," 172–73.

102. David Finkelhor, "The Victimization of Children: A Developmental Perspective," *American Journal of Orthopsychiatry* 65, no. 2 (1995): 179–81.

4

Psychological Maltreatment

◆ ◆ ◆

A CHILD'S NEEDS

IT WOULD BE NAÏVE TO EXPECT EVERY CHILD to have the perfect child-hood. However, when a child does face some type of unpleasant experience, they usually look for that safety net that most children can find in the comfort of their home. Children, like adults, have basic needs and desires and look forward to fulfilling their dreams through self-actualization as suggested through Maslow's Hierarchy of Needs.[1] Unfortunately, psychological maltreatment can happen in what is supposed to be the safety of their own home, preventing children from obtaining those basic needs.

PSYCHOLOGICAL MALTREATMENT

Psychological maltreatment is a significant problem where children can face adverse physical and mental health ailments resulting from the experiences of emotional abuse. As detrimental as this type of abuse can be, it does not appear to stir up the same type of emotion or outrage as that of physical or sexual abuse. One explanation as to why researchers focus on physical and sexual abuse is that physical abuse and to a lesser degree sexual abuse can show an immediate and observable harm.[2] Another factor that may explain this lack of interest from researchers and the general public is that its definition is somewhat ambiguous. Psychological maltreatment is underrecognized and is considered as a lower level of priority in social services.[3] However, psychological maltreatment is the most harmful type of abuse with long-lasting consequences. Additionally, the general public may not recognize the seriousness of this kind of abuse and may not be able to identify this particular behavior as psychological maltreatment but rather that of suboptimal parenting.[4] There is a challenge in determining what behaviors constitute psychological maltreatment as it is the most ambiguous form of child abuse, and most parents to some degree treat their children in an inappropriate way occasionally, saying or doing something they may regret later.[5] Furthermore, unlike other types of abuse, the physical indicators may not be as apparent and therefore not as obvious. Finally, the controversy in defining psychological maltreatment is that the definition is not so broad as to identify everyone as a victim, thus failing to provide clear guidelines for recognizing this unique type of maltreatment.[6] In creating a definition relating to this type of abuse, it must have criteria that demonstrate how the maltreatment will result in mental and psychological consequences for the child's developmental functioning, and these indicators can act as evidence of harm that may not be recognized for an extended period of time.[7]

There is significant research that discusses the challenges of defining psychological maltreatment, as there is no "line in the sand" that separates maltreatment from bad parenting. However, it is still important to attempt to distinguish between the two, as they may co-occur and eventually lead to psychological maltreatment as this abusive behavior is characterized by chronic, severe, and escalating patterns of emotional abuse.[8] The concept itself is vague as it usually refers to a pattern of behavior that causes some type of mental injury. Psychological maltreatment may be the most complex type of abuse to define and is not easily identifiable.[9] To expound on the difficulty of defining psychological maltreatment is the fact that it is used synonymously with emotional abuse and though different, these terms are related as they refer to the same type of behavior.[10] The term "psychological maltreatment" is preferable as it is more inclusive of all affective and cognitive aspects of child maltreatment.[11] Although there is no universal definition of psychological maltreatment, there have been prominent organizations that are dedicated to the care of children who have addressed the issue of defining this type of maltreatment. Although their goals in the care of psychological maltreatment may be similar, their definitions may vary.

THE AMERICAN PROFESSIONAL SOCIETY ON THE ABUSE OF CHILDREN

The American Professional Society on the Abuse of Children (APSAC) defined psychological maltreatment as "a repeated pattern or extreme incidents of caretaker behavior that thwart the child's basic psychological needs (e.g., safety, socialization, emotional and social support, cognitive stimulation, respect) and convey a child is worthless, defective, damaged goods, unloved, unwanted, endangered, primarily useful in meeting another's needs, and/or expendable."[12] APSAC classifies psychological maltreatment through six major subtypes: (1) spurning, (2) terrorizing, (3) isolating, (4) exploiting/corrupting, (5) denying emotional responsiveness, and (6) mental health, medical, and educational neglect.[13]

SUBTYPES OF PSYCHOLOGICAL TREATMENT

Spurning

There is an old adage that states "Sticks and stones can break my bones, but names will never hurt me," but in reality, words can and do cause harm, and this hurt is exemplified when verbal abuse is administered from a parent or a primary caretaker who the child looks up to. Spurning can come in different formats which include, but are not limited to, belittling, degrading, ridiculing, and publicly humiliating the child. Making fun of a child or shaming them can be destructive and demoralizing which can create guilt, doubt, or inferiority.[14] One example of spurning is when a child is looking for praise for an assignment completed at school and the caretaker responds negatively by insulting their work, or calling the child "stupid." Another example, related to humiliating a child, would be telling their child's friends that they wet the bed as the parent deliberately tries to embarrass their child.

Terrorizing

There are many different facets of domestic violence where someone causes a domestic partner to live in fear as they are constantly subjected to being terrorized by someone who is supposed to love them. Unlike children, and although difficult to have the courage to pursue, an adult has remedies at their disposal where they are able to seek options so that they no longer live in fear. An adult can seek a restraining order or even move out of the house to live with other family members or even seek the safety of a shelter. However, these options are not available to children unless another person intervenes on their behalf so they don't have to live in fear. Unfortunately, the very person that should advocate for the child (as a parent is supposed to provide safety for their children) is the one who is placing the child in fear. Terrorizing is the threatening of a child or the child's loved ones or possessions. One subcategory of terrorizing could include the destruction of property. The destruction of a child's property demonstrates the abuser's control over the child.[15] The killing of a child's pet, for example, would only amplify the power of the abuser in the child's mind, indicating he has power to control life and death. Although many threats may appear "hollow" to other adults who witness this verbal assault and may not take the threat seriously as they feel the caretaker would never impose such an outrageous act, in the child's mind those threats are real, giving the child legitimate concern. Various types of terrorizing create an atmosphere in which the child is continuously living in fear. In some circumstances, the threat can reach the level for criminal intervention where the child's caretaker could be charged with criminal threatening. However, this type of abuse occurs primarily behind doors, which may never come to the attention of the criminal justice system, as many parents may restrain such behavior in a public setting.

Isolating

Isolating is the confining of a child and not allowing them to associate with others. Isolating, like other subcategories of maltreatment, needs to exhibit a pattern of behavior to be considered maltreatment. For instance, a child being sent to their room for misbehavior would not be considered maltreatment, but if there was a pattern where the child is continuously isolated from socializing or contact with other children or adults, that pattern of behavior could indicate psychological maltreatment. Other forms of isolating can result from an overprotective parent. A parent or caretaker who has been a victim of abuse in their own life may be excessively concerned that their child may face the same type of victimization, thus fearing leaving their child somewhere without their own personal supervision. In most cases of isolation, it may be unlikely that law enforcement would intervene as it may not rise to the level of criminal behavior of abandonment. However, it is not uncommon for parents who are involved in criminal activity to limit their child's socialization in fear that their criminal activity may be exposed through the discourse of their children. In other circumstances, the police may be called to check on the physical welfare of a child.

Exploiting/Corrupting

This is encouraging a child to develop or engage in inappropriate behavior. This can involve encouraging delinquent behavior or victimizing them through various types of exploitation. This type of behavior can result from modeling the parent's activities or encouraging a child to commit delinquent acts such as stealing or selling drugs on the behalf of their caretakers. Parents are quite aware that the juvenile justice system is based on rehabilitation and not on punishment, so the consequences of a juvenile committing a crime are significantly lower than that of an adult. Additionally, a parent may exploit the child by allowing them to engage in illegal sexual activity such as prostitution or child pornography that will suit the parent's financial ambitions. This category of psychological maltreatment is the most likely type of abuse that will generate a law enforcement response, not only because of the objectivity of a criminal act, but also due to its discovery. Unlike most forms of psychological maltreatment, evidence of exploiting or corrupting will be discovered outside the child's home, making it easier to detect. Law enforcement may intervene by charging the juvenile with a delinquent act. It is unclear, however, if law enforcement will report this as psychological abuse as the child may not want to implicate their caretaker. In addition, law enforcement may choose not to file a juvenile petition alleging criminal behavior, but instead have Child Protective Services file a petition for neglect, thus focusing on the parent as the offender and not the child. The English Common Law doctrine of *parens patriae* allows the state to act as the parent.[16] With this authority, the courts, if they feel the child's home is conducive to more corrupting behavior, can have the parent's custody rights terminated. Finally, this type of corruption often leads the child into further criminal acts as they enter adulthood.

CASE STUDY #1 (WOMAN PROVIDES SEX AND DRUGS FOR CHILDREN)

Law enforcement had been receiving multiple complaints of teenagers partying at a local condominium. The resident, Selena Dross, was a single mother of two children, a daughter aged fourteen and a son aged seven. The complaints that were filed reported that neighbors observed teenagers entering the condo on a regular basis carrying alcohol and that there was a constant odor of marijuana coming from the premises. It had also been reported that the fourteen-year-old daughter would invite boys from the neighborhood to come to the residence to party with the permission of Selena, who would be present. Teenagers in the neighborhood reported to the police that sometimes Selena would purchase alcohol and marijuana for the teenagers and would "party" alongside of them. This was done in the presence of the seven-year-old boy and at times the boy was given alcohol. There were also several allegations of how the mother would allow her daughter to engage in sex with multiple teenagers while she was still at the residence (the teenage daughter would not cooperate in the investigation). A teenager who attended one of the parties reported that on one occasion Selena was intoxicated, had four teenage boys line up, and in the presence of her daughter perform oral sex on them while singing "lollipop, lollipop." These incidents were reported to social services, but law enforcement was advised that there wasn't adequate evidence to justify removing the children from the house. A few weeks later, a male suspect repeatedly stabbed another man and fled the scene using Selena's residence as a hideout. The suspect was arrested for attempted murder and although rarely done, law enforcement filed a civil complaint of child neglect, and not psychological maltreatment.

Denying Emotional Responsiveness

This is when a parent or caretaker shows no emotional reaction to or do not express any affection for their child. Emotional intimacy is knowing that you have someone you can share your feelings with; you are able to open up to that person through words or even just a certain look.[17] Unfortunately so many children are deprived of what most people may believe is a natural bond between a parent and their child. Even with this type of abuse being so detrimental, it is still a difficult category to measure and respond to. There are some parents who are naturally more nurturing than other parents, but there is a unique challenge when you try to classify it as maltreatment. How do you measure how much love a child is supposed to have before it can be categorized as maltreatment? In contrast to exploiting/corrupting, this category of maltreatment is the least likely to generate a criminal investigation. When an adult denies a child's emotions, they are sending a message that their emotions are wrong and the child is wrong for experiencing them.[18] To make matters worse, children are left with the feeling that their emotions are not important, which can affect a child's self-esteem.[19]

Mental Health, Medical, and Educational Neglect

This type of neglect refers to when a parent fails to provide them with any of the necessary services in any of these areas. There are a significant amount of children who suffer from different mental health issues such anxiety, depression, psychosis, and even more common mental health issues such as attention deficit disorder. Each one of these conditions requires extra supervision and support where it is important to the parent to seek out the appropriate medical care such as counseling through a psychiatrist or psychologist and obtain the appropriate medication if warranted. Children with special needs may require special attention or services to meet their educational challenges. If a child is failing in school and is not getting the appropriate assistance, then the parent must advocate for that child and seek the appropriate accommodations such as an Individual Educational Plan so that the child can be successful in school. However, there are many parents who may not have the knowledge or willingness to assist their child with special needs. It is expected that parents know how to adequately care for their children, but actual parenting skills are based on emotional maturity, their positive attitude toward their children, their knowledge of child development, their coping skills, and the treatment received from their own parents. These abilities could be supplemented through extended social support networks such as grandparents, friends, or neighbors.[20] This type of abuse is commonly classified under the category of neglect.

THE AMERICAN ACADEMY OF PEDIATRICS

The American Academy of Pediatrics is a prominent medical institution within the United States that is responsible for the physical, mental, and social health of infants, children, adolescents, and young adults; this agency has addressed the challenges of defining psychological maltreatment or emotional maltreatment, as the terms are often used interchangeably.[21] In the *Psychological Maltreatment of Children—Technical Report*, psychological maltreatment has been defined as repeated patterns of damaging interactions between parents(s) and child that becomes typical of the relationship.[22] They then describe behaviors—spurning; terrorizing; exploiting/corrupting; denying emotional responsiveness; neglecting mental health, medical, and educational needs; and isolating—that are consistent with APSAC's (2017) indicators of psychological maltreatment. In addition, the behavioral indicators of unreliable or inconsistent parenting, rejecting, and witnessing intimate partner violence are cited as behavioral indicators.

Rejecting

This can involve a parent who shuns, avoids, or pushes away their child, thus making their child feel that they are not wanted. This category of maltreatment may be neglectful or abusive.[23] The effects of rejection are devastating as a child feels that they are not loved, and these feelings can last a lifetime. To exacerbate the emotions of feeling rejected, the child in many cases will naturally assume most of the blame.[24] One of the long-term consequences associated with rejection is that these children often grow up expecting the same type of rejection from other people. They may settle for relationships where they are willing to tolerate the lack of compassion, nurturing, or even rejection that they may consider commonplace.

Unreliable or Inconsistent Parenting

The parent makes contradictory and ambivalent demands, creating unnecessary confusion for the child. This inconsistency may be the result of emotionally immature parents who are either loving or detached, depending on their mood. Growing up with an inconsistent parent undermines a child's sense of security, keeping the child on edge. A child may believe that these changing moods of a parent are somehow the child's fault.

Witnessing Intimate Partner Violence

There is significant research on the negative effects of witnessing domestic violence, which will be discussed in chapter 10—the detailed comprehensive discussion will include the psychological maltreatment of children.

THE CENTERS FOR DISEASE CONTROL AND PREVENTION

The Centers for Disease Control and Prevention (CDC) is a federal agency and the leading national public health institute. The CDC defines psychological maltreatment as:

> intentional caregiver behavior that conveys to a child that he or she is worthless, flawed, unloved, unwanted, endangered, or valued only in meeting another's needs. Psychologically maltreating behaviors may include blaming, belittling, degrading, intimidating, terrorizing, restraining, confining, corrupting, exploiting, spurning, or otherwise behaving in a manner that is harmful, insensitive to the child's developmental needs, or can potentially damage the child psychologically or emotionally.[25]

The CDC, APSAC, and the Academy of Pediatrics have similarities in their definitions, and they provide similar subcategories as examples of this maltreatment. However, the CDC appears to be unique as they focus on the "intentional caregiver behavior," which can be controversial as the intent of the abuser is not always specified in operational or legal definitions when identifying this type of abuse. The lack of uniformity in defining psychological maltreatment continues as we examine how psychological maltreatment is defined through an international perspective.

UNITED NATIONS

In 1959, the Declaration on the Rights of a Child was adopted and was considered the first international consensus on the rights of a child, although it was not legally binding.[26] Definitions of child abuse were developed, including psychological maltreatment. In 2011, the United Nations, through the committee on the Rights of a Child, addressed psychological maltreatment through a legal analysis in Article 19. It categorizes psychological maltreatment under the categories of neglect and mental violence. These are specifically addressed in sections 20 and 21:

> **Neglect or negligent treatment (20).** Neglect means the failure to meet children's physical and psychological needs, protect them from danger, or obtain medical, birth registration or other services when those responsible for children's care have the means, knowledge and access to services to do so. It includes: 8 CRC/C/GC/13 (a) Physical neglect: failure to protect a child from harm,including through lack of supervision, or failure to provide the child with basic necessities including adequate food, shelter, clothing and basic medical care; (b) Psychological or emotional neglect: including lack of any emotional support and love, chronic inattention to the child, caregivers being "psychologically unavailable" by overlooking young children's cues and signals, and exposure to intimate partner violence, drug or alcohol abuse; (c) Neglect of children's physical or mental health: withholding essential medical care; (d) Educational neglect: failure to comply with laws requiring caregivers to secure their children's education through attendance at school or otherwise; and (e) Abandonment: a practice which is of great concern and which can disproportionately affect, inter alia, children out of wedlock and children with disabilities in some societies.
>
> **Mental violence (21).** "Mental violence," as referred to in the Convention, is often described as psychological maltreatment, mental abuse, verbal abuse and emotional abuse or neglect and this can include: (a) All forms of persistent harmful interactions with the child, for example, conveying to children that they are worthless, unloved, unwanted, endangered or only of value in meeting another's needs; (b) Scaring, terrorizing and threatening; exploiting and corrupting; spurning and rejecting; isolating, ignoring and favoritism; (c) Denying emotional responsiveness; neglecting mental health, medical and educational needs; (d) Insults, name-calling, humiliation, belittling, ridiculing and hurting a child's feelings; (e) Exposure to domestic violence; (f) Placement in solitary confinement, isolation or humiliating or degrading conditions of detention; and (g) Psychological bullying and hazing by adults or other children, including via information and communication technologies (ICTs) such as mobile phones and the Internet.[27]

The definitions that are in use today generally include a pattern of behavior that includes both acts of commission and omission judged by a community and professional standards that are believed to be psychologically damaging.[28] These various definitions, used by organizations and researchers, form a basis for identifying psychological maltreatment. Creating an operational definition involves taking an abstract concept and defining it in terms of operations or behaviors that can be observed. Criticism of operational definitions include that they are too broad and that some aspects within these definitions should not be classified as psychological maltreatment.[29] In addition, applying these concepts in order to formally intervene on a child's behalf is considerably more challenging as you are required to act based on the laws within your jurisdiction.

LEGAL DEFINITIONS

Just as there are no universal definitions of psychological maltreatment, there are varying legal definitions of psychological maltreatment throughout the United States. Some states require that the abuser was intentionally causing harm. The inconsistency continues with state terminology as states refer to the harm imposed as emotional maltreatment, psychological harm, or mental injury. These terms, depending on the state, may limit these references as just a phrase, whereas others will expand on the definition detailing what is required to prove that harm.[30] Some states require proof of mental injury using narrow definitions, whereas other states require injuries to be substantial and observable, which may take years to occur.[31] Although most states address psychological abuse, there are several states that don't address psychological neglect, in that psychological neglect must be inferred within the state statutes.[32] There are some states that don't identify psychological maltreatment within their statutes. For example, Georgia and Washington identify neglect, sexual, and physical abuse, but there is no mention of psychological maltreatment. Finally, from a legal perspective, although most states identify psychological maltreatment within their statutes, it is often considered an intangible activity and there may be a reluctance to prosecute. When states do prosecute psychological maltreatment cases, it is not uncommon for those accused to challenge the language in the statute as being too vague. Courts, however, have consistently turned back these challenges.[33]

MEASURING PSYCHOLOGICAL MALTREATMENT

Measuring psychological maltreatment is difficult as some aspects may be very subtle and unnoticed, especially when your observations may be limited to what you believe is an isolated incident, thus not witnessing a pattern of behavior to properly identity this type of abuse. Although there are unique challenges in identifying psychological maltreatment, it is considered the most prevalent form of abuse.[34] It should also be noted that psychological maltreatment is commonly associated with other types of abuse.[35] Although this type of abuse is commonly associated with other acts of abuse, it may be neither properly identified or reported. For instance, if an adult manipulates a child into engaging in sex with them and the sexual abuse is discovered, the only abuse that might be reported is the sexual act, and the "exploiting," a category of psychological maltreatment, is never registered. The same concept applies to neglect. Neglect is the most commonly reported type of abuse. One of the common subcategories of neglect is supervisory neglect. Within this category, there is a failure to adequately supervise a child by leaving them alone or abandoning the child.[36] Either action would be reported as a form of neglect even though this action by the caretaker is "denying emotional responsiveness"; by their actions, they are not displaying any affection for the child. Finally, striking a child with such force that causes substantial injury while stating "I wish you were never born" will most likely be reported as physical abuse, and the injuries sustained may eventually go away, but those hurtful words that a child may never forget are unlikely going to be reported as psychological maltreatment. With all the challenges in identifying and reporting psychological maltreatment, these allegations have been reported and documented. The Department of Health and Human Resources records report of psychological maltreatment as an individual report and in combination with another form of abuse. These reports are released on an annual basis (see table 4.1).

Table 4.1   Maltreatment Type Combinations, 2016[1]

Maltreatment Type Combinations	Maltreatment Type	Maltreatment Type, Percent
Single Type		
Neglect includes medical neglect	423,007	63.0
Other/unknown	20,258	3.0
Psychological or emotional maltreatment	15,504	2.3
Sexual abuse	44,468	6.6
Two Types		
Neglect and "other"/unknown	23,182	3.5
Neglect and physical abuse	34,606	5.2
Neglect and psychological maltreatment[2]	12,858	1.9
Neglect and sexual abuse[3]	9,079	1.4
Physical abuse and "other"/unknown	681	0.1
Physical abuse and psychological maltreatment[4]	5,109	0.8
Physical abuse and sexual abuse[5]	1,430	0.2
Sexual abuse and psychological maltreatment[6]	425	0.1
Three Types		
Neglect, physical abuse, and psychological maltreatment	3,178	0.5
Neglect, physical abuse, and "other"/unknown	1,207	0.2
Neglect, physical abuse, and sexual abuse[7]	980	0.2
Remaining combinations	**1,104**	**0.2**
National	**671,622**	**100.0**

1 U.S. Department of Health & Human Services, Administration for Children and Families, Administration on Children, Youth and Families, Children's Bureau. (2018). Child maltreatment 2016. Available from https://www.acf.hhs.gov/cb/research-data-technology/statistics-research/child-maltreatment.
2 Includes 155 victims with a combination of neglect, psychological maltreatment, and "other"/unknown.
3 Includes 359 victims with a combination of neglect, sexual abuse, and "other"/unknown.
4 Includes twenty-four victims with a combination of physical abuse, psychological maltreatment, and "other"/unknown.
5 Includes twenty-six victims with a combination of physical abuse, sexual abuse, and "other"/unknown.
6 Includes nine victims with a combination of sexual abuse, psychological maltreatment, and "other"/ unknown.
7 Includes one victim with a combination of neglect, physical abuse, sexual abuse, and "other"/unknown.

INDICATORS OF PSYCHOLOGICAL MALTREATMENT

There is no simple test that can be administered to determine whether a child has been psychologically abused.[37] However, there can be both physical and mental health indicators through psychological testing to support that a child has been a victim of psychological abuse. Psychological testing can, however, provide potentially useful information about someone's emotional, behavioral, and cognitive functioning, which can possibly be associated with psychological maltreatment. It should also be noted that psychological testing is not diagnostic and should only occur in the context of a more comprehensive assessment of a person's overall psychological functioning and can be used in conjunction with other sources of data that are gathered during the evaluation.[38] Indicators may vary based on the duration of the abuse and the child may act differently if the abuse is followed by periods of positive parent-child relationships in comparison to a child who has always experienced a poor relationship with their parents.[39] Unfortunately, even with the collection of information through a comprehensive analysis, it can be challenging to form a definitive correlation through some type of indicator and conclusively state that it was a result of psychological maltreatment. For instance, if a child sustains a fracture, you could easily associate it with who the child alleges to have used such a level of force to cause that type of injury. With psychological abuse, the indicators may be very subtle and possibly not recognized; if an indicator is recognized, the observer may not be able to form a relationship between the particular indicator and its causation. For example, if a child suffers from anxiety, it would be extremely difficult to say that diagnosis was the result of parental care. It is just as challenging, if not more so, as the fracture, where you can tie the injury to one act of physical abuse: you would have to prove a pattern of behavior by the caretaker and prove that pattern of behavior resulted in the diagnosis of anxiety. As difficult as it is to identify indicators, research has identified several conditions that are consistent with psychological maltreatment.

BRAIN FUNCTION AND OTHER PHYSIOLOGICAL INDICATORS

Psychological maltreatment can have a direct effect on how a child's brain functions. The American Academy of Pediatrics reports that toxic stress is a significant threat to a child's healthy neurological development.[40] The brain has a dynamic neural system that has the ability to adapt and change based on novel experiences. It is particularly vulnerable to psychological abuse. Psychological abuse by caretakers can alter the structure and efficiency of the child's brain and the body's neurobiological system, keeping the child in an alert and stressful state.[41] Children living in emotionally abusive environments can acquire long periods of stress, which can adversely influence the brain's architecture.[42] A neglected child who experiences insufficient stimulation and therefore fewer connections between the neurons can lead to learning disabilities.[43] All the repercussions of psychological maltreatment and its effect on the brain can have a direct correlation to a child's cognitive abilities.

Finally, the impact of psychological wounds activates the same regions of the brain as pain caused from physical wounds.[44] In addition to brain function, there are other adverse biological changes resulting from psychological maltreatment, including allergies, asthma, headaches, and respiratory ailments. There is also a condition referred to as non-organic failure to thrive, which identifies children whose rate of weight gain is much lower than other children of similar age or gender. This results as the child's physical growth has ether decelerated or the child's growth has been suspended. This should not be confused with organic failure to thrive, which is an underlying medical condition and may not be related to maltreatment. This condition, when identified as a form of abuse through earlier studies, was identified as a result of neglect.[45] It was through later studies that this condition has been identified as the result of emotional neglect as the parent and child lose their emotional bond.

BEHAVIORAL INDICATORS

Children who have been victims of psychological maltreatment have challenges socializing and developing friendships with their peers. The verbal abuse that they experienced as a child can become learned behavior where they could become abusive to their friends, thus alienating themselves. This inappropriate behavior can include aggression, conduct problems, disruptive classroom behavior, hostility, and anger.[46] Other behavioral indicators can be the reaction of the children to their caretaker's abuse. Some may have self-blame, believing that they have done something wrong and deserve this type of emotional abuse. They yearn for their parent's affection and continuously try to please their parents in the hope of acceptance. This rejection can lead to other behavioral indicators such as substance abuse, running away, eating disorders, self-mutilation, or attempts on their lives. Finally, some behavior indicators may be extremely subtle or even hidden as some children will try and suppress their negative emotions.

LONG-TERM EFFECTS

Resiliency is the ability to come through negative experiences in life relatively unscathed or even thrive in the face of adversity.[47] Children can be extremely resilient where they can tolerate an onslaught of verbal abuse and other forms of psychological maltreatment through their entire childhood. Through this exposure, they will often display no physical or behavioral indicators as they are able maintain a healthy disposition even though they have been exposed to a type of victimization. They can use this inner strength and carry their resiliency into their adulthood, making their childhood history just an irrelevant memory. They don't have illusions of family perfection and want to pursue the truth.[48] These children are able to move forward and have a productive and successful adult life, including forming new relationships. Unfortunately, there are different levels of resiliency where children may be unable to cope with their victimization and those haunting memories stay with them through their adulthood. The ability to cope with childhood experiences also depends on the severity and the duration of the abuse. One of the long-term consequences of psychological maltreatment is the difficulty or inability to form an interpersonal relationship with another adult.[49] Fortunately for some, forming a relationship with a reliable adult can help with their resilience in an indirect way, although the lingering trauma may haunt them in other ways, such as anxiety, depression, or bad dreams.[50]

Other victims of psychological abuse may never find that supportive relationship as their childhood experiences hamper them from forming that bond. Specific long-term effects can include mental illness such as bipolar disorder or depression. Personality disorders can include being narcissistic, obsessive-compulsive, and paranoid. Additionally, long-term effects can include eating and sleeping disorders.[51] Long-term effects can also include physical repercussions for psychological maltreatment including hypertension, somatic complaints, and high mortality in adulthood.[52] In addition to these physiological changes resulting from psychological maltreatment, other long-term consequences include damage to their mental health: slowly eroding their self-worth and self-esteem can lead to educational failure and potential criminal behavior.[53] Furthermore, psychological maltreatment can result in dwarfism due to growth failure.[54] Finally, the long-term implications of psychological maltreatment are not solely based on what your caretaker did to you, but also includes what they failed to do. Acts of omission (denying emotional responsiveness) have been associated with personality disorders such as paranoid, schizoid, and avoidant.[55]

OFFENDERS

Children can't pick their parents, and although no parent is without flaws, abusive parents can be detrimental to a child's well-being. When there are psychological issues affecting the parent to the point of being abusive or neglectful, it can have a lasting negative effect throughout a child's life. There are certain factors that can identify why a parent may be emotionally abusive to their own children. The National Incidence Study is a congressionally mandated research effort that provides periodic research providing information to determine how prevalent child abuse is in the United States. The fourth National Incidence Study found that the biological parents are the primary perpetrator, accounting for 73 percent of all emotional abuse cases and 90 percent of reported emotional neglect cases. Moreover, it was reported that females are twice as likely to be perpetrators of emotional neglect. However, males were more likely (60 percent) to be the perpetrator of emotional abuse.[56] There are benefits to having both parents in the household, as one parent can compensate for the shortcomings of the other parent. Although there are unique stressors associated with single parenthood that can lead to psychological maltreatment, there are also benefits of having one caretaker. One caretaker may include a close harmonious family and provide emotional stability.[57] There is other research that addresses the stepparent, and although many stepparents provide excellent and devoted care, there is substantial evidence that they too pose a risk toward children.[58] Additionally, an offender's perception of caretaking can contribute to psychological maltreatment. For instance, the traumatizing narcissist who is someone who cannot foster or tolerate intersubjectivity only feels alive and loved when their point of view is the only valid perception, using the child for the sole purpose as a gratifying object. As long as the child affirms the parent's beliefs, the child is accepted and loved.[59] Other dynamics to consider are the personality of the offender, as this attribute can itself be a causation of abuse. The personality of the offender (including maturity) can also be a contributing factor to abuse. Lindsay Gibson, a clinical psychologist, categorizes four main types of emotionally immature parents who are especially likely to cause feelings of insecurity in their children:

1. **Emotional parents** are run by their feelings, swinging between overinvolvement and abrupt withdrawal. They are prone to frightening instability and unpredictability. Overwhelmed by anxiety, they rely on others to stabilize them. They treat small upsets like the end of the world and see other people as either rescuers or abandoners.
2. **Driven parents** are compulsively goal-oriented and super busy. They can't stop trying to perfect everything, including other people. Although they rarely pause long enough to have true empathy for their children, they are controlling and interfering when it comes to running their children's lives.
3. **Passive parents** have a laissez-faire mindset and avoid dealing with anything upsetting. They're less obviously harmful than the other types but have their own negative effects. They readily take a backseat to a dominant mate, even allowing abuse and neglect to occur by looking the other way. They cope by minimizing problems and acquiescing.
4. **Rejecting parents** engage in a range of behaviors that make you wonder why they have a family in the first place. Whether their behavior is mild or severe, they don't enjoy emotional intimacy and clearly don't want to be bothered by children. Their tolerance for other people's needs is practically nil, and their interactions consist of issuing commands, blowing up, or isolating themselves from family life. Some of the milder types may engage in stereotyped family activities but still show little closeness or real engagement. They mostly want to be left alone to do their thing.[60]

CASE STUDY #2 (MOTHER SHOOTS HERSELF AFTER LOSING CUSTODY)

Madeline Brickley, a divorced mother with one child, lived in a local condominium. Although never having an official psychiatric examination, she seemed to be suffering from paranoia. Law enforcement was notified by Child Protective Services that Madeline had a ten-year-old son who was not attending school and was not allowed to visit his father. Through phone discussions with Child Protective Services and law enforcement, it became clear that Madeline would never leave the house because she believed the mafia was out to get her—if they left the house, she believed they would be murdered. Both agencies tried to convince her that she was not in any danger, as she had never had any contact with organized crime, so there was no reason they would want to harm her in any way. Unfortunately, reasoning with Madeline did not work as she would not leave her house (with the exception of sneaking out to get groceries), isolating herself and her son from any contact. She took the additional measures of barricading both doors to her residence. Law enforcement obtained an emergency protective order to remove the child and temporally place the child in the custody of his father until there was a judicial review. Law enforcement was unable to convince Madeline to open the door despite informing her of a court order. Police officers then forcibly knocked down the front door and removed the child and returned him to his father. The next day, there was a judicial hearing to determine temporary custody of their child pending a possible psychiatric evaluation. The court ruled that the ten-year-old boy could stay with his father until Child Protective Services evaluated the home environment to determine physical custody of the child. On that same afternoon, Madeline drove on a highway during rush hour, pulled over onto the breakdown lane, took out a gun, and shot herself in the chest in front of passing motorists.

VICTIMS

It is clear that any child can be a victim of psychological maltreatment as the social influences a caretaker experiences or the individual traits a caretaker possesses can affect the way they care for all their children. However, in some circumstances, the parent may single out an individual child. This is referred to as the "Cinderella syndrome," where a specific child of the family is abused or rejected while the rest of the family adequately cared for.[61] Sometimes a child may be singled out due to the child's behavior. For example, a child with a difficult temperament or even a personality disorder may be targeted for psychological maltreatment.[62] Some children may be targeted due to the circumstances of their existence. For example, if a child's birth is the result of a rape, the mother died giving birth, or the child was the result of infidelity, despite these circumstances being no fault of the child, they are targeted as their presence reminds the caretaker of that unpleasant history.[63] Other children may be targeted due to their disabilities as the caretaker may be frustrated with the additional work and emotional drain associated with raising a child with these challenges. In addition to demonstrating a causation for psychological maltreatment, the targeting of an individual based solely on their disability is one of the categories listed under hate crime legislation.

CAUSATION

Determining the causation of psychological maltreatment can be a difficult task, but there are still plausible theoretical perspectives of why caretakers engage in this type of abuse. However, to add to the complexity in determining causation, some acts of abuse may be the result of multiple factors, making an analysis for cause even more difficult. We will now address some of the intraindividual and sociological explanations for psychological maltreatment.

Intraindividual Theories

The intraindividual approach views child maltreatment as the product of some type of internal defect inside the abuser.[64] One of the key factors for causation within this theory is mental illness. Mental illness refers to a broad spectrum of mental health conditions that can include, but are not limited to, depression, anxiety, or bipolar disorder. The challenge of raising a child can be overwhelming and, in some cases, too much to bear as one faces their own challenges of mental illness. The containment theory, by Walter C. Reckless, was introduced as a causation of juvenile delinquency, but the same principles of positive self-concept, tolerance for frustration, and the ability to set realistic goals[65] can be applied to parenting as well. Parents who suffer from mental illness may find themselves succumbing to the internal pushes within their containment that may create restlessness or a hostile attitude, which can in turn be directed toward their children. In some extreme types of mental illness such as postpartum psychosis, the parent may be unaware of their actions and unable to appreciate the wrongfulness of their behavior.[66] Although mental illness is a significant factor in the maltreatment of children, most people who do abuse their children are not suffering from some type of major mental illness. The strongest relationship between mental illness and child maltreatment is depression.[67] Substance abuse is another significant factor in the maltreatment of children. In some cases, substance abuse is in direct correlation with mental illness, as parents who are suffering from mental illness may abuse drugs as a coping mechanism. The risks associated with drug abuse cannot be accurately predicted as each user has their unique sensitivity to a drug.[68] Because the reactions to various substances can be unpredictable, the risk for psychological maltreatment are significant. The direct effects of the drugs or the withdrawal from those drugs can cause parents to act out of anger or frustration. Abuse of drugs can cause disinhibition, which is the loss of the ability to suppress behaviors or impulses.[69] It should be noted that parental substance abuse is frequently associated with all types of maltreatment, and almost 80 percent of families that come in contact with Child Protective Services have some sort of substance abuse problem.[70]

Sociological Theories

Emile Durkheim, considered the father of sociology, focused on how social forces and conditions influence attitudes and behaviors.[71] These principles are still discussed today as primary factors on the way one conducts themself in a particular situation. A parent's behavior can certainly be influenced by social factors. Some parents raise their children by the same standards they were raised, despite the fact that their own upbringing may have been considered abusive.

Abusive parents learn abusive behavior, thus the child abuse becomes an inter-generational phenomenon.[72] Parents can also learn to be abusive as they realize the power they have over their children. This is referred to as the control balance theory. When people are very controlling, they are more likely to engage in deviant behavior.[73] Ecological theories address environmental conditions that can elicit stressful behavior such as family structure or economic deprivation.[74] These environmental conditions, which a child has no control over, create a climate conducive to psychological maltreatment. Other aspects of the ecological theories include the abnormalities of a parent-child relationship.[75] These abnormalities that can lead to abuse or neglect include:

1. Inappropriate parental expectations
2. Lack of empathy toward the child's needs
3. Parental belief in physical punishment
4. Parental role reversal.

Finally, the structure of a neighborhood can affect the rate of maltreatment. Living in a less than desirable neighborhood can cause a parent frustration or stress, which can lead to the maltreatment of their child. Structural aspects such as poverty, a population with a high transitional rate, and a concentration of single parent families who are burdened with finding appropriate childcare can be factors that can enhance the potential for child abuse.[76]

CONCLUSION

Psychological maltreatment is considered the most common form of abuse because it almost always appears with other forms of abuse. However, psychological maltreatment is significantly underreported. One of the factors that contribute to underreporting is that this type of abuse is difficult to identify. Although there is no universal definition of what constitutes psychological maltreatment, APSAC defined it as a repeated pattern or extreme incidents of caretaker behavior that thwart the child's basic psychological needs (e.g., safety, socialization, emotional and social support, cognitive stimulation, respect) and convey a child is worthless, defective, damaged goods, unloved, unwanted, endangered, primarily useful in meeting another's needs, and/or expendable,"[77] and provides examples of what constitutes psychological abuse. Other prominent agencies have also created their own definition for psychological maltreatment. Unfortunately, even with these definitions to assist in understanding and identifying of this type of abuse, a pattern of behavior must be observed in order to properly classify the caretaker's behavior as abusive. These obstacles further contribute to the underreporting of this type of abuse. With the unique challenges of identifying this abuse and reporting it to the proper authorities, children are unfortunately subjected to years of mistreatment and face long-term consequences as the effects of psychological maltreatment can be detrimental.

REVIEW QUESTIONS

1. Why is psychological maltreatment so difficult to identify?

2. What are the underlying causes of psychological maltreatment?

3. Why is psychological maltreatment so difficult to measure?

4. What are the physiological and psychological consequences of psychological maltreatment?

5. Why do some children respond differently to psychological maltreatment?

KEYWORDS

National Incidence Study: A congressionally mandated, periodic research effort to assess the incidence of child abuse and neglect in the United States

American Professional Society on the Abuse of Children (APSAC): A non-profit, national organization focused on addressing the needs of professionals engaged in all aspects of investigations and services for maltreated children and their families

operational definition: Identifies one or more specific, observable events or conditions such that any other researcher can independently measure and/or test for them

resiliency: A human ability to recover quickly from disruptive change or misfortune without being overwhelmed or acting in dysfunctional or harmful ways

parens patriae: A doctrine that grants the inherent power and authority of the state to protect persons who are legally unable to act on their own behalf

NOTES

1. Abraham H. Maslow, *Motivation and Personality* (New York: Harper and Row, 1954), 35–280.

2. Cindy L. Miller-Perrin and Robin D. Perrin, *Child Maltreatment: An Introduction*, third edition (Thousand Oaks, CA: Sage, 2013), 187.

3. S. Hamarman, K.H. Pope, and S.J. Czaja, "Emotional Abuse in Children: Variations in Legal Definitions and Rates across the United States," *Child Maltreatment* 7, no. 4 (2002): 310.

4. P.K. Trickett, F.E. Mennen, K. Kim, and J. Sang, "Emotional Abuse in a Sample of Multiply Maltreated, Urban Young Adolescents: Issue of Definition and Identification," *Child Abuse & Neglect* 33, no. 1 (2009): 28.

5. Cindy L Miller-Perrin, Robin D. Perrin, and Claire M. Renzetti, *Violence and Maltreatment in Intimate Relationships* (Thousand Oaks, CA: Sage, 2018), 157–68.

6. S.N. Hart, M.R. Brassard, H.A. Davidson, E. Rivelis, V. Diaz, and N.J. Binggeli, "Psychological Maltreatment," in J.E.B. Myers (ed.), *The APSAC Handbook on Child Maltreatment*, third edition (Thousand Oaks, CA: Sage, 2011), 125–44; S.N. Hart, M.R. Brassard, and H.C. Karlson, "Psychological Maltreatment," in J.N. Briere, L.A. Berliner, J. Bulkley, C.A. Jenny, and T.A. Reid (eds.), *The APSAC Handbook on Child Maltreatment* (Thousand Oaks, CA: Sage, 1996), 72–89.

7. Danya Glaser, "Emotional Abuse and Neglect (Psychological Maltreatment): A Conceptual Framework," *Child Abuse & Neglect* 26, no. 6-7 (2002): 699–702. Monica L. McCoy

and Stephanie Keen, *Child Abuse and Neglect*, second edition (New York, NY: Psychology Press 2014), 126.

8. David A. Wolfe and Caroline McIsaac, "Distinguishing between Poor/Dysfunctional Parenting and Child Emotional Maltreatment," *Child Abuse & Neglect* 35, no. 10 (2011): 805–06.

9. Hart, Brassard, Davidson, Rivelis, Diaz, and Binggeli, "Psychological Maltreatment," 125–44.

10. McCoy and Keen, *Child Abuse and Neglect*, 126.

11. M.R. Brassard and L. McNeill, "Child Sexual Abuse," in M.R. Brassard, R. Germain, and S.N. Hart (eds.), *Psychological Maltreatment of Children and Youth* (New York: Pergamon Press, 1987), 69–88. American Professional Society on the Abuse of Children. (2017). *The Investigation and Determination of Suspected Psychological Maltreatment of Children and Adolescents: Practice Guidelines.* 4–6. Available from https://apsac.memberclicks.net/.../apsa%20guidelines%20psychological%20maltreatm.

12. American Professional Society on the Abuse of Children, *The Investigation and Determination of Suspected Psychological Maltreatment of Children and Adolescents*, 4.

13. American Professional Society on the Abuse of Children, *The Investigation and Determination of Suspected Psychological Maltreatment of Children and Adolescents*, 4–6.

14. Robin Grille, *Heart to Heart Parenting* (Asheville, NC: Vox Cordis Press, 2012).

15. Kimberly A. McCabe and Daniel G. Murphy, *Child Abuse: Today's Issues* (Boca Raton, FL: Taylor & Francis, 2016), 88.

16. A.S. Garner and J.P. Shonkoff, "Early Childhood Adversity, Toxic Stress, and the Role of the Pediatrician: Translating Developmental Science into Lifelong Health," *Pediatrics* 129, no. 1 (2012): 225.

17. Lindsay C. Gibson, *Adult Children of Emotionally Immature Parents: How to Heal from Distant, Rejecting, or Self-Involved Parents* (Oakland, CA: New Harbinger Publications, 2015).

18. L.G. Katz and S.J. Katz, *Intellectual Emergencies* (Lewisville, NC: Kaplan Press, 2009).

19. Grille, *Heart to Heart Parenting*.

20. Lauren R. Shapiro and Marie Helen-Maras, *Multidisciplinary Investigation of Child Maltreatment* (Burlington, MA: Jones & Bartlett Learning), 137–43.

21. R. Hibbard, J. Barlow, H. MacMillan, C.W. Crawford-Jakubiak, E.G. Flaherty, and R.D. Sege, "Psychological Maltreatment," *Pediatrics* 130, no. 2 (2012): 372–78.

22. S.W. Kairys and C.F. Johnson, "The Psychological Maltreatment of Children—Technical Report," *Pediatrics* 109, no. 4 (2002): 1.

23. Naomi H. Griffith and Janet S. Zigler, *The Unkindest Cut: The Emotional Maltreatment of Children* (Nashville, TN: Red Clay & Vinegar, 2002), 188–210.

24. Patricia Love and Jo Robinson, *The Emotional Incest Syndrome: What to Do When a Parent's Love Rules Your Life* (New York, NY: Bantam Books, 1990), 40.

25. R.T. Leeb, L. Paulozzi, C. Melanson, T. Simon, and I. Arias, *Child Maltreatment Surveillance: Uniform Definitions for Public Health and Recommended Data Elements* (Atlanta GA: Centers for Disease Control and Prevention, National Center for Injury Prevention and Control, 2008), 11.

26. Yanghee Lee and Sangwon Kim, "Child Maltreatment in the Context of Child Rights: Obligations Under the UN Convention on the Rights of the Child," in J.B. Klinka and J.R. Contente (eds.), *The APSAC Handbook on Child Maltreatment*, fourth edition (Thousand Oaks, CA: Sage, 2018), 79–94.

27. United Nations. (2011). Convention on the Rights of a Child. Available from http://www2.ohchr.org/english/bodies/crc/docs/CRC.C.GC.13_en.pdf.

28. Alan R. Kemp, *Abuse in Society: An Introduction* (Long Grove, IL: Waveland Press 2017), 101.

29. Kemp, *Abuse in Society: An Introduction*, 102.

30. Griffith and Zigler, *The Unkindest Cut*, 91–108.

31. J.D. Weaver, "The Principle of Subsidiarity Applied: Reforming the Legal Framework to Capture the Psychological Abuse of Children," *Virginia Journal of Social Policy and the Law* 18 (2011): 247–318.

32. McCoy and Keen, *Child Abuse and Neglect*, 124–25.

33. Griffith and Zigler, *The Unkindest Cut*, 127–57.

34. Hibbard, Barlow, MacMillan, Crawford-Jakubiak, Flaherty, and Sege, "Psychological Maltreatment," 372–78; N. Binggeli, S. Hart., and M. Brassard, *Psychological Maltreatment of Children* (Thousand Oaks, CA: Sage, 2001); Brett Drake and Melissa Jonson-Reid, "Defining and Estimating Child Maltreatment," in J. Bart Klika and Jon R. Conte (eds.), *The APSAC Handbook on Child Maltreatment*, fourth edition (Thousand Oaks, CA, 2018), 29; Evin M. Daly, *Child Abuse: What You Need to Know*, second edition (Miami, FL: Parker Publishing, 2017), 11.

35. Douglas E. Abrams, Susan V. Mangold, and Sarah Ramsey, *Children and the Law: In a Nutshell*, sixth edition (St Paul, MN: West Academic, 2018); F. Leeson and R.D.V. Nixon, "Therapy for Child Psychological Maltreatment," *Clinical Psychologist* 14, no. 2 (2010): 31; M.W. Schneider, A. Ross, J.C. Graham, and A. Zielinski, "Do Allegations of Emotional Maltreatment Predict Developmental Outcomes Beyond That of Other Forms of Maltreatment?" *Child Abuse & Neglect* 29, no. 5 (2005): 528; Hart, Brassard, and Karlson, "Psychological Maltreatment," 72–89; Angelika H. Claussen and Patricia M. Crittenden, "Physical and Psychological Maltreatment: Relations Among Types of Maltreatment," *Child Abuse & Neglect* 15, no. 1-2 (1991): 5–18; Dianne Prinz Callin, *The Last Bastion: Child Abuse and Child Neglect in the Brotherhood of America's Schools* (Helmet, CA: RFK Publishing, 2017), 39.

36. McCabe and Murphy, *Child Abuse: Today's Issues*, 88.

37. Hart, Brassard, Davidson, Rivelis, Diaz, and Binggeli, "Psychological Maltreatment," 125–44.

38. S.N. Hart, M.R. Brassard, A.J.L. Baker, and Z.A. Chiel, "Psychological Maltreatment of Children," in J.B. Klinka and J.R. Contente (eds.), *The APSAC Handbook on Child Maltreatment*, fourth edition (Thousand Oaks, CA: Sage, 2018), 154.

39. Dorota Iwaniec, Emma Larkin, and Siobhan Higgins, "Research Review: Risks and Resilience in Cases of Emotional Abuse," *Child & Family Social Work* 11, no. 1 (2006): 75–77.

40. A.S. Garner and J.P. Shonkoff, "Early Childhood Adversity, Toxic Stress, and the Role of the Pediatrician: Translating Developmental Science into Lifelong Health," *Pediatrics* 129, no. 1 (2012): e224–e231.

41. Tuppett M. Yates, "The Developmental Consequences of Child Emotional Abuse: A Neurodevelopmental Perspective," *Journal of Emotional Abuse* 7, no. 2 (2007): 18–19; D.B. Bugental, G.A. Martorell, and V. Barraza, "The Hormonal Costs of Subtle Forms of Infant Maltreatment," *Hormones and Behavior* 43, no. 1 (2003): 237–44.

42. E. McCroy, S.A. De Brito, and E. Viding, "The Impact of Child Maltreatment: A Review of Neurobiological and Genetic Factors," *Frontiers in Psychiatry* 2, no. 48 (2011): 3–5.

43. Celia Doyle and Charles Timms, *Child Neglect & Emotional Abuse: Understanding, Assessment & Response* (Thousand Oaks, CA: Sage, 2014), 39.

44. Amy J.L. Baker and Mel Schneiderman, *Bonded to the Abuser: How Victims Make Sense of Childhood Abuse* (Lanham, MD: Rowman & Littlefield, 2015), 92.

45. Abrams, Mangold, and Ramsey, *Children and the Law: In a Nutshell*, 115–16.

46. Miller-Perrin and Perrin, *Child Maltreatment: An Introduction*, 204.

47. M.M. Tugade, "Positive Emotions, Coping & Resilience," in S. Folkman (ed.), *Oxford Handbook of Stress, Health, and Coping* (New York, NY: Oxford University Press, 2011), 186–99.

48. Love and Robinson, *The Emotional Incest Syndrome*, 139.

49. N. Bigras, N. Godbout, and M. Herbert, "Identity and Relatedness as Mediators between Child Emotional Abuse and Adult Couple Adjustment in Women," *Child Abuse & Neglect* 50 (2015): 85–93; S.A. Riggs, A.M. Cusimano, and K.M. Benson, "Childhood Emotional Abuse and Attachment Processes in the Dyadic Adjustment of Dating Couples," *Journal of Counseling Psychology* 58, no. 1 (2011): 128; S.A. Riggs and P. Kaminski, "Childhood Emotional Abuse, Adult Attachment, and Depression as Predictors of Relational Adjustment and Psychological Aggression," *Journal of Aggression, Maltreatment & Trauma* 19, no. 1 (2010): 77.

50. Gibson, *Adult Children of Emotionally Immature Parents*, 22; McCoy and Keen, *Child Abuse and Neglect*, 144–45.

51. M.R. Brassard and K.L. Donovan, "Defining Psychological Maltreatment," in M.M. Feerick, J.F. Knutson, P.K. Trickett, and S.M. Flanzer (eds.), *Child Abuse and Neglect: Definitions, Classifications, and a Framework for Research*, (Baltimore, MD: Paul H. Brooks, 2006), 151–97.

52. Hart, Brassard, Davidson, Rivelis, Diaz, and Binggeli, "Psychological Maltreatment," 125–44; Hart, Brassard, and Karlson, "Psychological Maltreatment," 72–89.

53. E. Greenfield and N. Marks, "Identifying Experiences of Physical and Psychological Violence in Childhood that Jeopardize Mental Health in Adulthood," *Child Abuse & Neglect* 34, no. 3 (2010): 169–70.

54. A. Muñoz-Hoyos, A. Molina-Carballo, M. Augustin-Morales, F. Contreras-Chova, A. Naranjo-Gómez, F. Justicia-Martínez, and J. Uberos, "Psychological Dwarfism: Psychopathological and Putative Neuroendocrine Markers," *Psychiatric Research* 188, no. 1 (2011): 96–101.

55. R. Waxman, M.C. Fenton, A.E. Skodol, B.F. Grant, and D. Hasin, "Childhood Maltreatment and Personality Disorders in the USA: Specificity of Effects and the Impact of Gender," *Personality and Mental Health* 8, no. 1 (2014): 38. 9

56. A.J. Sedlak, J. Mettenburg, M. Basena, I. Petta, K. McPherson, A. Greene, and S. Li, *Fourth National Incidence Study of Child Abuse and Neglect (NIS-4): Report to Congress* (Washington, DC: U.S. Department of Health and Human Services, Administration for Children and Families, 2010).

57. Shapiro and Maras, *Multidisciplinary Investigation of Child Maltreatment*.

58. H.A. Turner, D. Finkelhor, and R. Ormrod, "Family Structure Variations in Patterns and Predictors of Child Victimization," *American Journal of Orthopsychiatry* 77, no. 2 (2007): 290. 2

59. Daniel Shaw, *Traumatic Narcissism: Relational Systems of Subjugation* (New York: Routledge, 2013), 1–88.

60. Gibson, *Adult Children of Emotionally Immature Parents*, 9.

61. Doyle and Timms, *Child Neglect & Emotional Abuse*, 83.

62. S. Laulik, J. Allam, and K. Browne. "Maternal Borderline Personality Disorder and Risk of Child Maltreatment," *Child Abuse Review* 25, no. 4 (2014): 301–02.

63. Doyle and Timms, *Child Neglect & Emotional Abuse*, 83–84.

64. William G. Doerner and Steven P. Lab, *Victimology*, seventh edition (Waltham, MA: Anderson Publishing 2015), 50.

65. Walter C. Reckless, "A New Theory of Delinquency and Crime," *Federal Probation* 25 (1961): 42–46.

66. S. L. Bienstock, "Mothers who Kill Their Children and Postpartum Psychosis," *Southwestern University Law Review* 32, no. 3 (2003): 451.

67. McCoy and Keen, *Child Abuse and Neglect*, 26.

68. Aric W. Dutelle, *An Introduction to Crime Scene Investigation*, third edition (Burlington, MA: Jones & Bartlett Learning, 2017), 329.

69. McCoy and Keen, *Child Abuse and Neglect*, 24–25.

70. Mark A. Winton and Barbara A. Mara, *Child Abuse and Neglect: Multidisciplinary Approaches* (New York: Pearson, 2001).

71. Emile Durkheim, *The Rules of Sociological Method* (New York: Free Press, 1962 [1895]).

72. C.S. Widom and H. W. Wilson, "Intergenerational Transmission of Violence," in J. Lindert and I. Leviv (eds.), *Violence and Mental Health* (New York: Springer, 2015), 27–45; S. Cox, J.M. Allen, R.D. Hanser, and J.J. Conrad, *Juvenile Justice: A Guide to Theory, Policy, and Practice* (Thousand Oaks, CA: Sage, 2014), 121–28.

73. C.R. Tittle. "Refining Control Balance Theory," *Theoretical Criminology* 8, no. 4 (2004): 397. 7

74. Ann W. Burgess, *Victimology: Theories and Applications*, second edition (Burlington, MA: Jones and Bartlett Learning, 2019), 91–92.

75. S. Bavolek, *The Nurturing Parenting Programs* (Washington, DC: Office of Juvenile Delinquency and Prevention, US Department of Justice, 2000).

76. C.J. Coulton, D.S. Crampton, M. Irwin, J.C. Spilsbury, and J.E. Korbin, "How Neighborhoods Influence Child Maltreatment: A Review of Literature and Alternative Pathways," *Child Abuse & Neglect* 31, no. 11-12 (2007): 1132–33.

77. The American Professional Society on the Abuse of Children. *Practice Guideline-The Investigation and Determination of Suspected Psychological Maltreatment of Children and Adolescents.* Available from https://www.apsac.org/single-post/2019/08/16/ APSAC-ANNOUNCES-REVISIONS-TO-ITS-DEFINITIONS-OF-PSYCHOLOGICAL-MAL-TREATMENT-AND-ADDS-A-CAUTIONARY-STATEMENT-REGARDING-USE-TO-SUP-PORT-PARENTAL-ALIENATION-CLAIMS.

5

Child Neglect

◆ ◆ ◆

CHILD ABUSE AND NEGLECT HAS MANY different meanings depending on what state or what country you are in. The Child Abuse Prevention and Treatment Act (CAPTA), as amended by the CAPTA Reauthorization Act of 2010, defines child abuse and neglect as "any recent act or failure to act on the part of a parent or caretaker which results in death, serious physical or emotional harm, sexual abuse or exploitation; or an act or failure to act, which presents an imminent risk of serious harm."[1] The National Incidence Study of Child Abuse and Neglect identified two standards in evaluating children of abuse: the Harm Standard and the Endangered Standard. The Harm Standard requires that a demonstrable harm has occurred to the child. The Endangered Standard identifies children at risk but who have not yet been harmed.[2] When we think about harm of a child, the mind goes more to physical abuse. Physical abuse tends to be more dramatic, noticeable, and gut-wrenching; so much so, that those that notice are driven to report. Neglect, on the other hand, can be subtle and less noticeable but just as deadly. Child neglect is overwhelmingly the most common reported form of child abuse at close to 75 percent of substantiated cases of abuse that are documented. Child neglect consists of many different facets. Child neglect is defined as the

> failure to provide for the development of a child in all spheres: health, education, emotional development, nutrition, shelter, and safe living conditions, in the context of resources reasonably available to the family or caretakers or has a high probability of causing harm to the child's health or physical, mental, spiritual, moral, or social development. This includes the failure to properly supervise and protect children from harm as much as feasible.[3]

It is important to recognize the subtleties (though they are sometimes not so subtle) of child neglect, know your role, and act on that role.

When trying to determine what makes a child at risk of neglect, several thoughts come to mind: lack of parenting skills, lack of social support, and low socioeconomic status are at the forefront. While all of these can be a factor of child neglect, they do not cause child neglect. Low socioeconomic status for years has been universally defined as a cause of child neglect, yet there are many impoverished families that do not neglect their children. Material poverty does impact the ability of a parent or caregiver to meet the needs of the children but does not constitute neglect if they are unable. Higher income certainly can ease the burden of the financial obligations such as clothing, housing, and nutrition but does not erase the chance of neglect.[4] The question arises as to how to tell the difference, and perhaps it is not possible every time. If we think in a close-minded way—that to neglect a child you must be poor—we have left out a large portion of the population. While poverty does not cause you to neglect your child, wealth does not ensure that you won't. As a society, the need is to figure out how to allocate the resources to at least properly assist with the basic needs.

CASE STUDY #1

Jack is a ten-year-old boy who presented for medical care for a burn to his leg. The burn had become infected because the injury had occurred five days previous. Jack was with his two siblings who were dirty; their clothes were tattered. The medical staff were angry that his parents did not seek care for the burn to Jack's leg. The medical staff also concluded that since the children were so dirty, the parents were neglectful. What are your thoughts? In speaking with Jack, he states that there is no heat or running water at the house. That his parents are working and trying hard but that they are having a rough time. Jack states that candles are lit in the home for light and he accidentally knocked one off the mantel five days ago and burned his leg. Jack did not want to tell his parents, and it was easy to hide since it was cold and he would wear long pants. When the burn began to drain and hurt more he told his parents and they immediately brought him to the hospital. Once the whole picture was displayed, it was clear that there was situational neglect due to life circumstances. Intentional neglect was not caused by either parent. Does the family need resources? Absolutely.

When we are thinking about what neglect is, it is important to remember that often the need is not met perfectly. There are many gray areas as to what constitutes neglect. Is the child receiving proper nutrition? Is the household properly cleaned? Are the clothes the child is wearing properly laundered? These are definitely questions that need to be considered; however, who is to say what is proper?

There are occasions in which gross neglect is obvious and the term "proper" is easily identified as lacking. In practice, whether in the criminal justice, medical, or other field, it is our job to apply the best knowledge obtained to determine if certain circumstances or patterns of behaviors or experiences are jeopardizing the child's well-being.[5] This can be a daunting task and requires knowledge on the different types of neglect that the child may face. When evaluating neglect of a child, we must take into consideration not just actual harm but also the potential harm that may ensue. Potential harm is important because it may be years before the impact of neglect is noticed.

HETEROGENEITY IN CHILD NEGLECT

When trying to decipher the impact of neglect, it is important to look at all aspects. Consideration needs to be given to the severity of neglect, chronic (repeated) episodes of neglect, frequency of neglect, intentionality of neglect, cultural considerations, and poverty.[6]

Severity of Harm

Severity of harm is determined by the actual or potential risk of harm from neglect. The greater the risk to the child, the more severe the neglect. Little is known about the behavioral impact on children based on the severity trajectory simply because the severity of neglect also coincides with the chronicity of neglect. Chronicity of neglect has been shown to have poorer childhood outcomes.[7]

Chronicity of Neglect

This means there is a pattern of needs not being met over a period of time.[8] Chronicity of neglect does seem to lead to poorer child outcomes including delinquency, aggression, anxiety, and depression.[9] It is difficult to assess exactly how long the neglect has occurred. It is possible to develop a timeline on reports to Child Protective Services (CPS). This statistic is only as good as the reports made. It is possible to evaluate when the first CPS report was made and compare that report to the last CPS report. The likelihood is that the extent of neglect was occurring prior to the first report being made. It is possible to talk with older siblings, family, or neighbors to get a greater understanding of the extent of the problem if they are aware and willing to divulge this information.

Frequency of Neglect

Frequency refers to the number of episodes of neglect. This number is also difficult to pinpoint. Most caregivers are not going to admit to how frequent neglectful events are occurring. Reports may be made to CPS, but the likelihood of those numbers being accurate is low. It is possible to obtain more information from older siblings, family members, or neighbors to get a greater understanding of the extent of the problem if they are aware and are willing to divulge this information.

Intentionality

Intentionality gives the illusion that parents or caretakers purposefully caused harm through neglect of the child. This is not the case in most circumstances.

Merriam-Webster Dictionary defines intentional as "done by intention or design."[10] To break it down more, what is done by intention? Intention is defined by Merriam-Webster Dictionary as the "determination to act in a certain way."[11] While some caregivers have purposefully neglected the child, it is important to try to decipher why. While it is impossible to positively say why one person acts one way and another person acts in another way, there are some suggestions for rationale for neglect.

1. *Infant neglect by young mothers:* Infant neglect consists of children from birth to one year old. This is one of the most abundant areas of child neglect with a major risk of long-term consequences. Neglect during this sensitive time period of growth can undermine neuronal development and alter brain growth and development.[12] To compound matters, infants that are born to adolescents mothers, especially under the age of eighteen years old, are at 2.4 times greater risk of being neglected.[13] The adolescent mother may not have intended to be neglectful of the child; however, the adolescent mother is facing challenges of her own. Young mothers are not developmentally ready to care for an infant; they may not have the parenting instincts that a more mature mother would have. The adolescent mother is more likely to be raising the infant as a single parent with less social support in an impoverished environment. Finally, the adolescent mother is at risk of having being maltreated herself. With these risk factors present, intentionality may be low; however, risk of neglect is high.

2. *Parent-child bonding:* Your first role model is your mother or your father or the person that is there to provide your basic needs. What happens if that supportive relationship is not present? When the caretaker is unable to provide emotional or physical needs for the child, what happens to the child? The child may be exposed to life-threatening situations through the lack of supervision from the caregiver. The child may grow up having a difficult time developing relationships, trusting others, and receiving emotional support. As the child ages, the lack of support from the caretaker leads to the child having greater academic struggles in school, poorer social interaction, and stunted development of psychopathology.[14] When parent-child bonding is hindered due to parental distress, the intentionality of neglect may be low; however, the risk of negative long-term consequences affecting the child is high.

3. *Disorganized neglect/living from crisis to crisis:* Imagine walking into a home in which clutter is everywhere, the electricity is shut off, children are yelling and fighting, and there seems to be no order anywhere; this is what you will find in a disorganized neglect household. The family functions under circumstances in which there are multiple problems, constant interruptions, and disorganization.[15] The way to capture the attention in the household is to be the one that makes the biggest scene, the one that is the noisiest. The attention that is being sought may have both positive and negative consequences. The neglectful parenting style

is inconsistent at best, only responding to the most immediate crisis situation. During infancy, the response to the child is variable. The caretaker may respond to the infant in a responsive way, in an angry way, or just ignore the child's signals completely if the signals are not intense enough to capture the caretaker's attention. As the child becomes older, they have begun to learn that in order to get the attention or at least a response, the child must act out. The child begins to learn that anger outbursts are the accepted way to get the attention, but also may cause the caretaker to become angry with them as well. This child will grow up thinking that these behaviors are appropriate. By organizing behaviors on feelings and not by planning ahead, caretakers fail to provide adequately for the needs of the child until that need becomes a situational crisis. The intentionality of disorganized neglect may be low; however, the impact will be lifelong on the children without professional guidance in providing direction on how to cope and plan ahead.

Cultural Context

With the ability to travel being so easy, technology in almost every room, and social media at your fingertips, the world has become a much smaller place. According to the U.S. Department of Homeland Security, over one million documented immigrants come to the United States each year.[16] Cultural diversity is not only in the big cities but also in the rural communities. With an increase in the melting pot of cultures, it is recognized that different cultures place different emphasis on child-rearing philosophies and as professionals working with the different cultures the need to become more culturally competent is absolute. To be culturally competent, the well-being of the child is the greatest consideration while understanding that different cultures have a variety of views in how to raise children. In some cultures, it is expected for young children to assist the family with raising younger siblings. Cultural child rearing can be evolving. It is unacceptable to look at a culture and assume, for example, that because you are Hispanic, you must raise your child one way or because you are of Chinese descent, you must raise your child another way. If you look at the various styles of child rearing in the United States alone, it is clear that styles are different between individual families. The universal goal, however, is to have your child grow up to be successful, but there is no cookie-cutter pattern that can be used. As you work with some cultures, it also cannot be assumed because of what is being taught as a cultural practice and is considered normative in that culture that it will not cause harm. For example, some cultural practices support the mistreatment of women and children under the patriarchal values and the hierarchy of power within the household.[17] In the United States, this pattern of behavior would not be accepted and would need to be reported to CPS and/or law enforcement. The challenge in being culturally competent is to determine if the behavior is only culturally different but does not cause neglect to the child or is the child's well-being at risk.

Poverty

As discussed earlier, poverty is linked to child abuse and neglect, but poverty is not the cause of abuse and neglect. The National Incidence Study of Child Abuse and Neglect evaluated risk of suffering harm in the Harm Standard neglect study that evaluated parents that are not employed but looking for employment, employed parents, and no parent employed (retired, unemployed and not looking for employment, maternity leave, homemaker, disabled, or on temporary assistance for needy families). The findings for this study are that children of unemployed parents were almost three times as likely to suffer neglect than a child of employed parents at a rate of 12.1 versus 4.1 children per one thousand. Children with no parent in the labor force were more than three times as likely to face neglect at a rate of 14.8 children per one thousand.[18]

CONTRIBUTORS OF NEGLECT

When delving into what neglect is and why neglect happens, there are no real answers. Two families can face the exact same challenges and the outcomes will be different. What can be focused on is what may contribute to neglect. All levels of society from the individual to the community and even the professional play an active role in working with parents and children that are victims of neglect.

1. *Parental characteristics:* Because neglect tends to focus on the mother as the primary contributor to child neglect, this text will begin with her and tie in the father. The mother tends to have co-existing issues ranging from problems with emotional health, intellectual disabilities, and/or substance abuse.[19,20] Many times the mother has experienced child maltreatment herself; when this is the case, the mother is more likely to develop prenatal depression and is at an even higher risk of postnatal depression.[21] While maternal depression is linked to child neglect, new research suggests that if the mother is willing to have CPS make home visits after the child is born, there is promise that recidivism in neglecting that child can be reduced.[22]

   Drug use: Drug use by parents is greatly impacting the care of the children. It is estimated that in the United States 246 million people between the ages of fifteen to sixty-four are using illegal drugs; this accounts for about one in twenty people. Within these households, around 8.3 million children are being raised with one or both parents using drugs. Parental drug use has been strongly correlated to child abuse and neglect. Children being raised in homes in which drug use is occurring are more likely to witness intimate partner violence, more likely to be hospitalized, and more likely to be living in poverty. CPS has to play an active role to assure that these children are safe. One of the solutions is to place the children with the grandparents. This is difficult for the grandparents to handle with, as they are dealing with issues of aging and now have to raise children again. About 2.4 million grandparents are raising 4.5 million children in the United States today. This is causing a negative impact to the parents, children, and the grandparents.[23]

Father's role: Less research has been conducted on what is the father's role in child neglect. What has been shown is the more support by the father, the more competent the child and that the child is more socially accepted.[24] It does appear that the father has a significant impact on the child no matter what the role is—minimally engaged or absent. While a father's presence impacts the child positively normally, a father's absence will have a negative impact. When a father is not in the home, research supports that the home is at risk of being more financially deprived. Financial deprivation does not mean that the child is neglected, but it does put that child at a higher risk. If the father is unemployed, the risk is greater of the father abusing the child. If the father is abusing substances as mentioned previously, the risk is greater for abuse and neglect of the child.[25]

2. *Child characteristics:* When discussing child neglect, child-loving people can easily jump to the defense and say "how can you do that to a child?" In reality, children can be difficult. Depending on the maturity level of the parent, the social support, mental health factors, and substance abuse by the caretaker, they may have a difficult time responding to the child.

Children have characteristics that may contribute to neglect. If children are considered difficult or not at the growth and developmental level of expectation of the parent (no matter how unrealistic that expectation may be), the child's risk of abuse and neglect increases. Normal events that can occur, such as a child with colic, a child waking up with nightmares, or toilet training, can all be triggers to abuse and neglect.[26]

> **Premature:** Low-birth-weight children and children that are affected by complicated pregnancies or complications at birth are at increased risk of non-accidental trauma and/or neglect. When children are premature or are born with complications, it may impact parent-child bonding, especially if the child has an extended stay in the neonatal intensive care unit. Research supports that mothers of premature infants interact differently compared to mothers who deliver at full term. Premature infants may have abnormalities in temperament, sleep/wake patterns, and the ability to adapt causing the child to be more "difficult." With a child that is perceived as more difficult, interaction and bonding between the child and caregiver may be altered. If the child has had to stay in the neonatal intensive care unit, barriers can develop in the bonding of the child and caregiver.[27] When all of these factors are taken into consideration, it has been found that these infants are at greater risk of non-accidental trauma. As medical providers, it is important to screen families for this risk and provide comprehensive resources to the families prior to the child being discharged home.
>
> **Special health care needs:** Some children that are considered more difficult can include children with special health care needs. The 1997 Federal Maternal and Child Health Bureau defines special health care

needs in children as "children who have chronic physical, developmental, behavioral, or emotional conditions and who require health and related services of a type or amount beyond that required by children generally."[28] It is estimated that 14 to 18 percent of children in the United States have a mental or physical disability.[29] Children with special health care needs are twice as likely to be abused and/or neglected. While it is hard to understand who would abuse or neglect a child, much less a disabled child, the fact is this happens much too often. Children with special health care needs are looked upon differently in society. Many people in the community disregard special needs children as unproductive members in society; therefore, they are perceived as less of a person. Children that are mentally challenged may be viewed as unable to comprehend pain; therefore, they are easily neglected. A child that is physically incapacitated may be restrained; if this is part of the normal routine, the child may not realize that abuse or neglect is occurring. If the child is being neglected, what are the options? It is difficult for a physically and mentally healthy child to come forward when being physically neglected, so imagine the lack of options with special needs children. These children tend to be isolated even more from the community, not be aware of what is normal, and do not have a person available to report it to. With the greater amount of time and care necessary for special needs children, they can be an easy target for abuse.

3. *Neighborhoods:* The condition, the makeup, and the economic status of the neighborhood can either act as a stressor to families at risk of child maltreatment or support that family. Consistent findings regarding neighborhood characteristics and the risk of maltreatment have been similar. When evaluating at-risk neighborhoods, poor economy, high male unemployment rates, and residential turnover are greatly associated with child maltreatment and neglect.[30]

4. *Professional characteristics:* Throughout this chapter, it will be clear that neglect is not always recognizable. The signs can be subtle. Medical care providers may see early indicators, but not really believe that the child is being neglected or give the caretakers the benefit of the doubt, preventing the neglect from being identified early.

    Example: A ten-week-old baby was referred to the hospital by his primary care physician. The call came in to the emergency department with the physician stating, "I have no suspicion of abuse because this is a good family."

    This physician had been treating this family for years, so when a potential abuse situation presented, he did not recognize the situation as abuse. In reality, it is not possible to identify who may abuse and/or neglect their child. When a full workup was completed on this child, he had ten fractures in different stages of healing.

Was the physician negligent and not complying with his duties and not seeing this situation as abuse? Many times, it is a lack of understanding and a lack of belief that neglect happens everywhere rather than intentional negligence on the part of the medical staff.

The medical staff then must report cases such as this to the Department of Social Services. The communication between the medical team and the legal/investigative team can be a challenge. The medical team speaks a language that the investigative team does not usually understand. The investigative team also speaks in a language that the medical team may not understand.

The challenge is to bring everyone to the table, to enhance communication between all agencies, and to learn to speak each other's language. It is helpful when the communities have a forensic nursing team available to evaluate the patient and provide a bridge to the gap between medical and investigative/legal.

Physical Environment

1. *Inadequate shelter:* Imagine going to a home with a six-month-old child, a four-year-old child, and an eight-year-old child. When arriving to the home, the door is on the hinges and will not close all the way. The mother steps out on the broken-down porch to speak to you and you ask to go inside. Reluctantly, she consents. When stepping inside, you walk into the living room. You notice that you must step very carefully because there are holes in the flooring. Some of the holes are covered by stained rugs. Trash is overflowing from the kitchen into the living room, with the cats and dogs living in the house trying to make their meals from the empty cans lying on the floor. Dog and cat feces are noted all over the floor, cabinets, and smeared on the walls. The children are running around in saggy, brown underwear with no other clothes; the infant's diaper is as full as possible before it overflows. Roaches and other bugs you have not yet identified are going up and down on the walls and floor even though it is the middle of the day. Multiple adults are in the house, but no one but you seems to notice the squalor.

   Many complaints are made to CPS regarding inadequate shelter. Families are homeless because of poverty; houses are in need of repair, but families are not financially able to make the repairs. Are the needed repairs necessary for the safety of the children inside the home? If so, this may be a safety issue. Is this a safety issue because of neglect or because of poverty? In the previous scenario, there are safety concerns with the home needing repair. In addition, there are safety concerns for things that could be controlled such as the garbage and the animals in the house.

   When CPS is notified of situations of neglect through inadequate housing, many may be screened out because a safety issue does not exist. Some may be screened in for resources to be provided but not a full CPS investigation.[31,32] When safety issues exist due to negligence and not poverty, an investigation by CPS is warranted. When a case is substantiated, the child welfare worker has to consider multiple factors to substantiate neglect.

2. *Unsanitary conditions:* Unsanitary conditions consists of garbage that has accumulated, animal and human feces on the floor and other objects around the home, no running water, and bugs and rodents that have infested the house.[33] When the house is dirty, it is difficult to keep the day-to-day life under control. Food preparation is tainted, and minor wounds can become infected and complicated. The question from the professional is, "why is the house dirty?" Is the dirty house because the caretakers are working two jobs and don't have time to clean? Perhaps the caretaker does not know how to properly clean the house. Is the caretaker in such a state of depression that they do not realize that the house is in disarray? Is the caretaker using drugs and alcohol and is too high to notice the conditions of the home? Multiple factors and considerations come into play when trying to determine if a house is unsanitary and why. Sometimes a dirty house is not just a dirty house. The worker's knowledge, education, and experience have to take all factors into consideration before deciding how to act.[34] Resources may be what are needed, the caretaker may need medical and/or mental treatment themselves, or it is in the best interest and safety of the child to be removed from the situation.

3. *Inadequate sleeping arrangements:* Children may suffer from chronic fatigue or noted to be falling asleep in class during school. Reports from teachers may range from not paying attention, daydreaming, not listening, and falling asleep. These may all be signs of inadequate sleeping arrangements in the home. The child's need for rest is not being met because, for example, there are too many people in the home, too much noise and stimulation in the home, too many people sleeping in the bed, or is no bed is available at all.[35] By having crowding issues in the household, the child may have personal boundary issues. When the child is forced to sleep in the bed with other adults, it may predispose them to being sexually assaulted. By not having personal space and/or privacy, the child may begin to display signs of shame, fear, or anxiety.[36]

Environmental Hazards

1. *Fire hazards:* A subtype of inadequate housing is fire hazards. Fire hazards can include exposed or frayed wiring, fuel containers that are stored in inappropriate areas, and combustible items too close to a heat source.[37] Bars going across the windows for safety from the neighborhood can also act as a death trap in case of a fire in the home.

Imagine a home with no heat source except a kerosene heater located in the center of the living room floor in the middle of winter. Everyone in the home is sleeping in the living room in an attempt to stay warm. The children have been playing around the heater during the day and have left the toys in the floor by the heater. The caretaker has been working all day and fell asleep reading a book. The book lands on the toys right next to the heat and becomes engulfed in flames.

Sadly, this is an all too common story. In this case, when you think back to the intentionality of the neglect, it would be considered low though the risk to the child is high.

2. *Substance accessibility and use:* The use of drugs for non-medical purposes has become a global problem. Drug use threatens public health with negative trends for the user and the family of the users. Drugs and chemicals that are within the child's reach are particularly hazardous to the children and the caretaker may be investigated for neglect.[38]

CASE STUDY #2

An eighteen-month-old presents to the emergency department with altered mental status. The child is awake and alert but is not acting right. The child is interacting with family and staff but is described as being kind of spaced out. The child presents smiling but his eyes are noted to be somewhat glazed over. A urine drug screen was collected and he tested positive for THC (marijuana). Parents admit to having brownies in the home with marijuana baked into the brownies. CPS and law enforcement were notified and responded to the hospital.

A mother wants to have a girl's night out with her friends and has a sixteen-year-old girl come over to babysit the one-year-old child. Mother does not want the child to act up while she is gone so she places Schnapps in the sippy cup. The child is noted by the sitter to be lethargic and the child begins to vomit. 911 is called and the child is brought into the hospital by emergency medical services limp with decreased responsiveness. Upon assessment the child's blood alcohol content was a 245 mg/dl (0.245). In this particular state, the legal alcohol limit for an adult is 0.08.

With these scenarios, both would be considered neglect: one through accessibility and one through direct action.

3. *Excessive hot water temperature:* Many of us enjoy a nice hot shower after a day's work and do not think about the temperature setting of the hot water heater. Having children in the home brings the need to know the hot water temperature to the forefront. An average household recommendation for the hot water heater setting is to be no higher than 125 degrees Fahrenheit (51.66 degrees Celsius). Water at greater than 130 degrees Fahrenheit will burn an adult and child at about the same degree. Water that is lower than 130 degrees Fahrenheit will burn a child only a slightly bit faster than an adult. If water is set at 150 degrees Fahrenheit, a child will get a full thickness burn in two seconds. Many times families do not understand the significance of the hot water settings and this should be used as an opportunity to teach to prevent a child from having significant burns.

Each year, CPS gets reports on over three million children that have been maltreated, in which two million are substantiated. Of those cases about 78.5

percent are reported for neglect.[39] Child neglect many times can be subjective depending on the culture, the caretakers, and the professional person working with the child. It may seem like neglect to one person but someone else may see the situation completely different. The impact on the child is going to range based on the developmental level of the child, the severity of the neglect, and the chronicity of the neglect.[40] The next part of the text is going to go into depth on the different areas of child neglect.

The U.S. government, over a period of many decades, began to recognize child abuse and neglect as a public health concern that has long-term consequences for the victims. In 1974 a Child Abuse Prevention and Treatment Act was established to define child maltreatment. The Child Abuse Prevention and Treatment Act states that maltreatment is "any recent act or failure to act on the part of the parent or caretaker which results in death, serious physical or emotional harm, sexual abuse or exploitation, or an act or failure to act which presents imminent risk of serious harm."[41] This federal act provides the minimal standards in which child abuse is defined. The individual states are given the leeway to further define child abuse and neglect within the state and based on the state laws established, the state investigates the crime of child abuse and neglect and determines how to hold the perpetrator accountable.

CHILD PHYSICAL NEGLECT

Child physical neglect is when the basic needs of the child are not being met. Basic needs include food, shelter, clothing, safety, adequate supervision, dental care, and medical care at a minimum. When evaluating at-risk children for child physical neglect, considerations must be made regarding the current at-risk situation and the potential for future harm. Research is trending to identify if child maltreatment affects the neurological makeup of the brain, and the research is supporting that it does. Child maltreatment is found to alter the neuroendocrine stress response and immune response in the brain.[42] The hippocampus, cerebral cortex, and cerebellum all have densely populated glucocorticoid receptors. The glucocorticoid receptors are highly susceptible to damage from an excess of glucocorticoids such as cortisol. Cortisol is released during periods of high stress. As research is evolving, it is supporting the fact that childhood neglect increases stress and the production of cortisol, therefore causing early damage to the limbic structures of the brain leading to alterations in the white matter of the brain, particularity in males.[43,44]

Inadequate Nutrition

CASE STUDY #3

A two-month-old presents to her primary care physician in the care of her mother for immunizations. On physical assessment, the child is noted to be malnourished and presents with symptoms of a cold. The primary care physician instructs the mother that the child is unable to receive her immuniza-

tions due to her current medical condition and that she needs to take the child straight to the emergency department. A few hours later, the primary care physician calls the emergency department to make sure the child has arrived; she had not. Police were called to go to the home for a well check. Emergency medical services was then called to transport the child to the hospital. The mother states that she did not take the child as instructed because her window was broken in her car and it would have been too cold to drive to the emergency department. Upon arrival, the child was emaciated, weighing only one pound more than her birth weight. She was described as looking like a little old woman because of the amount of loose, wrinkled skin on her body. The mother states that she feeds the child every few hours but that she keeps throwing it back up. Note that the mother did not take the child to the primary care physician for this earlier in the day.

Malnutrition is the main factor in growth failure. When assessing victims of inadequate nutrition, it is rare that it is to the extent that it becomes fatal to the child; if it does it is considered one of the most severe forms of child abuse.[45] When evaluating the nutritional status of the child it helps to know what is the expected weight of the child especially during the first year of life.

Birth to four months old = ¾ kilogram weight gain per month
Five to eight months old = ½ kilogram weight gain per month
Nine to twelve months old = ¼ kilogram weight gain per month

An infant's body mass consists of about 75 percent water; this is the highest percent of body water than at any other time period of life. An infant's diet consists solely of breastmilk or formula for the first six months of life. Breastmilk or formula will satisfy the hydration and nutritional requirements of the infant. Infants average about 780 milliliters per day. As solid food is introduced, the fluid intake will decrease to 120 kilograms per day and continues to decrease as solid foods increase.[46]

Inadequate nutrition can come from food that is lacking nutritional value, food that is prepared but is inappropriate for the child's age and development, or simply a lack of food altogether. A retrospective study was completed by Laura Night and Kim Collins. In this study, children that died from malnutrition/starvation ranged from the ages of six weeks old to eighteen months old, with the average age being six months. The mother during this time period is seen as the primary caretaker which correlated with this study's findings that the mother was the perpetrator in all of the malnutrition/starvation cases reviewed.[47]

Common findings that are seen from the child that is malnourished/starved are:

1. *Skin tenting:* Pinch an area of skin between the thumb and index finger, and let it loose. Healthy skin will immediately return to its normal state. When dehydrated, the skin will slowly return to its normal state (more than two seconds).[48]

2. *Wrinkled loose skin.*
3. *Sunken fontanelles:* Fontanelles are referred to as "soft spots." They are the area of the skull that has not fully ossified.[49] Typically, when assessing for hydration of infants, the anterior and posterior fontanelle is palpated. If the infant is dehydrated, the fontanelle will be sunken. The anterior fontanelle is an unossified area of the scalp located at the juncture of the frontal, coronal, and sagittal sutures.[50] The posterior fontanelle is an unossified area of the scalp located at the sagittal and lambdoidal suture.[51]
4. *Sunken ocular globes (eyes that are sunken in appearance).*
5. *Depressed cranial sutures.*
6. *Focal alopecia (localized area of baldness).*
7. *Prominent ribs and bony planes.*
8. *Loss of muscle tone.*
9. *Loss of adipose tissue (fat).*
10. *Demineralization to bones.*
11. *Decrease urine output.*
12. *Empty stomach content on autopsy.*
13. *Children that have died tend to be lower than the fifth percentile on the growth chart.*

Failure to Thrive

When evaluating children for inadequate nutrition, failure to thrive (FTT) is a catchall term. FTT describes children that have inadequate nutrition and are unable to maintain growth and development when their weight for age drops by 3 to 5 percent or crosses two major growth percentiles.[52]

FTT has been listed under two causes: organic (medical) versus non-organic (psychosocial). As research has progressed, FTT is difficult to place in a tidy little box of causes. While there may be an organic cause initially, psychosocial factors can cause the situation to worsen. Medically, it is important to assess the child and attempt to find out if there is an organic issue that is causing the malnutrition while keeping an open mind of other circumstances that may be at play.

There are four main categories of FTT depicted by Deborah Lowen.[53] These categories are listed in the following.

Category 1: Inadequate Caloric Intake
Poor Quality or Caloric Content

- Breastfeeding problems: poor latch, poor letdown, inadequate milk supply
- Formula problems: incorrect preparation or supply
- Poor nutritional content: excess juice or water, unusual diets, fixed beliefs
- Grazing
- Inadequate quantities of food given: poverty, food insecurity, neglect
- Medical child abuse: formally referred to as Munchausen syndrome by proxy

Feeding Difficulties

- Oromotor dysfunction
- Neurological impairment
- Gastroesophageal reflux
- Esophageal strictures
- Poor dentition
- Anorexia from various causes
- Parent-child conflict: temperament, autonomy struggles

Category 2: Inadequate Absorption and/or Excess Losses
Persistent Vomiting

- Pyloric stenosis
- Central nervous system disease
- Gastrointestinal obstruction
- Rumination
- Psychogenic vomiting

Gastrointestinal Disease

- Celiac disease
- Cystic fibrosis
- Protein allergies
- Lactose intolerance
- Infection
- Liver disease
- Short gut

Category 3: Increased Caloric Requirements
Cardiorespiratory Disease

- Congenital heart disease
- Acquired heart disease
- Chronic lung disease
- Cystic fibrosis
- Obstructive sleep apnea

Chronic Infection

- Human immunodeficiency virus/acquired immune deficiency syndrome
- Tuberculosis
- Urinary tract infections

Other

- Malignancy
- Hyperthyroidism
- Excess activity

Category 4: Defective Utilization

- Inborn errors of metabolism
- Diabetes mellitus
- Congenital adrenal hyperplasia

It is obvious that there are many medical causes of FTT and a workup is required. For the purpose of the neglect of children, it is not the intent of this text to identify what all of these organic factors mean, but to advise that these processes can affect the nutrition status of a child being evaluated.

The non-organic factors are the factors that can be related to child abuse. As the child is being medically evaluated for the cause of FTT, the practitioner should simultaneously be completing a psychosocial analysis to evaluate for other possible causes. Some common risk factors seen in this psychosocial analysis are very similar to what has been described throughout this chapter. Some risk factors include:

1. Mental health of the caregiver: history of depression, marital status, stress in the home
2. Mental retardation of the parent or caregiver
3. Young, single mothers with poor social network
4. Alcohol and/or substance abuse
5. Prior history of child abuse in the family
6. Poverty
7. Parents that are overly focused on careers and are frequently away from the home
8. Do not follow medical advice
9. Unrealistic view of normal growth and development
10. Premature infant or low-birth-weight infant.[54]

CASE STUDY #4 (CONCLUSION)

When taking into account the infant's presentation, a medial workup was completed and confirmed that this child had an organic reason for her failure to thrive. While you can have a medical explanation, it is necessary to evaluate the entire picture. Had the mother really being feeding the child as she said? If the child had been losing weight, why didn't she take her to the primary doctor? When she did take her to the primary doctor, why didn't she state that she had concerns about the child's weight loss instead of presenting for immunizations? At first, I was going to give the mother the benefit of the doubt—maybe this was her first child—it was her third. Maybe she did not know how to handle medical complications in an infant: her other two children had medical problems and had to receive specialized care. This was a case in which there was an organic cause exacerbated by non-organic means of neglect.

When talking with the caretaker (typically the mother) about the signs of maltreatment, the response in regard to duration will tend to be minimized. When the story is documented and an investigation initiated, many inconsistencies are found in the story. In an effort to try to get the best foundation for intake regarding the child, a feeding history needs to be documented.[55] Find out from the caregiver what the child has been eating, how often the child eats, what amount (especially with formula) the child eats in a sitting, and when the last time the child had a normal bottle/meal was.

Childhood Obesity

When discussing inadequate nutrition, the first thought is usually being malnourished from undernutrition. In recent years the focus is also turning to children that are obese. In determining obesity, a comparison is made with weight versus height, or calculating a body mass index. A body mass index that is 95 percent or greater is considered obese.[56] In 2003, the Surgeon General released a statement to the U.S. House of Representatives regarding the obesity crisis of children in America.[57] Childhood obesity is now at a rate of about 30 percent of children in thirty states.[58] Is this the child's fault? The answer is no; childhood obesity is linked to the parents or caretakers. Children learn by example. When children are young, the parents are the ones to help them recognize healthy foods and to acquire a taste for those foods. The parents are the ones that set the child's plate, setting the standard for what is a normal portion of food. Finally, the parent is the one that encourages the child to exercise and to limit the amount of time watching television and/or playing video games. If the parent does not set a healthy example for the child, the likelihood of childhood obesity rises.

While some may argue that the parent has the right to make decisions for the child, the courts agree to a point. The courts have taken a stance that if the decisions that are being made cause a potential life-threatening situation for the child, then intervention will be necessary, even to the point of placing the child in foster care. In 1992 the Iowa Court of Appeals upheld the removal of a ten-year-old child that was five foot, three inches tall and weighed 290 pounds. The child was admitted to the hospital for morbid obesity with severe yeast infections in her skin creases on her abdomen, and she had an infantile personality disorder. The mother had the option to have the child placed back with her after the child received long-term care regarding her physical and mental disorders. The mother refused the care and lost custody of the child.[59]

In another example, a sixteen-year-old boy was in the care of his mother. This boy was five foot, three inches tall and weighed 451 pounds. The school had noted that he had an increase in absenteeism and had gained one hundred pounds within the year; the school reported this to the Department of Social Services. The mother was morbidly obese herself and unable to leave the house because of this. Since she was homebound, she was not able to provide or participate in his medical care; he was removed from the home. The courts were clear that the removal was not because of the obesity but because of the life-threatening condition of his health directly related to obesity. At sixteen years old, this boy was already dealing with an enlarged liver, high blood pressure, respiratory problems causing a need for oxygen therapy, insulin resistance, sleep apnea, knee problems, and depression.[60]

There are physical disorders that are directly related to childhood obesity, disorders that you think of occurring in adulthood. With the risk of being morbidly obese at such a young age, these disorders are being seen in childhood.[61]

Physical disorders for childhood obesity:

1. Cardiovascular disease risk:
   a. High cholesterol
   b. High blood pressure
   c. Abnormal glucose tolerance
2. Childhood obesity is a strong predictor of type 2 diabetes in youth
3. Asthma
4. Enlarged liver/fatty liver

Psychosocial disorders for childhood obesity:

1. Decreased self-esteem
2. Decreased self-image (especially in adolescent girls)
3. Depression
4. Peer rejection
5. Increased likelihood (two to three times greater than a normal weight child) to contemplate suicide
6. Less likely to receive higher education
7. Less likely to marry
8. More likely to be impoverished

Those at highest risk of childhood obesity have been found to be Mexican American boys, African American girls, and low-income households with poorly educated parents.[62]

With the discussion of obesity, claims have been made that the cause is from a genetic disorder. A rare genetic disorder (now identified as a genomic disorder) has been identified that does cause childhood obesity: Prader-Willi syndrome, which is caused by a malfunction in the hypothalamus. As a newborn, the suck reflex is poor causing a child to fail to gain weight and grow. Between the ages of one to six, the child develops an insatiable appetite and if weight is not closely monitored, the child will become obese.[63]

Medically, it is important to know how to respond to children that are undernourished as well as overnourished. Be prepared to rule out medical causes and intervene in the psychosocial issues that may be contributing to the neglect.

DENTAL NEGLECT

Dental neglect is not a type of neglect that is at the top of the list when discussing child neglect, but is an important precursor and should be considered. When assessing children that have been abused, it is found that they are more likely to have untreated dental disease than children that are not abused. If dental neglect is noted sooner and addressed, it could potentially decrease the risk of child abuse and neglect. Dental neglect is defined by the Academy of Pediatric Dentistry as "the willful failure of parent or guardian to seek and follow through with treatment necessary to ensure a level of oral health for adequate function and freedom from pain"[64]

Primary teeth are composed of twenty teeth emerging from the age of seven months to three years. Permanent teeth begin to erupt around the age of six. Parents or caregivers may feel that the primary teeth are not important since the child will be losing these teeth anyway. It is important to educate the caregivers on care of both primary and permanent teeth. Dental caries is the most common culprit of dental neglect and can be prevented with proper oral care; it is five times more common than asthma.

Without proper care and treatment, whether it is the primary or permanent tooth, the child is at risk for pain, loss of function, and infections; if infection is severe enough it can become life threatening. In addition, learning, communication, and nutrition is affected dental neglect.

Dental neglect incorporates many factors that may place a burden on the family. Dental care is not cheap, and many families do not carry dental insurance. When the family is trying to decide between getting food on the table versus having the child's teeth cleaned, food is going to win. While lower socioeconomic status does not cause dental neglect, it may contribute. As medical professionals, it is important to educate on proper oral care and nutrition to enhance proper care and decrease the likelihood of dental neglect.

There are three phases of intervention.

1. Phase one: Preventative dental team management—The dental team will share the concerns with the parents and provide resources to meet the child's needs. A plan of care will be established with necessary dental treatment for the child. The initial treatment will include pain management and discussion on preventative care. If concerns remain, then the team will need to go to the second phase.
2. Phase two: Preventative multi-agency management—The dental team will work with other professionals such as primary care physician, school

nurse, and social worker to share information and develop a joint plan of action. If concerns are not addressed, then the team will need to go to the third phase.

3. Phase three: Child protection referral—If recommendations are not being followed and it is felt by the team that the child is suffering harm or deteriorating, then a report will need to be made to CPS. If at the onset clear signs of neglect are noted, immediate report to CPS is warranted and phases one and two are skipped.[65]

This is an excellent opportunity for greater communication sharing between dentistry, doctors, nurses, and social services, all in the best interest of the child.

MEDICAL NEGLECT

Medical neglect is the failure to provide medical treatment or care and/or failure to seek medical care in a timely manner. The determination of medical neglect can be difficult. When investigating if medical neglect has occurred, don't lose sight of the ultimate goal—protecting the child from actual or potential harm, not blaming the parent.

What is medical neglect? A parent that chooses to not immunize their child? A child that is ill but the parents have no health insurance and are not working so they decide not to go to the doctor and the child becomes progressively worse? By the time the parent recognizes that medical care is necessary, the child is too ill and dies. How about the child involved in a bad motor vehicle collision and due to religious beliefs, the parent refuses blood transfusions that may save the child's life? When does a parent's right to choose what is in the best interest of the child turn into medical neglect? A parent being non-compliant or not adhering to the treatment regimen prescribed is not medical neglect; it becomes medical neglect when it causes permanent harm or death to the child.

In addition to what is listed here, factors that may constitute medical neglect are:

1. Acute illness in which there is a delay in seeking health care. This delay is greater than what a "reasonable parent" would bring their child in for. This delay causes the illness to become serious and/or cause death.
2. Child with a chronic illness in which the parent is not following the proper treatment regimen, causing adverse consequences to the child's health.
3. Not seeking assistance for obvious developmental delays.
4. Delay in medical care for an obvious injury to the child (i.e., fracture, burns).

At times the thought could be that the parents just did not know better. That is why the consideration is what would a reasonable parent think.

CASE STUDY #5

A four-year-old almost catatonic child presents to the emergency department with a leg fracture. The mother is present but does not participate in the child's care at this time, nor does she attempt to console the child. The child is not talking about what caused the fracture. On a head-to-toe assessment, the child is covered in bruises to the face, extremities, abdomen, and back. So you think well at least the mother brought the child in for the leg fracture. On a careful medical history dissection, up until one year prior the mother brought this child to the emergency department for a cough, earache, stomachache, etc. The mother used the emergency department as her primary care physician for multiple complaints over the first three years. The mother does not bring the child in for any of the bruises until he had a fractured leg. This case was investigated by a multi-disciplinary team. In that year, the mother was dating a man that was physically abusive to the child, and that is when the medical care ended. Is this mother aware of when and how to get treatment? The proof is there in the first three years. This mother chose to medically neglect the needs of her child to protect her boyfriend.

Poisoning

Poisoning is an emergency worldwide. Most poisonings in children are accidental. The most common setting is in the home where children have easy access. Common poisoning agents include pesticides, drugs, household cleaners, and plants. There has also been an increase in alcohol intoxications.[66] Children younger than one year old had the highest number of incidents of unintentional poisonings, typically from improper dosing of medication or access to medication that is not properly childproofed.

While accidents can happen, caregivers may be held accountable for unintentional poisonings if the child is exposed to unsafe conditions that may lead to a poisoning, whether it is from pure neglect in childproofing the house (i.e., cocaine left on the coffee table) or improper supervision.

Some additional forms of neglectful intoxication include:[67]

1. Environments that are not childproof with easy access to caustic chemicals. This can include chemicals left in the reach of the child or chemicals that are improperly labeled and placed in storage containers that do not alert the potential harm of ingesting the substance.
2. Drug use with drugs and drug paraphernalia left behind in the reach of the child. As different drugs become popular, there are varied risks with those drugs. For example, methamphetamine is becoming an epidemic. This drug can be made in the home. During the process of synthesis with the acids and bases used for the drugs, contaminates are released and will adhere to all types of surfaces. Children within the home where these drugs are being manufactured can become intoxicated just from being in the home and touching the surfaces on which the contaminants lie.

3. A serious poisoning to infants is water toxicity. Parents may improperly mix formula or give bottles of water to the child instead of formula, resulting in hyponatremia (low sodium levels), causing seizures.

Child intoxications are one of the most covert forms of maltreatment and should be considered when treating the child medically. Because this can be easily missed in children, the recommendation should be that when treating children with an apparent life-threatening event, toxicology screening should be included in the routine exam.

EMOTIONAL NEGLECT

With all forms of neglect, the risk factors can be subtle. No acts of neglect can be as subtle as emotional neglect. Emotional neglect has no visible findings and the hurt goes much deeper than the skin. A consensus has not been made as to what exemplifies emotional abuse, but research supports the fact that emotional or psychological abuse is the most developmentally destructive form of abuse. A standard definition has not been developed on what qualifies as emotional abuse or neglect Some definitions include "psychological tactics aimed at undermining emotional security and sense of self that includes guilt induction, and exertion of power through psychologically coercive means" and a "repeated pattern of behavior that conveys to children that they are worthless, unloved, unwanted, only of value in meeting another's needs, or seriously threatened with physical or psychological violence."[68] As traumatizing as emotional abuse and/or neglect is by itself, it usually is accompanied with other forms of abuse and/or neglect.

There are several forms in which emotional neglect may occur:

1. The caregiver is emotionally unavailable and unresponsive to the child. The caregiver does not acknowledge the existence of the child.
2. The interaction of the caregiver to the child is that of hostility, blame, and/or rejection. The child is targeted for whatever reason the caregiver has identified (special needs, gender, personality, physical traits, etc.) as being deserving of this negative treatment.
3. Developmentally inappropriate or inconsistent interactions with the child. The expectations of the child are above or below the child's developmental capacity. This category of emotional neglect also incorporates children as a witness to domestic violence.
4. Failure to allow for the individuality of the child. The caregiver enforces their beliefs and wishes on the child and does not allow for the child to develop their own reality. An all too common example of this is parents in a custody battle, using the child as a pawn for their own gain.
5. Caregivers isolating the child from others.[69]

Emotional abuse has the potential of lifelong impact of behavioral side effects that may begin in childhood, adolescence, or adulthood and continue throughout that person's life. Research conducted to evaluate the long-term implications of emotional abuse and neglect concluded that children exposed to emotional abuse are more likely to develop depressive and anxiety disorders than non-abused children. Children that are emotionally neglected are 2.5 times more likely to develop eating disorders, are 1.27 times more likely to have problem drinking behaviors, and 1.4 times more likely to use drugs than those that were not abused as a child. These same children are more than three times as likely to complete suicide in their lifetime.

From a medical standpoint, emotional abuse may be difficult to identify in a routine doctor visit, but it may not. The medical team needs to be vigilant in listening and seeing what is being presented. Read between the lines; ask the questions. Identify the risk factors, and provide education to the families on skills needed to care for the children. Provide resources for families that need help. Finally, don't be afraid to involve CPS where there are concerns of neglect of the child.

SUPERVISORY NEGLECT

The American Academy of Pediatrics "believes that supervisory neglect occurs whenever a caregiver's supervisory decisions or behaviors place a child in his or her care at significant risk for physical, emotional, or psychological harm."[70] The main categories of supervisory neglect include:

1. Leaving a child home alone
2. Not watching a child closely enough
3. Failure to provide adequate substitute child care
4. Allowing a child to participate in harmful behaviors
5. Leaving children unattended in the vehicle.

When evaluating cases of supervisory neglect, young children are more likely to be harmed when they are not being watched closely enough. Older children are more likely to act out and participate in deviant behavior with inadequate supervision.[71] Supervisory neglect can occur for multiple different reasons: lack of knowledge of the caregiver and/or alcohol or drug related seem to be the most common.

CASE STUDY #6

Mom and Dad are recently separated. Mom works night shift from 10:00 p.m. to 7:00 a.m. There are six children in the family. The oldest child is a boy that is twelve years old. The younger children range from two to six years old. The older male is left in charge of the children while the mother is at work. The family lives in a two-story house. The bedrooms are on the second floor, and the house is heated by a wood stove on the first floor. All of the children were asleep on the second floor when the older child noted smoke. The phone was on the first floor, so the child could not call for help. The flames erupted, blocking all door exits to the house. The older child wakes his siblings up and throws the older children out of the window of the second floor. He holds the younger children in his arms as he jumps out the window. The older male then gets to the pickup truck in the driveway and drives to a neighbor's house to call 911. No child in this case study had fatal injuries. They had bumps, bruises, and minor broken bones. Is this supervisory neglect? When determining if a child can stay home alone and care for other children, an exact age is not dictated by the law. The child has to show good judgment and be able to handle situations; this child did that by saving his life and that of all of his siblings.

Caregivers that leave children home alone tend to have poor judgment, fewer adults living within the home, and/or work outside of the home. At times financial restraints leave caregivers with the feeling that choices are limited. Childcare is expensive, so the caregiver may feel like they do not have options. The caregiver can't afford to put the child in childcare to go to work and the caregiver can't afford to not work. Does this make it okay to leave children home alone? Absolutely not. This does need to be reported to CPS. CPS can then offer appropriate parental training and resources.

Leaving children with inadequate substitute caregivers is also problematic. The caregiver does have someone stay with the children, but that person may not be an appropriate choice. The substitute caregiver may be too young, have mental health problems, abuse alcohol and drugs, or may be an abuser themselves. Even if the care needed is for only a brief amount of time, negative consequences such as physical and sexual abuse can occur in a short amount of time. Children that have been left with inadequate supervision tend to be at the greatest risk of harm.[72]

Abandonment is also a form of supervisory neglect. Abandonment of a child can be emotional or physical abandonment. Infants can be abandoned and left to die (infanticide). Infants or children can be left in places where they are likely to be found and care provided for the children. Children can be "thrown away" by the caregivers. Throwaway children are thrown out of the home, locked out, or refused admittance back in the home after the child has run away, gotten pregnant, or committed an act that the parents did not approve of or accept. Abandonment of a child has long-term consequences from childhood to adulthood:

1. When a child is abandoned by the parent or caregiver, the child tends to operate in a more confused and emotionally stressed state.
2. Sense of trust in others becomes greatly altered.
3. Once the child has reached adulthood, the child may have limited perspective on what is right and wrong.
4. As an adult, they may have difficulty bonding and caring for their own children.
5. Abandoned children are more likely to have juvenile delinquency issues. If they do become juvenile delinquents, as adults, these children are more likely to develop antisocial behaviors.[73]

To overcome supervisory neglect and abandonment, these children will need intensive counseling.

EDUCATIONAL NEGLECT

Educational neglect, like many other forms of neglect, has multiple different versions of what may be considered neglect. Educational neglect can range from failing to enroll a child in school, neglecting the learning needs of a child, or allowing truancy behaviors. Educational neglect incorporates both active roles of neglect of the parent as well as passive roles. In a young child, educational neglect is typically seen as a lack of support from the parent or caretaker in the learning role of the child (i.e., not knowing alphabet, colors, shapes, etc.). In the older child, educational neglect will typically be noted by truancy issues. Truancy is monitored by school officials and is a more easily observed sign of neglect. Truancy is many times closely associated with poverty, so the question is should the child (parent) be punished or do the child welfare workers and school administration need to think outside of the box to help develop a solution. Truancy is a sign of trouble for that child; intervention would be a positive to guide the child to a better future. Children who have experience educational neglect are more like to take remedial classes in school and to have problems in school.[74] Children with truancy issues are more like to be dealing with family poverty, mental health issues, homelessness, substance abuse issues, and crime. These children are trying to survive day to day.

Educational neglect is so much more than not going to school. Children are dealing with real-life issues that some people can't imagine. In order for the children to have a chance at success later, school continues to need to be a priority. The No Child Left Behind Act requires that school districts monitor and report attendance rates. For the success of the child, parents and children need to be held accountable in getting the child to school and/or assuring the child is going to school. Research supports that attending school provides better outcomes for the child, including more likely to achieve full-time work and less likely to be impoverished as an adult.[75]

PROVIDER'S ROLE

There are multiple reasons that providers are hesitant to report child neglect, which can range from not wanting to ruin the relationship between the provider and the family, not recognizing the symptoms of child neglect, and finally not wanting to go to court. The fact remains: the provider has to be a voice for the child.

A provider should be able to express the concerns of the child to the family without blaming the family. Listen to what is being said and offer appropriate resources to the family. Set specific outcomes and follow up to assure that the objectives have been met. If not, ask why. If the family is not following through with the medical care, CPS will need to be notified and become involved with the family, for the well-being of the child. It is the responsibility of the providers to know and understand the reporting mandates for professionals and abide by those mandates.

In conclusion, child neglect is the most commonly reported type of child abuse second only to emotional abuse. Many contributing factors can lead to neglect; some factors are intentional but many are not. The challenge is to recognize that neglect is occurring, how to protect the child, and how to guide the parents to resources that they may need. The next challenge is to have a community in which the professional agencies are all on one page. The medical staff can discuss concerns with CPS and law enforcement, and have a working relationship and understanding on what is in the child's best interest.

REVIEW QUESTIONS

1. What are some contributors to neglect?

2. Compare and contrast emotional neglect and physical neglect.

3. Discuss factors that can make the investigation of medical neglect difficult.

4. Describe challenges of the professional agencies when reporting, investigating, and prosecuting neglected children.

KEYWORDS

Child neglect: A deficiency in meeting the basic needs of a child.
Harm Standard: Demonstrable harm has occurred to a child.
Endangered Standard: A child has not been harmed, but has been deemed at risk of harm.
Intentionality: One's own determination to act in a specific manner.

NOTES

1. U.S. Department of Health and Human Services. (2016). Child Maltreatment. Available from https://www.acf.hhs.gov/cb/research-data-technology/statistics-research/child-maltreatment.

2. U.S. Department of Health and Human Services. (January 15, 2010). Fourth National Incidence Study of Child Abuse and Neglect. Accessed on March 27, 2019. Available from https://www.acf.hhs.gov/opre/resource/fourth-national-incidence-study-of-child-abuse-and-neglect-nis-4-report-to.

3. Marije Stoltenborgh, Marian J. Bakermano-Kranenberg., and Marinus H. van Ijzendoorn, "The Neglect of Child Neglect: A Meta-analytic Review of the Prevalence of Child Neglect," *Sociology Psychiatry Psychiatric Epidemiology* 48 (2013): 345–55.

4. Anna Gupta, "Poverty and Child Neglect—The Elephant in the Room?" *Families, Relationships and Societies* 6, no. 1 (2017): 21–36.

5. Howard Dubowitz, "Epidemiology of Child Neglect," in Carole Jenny (ed.), *Child Abuse and Neglect: Diagnosis, Treatment, and Evidence* (St. Louis: Elsevier Saunders, 2011), 28–38.

6. Dubowitz, "Epidemiology of Child Neglect."

7. Svetlana Yampolskaya, C. Hendricks Brown, and Mary J. Armstrong, "Heterogeneity in Trajectories of Child Maltreatment Severity—A Two-Part Growth Mixture Model," *Violence and Victims* 30, no. 5 (2015): 916–32.

8. Dubowitz, "Epidemiology of Child Neglect."

9. Dubowitz, "Epidemiology of Child Neglect."

10. Merriam-Webster Dictionary, "Intentional." Accessed August 16, 2018. Available from https://www.merriam-webster.com/dictionary/intentional?src=search-dict-box.

11. Merriam-Webster Dictionary, "Intention." Accessed August 16, 2018. Available from https://www.merriam-webster.com/dictionary/intention?src=search-dict-box.

12. Jessica D. and M. Ann Easterbrooks, "The Moderating Effect of Relationships on Intergenerational Risk for Infant Neglect by Young Mothers," *Child Abuse and Neglect*, 45 (2015): 21–34.

13. Bartlett and Easterbrooks, "The Moderating Effect of Relationships on Intergenerational Risk for Infant Neglect by Young Mothers."

14. Sara R. Berzenski, David S. Bennett, Victoria A. Marini, Margaret W. Sullivan, and Michael Lewis, "The Role of Parental Distress in Moderation, the Influence of Child Neglect on Maladjustment," *Journal of Child Family Studies* 23 (2014): 1325–36.

15. Patricia M. Crittenden, "Child Neglect Causes and Considerations," in Howard Dubowitz (ed.), *Neglected Children: Research, Practice, and Policy* (Thousand Oaks: SAGE Publications, Inc., 1999), 47–68.

16. Dinko S. Aleksandrov, Alisha R. Bowen, and Jay Colker, "Parent Training and Cultural Considerations," *The Journal of Individual Psychology* 77, no. 2 (2016): 77–89.

17. Aleksandrov, Bowen, and Colker, "Parent Training and Cultural Considerations."

18. U.S. Department of Health and Human Services. Fourth National Incidence Study of Child Abuse and Neglect.

19. Dubowitz, "Epidemiology of Child Neglect."

20. Howard Dubowitz, "Tackling Child Neglect: A Role for Pediatricians," *Pediatric Clinics of North America* 56 (2009): 363–78.

21. Christina G. McDonnell and Kristin Valentino, "Intergenerational Effects of Childhood Trauma: Evaluating Pathways Among Maternal ACEs, Perinatal Depressive Symptoms, and Infant Outcomes," *Child Maltreatment* 21, no. 4 (2016): 317–26.

22. Melissa Jonson-Reid, Brett Drake, John N. Constantino, Mini Tandon, Laura Pons, Patricia Kohl, Scott Roesch, et al., "A Randomized Trial of Home Visitation for CPS-Involved Families: The Moderating Impact of Maternal Depression and CPS History," *Child Maltreatment* 23, no. 3 (2018): 281–93.

23. Tobi Delong-Hamilton, Kathryn Krase, and Kimberly Bundy-Fazioli, "Exploring Child Welfare Workers' Experiences in Neglect Cases: A Qualitative Study," *Journal of Public Child Welfare* 10, no. 1 (2016): 21–38.

24. Howard Dubowitz, "Epidemiology of Child Neglect."

25. Howard Dubowitz, "Where's Dad? A Need to Understand Father's Role in Child Maltreatment," *Child Abuse & Neglect* 30 (2016): 461–65.

26. Samantha Schilling and Cindy W. Christian, "Child Physical Abuse and Neglect," *Child Adolescent Psychiatric North American Journal* 23 (2014): 309–19.

27. Andrea Doud, K. Lawrence, M. Goodpasture, and K. Zeller, "Prematurity and Neonatal Comorbidities as Risk Factors for Nonaccidental Trauma," *Journal of Pediatric Surgery* 50 (2015): 1024–27.

28. Angelo P. Giardino, Karen M. Hudson, and Judith Marsh, "Providing Medical Evaluation for Possible Child Maltreatment to Children with Special Health Care Needs," *Child Abuse & Neglect* 27 (2003): 1179–86.

29. Edward Traisman, "Recognizing Maltreatment in Children with Special Needs," *Pediatric Annals* 45, no. 8 (2016): 273–77.

30. Claudia Coulton, D. Crampton, M. Irwan, J. Spilsbury, and J. Korbin, "How Neighborhoods Influence Child Maltreatment: A Review of Literature and Alternative Pathways," *Child Abuse & Neglect* 31 (2007): 1117–42.

31. Michael S. Wald, "Beyond CPS: Developing an Effective System for Helping Children in Neglectful Families," *Child Abuse & Neglect* 41 (2015): 49–66.

32. Sarah A. Font and Emily J. Warren, "Inadequate Housing and the Child Protection System Response," *Children and Youth Services Review* 35 (2013): 1809–15.

33. U.S. Department of Health and Human Services. Fourth National Incidence Study of Child Abuse and Neglect.

34. Delong-Hamilton, Krase, and Bundy-Fazioli, "Exploring Child Welfare Workers' Experiences in Neglect Cases."

35. Wayne I. Munkel, "Neglect and Abandonment," in Elaine Steinborn (ed.), *Quick-Reference Child Abuse for Healthcare Professionals, Social Services, and Law Enforcement* (St. Louis, MO: G.W. Medical Publishing, Inc., 1998), 259–82.

36. Munkel, "Neglect and Abandonment."

37. Munkel, "Neglect and Abandonment."

38. Munkel, "Neglect and Abandonment."

39. Samantha Schilling and Cindy W. Christian, "Child Physical Abuse and Neglect," *Child Adolescent Psychiatric North American Journal* 23 (2014): 309–19.

40. Ann L. O'Sullivan and Angelo P. Giardino, "Clinical Aspects of Child Neglect," in Kristin Feeherty and Ann Przyzycki (eds.), *Nursing Approach to the Evaluation of Child Maltreatment* (St. Louis, MO: G.W. Medical Publishing, Inc., 2003), 251–88.

41. Schilling and Christian, "Child Physical Abuse and Neglect."

42. Schilling and Christian, "Child Physical Abuse and Neglect."

43. Martin H. Teicher and Jacqueline A. Samson, "Annual Research Review: Enduring Neurobiological Effects of Childhood Abuse and Neglect," *Journal of Child Psychology and Psychiatry* 57, no. 3 (2016): 241–66.

44. India Tendolkar, Johan Martensson, Simone Kuhn, Floris Klumpers, and Guillen Fernandez, "Physical Neglect during Childhood Alters White Matter Connectivity in Healthy Young Males," *Human Brain Mapping* 39 (2018): 1283–90.

45. Ann H. Ross and Chelsey A. Juarez, "A Brief History of Fatal Child Maltreatment and Neglect," *Forensic Science Med Pathology* 10 (2014): 413–22.

46. Bridget Benelam, "Recognizing the Signs of Dehydration," *Practice Nursing* 21, no. 5 (2010): 230–35.

47. Laura D. Knight and Kim A. Collins, "A 25-year Retrospective Review of Deaths due to Pediatric Neglect," *The American Journal of Forensic Medicine and Pathology* 26, no. 3 (2005): 221–28.

48. Richard Omore, Jacqueline E. Tate, Ciara E. O'Reilly, Tracy Ayers, John Williamson, Feny Moke, Katie A. Schilling, et al., "Epidemiology, Seasonality and Factors Associated with Rotavirus Infection Among Children with Moderate-to-Severe Diarrhea in Rural Western Kenya, 2008-2012: The Global Enteric Multicenter Study," *PLOS One* (2016): 1–17.

49. Eiji Yanagisawa and John K. Joel, "Anterior and Posterior Nasal Fontanelles," *Ear, Nose & Throat Journal* 80, no. 1 (2001): 10–11.

50. Yanagisawa and Joel, "Anterior and Posterior Nasal Fontanelles."

51. Omore, Tate, O'Reilly, Ayers, Williamson, Moke, Schilling, et al., "Epidemiology, Seasonality and Factors Associated with Rotavirus Infection Among Children with Moderate-to-Severe Diarrhea in Rural Western Kenya, 2008-2012."

52. Nancy S. Harper, "Neglect: Failure to Thrive and Obesity," *Pediatric Clin North America* 61 (2014): 937–57.

53. Deborah E. Lowen, "Failure to Thrive," in Carole Jenny (ed.), *Child Abuse and Neglect: Diagnosis, Treatment, and Evidence* (St. Louis: Elsevier Saunders, 2011), 547–62.

54. Robert W. Block, Nancy F. Krebs, Committee on Child Abuse & Neglect, and Committee on Nutrition, "Failure to Thrive as a Manifestation of Child Neglect," *American Academy of Pediatrics* 116, no. 5 (2005): 1234–37.

55. Knight and Collins, "A 25-year Retrospective Review of Deaths due to Pediatric Neglect."

56. U.S. Department of Health and Human Services. Fourth National Incidence Study of Child Abuse and Neglect.

57. U.S. House of Representatives, Testimony before the Subcommittee on Education Reform. "The Obesity Crisis in America," statement made by Richard H. Carmona, Surgeon General, July 16, 2003. Accessed August 25, 2018. Available from https://www.surgeongeneral.gov/news/testimony/obesity07162003.html.

58. Jenna T. Hayes and Lorie L Sicafuse, "Is Childhood Obesity a Form of Child Abuse? Factors to Consider in Judicial Rulings," *Judicature* 94 (2010): 20–28.

59. Lizet Dominguez, "Childhood Obesity as Child Abuse: Criminalizing Parents for Raising Obese Children," *Child and Family Law Journal* 2 (2014): 105–22.

60. Dominguez, "Childhood Obesity as Child Abuse."

61. Dubowitz, "Epidemiology of Child Neglect."

62. Dubowitz, "Epidemiology of Child Neglect."

63. Susan A. Vitale, "Parent Recommendations for Family Functioning with Prader-Willi Syndrome: A Rare Genetic Cause of Childhood Obesity," *Journal of Pediatric Nursing* 31 (2016): 47–54.

64. David Katney and S. Fournier, "Considerations in Identifying Pediatric Dental Neglect and the Legal Obligation to Report," *Journal of American Dental Association* 147, no. 10 (2016): 812.

65. Jenny Harris and A. Whittington, "Dental Neglect in Children," *Paediatrics and Child Health* 26, no. 11 (2016): 478–84.

66. Ricardo J. Dinis-Oliverira and T. Magalhaes, "Children Intoxications: What is Abuse and What is Not Abuse" *Trauma, Violence & Abuse* 14, no. 2 (2012): 113–32.

67. Sara R. Berzenski, David S. Bennett, Victoria A. Marini, Margaret W. Sullivan, and Michael Lewis, "The Role of Parental Distress in Moderation, the Influence of Child Neglect on Maladjustment," *Journal of Child Family Studies* 23 (2014): 1325–36.

68. Diana English, R. Thompson, C. White, and D. Wilson, "Why Should Child Welfare Pay More Attention to Emotional Maltreatment," *Children and Youth Services Review* 50 (2015): 53–63.

69. Danya Glaser, "How to Deal with Emotional Abuse and Neglect—Further Development of a Conceptual Framework (FRAMEA)," *Child Abuse & Neglect* 35 (2011): 866–75.

70. Kent P. Hymel, "When is Lack of Supervision Neglect?" *American Academy of Pediatrics* 118, no. 3 (2006): 1296–97.

71. Bridget Freisthler, M. Johnson-Motoyama, and N. Kepple. "Inadequate Child Supervision: The Role of Alcohol Outlet Density, Parent Drinking Behaviours, and Social Support," *Children and Youth Services Review* 43 (2014): 75–84.

72. Michael S. Wald, "Beyond CPS: Developing an Effective System for Helping Children in Neglectful Families," *Child Abuse & Neglect* 41 (2015): 49–66.

73. U.S. Department of Health and Human Services. Fourth National Incidence Study of Child Abuse and Neglect.

74. Melissa V. Wert, B. Fallon, N. Trocme, and D. Collin-Vezina, "Educational Neglect: Understanding 20 Years of Child Welfare Trends," *Child Abuse & Neglect* 75 (2018): 50–60.

75. Sarah A. Font and Emily J. Warren, "Inadequate Housing and the Child Protection System Response," *Children and Youth Services Review* 35 (2013): 1809–15.

6

Child Fatalities, Fetal Abuse, and Missing Children

◆ ◆ ◆

CHILD FATALITIES

THERE ARE FEW THINGS IN THIS WORLD that generate such emotions as the death of a child. Even the strongest of individuals can fall to their knees in sorrow. This sorrowfulness can easily turn to anger and confusion when it is determined that a child's death could have been prevented. In response to dealing with these unnecessary and preventable fatalities, the Protect Our Kids Act of 2012 established the Federal Commission to Eliminate Child Abuse and Neglect Fatalities (CECANF). In 2018, CECANF released a progress report to show that this organization has been influential by recently passing two pieces of legislation in preventing child fatalities. The first being the Comprehensive Addiction and Recovery Act, which ensures that Child Protective Services (CPS) has a safety plan in place for infants who are born affected by substance abuse or suffering from fetal alcohol spectrum disorder. The other piece of legislation that passed, known as Talia Law, requires the Department of Defense to report child abuse to CPS. Other bills that have been recommended by CECANF that are currently in front of Congress for review include the Family First Prevention and Services Act and the Maternal, Infant, and Early Childhood Home Visiting Program. This organization continues to strive to create programs and pass legislation to reduce child fatalities. Unfortunately, the number of child fatalities is still staggering.

CHILD FATALITY STATISTICS

CECANF acknowledges that child fatalities are still a significant problem in our society noting how the National Child Abuse and Neglect Data System (NCANDS) estimated that there were 1,670 child fatalities in 2015 resulting from abuse or neglect, noting that the actual amount may be double or even more than that.[1] Research has shown that children are at greatest risk of dying from maltreatment before the child reaches four years of age. Additionally, 40 percent of the children who are victims of fatal maltreatment are under the age of one.[2] Race was also a significant factor in child fatalities. In a 2014 report, African American children died from child abuse and neglect at a rate two and a half times the rate of white or Hispanic children.[3]

CECANF found that NCANDS does not have a standardized reporting system for abuse and neglect fatalities across the United States, noting that nearly half the states included child fatality data only from reports from CPS. This is not an accurate account of child fatalities because not all children who died had prior contact with these agencies.[4] There are cases of child fatalities that may have been the result of child abuse or neglect. However, these same cases of possible abuse may have been ruled accidental or death by natural causes. This inaccurate diagnosis may explain why the data on child fatalities are considered significantly underestimated. See the following two figures and tables 6.1 to 6.3 for child abuse fatality statistics from 2013 to 2017.

SUDDEN INFANT DEATH SYNDROME

Sudden infant death syndrome (SIDS) is defined as the unexpected death of an infant younger than one year of age that remains unexplained after a thorough investigation, including the performance of an autopsy and a review of the circumstance of death and the clinical history of the child.[5] Although there have been several definitions proposed since this condition was first defined in 1969, there are only a few that are accepted internationally. Additionally, interpretations of these definitions have been numerous, inconsistent, and idiosyncratic.[6] It is difficult to diagnose why a baby has stopped breathing, acknowledging that some deaths have resulted from asphyxia or deliberate smothering by the parent or caretaker.[7] Although SIDS is associated with when a child is placed in a crib during sleep time, SIDS can also occur in infant seats, car seats, or while in their parents' bed. SIDS is not a positive finding, but a diagnosis that is made when there is no other medical explanation for the abrupt death of what appeared to be a healthy infant.[8]

Children that die from SIDS are usually between one to five months of age, with the most common between two to four months. Males are at greater risk at a rate of 2:1 compared to females. While there is no answer as to the cause of SIDS or SUIDS (sudden unexplained infant death syndrome), there are factors that have been associated to increase the risk of death. These factors include:

- Premature births
- Low birth weight
- Lower socioeconomic status
- Young maternal age
- Short intergestational level
- Exposure to cigarette smoke.

Table 6.1 Child Fatality Rates per 100,000 Children, 2013–2017[1]

Year	Reporting States	Child Population of Reporting States	Child Fatalities from Reporting States	National Fatality Rate per One Hundred Thousand Children	Child Population of all Fifty-two States	National Estimate of Child Fatalities
2013	51	74,116,816	1,548	2.09	74,378,641	1,550
2014	51	74,081,066	1,585	2.14	74,339,990	1,590
2015	49	70,432,795	1,589	2.26	74,360,792	1,680
2016	49	72,028,582	1,699	2.36	74,352,938	1,750
2017	50	72,689,585	1,688	2.32	74,312,174	1,720

Data are from the Child File and Agency File. National fatality rates per one hundred thousand children are calculated by dividing the number of child fatalities by the population of reporting states and multiplying the result by one hundred thousand.

If fewer than fifty-two states reported data, the national estimate of child fatalities is calculated by multiplying the national fatality rate by the child population of all fifty-two states and dividing by one hundred thousand. The estimate is rounded to the nearest ten. Because of the rounding rule, the national estimate could have more or fewer fatalities than the actual reported number of fatalities.

[1] U.S. Department of Health & Human Services, Administration for Children and Families, Administration on Children, Youth and Families, Children's Bureau. (2019). Child Maltreatment 2017. Available from https://www.acf.hhs.gov/cb/research-data-technology/statistics-research/child-maltreatment.

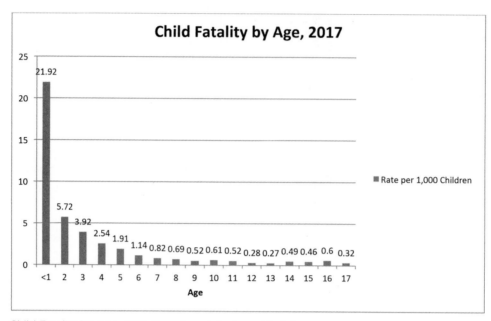

Child Fatality by Age, 2017; Based on data from 44 states
"U.S. Department of Health & Human Services, Administration for Children and Families, Administration on Children, Youth and Families, Children's Bureau. (2019). Child Maltreatment 2017. Available from https://www.acf.hhs.gov/cb/research-data-technology/statistics-research/child-maltreatment.

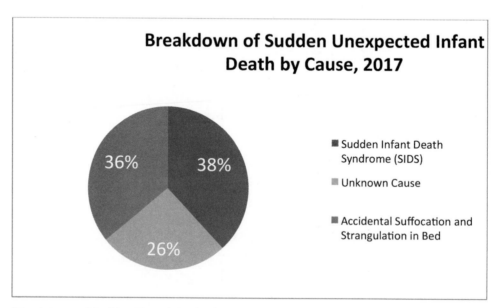

"Breakdown of Sudden Unexplained Infant Death by Cause, 2017 According to the Centers for Disease Control and Prevention (CDC)"
Source: CDC/NCHS, National Vital Statistics System, Compressed Mortality File

Table 6.2 Child Fatalities by Sex, 2017[1]

Sex	Child Population	Child Fatalities	Child Fatalities Percent	Child Fatalities Rate per One Hundred Thousand Children
Boys	29,606,586	792	57.9	2.68
Girls	28,359,358	573	41.9	2.02
Unknown	—	3	0.2	N/A
National	57,965,944	1,368	100.0	—

Based on data from forty-four states. Data are from the Child File. There are no population data for unknown sex and therefore no rates.
1 U.S. Department of Health & Human Services, Administration for Children and Families, Administration on Children, Youth and Families, Children's Bureau. (2019). Child Maltreatment 2017. Available from https://www.acf.hhs.gov/cb/research-data-technology/statistics-research/child-maltreatment.

Ethic groups at higher risk are:

- African American
- Native American
- Alaskan Natives
- Australian aboriginal
- Maori[9]

There have been multiple hypotheses regarding why infants are dying from unknown causes. Wedgewood first mentioned a multiple contingency hypothesis

Table 6.3 Child Fatalities by Race and Ethnicity, 2017[1]

Race and Ethnicity	Child Population	Child Fatalities	Child Fatalities Percent	Child Fatalities Rate Per One Hundred Thousand Children
Single Race				
African American	8,556,624	416	31.5	4.86
American Indian or Alaska Native	486,121	15	1.1	3.09
Hispanic	12,512,722	199	15.1	1.59
Pacific Islander	89,418	4	0.3	4.47
Unknown	—	63	4.8	N/A
White	30,122,748	554	41.9	1.84
Multiple Race				
Two or More Races	2,284,306	56	4.2	2.45
National	**56,333,950**	**1,321**	**100.0**	**—**

Based on data from forty-two states. Data are from the Child File. The multiple race category is defined as any combination of two or more race categories. Counts associated with specific racial groups (e.g., white) are exclusive and do not include Hispanic.
States with more than 25.0 percent of victim race or ethnicity reported as unknown or missing are excluded from this analysis. This analysis includes only those states that reported both victim race and ethnicity.
1 U.S. Department of Health & Human Services, Administration for Children and Families, Administration on Children, Youth and Families, Children's Bureau. (2019). Child Maltreatment 2017. Available from https://www.acf.hhs.gov/cb/research-data-technology/statistics-research/child-maltreatment.

in 1972 that described three areas that put infants at risk. Filiano and Kinney expanded upon the multiple contingency hypothesis, discussing three overlapping factors that are required for a child to succumb to SIDS; this hypothesis is referred to as triple risk model. The triple risk model contends that infants need to be in a critical development period, be a vulnerable infant, and be exposed to some type of exogenous stressors. Exogenous stressors are defined as prone sleeping, co-sleeping, and soft bedding.[10] While this model does not give the needed answers as to what causes SIDS, it does open the door for further research.

In 1992, based off of the exogenous stressor hypothesis, a media campaign titled "Back to Sleep" was started. The "Back to Sleep" campaign promoted infants being placed on their backs rather than on the abdomens. After this campaign was instituted, statistics showed a decrease in babies succumbing to SIDS by 38 percent. While the numbers have drastically declined, the Centers for Disease Control and Prevention reports that in 2016, the United States had 3,607 sudden unexplained infant deaths.[11]

In the past decade, the rate of SIDS has dropped significantly. One factor that can be attributed to this is how child deaths are now being evaluated. The term sudden unexplained death of infancy is often used in lieu of SIDS, although there is no universal agreement on the use of the term.[12] Classifying a child's death as SIDS is based on an objective investigation. Professionals investigating SIDS cannot approach grieving parents with the presumption of guilt or suspicion, as that can in turn lead to misguided and hurtful accusations. However, these same investigators would be remiss if they believed that a parent would never kill their own child.[13] An autopsy can help address the concerns of a grieving parent as well as be an invaluable tool in assisting investigators if there was any indication of child maltreatment. In one study, 83 percent of parents found that autopsies helped them cope better with their child's death.[14] Today, the cause of SIDS remains unknown, and physical abuse or neglect still may not be identified as the causation of a child's death. To help reduce the occurrence of death outside of child maltreatment, research has identified methods in reducing the likelihood of SIDS, although accidental suffocation and strangulation can still occur. Some of the methods to reduce the occurrence of SIDS include:

- Firm sleeping surface
- Avoid overheating (blankets, head coverings, excess clothing)
- Encourage breastfeeding (provides immunoglobulins and cytokines that help shield infants during the most vulnerable period for SIDS)
- Room sharing with parents
- Optimizing pre- and postnatal care
- Supine position.[15]

There are four types of accidental suffocation and strangulation in bed:

1. Suffocation: This can result from loose bedding, pillows, or stuffed animals or toys that are near or covering the nose and mouth of the child.

2. Overlay: This can occur when another person rolls on top or against the infant while the infant is sleeping.
3. Wedging or entrapment: This occurs when the infant is wedged between two objects such as a mattress and wall.
4. Strangulation: This can occur when an infant's head and neck become caught between the crib railings.[16]

CLASSIFICATIONS OF HOMICIDE

The term homicide is the act of killing of one person by another. Our criminal justice system breaks down homicide into different categories depending on the circumstances that led to an individual's death. For instance, the term "first-degree murder" refers to the intentional killing of another person that was considered premeditated. "Second-degree murder" refers to the intentional killing of an individual where the act may have been done spontaneously or in the heat of passion. Our criminal justice system also categorizes homicide where the individual did not intentionally try to kill someone else but still their actions caused the death of another. Depending on the jurisdiction, homicides that were committed without intent may be referred to as either "negligent homicide" or "involuntary manslaughter." These various terms of homicide can be used when charging an offender whether the victim was a child or an adult. However, in the United States the penalty may be more severe if a child is intentionally murdered, as several states have the intentional killing of a child as an aggravating factor that warrants stronger sanctions including the death penalty.

Children are killed every day by strangers, gang violence, and school shootings, and these tragedies have been met with an aggressive response whether through enhanced penalties against the perpetrator or through a forceful law enforcement response. Unfortunately, the dynamics of child fatalities within a family may not be as easily deterred through enhanced penalties or through aggressive law enforcement measures, especially when the perpetrator is the caretaker of the child. The focus of this chapter is to address how and why child fatalities occur within a family setting. To address this issue, one must understand that the terminology when discussing child homicides within the family is different from other types of homicide.

Filicide

In general terms, filicide refers to parents killing their own child. The term "child," for the purposes of this chapter, refers to someone under the age of eighteen. The -cide in filicide originated from the Latin -cida which mans to cut or kill, and fili- was derived from the Latin filius and filia, which mean son and daughter, respectively.[17] Dr. Phillip Resnick, a forensic psychiatrist, was the first one to classify filicide by age creating the category of neonaticide and infanticide. *Neonaticide* refers to homicide committed in the first twenty-four hours after the child's birth, and *infanticide* refers to the parents killing their child within the first year of the child's life. There are approximately twenty countries that have infanticide laws

(Australia, Austria, Brazil, Canada, Colombia, Finland, Germany, Greece, Hong Kong, India, Italy, Japan, Korea, New Zealand, Norway, Philippines, Sweden, Switzerland, Turkey, and the United Kingdom). The majority of these countries have reduced penalties for mothers killing their children when they are under the age of one.[18] The concept of having reduced penalties is based on the concept that many governments recognize that mothers who kill their children within the first year of life may be suffering from some form of mental illness. *Familicide* involves killing your spouse and your children, which tends to be more of a male crime as the females will usually kill only their children.[19]

Premeditation

Kieran O'Hagan reports how most cases of filicide occur as the result of premeditation. Male perpetrators will usually choose a day in which they have contact visits in cases where the parents are separated. Female perpetrators will often choose to kill their children at night when the father is absent and they have complete control over their environment. There is a sinister manifestation in how the premeditation evolves. Children are lied to repeatedly and lured into isolated areas. Many male and female perpetrators will claim mental illness for their actions, but that does not preclude the fact that these acts were completed through meticulous planning.[20] O'Hagan provides examples of premeditation through various case studies:

- A mother preparing to kill her two children, ages five years and eleven months, asked the oldest child if she would prefer to live a few happy days with her mother or a long time without her mother. The child incapable of understanding what the mother meant said she would prefer to stay with her mother. The child, along with younger sibling, was then asphyxiated.
- A father during a contact visit announced that he was taking his three very young children to the zoo. Then he kills them and himself via carbon monoxide poisoning in the car. He leaves a revenge note for his wife.
- A mother uncharacteristically took her two teenage children shopping before stabbing both of them thirty-seven and twenty-nine times, respectively.
- A father called to take his four children on an access outing. He bought them sweets. They were eating the sweets at the same time he was poisoning them and himself with carbon monoxide.
- A mother, who had been planning the killing for months with the help of internet sites, took a bath with her eleven-year-old son and drowned him. He tried resisting and escaping, leaving bite marks on her fingers.
- A father, on the day his wife left him, persuaded his teenage son to go on an errand so that he would have sufficient time to kill a much younger son and a disabled daughter.

These are just a few examples of how these horrifying acts are planned out and are formulated through the betrayal of trust that a child has for their parents.[21]

Child murder is not common, but it is still considered the most common reason for child death in developed countries.[22] Although men commit the vast majority of homicides in general, the act of neonaticide and infanticide are primarily committed by women.[23] In the United States, women commit the crime of filicide as frequently as men when it is their children.[24] When women do kill their children they are more likely to suffer with some type of depression disorder compared to men. Men who kill their children are more likely to have maltreated their children prior to their death. In one study of family members who kill their children, twenty-two of them being women and twenty-four men, there was an outstanding difference in the offender's relationship with the child. In all the cases examined, the biological mother was the perpetrator of the homicide. However, when the children were killed by men, less than half of the perpetrators were the biological father.[25] The method of murder can also vary between biological parents and stepparents. Filicide by stepparents may be fueled by bitterness and resentment and therefore may involve more force or prolonged beatings, whereas the natural parent is less likely to use methods of killing that prolong death or cause extended or extensive pain.[26]

There have been some high-profile cases that have garnered a lot of media attention as the public is in disbelief that a parent could kill their own child. For instance in 2001, Andrea Yates of Texas drowned all five of her children in a bathtub. Shortly after murdering her children, she called the police to report her crime. She was initially convicted of murder until her conviction was overturned due to mental illness. She was then sentenced to North Texas State Hospital for treatment. Another high-profile case that garnered significant attention was in 1994 when Susan Smith of South Carolina claimed that her two children were abducted by a black man. She was seen on television crying and pleading for the safe return of her children. She later confessed to murdering her two children by driving them into a lake while they were strapped in their car seats.

Fratricide, which is the killing of a brother or sister, is considered the rarest form of any family homicide as it accounts for only 1.5 percent of the total amount of criminal deaths in the United States. When it does occur, it is estimated that female perpetrators account for 15 percent of the cases.[27]

Filicide-Suicide

Fathers and mothers are capable of taking their life and the life of their children, although the reasons are strikingly different. Men are more likely to commit filicide-suicide because they are going through a custody battle, and on occasion, will kill their wife as well. Additionally, a perpetrator may kill one or more children as a desire to hurt their former partner; although either parent may commit this act, it is more likely to take place by the father.[28] In one study, men who committed filicide-suicide were suffering from depression associated with conjugal separation.[29] Maternal filicide-suicide can also occur through the different sentiment that a mother feels toward their children. For instance, in some circumstances a mother may feel that once they are gone that there will not be anyone else to care for their child. Others perceive that they need to save themselves and their children from circumstances that the mother believes are intolerable for both her and her children. For example, there have been cases where the male partner abuses his spouse through physical violence, and the mother will take her life and the life of the children to save them from enduring physical abuse. Finally, in certain cases, the mother will take her life and the life of the child as the result of separating from the child's biological father.[30]

Suicide

Suicide refers to taking one's own life. There is a correlation between child abuse and suicide as well as suicidal ideation, which refers to having thoughts of completing suicide. Given the potential lethality of suicide attempts and suicidal ideation, a fair amount of research has been conducted to examine factors that increase risk of these behaviors.[31] There have been numerous studies of adolescents who have either attempted suicide or have had suicidal ideation that are associated with all four types of abuse (physical, sexual, emotional, neglect). Most research shows that each form of child maltreatment maintains an independent association with adolescent suicidal ideation and behavior. Research also suggests that sexual abuse and to a lesser degree physical abuse may be a stronger influence with males compared to females as causation for suicidal attempts.[32] There are long-term effects of child abuse that continue far into their adulthood where they still can't cope with the victimization they experienced as a child. Research has also revealed that adults with at least one type of harmful childhood experience were two to five times more likely to attempt suicide. Women are three times more likely than men to attempt suicide. However, men are more successful in completing suicide.[33]

CHILD FATALITIES AROUND THE WORLD

In general, homicides are likely to be underreported especially from countries with an inadequate monitoring system or that are under some form of conflict. However, it is estimated that ninety-five thousand children are murdered annually around the world, with the majority of victims living in middle-income or low-income countries. One examination of thirty-five countries that provided data on child murders revealed that in more than half of the reported murders the perpetrator was the parent and that 58 percent of those victims were girls compared to 46 percent for boys. A total of 3 percent of the children were killed by another family member, 12 percent by an acquaintance, 2 percent of child homicides were committed by a stranger, and 9 percent of the perpetrators were listed as unknown.[34]

HONOR KILLINGS

Honor killings originated as a patriarchal custom in Muslim, Sikh, and Hindu cultures.[35] In certain cultures, the killing of a family member is considered acceptable if they bring shame to the family. Honor killings in some circumstances can result from just mere suspicion or rumors that a female relative has defied cultural norms by being disobedient or has been misbehaving.[36] Daughters and sisters who are seen rebelling against their fathers or brothers may be killed as the perpetrator attempts to restore authority and resolve the perceived shame that the victim may have brought to their family.[37] Other acts of misbehavior by a Muslim daughter that can cause humiliation to the family include not wearing a hijab, having a non-Muslim boyfriend or male friend of any origin, or being sexually active. Additional infractions can include rejecting an arranged marriage, aggressively seeking employment, or attempting to simulate Western culture.[38] Women and girls are considered property in some cultures and are expected to follow the rules of their fathers or husbands. Men are usually the perpetrators of honor crimes, but other perpetrators can include sisters, neighbors, or friends. Mothers have been known to commit honor crimes as well when their daughter has been involved in sexual activities. Mothers have also indirectly participated in honor killings by luring their daughters back into to their home under the direction of their husband.[39] A female's value is based on their purity. As a result of this indicator of worth, women and girls who are victims of rape or sexual assault are still at risk of death via an honor killing.[40] It is difficult to measure the number of honor killings that actually occur as the family may falsely report the death as a suicide.[41]

NEGLECT

Neglect is the number one cause of child fatalities.[42] Deaths as a result of *external causes* can in most cases be considered preventable. Cases of *drug overdoses* or *accidental shootings* can be deemed as neglect as many cases are the direct result of poor supervision. For instance, a child could lose their life when the caretaker fails to read the directions on the medication that is being dispersed to their child or a caretaker leaves a loaded weapon within reach of their child. *Drowning* is another cause of death that can be associated with neglect. A young child could easily drown in a bathtub without the appropriate supervision. Failing to place a fence around an in-ground pool or failure to secure a pool ladder are also examples of how drowning can be associated with neglect. Other forms of neglect that may lead to death can include *hyperthermia* or exposure to extreme heat.[43] This can happen, for example when a child wanders outside in extreme temperatures without their parents' knowledge or if a child is left in a vehicle under extreme heat. In many of these cases, an investigation may conclude that the death was accidental. However, there have been some cases where the caretaker deliberately leaves the child in the vehicle in extreme heat and pretends the act was accidental: Justin Harris, in June 2014, was charged with murder for leaving his twenty-two-month-old son in his car for approximately seven hours.[44] From 1998 to 2017, an average of thirty-seven children died annually from heat exposure in hot cars. Some of these deaths resulted from children accidently locking themselves in the car or trunk. Other children died after being left in the car by their caretaker, and in rare cases, the child is deliberately left in the vehicle.[45] Other factors relating to death by neglect include *home fires*. A caretaker who fails to have smoke detectors in their home or doesn't replace batteries can be a factor in a child's unnecessary death. Additionally, leaving a child with access to matches or a lit candle can be contributing factors to a child's death with home fires.[46]

PHYSICAL ABUSE

Physical abuse is the second-leading cause for child fatalities. The most common type of physical abuse that leads to death is the result of head trauma. Fatal physical abuse can be a one-time incident or the result of a history of physical abuse.[47]

CASE STUDY #1

A twenty-month-old female was brought into the hospital for decreased level of responsiveness. The mother reported that the child was clumsy and had fallen off the bed three times. The same child had been evaluated when she was one month old for injuries and placed in foster care. The child had been reunited with her mother a year later.

On examination, the child was diagnosed with possible diffuse axonal injury. Thirty soft tissue findings were documented on physical examination, including looped patterned injuries and burns. On visual examination, the abdomen was sunken with loose skin appreciated; the evaluation of her medical record revealed a weight loss of three pounds over 1.5 months. Through medical technology, the child was able to survive three days before succumbing to her injuries. The mother confessed to beating the child. The medical examiner listed hypernatremia (sodium poisoning) as the cause of death.

SEXUAL ABUSE

Although rare, there are cases where sexual assault can lead to a child's death. For example, in 1998 Steven Smith of Lucasville, Ohio, was charged with the rape and murder of his girlfriend's six-month-old infant. Expert witnesses testified that the child died from suffocation as Smith lay on top of her in an attempt to have sex. Steven Smith was convicted of this child's death and was executed in 2013 for this offense. Children can also die from the medical implications associated with sexual abuse whether the abuse occurs within the household or in the community. The Centers for Disease Prevention and Control reported that 7 percent of students reported that they were physically forced to have sex, increasing the chances of obtaining sexually transmitted infections and human immunodeficiency virus. This report also revealed that the use of condoms among students has decreased, putting more students at risk.[48]

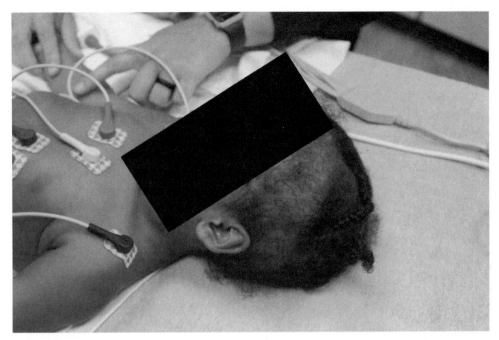

Abrasions noted to the face and eye

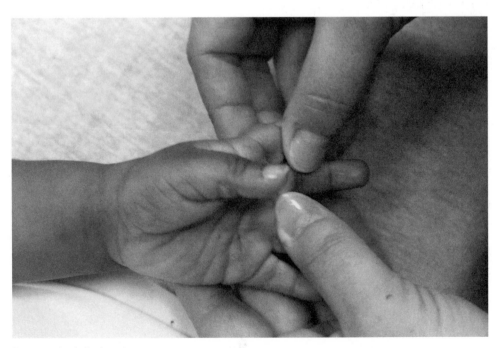

Burn to the left thumb

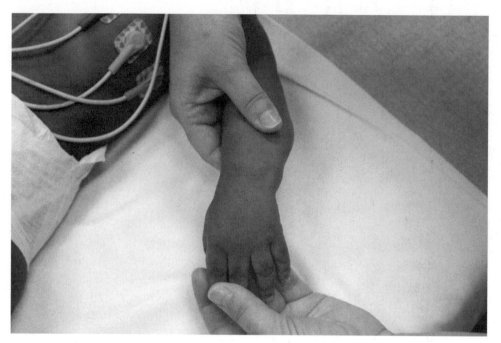

Bruising to the left wrist and left hand

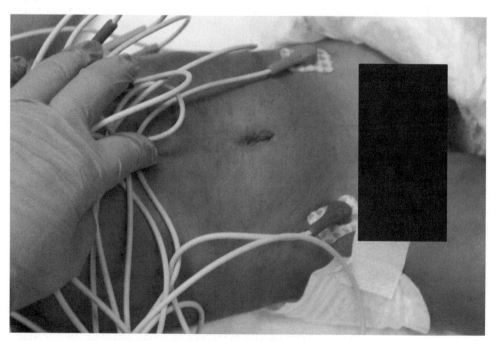

Loose skin noted over the abdomen with documented weight loss over 1.5 months

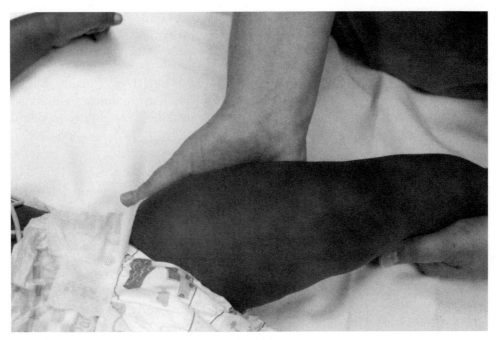

Looped patterned injury to the anterior left thigh

DEATH INVESTIGATIONS

Prior to the role in the investigative phase of any child homicide, there are certain responsibilities of the first responder who is usually the uniformed officer who arrives on the scene on the report of a seriously injured or deceased child.

First Responder

On the assumption that medical personnel are treating an injured child, the responsibility of the first responder should include the following:

1. Secure the crime scene or the location where the child was injured. The crime scene may involve more than one room or involve the outdoors.
2. The officer should assess the situation and request additional support if necessary. Additional support can include crisis counselors, personnel from the coroner's or medical examiner's office, and the notification of investigators who will conduct the investigation.
3. First responders should clear all individuals from the scene and make sure no unauthorized people enter the area so that no evidence is tampered with or removed.
4. First responders should be observant and write down their observations, which can include conversations with the people who are at the scene.
5. It is not the responsibility of the first responder to conduct a thorough investigation, but they should identify who discovered the child and find

out whether anyone attempted first aid or moved or dressed the child. They should also obtain all the names of those present and their relationship to the child. No one should be able to leave the scene until this information is obtained.

6. Once the scene is secure, one officer should be in charge of maintaining a log of all personnel who enter the scene. The first responder should also ensure that nobody disposes of any items until the scene is processed and photographed.[49]

The Investigator

Conducting a homicide investigation can be a daunting task as family members are completely distraught and filled with grief. The investigator should be prepared when asking questions as it can in some cases acquire a volatile response. It is the responsibility of the investigator to be objective, but also compassionate to those who have lost a child. The investigator must understand that the emotions of grief that are displayed can quickly turn to anger if your questions toward the caretakers are presented in a way that casts suspicion on those who are grieving. The explosive response can result from sincere anger that they are under suspicion or a carefully acted display of insincere rage that is used to deceive the investigator. It is important that the investigator gathers sufficient evidence before making accusatory comments to anyone that may be involved.

An investigation of a sudden and unexplained death of a child should be conducted in three phases. The investigation involves processing the scene of the death, an autopsy, and a collateral history from professionals who have had contact with the deceased.[50] The investigator should process the scene as a "crime scene," even if the initial evaluations of the child's death do not appear to be the result of maltreatment. Photograph the scene, and record and seize any physical evidence that might be related to the child's death. For instance, a baby bottle in and of itself should not garner suspicion, but it should be seized as potential evidence, as the contents of the bottle may have caused the child's death. There have been cases of Munchausen by proxy where the caretaker has poisoned their child by adulterating their formula. The investigator should also look for trace evidence. DNA or fingerprint evidence will have limited value because the parents have access to the child; however, trace evidence could become invaluable if it traces back to an individual who should not have been in contact with the child.[51] In some circumstances, there is a delayed death between the time the child sustains a fatal injury and the subsequent death. In these situations, the investigator may be called to the hospital as the result of injuries that led to the child's delayed death, or the parents may have tried to conceal the injury, and the death resulted from the parents failing to seek medical care. One of the most common types of fatal injury maltreatment deaths include brain trauma from shaken baby syndrome. Other example of delayed deaths can occur when a child is scalded from a burn and suffers from an infection or other medical complications arising from these injuries.[52] The autopsy should be done by a pathologist who is familiar with the causes of childhood death. A complete autopsy will include an internal and external examination, a historical examination, a test for toxins, a microbiological test, and metabolic screening for genetic conditions.[53] Additionally, most infant deaths should include a skeletal survey, and those crucial organs such as the brain, eyes, or heart should be sent to pathological specialists for evaluation.[54] Unfortunately, not all states have thorough autopsy practices. A study among states from 2010 to 2012 showed the inconsistency in autopsies in their testing procedures, especially in blood chemistry and genetic testing.[55] Before an investigator concludes their investigation, they should have autopsy results, the examination of any physical evidence, and a complete review of the child's history. The investigator should also have all their interviews complete with any potential witnesses, have their statements recorded, and forward their findings to the prosecutor to see if charges are warranted in the child's death. It should be noted that in most child maltreatment cases there is a lack of witnesses or any direct evidence that links a suspect to a crime. The investigator must rely on circumstantial evidence to show that the death was not accidental and prove that the suspect in their investigation was the only one who could have been responsible for the child's death.[56]

Child Death Review Teams

Child death review teams evolved from the concept that was developed by Dr. Michael Durfree in 1978 as he had made the observation that child maltreatment deaths were being missed because he found that information was not being shared among the various agencies.[57] The child death review team was originally developed to improve identification and prosecution of cases involving fatal abuse or neglect. The National Center for Child Death Review established ten objectives ranging from the investigation of a child's death to its prevention:

1. Ensure the accurate identification and uniform, consistent reporting of the cause and manner of every child death.
2. Improve communication and linkages among local and state agencies and enhance coordination of efforts.
3. Improve agency responses in the investigation of child deaths.
4. Improve agency responses to protect siblings and other children in the homes of deceased children.
5. Improve criminal investigations and the prosecution of child homicides.
6. Improve delivery of services to children, families, providers, and community members.
7. Identify specific barriers and system issues involved in the deaths of children.
8. Identify significant risk factors and trends in child deaths.
9. Identify and advocate for needed changes in legislation, policy, and practices and expanded efforts in child health and safety to prevent child deaths.
10. Increase public awareness and advocacy for the issues that affect the health and safety of children.[58]

Although there is a National Center for Child Death Review and Prevention, there isn't consistency in the use of child death review teams as each state is different in their protocol. Some states review cases as a state review, some states have a county review only, and others have both. A review of a child's death is mandated in thirty-seven states. The funding of these programs also varies between states. The jurisdiction of the review function varies as well but generally there has been a move away from child welfare/justice toward reviews being conducted by public health community. Furthermore, most child death review teams review all deaths up to the age of eighteen.[59] Canada is similar to the United States as each province/territory is different and their reviews are mandated at the provincial level. In contrast, England and Wales have a nationally funded review system.[60] One of the primary goals of any death review team is to determine risk factors for child fatalities so that possible preventative measures can be implemented. Child death review teams are primarily made up of, but not limited to, the following representatives: a pediatrician, medical examiner, prosecuting attorney, social worker, mental health professional, law enforcement, and nurses.[61]

RISK FACTORS FOR CHILD FATALITIES

Mental Illness

There is a significant correlation between mental illness and filicide. In one study of 119 filicide perpetrators, 40 percent had a history of mental illness, which was more common with maternal filicide representing 66 percent of the offenders. Mothers were also more likely to be suffering from mental illness at the time of the offense. Overall, the most common diagnosis was affective disorder.[62] Dr. Phillip J. Resnick, who is recognized as a leading authority in forensic psychology, developed five categories describing the motives of why a parent would kill their child:

1. **Altruistic filicide:** The parent kills their children because they believe that it is in the best interest of the child. For instance, a mother may kill her child so that the child will no longer have to endure physical or sexual abuse, or that a parent may believe that we live in such a cruel and dangerous world that the parent does not want to see their child raised in such an unfavorable environment.
2. **Acutely psychotic filicide:** The parent is experiencing some type of psychosis that placed the child in danger for no apparent motive. The perpetrator could be experiencing hallucinations or hearing voices, thus believing the child is a threat and needs to be killed. Evidence of psychosis can be used to determine whether the parent is legally competent to participate in a criminal proceeding.[63]
3. **Unwanted child filicide:** A parent can become resentful of their own child's existence and kill their own child. A child's birth may have been the result of a rape and the child's existence is a constant reminder of the

assault. Other factors that can contribute to this type of filicide include infidelity. A child born that is the direct result of a marital affair is a constant reminder of your spouse's infidelity. In some circumstances, a parent may kill their own child because of their disability and the work associated with caring for them.

4. **Accidental filicide:** Accidental filicide can be the direct result of physical abuse or neglect where, although the parents did not intend to kill their child, the death was still the result of their actions or neglectful inaction. More filicides occur due to fatal maltreatment than because of maternal psychiatric illness. Many cases of fatal maltreatment filicide never come to psychiatric attention

5. **Spouse revenge filicide:** This type of filicide can be the direct result of a parent's anger over a separation or a child custody dispute. The purpose of this type of homicide is to make the other parent suffer.[64]

Other Factors for Child Fatalities

The most common reason given by parents and caretakers who fatally injure their child was that they lost patience when the child would not stop crying. Furthermore, it was common for abusers to kill their children for bedwetting, fussy eating, and disobedient behavior.[65] Other factors include:

1. Children who have special needs that may increase caregiver burden
2. A parent's young age, low education and income, and single parenting
3. Non-biological caregivers in the home
4. Children with emotional and health problems
5. Intimate partner violence
6. Lack of suitable childcare
7. Substance abuse and/or mental health issues among caregivers
8. Parents and caregivers who do not understand children's needs and development or how to parent
9. Parent history of being a victim of child maltreatment.[66]

PERPETRATORS OF CHILD FATALITIES

Fathers and a mother's boyfriend are most often the perpetrator in abuse that leads to death. Mothers are more often the perpetrator when the fatality is the result of neglect. A total of 79 percent of child fatalities involve parents either acting alone, together, or with other individuals. Non-parent perpetrators are responsible for 16 percent of child fatalities, whereas unknown perpetrators account for 5 percent of child fatalities.[67]

FETICIDE

Feticide is the act that causes the death of a fetus. Thirty-eight states currently recognize the unborn child as a homicide victim. Of the thirty-eight states that recognize fetal homicide, two-thirds of those states apply that principle through-out the period of prenatal development. Feticide laws do not apply to legally induced abortions, although unlawful abortions may be considered feticide.[68] In 2015, Indiana resident Native American Purvi Patel became the first person in the United States to be charged and convicted for the crime of feticide for a self- induced abortion. However, this conviction was overturned in 2016.[69] In addition to individual state laws addressing the rights of the fetus, the federal government through the Unborn Victims of Violence Act of 2004 recognizes an embryo or fetus as a legal victim. This law, also known as Laci and Conner's Law, was introduced in memory of Laci and Conner. Laci Peterson of California, who was pregnant with Conner, was murdered by Laci's husband Scott Peterson, who was convicted of double homicide for the murder of Laci and the fetus Conner. This act specifies that when a criminal attacks a pregnant women and kills her and her unborn child, the offender has claimed two human victims.[70] This legislation was praised by those who supported the life of a fetus, whereas others were concerned that it was taking away some of the reproductive rights of women. The rights of the fetus have also come into question when the fetus is in danger by direct action or inaction of the mother.

FETAL ABUSE

A fetus is considered an offspring of a mammal that takes on the form of that mammal (e.g., human being). An embryo develops into a fetus at some point between six to nine weeks of gestation. Fetal abuse is an umbrella term that describes any behavior that would put that fetus at risk of harm. Behaviors can range from malnutrition, ingestion of chemicals or alcohol, to physical abuse.

There has been a great amount of discussion of women's rights versus fetus rights. States across the United States are disagreeing. Some states, like New York, have legalized late-term abortion. Virginia Governor Northam has been quoted recently on the news that he supported delivering the baby and then asking the mother if she wants resuscitation to be given to the baby. The state of Georgia just ruled that abortions will not be legal after a heartbeat can be heard at six weeks of the pregnancy. Without states having a consensus on when a fetus is considered a living being, it is difficult to determine what is considered fetus abuse, who can abuse the fetus, and how far along is the fetus before abuse can be decided. Since *Roe v. Wade (*419 U.S. 113, 1973) the woman's liberty of personal privacy takes priority over the viability of the fetus and the state is not allowed to interfere.[71]

Substance Use as a Form of Fetal Abuse

Drug use is on the rise across the nation; unfortunately, pregnant women are included in this trend. Evaluating Medicaid data in 2012, 1.1 million completed births occurred in the United States. Of those births, 21.6 percent of mothers had filled an opioid prescription during their pregnancy.[72] This is what we know about legally filled prescriptions: it is hard to say how many women have illegally used opioids at some point during or throughout the pregnancy. The increased usage of opioids has also caused a notable increase in infants born with neonatal abstinence syndrome. While there are debates on the different effects of various drugs on the fetus, what we know for sure is the drugs are passed on to the fetus. Substances will remain active longer in the fetus than in the maternal system. The mother that is on drugs is more likely to be malnourished because the focus is on the drugs and not adequate nutrition for the pregnancy, which in turn leads to babies born with a low birth weight.

Cigarettes have been associated with poor pregnancy outcomes. Women that smoke during pregnancy are at risk of poor fetal growth, increased placenta abruption, and later intrauterine death.

Common adverse effects of drugs and cigarettes on a fetus are:

1. Intrauterine growth restriction
2. Antepartum hemorrhage
3. Preterm labor
4. Neonatal abstinence syndrome.

Alcohol as a Form of Fetal Abuse

Drinking during pregnancy is the leading cause of preventable fetal deaths, malformations, and neurodevelopmental problems. Women that drink alcohol during pregnancy are at a 33 percent greater risk of developing placental abruption.[73]

It is estimated that 0.2 to 1.5 per one thousand live births are associated with fetal alcohol syndrome. While not every woman that drinks has a child with fetal alcohol syndrome, many children are affected when mothers drink alcohol. Research has not been able to correlate why some children are born symptomatic and others are not.

Signs of fetal alcohol syndrome are:

- Mental retardation (alcohol is the third-leading cause of mental retardation in children)
- Low birth weights
- Head and face abnormalities; characteristic flat nasal bridge
- Growth deficiency
- Withdrawal at birth.

Domestic Violence as a Form of Fetal Abuse

Domestic violence is known to either begin or become worse when a woman becomes pregnant. Domestic violence is a significant contributor to perinatal and maternal morbidity and mortality.[74] Domestic violence can cause fetal distress and fetal demise, especially when abdominal blows occur during the third trimester. Domestic violence can be direct to the woman or can have an indirect impact.

Some indirect impacts of domestic violence can affect the way in which pregnancy care is obtained. When domestic violence is in the home, the woman is more likely to have delayed presentation in receiving prenatal care. The woman is also more likely to abuse drugs and alcohol during the pregnancy.

There are four themes that have been identified as possible reasons of violence during the pregnancy:

1. The domestic partner is jealous of the future child.
2. Pregnancy-specific violence occurs but it is not directed toward the fetus.
3. The domestic partner has anger to the fetus.
4. It is just normal violence within the relationship.[75]

Fetal abuse can occur directly by the mother or indirectly by the mother. Fetal abuse can occur from the father or significant other in the life of the mother. There are a variety of methods of fetal abuse as well as a variety of versions of how laws interpret the abuse. It continues to be a challenge from state to state on what is considered fetal abuse, what will be prosecuted, and if any prosecution will occur at all.

CHILD ABDUCTIONS

There have been several high-profile child abductions that have garnered significant media attention. For example, the case of Charles Lindbergh, who in 1932 had his baby kidnapped from their mansion in Hopewell, New Jersey, or the case of Polly Klaas, who in 1993 was kidnapped at knife point while attending a slumber party in her mother's home in Petaluma, California. Although these cases received noteworthy attention, they do not depict an accurate account of child abductions. In both these cases, the child was abducted by strangers; in reality, stranger abductions, although extremely dangerous, are still considered rare. Although this type of abduction is infrequent, some refer to this as a parent's worst nightmare. In response to the Polly Klaas abduction and murder and the abductions of children throughout the country, the Polly Klaas Foundation was formed as a non-profit agency. The Polly Klaas Foundation is dedicated to the safety of children, the recovery of missing children, and the support of public policies to keep children safe within their communities.[76] Other high-profile child abductions include the abduction and murder of Adam Walsh, who in 1981 was kidnapped while in a Sears department store in Hollywood, Florida. This case also garnered significant media attention and to this day, department stores throughout the country have a protocol response referred to as "Code Adam" whenever a child is missing within a store. In 1984, John Walsh and Reve Walsh, the parents of Adam Walsh, and other child advocates founded the National Center for Missing and Exploited Children (NCMEC), which is a private non-profit organization that serves as a national clearinghouse and resource center for information on missing and exploited children. In 2017, the Federal Bureau of Investigation reported that there were 464,324 children reported missing that year and that NCMEC assisted law enforcement in over twenty-seven thousand cases. The types of cases comprise:

1. 91 percent endangered runaways
2. 5 percent family abductions
3. 3 percent critically missing young adults ages eighteen to twenty
4. 1 percent by non-family abductions.[77]

RUNAWAY/THROWAWAY CHILDREN

There are also a significant number of children who are missing with no record that they are gone. An inattentive parent may be unaware that they are missing or the parent deliberately neglects to notify authorities of their absence. When a child is reported missing, law enforcement is required to take a report and enter the child's information into the National Crime Information Center (NCIC). The information about the missing child will include the physical characteristics of the child, what they were wearing, and any other distinguishing characteristics that can help in identifying a child that is unaccounted for. Parents' decision to report a missing child varies considerably especially with a child's age. A young child would more likely be reported immediately compared to an older child. With an older child who is unaccounted for, the parent may check with their child's friends before calling law enforcement as some children may have just neglected to inform their parents of their current whereabouts. However, parents who may not want to come across as alarmists may unwittingly place their child in danger as the potential for harm increases with every moment of unaccountability. Although law enforcement clearly recognizes the potential harm of a missing child, it is not uncommon for some law enforcement officers to become annoyed with missing child complaints that involve adolescents. In many occasions where the child has in their parent's eyes "disappeared," the child returns home before the officer has even had the opportunity to finish their report and enter the child in NCIC as missing. This scenario clearly has an adverse effect on collecting accurate data on missing children. Other factors that can skew the actual number of missing children are "throwaway" children. Children who are considered throwaways are at a higher risk of danger as, unlike runaways or missing children, no one is looking for them. Throwaway children can be classified as children who have been abandoned or are "kicked out" of their own house because of their behavior or other factors. The parents will not report this as the parent is responsible for their child up to the age of eighteen and therefore could be charged with neglect if law enforcement becomes aware of their actions.

Both runaway and throwaway children are vulnerable to abduction and in some cases become victims in sex trafficking. It is estimated that one in seven runaways become victims of sex trafficking.[78]

FAMILY ABDUCTIONS

The National Incidence Studies of Missing, Abducted, Runaway, and Throwaway Children defines family abduction "as the taking or keeping of a child by a family member in violation of a custody order, a decree, or other legitimate custodial rights, where taking or keeping involved some element of conceal-ment, flight, or intent to deprive a lawful custodian indefinitely of custodial priv-ileges."[79] In 1968, the Uniform Commissioners promulgated the Uniform Child Jurisdiction Act. The law was designed to discourage interstate kidnapping of children by non-custodial parents. Prior to the implementation of this act, it was common for non-custodial parents to take their children across state lines to find a sympathetic court to reverse an unfavorable custodial order.[80]

Perpetrator

In one study of 13,052 children who were victims of a family abduction, the per-petrator was the parent in 90 percent of the cases, and the family had a history of violence or other family dysfunction.[81]

Motives

The perpetrator may abduct the child from the other parent as they feel they are doing it for the child's safety, as the spouse may be a victim of physical abuse or witness their own child being a victim of physical or sexual abuse. In other cases, a parent may abduct the child after losing a custody battle or flee with the child in the belief that they will lose a custody battle. In some cases where the child has dual citizenship, a parent can take that child out of the United States, and the child's return is not always guaranteed even if the child has been located. The International Kidnapping Crime Act of 1995 states that it is a federal offense if a parent abducts a child from the United States and takes them to another country. Research has indicated that the vast majority of these child kidnapping cases occur within the context of divorce.[82] However, this law has little significance if the parents flee to a country that will not extradite to the United States.

Although abductions by family members are defined by statute as a crime, the perception of these crimes is not taken as seriously as that of non-stranger abduction as there is a belief among some of the public and law enforcement that the children are not endangered when they are with a family member.

NON-FAMILY ABDUCTIONS

A non-family abduction can be defined as an episode in which a non-family per-petrator takes a child by the use of force or threat of bodily harm or detains the child for a substantial period of time in an isolated place by the use of physical force or threat of bodily harm without lawful authority or parental permission.[83] Although the act of non-family abductions is rare, they generate a substantial amount of warranted fear as the consequences of being abducted by a non-fam-ily member are severe. In one study of stereotypical kidnappings by strangers or a slight acquaintance, 40 percent of the children were killed and another 4 percent were never recovered. Teenagers were the most likely victims, and nearly half of the children abducted were sexually assaulted.[84] In another study of 105 children in 2011, the most common ages of victims were between twelve and sev-enteen, were girls, and were white. Half of the stereotypical kidnapping victims were sexually assaulted. The perpetrators were mostly males between the ages of eighteen and thirty-five, and 70 percent of them were unemployed.[85] The danger associated with non-family abductions creates justifiable fear for any parent, and these fears are only heightened through media to sensationalize crime. There is also evidence that there is a significant difference in the amount of media coverage depending on the abductee's race. The media routinely ignore the problem of missing minority children, especially if the child was from a lower-income urban neighborhood.[86] In contrast, not only does stranger abduction of white girls garner significantly more media attention, these non-family abductions of white girls have also led to policy and legislative reform. The witnessed abduction of nine-year-old Amber Hagerman occurred 1996 while she was riding her bicycle in Arlington, Texas. Although authorities conducted a search of the area, her body was not discovered until four days later, miles from where she had been reported to have been abducted. She had been sexually assaulted and stabbed to death. People in the area were asking why there wasn't a system where the public could be immediately notified if a child was abducted. In response to community demands, local broadcasters and law enforcement set up a system in Texas that year where the public could be notified if a child was abducted and in danger. This is the case that initiated what is commonly referred to as the Amber Alert system. However, it was the abduction of Elizabeth Smart that gained national attention and the need to expand the Amber Alert system. Elizabeth Smart, at age fourteen, was kidnapped right from her bedroom in Salt Lake City, Utah, and was held by her captives for nine months. Elizabeth stated during this horrible ordeal that over that period of nine months, her abductor "Brian Mitchell would rape me every day, sometimes multiple times a day. He would torture me in ways that are impossible to describe, would starve and manipulate me like I was an animal."[87] In response to this high-profile abduction, the Protect Act, signed into law in 2003 by President George W. Bush, established the National Amber Alert coordinating system that encourages all states to participate. Prior to 2002, only four states had a statewide Amber Alert plan.[88] This notification system eventually went nationwide and is known as an Amber Alert in honor of Amber Hagerman. Today, the Amber Alert system is being used in all fifty states, the District of Columbia, and the U.S. Virgin Islands.[89] The current system uses electronic highway signs and radio and television broadcasts. The Amber Alert system continues to expand as social networks such as Facebook in partnership with the NCMEC will alert Facebook users through news feeds and notifications are pushed to cellphones.[90]

The Department of Justice recommended criteria for initiating an Amber Alert:

- There is reasonable belief by law enforcement that abduction has occurred.
- The law enforcement agency believes that the child is in imminent danger of serious bodily injury or death.
- There is enough descriptive information about the victim and the abduction for law enforcement to issue an Amber Alert to assist in the recovery of the child.

- The abduction is of a child aged seventeen years or younger.
- The child's name and other critical data elements, including the Child's Abduction Flag have been entered into the (NCIC).
- The child's abduction is flagged as it entered into the NCIC system.[91]

JENNIFER'S LAW ACT OF 1997

This act amends the Omnibus Crime Control and Safe Streets Act of 1968. Under this amended legislation, the Federal Bureau of Investigation is granted easier access to cross-reference indexes of missing persons of those of unidentified persons and requiring:

> immediate reporting by a State's authorities of every unidentified person found in that State's jurisdiction, to the National Crime Information Center (NCIC) and to the State's law enforcement authorities; the subsequent entry of a complete profile of the unidentified person; the entry of an NCIC or other appropriate number on all unidentified persons' death certificates; and (4) the retention of all such records pertaining to unidentified persons in the NCIC and with appropriate State agencies until the person is identified.[92]

HOSPITAL ABDUCTIONS

The NCMEC reported that from 1965 to December 2018, 140 children were abducted from health care facilities.[93] Ensuring the safety of every infant that is born should be every hospital's top priority. One of the most important measures that can be taken in preventing infant abduction is parent education. Medical staff should instruct parents about visitation guidelines, the safety procedures that are in place, and how to properly identify hospital staff. Additionally, it is important for medical staff to introduce the replacing staff at the end of every shift. Security systems should also be installed where an alarm is triggered should the baby be removed from a secured area. An emergency plan should also be in place if and when an infant is ever abducted. Some health care facilities implement protocols such as a "code purple," which creates a coordinated response from hospital staff who are instructed to monitor all exits according to their specific policy and procedures. Hospitals should have periodic drills to ensure an efficient response.[94]

FETAL ABDUCTIONS

Fetal abductions involve forcefully removing a fetus from the mother's womb. Although extremely rare, this is a horrific crime that generates significant public concern. Of the eighteen U.S. fetal abductions that were documented by the NCMEC, four of the crimes occurred between 1983 and 2003, but there has been a dramatic increase in the rate for fetal abductions since that date where the last fourteen abductions occurred after 2003. It has been suggested that the rise in fetal abductions is due to the accessible information on how to perform a caesarean procedure.[95]

Most information relating to fetal abductions comes from journalists working for newspapers, television, radio stations, or magazines.[96] For example, the *New York Post* reported on November 20, 2015, that Ashleigh Wade of New York sliced the throat of her long-term friend Angelikque Sutton who was nine months pregnant, killing the mother and forcefully removing the fetus from her womb. Wade was charged with murder; it had been reported, prior to the abduction, that she previously had told neighbors that she was due to give birth next week.[97] There are several reported news stories of fetus abductions, but very little research. However, in a study of nine fetal abductions or attempted fetal abductions, an abductor profile and motives were assessed.

Abductor Profile

The primary offender was female and between the ages of nineteen and forty. All the females faked their pregnancy as they put on weight and dressed in maternity clothing. The offenders had preselected and stalked their victims. In some of the cases, the perpetrator would attempt to befriend them before the abduction.

Motives

The primary motivation was to sustain a relationship with a male partner by providing them with a child; the majority of them convinced the partner that they were pregnant.[98]

The offender can be charged with both murder/feticide or kidnapping, depending whether the pregnant mother and/or the fetus survives the abduction. When an offender commits such a heinous criminal act, no matter how disturbing the act is, the insanity defense is rarely successful, which suggests that most perpetrators of fetal abduction are ruled sane and ultimately face criminal sanctions. Although some may be later diagnosed with multiple personality disorders, they were still able to plan out their abductions, making them culpable for their actions. Other types of mental illness, such as psychosis, may have been present in which there may be a delusional belief that one is pregnant; however, the majority of perpetrators made attempts to feign pregnancy, indicating that they were of sound mind when they committed their offense.[99] It is important to reemphasize that, as horrendous as these crimes are, they are still considered extremely rare.

CONCLUSION

The ultimate form of child maltreatment is the abuse that leads to the death of a child. Statistics on child fatalities clearly indicate that most child fatalities occur in the child's first year of life. To address the magnitude of child fatalities, child death review teams have been formed not only to determine the causation of a child's death but to seek preventive measures with child fatalities. One of the

188 ◆ Chapter 6: Child Fatalities, Fetal Abuse, and Missing Children

reasons/diagnosis for so many child fatalities is SIDS, which happens to apparently healthy children who have died without any explanation. However, some children who have died under the diagnosis of SIDS may have actually died as a result of their caretaker's neglect or abuse. Other forms of child fatalities may be the direct result of mental illness of the caretaker, whereas other children may be killed through cultural expectations such as honor killings. This chapter also discussed how child fatalities can occur through fetal abuse where the mother fails to properly care for her fetus during pregnancy. One of the more commonly recognized repercussions of fetal abuse is fetal alcohol syndrome where the child is born with abnormalities associated with too much alcohol consumption during pregnancy. In addition to child fatalities and fetal abuse, this chapter covered the varying categories relating to missing children, including child abductions. Family abductions are more common than that of stranger abductions, and although stranger abductions are considered relatively rare, they generate a significant amount of fear which in turn has prompted government officials to initiate an Amber Alert system to help locate children who have been abducted. Finally, although extremely rare, some individuals will attempt to steal the fetus from the mother, which in many cases leads to the mother's death.

REVIEW QUESTIONS

1. How did the Amber Alert system originate?

2. Why are statistics on throwaway children difficult to measure?

3. Why are child fatalities from external factors considered the most preventable?

4. What is the role of a child death review team?

5. Why would an honor killing be difficult to identify?

KEYWORDS

Sudden infant death syndrome (SIDS): The unexplained sudden death of an infant under one year of age.

Filicide: The killing of a child by their parent or caretaker.

Neonaticide: The act of killing a child within twenty-four hours of birth.

Infanticide: The act of killing of a child under one year of age.

Familicide: The murder of an entire family.

Feticide: An act that causes the death of a fetus.

Honor killings: The practice by some countries of killing a family member who has brought shame to the family.

Child death review teams: Team of individuals who review the causes of child fatalities in order to prevent harm to other children.

Fetal abduction: The taking of the fetus from a human's womb without her consent.

Suicide: The act of deliberately taking one's own life.

Suicidal ideation: The thought of committing suicide.

Family abduction: The taking or keeping of a child by a family member in violation of a custody order, a decree, or other legitimate custodial rights, where taking or keeping involved some element of concealment, flight, or intent to deprive a lawful custodian indefinitely of custodial privileges.

Non-family abduction: An episode in which a non-family perpetrator takes a child by the use of force or threat of bodily harm or detains the child for a substantial period of time in an isolated place by the use of physical force or threat of bodily harm without lawful authority or parental permission.

Neonatal abstinence syndrome: The sudden discontinuance of fetal exposure to substances used by the mother during the pregnancy that results in withdrawal syndrome in the newborn.

Diffuse axonal injury: Shearing injury to the axons within the brain that occurs from shifting and rotating within the skull. Diffuse axonal injury causes injury to multiple areas of the brain resulting in an unresponsive state.

Hypernatremia: Electrolyte imbalance resulting in an elevated serum concentration.

NOTES

1. Amy Harfeld, Christina Riehl, and Elisa Weichel. Steps Forward: First Progress Report Within Our Reach, A National Strategy To Eliminate Child Abuse And Neglect Fatalities, The Final Report Of The Federal Commission To Eliminate Child Abuse And Neglect Fatalities. (2018), 5–10. Available from http://www.alliance1.org/web/resources/pubs/steps-forward-progress-report-national-strategy-eliminate-child-abuse-neglect-fatalities.aspx.

2. Bill Walsh, *Investigating Child Fatalities: Portable Guides to Investigating Child Abuse* (Middletown, DE: Office for Justice Programs, 2005), 2.

3. Commission to Eliminate Child Abuse and Neglect Fatalities. *Within Our Reach: A National Strategy to Eliminate Child Abuse and Neglect Fatalities.* (2016), 25. Available from https://www.acf.hhs.gov/sites/default/files/cb/cecanf_final_report.pdf.

4. Tricia D. Gardner, Betty Wade Coyle, and Theresa Covington, "Child Death Review in the United States: A Multidisciplinary Process to Better Count, Understand, Respond to, and Prevent Child Abuse and Neglect Fatalities," in J. Bart Klika and Jon R. Conte (eds.), *The APSAC Handbook on Child Maltreatment*, fourth edition (Thousand Oaks, CA: Sage, 2018), 407–08; Peter Jaffe, Jordan Fairbairn, and Katherine Reif, "Children at Risk of Homicide in the Context of Intimate Partner Violence," in Jacquelyn C. Campbell and Jill Theresa Messing (eds.), *Assessing Dangerousness: Domestic Violence Offenders and Child Abusers*, third edition (New York, NY: Springer Publishing, 2017), 181.

5. H.F. Krous, J.B. Beckwith, R.W. Byard, T.O. Rognum, T. Bajanowski, T. Corey, and E.A. Mitchell, "Sudden Infant Death Syndrome and Unclassified Sudden Infant Deaths: A Definitional and Diagnostic Approach," *Pediatrics* 114, no. 1 (2004): 234.

6. Lisbeth Lund Jensen, Marianne Cathrine Rohde, Jytte Banner, and Roger William Byard, "Reclassification of SIDS Cases—A Need for Adjustment of the San Diego Classification?" *International Journal of Legal Medicine* 126, no. 2 (2012): 271.

7. Cindy L. Miller-Perrin and Robin D. Perrin, *Child Maltreatment: An Introduction*, third edition (Thousand Oaks, CA: Sage, 2013), 312.

8. Michael D. Lyman, *Criminal Investigation*, third edition (New York, NY: Pearson, 2018), 238.

9. Henry F. Krous and Roger Byard, "Sudden Infant Death Syndrome or Asphyxia," in Carole Jenny (ed.), *Child Abuse and Neglect: Diagnosis, Treatment and Evidence* (St. Louis, MO: Elsevier Saunders, 2011), 337–45.

10. Jade Spinelli, Lyndsey Collins-Praino, Corinna Van Den Heuvel, and Roger Byard, "Evolution and Significance of the Triple Risk Model in Sudden Infant Death Syndrome," *Journal of Pediatrics and Child Health* 53, no. 2 (2017): 112–15.

11. Centers for Disease Control and Prevention. Accessed on 03-09-2019. Available from https://www.cdc.gov/sids/data.htm.

12. Scott D. Klugman and Francie J. Julien-Chinn, "Evaluating Risk Factors for Fatal Child Abuse," in Jacquelyn C. Campbell and Jill Theresa Messing (eds.), *Assessing Dangerousness: Domestic Violence Offenders and Child Abusers*, third edition (New York, NY: Springer Publishing, 2017), 93.

13. Miller-Perrin and Perrin, *Child Maltreatment: An Introduction*, 314.

14. M.M.T. Vennemann, C. Rentsch, and T. Bajanowski, "Are Autopsies of Help to Parents of SIDS Victims," *International Journal of Legal Medicine* 120, no. 6 (2006): 352.

15. Mazal Maged and Denise Rizzolo, "Preventing Sudden Infant Death Syndrome and Other Sleep Related Infant Deaths," *Journal of the American Academy of Physician Assistants* 31, no. 11 (2018): 27–28.

16. Evin M. Daly, *Child Abuse: What You Need to Know*, second edition (Miami, FL: Parker Publishing, 2017), 245.

17. Kieran O'Hagan, *Filicide-Suicide: The Killing of Children in the Context of Separation, Divorce and Custody Disputes* (New York, NY: Palgrave, 2014), 34.

18. Susan Hatters Friedman and Phillip J. Resnick, "Child Murder by Mothers: Patterns and Prevention," *World Psychiatry* 6, no. 3 (2007): 139.

19. Suzzanne Levelle, Jacques D. Marleau, and Myriam Dube, "Filicide: A Comparison by Sex and Presence or Absence of Self-destructive Behavior," *Journal of Family Violence* 22, no. 5 (2007): 293.

20. O'Hagan, *Filicide-Suicide*, 100.

21. O'Hagan, *Filicide-Suicide*, 101.

22. Pamela Kulbarsh, "Filicide: The Unfathomable Crime," 2015. *Officer.com*. Available from https://www.officer.com/investigations/article/12052216/filicide-the-unfathomable-crime.

23. Stacy L. Mallicoat, *Women and Crime: Core Concepts* (Thousand Oaks, CA: Sage, 2018), 148; Christine Alder and Ken Polk, *Child Victims of Homicide* (New York, NY: Cambridge University Press, 2001), 3–4.

24. Kulbarsh, "Filicide: The Unfathomable Crime."

25. Alder and Polk, *Child Victims of Homicide*, 68.

26. Viviana A. Week-Shackelford and Todd K. Shackelford, "Methods of Filicide: Stepparents and Genetic Parents Kill Differently," *Violence and Victims* 19, no. 1 (2004): 76.

27. Denise Kindschi Gosselin, *Heavy Hands: An Introduction to the Crimes of Family Violence*, fourth edition (Upper Saddle River, NJ: Pearson, 2010), 127.

28. Jaffe, Fairbairn, and Reif, "Children at Risk of Homicide in the Context of Intimate Partner Violence," 189.

29. Levelle, Marleau, and Dube, "Filicide: A Comparison by Sex and Presence or Absence of Self-destructive Behavior," 293.

30. Alder and Polk, *Child Victims of Homicide*, 46–49.

31. Adam B. Miller, Christiane Esposito-Smythers, Julie T. Weismoore, and Keith D. Renshaw, "The Relation Between Child Maltreatment and Adolescent Suicidal Behavior: A Systematic Review and Critical Examination of the Literature," *Clinical Child and Family Psychology* Review 16, no. 2 (2013): 147.

32. Miller, Esposito-Smythers, Weismoore, and Renshaw, "The Relation Between Child Maltreatment and Adolescent Suicidal Behavior," 12–13.

33. Daly, *Child Abuse: What You Need to Know*, 223–24.

34. Heidi Stocki, Bianca Dekel, Alison Morris-Gehring, Charlotte Watts, and Naeemah Abrahams, "Child Homicide Perpetrators Worldwide: A Systematic Review," *BMJ Pediatrics Open* 1, no. 1 (2017): 4.

35. Ann Wolbert Burgess, *Victimology: Theories and Applications* (Burlington, MA: Jones & Bartlett, 2019), 343.

36. Recep Dugan, "The Dynamics of Honor Killing and the Perpetrator Experiences," *Sage Journals* 20, no. 1 (2016): 60.

37. Jaffe, Fairbairn, and Reif, "Children at Risk of Homicide in the Context of Intimate Partner Violence," 186; Murray A. Straus, Richard J. Gelles, and Suzanne K. Steinmetz, *Behind Closed Doors: Violence in the American Family* (New Brunswick, NJ: Anchor Press, 2006), 78.

38. Gosselin, *Heavy Hands*, 7.

39. Lindsey N. Devers and Sarah Bacon, "Interpreting Honor Crimes: The Institutional Disregard Towards Female Victims of Family Violence in the Middle East," *International Journal of Criminology and Sociological Theory* 3, no. 1 (2010): 360–61.

40. Mallicoat, *Women and Crime*, 176–77.

41. Leah E. Daigle and Lisa R. Muftic, *Victimology* (Thousand Oaks, CA: Sage, 2016), 123; Anthony Walsh and Cody Jorgensen, *Criminology: The Essentials*, third edition (Thousand Oaks, CA: Sage, 2018), 4.

42. Daly, *Child Abuse: What You Need to Know*, 219.

43. Debbie Scott, "Reporting Fatal Neglect in Child Death Review," *Trauma, Violence and Abuse* (2018): 8.

44. Eliott C. McLaughlin and Dana Ford, "Police: Father was Sexting as Son was Dying in Hot Car," *CNN*, January 6, 2015. Available from https://www.cnn.com/2014/07/03/justice/georgia-hot-car-toddler-death/index.html.

45. A.J. Willington, "More than 36 Kids Die in Hot Cars Every Year and July is Usually the Deadliest Month," *CNN*, July 3, 2018. Available from https://www.cnn.com/2018/07/03/health/hot-car-deaths-child-charts-graphs-trnd/index.html.

46. Scott, "Reporting Fatal Neglect in Child Death Review," 8.

47. Daly, *Child Abuse: What You Need to Know*, 220.

48. Centers for Disease Control and Prevention, "CDC Releases 2017 Youth Risk Behavior Survey (YRBS) Results." Accessed on January 27, 2019. Available from https://www.cdc.gov/nchhstp/dear_colleague/2018/dcl-061418-YRBS.html.

49. Walsh, *Investigating Child Fatalities*, 11.

50. Scott D. Krugman and Francie J. Julien Chinn, "Evaluating Risk Factors for Fatal Child Abuse," in Jacquelyn C. Campbell and Jill Threresa Messing (eds.), *Assessing Dangerousness: Domestic Violence Offenders and Child Abusers*, third edition (New York, NY: Springer Publishing, 2017), 92.

51. Walsh, *Investigating Child Fatalities*, 5; Krugman and Chinn, "Evaluating Risk Factors for Fatal Child Abuse," 92.

52. Walsh, *Investigating Child Fatalities*,. p.4

53. Krugman and Chinn, "Evaluating Risk Factors for Fatal Child Abuse," 92.

54. Krugman and Chinn, "Evaluating Risk Factors for Fatal Child Abuse," 92.

55. Alexa B. Erck Lambert, Sharyn E. Parks, Lena Camperlengo, Carri Cottengim, Rebecca L. Anderson, Theresa M. Covington, and Carrie K. Shapiro-Mendoza, "Death Scene Investigation Autopsy Practices In Sudden Unexpected Infant Deaths," *The Journal of Pediatrics* 174 (2016): 88.

56. Walsh, *Investigating Child Fatalities*, p.6

57. Gardner, Coyle, and Covington, "Child Death Review in the United States," 405; Lyman, *Criminal Investigation*, 233.

58. National Center for Child Death Review, *A Program Manual for Child Death Review*, 5. Accessed March 23, 2019. Available from https://www.ncfrp.org>NCRPCD-Docs.

59. Sharon Vincent, "Child Death Review Processes: A Six Country Comparison," *Child Abuse Review* 23 (2014): 119.

60. Sharon Vincent, "Child Death Review Processes," 119.

61. Kindschi, *Heavy Hands*, 128.

62. Sandra M. Flynn, Jenny J. Shaw, and Kathryn Abel, "Filicide: Mental Illness in Those Who Kill Their Children," *PLoS One* 8, no. 4 (2013): e58981.

62

63. Mallicoat, *Women and Crime*, 299.

64. Friedman and Resnick, "Child Murder by Mothers: Patterns and Prevention," 139; O'Hagan, *Filicide-Suicide*, 63.

65. Daly, *Child Abuse: What You Need to Know*, 222.

66. The National Center for Fatality Review and Prevention. Available from www.ncfrp. org.

67. Daly, *Child Abuse: What You Need to Know*, 221.

68. C.L. Evans, *Fetal Abductions: An Insight into the Abduction of an Unborn Child* (Morrisville, NC: Lulu Press, 2017).

69. Robert Franklin, "Indiana Court Tosses Purvi Patel's 2015 Feticide Conviction," *Associated Press*, July 22, 2016.

70. National Right To Life, "Key Facts on the Unborn Victims of Violence Act," April 1, 2004.

71. Monica L. McCoy and Stefanie M. Keen, *Fetal Abuse in Child Abuse and Neglect* (New York, NY: Psychology Press, 2014), 189–209; M.H. Aliyu, O. Lyncy, P.N. Nana, A.P. Wilson, P.J. Marty, and H.M. Salihu, "Alcohol Consumption during Pregnancy and Risk of Placental Abruption and Placenta Previa," *Maternal Child Health Journal* 15 (2011): 670–76.

72. Verena E. Metz, Q. Brown, S. Martins, and J. Palamar, "Characteristics of Drug Use Among Pregnant Women in United States: Opioid and Non-Opioid Illegal Drug Use," *Drug and Alcohol Dependence* 183 (2018): 261–66.

73. McCoy and Keen, *Fetal Abuse in Child Abuse and Neglect*; Aliyu, Lyncy, Nana, Wilson, Marty, and Salihu, "Alcohol Consumption during Pregnancy and Risk of Placental Abruption and Placenta Previa."

74. Nicola Graham-Kevan and John Archer, "Violence During Pregnancy: Investigating Infanticide Motives," *Journal of Family Violence* 26 (2011): 453–58.

75. Graham-Kevan and Archer, "Violence During Pregnancy: Investigating Infanticide Motives."

76. Polly Klaas Foundation. Accessed July 17, 2018. Available from http://www.pollyklaas. org/about/pollys-story.html.

77. National Center for Missing and Exploited Children, "Key Facts." Available from http://www.missingkids.com/keyfacts.

78. National Center for Missing and Exploited Children, "Key Facts."

79. Heather Hammer, David Finkelhor, and Andrea J. Sedlak, "Children Abducted by Family Members: National Estimates and Characteristics," U.S. Department of Justice, October 2002, 2.

80. Uniform Law Commission, "Child Custody Jurisdiction and Enforcement Act Summary." Available from www.uniformlaws.org; Patricia M. Hoff, "The Uniform Child-Custody Jurisdiction and Enforcement Act," U.S. Department of Justice.

81. David Finkelhor, Megan Henly, Heather Turner, and Sherry Hamby, "Family in a National Sample of US Children," *Child Abuse and Neglect* 67 (2017): 403–07.

82. Kindschi, *Heavy Hands*, 125.

83. David Finkelhor, Heather Hammer, and Andrea J. Sedlak, "Nonfamily Abducted Children: National Estimates and Characteristics," U.S. Department of Justice, October 2002.

84. Finkelhor, Hammer, and Sedlak, "Nonfamily Abducted Children: National Estimates and Characteristics," 2.

85. Janis Wolak, David Finkelhor, and Andrea J. Sedlak, "Child Victims of Stereotypical Kidnappings Known to Law Enforcement in 2011," U.S. Department of Justice, June 2016.

86. Leigh Moscowitz and Spring-Serenity Duvall, "Every Parent's Worst Nightmare: Myths of Abductions in US News," *Journal of Children and Media* 5, no. 2 (2011): 147–63.

87. Chris Stewart, *My Story: Elizabeth Smart* (New York, NY: St Martin's Press, 2013), 46.

88. U.S. Department of Justice, "Department of Justice Announces Amber Alert Awareness Campaign Commemorating Amber Hagermann and the Success of the Amber Alert System." Available from https://www.amberalert.gov/newsroom/pressreleases/ojp_05_0113.htm.

89. U.S. Department of Justice: Office of Justice Programs, "Amber Alert: 21 Years of Progress in Recovering Abducted Children." Available from www.amberalert.gov.

90. Donna Leinwand Leger, "Facebook to Post Amber Alerts for Missing Children," *USA Today*, January 13, 2015.

91. Department of Justice: Office of Justice Programs, "Amber Alert: Americas Missing Broadcast Emergency Response." Available from www.amberalert.gov.

92. Congress.gov, "Jennifer's Law Act of 1997." Accessed March 5, 2019. Available from https://www.congress.gov/bill/105th-congress/house-bill/2850.

93. National Center for Missing and Exploited Children, "Infant Abductions." Accessed February 24, 2019. Available from http://www.missingkids.com/theissues/infantabductions.

94. Jacqueline Hiner, Jeannine Pyka, Colleen Burks, Lily Pisegna, and Rachel Ann Gador, "Preventing Infant Abductions: An Infant Security Program Transitioned Into an Interdisciplinary Model," *The Journal of Perinatal & Neonatal Nursing* 26, no. 1 (2012): 48–49.

95. Evans, *Fetal Abductions*.

96. Kerry Arquette, "Fetal Attraction: A Descriptive Study of Patterns in Fetal Abductions" (Thesis, Regis University, 2012).

97. Kevin Fasick and Jennifer Bain, "It's My Baby! Woman Rips Infant from Mom's Womb, Parades as Her Own," *New York Post*, November 20, 2015.

98. Vernon J. Geberth, "Homicides Involving the Theft of a Fetus from a Pregnant Victim," *Law and Order* 54, no. 3 (2006).

99. Evans, *Fetal Abductions*.

7

Investigating Child Abuse

◆ ◆ ◆

BEFORE AN ALLEGATION OF ABUSE IS REVEALED, whether through suspicion of responsible adults or from the child themselves, the U.S. Department of Justice recommends that law enforcement agencies have protocols and procedures in place in order to have an effective response. Failure to investigate a disclosure properly can result in a victim's complaints being dismissed in court as the direct result of an ineffective investigation, or in some cases, an innocent person being falsely accused with the potential of an unjust conviction. Investigators should be trained and experienced in objectivity when investigating allegations of child abuse including how to properly interview a child who is a possible victim and/or a suspected offender. Moreover, law enforcement agencies must establish policies and procedures on how to properly investigate child maltreatment allegations. Furthermore, agencies should provide protocols, guidelines, and training to assist in the decision-making process, but officers must still be aware that they may face unique situations where the officer's own judgment may be the only guide as to what action is needed.[1] This chapter will explore some of the aspects of investigating child abuse, which begins on the day of disclosure.

THE DISCLOSURE

An investigation cannot begin until the child makes a declaration of abuse or there is suspicion based on behaviors or medical indicators. Suspicious behavior can include a child displaying sexual behavior inappropriate for their age or a distraught child found alone with an adult without a justifiable reason. Sexually inappropriate behavior certainly warrants suspicion, but investigators should be cautious when evaluating the importance of sexual behavior. Children's easy access to various media outlets provides them with knowledge of sexual acts without actually experiencing any direct victimization. Other forms of suspicion can arise from medical examinations, whether through tearing, bruising, or some other physical indicator consistent with child abuse. It is the investigator's responsibility to determine whether these suspicions are justified. Other forms of disclosure are the direct result of a child reporting that they have been abused. The emotions surrounding a child's disclosure make the investigation more challenging as family members want an immediate resolution to these allegations while demanding justice against the accused. However, there may be individuals who are cynical about the allegation and may become protective of the alleged perpetrator. These emotions play a significant factor when interviewing a child, which will be discussed later on in this chapter.

ADULT DISCLOSURE

The statute of limitations is legislation which allows victims of child abuse to seek justice well after they enter adulthood. Although this is a valuable outlet for victims of abuse to find resolution, there are also some unique challenges in investigating these offenses that may have occurred decades earlier. Acquiring physical evidence is rare in sexual abuse cases and may be non-existent in many of the allegations made by adults. Although research supports how victims can give details of traumatic events of years previous, there remains the possibility that memories of the event may be distorted despite the belief that their recollection is extremely accurate. This can occur with various venues including disclosures through repressed memory. Other challenges investigators face with late disclosures are locating witnesses or even suspects as they could be living well out of the investigator's jurisdiction or may be deceased. Even if the investigator is able to overcome all the obstacles of a late disclosure and is able to establish probable cause, the challenge of obtaining justice can be even more elusive when the victim proceeds through the judicial system.

CASE STUDY #1 (WOMAN DISCLOSES ABUSE)

Colleen, a twenty-four-year-old woman, reported to law enforcement that she was sexually abused when she was fourteen years old by a woman who was eight years older. She described the abuse in detail and expressed how it has affected her mental health and that it was only last year where she was able to have a heterosexual relationship. Coleen was adamant about wanting to press charges against her abuser. Law enforcement was able to track down the accused, Martha, who was now living in a different state and now identified herself as Martin: this individual was in the process of having a sex change. Martin denied any abuse, and there was no corroborating evidence to support the victim's allegation. Local prosecutors would not support bringing charges.

PREDICTORS OF NON-DISCLOSURES

Kathleen Faller reports how several studies have documented predictors of non-disclosure of sexual abuse during forensic interviews:

> *Gender:* The disclosure rate of boys is usually lower when compared to girls who have been sexually abused. Boys not only have to struggle about disclosing sexual abuse, but since most perpetrators are men, the boys have an additional burden in disclosing same gender sexual activity.
>
> *Proximity to the relationship of the offender:* Studies have shown that the closer the relationship between the victim and the offender, the less likely the disclosure will come forth.
>
> *Non-supportive, non-offending caregiver:* Having a non-supportive parent or caretaker will reduce the chances of a child bringing the allegations to light. Additionally, if the victim does disclose to a non-supportive parent, there is a higher probability that the child will not make a disclosure during a forensic interview. This non-supportive caregiver can also contribute to the child recanting their statement of abuse.
>
> *Age of victim:* Studies have shown that both very young children and adolescents are less likely to disclose their abuse. Younger children may lack the communication skills to make the appropriate disclosure or they may not be knowledgeable as to what constitutes sexual abuse. Adolescents may be less likely to disclose their abuse as they may be fully aware of the negative consequences once their secret is exposed.
>
> *Race and ethnicity:* There is a general recognition amongst practitioners that children from non-dominant racial or ethnic groups may be less likely to disclose their abuse. Despite the importance of race and ethnicity, there is little research that addresses whether there are racial/ethnic barriers when the interviewer and the interviewee are of different ethnic groups. There are some studies that have addressed racial/ethnic barriers resulting in inconsistent findings.
>
> *No prior disclosure:* Children who have not made a disclosure of sexual abuse to anyone prior to a forensic interview are less likely to disclose their victimization. Forensic interviews are conducted when there is a suspicion of abuse, whether that suspicion arose from the child's previous disclosure or through behavioral or physical indicators.[2]

WHO INVESTIGATES?

Investigating child abuse is a team effort. Agencies throughout the country have formed task forces containing multiple disciplines to investigate child maltreatment. This is referred to as the "multidisciplinary team approach," which is the most effective way to investigate child maltreatment as professionals respond through interagency coordination and planning. Social workers, medical personnel, therapists, prosecutors, judges, and police officers all have an important role to play. All these members are working together with a common goal, which is acting in the best interest for the welfare of the child, and ideally each member communicates with mutual respect toward one another. All members of a multidisciplinary team have an obligation to appreciate what the other professionals are seeking to accomplish, and each member should understand how their activities interrelate. Each and every member of this team must have clearly defined roles in order for them to carry out their responsibilities effectively.[3] Although each member of the team and their roles may be deemed equally vital, the two primary investigators for child abuse are law enforcement and social services. In some cases, law enforcement and social services will work together; in other instances, only one agency will be involved. Social services will not investigate child abuse unless it involves a family member or an agency that is responsible for the care of children. However, even in cases of extrafamilial abuse, social services will still assist law enforcement when requested. Law enforcement will usually only investigate a child abuse allegation that rises to the level of a crime or any circumstances which lead them to believe that a child is in danger. However, law enforcement may aid child protective services by assisting in home visits where there is potential for violence or in any situation where a child may have to be placed in protective custody.

Almost all cases of sexual abuse are investigated by police including allegations of sexual abuse between very young children who are not old enough to face criminal sanctions. Although there may be no intention of prosecuting a young child, it is important for the police to inquire where the children learned this deviant behavior because there is a potential that a small child who is being sexually aggressive may have been a victim of abuse themselves. In cases when the alleged offender is too young to prosecute, the police may defer to social services for intervention. The police do not investigate all allegations of physical abuse. Law enforcement may only elect to investigate physical abuse that results in severe injury. Injury that is not considered severe (minor bruising) may fall under the heading of corporal punishment depending on the reason for the discipline. Social services, in contrast, may become involved to provide services for the family including counseling or establishing a program to ensure the child's safety. Law enforcement may investigate neglect depending on the severity, but usually this type of complaint is handled by the patrol division who will initiate the inquiry and determine if a police specialist is warranted. In contrast, neglect is the most common form of abuse reported to social services and investigated by the agency.

Psychological abuse is rarely investigated by police or social services as an individual complaint as it usually coincides with another kind of abuse allegation. Law enforcement may intervene in psychological abuse, especially if it involves encouraging a child to engage in criminal behavior. Some of the more commonly referred charges under these circumstances would be "contributing to the delinquency of a minor" or "endangering the welfare of a child." No matter what the allegation of abuse may be, the investigation has to have the jurisdiction to investigate. In other words, the investigator must have the legal authority to conduct an investigation in a community. For law enforcement, it is not where the child lives but where the crime allegedly took place. However, it is not uncommon for larger departments, which may have adequate resources to handle particular types of child abuse allegations, to assist smaller communities. The same principles apply to social services as they investigate cases within a certain jurisdiction. On occasion, social services will make exceptions as another agency may have a conflict of interest in a case or the family resides within in their jurisdiction, and may offer services to assist a primary agency.[4] Federal law enforcement also plays a pivotal role in assisting other agencies, not only by having more powerful jurisdictional authority, but in sponsoring training in the investigation of abuse.

WHAT IS INVESTIGATED?

The word "investigate" means a systematic examination to conduct an official inquiry. For law enforcement, this term would be used to investigate a crime.[5] Law enforcement and social services will investigate any viable allegation of abuse including psychological, sexual, physical, and neglect. Some allegations are reported directly to law enforcement, whereas the majority of cases are sent directly to social services, who in turn will turn the information over to law enforcement when applicable. Very few states require social services to report all allegations of abuse to law enforcement.[6] Social services has a "screen out" process where, based on the facts of the allegation, they determine what will be investigated as some complaints do not fall under the heading of child abuse. For example, some callers may report that a child is showing behavioral issues that are concerning, but that concern does not indicate that it is necessarily child maltreatment. Other allegations of maltreatment can be made while staying anonymous, and although this is permissible in most states, the allegation may not comprise enough adequate information to warrant an investigation as the caller is unwilling or unable to explain how they are aware of the suspected case of abuse.

Table 7.1 Total Referral Rates, 2013–2017[1]

Year	National Estimate/Actual Screened-in Referrals	National Estimate of Screened-out Referrals	National Estimate of Total Referrals	Child Population of All Fifty-two States	Total Referrals Rate per 1,000 Children
2013	2,102,660	1,495,000	3,598,000	74,378,641	48.4
2014	2,163,450	1,554,000	3,717,000	74,339,990	50.0
2015	2,237,754	1,651,000	3,889,000	74,360,792	52.3
2016	2,327,000	1,718,000	4,045,000	74,352,938	54.4
2017	2,359,911	1,776,000	4,136,000	74,312,174	55.7

Screened-out referral data are from the agency file and screened-in referral data are from the child file. The national estimate of total referrals is the sum of the actual reported or estimated number of screened-in referrals plus the number of estimated screened-out referrals. The sum is rounded to the nearest thousand. The national total referral rate is calculated for each year dividing the national estimate of total referrals by the child population of all fifty-two states and multiplying the result by one thousand.

[1] U.S. Department of Health & Human Services, Administration for Children and Families, Administration on Children, Youth and Families, Children's Bureau. (2019). Child Maltreatment 2017. Available from https://www.acf.hhs.gov/cb/research-data-technology/statistics-research/child-maltreatment.

Tiffany Vassar (left) & Brooke Maynard (right) work in the investigative unit for Child Protective Services for the Commonwealth of Virginia

THE ROLE OF THE INVESTIGATOR

The primary role of the investigator, no matter which agency they work for, is to determine if abuse actually occurred and make sure the child is no longer in danger via protective custody or some other action ensuring safety. The goal after these objectives varies depending on the agency. If law enforcement determines that a crime has indeed occurred, they will continue their investigation in order to build a case against those accused and ensure their accountability. In contrast, social services, once confirming abuse, will focus on what services are needed to help the child recover from any possible trauma and establish that the child is residing in a safe environment.

THE SOCIAL WORKER

Working as a social worker can be a frustrating but rewarding career, especially for those who are dedicating themselves to the protection of children. Social workers are an integral part of the team who collaborates with other professionals in the common goal of protecting children. A social worker can be constantly put under a microscope by the public: the public either accuse them of failing to protect children or claim that they are acting as "gestapo" being too aggressive, thus violating the rights of parents. Due to the strict laws of confidentiality within social work, those who are accused of wrongdoing are unable to defend themselves, no matter (despite) how ludicrous the allegation may be. Tiffany Vassar and Brooke Maynard provide a brief synopsis of a day in the life of a social worker:

The process of investigating child abuse and/or neglect begins with a referral that alleges abuse and/or neglect has taken place. This will start with our intake worker. For a complaint to be valid it has to meet the definition of abuse and/or neglect, the person must be under the age of 18, the alleged abuser must be a caretaker and we must have jurisdiction to investigate. In 2018, we validated 74% of the complaints reported to intake.

Once an accusation is validated it is then assigned to an investigator. Our intake worker will contact law enforcement and our Commonwealth attorney if the allegation could result in any criminal charges, even a misdemeanor charge. If the police decide to work along with Child Protective Services we will proceed together. Our CPS always proceeds with the Police Department taking the lead. The first step is to interview the alleged victim or victims along with any siblings. We then speak with all caretakers, alleged abusers and any others listed in the referral.

After interviews are complete safety of the alleged victim is determined. If we feel there is abuse and/or neglect one option is we can proceed with a safety plan. A safety plan is a plan between the agency and the parent/caretaker. It lists what services need to be in place along with any expectations the agency has of the parents. An example could be they will not use any physical discipline. This safety plan will be followed up with the parents and the CPS investigator assigned.

If it is determined that a child is not safe to go back to the caretaker/parent then the CPS Investigator's first step is to look into relative placements. These are where the worker engages the family to place the child/children with a relative until the safety concern is no longer an issue. In the occasion that a child/children are in imminent risk and there is no placement or a safe placement cannot be made then an emergency removal is done and the child/children are placed in foster care. Placing a child in foster care is a last resort but is done to keep a child safe.

If a child is placed in foster care then the worker has to file an emergency removal affidavit immediately with the Juvenile & Domestic Court. There will be an ex parte hearing for a Judge to hear the complaint that abuse and/or neglect has occurred. At that time there is another hearing scheduled which is referred to as the "5 day hearing." At this hearing, the parents will be notified and be present with attorneys appointed for them as well as an attorney for the child/children known as the Guardian ad litem. We have 45 days to investigate and close a case from the date the case was reported and initiated. We are allowed to request a 15 day extension if necessary, and are allowed a 90 day extension when we are working in conjunction with law enforcement.[7]

THE TRAINING

Child abuse investigation can be detrimental to the child, especially when the investigator is ill equipped to handle such a difficult and emotionally draining assignment. Although most investigators should have specific training to respond to the unique field of child maltreatment, this is not always the case. The criminal justice system, specifically its law enforcement officers, are on many occasions not properly trained and are unprepared to handle complex cases. It is imperative that child maltreatment cases should only be investigated by a highly trained law enforcement officer who has received the appropriate training to handle such sensitive cases. There are different levels of abuse where some cases may be initiated by patrol officers and then forwarded to detectives pending the severity of the case. A typical call that may be resolved through the patrol division is supervisory neglect. It is not uncommon for police to receive calls that a child is left at home without any adult supervision. The patrol officer responds to ensure the child isn't in imminent danger and notifies social services if warranted. In smaller departments, even where the allegation of abuse is more complex, patrol officers may have to handle the entire case due to their limited resources, including the lack of training that is required to effectively and thoroughly respond to child maltreatment complaints. Although there is ample training available in the field of child abuse, not all law enforcement officers are afforded these essential opportunities. A research project was conducted in 2017 to determine if police officers who graduate from the police academy are adequately prepared to investigate or even recognize the indicators of child abuse. An examination of several police academies from multiple jurisdictions revealed by reviewing the police academy itinerary that there was minimal training specifically dedicated to the topic of child abuse, and in some cases, no specified training was afforded despite that the academies seem to keep increasing the length of time of instruction to accommodate the ever-increasing expectations of incoming recruits.[8] The lack of training is not an issue that is exclusive to law enforcement. Social workers are put into situations involving child maltreatment fresh out of college, leaving them susceptible to making mistakes at the cost of the children. It is important for both law enforcement and social services to have "green" investigators work alongside seasoned investigators until they are capable of mastering the skills needed. This does not mean that highly trained individuals will not make mistakes, but the goal is to minimize the frequency of these errors in order to optimize the outcomes and properly safeguard the young and vulnerable in society. In some cases, professionals such as highly trained forensic nurses or other medical personnel can confirm an injury, but in many cases they cannot distinguish between accidental injury and deliberate abuse. These cases are referred to as the "gray cases," which emphasizes the point of how even highly trained individuals cannot resolve the validity of some child abuse allegations.[9]

THE EMERGENCE OF THE POLICE SPECIALIST

Within the law enforcement community there are typically those who maintain order and those who investigate crime. This is not necessarily the case within smaller limited departments where officers are expected to take the role of generalist. In larger departments, however, specialists are used, especially in the case of crimes against children. Some departments refer to these specialists as the special victims unit. Most detectives who are specialists in a particular area were former patrol personnel who worked their way up through the ranks and understand the value of the patrol division as being a valuable resource in their investigations.[10] Some departments may use patrol officers in child abuse investigations;

others may have strict policies against it. In addition to the limited training a patrol officer may have, the uniform itself can be a detriment. Although most children (especially younger children) admire the police, there are some who are fearful of the police (law enforcement). This problem is only enhanced when parents jokingly or deliberately point to a uniformed police officer and say to their child, "You better behave or the police are going to arrest you!" Some sex offenders may use this fear, created by the child's parents or caretaker, to their advantage telling the child that the police will arrest them if they discover what they have done.

THE INTERVIEW

Interviewing a child to solicit information is considerably more challenging than any standard interview, especially when the case involves child abuse. It is extremely important that the interviewer is not biased as a presumptive attitude can lead to false allegations or an offender escaping justice. There are some basic skills in being a good interviewer such as being a good listener. It can be easy for someone, especially when dealing with children, to focus so much on what they have to say that they don't hear what the child is verbalizing. In order to conduct a proper interview, it is beneficial to develop a rapport with the child, especially when expecting the child to confide a potentially uncomfortable topic. Building a connection with a child can be accomplished by discussing topics interesting to the child. This is easier for an interviewer who has young family members and is cognizant of what is popular among children. It can be awkward if the child brings up something of interest to them, and the interviewer is not familiar with the subject.

SECRET INTERVIEWS

In some circumstances, interviews of children can occur without the consent or knowledge of the parents or caretakers. This practice is usually employed when the suspicion of abuse involves a family member, as there is concern that the family member may hinder the investigation, the child is in immediate danger, or other criteria. Most interviews that the investigating officials wish to keep secret are conducted at the child's school through the lawful cooperation of school officials. The twenty-three states where no parent or guardian permission is needed to interview the child within specific criteria are as follows: Arizona, Arkansas, Connecticut, Delaware, Florida, Indiana, Kansas, Maine, Maryland, Missouri, Mississippi, Montana, New Hampshire, New Jersey, New York, Ohio, Oregon, Tennessee, Texas, Utah, Vermont, Washington, and West Virginia. The following eighteen states have few or no restrictions on interviewing children without parental consent: Alaska, Hawaii, Idaho, Illinois, Iowa, Kentucky, Louisiana, Michigan, Minnesota, Nebraska, Nevada, New Mexico, North Dakota, Oklahoma, Rhode Island, South Carolina, Virginia, and Wisconsin. The law of non-consent is not addressed in statute or policy in these following states: Alabama, California, Colorado, Georgia, Massachusetts, North Carolina, Pennsylvania, and Wyoming. Iowa and New Mexico are the only states that require the child's consent in order to conduct an interview.[11] The support of legislators and school officials is crucial as these "secretive" interviews are only conducted when it is in the best interest of the child.

SUGGESTIBILITY

The Misinformation Effect was introduced in the 1970s through a series of studies by Elizabeth Loftus and her colleagues, which ushered in a new era of psychological research on memory. It is considered one of the most influential findings in experiential psychology. The results of these studies revealed that misleading post-event suggestions introduced after an eyewitness event are highly likely to contaminate the memory of a witness, producing in some cases confident recollections of an event that never occurred. The critical manipulation of questioning includes false or misleading suggestions that typically come in the form of presuppositions or leading questions.[12] As research continues to support how suggestibility can influence the accuracy of an event, it is crucial that an investigator avoid such methods to ensure the accuracy of a victim's testimony. When the investigator is about to initiate their questioning they should explain to the child, in general terms, why they are there without getting into specifics to avoid any suggestibility. Children are extremely prone to suggestibility.[13] Children with intellectual disabilities (which refers to cognitive difficulties or lower IQ) are not only more susceptible to abuse but also to suggestibility during an investigative interview. A child with an IQ less than seventy would generally be considered intellectually disabled.[14] However, chronological age remains the single most powerful predictor of suggestibility as the older the child is the less likely they are to be influenced.[15] It is important for the interviewer to ask open-ended questions and only use closed-ended questions under specific guidelines. To ask specific closed-ended questions may be deemed leading and suggestive to the child. A defense attorney can bring up a concern that an interviewer asked closed-ended questions and use this against the victim, arguing that the investigator put those thoughts in the child's head. The defense attorney can then call for a "Taint Hearing," which is discussed in chapter 14.

No matter how well trained an interviewer may be in avoiding suggestibility, the interview might have been tainted before it even started. An investigator should attempt to conduct an interview as soon as possible after hearing the initial disclosure. Current research has revealed how a single suggestive interview can have equally detrimental effects as multiple interviews when "(1) the strength of the original memory trace is weak or the memory is of repeated events and (2) the timing of the misinformation occurs relatively close to the original event compared from the time of the memory test. These findings illustrate the importance of evaluating every interview with a child, as even one biased interviewer can taint a child's testimony."[16] Unfortunately, some adults who have access to the child may conduct their own inquiry as a concerned community member or a protective family member and may instinctively ask questions out of concern, which can alter the accuracy of the investigation. Additionally, some family members or members of the community may discourage or even threaten a child not to say anything, even if they believe the allegations to be true. Other forms of suggestibility can come through repeated questions.

Repeated Questions

Child forensic interviewers often to try clarify details previously mentioned by children or to encourage children who may be reluctant to disclose. This can be problematic as it can show inconsistency in the child's statements. Other specific problems associated with repeated questions is that studies have shown that some children can believe that something really happened to them just by repeatedly being asked the same question.[17] Still other research has shown that repeated questions can encourage a child to change their answer. For instance, if an interviewer repeatedly asks the same question over and over again, especially if the child has truthfully answered the question, the child may change their answer just to please the interviewer as they feel they their previous answer was not acceptable. Some of the reasons for repeated questions include:

- **No apparent reason:** The child answered the question in a clear and unequivocal manner, but the interviewer asks the question again nonetheless.
- **Challenge:** The interviewer casts doubt on the truthfulness of the child's previous statement.
- **Child clarification:** The interviewer did not understand what the child was saying.
- **Interviewer clarification:** The child did not understand the question so the interviewer repeats or rephrases question.
- **Digression:** The child was resistant or provided an irrelevant response. For repeated questions to be coded as digression, the child must have provided a forensically relevant response to the initial question and is given the opportunity to change their answer.
- **Compound:** The interviewer prompted the child with a great deal of information in a single utterance, and the child did not respond in detail to clarify their response.[18]

SUGGESTIVE THERAPY

In some cases, a child denies or fails to disclose their victimization even though there is strong suspicion that the abuse occurred. Children in these cases may be assumed to be in a stage of denial and should be referred to someone for therapy to help them disclose. This technique is inadvisable because even if suspicion is strong, there is the possibility that the child was not a victim. If the therapy has a covert goal of producing evidence in a legal proceeding, it will inevitably be challenged as suggestive questioning by therapists. Additionally, unlike a child forensic interview, these sessions are probably not recorded.[19]

TECHNIQUES OF FORENSIC INTERVIEWING

There are numerous ways to conduct a forensic interview, and there isn't one exclusive set of specific techniques that is universally accepted by experts in the field. Some of the forensic interviewing models today include the child cognitive interview, step-wise interview, and narrative elaboration. All three of these methods have been shown to be more effective in helping children recall information than the standard techniques that are often used with adults. Despite the different styles of interviews, there are some common characteristics that are implemented such as the introduction phase, rapport building, developmental assessment, certain guidelines, and competency assessment.[20]

ANATOMICALLY DETAILED DOLLS

These dolls, first introduced in the 1970s, have genitalia and other sexual features and are used for two primary reasons in child sexual abuse cases. The first reason these dolls may be used is due to the child's limited cognitive and language skills; the second involves the potential emotional reactions of the child. With respect to the first reason, these dolls serve as cues or props to help a young child accurately explain their experiences. Anatomical dolls can also be utilized to aid in reducing a child's fear and embarrassment by not having to verbally express their victimization.[21] There is no conclusive evidence that anatomically detailed dolls elicit more information, and the results of their reliability are questionable. Several concerns have been raised over the use of these dolls. In one study of the reliability of anatomically detailed dolls, three-year-old children who received routine medical exams were assessed. In this study, half the children received a genital examination and the other half did not. The result of the study showed that children were inaccurate about reporting genital touching despite how the questions were presented. The dolls only increased the inaccurate reporting with the children falsely showing the doctor inserting his finger into the anal or genital cavity. Due to the controversy in the use of anatomically correct dolls, some jurisdictions have banned their use as legal evidence, until scientific data can attest to its validity.[22]

MEMORY SOURCE MONITORING

Source monitoring is the process of identifying the origin of one's knowledge or event memories. Faulty source monitoring can lead to children reporting that they experienced events or saw something that they actually heard from an adult, something they watched on television, or something they just imagined. Young children are more likely than older children or adults to have difficulty in distinguishing what they truly experienced instead of what they may have seen or heard.[23] After it is established that the child is indeed a victim, the investigator needs to inquire further by putting the appropriate facts in order to protect the child from further abuse and to make the offender accountable for their actions.

GETTING THE FACTS

Once a child discloses, the investigator has to obtain additional information for clarity and establish facts for potential prosecution. For instance, if a child says that someone touched his "pee pee," the investigator needs to clarify with the child what they are referring to. Although there is a strong likelihood that the child is talking about their genitalia, you don't want to be surprised later on in the investigation or even during trial that the term indicated something else and no crime was committed.

For purposes of potential prosecution, the investigator must establish where and when the abuse took place. Unfortunately what may be a rather easy task with adult victimization can be rather challenging when interviewing children. A young child, for example, is not going to report that on November 4 at 1755 hours they were sexually assaulted at 12 Mayflower Dr. Younger children, especially, will be unable to give such precise details. The judicial system realizes this and allows prosecutors to charge an offender of child abuse by stating that the offense took place on or about November 4. Some jurisdictions allow a prosecutor to charge an individual with an act that occurred over a two-year time frame, although it is better for all parties to narrow the time frame as close to the date as possible in order to provide fairness to the judicial process.[24] However, determining the location is paramount as you cannot charge someone in an offense if you can't determine the jurisdiction where the alleged crime occurred. To help establish these facts it is important to ask the child questions that they can associate with times and locations. For instance, "Do you know what season it occurred in?" Was it winter, summer, etc.? Were you in school when the abuse took place? How old were you when this happened? Other methods to narrow down the time are by using special events. Did it happen around your birthday, Christmas, Halloween? For the purpose of this discussion, the child may state, "It happened a few days after Halloween." But they can't state the exact date. If the child says it happened over Grandpa's house, then the investigator can look up the address of the grandfather who happens to live at 12 Mayflower Drive. Establishing a time of day employs the same principles of questioning, such as "Was it morning, afternoon, or night?" The child reveals that it happened just before supper. Based on the facts provided by the child, the court complaint can now state that on or about the evening of November 4 at 12 Mayflower Drive the defendant committed the crime of sexual assault.

The investigator also needs to get specific facts about the sexual act to support a charge for a particular crime. For instance, a disclosure that describes penetration of an orifice can substantially change the severity of the charge. Obtaining important facts can not only bring a perpetrator to justice, but can also help those who are falsely accused. Collecting crucial facts during an interview is only part of an investigator's responsibility. In most child sexual abuse cases there is rarely any physical evidence so the investigator must attempt to develop corroborating evidence.

SUPPORT PERSONS

There is a debate as to whether a support person should be present during an official interview by law enforcement, social services, or anyone working in an official capacity when they interview a child for possible sexual abuse or other form of maltreatment. A support person can include a family member, counselor, school official, or anyone who would make the child feel more at ease during an interview. There is limited evidence to support that a child is unwilling to talk with authorities without the presence of a supportive person; however, support persons have been allowed to sit in during an interview with the understanding that they are not to interject during the process. It can be detrimental, however, if a support person is allowed to be present and their presence alters the accuracy of the proceeding. For instance, a child may not want to disclose any graphic details in front of a family matter due to their own embarrassment or they may be concerned that the family member will be angry or upset in some way once hearing the details of the abuse. Additionally, if an interviewer is suspicious about the validity of an allegation and questions a child for clarification, a support person may become upset and come to the child's defense. Another aspect of using a support person is to consider whether this person is neutral to the investigation. They may not believe the child and interject their thoughts during the process. This "support" person may also be involved with the abuse or want to protect the person accused. A forensic interviewer must consider all of these possibilities before allowing a person to sit in for support.

CASE STUDY #2 (MOTHER STAYS DURING INTERVIEW)

Barry, a ten-year-old boy, comes directly to the police station with his mother with the suspicion of sexual abuse. A patrolman greets them at the front foyer where the mother briefly addresses her suspicion with the officer. The officer, with good intentions but without any specialized training in interviewing children who may have been abused, decided to conduct the interview himself. He brought the child along with mother to one of the interview rooms for questioning. As the officer questioned the boy in front of his mother, the boy began to give graphic details of how he was sexually abused by his father. The mother, soon after hearing these details, started screaming in grief and crying uncontrollably. Barry could see how much his disclosure upset his mother and declined to say anything further. A trained detective was called in to assist in the investigation and explained to the mother that he would prefer that she wait outside. The trained detective knew that his training instructed him to avoid having family in during questioning unless the child was adamant about having a support person there for comfort. When the trained investigator interviewed Barry alone, Barry admitted to his victimization but would not give any details of the abuse, stating that he didn't want to upset his mother anymore. Due to the lack of cooperation of the victim and no corroborating evidence to support an allegation, this case never went forward for prosecution.

REACTION TO DISCLOSURE

It can be extremely difficult to conceal one's emotions when hearing a child give graphic details of the abuse they encountered. Although you may be pleased that a child is willing to disclose to you, giving you a factual description of what occurred, it can be detrimental if there is a display of an inappropriate response to their disclosure. For instance, after a child describes some abuse, you respond by saying "you're doing a good job." The child may perceive this as an invitation to give more information whether true or not as it is pleasing the interviewer. A trained interviewer should be able to hear graphic details of abuse without showing any display of emotion. A child witnessing an interviewer being upset, just as can happen in the case of a support person, can deter the child from disclosing any more graphic but important information. This purposeful lack of display of emotions does not mean that the interviewer is jaded or is not passionate about protecting children, but instead they understand the value of keeping emotions in check.

NUMBER OF INTERVIEWERS

When an interview is being conducted, a decision must be made as to how many people should be involved in interviewing a child. The advantages of having more than one person conducting an interview is that one of the interviewers may address an issue that the other interviewer neglected to see or address. One of the challenges, however, in having more than one interviewer in the room is the difficulty of having a child build a rapport with both adults and then be willing to disclose their abuse. A tactic to address this potential problem is by having a second person in the room taking notes while the primary investigator conducts their interview. Whoever conducts the interview should have forensic training on how to properly conduct an interview to avoid any unnecessary mistakes. Finally, agencies with adequate resources can conduct an interview while using a two-way mirror for other professionals such as social services, victim advocates, and prosecuting attorneys, and also give protective family members an opportunity to observe. Under this format, the interviewer will either have an ear piece installed where they can have questions "fed" to them while they are actively conducting the interview, or they can step out of the room to speak with other professionals who may want a particular question asked or to go back to an earlier statement for clarification. This method not only helps create a more comprehensive interview but also helps in limiting the need for additional interviews.

However, there is no consensus as to whether an interview should be restricted to one session. On the other hand there is little evidence that the testimony of a child is affected adversely by repeated non-suggestive interviews, which can afford the interviewer an additional chance to clarify a child's account of what took place. Then again, repeated suggestive interviews can degrade accuracy, and multiple interviews provide opportunities for children to be questioned informally but suggestively through conversations with parents, grandparents, or other adults between official forensic interviews. This has the potential to pollute the accuracy of the disclosure.[25] Another important factor to consider is whether subjecting a child to multiple interviews is in the best interest of the child. Professionals must evaluate whether having the child repeat traumatic events in a non-therapeutic setting is beneficial to the child.

TALKING TO CHILDREN—LANGUAGE USED

Adults tend to dominate conversations with children and encourage children to expand on their own comments, then asking specific questions. One of the primary goals of an interview is to listen after asking open-ended questions that allow a child to share their experience. When an interviewer does ask questions, they should use a vocabulary that the child understands. There are many reasons why children misunderstand words, especially if it is a word that is rarely used around them. Also, words have different connotations with children, such as the word "touch." If you ask a child if someone touched them, they may automatically associate the word touch with their hands or someone else's hands, although sexual contact can still occur through other means. Children can be very literal so your choice of words can have a completely different meaning among children, as described in this exchange involving a 5-year-old girl. This was first recounted by Berliner and Barbieri and it emphases the point of how literal interpretation can be problematic:[26]

Defense attorney: And then you said you put your mouth on his penis?
  Child: No.
  Defense attorney: You didn't say that?
  Child: No.
  Defense attorney: Did you ever put your mouth on his penis?
  Child: No.
  Defense attorney: Well, why did you tell your mother that your dad put his penis in your mouth?
  Child: My brother told me to.
  Note: Looking at this narrative, you would think that the child is recanting his previous allegation and the case would be dismissed. See what follows!
  Prosecuting attorney: Jennie, you said that you didn't put your mouth on daddy's penis. Is that right?
  Child: Yes.
  Prosecuting attorney: Did daddy put his penis in your mouth?
  Child: Yes.
  Prosecuting attorney: Did you tell your mom?
  Child: Yes.
  Prosecuting attorney: What made you decide to tell?
  Child: My brother and I talked about it, and he said I better tell or dad would just keep doing it.[27]

CORROBORATING EVIDENCE

Corroborating evidence is evidence that confirms or gives support to a statement or theory. An aspect of corroborating evidence is physical evidence that supports abuse. In chapter 2, various types of physical injuries are described that can support the allegation of physical abuse, such as burns, bruises, fractures, etc. The same principles of evidence apply with sexual abuse cases as well. Chapter 3 describes physical indicators that are consistent with victims of sexual abuse. However, physical evidence is not strictly relating to physical indicators on the child's body to support a child's testimony, but to other physical evidence that might be at a crime scene or from some other facet. It is important to gather as much information as possible from a child during a forensic interview so that the investigator can look for and gather as much evidence as possible and avoid having a case that revolves solely around a child's word against that of the accused.

Corroborating evidence can also be obtained through behavioral indictors, such as witnesses stating how they observed a child get upset each time they were to go to a particular relative's house. Other indicators can include statements of those who made observations of unusual trends in behavior: for instance, if a child reports that over the last six months she was forced to perform fellatio on her uncle and the parents also observed that during that same time period their daughter began to have an obsession with brushing her teeth. This behavior of obsessive hygiene may be used as corroborating evidence. Additionally, a mental health worker who specializes in behavioral effects of child maltreatment victims could advise an investigator that the child's overall mental health appears consistent with someone who was a victim of abuse.

CASE STUDY #3 (HERPES)

Maegan, age fourteen, babysat for a couple's two-year-old child on multiple occasions when the parents (Jim and Alicia) went out for leisure or they were both scheduled to work. On one such occurrence, Jim called Maegan, asking her to babysit, since both parents had to work (although there was no evidence the father was ever scheduled to work). When Maegan arrived at the home, Alicia had already left for work, but Jim stated that his place of employment called to say that he was no longer needed. Jim proceeded to tell Maegan that since she already came over he would still have her babysit while he got some work done around the house. He was now alone with his potential victim. Jim decided to sit on the couch with Maegan, where they both started to become flirtatious. Eventually Maegan agreed to perform fellatio on this man even though she was under the age of consent. She later felt coerced for what had happened and reported it to the police. The investigator asked Maegan about the details of how the fellatio took place. Through this discussion, the fourteen-year-old babysitter was able to state that Jim had some "pimples" on the stem of his penis. This description was later confirmed by law enforcement that discovered that the "pimples," as she described them, were actually herpes, which was used as corroborating evidence to support the allegation of sexual abuse.

PHYSICAL ABUSE INVESTIGATIONS

Unlike sexual abuse investigations, physical abuse investigations leave a vast array of information through the injuries the child suffered. However, the injuries themselves are not always conclusive to physical abuse, as the investigator needs to determine whether the injuries sustained were accidental or the result of physical abuse. Battered child syndrome is defined as injuries sustained by a child as a result of repeated beatings or mistreatment. Law enforcement has an important role in uncovering cases of battered child syndrome and must collect the appropriate information surrounding the reported injury, which requires interviewing potential witnesses including medical personnel and the caretaker of the child to determine what caused the child's injuries. When battered syndrome is suspected, the investigator should take the following steps:

- Collect information about the acute injury that led the person or agency to make the report.
- Conduct interviews with medical personnel who are attending the child.
- Review medical records from a doctor, clinic, or hospital.
- Interview all persons who had access to or custody of the child during the time in which the injury or injuries allegedly occurred. Caretakers should always be interviewed separately.[28]

THE FORENSIC NURSE

The role of a sexual assault nurse examiner evolved throughout the United States in the late 1990s.[29] Today, many nurses take on a more inclusive role of evaluating victims of crimes in addition to sexual offenses. These nurses are referred to as forensic nurses. The forensic nurse role can vary from site to site and state to state. Forensic nurses are involved with evaluation of patients and evidence collection above and beyond that of sexual assault. The forensic nurse role incorporates sexual assaults, but also domestic violence, child physical abuse and neglect, elder abuse and neglect, pediatric deaths, malicious wounding type crimes, car versus pedestrian, and other cases that may have a criminal aspect to them.

Although most sexual abuse cases do not have physical evidence to support their allegation, when physical evidence is available, the forensic nurse's role is paramount, as they can not only properly identify the physical evidence, but are trained on how to retrieve it and record it as evidence so that it can be properly introduced in court. Furthermore, a forensic nurse is instrumental in clearing the name of those who have been falsely accused as the forensic nurse can identify medical mimickers that are sometimes mistaken as evidence of abuse. Additionally, in some circumstances, forensic nurses may be called upon to review child pornography in order to give a professional opinion as to the age of the victim. The role of the forensic nurse expands outside of a medical facility as they are required frequently to appear in court to testify to their findings. Please see the photograph of a physical evidence recovery kit that forensic nurses use in the Commonwealth of Virginia for the collection of forensic evidence.

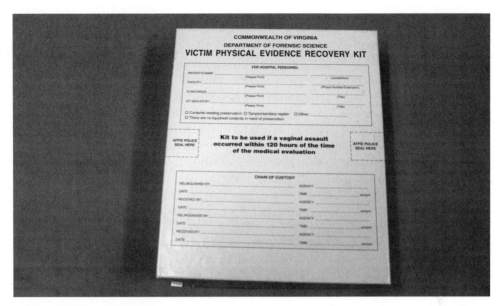

Physical Evidence Recovery Kit

SEXUAL ABUSE INVESTIGATIONS

In direct contrast to physical abuse investigations, physical evidence relating to child sexual abuse is rare, especially because so many allegations of sexual abuse are disclosed long after the abuse has occurred. However, this does not mean that physical evidence is not available. A trained investigator can not only obtain evidence from the victim, but also through crime scene investigations long after the reported abuse has taken place.

CASE STUDY #4 (RAPE OF A FOUR-YEAR-OLD)

A pediatrician had contacted law enforcement after conducting a medical exam of a four-year-old child (Cindy); it was discovered that she had contracted chlamydia. Police interviewed Cindy who told police that her uncle (Donnie) would take off her clothes and put his "private in her pee pee hole." The uncle, who had just been released from prison and was on parole for larceny, denied the allegation, stating how "he loves his niece and he would never do such a thing." His parole officer violated his parole based on the allegation, and Donnie was sent back to prison on the larceny charge. Law enforcement then obtained a search warrant for a urethral cell sample from the uncle, which turned up positive for chlamydia. He was charged with sexual assault but was given only a suspended prison sentence as the prosecutors were extremely concerned that the child would be unable to pass a competency hearing. We will discuss competency hearings in chapter 14, which will address court proceedings involving children.

INTERVIEWING/INTERROGATING A SUSPECT

There is a distinction between interviews and interrogations. An interview should precede any interrogation to learn about the suspect in an attempt to build a rapport. Interrogations in contrast lead the conversation with goal of obtaining confessions, admission, or inconsistencies. The ultimate objective of any investigator is to seek the truth, which includes clearing the falsely accused. If the accused is guilty of an offense, the investigator will work to achieve three goals. The first is a confession where the interviewee totally admits to the allegation against them. Second is an admission, which is short of a confession but can be used against the accused. For instance, the suspect may deny ever having had sex with a certain child, but acknowledges that they were alone with the child giving them ample opportunity to commit the offense. The third goal is finding an inconsistency. Inconsistency is basically catching the accused in a lie, thus giving the victim more credibility in their disclosure. For example, if an accused individual states they never saw that child before and, despite there being no witnesses to sexual abuse, there are witnesses that can say that they have seen the accused with the child, the accused's credibility is ruined.

No matter what the objective for questioning, the law enforcement officer must understand the legality of their interrogation. It can be extremely disheartening for a police officer, a prosecutor, and most especially the victim and their family to hear that the accused offender admitted to the offense, but the confession was dismissed due to the court's ruling that it was obtained illegally. If interviewing a suspect of a crime and that suspect is not free to leave or they have the impression that they are not free to leave, they should be advised of their Miranda rights to avoid the potential of losing an acquired confession. A trained investigator can advise someone of their rights and present it in a way where the suspects still feels comfortable in talking to the investigator and waives their rights, allowing the interviewer to legally conduct the interview. Once the legality of the interview is resolved, the challenge of the interview itself is presented.

Interviewing a suspect of a crime can be challenging, but questioning a suspect of sexual abuse can be a daunting task, as some child molesters are some of the most intelligent, charismatic individuals ever encountered. Consider the craftiness and the ability to deceive used by child molesters. They have already displayed that they are sly enough and can manipulate a child to engage in sexual activity while ensuring they maintain their silence. Additionally, these offenders are so manipulative that they are able to convince parents to allow them access to their children. How many parents naïvely give molesters access to their children, thinking that this charismatic individual is responsible and caring around children? It is this type of deviant behavior and the repercussions of being identified as a child sexual predator that makes confessions in these types of cases even more challenging. The investigator has to be just as manipulative as the offender in order to seek the truth. The legality of deceptive interrogation tactics by law enforcement was affirmed by the U.S. Supreme Court in *Frazier v. Cupp* (394 U.S. 731). *Frazier v. Cupp* allowed police in this case to lie to suspects in what evidence they had in order to solicit a confession. This case was considered a landmark decision allowing police to use deceptive practices as part of their investigative techniques.

Tactics such as persuasive themes and arguments can assist in obtaining a confession. Certain themes and arguments remain universally available, such as:

- Minimizing the crime
- Blaming the victim
- Decreasing the shamefulness of the act
- Increasing guilt feelings
- Appealing to the subject's hope for a better outcome.[30]

CASE STUDY #5 (POLICE MANIPULATION)

A man, approximately forty years old, was accused of fondling the vaginal area of a six-year-old child at a community pool. The police called the suspect in for questioning. He said that he knew the girl because they were neighbors, but that he never touched her. The officer pretended to understand what the accused may have been thinking and employed a tactic of deception in order to obtain the truth. The officer told the accused that he couldn't condone what he did because of his position, but understood why he did what he was accused of. The officer told the accused that he found girls that age attractive too, implying how their skimpy bathing suits should not be allowed in public venues as they are just acting promiscuous. The officer continued his deception by stating how he felt the child's figure can sometimes be enticing, and he got the offender to admit that he was attracted too, but continued to deny the contact. The deception continued as the officer tried to minimize the act by saying that some of these children are very seductive, and he made a point to ask the accused whose idea it was. The offender never admitted to assaulting this child, but he did state that there could have been some incidental contact that she may have initiated. Some readers may find this actual scenario disturbing in that a police officer can communicate in that fashion, but it is important for society to know that an investigator should use whatever tool is necessary to protect a child and bring a perpetrator to justice.

CRIME SCENE INVESTIGATION

An investigator should treat any location of where alleged abuse occurred as a crime scene (even if the abuse happened in the past). They should secure any instrument of abuse or any other form of corroborating evidence that the child identifies at the scene.[31] What can physical evidence at a crime scene do?

- Prove the elements of a crime or reveal that a crime has been committed
- Place the suspect at the scene
- Eliminate innocent persons
- Lead to a suspect's confession

- Support witness testimony
- Positively impact juries in a criminal case.[32]

Photography

Documenting a crime scene is critical in that any evidence seized, no matter how valuable, cannot be introduced in court unless it is legally obtained. One of the first steps at any crime scene is photographing any evidence before it is moved. A systematic series of photographs is the best way to document a crime scene and any physical evidence to show where the crime occurred.[33] This helps the prosecution argue against any defense motion that evidence wasn't properly seized or that the evidence presented did not come from the crime scene. Once items have been photographed, the investigator can begin the process of evidence retrieval, which can be minuscule in size but enormous in value.

Locard's Exchange Principle

The concept of Locard's exchange principle states that whenever two objects come in contact with one another, there will be a cross-transfer of material. Trace evidence can be defined as any evidence that is small and which would require microscopic analysis in order for proper identification.[34] Hair would be an appropriate example of how Locard's exchange principle works. If someone sexually abuses a child, they may leave a trace sample of their hair at the scene or leave with a sample of the child's hair by making contact with them at the time of the assault.

Hair

Hair is an extremely important piece of evidence, especially in relation to sexual assault cases as traces of hair found can be on the victim, the suspect of a crime, an individual's clothing, a vehicle, or any location where the crime may have occurred. However, the analysis of hair does have some forensic limitations. An individual hair sample will not result in the definitive identification of a person unless the hair has the root attached, which can be analyzed for DNA.[35] Hair can draw some conclusions without the specific identification of an individual such as the race of the individual, where on the body the hair came from (head, face, pubic area), and whether the hair is damaged or altered such as bleaching or dyeing of the hair. The majority of forensic work involves comparing and differentiating hairs from both the head and pubic regions.[36]

Prints

Prints are extremely valuable in criminal investigations as they supply even more definitive identification than that of DNA: there are no two people in the world with the same fingerprints but identical twins can have the same DNA. However, fingerprints have very limited value in familial sexual abuse cases where the assault took place in the child's home. It would not be unusual for parents or other family members to have their fingerprints all over the house where the child resides, including the child's bedroom. Nevertheless, prints can still have evidentiary value, even though it may be considered circumstantial at best. For instance, if a child alleges that her father would use lubricant on her prior to having intercourse, the father's prints on a container of lubricant can still have substantial value, especially if the lubricant is found in the child's room and only the father's prints are identified.

Saliva

Saliva is an important element of evidence that can easily be overlooked by an investigator as it is usually invisible to the naked eye. Saliva is a good source of DNA and can be found almost anywhere in a criminal investigation including on cigarettes, bottles left at the scene, or on the victim themselves from bite marks and on clothing. "It is difficult to collect saliva stains from skin, clothing, paper or other inanimate objects since it remains invisible and substrate on which saliva is deposited, mainly skin, cannot be submitted directly to extraction procedures."[37]

Semen

Seminal traces can usually be found on the underclothing of the suspect or the victim or both suspect and victim. Seminal traces can also be discovered in bedding, mattresses, automobile cushions, or any place where the assault occurred. Ultraviolet light or an acid phosphatase color test can be used in identifying semen on these surfaces.[38]

Vaginal Secretions

Vaginal secretions, another form of valuable evidence in sexual assault cases, can react to the acid phosphate color test, but not at the same speed as semen.[39] The ability to definitively identify vaginal epithelia or their secretions as a source of DNA would significantly assist in many sexual assault investigations. A penile swab of the suspected offender could prove indicative of someone who recently had sexual intercourse.[40] An investigation of familial sexual abuse is more challenging as one has to be leery of cross-contamination. For instance, if a child states that the perpetrator ejaculated on her bedsheets or over her underwear, but the bedsheets and the clothing have already been put in the hamper by the time a search of the residence is conducted, they have been subject to cross-contamination, thus limiting any evidentiary value.

Blood

Blood can be a valuable indicator of sexual assault, and traces of blood can occur if there is resistance to the sexual abuse or through tearing that can result from penile or digital penetration. Blood samples can contain a large quantity of DNA which may tie a perpetrator to a child. It should be noted, however, that most forms of sexual abuse occur through manipulation and not through physical force, which is more likely to leave traces of blood evidence.

COMBINED DNA INDEX SYSTEM (CODIS)

The Combined DNA Index System (CODIS) is an electronic database of DNA profiles administered by the Federal Bureau of Investigation. The DNA Identification Act of 1994 gave the Federal Bureau of Investigation the authority to establish a National DNA Index System. The Federal Bureau of Investigation website has several indexes that help to categorize the profiles entered into CODIS including:

- **Convicted offender:** DNA profiles of convicted persons
- **Arrestees:** If state law allows collection
- **Forensics:** Contains DNA profiles developed from crime scene evidence such as semen or blood
- **Missing persons:** DNA reference from missing persons
- **Unidentified humans (remains):** DNA developed from unidentified humans or remains
- **Biological relatives of missing persons:** Contains DNA from families of missing persons.[41]

CODIS can be instrumental in assisting local law enforcement with missing children and solving child abuse cases. Although the vast majority of sexual abuse cases involve perpetrators the children know, the value of CODIS in solving stranger sexual assault is astronomical.

HANDLING OF EVIDENCE

The proper retrieval of evidence from a crime scene is only one phase in the correct handling of evidence. The various types of evidence must be marked appropriately, indicating the location, date, and time when it was collected. The evidence should have a case number assigned to it as it follows the chain of custody. Every person who handles the evidence, including lab personnel, must record the date and time that it was in their possession. Any gap in the records within the chain of possession can prevent this vital evidence from ever being introduced in court.

CRIMES AND TECHNOLOGY

Although the desire to hurt and exploit children hasn't changed over time, the methods of abuse have certainly evolved. Child predators are using technology to access children more readily through solicitation. These predators are able to live in a virtual world of secrecy as they exploit children through child pornography whether using their desktop, laptop, or mobile computers.

Child Pornography

The internet allows individuals to obtain vast amounts of pornography from all over the world. Child pornography can be easily distributed via the internet by uploading it onto websites, instant messages, chat rooms, and peer-to-peer networks. Officers work undercover in the digital world in an attempt to lure predators to justice. Some of the techniques include entering chat rooms and requesting child porn pictures or establishing internet sites claiming to have child pornography but are really designed to identify the IP address or credit card number of those who access the site.[42]

With such convenience, abusers can exploit children from work or in the comfort of their homes. Cybercrime is a general term used to describe crimes committed through the use of a computer, including crimes such as solicitation of a minor, child pornography, and child trafficking. There could be plenty of physical evidence that may be found on any suspect's computer, and although the investigator may have all the probable cause and legal authority to conduct a search warrant on a computer, the execution itself must be done by a trained investigator with substantial knowledge in computer forensics. When an item is not seized properly, vital evidence may be destroyed. The fast-growing industries involved in computer crimes require investigators to continually update their knowledge as offenders are constantly seeking ways to circumvent laws and computer systems. Seizing a computer is a highly technical endeavor that requires specific training.[43] In response to the evolving technical advances with computer crimes, the government developed a task force specifically designed to combat abuse through technology.

> The Internet Crimes Against Children Task Force Program (ICAC) is a national network of 61 coordinated task forces representing more than 4,500 federal, state, and local law enforcement and prosecutorial agencies. These agencies are engaged in both proactive and reactive investigations, forensic examinations, and criminal prosecutions. By helping state and local agencies develop effective, sustainable responses to online child victimization—including responses to child sexual abuse images, the ICAC Program has increased law enforcement's capacity to combat technology facilitated crimes against children at every level.
>
> The ICAC Program was developed in response to the increasing number of children and teenagers using the Internet and other technology, the proliferation of child sexual abuse images available electronically, and the heightened online activity by predators seeking unsupervised contact with potential underage victims. Because ICAC Members understand that arrests alone cannot resolve the problem of technology-facilitated child sexual exploitation, the ICAC Program is also dedicated to training law enforcement officers and prosecutors, as well as educating parents and youth about the potential dangers of online activity.[44]

Investigator Chauncey Wilder is a certified law enforcement officer in the State of Virginia and a task force officer on the (Southern Virginia) Internet Crimes Against Children Task Force. He has been on the task force for ten years, with his first seven years as an investigator where he instructed peer-to-peer investigations

Chauncey Wilder, Internet Crimes Against Children (ICAC) Investigator

around the country. Chauncey has spent the last three years as a full-time computer forensic examiner, obtaining certifications such as Encase Certified Examiner, Forensic Explorer Certified Examiner, and XRY mobile forensics.[45]

> Since joining the agency in 2008 I have seen the (SOVA ICAC) task force expand from less than a handful of investigators to well over a dozen in 2019. We are responsible for conducting proactive and reactive investigations. Our investigations primarily include online chatting, peer to peer file sharing and cybertips received from the National Center for Missing and Exploited Children (NCMEC). The agency also houses a full-time forensic lab with four full time forensic examiners, including me that receive evidence submitted for examination from various affiliate agencies throughout Southern Virginia.
>
> In my years on the task force, I have witnessed some of the most horrific acts that can be committed against children. Offenders often digitally record their sexual exploitation of children and share it online for others to see. Many offenders seek "like minded individuals" to help validate their sexual fantasies and the abuse of children. Offenders come in all shapes, sizes, ethnicities and socioeconomic backgrounds. There have been school teachers, church leaders, politicians, daycare workers, police officers, lawyers etc., all arrested for the sexual exploitation of children. There is no magic wand for spotting a predator. The best way to protect our children online is through education, awareness and diligent proactive supervision.
>
> Another huge part of the ICAC mission is to train officers and prosecutors on the high-tech crimes of online child sexual exploitation, which is forever changing. It is important that officers involved with working these types of crimes be aware of how suspects locate victims online and the steps they take to cover their tracks. Additionally, officers must be aware of how to conduct these investigations correctly and in a safe manner. This coupled with the public awareness and community outreach component has been one of the most important parts of the task force.
>
> I personally believe that one of the hardest parts of the job is not only witnessing the abuse of children, but also seeing good, hard-working officers leave the task force program, nationwide. Promotions, transfers, relocations, etc., have all played a factor in losing these professionals; however, many leave because they could not bring themselves to look at another image of children being sexually abused or suffering. Our local office is like a family. We all know one another's spouses, children and sometimes even the names of their pets. We watch out for each other. If one of us is having a difficult time with the job or personal life, we always know there is someone in the office that we can confide in for help or guidance. Some of the most intelligent and noble individuals I have ever known, have served on the ICAC task forces nationwide, and I am supremely grateful to have worked beside them.[46]

INVESTIGATING HUMAN TRAFFICKING

Although human trafficking does not require smuggling or movement of its victims, interstate as well as transnational movement of victims is a significant part of this secretive industry. Due to the complexity of multiple jurisdictions that can be involved in human trafficking, the federal government has taken the lead in addressing this crime. In 2007, the Civil Rights division created the Human Trafficking Prosecution Unit (HTPU) to consolidate the expertise of some of the nation's top human trafficking prosecutors. HTPU prosecutors work closely with law enforcement agencies to streamline fast-moving trafficking investigations and identify multi-jurisdictional trafficking networks. The Bureau of Justice Assistance has funded forty-two human trafficking task forces to bring together federal, state, and local law enforcement agencies, government agencies, as well as non-governmental agencies that provide victim assistance in trafficking investigations.[47]

Investigations of human trafficking usually originate from:

- Citizen complaints
- The National Human Trafficking Resource Center Hotline
- A referral from local law enforcement
- Referral from non-governmental organizations
- Proactive victim recovery operations
- Outreach to state government and community entities.[48]

CONCLUSION

Investigating child abuse is stressful for anyone fighting to protect the child, and the investigations are unique and complex. Due to the complexity of investigating child abuse, a multi-disciplinary team approach is an absolute necessity as no sole investigator should be responsible for handling such cases alone. This team approach can include law enforcement, child protective services, mental health services, victim advocacy, the judicial system, and the medical community. Every individual on the team may have extensive training in an area of child abuse investigations including interviewing techniques. The interviewer cannot be biased and must approach the interview in a manner that is not suggestive. Suggestive interviewing can only cloud the accuracy of the child's statement. Upon completion of an appropriate interview, investigators must look for corroborating evidence to either support the child's testimony or refute the child's claims. The ultimate goal of any investigator is always to determine the truth. The same principles of finding the truth will apply when an investigator interviews anyone accused of child maltreatment. It is equally important, if not more vital, to clear the name of one falsely accused as it is to gather evidence against those believed to be guilty. When an investigator does collect evidence, it may be the result of the examination of a crime scene where a vast array of forensic evidence such as semen, blood, hair, saliva, or any other form of trace evidence may associate the victim with the offender. Not all physical evidence is located at a crime scene. In some cases, the physical evidence may be with the body or clothing of the child. In these cases, forensic nurses are specifically trained not only in how to identify forensic evidence, but also to properly document and retrieve the evidence as well. Child abuse comes in different forms, and investigators continually have to evolve with the different aspects of abuse in order to investigate them properly. Technology has become the new venue used to exploit and abuse children, and investigators now must continue to receive specific training and work together as they form teams such as ICAC in order to have the most appropriate and effective response.

REVIEW QUESTIONS

1. Does the number of child abuse interviews affect the accuracy of the disclosure? If so, why?

2. How does Locard's Exchange Principle apply to sexual assault investigations?

3. How is CODIS used in crime scene investigations?

4. Why are open-ended questions important when interviewing a child?

5. What are the controversies in using anatomically detailed dolls?

KEYWORDS

Corroborating evidence: Evidence that confirms or gives support to a statement or theory.
ICAC: Internet Crimes Against Children.
Locard's Exchange Principle: A principle that states that whenever two objects come in contact with one another, there will be a cross-transfer of material.
CODIS: The Combined DNA Index System.
Memory source monitoring: The process of identifying the origin of one's knowledge or event memories.
Battered child syndrome: Injuries sustained by a child as a result of repeated beatings or mistreatment.

NOTES

1. Carl B. Hammond, Wayne Promisel, Jac R. Shepherd, and Bill Walsh, "Law Enforcement Response to Child Abuse: Portable Guides to Investigating Child Abuse," U.S. Department of Justice, 2014, 4.

2. Kathleen Coulborn Faller, "Disclosure Failures: Statistics, Characteristics, and Strategies to Address Them," in William T. O'Donohue and Matthew Fanetti (eds.), *Forensic Interviews Regarding Child Sexual Abuse: A Guide to Evidence-Based Practice* (Springfield, MO: Springer, 2016), 127–28.

3. Hammond, Promisel, Shepherd, and Walsh, "Law Enforcement Response to Child Abuse: Portable Guides to Investigating Child Abuse," 3.

4. Brooke Maynard, email message to author, January 17, 2019.

5. Aric W. Dutelle and Ronald F. Becker, *Criminal Investigation*, fifth edition (Burlington, MA, 2019), 3.

6. Steven G. Brandl, *Criminal Investigation*, fourth edition (Thousand Oaks, CA: Sage, 2019), 341.

7. Tiffany Vassar and Brooke Maynard, email message to author, January 4, 2019.

8. Daniel G. Murphy, "Child Abuse: Colleges are Failing to Properly Educate Students in a Criminology/Criminal Justice Curriculum," paper presented at the annual meeting for the

Academy of Criminal Justice, New Orleans, Louisiana, February 13–17, 2018; Debra A. Poole and Michael E. Lamb, *Investigative Interviews of Children: A Guide for Helping Professionals* (Washington, DC: American Psychological Association, 1998), 30.

9. Barbara H. Chaiyachati, Andrea G. Asnes, Rebecca L. Moles, Paula Schaeffer, and John M. Leventhal, "Gray Cases of Child Abuse: Investigation Factors Associated with Uncertainty," *Child Abuse & Neglect* 51 (2016): 91.

10. Michael D. Lyman, *Criminal Investigation*, third edition (New York, NY: Pearson, 2018), 14.

11. Jeffrey McCabe, "Child Welfare Interviews at School: A Review of Statutes and Policies," *Child and Adolescent Social Work Journal* 35, no. 4 (2018): 343–44.

12. Quin M. Chrobak and Maria Zaragoza, "The Misinformation Effect: Past Research and Recent Advances," in Anne M. Ridley, Fiona Gabbert, and David J. La Rooy (eds.), *Suggestibility in Legal Contexts: Psychological Research and Forensic Implications* (Malden, MA: Wiley-Blackwell, 2013), 22.

13. Monica L. McCoy and Stefanie M. Keen, *Child Abuse and Neglect*, second edition (New York, NY: Psychology Press, 2014), 251.

14. Kama London, Lucy A. Henry, Travis Conradt, and Ryan Corser, "Suggestibility and Individual Difference in Typically Developing and Intellectually Disabled Children," in Anne M. Ridley, Fiona Gabbert, and David J. La Rooy (eds.), *Suggestibility in Legal Contexts: Psychological Research and Forensic Implications* (Malden, MA: Wiley-Blackwell, 2013), 138.

15. Stephen Ceci, Amelia Hritz, and Caisa Royer, "Understanding Suggestibility," in William T. O'Donohue and Matthew Fanetti (eds.), *Forensic Interviews Regarding Child Sexual Abuse: A Guide to Evidence-Based Practice* (Springfield, MO: Springer, 2016), 147.

16. Amelia Courtney Hritz, Caisa Elizabeth Royer, Rebecca K. Helm, Kayla A Burd, Karen Ojeda, and Stephen J. Ceci, "Children's Suggestibility Research: Things to Know Before Interviewing a Child," *Anuario de Psicologia Juridicia* 25, no. 1 (2015): 8.

17. McCoy and Keen, *Child Abuse and Neglect*, 253.

18. Samantha Andrews and Michael Lamb, "The Effects of Age and Delay on Responses to Repeated Questions in Forensic Interviews with Children Alleging Sexual Abuse," *Law and Human Behavior* 38, no. 2 (2014): 173–74.

19. Misty C. Duke, Elizabeth R. Uhl, Heather Price, and James M. Wood, "Avoiding Problems in Child Abuse Interviews and Investigations," in William T. O'Donohue and Matthew Fanetti (eds.), *Forensic Interviews Regarding Child Sexual Abuse: A Guide to Evidence-Based Practice* (Springfield, MO: Springer, 2016), 229.

20. Lyman, *Criminal Investigation*, 241.

21. Anne Hungerford, "The Use of Anatomically Detailed Dolls in Forensic Investigations: Developmental Considerations," *Journal of Forensic Psychology Practices* 5, no. 1 (2005): 77.

22. Maggie Bruck, Stephen J. Ceci, Emmett Francouer, and Ashley Renick, "Anatomically Detailed Dolls Do Not Facilitate Preschooler's Reports of a Pediatric Examination Involving Genital Touching," *Journal of Experimental Psychology: Applied* 1, no. 2 (1995): 95.

23. Poole and Lamb, *Investigative Interviews of Children*, 43.

24. Mark Krueger, "Forensic Interviewing and Charging: A Prosecutor's Perspective," in William T. O'Donohue and Matthew Fanetti (eds.), *Forensic Interviews Regarding Child Sexual Abuse: A Guide to Evidence-Based Practice* (Springfield, MO: Springer, 2016), 73.

25. Poole and Lamb, *Investigative Interviews of Children*, 56.

26. Poole and Lamb, *Investigative Interviews of Children*, 160–63.

27. Lucy Berliner and Mary K. Barbieri, "The Testimony of the Child Victim of Sexual Assault," *Journal of Social Issues* 40, no. 2 (1984): 132.

28. Lyman, *Criminal Investigation*, 235; Office of Juvenile Justice Delinquency and Prevention. Accessed January 19, 2019. Available from https://www.ojjdp.gov/pubs/243908.pdf; Douglas E. Abrams, Susan Vivian Mangold, and Sarah H. Ramsey, *Children and the Law: In a Nutshell*, sixth edition (St. Paul, MN, West Academic, 2018), 118.

29. Linda E. Ledray and Diana Faugno, "SANE: Advocate, Forensic Technician, Nurse?" *Journal of Emergency Nursing* 27, no. 1 (2001): 91.

30. Dutelle and Becker, *Criminal Investigation*, 166.

31. Hammond, Promisel, Shepherd, and Walsh, "Law Enforcement Response to Child Abuse: Portable Guides to Investigating Child Abuse," 6–7.

32. Lyman, *Criminal Investigation*, 45.

33. James E. Girard, *Criminalistics: Forensic Science, Crime, and Terrorism*, fourth edition (Burlington, MA: Jones & Bartlett, 2018), 8.

34. Aric W. Dutelle, *An Introduction to Crime Scene Investigation*, third edition (Burlington, MA: Jones & Bartlett, 2017), 191–92.

35. Girard, *Criminalistics*, 80.

36. Dutelle, *An Introduction to Crime Scene Investigation*, 208.

37. Susmita Saxena and Sanjeev Kumar, "Saliva in Forensic Odontology: A Comprehensive Update," *Journal of Oral and Maxillofacial Pathology* 19, no. 2 (2015): 263.

38. Lyman, *Criminal Investigation*, 206.

39. Lyman, *Criminal Investigation*, 206.

40. Eric K. Hanson and Jack Ballantyne, "Highly Specific mRNA Biomarkers for the Identification of Vaginal Secretions in Sexual Assault Investigations," *Science and Justice* 53, no. 1 (2013): 15.

41. Dutelle, *An Introduction to Crime Scene Investigation*, 227.

42. Brandl, *Criminal Investigation*, 433.

43. Dutelle and Becker, *Criminal Investigation*, 322–23.

44. Internet Crimes Against Children, ICAC Task Force Program. Accessed February 24, 2019. Available from https://www.icactaskforce.org/about-us.

45. Chauncey Wilder, email message to author, February 6, 2019.

46. Chauncey Wilder, email message to author, February 6, 2019.

47. U.S. Department of Justice: Human Trafficking Prosecution Unit. Accessed February 8, 2019. Available from https://www.justice.gov/crt/human-trafficking-prosecution-unit-htpu.

48. Federal Bureau of Investigation, "What We Investigate." Accessed February 8, 2019. Available from https://www.fbi.gov/investigate/civil-rights/human-trafficking.

8

False Allegations

◆ ◆ ◆

THE CONCEPT OF FALSE ALLEGATIONS DATES back to biblical times as the ninth commandment states that you shall not bear false witness against thy neighbor. Throughout our history, false allegations have been made against the innocent for a vast array of reasons, including but not limited to vengeance, personal gain, or misunderstanding. Not only do the reasons for accusations vary, but the type of accusation varies as well. Although any false allegation can cause some type of harm to the accused, there are few allegations that can carry the same stigma as that associated with being accused of child abuse. Additionally, this type of allegation can easily be made, but in so many instances, it can be extremely difficult to refute. How does someone who has legitimate access to a child defend the accusation that they inappropriately touched a child? Are adults afraid to be alone with children because of fear of accusations?

There are several organizations, schools, youth sports, scouting, etc., that have implemented policies that discourage adults from being alone with a child as a precautionary measure against false allegations and for the protection of the children. For once an allegation is made that has any potential merit, there is an immediate criminal justice response that can result in a formal investigation. Before an allegation begins, the accused may be already convicted in the "court of public opinion." When an investigation does ensue, the stress and stigma of the investigative process can be detrimental, even if there are no formal charges being brought forward. In some circumstances, charges may be brought forward only to be dropped as the child recants the allegation or the investigator feels there isn't enough evidence to prove the allegation. A mere accusation of child abuse can leave permanent damage to the accused as their reputation will always be in question. It is not uncommon for an employer to dismiss an employee solely on such an accusation because the employer wants to maintain a positive image of their company.

For those who are removed from their job, this will create a financial burden. This monetary strain is enhanced when the accused may have used all their financial resources to prove their innocence, and yet even if they are successful in defending themselves against criminal charges, one's reputation can be tarnished permanently. For those who are wrongly convicted, the repercussions are even more devastating. The concept of being incarcerated for an offense that one did not commit can be detrimental, but the repercussions are dramatically heightened when falsely accused of a sexual offense, especially if the sexual offense is against a child. Those individuals who are incarcerated for a sex crime must be segregated from the rest of the inmate population as the label of being a sex offender carries a stigma even within the inmate community. This form of segregation is administered as an attempt of providing safety among the sex offender population. The possibility of being falsely convicted through a civil proceeding is even higher. Unlike a criminal proceeding, child protection services can bring forth charges and in many cases, their burden of proof is just a preponderance of evidence. The falsely accused may find little comfort in the fact that they cannot be incarcerated with a finding of guilt—a civil proceeding may order the accused to stay away from their own child. Whether it be a criminal complaint or a civil complaint that is issued, an accusation can tear a family apart, not only through the emotional turmoil associated with the allegation, but the claim of abuse can lead to spousal separation and eventually custody battles.

MEASURING FALSE ALLEGATIONS

Many accusations of child maltreatment conclude with a finding of "unsubstantiated" or "unfounded," which doesn't exonerate the accused but merely states that there is insufficient evidence to sustain the allegations. The International Chiefs of Police defined false allegations of sexual assault as:

> The determination that sexual assault is false can be made if the evidence establishes that no crime was committed or attempted. This determination can be made only after a thorough investigation. This should not be confused with an investigation that fails to prove a sexual assault occurred. In that case the investigation would be labeled unsubstantiated. The determination that a report is false must be supported by evidence that the assault did not happen.[1]

Because so many investigations can be found inconclusive, it is difficult to measure the true number of false allegations.[2] A child recanting their allegations may be one of the few methods available to prove a false allegation, although the retraction may be the result of threats and manipulation.[3] With or without an accused individual being completely exonerated, there will always be those who believe that they are guilty nonetheless and will use this belief to spread rumors, labeling that person as an offender, which can ultimately lead to being be shunned by their family and community.

WHY DO ALLEGATIONS OCCUR?

It is important to note that some false allegations are the result of deliberate deception, whereas others are the result of a misunderstanding where a person with good intentions unwittingly makes a false allegation. Whatever the reason for the accusation, victims of false allegations may suffer from psychological distress, which includes symptoms such as shock, excessive fear, angry outbursts, confusion, and anxiety.[4]

DERIVATIVE VICTIM

In addition to all the repercussions associated with being falsely accused, it should be noted that there are derivative victims associated with false allegations. The accused's family may also be ostracized for the sole reason that they are related to the accused. For example, neighbors may no longer allow their child to play with the children of an accused abuser in fear of their child being victimized. And let us not forget the financial challenges, as the one who was accused may have been the primary wage earner and was terminated from their employment based on the accusation. Furthermore, when it is discovered that prior cases of child abuse are deemed false, future cases of actual child abuse may result in disbelief by jurors or investigators as they may have become cynical and do not believe the truthfulness of any child.

CASE STUDY #1 (TEACHER FALSELY ACCUSED)

Jenna was a second-grade student who complained to school authorities that Mr. Tocci had rubbed her vaginal area over her clothing in the classroom while he assisted her with her schoolwork. She alleged that this happened on more than one occasion while class was in session. Jenna stated that she didn't think that any of the other students saw what was happening. The school district put Mr. Tocci on administrative leave until an investigation was conducted. An examination of the classroom room showed that the desk and chairs were in columns and that they were fairly close to one another. The desk and chairs themselves were extremely small to accommodate the small stature of students in that grade level. An attempt was made to place a hand on the top of the chair to simulate touching the child's vaginal area. It was discovered that the investigator almost had to be in the prone position in order to place his hand on the chair because these small desks and chairs were so very low to the ground, making it impossible to discreetly touch a child in that area without bringing substantial attention to the accused. A follow-up interview with Jenna revealed that she saw her mother smile at Mr. Tocci during a parent/teacher conference and thought that her mother was going to leave her father because of what she witnessed. Although she did not recant her allegation, Jenna admitted that she didn't like Mr. Tocci because he was going to "steal her mother." Despite the fact that there were insufficient grounds to allege misconduct with Mr. Tocci, rumors spread rapidly throughout the community and parents demanded that their child not be in his class. Mr. Tocci was forced to resign.

MANDATORY REPORTING LAWS

Today all fifty states of the United States have enacted child victimization reporting statutes mandating the reporting of child maltreatment.[5] Although the states may vary on what defines child maltreatment, the concept of these laws is to require professionals who work with children to report suspected abuse. These professionals are deemed mandatory reporters as they may work with children; it doesn't necessarily indicate they fully comprehend what child abuse entails. They can be guilty of failing to recognize abuse or falsely accusing someone of abuse. There are also barriers to reporting suspected or confirmed cases of child abuse. These barriers include lack of training from professionals in identifying child abuse and understanding the process of reporting alleged abuse.[6] For instance, educators are consistently the primary reporters of suspected child abuse. However, school personnel may not feel comfortable reporting child abuse as they lack knowledge on how to identify it. There were several studies that indicate that educators do not receive adequate training on child abuse during their college education or in-service training. This not only can lead to underreporting but also to overreporting of suspected child abuse.[7] The medical community has been identified as one of the mandated reporter groups that lack training in child abuse and neglect. Studies have shown that there is either insufficient training for medical personnel, including those specializing in pediatrics, or that personnel may be being misinformed about the specific issues relating to child abuse.[8]

In addition to states mandating professionals working with children as reporters, some states will designate "any other person" as a mandated reporter as well, thus requiring laypersons without any training relating to child abuse to report abuse. Although the intent of mandatory reporting laws is to ensure that allegations of abuse are brought to light and the appropriate authorities are informed so that they can investigate the allegations, the laws may create an unanticipated repercussion. Because most states specify in their statutes that there is a penalty for failure to report child abuse even if it only suspected, some reporters may be inclined to convey their suspicion of abuse in fear of facing the consequences of failing to act. A mandated reporter who fails to report child maltreatment can be held criminally liable, resulting in a misdemeanor charge.[9] The laws do not require that the reporter be certain that abuse has actually occurred, but instead lowers the requirement to mere suspicion. Because suspicion is such a low burden to reach, a potential reporter may feel obligated to report to avoid any legal repercussions. In fact, the reporter of abuse will be found immune from liability if the allegation, although false, was made in good faith. Additionally, some states permit victims of abuse to seek tort action against mandated reporters who failed to report cases where there was reasonable suspicion child abuse had occurred.[10]

Overall, the consensus of those working in child protective services is that there is more of a problem of underreporting than that of overreporting.[11] To address the problem of unnecessary reports of abuse, child protective services has a screening process for allegations of abuse. If child protective services feels there are insufficient grounds to conduct an investigation, the case will be screened out, and the accused will not be subject to further inquiry. However, depending on the jurisdiction, the accused's name will nevertheless be placed on file for a designated period of time. Finally, it should be noted that mandated reporters are not exclusively those who may make false allegations. Anyone suspecting abuse can notify the appropriate authorities. This process allows for a greater misunderstanding, and it opens the door to those who choose to make a false allegation out of spite.

WHO MAKES FALSE ALLEGATIONS?

Children

Although most false allegations originate with adults, some are the results of a direct disclosure from the child. A child can make a false allegation based on three factors. (1) The allegation is completely false and none of the alleged events occurred. (2) A child is a victim of abuse, but the child accuses someone rather than the actual perpetrator, which is referred to as *perpetrator substitution*. (3) The child's allegation is only partially true in that some of the events the child describes actually occurred.[12] Although false statements can be categorized under these three factors, the reasons for making false statements are numerous. Some children will make false statements as they are unable to separate fact from fantasy.[13] According to Michael Robin, fantasized incest is more common in preadolescent or adolescent girls who project sexual wishes onto a parent, usually the father or a father substitute. These children with severe ego impairment are more likely to confuse sexual fantasies with reality.[14] When exploring the possibility that younger children are fantasizing, it is not uncommon for an investigator to ask a younger child during an interview if they know the difference between the truth and a lie. In contrast, an older child may make a false allegation as a form of revenge. Overall, children are rarely the source of intentional false allegations.[15]

Factors That May Influence Children in Truth-Telling

Intrapersonal variables and external influences are two factors that might influence whether a child is being truthful.[16] Intrapersonal variables can include developmental sophistication, a child's memory, and the ability of the child to communicate. A child's age certainly is not a definitive analysis of their level of sophistication as the general intelligence or even the "street smarts" vary considerably among children. A brighter child may be more articulate in explaining what happened, thus providing the investigator the appropriate evidence to alleged abuse. However, the more sophisticated a child may be, the more likely that they can use their intelligence to deceive the investigator. A child's ability to provide an account of what occurred is another variable to be considered. No matter how well intentioned a child may be, children differ in their ability to retrieve relevant information. A child may inadvertently provide false information due to their limited ability to properly recall events. Additionally, the child needs to be able to properly communicate what they have recalled. It is not unusual for younger children to resort to physical actions in order to communicate, rather than words to express themselves.[17] Some children can easily convey what has happened to them despite being under stressful circumstances, whereas others are more reticent by nature.[18] External influences can also be a factor regarding a child's recollection. These influences can lead to false allegations through suggestibility or the child may be reluctant to disclose abuse due to fear or inducements. Suggestibility refers to errors that arise when the child is exposed to information that is false or pressures to encourage a particular type of answer.[19] It is the responsibility of the child abuse investigator to examine the possibility of these influences in determining whether child maltreatment indeed occurred.

Parents

Parents can certainly be influential in their child's life through their suggestibility. Unfortunately, this influence can lead to false allegations. The family dynamics can be a factor when alleging abuse. The act of parents separating or seeking divorce can be substantial factors in relation to child maltreatment allegations. For instance, one parent may believe that the other parent has abused their child and file for custody of the child with the intentions of protecting their child from future abuse. Some of these false allegations can originate from misinterpretations or overinterpretations of a young child's comments.[20] But there are those spouses who may deliberately create false allegations due to vengeance, vindictiveness, and hostility over the marital breakup.[21] Still other parents may make false allegations because they are psychologically troubled or there might be a financial incentive.[22] Some may justify making false allegations as they rationalize their behavior believing they are the better parent and the greater good of having custody outweighs their deviant behavior. This concept is addressed in the expansion of the neutralization theory as the offender justifies their act for the sake of necessity.[23] Additionally, one of the tactics to create a false allegation is to attempt to alienate their child from the other parent by using their influence to create the suggestibility of child maltreatment. The alienating parent may verbalize things to their child that place false memories of harm or misinterpret events to create that impression.[24] The child unfortunately may now unwittingly make a false allegation against their parent. Others parents may blatantly make false allegations under the belief that this would be the fastest way to ensure sole custody. The targeted parent may make concessions during a custody battle or may even consider relinquishing custody in response to the stress and fear produced by an investigation of maltreatment.[25] A judge can find themselves in a difficult position when allegations of abuse are made. The decision a judge makes has the potential of either destroying a family when an innocent person is kept from seeing their own child or a child may be returned to a place of abuse if judgment is made from being skeptical of the allegations.

THE INVESTIGATOR

Although there are several professionals that assist in the investigation of a child maltreatment complaint, child protection services and law enforcement are the two primary agencies that are called to intervene. The goals between the two agencies may differ, but they both are in search of the truth and want to determine if the reported abuse actually occurred. There is extensive training available to properly conduct interviews of children who have been reported as abused. However, it is not uncommon for investigators with limited training to conduct such sensitive investigations. For those investigators with extensive training in child abuse investigations and who are responsible for interviewing children, there are still significant factors that can lead to believing false allegations. A properly trained interviewer understands the importance of objectivity; however, training alone may give the investigator a false sense of objective security.[26]

Objectivity is essential in any investigation as bias can cloud the judgment of any investigator, which can be detrimental to the accused. For example, if the interviewer has a preconceived belief that a child would never lie about abuse, they may be more inclined to miss indicators that the abuse did not in fact occur. It is important that the investigator not only tries to corroborate a child's testimony, but every effort should be in an attempt to disprove what a child has said as the ultimate goal is to find the truth. An interviewer's preconceived ideas as to what occurred can also influence the type of questions they ask witnesses.[27]

In addition to the importance of objectivity, it is also possible that law enforcement or child protective services may feel pressured to conclude the investigation as the accused may have been removed from the household or the child had been placed in protective custody since those involved need to be separated until the investigation is completed.

The pressure for a resolution specifically affects child protective services, as the agency has designated timelines when conducting an investigation: "In 28 states, The District of Columbia, Guam, and the Northern Mariana Islands, laws also specify a timeframe for completing the investigation or assessment, generally between 30 and 60 days."[28] Artificial deadlines or actual deadlines to complete an investigation can be conducive to an ineffective investigation and possibly coming to an erroneous conclusion that can be detrimental to the accused or it may place a child in danger. Additionally, it is essential that the investigator doesn't allow the sentiments and the sense of urgency in the child's family, affect the objectivity of their investigation. Although the importance of objectivity can never be overstated, it can be extremely difficult to be unbiased when dealing with something which generates such raw emotion as that of child sexual abuse.[29] To avoid the potential of being prejudiced during an interview, the investigator may repeat some open-ended questions that can be beneficial to ensure clarity and consistency in what the child is reporting. However, if the interviewer persists in asking the same closed ended questions, the child may interpret that as a request for a different answer.[30] This investigative mistake may cause the child to make a false allegation in an attempt to satisfy the investigator.

THE MEDICALIZATION OF CHILD MALTREATMENT

The mid-1940s represents the time period that the medical community's attention was directed toward child maltreatment.[31] Investigators were beginning to rely on the medical community to assist in the diagnosis and treatment in cases of child maltreatment. The advances in medical care have proven essential not only in corroborating evidence to support allegations of abuse, but also as a resource to assist those who have been falsely accused. The medicalization of child maltreatment is categorized through both the mental and physical health of a child. Although the medical community is an essential component in the child maltreatment response, it can in some cases contribute to a false allegation. For many years physicians have testified in criminal and family courts, diagnosing the symptoms or injuries that they have concluded have resulted from deliberate abuse of a child. Such testimony provides a classic example of a scientific hypothesis as medical professionals testify to their opinion on child maltreatment. It has only been in the last few years that the legal, medical, and scientific communities have confronted the question of the strength of the evidence to support the hypothesis.[32]

MENTAL HEALTH PROFESSIONALS

"Many types of mental health professionals may be involved in child maltreatment cases, including psychiatrists, forensic psychiatrists, child psychiatrists, psychiatric nurses, psychiatric social workers, clinical psychologists, child psychologists and/or educational psychologists."[33] As most cases of sexual abuse leave no physical evidence, the various subspecialties in psychology may be asked to provide insight based on behavioral indicators that an alleged victim of child abuse is displaying. There is significant concern from both the general public as well as the legal world in relation to psychological expertise, and this critique is leveled from criticism in the mental health profession itself.[34] Professionals in the field of mental health are rendering opinions of whether some behavioral indicators are consistent with someone who has been abused. Psychological or behavioral indicators of child abuse may include depression, self-destructive behavior, anxiety, posttraumatic stress disorder, acute stress disorder, mood disorders, substance abuse, as well as personality and eating disorders. Although there is significant research to indicate that these symptoms are consistent in victims of child abuse, they may also be the result of something other than abuse as there is disagreement among professionals regarding the effects of child abuse in later development.[35] It should also be noted that many children are assessed months or even years after the abuse occurred. This long time gap makes it challenging to determine if the problems assessed in maltreated children are a result of the abuse or they existed beforehand.[36] In fact, there is significant research that demonstrates a substantial group of child abuse victims do not have any of these symptoms,[37] amplifying the debate among mental health professionals on the effects of child abuse. Finally, it is important to note that a mental health professional is not a finder of fact; rather, they provide an assessment. They can express their opinions or recommendations, weighing data that supports or refutes allegations of maltreatment, but it is beyond their psychological expertise to determine with certainty that child abuse has occurred.[38] The controversy of mental health assessment is highlighted when addressing repressed memory.

REPRESSED MEMORY

Memory is based on sense receptors, and one experiences events through senses, such as hearing, seeing, or touching.[39] The controversy is whether memories can actually be repressed. Psychoanalyst Sigmund Freud (1856–1939) first proposed the theory of repression, which hypothesizes that the mind can reject unpleasant memories by banishing them into the unconscious, thus allowing the victim of a traumatic experience such as child abuse to forget that the maltreatment occurred.[40]

In recent years, psychologists have developed broader, more diverse definitions of repression including lack of conscious memory to a traumatic event or the lack of awareness of appropriate feelings as a result of a traumatic event. The concept of repressed memory is extremely controversial as repression is not clinically observable, but its existence is inferred.[41] Repressing memories of traumatic events concerns a complex system of cognitions and emotions that are mainly limited to a theme or an event such as child abuse.[42] There is a debate within the mental health community as to whether some of these memories are fueled by suggestive therapeutic practices.[43] Research suggests that adults, like children, can be manipulated. Critics of repressed memory argue that therapists may communicate (perhaps inadvertently) by suggesting to their clients that child sexual abuse is very common, which might explain their psychological struggles and that memories are often repressed.[44] A false memory is more likely to occur when an acknowledged expert in trauma treats incest victims almost exclusively.[45] The problem is amplified when both the therapist and the patient believe treatment will not be successful unless traumatic memories are uncovered. Other researchers argue that children cannot ever forget such horrific events, and they dismiss the concept of repressed memory. There are those who believe that abuse victims who have false memories are suffering from a disorder referred to as false memory syndrome.[46] The controversy continues as other professionals in the mental health community argue that there is no such disorder in that it was just a condition created by organizations representing those who have been falsely accused.[47] There is also considerable controversy on how accurate a person's memory can be. Clinical psychology has traditionally viewed memories as perceptions to be processed, evaluated, and healed. Memories may not always be accurate accounts of what actually happened, but we assume our eyewitness accounts are true because that is how we remembered them.[48] No matter how strongly we believe our memory, it still doesn't completely validate that the event occurred. The process of repression and dissociation can occur when one has no way to release emotions and they feel completely helpless and powerless. There may be an extreme fear that those who have experienced trauma may be retraumatized and that the feelings of helplessness will be overwhelming. If someone is subjected to repetitive abuse, this abuse is more likely to be repressed than compared to a one-time incident of child abuse.[49]

CRIMINAL JUSTICE RESPONSE TO REPRESSED MEMORY

Opinions vary as to the legitimacy of repressed memories in the criminal justice system as well. From a legal perspective, the scientific validity of repressed memory is substantial due to the fact that recovered memories may serve as the impetus for an alleged victim's desire to pursue criminal and/or civil charges against the accused abuser.[50] Unfortunately, this legal remedy has created an environment where alleged abusers have been falsely accused.

Child abuse allegations are not the only allegations associated with repressed memory. In 1990, Eileen Franklin-Lipsker became the first person in history to prosecute successfully on the basis of recovered memory. Under hypnosis, she saw herself looking back twenty years and witnessing her father sexually assault and murder a small child.[51] Eileen's testimony was so convincing despite having little other evidence that her father was convicted of murder. This conviction was overturned and not retried due to insufficient evidence. This potential injustice is highlighted with the creation of the False Memory Syndrome Foundation that advocates for victims of false allegations.[52] The criminal justice system has convicted individuals based on the victim's recovered memory,[53] whereas some states are skeptical of recovered memory testimony. For example, the Delaware criminal code states, "No prosecution under this subsection shall be based upon the memory of the victim that has been recovered through psychotherapy unless there is some evidence of the corpus delecti [essence of the crime] independent of such repressed memory."[54] The courts have also addressed repressed memory in civil litigation. Some courts have recognized that trauma can unconsciously repress a victim's memory and allow an alleged victim to file suit through a delayed discovery rule, which is addressed in the statute of limitations.[55] Several states have no statute of limitations when it comes to bringing criminal child abuse complaints forward, allowing cases of claimed repressed memory to be tried.

CONCLUSION

False allegations can have a devastating effect on anyone who is falsely accused, especially with allegations that carry a stigma like child abuse. False allegations can occur out of spite or vengeance, or can be just the result of a misunderstanding. Either way, the repercussions are severe, as the falsely accused can have their reputation tarnished forever. Allegations of abuse may come directly from the child or another family member. Additionally, false allegations can arise from professionals that, although they have specific training in child abuse, allow their emotions to take over their objectivity, resulting in an ineffective investigation to the detriment of the accused. Finally, the controversial disclosure resulting from repressed memory has questioned the validity on whether their memory of abuse is accurate or if it is the result of suggestibility from professionals that are supposed to be objective in their inquiry.

REVIEW QUESTIONS

1. How does medical evidence assist someone who has been falsely accused?

2. How can investigators' bias lead to false allegations?

3. How does the neutralization theory apply to custody battles?

4. Why can't a mental health professional give a definitive diagnosis that a child has been abused?

5. How can mandatory reporting laws lead to false allegations?

KEYWORDS

Repressed memory: The mind can reject unpleasant memories by banishing them into the unconscious, thus allowing the victim of a traumatic experience such as child abuse to forget the maltreatment occurred.

False Memory Syndrome Foundation: Foundation that supports victims of false allegations.

Mandatory reporting laws: Statutes requiring certain individuals to report suspicion of child abuse.

Derivative victim: A victim who is indirectly victimized through another's victimization.

NOTES

1. David Lisak, Lori Gardiner, Sarah C. Nicksa, and Ashley M. Cote, "False Allegations of Sexual Assault: An Analysis of Ten Years of Reported Cases," *Violence Against Women* 16, no. 12 (2010): 1319; Ann Wolbert Burgess, Cheryle Regehr, and Albert R. Roberts, *Victimology: Theories and Applications*, second edition (Burlington, MA: Jones & Bartlett, 2013), 392–93.

2. Bonnie L. Davis Kenaley, "Child Victimization," in Lisa Growette Bostaph and Danielle D. Swerin (eds.), *Victimology: Crime Victimization and Victim Services* (Frederick, MD: Wolters Kluwer, 2017), 255; Debra A. Poole and Michael E. Lamb, *Investigative Interviews of Children: A Guide For Helping Professionals* (Washington, DC: American Psychological Association, 1998), 17.

3. Philip Rumney and Kieran McCartan, "Purported False Allegations of Rape, Child Abuse and Non-Sexual Violence: Nature, Characteristics and Implications," *Journal of Criminal Law* 81, no. 6 (2017): 505.

4. Michael Robin, *Assessing Child Maltreatment Reports: The Problem of False Allegations* (Binghamton, NY: Haworth Press, 1991), 25; Poole and Lamb, *Investigative Interviews of Children*, 19.

5. Kenaley, "Child Victimization," 252; Douglas E. Abrams, Susan Vivian Mangold, and Sarah H. Ramsey, *Children and the Law: In a Nutshell*, sixth edition (St. Paul, MN: West Academic Publishing, 2008), 94.

6. A.M. Pietrantonioa, E. Wright, K.N. Gibson, T. Alldred, D. Jacombson, and A. Niec, "Mandatory Reporting of Child Abuse and Neglect: Crafting a Positive Process for Health Professionals and Caregivers," *Child Abuse & Neglect* 37, no. 2-3 (2013): 104–05.

7. Cynthia Crosson-Tower, *The Role of Educators in Preventing and Responding to Child Abuse and Neglect* (Washington, DC: National Clearinghouse on Child Abuse and Neglect Information, 2003), 9; Maureen C. Kenny. "Training in Reporting of Child Maltreatment:

Where We Are and Where We Need to Go," in Ben Mathew and Donald C. Bross (eds.), *Mandatory Reporting Laws and the Identification of Severe Child Abuse and Neglect* (New York, NY: Springer, 2015), 330; Allison N. Sinanan, "Bridging the Gap of Teacher Education about Child Abuse," *Journal of Educational Foundations* 25, no. 3-4 (2011):60.

8. Kenny, "Training in Reporting of Child Maltreatment," 331.

9. Leah E. Daigle and Lisa R. Muftic, *Victimology* (Thousand Oaks, CA: Sage, 2016), 197.

10. Abrams, Mangold, and Ramsey, *Children and the Law: In a Nutshell*, 99–100.

11. R. Gilbert, A. Kemp, J. Thoburn, P. Sidebotham, L. Radford, D. Glaser, and H.L. MacMillan, "Recognizing and Responding to Child Maltreatment," *Lancet* 373, no. 9658 (2009): 167–80.

12. John C. Yuille, Monica Tymofievich, and Davide Marxsen, "The Nature of Allegations of Child Sexual Abuse," in Tara Ney (ed.), *True and False Allegations of Child Sexual Abuse: Assessment and Case Management* (New York, New York: Brunner/Mazel Inc, 1995), 23.

13. Marcia K. Johnson and Mary A. Foley, "Differentiating Fact from Fantasy: The Reliability of Children's Memory," *Journal of Social Issues* 40, no. 2 (1984): 37; Arlys Norcross McDonald, *Repressed Memories: Can You Trust Them?* (Grand Rapids MI: Flemming H. Revell Publishing, 1995), 103.

14. Robin, *Assessing Child Maltreatment Reports*, 184.

15. N. Trocme and N. Bala, "False Allegations of Abuse and Neglect when Parents Separate," *Child Abuse & Neglect* 29, no. 12 (2005): 1334.

16. Nancy W. Perry, "Children's Comprehension of Truths, Lies, and False Beliefs," in Tara Ney (ed.), *True and False Allegations of Child Sexual Abuse: Assessment and Case Management* (New York, New York: Brunner/Mazel Inc, 1995), 85.

17. Marjorie J. Kostelnik, Anne K. Soderman, Alice Phipps Whiren, and Michelle L. Rupiper, *Guiding Children's Social Development & Learning: Theory and Skills*, ninth edition (Boston, MA: Cengage, 2018), 303.

18. Perry, "Children's Comprehension of Truths, Lies, and False Beliefs," 85.

19. Poole and Lamb, *Investigative Interviews of Children*, 48.

20. Poole and Lamb, *Investigative Interviews of Children*, 19.

21. James N. Bow, Francella A. Quinnell, Mark Zaroff, and Amy Assemany, "Assessment of Sexual Abuse Allegations in Child Custody Cases," *Professional Psychology: Research and Practice* 33, no. 6 (2002): 566; Steven G. Brandl, *Criminal Investigation*. (Thousand Oaks, CA: Sage, 2019), 331.

22. Cindy L. Miller-Perrin and Robin D. Perrin, *Child Maltreatment: An Introduction* (Thousand Oaks, CA: Sage, 2013), 292.

23. Nicole Shoenberger, Alex Heckert, and Druann Heckert, "Techniques of Neutralization Theory and Positive Deviance," *Journal of Deviant Behavior* 33, no. 10 (2012): 774–91; McDonald, *Repressed Memories*, 74.

24. Amy J.L. Baker and Paul R. Fine, *Surviving Parental Alienation: A Journey of Hope and Healing* (Lanham, MD: Rowman & Littlefield, 2014), 10.

25. Baker and Fine, *Surviving Parental Alienation*, 10.

26. Tara Ney, *True and False Allegations of Child Sexual Abuse: Assessment and Case Management* (New York, NY: Brunner/Mazel Publishers, 1995), 9.

27. L. Shapiro and M. Helen-Maras, *Multidisciplinary Investigation of Child Maltreatment* (Burlington, MA: Jones & Bartlett, 2016), 221.

28. Making and Screening Reports of Child Abuse and Neglect. Child Welfare Information Gateway. Available from https://www.childwelfare.gov/pubPDFs/repproc.pdf.

29. Dianne L. Martin, "Lessons About Justice from the Laboratory of Wrongful convictions: Tunnel Vision, the Construction of Guilt and Informer Evidence," *UMKC Law Review* 70, no. 2 (2002): 848; Robin, *Assessing Child Maltreatment Reports*, 96.

30. Michael Siegal, Lorraine J. Waters, and Leigh S. Dinwiddy, "Misleading Children: Casual Attribution for Inconsistency Under Repeated Questioning," *Journal of Experimental Child Psychology* 45, no. 3 (1988): 454.

31. Clifford K. Dorne, *Child Maltreatment: A Primer in History, Public Policy and Research*, second edition (Albany, NY: Harrow and Heston, 2001), 33.

32. Anna Kirkland, David Moran, and Angela K. Perone, "Child Abuse Evidence: New Perspectives from Law, Medicine, Psychology & Statistics: Introduction," *University of Michigan Journal of Law Reform* 50, no. 3 (2017): 669.

33. Dorne, *Child Maltreatment*, 46.

34. Gary B. Melton, John Petrila, Norman G. Poythress, Christopher Slobogin, Randy K. Otto, Douglass Mossman, and Lois O. Condie, *Psychological Evaluations for the Courts: A Handbook for Mental Health Professionals and Lawyers*, fourth edition (New York, NY: Guilford Press, 2018), 4.

35. Monica L. McCoy and Stefanie M. Keen, *Child Abuse & Neglect*, second edition (New York, NY: Psychological Press, 2014), 181.

36. Stephen Meyer, *Child Abuse and Domestic Violence: Information Plus* (Farmington Hills, MI: Cengage, 2017), 53.

37. McCoy and Keen, *Child Abuse & Neglect*, 187.

38. Jennifer Wheeler, "Psychological Assessment of the Child and the Family," in J. Bart Klika and Jon R. Conte (eds.), *The APSAC Handbook on Child Maltreatment*, fourth edition (Thousand Oaks, CA: Sage, 2018), 166.

39. McDonald, *Repressed Memories*, 43–44.

40. Meyer, *Child Abuse and Domestic Violence*, 91; Lenore Terr, *Unchained Memories: True Stories of Traumatic Memories, Lost and Found* (New York, NY: Harper Collins Publishing, 1994), 6.

41. Barbara L. Coleman, Michael J. Stevens, and Glenn D. Reeder, "What Makes Recovered-Memory Testimony Compelling to Jurors?" *Law and Human Behavior* 25, no. 4 (2001): 319; McDonald, *Repressed Memories*, 54.

42. Bert Garssen, "Repression: Finding Our Way in the Maze of Concepts," *Journal of Behavioral Medicine* 30, no. 6 (2007): 476.

43. Lawrence Patihis, Lavina Y. Ho, Ian Tingen, Scott O. Lilienfeld, and Elizabeth F. Loftus, "Are the 'Memory Wars' Over? A Scientific-Practitioner Gap in Beliefs about Repressed Memory," *Psychological Science* 25, no. 2 (2014): 519; Terr, *Unchained Memories*, 160.

44. Miller-Perrin and Perrin, *Child Maltreatment: An Introduction*, 301.

45. Terr, *Unchained Memories*, 160.

46. Miller-Perrin and Perrin, *Child Maltreatment: An Introduction*, p.294

47. Terr, *Unchained Memories*, 164.

48. McDonald, *Repressed Memories* p.19

49. McDonald, *Repressed Memories* p.33

50. Meyer, *Child Abuse and Domestic Violence*, 91.

51. James R. Kincaid, *Erotic Innocence: The Culture of Child Molesting* (Durham, NC: Duke University Press, 1998), 253.

52. Miller-Perrin and Perrin, *Child Maltreatment: An Introduction*, 194.

53. McCoy and Keen, *Child Abuse & Neglect*, 179.

54. Meyer, *Child Abuse and Domestic Violence*, 92.

55. Alan R. Kemp, *Abuse in Society: An Introduction* (Long Grove, IL: Waveland Press, 2017), 237.

9

Medical Mimickers

◆ ◆ ◆

MEDICAL MIMICKERS OF CHILD ABUSE

PROVIDERS HAVE AN ETHICAL AND LEGAL responsibility to recognize and report suspected child abuse. While this sounds like a simple responsibility, it is not. In the medical arena, presentation is not always clear when evaluating patients. What may appear initially as abuse may actually be a medical situation. While an investigation may be occurring, the provider is actively taking care of the patient and trying to determine if they are being abused or if there a medical mimicker that makes it appear that way. Differentiating these conditions may be challenging and the provider will need to be aware of alternate diseases and processes and be willing to consider alternative diagnoses. This chapter is going to specifically discuss medical mimickers of child physical abuse and medical mimickers of child sexual abuse that may challenge the provider in trying to determine a medical condition versus an abusive situation. This chapter will not be able to cover all of the possible medical mimickers, nor does it rule out abuse because a mimicker is present. When evaluating children and attempting to rule in or out the possibility of abuse, it is important to have an explanation of the injury, to note the location of that injury, chart the growth and developmental level of the child, obtain a thorough medical and family history, and complete a head-to-toe assessment. A full examination also includes diagnostic indicators to help determine if the suspicious finding is actually a medical mimicker.

MEDICAL MIMICKERS OF CHILD PHYSICAL ABUSE

Allergic Contact Dermatitis

Contact dermatitis reactions occur from an exposure to some external agent that reacts with the skin. External agents can range from a vast array of exposures such as cosmetics, hair products, sunscreen, and medications. Exposures could also occur from close contact with someone else, such as a caregiver, that causes a reaction. The severity of the reaction depends on the chemical agent, the duration of the exposure, and the susceptibility of the person to that agent.

Contact dermatitis has two major types of reactions:

1. Irritant contact dermatitis: Damage to the skin from an exposure to an agent that causes a reaction that occurs faster than the skin can repair. No prior sensitization to the exposure agent is necessary.
2. Allergic contact dermatitis: A delayed hypersensitivity that occurs from an exposure to an allergen. Allergic contact dermatitis occurs to those previously sensitized to the allergen.

Itching is the primary complaint of allergic contact dermatitis. The patient may also experience burning, stinging, and pain. Further reactions can appear, such as a well-circumscribed lesion that is erythematous. These reactions can appear patternlike or with a linear distribution, and may create lesions that simulate blisters from burns, thereby causing the provider to incorrectly diagnosis as an abusive injury.[1]

Anorexia Nervosa

Anorexia nervosa is a potentially life-threatening disorder that has historically been recognized as occurring predominately in adolescents. We are in the age of being thin as being in, and self-esteem issues and altered body image have become more notable in the younger population as well, causing a rise in this disease process in prepubescent children. This a serious disease process that can lead to major medical complications and/or death if recognition and intervention is not successfully implemented. In addition to being a major medical issue, psychological issues also need to be considered. Anorexia nervosa is classified in the fifth version of the *Diagnostic and Statistical Manual of Mental Disorders*.

The literal definition of anorexia nervosa is a neurotic loss of appetite. Those with anorexia nervosa have a fear of gaining weight. Multiple ways to prevent weight gain can include behaviors such as food restriction, binge eating/purging, overuse of diet pills or laxatives, and overexercising. There are children/adolescents that are anorexic and those that develop atypical anorexia nervosa. There are several differences between the two, but with anorexia nervosa, the child appears malnourished; with atypical anorexia nervosa, the child may be of normal weight or even overweight. In atypical anorexic nervosa, although not as evident externally, the child is also malnourished due to the amount of weight loss that occurs in a small amount of time which the body is unable to compensate for. The question is why would this be a medical mimicker?

When evaluating a child/adolescent that has anorexia nervosa, the child may appear as a failure to thrive. Why does the child appear malnourished? Is it because this child has been chosen by the family as the outcast, like the child that was locked in her closet and starved and abused by her mother, father, grandmother, and siblings? Or does this child have a medical and/or psychological reason for being malnourished?

There is still a great debate on what body weight a child should be classified as having anorexia nervosa. The current *International Statistical Classification of Diseases and Related Health Problems–10* guideline for diagnosing anorexia nervosa in a child or adolescent is "a body weight of at least 15% below the expected body weight for age and height."[2] The major cause of medical complications for anorexia nervosa is the imbalance between energy intake and requirements, which leads to a hypometabolic state. The body slows down to try to compensate for the lack of fuel supply. Some common medical complications are bradycardia, orthostatic hypotension, and increased vagal tone. When purging behaviors are also present, as seen with atypical anorexia nervosa, the child/adolescent may develop electrolyte imbalances such as hypokalemic hypochloremic metabolic alkalosis. Hyponatremia may also develop if large amounts of water intake are consumed with the intent of curbing hunger or trying to falsify the low body weight when having to weigh in.[3]

Another complication that can raise suspicion for abuse is the fracture risk. A symptom that commonly presents is amenorrhea. Amenorrhea occurs due to the body attempting to conserve energy, resulting in central hypothalamic suppression, causing hypogonadotropic hypogonadism, with decreased luteinizing hormone, follicle-stimulating hormone, and estradiol. The decrease in estrogen predisposes that teen to osteopenia and osteoporosis.[4] Bone mass acquisition peaks during adolescence. If the adolescent develops amenorrhea and is deficient in the production of the bone mass, premature fracturing of bones may result.

When a child/adolescent presents with what appears to be anorexic nervosa, the provider will need to get a good history from both the child and the caregivers. To complicate this diagnosis more is the question of what precipitated the anorexic behaviors. Did the child develop an eating disorder from watching the caregiver's diet? Are the caregivers obese and have co-morbidities that caused the child to become fearful and develop an eating disorder? Several studies have been conducted to evaluate if a precipitating factor could actually be abuse. Carter, Blackmore, and Woodside evaluated seventy-seven patients that were admitted with anorexia nervosa and discovered that 48 percent of those patients reported a history of being sexually abused as a child.[5] Another study conducted by Racine and Wildes evaluated 188 patients that were either receiving in-patient treatment or day hospital treatment for anorexia nervosa. In this study, the authors concluded that child emotional abuse was prevalent in the history of the patients being treated for eating disorders.[6]

Treatment

Diagnostic screening should include:

1. Complete blood count
2. Comprehensive metabolic panel
3. Urine analysis (to assess for dehydration of water loading)
4. Stool guaiac (assess for inflammatory bowel disease or abuse laxatives/enemas)

5. Urine pregnancy test
6. Electrocardiogram (potential arrhythmias that may develop)
7. Mental health evaluation.

Additional labs to consider include those that will assess nutritional status such as albumin, pre-albumin, and transferrin. If the patient has amenorrhea, evaluate luteinizing hormone, follicle-stimulating hormone, estradiol, and pro-lactin.[7]

Screening for child physical, emotional, and sexual abuse should be considered.

Car Seat Burns

There is little research that has been conducted on car seat burns in infants. On a hot, sunny day, the interior of a car can heat up to one hundred degrees Celsius, which means the metal parts of the car seat as well as the plastic on a car seat will also get hot. When a child is placed in the car seat and buckled in, the child has limited range of motion to move away from the hot components of the car seat and can sustain a burn.

If a child is brought in with burns and no history is given except riding in a car, it is helpful if the car seat can be brought into the facility. The provider or investigator can then compare the exposed parts of the car seat to the injury identified to see if the burn is consistent with the portion of the car seat that would have had an extreme rise in temperature.

Coining

Coining is a Southeast Asian folk remedy. I (A. Rasmussen) have also seen this cultural practice in the Native American population. The purpose of coining is believed to rid the body of the "bad winds" that cause fever, seizures, chills, headaches, cough, vomiting, etc. The terminology is different based on geography. The Vietnamese refer to the coining process as *cao gio* or "scratch the wind." The Chinese say *cheut sah* or *quat sha* if a spoon is used. The symptomatic area is massaged with a medicated oil, then rubbed in a linear fashion with the edge of a coin or other object. The area is rubbed until ecchymosis develops. Once the ecchymosis has resolved, the child may continue to have hyperpigmented areas on the skin.[8]

Some believe that the practice of coining increases circulation and body warmth, stimulating trigger points and increasing the rate of respiration.[9] Coining is typically not painful and may even be considered pleasant.

Cupping

Cupping is a folk remedy that was used in ancient cultures. In the United States, it has been talked about in child abuse trainings as to what may appear as abuse but really is a cultural practice. The belief is that cupping will provide relief for pain, fever, poor appetite, and congestion. For many years this has been discussed but not seen that often. The placement of the cups depends on the symptoms that are being treated. Successful cupping occurs by creating a vacuum in the cup. In ancient cultures this was most classically completed by saturating a cotton ball with alcohol, placing it on a stick, and then putting the cotton ball in a glass cupping jar to burn oxygen, which created the vacuum. The cotton ball is then removed from the cup and the cup is placed immediately on the skin. The vacuum in the cup draws up the skin, creating what could be mistaken for a burn. This is considered dry cupping.[10] In 2016, this all changed with Michael Phelps in the Summer Olympics. Michael Phelps came out to the swimming competition with circular red to purple bruises for the whole world to see. Now athletes are using this practice to help loosen the muscles and relieve pain. It no longer is something you see only in other cultures such as Russian immigrants, Asian cultures, and Mexican American cultures. The cupping method has also evolved. Heat is not the main source of cupping; air pumps can now be used to suction the skin into the cup. This process only lasts a few minutes but causes the capillaries that lie just beneath the skin

Air pump used for cupping. Note the suction within the cup, pulling the skin into the cup.

to break leaving circular bruises. If you don't recognize this practice, it can easily be mistaken for abuse.

In wet cupping, small cut marks are made in the skin, which produces bleeding. This process is referred to as scarification.[11]

Cutting

Self-harming behaviors are considered deliberate destruction of body tissue without conscious suicidal intent. Self-harming behaviors are most often seen from cutting or carving on the body, which is what will be discussed here. Other forms of self-harm may include burning, biting, pulling out hair, and picking at the skin, including scratching and picking scabs. The self-harming behavior of cutting is most prevalent in the adolescent population, with the age of onset typically ranging from twelve to fourteen years of age.[12] Self-harming behaviors have increased by 150 percent over the past twenty years.

Cutting behaviors are when superficial cuts are made to the body in an attempt to reduce emotional pain and/or cope with overwhelming emotions. Cutting is typically on the arms, but it may be seen in other areas of the body such as the legs or abdomen. Cutting is not usually due to suicidal ideation but is used as a coping mechanism. It is believed that the reason for the onset of cutting behaviors is due to previous physical, sexual, or emotional harm either to the child that has started the cutting behaviors or has been witnessed by that child.

Typically, the injuries will just need wound cleaning and antibiotic ointment; treatment will depend on the severity of the injury. Suicidal ideation should be addressed, and mental health counseling instituted to help the child identify additional coping mechanisms.

Eczema

Atopic dermatitis, commonly known as eczema, is a chronic, relapsing skin condition that effects about 10 to 20 percent of children in developed countries. Eczema will typically appear within the first year of life. There is a strong genetic component, but it is believed that environmental factors can also influence the condition. In healthy skin, the stratum corneum (the outer layer of the epidermis) provides a strong barrier that controls transepidermal water loss and stops the influx of allergens and irritants. In eczema, the structural integrity of the stratum corneum is altered, causing a skin barrier breakdown.[13]

Eczema is an inflammatory reaction of the skin. Irritation from soaps, fabrics, overheating at night, contact with water, and contact with dust are just some of the environmental irritants that could be responsible for a flare up. The most common complaint with eczema is itching. The itching can be so bad that it will affect the sleep of the child as well as the caregiver. As the child scratches, it stimulates the production of cytokine which causes more itching and can further erode the skin barrier, allowing for the introduction of infection. A universal characteristic of eczema is dry skin with fine scaling and roughness on palpation.[14] Lesions can be acute and subacute; there is also a chronic component to this condition. The acute and subacute lesions are characterized by erythematous papules and vesicles with excoriations and serous exudate. Chronic lesions have lichenified plaques and papules with excoriations. The areas can be cracked, oozing, and/or bleeding. To identify the amount of area affected, the provider can use the rule of nines. Three classic stages are noted with eczema: infantile, childhood, and adulthood.[15]

Infantile eczema usually will become symptomatic around three months of life. The pattern for infantile eczema is to affect the face and the scalp first and then spread to the extensor surfaces of the limbs and trunk in symmetrical distribution. By the age of two to three years old, the pattern of distribution changes. During the toddler years, lesions primarily are seen at the flexor sites such as the wrists, antecubital fossae, popliteal fossae, and anterior ankles. By the time the child reaches puberty, the distribution involves the face, hands, back, wrists, and dorsal feet.[16]

Caring for children with eczema can be time-consuming for the caregiver and uncomfortable for the child. This can make it easy for families to not adhere to the treatment regimen, which is the main cause of failure in treating this condition. When a child presents especially during a flare up, a history is important to obtain. Some information that should be gathered includes the following:

1. Time of the onset, pattern, and severity
2. Response to previous and current therapies
3. Possible trigger factors: irritants (soaps, detergents, shampoos) or allergens (pets, dust)
4. Food allergies
5. Growth and development

6. Personal and family history of atopic diseases
7. Impact of eczema on the caregivers.[17]

Diagnosis is based on clinical signs and symptoms. There is no definitive diagnostic test or lab study to identify eczema. There is no cure for eczema, so treatment is based on symptoms during the flare up and prophylactic care to try and increase the amount of time between flare ups. Emollients should be used to help maintain moisture to the skin; emollients should be used even when the skin is clear. Topical corticosteroids are used for anti-inflammatory, antiproliferative, immunosuppressive, and vasoconstrive properties. Topical corticosteroids come in various potencies and should be used in accordance with the severity of the eczema flare up.

Some adjunct therapies that are recommended are as follows:

1. Use an occlusive bandage. The occlusive bandage will improve skin hydration for the child.
2. Wrap the limbs in wet to dry bandages. This process improves hydration, prevents excoriation, and soothes the itching for the child.
3. Bleach baths: Dilute 150 milliliters of bleach in ten centimeters of water in an adult bathtub, or use two milliliters of bleach for every one liter of water in a baby tub. This has been shown to reduce the rates of secondary infections. Soak up to ten minutes two to three times a week.
4. Phototherapy: This is useful for children with widespread eczema that is resistant to conventional treatment. Ultraviolet B radiation provides an immunosuppressive effect to the skin. Patients can attend three times a week for treatment lasting between thirty seconds to ten minutes.[18]

Why is this considered a medical mimicker? The skin lesions can be difficult to manage and can be widespread over the child. At this point, the medical providers and investigative team would have to consider if this a medical issue or is the caregiver negligent, or both?

CASE STUDY #1

A three-year-old male arrives to the emergency department. The child is covered from head to toe with eczema. The child was scratching all over; his face was expressionless, as he stared blankly at the caregivers. The child was in so much pain, he was unable to move on his own and the nursing staff had to physically help him to change positions. The nursing staff helped, because his mother did not stay by his side; she went to the waiting room and left the child alone. When the mother was notified that social services was contacted, she turned to her friend and said, "I told you I should have just let him die at home." This child's eczema was so out of control, he was admitted to the hospital for treatment, including pain management. The child ultimately had to be transferred to a burn unit and be treated as if he was a burn patient.

While this is a medical issue, this case study also shows how medical mimickers can also have a child physical or neglect component. While the provider is busy caring for the child, it may be necessary to conduct a simultaneous investigation.

Ehlers-Danlos/Hypermobility Syndrome

Ehlers-Danlos syndrome (EDS) is a hereditary, connective tissue disorder that is characterized by hypermobile joints and fragile skin. EDS affects collagen synthesis and structure, which can lead to extensive cutaneous injury. There are twelve subtypes of EDS, but classic EDS is known as EDS 1 and 2, which commonly affect the joints and the skin. EDS affects about one in five thousand people, and its symptoms can easily be mistaken for child abuse.

Clinical manifestations of EDS are:

1. Smooth lax (hyperextensibility) skin
2. Fragile skin: minor trauma can cause gaping wounds ("fishmouth" wounds) that will leave cigarette paper-like scars
3. Poor wound healing
4. Hypermobility of joints.

The skin is noted to tear easily and may have prolonged bleeding even with normal coagulation studies. Recurrent bruising to the same areas is common, causing a characteristic brownish discoloration to the skin. Diagnosis can be made in the majority of the cases with an accurate family history and clinical examination.[19,20]

Hair Tourniquets

Hair tourniquets are also referred to as ischemic hair syndrome and toe tourniquet syndrome. This it typically accidental; however, non-accidental trauma needs to be considered. A hair or fiber encircles the appendage of an infant, typically younger than six months old. The hair or fiber could affect fingers, toes, penis, female genitalia, and even the neck.

An average person loses fifty to one hundred strands of hair per day. Childbirth puts stress on a woman and can cause an increase in the loss of hair averaging more than one hundred strands of hair per day for up to six months after delivery; peak hair loss is after two months. This condition is called telogen effluvium.[21] The hairs that fall out can wrap around an appendage without the caregiver realizing that this has occurred. Fibers from clothing can also encircle appendages without being noticed, causing unintentional tourniquets to develop.

The classic symptom is irritability in the child. Without a thorough head-to-toe assessment, the reason for the irritability could be missed and the child released home. The appendage will become edematous and red. The fibers tend to be thin and can easily be overlooked or unable to view due to the swelling. If the fiber can be seen, it needs to be removed immediately with careful consideration that the fiber does not break and remain in the wound. This fiber can cause lacerations and the appendage can become ischemic and gangrenous if not treated promptly. If the causative agent is embedded and unable to be viewed, the child may need to have it explored and removed surgically. Once the fiber is removed, the child experiences immediate pain relief. Treatment specific to the wound would need to be considered.

Hemangiomas

Hemangiomas are a non-malignant growth of vascular endothelial cells that are present on the skin and other organ systems. Hemangiomas can be mistaken for bruising due to their red-purple discoloration. Congenital hemangiomas are present at birth, and infantile hemangiomas develop later in infancy.[22]

Hemangiomas normally do not require treatment; however, treatment depends on the location. Many hemangiomas develop on the face and may cause complications and/or need for cosmetic intervention. Providers should document these areas when they are noticed so that if it reported as a possible child abuse, medical records will reveal the history and help rule out the complaint.

Hemophilia

Hemophilia is a rare genetic (X-linked) bleeding disorder caused by a lack of specific clotting factors in the blood. There are two forms of hemophilia: hemophilia A, which is a deficiency in clotting factor VIII, and hemophilia B, which is a deficiency in clotting factor IX.[23] Hemophilia A is the most common disorder and is seen in about one in five thousand male births. Hemophilia B is seen in about one in thirty thousand male births.

Pediatric patients that present to their health care provider will have excessive bruising and bleeding, which may be misdiagnosed as child abuse. Bleeding in patients with a history of hemophilia can occur in the joints, muscle, soft tissue, and mucous membranes. In males, the first sign of hemophilia can occur during circumcision. It is important to get a thorough medical and family history when assessing these patients. Lab values will be significant for a prolonged partial thromboplastin time. The current treatment for hemophilia is to give recombinant formulations of FVIII and FIX.

CASE STUDY #2

A ten-year-old male was reported by a neighbor being seen on the front porch being poked with a broomstick handle by his grandmother. This child has a documented history of hemophilia. On evaluation, the child had circular bruises over his chest, abdomen, and back that were consistent with the size of a broom handle. In talking to the child, he stated that he liked to sleep with his "quarters" and kept them in his bed. It was later determined that the bruises were caused by the pressure of the coins when he slept on them.

Ink Stains

Ink, food coloring, dyes from clothing, and paints can absorb into the skin, appearing like a bruise. Forensic nurses may be notified by social services on numerous occasions to evaluate a bruise on a child. When evaluating the area that is concerning for a bruise, it can appear to have many times a bluish discoloration, but the area is not tender to palpation to the child. The child does not typically disclose a traumatic event that would have caused the bruise. A careful history should be obtained so as to not overlook any details that would be concerning for abuse. Soap and warm water to clean the area will allow the discoloration to disappear. Some stains will not be removed with soap and water, but alcohol has proven to be effective in removing these stains.

Laxative-Induced Dermatitis

Due to concerns of cancer, the composition of oral over-the-counter laxatives changed from phenolphthalein to senna in 1999. Laxative-induced dermatitis is a fairly new phenomenon related to the ingredient senna. Over-the-counter laxatives such as Ex-Lax contain chocolate squares wrapped in foil, which is very tempting to children. As of research today, the encounters of laxative-induced dermatitis have all been from accidental overdosing except for one.[24]

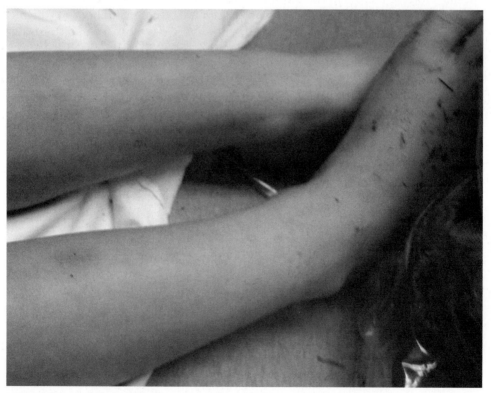

Ink stain from a blue marker.

When children are exposed the laxatives, diarrhea develops. If diapers or pull-ups are on the child, it exacerbates the situation by containing the stool next to the skin. Children present with what initially appears like first- and second-degree scald burns to the buttocks. Research is still evolving in trying to decipher the cause. It has been noted that prior exposure to senna without a reaction does not cancel out the risk of reacting after another exposure. The length of exposure is unknown. The mechanism of skin breakdown remains unknown; a hypothesis is the irritant effect of the digestive enzymes within the stool serve as an irritant to the skin along with senna being an irritant.[25]

Characteristics of laxative-induced dermatitis include a diamond-shaped lesion on the buttocks with linear borders that align with the diaper line. Sparing of the perianal tissue and gluteal cleft is also noted as a common characteristic.[26]

Menkes Disease

Menkes disease is a potentially fatal x-linked recessive neurodegenerative disorder of copper transport gene caused by the mutation of ATP7A. Early detection is crucial for treatment to enhance the chance of survival. Menkes effects about one in one hundred thousand births. The challenge to early detection is that the infant has normal development for the first two to three months after birth. After the initial few months, the child will begin to show signs of failure to thrive, developmental delays, hypothermia, hypotonia, and seizures.[27]

Characteristic features include the following:

1. Pudgy cheeks
2. Cupid's bow of the upper lip
3. Sparse kinky hair
4. Horizontal eyebrows
5. Lax skin and joints
6. Wormian bones
7. Inguinal hernias
8. Diverticula of bladder and ureters.

The first presentation to a medical provider may be seizures. On imaging of the head, subdural hemorrhages are noted; child abuse is suspected. Additional findings of this disease process that can mimic child abuse are rib fractures, metaphyseal spurs on the long bones, and c-spine deformities. Retinal hemorrhages, however, are not correlated with Menkes disease. Bony deformities with Menkes are caused from low bone mineral density. X-rays need to be read by a pediatric radiologist to help comprehend the findings from diagnostic testing.

Early detection is key. Testing can be completed by microscopically examining scalp hairs for the characteristic pili torti (short, brittle, twisted hair). Once the child has been diagnosed with Menkes disease, subcutaneous injections of copper-histidine may improve long-term outcomes.[28]

Mongolian Spots

Mongolian spots are a form of congenital dermal melanocytotis, a pigmented area of the skin. Mongolian spots are the most common form of birthmarks in children. Children are born with this hyperpigmentation, or it can develop within the first few weeks of life. As the child ages, the hyperpigmented tissue fades; by early childhood, it has usually completely disappeared. Mongolian spots are more prevalent in children of Polynesian, Indonesian, East Asian, and African origin. The most common area for Mongolian spots to appear is the lumbosacral area and the buttocks; however, it can be seen anywhere on the body.

Mongolian spots are non-tender to the touch. Mongolian spots are non-blanchable and have a blue/grey appearance. These spots can be easily mistaken for bruises and start a child abuse investigation. Most Mongolian spots do not need any action from the provider except for documentation. It is important to have these areas documented in the medical record from the time of appearance to prevent undue trauma to the family from having to go through a child abuse investigation. If this has not been completed or the child has been sent to have these areas documented for possible abuse, have the caregiver return for a recheck in two weeks. In this time, if these areas are bruises, they will have healed; if it is hyperpigmentation to the skin, the area will remain unchanged. At that point, make sure to document the findings in the medical record.

Osteogenesis Imperfecta

Imagine a two-year-old, running down the hall in their house, falls and begins to cry, complaining of leg pain. On evaluation, a right leg x-ray reveals a femur fracture. Concerns are raised for child abuse because the mechanism does not account for the injury. A skeletal survey is completed and multiple fractures in various stages of healing are noted. The caregivers deny any previous trauma. An investigation ensues as the medical staff are trying to find out if other causes could be responsible for the fractures. This is a story given the forensic nurse by an emergency department physician. The child has a history of osteogenesis imperfecta (OI); however, the family also has a history of physically and sexually abusing their children. It can be difficult to rule out medical versus abuse sometimes.

OI is a rare heritable connective tissue disorder characterized by varying degrees of bone mass that can cause an increase in the risk of fractures and can lead to substantial growth deficiency. This disorder is often referred to as "brittle bone disease." Approximately 90 percent of cases can be linked to defects in the COLIA 1 and COLIA 2 genes,[29] which are two genes that code for proteins.

OI has both clinical and radiographic findings. Depending on the age and severity of OI, skeletal features may be associated. Some features that may be seen with OI include:

1. Macrocephaly (overly large head)
2. Flat midface and triangular facies (due to underdevelopment of facial bones)

3. Dentinogenesis imperfecta (teeth may appear translucent, blue, or amber in color)
4. Chest wall deformities (pectus excavatum or carinatum)
5. Barrel chest
6. Scoliosis (80 percent of the time)
7. Kyphosis
8. Short stature
9. Wormian bones.

Other clinical indicators include:

1. Blue or grey sclerae
2. Hearing loss
3. Decreased pulmonary function
4. Cardiac valvular regurgitation
5. Joint instability.

Clinical manifestations vary based on the type of OI the person has.

- *Type 1:* Most common form of OI. There is minimal amount of bone fragility, and stature may be normal. Fractures occur more often, once the child begins to ambulate. Typical fractures seen with this form of OI include long bones, ribs, and hands and feet. Fractures heal at a normal rate. Blue sclerae are commonly seen. During periods of rapid growth such as puberty, vertebral compression fractures may occur.[30]
- *Type II:* Type II is a lethal form of OI that is associated as occurring in utero or early infancy. Children with type II have blue or grey sclerae and broad bones with decreased bone density. Pulmonary failure as a result of multiple rib fractures is the most common cause of mortality with this type of OI. Other causes of death to note with type II OI are related to central nervous system malfunctions as well as hemorrhages.[31]
- *Type III:* Type III OI is a severe form of OI that children may survive. Type III has many of the "typical" clinical manifestations such as the blue sclerae, dentinogenesis imperfecta, triangular facies, and short stature. These children have a difficult time with having multiple fractures at birth and the development of long bone fractures. By the time the children reach adulthood, they usually will require the use of a wheelchair. Respiratory complications are the major cause of mortality in type III OI.[32]
- *Type IV:* Type IV OI can be hard to distinguish between medical condition versus child abuse. These children do not always present with the clinical manifestations as seen in the other types of OI; they can range from mildly symptomatic to complicated. Classic symptoms such as blue sclerae are rare. At the time the child presents with their fracture for the first time, radiographs may be normal. The one sign that is common to see in type IV OI is translucent teeth, but if a child presents prior to eruption of teeth, this sign will not be obvious. In the other types of OI, there may

be a family history; type IV OI can have spontaneous mutations, so there will be no family history.[33]

- *Type V:* Type V OI has an autosomal development inheritance pattern. Blue sclerae and dentinogenesis imperfecta is not common. The classic sign for Type V is callus formation. When patients with type V OI fracture a bone, the soft tissue around the area will be firm and warm to palpation and often viewed as part of the inflammatory process or a malignancy. With repeated fractures of the same area, especially to bones such as the radius and ulna, limitation of movement may develop due to the callus formation. Repeated fractures to the radius and ulna cause patients to have a decreased ability to place the arm in a pronation or supination position. DNA and protein screening of type 1 collagen is negative.[34]

- *Type VI:* Type VI OI is an autosomal recessive form that has moderate to severe bony deformity and fragility. DNA and protein screening of type 1 collagen is negative. Bone biopsy is the only form of diagnosis that will reveal a mineralization defect within the bony matrix. Clinically, these patients will not usually have the blue sclerae or dentinogenesis imperfecta. The patients are noted to have an excessive osteoid accumulation even though calcium and phosphate metabolism is normal.[35]

- *Type VII:* Type VII OI is inherited through autosomal recessive mode. Type VII has moderate to severe bony deformities and will usually present in infancy through rhizomelia (shortened limbs) and coxa vara.[36]

Testing for OI includes the following:

1. Skeletal survey to identify all the fractures
2. Basic bone biochemistry to rule out possible defects in bone mineralization
3. Bone biopsy
4. Screening for mutations in COLIA 1 and COLIA 2 (for unusual or difficult cases).

When trying to distinguish between OI and non-accidental trauma, first identify the outward clinical signs. Does the child present with blue sclerae and/or dentinogenesis imperfecta? With the genetic ties with this disease, also pay close attention to the family member to identify if they are presenting with clinical signs that may indicate bone fragility. Identify if the family has a history of hypermobility of the joints, which can also be a sign of OI. What are the fractures that the child presents with? Typically, OI fractures occur to the long bones. Classical metaphyseal lesion fractures are uncommon in OI unless the child has a bone mineralization problem. Rib fractures can occur in OI but this is not a common fracture. On x-ray, does the child have an excessive number of wormian bones, which do indicate the possibility of OI? All of the signs and symptoms have to be taken into consideration. While OI is being ruled in or out, an investigation will need to occur simultaneously. Just because OI has been ruled in, child abuse cannot be ruled out.

Temporary Brittle Bone Disease

We would be amiss to leave out the *condition* of temporary brittle bone disease. This is a controversial issue that claims that children can have a temporary collagen defect due to copper deficiency or other deficiencies that can lead to fractures that cannot be explained. Experts claim that this is a condition that exists; however, scientific evidence to support this condition is lacking. Be aware that some experts have and will make this claim; without research to support, this issue is considered a non-existent condition.

Phytophotodermatitis

Phytophotodermatitis is a non-immunologic skin reaction that occurs from exposure to a phototoxic substance and ultraviolet light (the sun). The reaction can range from a minor dermatitis to what may appear as a major burn. Phototoxic substances can range from plants such as parsnip or hogweed, but in the United States it is most commonly seen after exposure to citrus juice such as lemons or limes in combination with being outside. The pattern can range from a dripping pattern if a child spills their juice or a handprint if the caregiver was touching a phototoxic substance (cutting up lemons for lemonade) and then touched the child. The rash can appear the next day, looking like a patterned injury.

Typically, the first sign is redness that may appear similar to a sunburn. The redness will appear within a day after the contact and then can erupt into vesicles or bullae that burst. A brownish hyperpigmentation appears that may last for months. Treatment for this phenomenon is wound management with moist dressings, local wound care, and anti-inflammatory pain relief medications.

Rickets

Rickets is a

> disease of children characterized by a failure or delay in endochondral calcification of the growth plates of long bones. This results in widening and splaying of the growth plates and leads to enlargement of the wrists and costochondral junctions, and the characteristic deformities of the lower limbs, notable genu varum (bow legs) and genu valgum (knock-knees).[37]

Rickets results in a lack of mineralization of the growth plates. The lack of mineralization causes bone fragility and muscle weakness. Vitamin D is a steroid hormone that increases serum calcium and phosphate and promotes mineralization of the bone matrix and the growth plate.

When discussing rickets, it usually is referred to as a disease resulting from a vitamin D deficiency. Vitamin D is absorbed through exposure to the sun. While this is true, it is not only a vitamin D deficiency but also a nutritional disorder that consists of a lack of calcium. In studying rickets across the globe, it has been noted that children may develop rickets when they consistently spend time outdoors but do not have calcium-enriched products readily available. On the other hand, children that have less exposure to the sun but have a higher intake of milk may not develop rickets.

Rickets is classified into three main types: calciopenic, phosphopenic, and inhibited mineralization.[38] Calcipenic rickets is associated with an increase in plasma parathyroid hormone concentration in response to low levels of plasma calcium. Phosphopenic rickets is associated with low plasma phosphate levels with normal parathyroid hormone and results from increased production or gain-of-function of FGF23, a phosphaturic hormone, or from a renal disorder that interferes with the reabsorption of phosphate. Inhibited mineralization directly affects the growth plate though calcium and phosphate levels remain normal.

Bone deformities are the classic sign of rickets with bowing of the femur and tibia. Infants with rickets may present with deformities of the forearms and bowing of the distal tibia.[39] As the child begins to ambulate, additional bowing of the leg may occur. On assessment, the knobby enlargements of the extremities can be palpated and visualized. If the rickets is from inhibited mineralization, growth of the child can be stunted.

When rickets is suspected, blood alkaline phosphatase should be drawn. Elevated alkaline phosphatase activity confirms rickets in patients that present with bony abnormalities. The cause of rickets needs to be identified, and based on what nutrient is lacking—vitamin D or calcium—supplemental replacements need to be given.

Scalded Skin Syndrome

Scaled skin syndrome is also referred to as Ritter's disease. This syndrome is caused by a commonly found bacteria on the skin, eyes, nares, umbilicus, and groin called *Staphylococcal aureus*. In an infant or young child, maternal anti-toxin antibodies are supposed to be a protector to prevent complications from this bacteria. A break in the skin allows *Staphylococcal* bacteria to enter systemically into the body and produce exfoliative toxins. If the maternal antitoxin antibodies do not protect the infant or child, the bacteria will enter into the bloodstream, and the toxins accumulate. If there is a failure in the renal excretion ability, the potential for developing scalded skin syndrome increases.

Characteristics of scalded skin syndrome can be mistaken as a burn in a child, causing suspicion of child abuse. The signs and symptoms have a quick onset, beginning with facial erythema. This will progress to bullae and exfoliation. If the superficial epidermis is invaded, generalized blanching is noted on assessment. The bullae or blisters will appear as small vesicles to large fluid-filled areas. This will develop into skin peeling, sometimes in large sheets, leaving exposed areas of tissue that appear red and moist, like the area has been scalded. The most severe areas tend to be creased areas such as the neck, axilla, and the groin.

On assessment, infants and children with scalded skin syndrome will have a Nikolsky sign. The Nikolsky sign is noted by rubbing of the skin that will cause exfoliation of the outer layer. Once the child has been identified, contact isolation needs to be implemented. Blood cultures need to be obtained prior to antibiotics being given. Gram staining and skin cultures should also be obtained. Pain management will need to be considered; even though a child at this age may not be able to express it, they will be experiencing pain. Meticulous wound care should be provided with the wounds wrapped in saline-soaked gauze or a soft silicone dressing. Penicillins are the first-line antibiotics to use.[40]

Scurvy

Vitamin C (also known as ascorbic acid) is a micronutrient essential in humans that plays a role in the maintenance of intercellular connective tissues, osteoid, dentine, and collagen. Unlike other mammals, humans do not have the ability to convert glucose into ascorbic acid, so the nutrients must be obtained through diet. Best sources of vitamin C are citrus fruits (oranges, lemons, limes, grapefruits, and melons) and vegetables (tomatoes, potatoes, green chilies, cabbage, broccoli, spinach, lettuce, cucumbers, and red peppers). Scurvy develops from a vitamin C deficiency.[41,42]

The recommended daily allowance of vitamin C for children one to thirteen years of age is fifteen to forty-five milligrams. For children fourteen to eighteen years of age, the recommended daily allowance increases to sixty-five to seventy-five milligrams. Newborn infants rely on maternal vitamin C absorption through placental transfer and breastmilk. Serum ascorbic acid levels become abnormal after forty-one days of vitamin C being absent from the diet. Scurvy is completely preventable and tends to be a forgotten disease. In modern health care, scurvy is still present. Several groups of children are at risk, including children that have had multiple blood transfusions causing an iron overload (seen in children with sickle cell anemia or thalassemia), children with neurologic disorders (autism or developmental delays), and children with bone marrow transplants or receiving chemotherapy treatment (due to decreased oral intake).[43]

Initial manifestations are fairly vague. These may include irritability, loss of appetite, and low-grade fever. Dermatological signs can develop later such as petechiae, ecchymosis, hyperkeratosis, and corkscrew hairs. Capillaries become fragile, causing the child to bruise and bleed easier. Gums become swollen and bleed with just a small amount of pressure.[44] Leg swelling and pain with walking can develop. Joints can fracture at the growth plate. All of these signs can be concerning for child abuse.

A thorough history needs to be obtained including a dietary history, along with a physical examination. Radiograph imaging can be helpful. There are classic radiographic signs of scurvy that can be diagnostic; if these are not present, scurvy cannot be ruled out. Classic signs include the following:

1. White line of Frankel: Irregular but thickened white line that appears at the metaphysis
2. Tummerfeld zone: A zone of rarefaction is a late sign located below the Frankel line in the metaphysis

3. Pelkan spurs: Associated with the healing fractures in the Tummerfeld zone is referred to as "beaks" located at the periphery of the zone of metaphyseal calcification; periosteal elevation is noted
4. Wimberger ring signs: Circular, opaque shadow in the growth centers that is often surrounded by a white line around the epiphysis.[45]

Labs should include assessing for micronutrient deficiencies by testing zinc, iron, folate, and vitamin B12 levels. Treatment includes vitamin C replacement at one hundred to three hundred milligrams daily until full recovery of clinical signs occurs.

Subcutaneous Fat Necrosis

Subcutaneous fat necrosis is a rare self-limiting disorder of the panniculus. The panniculus is a layer of fatty and fibrous tissue that lies just beneath the outer layer of the skin. This disorder will typically affect infants that are full-term and will develop within the first few weeks of life up to about six weeks old. Painful bumps or nodules will develop beneath the skin (panniculitis) that are characterized by firm, red or purple subcutaneous nodules and plaque that will typically develop over the trunk, buttocks, cheeks, and extremities.

It is unclear of the cause of this disorder; contributing factors have been identified. It is hypothesized that neonatal distress may interfere with the normal blood supply to the fat tissue, which creates an environment of hypoxia and hypothermia leading to inflammation and necrosis.[46]

Neonatal fat has a higher melting point than that of an adult. Neonatal fat contains a higher percentage of fatty acids or saturated fat that will solidify and crystallize the adipose tissue when exposed to colder conditions.[47] Neonatal risk factors are perinatal asphyxia, meconium aspiration, cord accidents, hypothermia, hypoglycemia, anemia, thrombocytosis, and lactic acid. Risk factors of the mother are preeclampsia, hypertension, gestational diabetes, cocaine and/or cigarette exposure, and the use of calcium channel blockers during pregnancy.[48]

Subcutaneous fat necrosis is typically self-limiting and without complications. Children with this disorder have to continue to be monitored to assure that complications do not develop later. Some complications are skin breakdown, hypoglycemia, anemia, thrombocytopenia, hypertriglyceridemia, and in rare situations hypercalcemia. Hypercalcemia can develop up to six months after the panniculitis develops. Hypercalcemia can be life-threatening. Signs of hypercalcemia are irritability, vomiting, polyuria, failure to thrive, seizures, low blood pressure, mental retardation, renal failure, and death.[49]

Treatment for this condition includes aggressive intravenous hyperhydration. Intravenous loop diuretics may need to be considered. Low calcium and low vitamin D formula along with oral corticosteroids are also used for treatment of this condition.[50]

Vitamin K Deficiency

Vitamin K deficiency was previously referred to as hemorrhagic disease. Vitamin K is a fat-soluble vitamin that activates factors II, VII, IX, and X. Vitamin K does not cross from the placenta to the fetus at levels needed in infancy, therefore supplemental intramuscular vitamin K is required within the first 24 hours of life. This is not an issue for most infants, as they are born in the hospital. Infants born at home may not receive this supplemental vitamin and will be prone to bleeding complications. When infants are born, coagulation factors are 30 to 60 percent less than that of an adult; without a supplement, the infant will begin to bleed within the tissue. Cutaneous bleeding can be noticed, with bruises appearing on the skin, and intracranial bleeds that may develop. When this infant presents to a medical provider, child abuse will be suspected.

Vitamin K deficiency presents in three forms:

1. Early onset of vitamin K deficiency presents within the first 24 hours of the infant's life. Early onset vitamin K deficiency can be correlated to medications that the mother was taking during the pregnancy. Some developing complications are catastrophic intracranial hemorrhages and visceral bleeding.
2. Classic vitamin K deficiency is rarely seen with the supplemental vitamin K that is given in the hospital. Classic vitamin K deficiency may develop within one to seven days after birth. Symptoms are usually less severe, including minor areas of ecchymosis, purpura, oozing around the umbilicus and the circumcision site, hematuria, and hematemesis.
3. Late onset is the most common type of vitamin K deficiency. This is primarily noted in breastfed infants (formula for babies is fortified with seven to ten times the daily recommended dose of vitamin K). Symptoms may develop from two to six months old. These children may present with ecchymosis, intracranial hemorrhages, and gastrointestinal bleeding. The infant may develop additional neurological symptoms such as coma, seizures, and/or paralysis.

Within the first twenty-four hours of life, the infant is to be given one milligram of vitamin K intramuscularly. If the child presents with classic or late onset symptoms, supplemental vitamin K should be given. This may need to be repeated an additional time. The provider may choose to given fresh frozen plasma instead of the vitamin K injection.[51]

Von Willebrand Disease:

Von Willebrand disease (VWD) is the most common inherited bleeding disorder and has an autosomal inheritance pattern, but is not to be confused with hemophilia. This disorder has a deficiency in Von Willebrand factor, Factor VIII, or both, causing a defect in platelet adhesion and aggregation. VWD is associated with mucosal bleeding. There may be a delay in the diagnosis of VWD, causing a child that presents with bruising from the prolonged bleeding associated with this disease to be referred for a child abuse investigation.

VWD is subdivided into three types with type 1 being the most common form. VWD is predominantly seen in the female population. When obtaining a history, common indicators that may clue the provider to test for this factor deficiency include a history of excessive bleeding with circumcision, bleeding after routine dental examinations, excessive menstrual bleeding, and prolonged bleeding with minor trauma.

It is important to obtain a good medical history and family history. Draw labs to test for abnormalities in the Von Willebrand factor or Factor VIII. Treatment consists of replacing the deficient factor so that it can bind to the collagen at the site of the vascular injury so that the platelet adhesion and aggregation can be stimulated.

When evaluating the patient, get a complete history from the caregiver. Find out prescribed medications that the child is taking, over-the-counter medications, and get a history of constipation and diarrhea and what treatment is given.

Treatment includes the following:

1. No more senna-based medication
2. Keep area cleaned
3. Wound management; if first- or second-degree burn a petroleum jelly may be used as well as antibiotic ointment.

MEDICAL MIMICKERS OF CHILD SEXUAL ABUSE

Anal Dilation

Anal dilation is associated with anal abuse. Of all children that report sexual abuse, about 29 percent of the females and 83 percent of males are anally abused. Signs of anal abuse are rare, due to the elasticity of the anal tissue that is made to expand to accommodate bowel movements. The question is, what is the significance of anal dilation on an examination of a child?

Sfriso et al. evaluated 230 children from the age of eight days old to 12.6 years old; 88 percent of the children in this group were younger than five years old. Fourteen patients of the 230 were noted to have reflex anal dilation. Reflex anal dilation is relaxation of the external and internal sphincter of the anus, allowing the examiner to be able to see into the rectum.[52] McCann et al. also completed a study evaluating 267 children in the prone knee-chest position for as long as four minutes. This study showed that 49 percent of the children showed signs of relaxed anal dilation after four minutes, with a smaller percentage of children showing complete dilation when only thirty seconds of traction was applied.[53] On a typical examination, traction should be held for thirty seconds or less. While these studies clearly indicate that anal dilation is significant for providing validity to a history of sexual abuse, the mere presence of anal dilation cannot predict that sexual abuse has occurred.

Anal Fissures

Anal fissures are a common, underappreciated issue in children that can occur at any age. An anal fissure is a tear in the anal mucosa extending from the anal verge toward the dentate line. The exact cause is not known, but some initiating factors have been identified. The first factor is hypertonicity of the internal anal sphincter along with ischemia that interferes with healing.

Anal fissures are thought to develop from anal canal trauma that occurs from a hard fecal mass (constipated stool) or bouts of diarrhea. This condition is painful and is exacerbated when the child defecates, which causes additional ischemia to the area. As the caregiver is concerned about the pain, they may also notice bright red blood coming from the anal area. At this point, the caregiver develops concerns of sexual abuse and presents to a provider for these concerns.

A thorough history needs to be obtained, including bowel habits of the child. Ask about history of constipation and/or diarrhea. When was the last time this occurred? How often does this occur? When did the child complain of pain? When was the anal bleeding noticed? How much blood has been observed?

Studies are being conducted on ointments that may be used to help with treatment of anal fissures from diltiazem ointment to nitroglycerin ointment. Conventional treatment for this condition is warm sitz baths, local application of analgesic ointment, stool softeners, and behavioral therapy.[54]

Perianal Redness

Perianal redness is a common finding in children that have been sexually abused, but it can also be seen also in non-abused children. Perianal redness can be from trauma, poor hygiene, skin disorders, excessive washing or wiping, and infections such as strep. Perianal redness may also be associated with parental neglect. It is important to get a good history; evaluate the age, growth, and development of the child; and perform a thorough physical assessment.

In both of these case studies, without getting a clear history, sexual abuse could have been suspected.

Anal Tags

Anal tags are fleshy areas of extra tissue found midline in the perianal region of the anus. This is a common finding in non-abused children.

Aphthous Ulcers

Aphthous ulcers are also known as canker sores. The sores are caused from an unknown origin but develop along the mucous membranes (mouth and genitalia). One factor that is suggested as a cause is the immune system is disturbed by an external factor and reacts abnormally against a protein that is in the mucosal tissue. The only causes are trauma, medications, and hormones (a woman may develop just before her period).[55] The sores occur in both males and females.

Characteristics of the sores are round or oval sores or ulcerations. Most of the time the sores are a minor nuisance and are painful. They are self-limiting

CASE STUDY #3

A three-year-old child is potty training and wiping herself. The child gets upset when caregiver attempts to help, so the caregiver allows the child to clean herself. Perhaps not great parenting, but a common story with caregivers. The child is not getting herself clean and develops perianal redness.

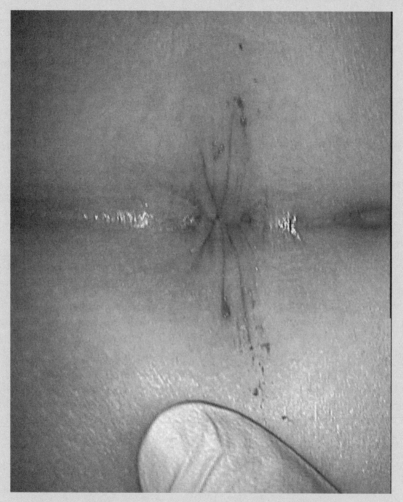

Note the perianal redness. This is not child abuse, but does warrant a discussion with the caregiver on assisting the child to wipe during this learning process.

CASE STUDY #4

A sixteen-month-old male is left in diapers for a prolonged period of time while the mother is on a cocaine binge. The perianal redness extends to the buttocks because of the contact of urine and stool in the diaper.

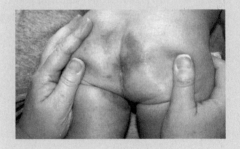

In this case, parental neglect is the cause of the perianal redness. Department of social services would need to be notified.

and will heal on their own. Treatment is symptomatic and best cared for by a topical corticosteroid.

Behcet Disease

Behcet disease is a chronic, relapsing, and remitting vasculitis that can affect all organ systems due to its association with the arteries and veins. There is no spe-

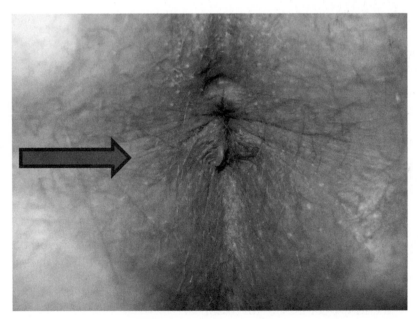

Perineal tag

cific test to determine if the disease is Behcet or something else, so diagnosis can be delayed. The hallmark symptom is ulcerations to the mucosal tissue similar to aphthous ulcers. The ulcers can be minor, less than ten millimeters, or major, greater than ten millimeters, in size. The ulcers can take a few weeks to heal and the patient may develop scarring. Behcet disease is seen more commonly in individuals between the age of twenty to forty years old but has been documented in children as well as the elderly. Males have a higher incidence of Behcet disease; ulcerations to the genitalia most notably are on the scrotum. Females with genitalia ulcerations from Behcet disease will generally be to the vulva.

This disease is more prevalent in Turkey, Japan, and Iran; however, there have been reports in North America. The ulcerations are painful and depending on the outbreak may affect activities of daily living. Mucosal ulcerations to the mouth will be painful, and it will become difficult to eat or swallow. Mucosal ulcerations to the genitalia will cause pain during sexual contact.[56] These ulcerations may be confused with herpes virus.

Bacterial Vaginosis

Bacterial vaginosis has proven to be a confusing vaginitis among providers. The etiology is unknown; however, it is identified as a sexually transmitted infection. While bacterial vaginosis is correlated with sexual activity and multiple sex partners, research also supports developing bacterial vaginosis with no sexual contact.

CASE STUDY #5

A three-year-old female is brought to her primary care provider for vaginal discharge; her mom can smell a fishy odor. The provider cultures the child and the culture results are bacterial vaginosis. The provider tells the caregiver that her child has been sexually assaulted and that she needs to go to the forensic office. The caregiver is distraught and crying, trying to figure out who would have sexually assaulted the child. The child has not made a disclosure and the caregiver had no suspicions of sexual assault until the provider told her that it had happened. A forensic evaluation is completed, with no signs of trauma. No story is given; the nurse then has to educate the caregiver on the fact that children have contracted bacterial vaginosis with no history of sexual abuse. Imagine the confusion and the doubt that the caregiver has.

Bacterial vaginosis is an alteration in the bacterial equilibrium of a female's vaginal flora. The number of lactobacilli is reduced, compromising its protective role to maintain the vagina's normal acidity level. With the reduced lactobacilli, an overgrowth of anaerobic pathogens develops. Symptoms of thin vaginal discharge and a fishy odor may begin to appear.[57]

While this is a vaginosis that appears in sexually active females, it also has been proven that bacterial vaginosis can also be present in prepubertal females with no allegations of sexual contact. Other factors that may contribute to bacterial vaginosis are excessive washing and douching. Research continues in trying to identify a clear etiology.

Constipation

Constipation is an underreported condition, so to know the actual statistics of how many children are affected is difficult; the estimated amount ranges from 0.7 percent to as high as 30 percent, depending on what research is being reviewed. Constipation is defined as an infrequent amount of bowel movements, typically fewer than three a week.

There are multiple types of constipation; the majority of children that have difficulty with constipation are from functional constipation, otherwise known as chronic idiopathic constipation.

Types of constipation include the following:

- *Atonic constipation:* This is an abnormal colonic response to stimuli to have a bowel movement. This form of constipation is thought to be from impairment of the pelvic splanchnic nerves that supply the distal colon. The interference that develops affects peristaltic function, causing the muscles to become sluggish.
- *Spastic constipation:* This is a form of irritable bowel syndrome and is due to constriction of intestinal muscles as a result of colonic spasms.
- *Obstructive constipation:* This is caused by obstruction of the passage of stool. The obstruction could be from adhesions that may develop from abdominal surgeries, scar tissue formation, or inflammation from chronic conditions such as Crohn's disease.
- *Functional constipation:* This form of constipation is not caused from any pathology that can be identified; the bowel is healthy, but the constipation ensues. Associated symptoms have to be documented to have been occurring for at least one month. Diagnostic criteria for infants up to the age of four have to have at least two of the following symptoms:
  o Two or less bowel movements per week
  o History of excessive stool retention
  o History of painful or hard bowel movements
  o Large fecal mass noted in the rectum
  o Large diameter stools which may obstruct the toilet
  o At least one episode a week of incontinence after the child has been toilet trained.

The major factors for functional constipation to develop is an unbalanced diet, inadequate amount of fluid intake, and a sedentary lifestyle.[58] Chronic constipation can be associated with anal dilation and with the passing of hard stools causing anal fissures. Both of these symptoms can be mistaken for sexual abuse.

The provider needs to complete a thorough history and physical. In obtaining the history, the provider needs to document the duration of the symptoms, frequency of bowel movements, and previous episodes of constipation. In addition, the provider should assess the nutritional habits of the child as well as any medications or supplements being taken.

Diastasis Ani

In order to recognize diastasis ani, the examiner needs to know and understand the normal anatomy of the anus and perianal area. When the external anal sphincter is closed, the perianal area takes on a wrinkled appearance. The tighter the contraction, the more wrinkles appear.

Diastasis ani is a congenital variant in which there appears to be an absence in muscle fibers in the midline of the external anal sphincter. Diastasis ani is noted at the 6 o'clock or the 12 o'clock position of the perianal tissue, and appears to be a wedge of flattened folds that could be misdiagnosed as anal scarring or anal swelling. This finding occurs more often in males than females.

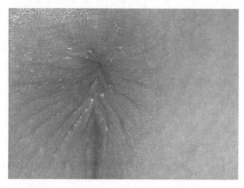

Normal perianal examination. Note the wrinkled appearance of the perianal tissue.

Enlarged Hymenal Opening

When girls are born, the mother's estrogen is passed along causing the hymenal tissue to be thickened and appear redundant. As the child ages, the estrogen levels decrease and the hymenal tissue becomes thinner. This typically will occur in the toddler age range. The caretaker does not know or understand the estrogenization process, but what the caretaker does see is a "vaginal opening that is larger than it should be." This is a very common complaint in which children are brought in for a forensic evaluation for fear that the child has been sexually assaulted. Many times, this fear is enhanced by an untrained examiner who confirms that the vaginal opening is larger than it should be.

The fact is hymenal sizes can vary. The same child can have a change in hymenal size depending on how relaxed the child is. As research continues, debates arise as to whether the horizontal measurement of the hymen indicates penetration or a history of penetration. No research as of this date has confirmed that hymenal width is an indicator of penetration or sexual abuse. A better indicator is the amount of hymen present and the appearance of the hymen between the posterior rim, which is three o'clock to nine o'clock.

Failure of Midline Fusion

Failure of midline fusion is mucosal exposure anywhere on the line from the fossa navicularis in females to under the scrotum in males that can extend to

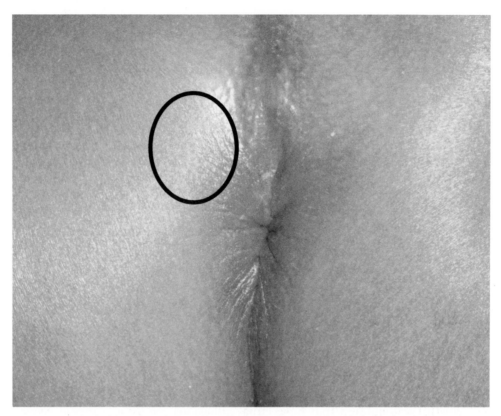

Note the wedge of flattened folds along the midline of the perianal tissue

the anus. This anomaly is a congenital finding that can easily be mistaken for a traumatic injury. To save confusion and unnecessary reports to investigative agencies, the medical provider needs to have accurate documentation within the chart regarding this anomaly. If the provider is unable to determine on the initial assessment whether the finding is failure of midline fusion or an acute injury, the child should return in two weeks for a follow-up examination. If no change to this area is noted, the provider can document that it is failure of midline fusion. A traumatic injury would be in the process of healing or completely healed within this time period. Failure of midline fusion typically will resolve by puberty.

Foreign Body

It is not uncommon for children to wipe and leave toilet paper behind. Toilet paper is a common culprit for foreign body in the vagina. Vaginal foreign body can lead to vaginal bleeding, foul odor, and discharge. The hymen is sensitive in prepubescent children, so on evaluation, the provider needs to be cautious to not touch the hymenal tissue. The proper technique for prepubescent children is to apply traction and separation to the labia majora. If the child is cooperative, the provider may be able to visualize the foreign body and use a genital irrigation to flush it out. If this process is not successful, a pediatric gynecologist may be consulted and/or the child may need to be taken to the operating room.

If repeated intentional insertions of foreign objects into the vagina by the child is reported, sexual abuse should be considered.

Labial Adhesions

Labial adhesions affect about 2 percent of females, developing within three months of age to three years old. Peak time of development is between thirteen to twenty-three months old. Since most labial adhesions are asymptomatic, this number may be higher. The etiology is not known but some suspected causes are inflammation or trauma that can erode the epithelium of the labia minora in the absence of estrogen causing the labia to fuse. The labia typically will stick together around the area of the posterior fourchette fusing until only a small opening is left for the urine to pass. Causes of inflammation can be the following:

- Poor hygiene
- Stool contamination
- Lichen sclerosis
- Frequent diaper rashes.

Trauma can also be a factor in the development of labial adhesions.[59] Trauma can be from multiple factors such as female circumcision or straddle injuries, or the trauma can be caused by sexual abuse.

Most of the children that have labial adhesions are asymptomatic. Symptoms that may develop can be urinary tract infections, pain during activity, post void dripping, abnormal urinary stream, and urinary retention.[60]

Topical estrogen cream should be applied three times a day for up to three or four weeks to help resolve labial adhesions. Betamethasone 0.05 percent can be applied twice daily with gentle traction during application to try separate the labia. If this does not work, the child may need to have the adhesion surgically separated.

While labial separation can be caused by non-sexual factors, it also can be caused by sexual abuse. It is important for the provider to get a good history to determine non-sexual causes that may account for the development of the adhesion. The provider should also note if there are any concerns of sexual abuse.

CASE STUDY #6

A two-year-old presents to the forensic office with a labial adhesion; estrogen was prescribed. The insurance company of the child refused to fill the prescription stating estrogen cream was for postmenopausal women. To get the prescription filled, the forensic nurse had to send a waiver on why she needed the cream as well as research articles to support the need for children with labial adhesions to obtain this medication.

Lichen Sclerosus

Lichen sclerosus typically develops in postmenopausal women between the ages of fifty and sixty years old. Ten to 15 percent of the time, however, lichen sclerosus will develop in prepubescent children. The development can happen in females as well as males, but it is more common in females at a rate of ten to one. Lichen sclerosus is a benign, chronic condition of the skin characterized by ivory or white shiny macules and papules that form hypopigmented plaque.[61] The origin of lichen sclerosus is unknown but is thought to be related to infections with *Borrelia* species to immunologic association with certain human leukocyte antigens.[62]

A classic sign of lichen sclerosus is the figure eight pattern that encircles the vulva and the anus. The hymen is usually spared. The skin affected by lichen sclerosus becomes thin and fragile. Acts as simple as wiping can cause bruising and excoriation. Fissures may also develop as a complication. The symptoms that develop can cause complaints such as vaginal bleeding, leading to suspicions of child sexual abuse. The child may complain of itching, pain with urination, and/or pain with bowel movements.

The physical evaluation of the anogenital area will usually be sufficient to diagnose a child with lichen sclerosus. Most cases are mild and education on avoidance of irritants, clothing, and activities that cause trauma is warranted. In addition, these children may need treatment with progesterone, topical estrogens, high-potency corticosteroids, immunosuppressants, and topical nonsteroidal anti-inflammatory agents.[63] Consideration should also be given for referrals to dermatology and pediatric gynecology.

Balanitis xerotica obliterans is a subcategory of lichen sclerosus that is limited to male genitalia. Balanitis xerotica obliterans is associated with destructive inflammation, phimosis, urethral stenosis, and squamous cell carcinoma. Balanitis xerotica obliterans does not normally affect children and it usually surfaces in adulthood.[64]

Linea Vestibularis

This is a normal variant of female genital examination. Linea vestibularis is characterized by white streaks that run from the inferior hymenal border to the posterior commissure. If white spots are noted instead of streaks, this is referred to as a partial linea vestibularis.

Molluscum Contagiosum

A common, benign viral skin infection that is noted more in children and immunocompromised adults. Lesions appear as pearly papules two to five millimeters in size with a centralized dimple or white, waxy core. Lesions appear on mucous membranes in infants, children, and adolescents. These lesions can appear as clusters in the anogenital area, making it easy to mistake for genital warts. These lesions are most commonly spread through non-sexual contact but can also be spread through sexual contact.

The lesions are most associated with swimming pools, living in close proximity, skin-to-skin contact, and tropical climates. Lesions are typically self-limiting but can last from six months to four years. The most common treatment is the use of corticosteroids for dermatitis and topical and oral antibiotics.[65]

Median Raphe

The median raphe is a midline structure in males and females that can be mistaken for trauma or scarring. This is a midline ridge that extends from the posterior commissure in females to the anus and in males from the penile shaft, scrotum, and perineum to the anus. The median raphe may be raised and may have a difference in coloration around the area; it represents the junction of the two halves of the perineum. This is a normal finding.

Pearly Penile Papules

Pearly penile papules are benign lesions that present in rows around the corona of the glans penis. The papules are pink or white dome-shaped or filiform papules that develop in late adolescence or early adulthood. About 14 to 18 percent of males are affected. While pearly penile papules are benign and do not contain the human papillomavirus, they can be mistaken for condyloma acuminate (genital warts). The papules are approximately one to two millimeters in diameter and one to four millimeters in height. They form a cobblestone pattern of one to two rows around the corona.

Circumcised males are less likely to develop these papules due to the likelihood of abrasion to that area, as the papules would be more exposed than those of an uncircumcised male. As the person ages, these papules tend to regress. No treatment is necessary for this condition; however, it can be an embarrassment for the male having others think that he has a sexually transmitted infection. For situations like this, cryotherapy or laser surgery may be used to remove the papules.[66]

Straddle Injuries

Straddle injuries are common in children. Children are active and are not so alert to what is ahead. Straddle injuries occur from a fall in which the child straddles an object, striking the urogenital area with the force of their own body weight, crushing the soft tissue between the object and the bony pelvis. The injuries that are received can range from bruises to hematomas, abrasions, and lacerations. With most unintentional straddle injuries, the expectation is the injuries will be more anterior and external. The labia majora in females protect the hymen and the vagina. Without a straddle or penetrating story, these two areas are rarely injured.

Straddle injuries can mimic child sexual abuse; therefore, sexual abuse has to be ruled out. If the child can give a clear history of the event and there are unbiased witnesses that have witnessed the event, the examiner can feel more confident that the mechanism of injury is a straddle injury. Common mechanisms causing straddle injuries include the center bar of a bicycle, furniture, gym bars, playground equipment, bathtubs, counter doors, and the edge of pools.

Toddler and preschool-aged children typically have self-limiting injuries that are non-penetrating. When obtaining the history of the event, find out what the child was wearing at the time the injury took place. Clothing can act as a barrier, preventing additional injuries, especially penetrating injuries. Common injuries to the female genitalia include abrasions, bruises, and lacerations to the labia majora and labia minora. Straddle injuries in males can cause scrotal lacerations, bruising, and tenderness. Penile injuries are less likely to occur. Males have a higher risk of urethral injury than do females.

Questions to consider on evaluation of a child with the complaint of a straddle injury include the following:

1. Can all of the anatomical structures be identified in a female examination?
   a. Clitoris
   b. Urethra
   c. Labia majora
   d. Labia minora
   e. Hymen
   f. Vagina
   g. Rectum
2. Do the injuries extend above the pelvic floor?
3. Is the hymen involved?
4. If the injury is a penetrating type injury, is it plausible that the straddled object could cause a deep penetration injury?[67]

CASE STUDY #7

A three-year-old female is being watched by her sixteen-year-old male cousin. The older cousin is making breakfast and is not watching the child. The child begins crying; the cousin runs in and then calls the mother. The child is brought to the emergency department with injuries noted in the following. The child cannot give a clear disclosure, which is a complication. There are no unbiased witnesses: the only other person at the home was the sixteen-year-old male cousin. The story was given that the child likes to take her diaper off and run around the house. The child had climbed onto the top of a dog kennel and fell, causing a straddle penetrating injury from the metal rod that closes the door of the kennel. While this needs to be treated as a potential sexual abuse case, forensic evidence collection was obtained in conjunction with medical care and an investigation. The investigators went to the scene and found the dog kennel exactly as described and concluded that this was a non-intentional straddle (with penetration) injury.

Venous Congestion

Venous congestion is a non-specific finding that occurs from the collection of venous blood in the venous plexus of the perianal tissue. This finding is thought to come from a temporary obstruction of blood flow. The tissue becomes blue or purple around the anus, which can be mistaken for a bruise. Venous congestion is positional and more commonly seen in the prone knee-chest position or when there is a prolonged examination.

Streptococcal Vaginitis or Perineal Streptococcal Dermatitis

It is not uncommon to have anogenital redness in children, especially prepubescent children. A condition that should be considered when a significant amount of redness develops and is noted during the examination is streptococcal infection. Streptococcal vaginitis is from typically Group A, beta hemolytic streptococcus, being passed from the nares or oral pharynx to the genital region. Streptococcus can grow in the vulvovaginal, penile, and anal area. The child will typical develop genital pain, pain with urination (leading to incontinence), and pain with defecation (leading to constipation). Additional symptoms that are common are itching and purulent discharge. One of the most characteristic signs of a streptococcal infection is sharply demarcated areas of redness. The area may become excoriated and develop erythematous lesions that can ooze. Bloody stools may be noted, and anal fissures can develop.

Bacterial cultures are to be collected from the area of outbreak: vulvovaginal, penile, or anal. It is best to culture the oozing lesions if at all possible. First-line treatment is penicillin or erythromycin.

Summer Penile Syndrome

Summer penile syndrome occurs in young boys. The cause is chigger bites or *Trombiculidae* mites. There is a rapid onset of penile edema and pruritus. It is most commonly seen in the spring and summer months. When completing a penile assessment, bites are typically noted. Symptoms are self-limiting and rarely involve urinary complications. Treatment is supportive care and may include topical antipruritic agents, topical corticosteroids, oral antihistamines, and cold compresses.

Urethral Prolapse

Urethral prolapse is a rare condition that has been reported worldwide. The cause is not known but tends to be more prevalent in children with African origin. Urethral mucosa prolapses appearing as red or cyanotic tissue. This tissue can be friable, and vaginal bleeding is a common complaint associated with this condition. The prolapse many times is large enough to obscure the hymen, therefore appearing as sexual abuse.

It is not clear as to whether treatment is necessary; at a minimum a consult should be made with pediatric urology or gynecology. Some journals suggest that a resection may be needed. Sitz baths, topical antibiotics, and estrogen creams can be utilized.

CASE STUDY #8

A three-year-old female presents to the emergency department with vaginal bleeding. Upon initial presentation, a red substance is noted on the underwear and an unusual vaginal examination is noted. The child denies any previous symptoms and denies being sexually abused. The child says that her two-year-old brother kicked her the day before. The mother denies that the child was around any male in the past few weeks. Upon further talking with the mother, it became clear the child had been alone with three different males in the period of the last two days. With the discrepancy in the stories, police and social services were notified.

Vulvovaginitis

The most common pediatric gynecologic condition is vulvovaginitis or genital redness and swelling. Additional symptoms are vaginal itching, and the child may have a brown to green discharge with the caregiver complaining of noticing a foul odor. The most common cause for this condition is poor hygiene. Fecal matter gets displaced into the vaginal area causing irritation. Additional causes can be chemical irritation, mechanical irritation, and trauma.

Prepubescent girls have a lack of estrogen. The lack of estrogen leads to a thinning of the vaginal epithelium with a decrease in lactobacilli. This causes the pH to be neutral and less protective. As the female becomes more estrogenized during adolescence, the pH becomes more acidic and protective of the vaginal flora.[68]

Yeast Infections

Yeast infections are typically caused by *Candida albicans*. Yeast infections in toilet-trained prepubertal children are rare. Children that are high risk are those that have just completed a broad-spectrum antibiotic, children with diabetes mellitus, or those who are immunocompromised. These children can begin to have a white, frothy discharge. This discharge and dysuria and lead to excoriation causing breaks in the skin that may bleed. The discharge and bleeding can mimic sexual abuse.

Yeast infections can be diagnosed through a wet mount. Treatment is topical or oral azoles.

CONCLUSION

In conclusion, trying to decipher what is a medical condition and what is a physical or sexual mimicker may not be as easy a task as you would think. It is the responsibility of the provider to objectively evaluate the findings, obtain a thorough history, and determine if a medical condition is mimicking an abusive injury. This may take multiple tests and be time-consuming. If there is a suspicion, as the mimicker is being ruled in or out, it is okay to initiate an investigation. The team can work together to determine abuse or mimicker. In the end, the safety of the child and the health of the child is what is important.

REVIEW QUESTIONS

1. Discuss questions that can be asked to caregivers that can rule in or rule out a physical mimicker.

2. Discuss questions that can be asked to caregivers that can rule in or rule out a sexual mimicker.

KEYWORDS

Physical indicators that may mimic abuse: Cutaneous indicators on the body that may mimic physical abuse.

Sexual indicators that may mimic abuse: Cutaneous indicators to the genital and anal area that may mimic sexual abuse.

NOTES

1. Cher-Han Tan, S. Rasool, and G. Johnson, "Contact Dermatitis, Allergic and Irritant," *Journal of Clinics in Dermatology* 32 (2014): 116–24.

2. Susanne Anderson, P. Lindgreen, and K. Rokkedal, "Grasping the Weight Cut-off for Anorexia Nervosa in Children and Adolescents," *International Journal of Eating Disorders* 51 (2018): 1347.

3. Lindsey Moskowitz and E. Weiselberg, "Anorexia Nervosa/Atypical Anorexia Nervosa," *Current Problems in Pediatric Adolescent Health Care* 47 (2017): 70–80.

4. Moskowitz and Weiselberg, "Anorexia Nervosa/Atypical Anorexia Nervosa."

5. Jacqueline Carter, C. Bewell, E. Blackmore, and D. Woodside, "The Impact of Childhood Sexual Abuse in Anorexia Nervosa," *Child Abuse & Neglect* 30 (2006): 257–69.

6. Sarah Racine and Jennifer Wildes, "Emotion Dysregulation and Anorexia Nervosa: An Exploration of the Role of Childhood Abuse," *International Journal of Eating Disorders* 48, no. 1 (2015): 55–58.

7. Moskowitz and Weiselberg, "Anorexia Nervosa/Atypical Anorexia Nervosa."

8. Karen Hansen, "Folk Remedies and Child Abuse: A Review with Emphasis on Caida De Mollera and Its Relationship to Shaken Baby Syndrome," *Child Abuse & Neglect* 22, no. 2 (1997): 117–27.

9. Hansen, "Folk Remedies and Child Abuse."

10. Hansen, "Folk Remedies and Child Abuse."

11. Hansen, "Folk Remedies and Child Abuse."

12. Tiffany B. Brown and Thomas Kimball, "Cutting to Live: A Phenomenology of Self-Harm," *Journal of Marital and Family Therapy* 39, no. 2 (2013): 195–208.

13. Jean Robinson, "The Management of Eczema in Children," *Community Practitioner* 88, no. 9 (2015): 33–35.

14. Nomathamsanqa Mathe and A. Loffeld, "The Management of Eczema in Children," *Paediatrics and Child Health* (2018): 1–7.

15. Andrew Sohn, A. Frankel, R. Patel, and G. Goldenberg, "Eczema," *Mount Sinai Journal of Medicine* 78 (2011): 730–39.

16. Robinson, "The Management of Eczema in Children."

17. Robinson, "The Management of Eczema in Children."

18. Robinson, "The Management of Eczema in Children."

19. Behareh Abtahi-Naeini, J. Shapouri, M. Masjedi, A. Saffaei, and M. Pourazizi, "Unexplained Facial Scar: Child Abuse or Ehlers-Danlos Syndrome?" *North American Journal of Medical Sciences* 6, no. 11 (2014): 595–98.

20. Amal Vadysinghe, C. Wickramashinghe, and C. Kaluarachchi, "Suspicious Scars: Physical Child Abuse vs Ehlers-Danlos Syndrome," *Autopsy Case Reports* 8, no. 1 (2018): 1–5.

21. R. Scott Strahlman, "Toe Tourniquet Syndrome in Association with Maternal Hair Loss," *Pediatrics* 111, no. 3 (2003): 687–87.

22. Ashley E. Kita and Jennifer L. Long, "Hemangioma," *Ear, Nose and Throat Journal* 95, no. 1 (2016): 19–20.

23. Joan McCarthy and Prasad Mathew, "Treatment of Hemophilia with Inhibitors: An Advance in Options for Pediatric Patients," *Journal of Emergency Nursing* 37, no. 5 (2011): 474–76.

24. Cherilyn C. Hall and Andrew D. DePiero, "Laxative Induced Buttock Dermatitis," *The Journal of Emergency Medicine* 40, no. 2 (2011): 212–13.

25. Hall and DePiero, "Laxative Induced Buttock Dermatitis."

26. Sabrina MacDuff, J. Sun, D. Bell, C. Lentz, and S. Kahn, "Accidental Burn by Intentional Laxative Use," *Pediatric Emergency Care* 32, no. 8 (2016): 541–43.

27. Rebecca J. Droms, J. Rork, R. McLean, M. Martin, L. Belazarian, and K. Wiss, "Menkes Disease Mimicking Child Abuse," *Pediatric Dermatology* 34, no. 3 (2017): 132–36.

28. Droms, Rork, McLean, Martin, Belazarian, and Wiss, "Menkes Disease Mimicking Child Abuse."

29. Kavon R. Golshani, M. Ludwig, P. Cohn, and R. Kruse, "Osteogenesis Imperfecta," *Delaware Medical Journal* 88, no. 6 (2016): 178–85.

30. Berkeley L. Bennett and Mary C. Pierce, "Bone Health and Development," in Carole Jenny (ed.), *Child Abuse and Neglect: Diagnosis, Treatment and Evidence* (St. Louis, MO: Elsevier Saunders, 2011), 260–74.

31. Golshani, Ludwig, Cohn, and Kruse, "Osteogenesis Imperfecta."

32. Golshani, Ludwig, Cohn, and Kruse, "Osteogenesis Imperfecta."

33. Golshani, Ludwig, Cohn, and Kruse, "Osteogenesis Imperfecta."

34. Golshani, Ludwig, Cohn, and Kruse, "Osteogenesis Imperfecta."

35. Golshani, Ludwig, Cohn, and Kruse, "Osteogenesis Imperfecta."

36. Golshani, Ludwig, Cohn, and Kruse, "Osteogenesis Imperfecta."

37. Ann Prentice, "Nutritional Rickets around the World," *Journal of Steroid Biochemistry and Molecular Biology* 136 (2013): 201.

38. Prentice, "Nutritional Rickets around the World."

39. A.S. Lambert and A. Linglart, "Hypocalcaemic and Hypophosphatemic Rickets," *Best Practice & Research Clinical Endocrinology & Metabolism* 32 (2018): 455–76.

40. Kourtney Hennigan and Cheryl Riley, "Staphylococcal Scaled Skin Syndrome: A Case Review," *Neonatal Network* (2016): 8–12.

41. Farahnaz Golriz, L.F. Donnelly, S. Devaraj, and R. Krishnamurthy, "Modern American Scurvy—Experience with Vitamin C Deficiency at a Large Children's Hospital," *Pediatric Radiology* 47 (2017): 214–20.

42. Anil Agarwal, A. Shaharyar, A. Kumar, M. Shafi, and M. Mishra, "Scurvy in Pediatric Age Group—A Disease Often Forgotten?" *Journal of Clinical Orthopaedics and Trauma* 6 (2015): 101–07.

43. Hennigan and Riley, "Staphylococcal Scaled Skin Syndrome."

44. Golriz, Donnelly, Devaraj, and Krishnamurthy, "Modern American Scurvy—Experience with Vitamin C Deficiency at a Large Children's Hospital."

45. Golriz, Donnelly, Devaraj, and Krishnamurthy, "Modern American Scurvy—Experience with Vitamin C Deficiency at a Large Children's Hospital."

46. Leire G. Lara, A. Villa, M. Rivas, M. Capella, F. Prada, and M. Ensenat, "Subcutaneous Fat Necrosis of the Newborn: Report of Five Cases," *Pediatrics and Neonatology* 58 (2017): 85–88.

47. Nicole Sterfanko and Beth Drolet, "Subcutaneous Fat Necrosis of the Newborn and Associated Hypercalcemia: A Systemic Review of the Literature," *Pediatric Dermatology* (2018): 1–7.

48. Agarwal, Shaharyar, Kumar, Shafi, and Mishra, "Scurvy in Pediatric Age Group—A Disease Often Forgotten?"

49. Lara, Villa, Rivas, Capella, Prada, and Ensenat, "Subcutaneous Fat Necrosis of the Newborn."

50. Subhabrata Mitra, J. Dove, and S. Somistery, "Subcutaneous Fat Necrosis in Newborns—An Unusual Case and Review of Literature," *European Journal of Pediatrics* 170 (2011): 1107–10.

51. Tonia Brousseau, N. Kissoon, and B. McIntosh, "Vitamin K Deficiency Mimicking Child Abuse," *The Journal of Emergency Medicine* 29, no. 3 (2005): 283–88.

52. Francesca Sfriso, S. Masiero, V. Mardegan, S. Bressan, and A. Aprile, "Reflex Anal Dilation: An Observational Study on Non-Abused Children," *Forensic Science International* 238 (2014): 22–25.

53. Joyce A. Adams, "Basic Anatomy of the Genitalia and Anus," in Glenn Whaley (ed.), *Medical Response to Child Sexual Abuse* (Saint Louis, MO: STM Learning, Inc., 2011), 9–40.

54. Muazea Cevik, M. Boleken, I. Koruk, S. Ocal, M. Balaioglu, A. Aydinoglu, and C. Korados, "A Prospective, Randomized, Double Blind Study Comparing the Efficacy of Diltiazem, Glyceryl Trinitrate, and Lidocaine for the Treatment of Anal Fissure in Children," *Pediatric Surgery International* 28 (2012): 411–16.

55. P.S. Ubiksha, "Various Remedies for Recurrent Aphthous Ulcer—A Review," *Journal of Pharmaceutical Sciences and Research* 6, no. 6 (2014): 251–53.

56. J.R. Nair and R.J. Moots, "Behcet's Disease," *Clinical Medicine* 17, no. 1 (2017): 71–77.

57. Ettedal A. Aljahdali, "Bacterial Vaginosis Awareness among Pediatric and Adolescent Age Groups in Saudi Arabia," *Journal of King Abdulaziz University* 24, no. 1 (2017): 33–42.

58. Lucille R. Ferrara and S. Saccomano, "Constipation in Children," *The Nurse Practitioner*, 42, no. 7 (2017): 30–34.

59. Govindarajan K. Kumar, "Labial Adhesions: An Office Problem in Pediatric Urology," *Pediatric Urology Case Report* 4, no. 1 (2017): 248–52.

60. Kumar, "Labial Adhesions."

61. Gail Horner, "Common Conditions that Mimic Findings of Sexual Abuse," *Journal of Pediatric Health Care* 23, no. 5 (2009): 283–86.

62. Lori Frasier, "Medical Conditions that Mimic Sexual Abuse," in Glenn Whaley (ed.), *Medical Response to Child Sexual Abuse* (Saint Louis, MO: STM Learning, Inc., 2011), 145–66.

63. Frasier, "Medical Conditions that Mimic Sexual Abuse."

64. Frasier, "Medical Conditions that Mimic Sexual Abuse."

65. Horner, "Common Conditions that Mimic Findings of Sexual Abuse"; Frasier, "Medical Conditions that Mimic Sexual Abuse."

66. Adam S. Aldahan, T. Brah, and K. Nouri, "Diagnosis and Management of Pearly Penile Papules," *American Journal of Men's Health* 12, no. 3 (2018): 624–27.

67. Kelly A. Sinclair and Jane F. Knapp, "Case Records of the Children's Mercy Hospital: A 12-year-old Girl with a Straddle Injury," *Pediatric Emergency Care* 27 (2011): 550–52.

68. Meredith Loveless and Ohmar Myint, "Vulvovaginitis—Presentation of More Common Problems in Pediatric and Adolescent Gynecology," *Best Practices & Research Clinical Obstetrics and Gynecology* 48 (2018): 14–27.

10

Domestic Violence and Dating Violence

◆ ◆ ◆

IT IS RARE FOR MORE THAN A COUPLE OF DAYS to go by without the news media reporting a woman being killed by her supposed "loved one." Domestic violence has plagued society, and it only seems to be getting worse, but despite all the media response to what happens with the adults in these situations, there seems to be a lack of coverage as to how violence within a family affects the children. The purpose of this chapter is not only to discuss dynamics of intimate partner violent behavior but also to address the effects this violence has on children. Both physical and psychological damage can be done to young ones in families of violence, which we will address in this chapter. We would be negligent if we fail to bring to light the sociological ramifications the children suffer as a result of living in a home surrounded by violence.

DEFINING DOMESTIC VIOLENCE

The Department of Health and Human Services defines domestic violence under criminal law (also referred to as intimate partner violence) as "any criminal offense involving violence or physical harm committed by one family or household member against another."[1] Statutes throughout the country have expanded the definition to be more inclusive identifying relationships outside of the family or household. Child abuse, although a distinct category from that of domestic violence, co-exists by the close personal nature of the victim-offender relationship.[2] Victims of intimate partner violence are usually women, but it is important to note that men, transgender people, or those in same sex relationships are also susceptible to victimization. As domestic violence can take place in diverse family structures in addition to the traditional nuclear family, domestic violence is also commonly referred to as family violence. The nuclear family of forty years ago was composed of parents of both sexes with one or more biological or adopted children. Today the term "family" may include blended families, families where both parents are of the same sex, or one-parent families created by choice or divorce, death of a partner, or unplanned pregnancy.[3] The term "violence" may also have a different understanding among families. For instance, some parents who use corporal punishment on their children consider their actions as appropriate behavior used in the best interest of the child, whereas other parents may consider spanking to be a form of violence and therefore abuse. The concept of child abuse has no precise guidelines when separating discipline from physical abuse to establish what is and what is not appropriate force in the eyes of the law, parents, and the community.[4]

CATEGORIES OF ABUSE

Domestic violence can involve neglect, physical, sexual, and psychological maltreatment, which are also the four main categories of child abuse. Other forms of domestic violence include economic abuse where the offender controls their partner's finances, thus creating a situation where the partner is dependent on their abuser. When the dominating partner has control of the purse strings, the care of the children may be less than optimal due to insufficient funds. Many adults in violent domestic relationships were subjected to the same forms of abuse as children, and in some cases the maltreatment was more severe. A significant difference that separates abuse of a child from that of an adult is the fact that an adult can legally leave an abusive relationship, but a child must rely on a responsible adult to provide them adequate safety. The reasons some adults remain in an abuse relationships include, but are not limited to, the abused adult is afraid to leave, they still love their abuser, their self-worth is diminished, they believe they can change the abuser's behavior, and/or they don't have the financial resources to leave. In some cases, those who have children may stay in the relationship claiming, "it is for the sake of the children." In other cases the final straw is when abuse is directed toward the children, then and only then is the abused willing to leave the abusive relationship. Other forms of domestic violence are demonstrated through power and control, as the abuser can use their own children in order to control their partner. The threat of removing a child from the custody of a parent is a powerful weapon in controlling one's partner. The Power and Control Wheel was created as a way to visualize and demonstrate the complexity of domestic violence. This illustration was developed by the Domestic Abuse Intervention Project in 1984 to help service providers and criminal justice officials understand the complex nature of domestic violence. The wheel shows the power and control abusers have over their victims.[5]

HOW DOES VIOLENCE OCCUR?

Domestic violence transpires in three phases, commonly referred to as the cycle of violence. Conceptualized as a cycle by Lenore Walker in 1979, the cycle of violence has taken on various forms and is found in many domestic violence websites. The initial phase is the tension phase. During this stage, the communication breaks down and pressure builds where the victim may feel like they must "walk on eggshells." Stress builds up within the perpetrator and they are no

Power and Control Wheel Illustration
Permission for display granted 1/24/19. From: mtendrup@theduluthmodel.org

longer able to hold back their anger. The aggression can take the form of physical, sexual, or emotional/psychological violence, or any combination thereof. When these types of aggression are exhibited, the cycle now enters the battery phase. The offender may feel remorse for causing harm to someone they claim to love, so they attempt to make amends by declaring how remorseful they are and trying to be especially thoughtful and caring in the future. The victim accepts the offender's apology and promises that the aggression will not happen again.[6] This final stage is referred to as the honeymoon phase. In reality, it is often not a final phase at all and the cycle continues. Unfortunately, the stressors that built the original tension reappear, which again leads to the battering phase, and then once again to the honeymoon phase.

This cycle of violence can occur on an intergenerational level as well. Children can learn abusive behavior by observing their abusive parent control their

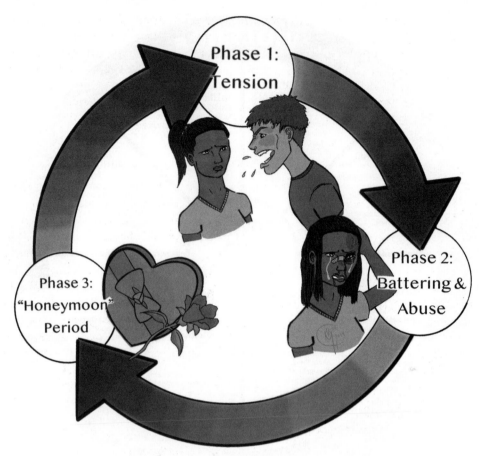

Cycle of Violence
Illustration Courtesy of Mollie Hubble University of Lynchburg

partner. Children seeing their parents using violence or threatening behavior can in their minds believe that these actions are acceptable conduct. This is consistent with Albert Bandura's Social Learning Theory that argues that aggressive tendencies are learned by a process of rewards and imitation of aggressive behavior.[7] In the case of domestic violence, children learn the rewards of controlling an intimate partner and therefore they become an abuser or, in some cases, a victim of domestic violence as they enter adulthood.

MEASURING DOMESTIC VIOLENCE

Attempting to estimate the magnitude of the problem of how often domestic violence occurs is a challenging task as most of these offenses occur behind closed doors and never come to the attention of law enforcement. Victimization surveys, as discussed in chapter 1, are an option when attempting to identify the frequency of domestic violence, but the mere fact of excluding anyone under the age of twelve from participating hinders the accuracy of any data under this format. Research has attempted to measure the level of domestic violence including the amount of exposure that children encounter. There have been multiple studies with varying results. One of the challenges in conducting these types of surveys is the terminology used. The terms "witnesses," "observed," or "exposed" can skew the results, therefore producing data based on the varying terms. Most studies are founded on a parent's report of children witnessing violence; rarely are there self-reporting tools for children to share their observations.[8]

CHILD NEGLECT DUE TO DOMESTIC VIOLENCE

Child neglect is another form of abuse that can be directly related to domestic violence. An abuser who is capable of harming others in their family may also lack the nurturing qualities needed in properly caring for and supervising a child. The abused partner, in contrast, may not be focusing on the needs of their child as they fail to take steps to protect their children from the abuser. Additionally, the battered partner fails to take the primary role of raising their children. Children in many cases are forced into reversed roles as by default, they have to become the caretaker of the abused parent and their younger siblings. Children who are neglected during childhood can face long-term consequences such as cognitive deficits, tendencies toward illegal behavior, psychiatric disorders, alcohol problems, and violence against their intimate partner.[9] Thus the pattern of abuse continues into the next generation.

SOCIAL PATTERNS OF FAMILY VIOLENCE

Strauss, Geles, and Steinmetz studied the social patterns of family violence. In their study they compared husbands whose parents did not have a history of violence toward one another to husbands who reported at least one instance of violence between his parents. Men who had seen their parent physically attack one another were three times more likely to hit their own wives during the study. Research has also shown that children learn at a young age to threaten their mothers who have been targeted by their fathers. A child who witnesses their mother being hit by their father can view physical violence as a way to achieve the goal of getting what they want, and therefore the appropriate thing to do. Surveys have indicated that many women are battered by both their husbands and their teenage children.[10] Intergenerational transmission suggests that children, especially boys who witness their father being abusive to their mother, are more likely to abuse their own intimate partner when they enter adulthood. The more severe and frequent the abuse toward the mother in front of children, the more likely boys will believe that men are superior to women, which can lead to an abusive adult relationship.[11]

PREGNANCY AND ABUSE

Each year, about 324,000 pregnant women in the United States are battered by their intimate partner. This rate is higher than pregnant women suffering from gestational diabetes or preeclampsia, which are two conditions pregnant women are routinely screened for. However, few physicians screen pregnant women for abuse.[12] This is unfortunate as a lot of abuse disclosures occur in a health care setting. There is conflicting research in national and international studies on the prevalence of interpersonal violence during pregnancy. Some researchers believe that the risk of violence increases from the time of conception to delivery, whereas other researchers believe that the level of violence decreases. Some other studies suggest that adolescents who are pregnant have a higher rate of pregnancy violence due to the fact that they live at home and are subject to violence from both their parents and their mate.[13] There is consistency, however, when addressing the repercussions associated with interpersonal violence during pregnancy. Babies exposed to interpersonal violence can be born underweight, premature, or experience fetal trauma leading to future long-term health and developmental problems.[14] The World Health Organization suggests that intimate partner violence in the United States is substantial during pregnancy. They point out that the risk of being killed by your intimate partner increases during pregnancy, although the link between pregnancy and homicide still needs to be explored further.[15]

STRESSORS IN THE HOUSEHOLD THAT CAN LEAD TO VIOLENCE

There are many stressors that can lead to violence. Many of these tensions are part of normal family life, but for anyone with a "short fuse," their reaction to stress can be detrimental to other family members. Stressors that are common with many families can cause tensions to rise, thus initiating the first phase in the cycle of violence.

Some of the stressors include:

- Troubles with one's boss
- Troubles with co-workers
- Laid off or fired from work
- Being arrested or convicted for something serious
- Experiencing the death of someone they cared for
- Foreclosure of mortgage or loan
- Pregnant or having a child born
- Serious illness or injury
- Problems with health or behavior of family member
- Sexual difficulties
- In-law troubles
- Poor financial status
- Separation or divorce
- Increase of work hours and responsibility
- Moving one's residence
- Child expelled or suspended from school
- Child participating in illegal activity.[16]

WITNESSING DOMESTIC VIOLENCE

It is estimated that 3.3 to 4.3 million children in the United States witness domestic violence within their home each year.[17] A child who witnesses domestic violence can experience both adverse physical and psychological consequences. A rare glimpse of a child being exposed to domestic violence was the case of Ulner and Susan Still. This case garnished national attention in 2003 when Ulner instructed his thirteen-year-old son to videotape him as he insulted his wife by calling her stupid and a heifer on multiple occasions. This child was forced to witness additional abuse as he had to continue videotaping as his father subsequently inflicted kicks and punches to his mother. The videotape was eventually used as evidence as Ulner Still was sentenced to thirty-six years in prison.[18] The judicial system understands the harm caused to children by witnessing domestic violence. For example, Idaho law states that penalties for domestic violence can be doubled if the act is committed in the presence of a child under the age of sixteen (Idaho Code 18-918).[19] The U.S. Health and Human Services with the Office of Women's Health reports that children who witness domestic violence can experience physical health problems such as diabetes, obesity, and heart problems.[20] Furthermore, other studies have shown that exposing children to domestic violence can have a direct effect on their physiology as their salivary cortisol levels can be altered while being exposed to stress.[21]

PSYCHOLOGICAL CONSEQUENCES

There are several ways children can suffer psychological consequences of being subjected to an environment of domestic violence such as posttraumatic stress disorder (PTSD). This disorder affects hundreds of thousands of people who have been exposed to violent crimes such as domestic violence and child abuse. The symptoms of PTSD may initially appear as part of a normal reaction to a traumatic event, whereas sometimes this disorder will not appear until months after an event or in the case of child victims witnessing domestic violence well into their adulthood.[22] The recognition of PTSD has been extremely helpful in treating traumatized victims. However, some may argue that the term has been overused or abused as it was never intended to be used as a synonym for one who is upset, frightened, or embarrassed.

SURVIVOR SYNDROME

Advanced levels of PSTD are better known as "survivor syndrome," which has symptoms similar to PTSD such as flashbacks, hypervigilance, and recurring dreams, but there are differences such as the trust factor, emotional regression, and death imagery. Emotional regression refers to victims who put themselves into adult roles under the pressure of having to pretend to have a normal adult life while feeling themselves emotionally back in their traumatic occurrences. Death imagery refers to suffering from a symbolic death. The victim feels more connected to death (his literal or symbolic dead loved ones) than to life and to the living.[23] Survivor syndrome was first documented as the result of the work done with Jewish survivors of the Holocaust. A domestic household can become a concentration camp–like environment through physical, mental, and emotional violence, and household members can face the illnesses associated with domestic survivor syndrome.[24] Symptoms of survivor syndrome in adult children of domestic violence include:

- Delayed reaction, usually of many years, from the occurrence of the trauma to obvious symptomatology such as high anxiety levels leading to withdrawal, despair, mental blockage, lower productivity level
- Emotional fixation or regression
- Immersion in death imagery
- Survivor's guilt
- Chronic depression
- Suppressed anger taking expression in workaholism or alcoholism
- Denial: a conscious attempt to "not remember" the painful experiences
- Perpetual grief, though unaware as to the loss being grieved
- Marital problems, though no specific cause known
- Re-experiencing of victimization in current times, on jobs, etc.
- Inability to experience pleasure.[25]

Children may also face anxiety and deal with this challenge by indulging in drug, alcohol, and promiscuous sexual behavior. A child's fatalistic perception of life due to domestic violence exposure can lead children to believe that they are doomed to a life of misery and unable to control their destiny.[26]

SIBLING ABUSE

Sibling abuse is considered the most common form of family abuse compared to violence toward children by parents and between the parents themselves. Sibling relationships can include biological siblings, half siblings (sharing one parent), step siblings, adoptive siblings, foster siblings, or fictive siblings (may not be biologically related, but are still considered siblings).[27] Sibling abuse can include physical, sexual, and emotional abuse, and in some cases neglect.[28]

Measuring Sibling Abuse

According to Straus, Geles, and Steinmetz, each year three out of every hundred children are kicked, bitten, or punched by their parents. In contrast, forty-two out of every hundred children aged three to seventeen kick, bite, or punch their sibling each year. They found that 15 percent of parents hit their children with an object, 10 percent of spouses use an object against each other, and an object is used 40 percent of the time when siblings strike one another.[29] It is difficult to measure the extent of sibling physical and emotional abuse as this type of behavior is often dismissed as normal sibling rivalry and is unattended by parents. Parents fail to distinguish between sibling abuse and sibling rivalry, leaving children to fight their own battles. The parents may deny any knowledge of an abused child and in some circumstances blame the abused child for what has transpired.[30]

Physical Abuse

Sibling physical abuse can take many forms but can be grouped into three main categories: common, unusual, and injurious. Common forms of abuse include hitting, slapping, shoving, punching, biting, hair pulling, scratching, and pinching. The second category is classified as unusual and may be thought of as frivolous by some when looked at initially, but tickling can be considered abusive under certain circumstances. Tickling can be pleasant when there is trust and mutual respect and the behavior ceases when requested. However, tickling becomes painful and abusive when a person does not have control over the situation. Perpetrators may pin their victims to the floor leaving the victim helpless and at the mercy of the more powerful sibling. The third category, injurious, occurs when sibling behavior becomes so aggressive that it leads to injury, such as smothering or suffocating the sibling.[31]

Age and Sex of Sibling

The age and the sex of the sibling is also a contributing factor in the frequency and the severity of violence. For instance, younger children have trouble resolving conflict through verbal communication so they resort to physical violence more often than older children. Teenagers may resort to using their size and greater physical strength to bully and assault their younger sibling. Boys are more likely to physically assault their sibling, whereas girls are more likely to verbally spar with one another. A study found that girls use less violence when compared to boys whether it is toward a brother or sister. However, when the brother is the perpetrator, the rate of violence is lower when the sibling is his sister. Families that are composed exclusively of male children have consistently more sibling violence than families made up of only female children. The rate of violence is dramatically different for older boys between ten and fourteen years of age in all boy families as the rate of violence is more than double the rate of girls.[32]

Emotional Abuse

Emotional abuse is so commonplace in some families that it is difficult for a parent to distinguish when it is happening. Name calling, for example, is an easy way to belittle or degrade a sibling. The name calling usually focuses on a sibling's attributes such as the victim's height, weight, intelligence, the inability to perform a certain task, or the lack of a skill. Other forms of emotional abuse include degradation, which is the attack on one's dignity or self-worth. Verbal attacks between siblings occur so frequently that parents tend to accept them as normal behavior.[33] In some families, where parents may target one child for abuse, other children may identify with their parent's aggression as giving implicit permission and encouragement to abuse their sibling. With other families, the parents may actively encourage some of the children to target one of their siblings.[34]

Sexual Abuse

Sexual abuse among siblings can occur in contact and non-contact forms. Contact forms include touching, fondling, attempted penetration, and intercourse. Examples of non-contact sexual abuse include exhibitionism, forcing a sibling to watch sexual behavior, taking pornographic picture of siblings, voyeurism, and sexual harassment.[35] Sibling incest is thought to occur more frequently than parent-child incest. An exaggerated sexual climate within the family or a rigidly oppressive sexual family environment only enhances the probability of sibling sexual abuse.[36] Research has indicated that girls are forced into sex by their brothers.[37] Older siblings threaten harm to younger siblings who do not comply with their sexual demands. A common method of dealing with sibling sexual abuse is the female sibling feigns sleep. By pretending to be asleep, the prospective victim provides themselves with a psychological defense from the emotional pain and suffering associated with the abuse. Unfortunately, this response works against victims who later attempt to prosecute their offender.[38]

Effects on Sibling Abuse Survivors

The long-term effects of being a victim of sibling abuse include, but are not limited to:

- Poor self-esteem
- Problems in relationships with the opposite sex
- Difficulty with interpersonal relationships
- Repeating the victim role in other relationships
- Continued self-blame
- Sexual dysfunction
- Eating disorders, alcoholism, and drug abuse
- Depression
- PTSD.[39]

PHYSICAL PUNISHMENT AND HUSBAND-WIFE VIOLENCE IN THE NEXT GENERATION

Parents who were frequently physically punished as children tend to use physical force against their own children, although there is no evidence to support that they use force or display violence outside of child rearing. People whose parents did not hit them as teenagers have the lowest rate of violent marriages. The more physical punishment one experienced as a child, the more likely domestic violence will occur when they are married. It is clear that those children who received physical punishment as teenagers are more likely to assault their wife or husband. Teenagers who received the most physical punishment have a rate of spousal abuse four times greater than those whose parents did not batter them.

This does not mean that all children who were beaten as a child will become husband or wife beaters, and nor does it mean that those who were not beaten as a child will never physically abuse their spouse as an adult. Research has shown that people who are violent toward their children tend to be violent toward their spouse. It should also be noted that couples who did not hit one another had the lowest rate of abusive behavior toward their children. Additional studies have also shown that the more violent parents are to their children, the more likelihood the children will be violent toward their siblings.[40] The laws also have differing standards depending on who is the aggressor and who is the victim. For instance, depending on the level of aggression, physical force against a child can fall under the category of corporal punishment; therefore, the parent is not subject to any sanctions. Keep in mind, however, this same parent could be charged with assault if the child is eighteen years of age even if it be only by one day. However, if a child strikes their parents, the child will most likely be deemed delinquent and subject to sanctions from the juvenile justice system.

THE ALCOHOLIC HOME ENVIRONMENT

The alcoholic home environment can remove feelings of intimacy, control, and trust. Children learn at a very young age that it's not okay to talk about what is happening in their home. There is a sense of loyalty and that you would be betraying your family if you discussed such private family problems. There are three roles most characteristic of children in alcoholic homes: the responsible one, the adjuster, and the placater. Some children may adopt some or all of these traits. The responsible one becomes self-reliant as they learn not to trust anyone. They rely totally on their own sense of responsibility. They stay busy, stay protective and responsible, and don't learn how to play or relax. The adjusting child learns how to detach themselves from chaos and the feelings that other family members experience. The placater is the more emotionally sensitive child and learns to do things that take care of the pain in order to survive. They try to lessen the pain for everyone else until they lose a sense of their own needs.[41] Additionally, the child may be afraid to speak of their own needs because their boundaries seem to be stepped on repeatedly, and they may learn not to confront the alcoholic, as it only results in a hostile response.

PROTECTING CHILDREN FROM VIOLENCE

Whether there is an alcohol home environment or just an environment conducive to violence, the abused partner (usually the mother) realizes that the violence that is directed toward them can easily be directed toward the children.

The following are examples of how a mother can protect her children from potential violence:

- Staving off fights with the abuser until the children are asleep or out of the house

- Lying to the abuser to protect the children (i.e., covering for a mistake the child may have made that could trigger abuse by the abuser)
- Getting the abuser mad at her to distract him from his anger at them (deflecting the anger of the abuser away from the child and onto themselves thus saving them from abuse)
- Putting them to bed early every night to avoid his late-night eruptions (moving the children's bedtime up to an earlier time to avoid the abuser and late-night interruptions)
- Leaving them with relatives or babysitters frequently to keep them out of the house so they aren't around him (bringing the children elsewhere to limit their time with the abuser)
- Enrolling them (the children) in activities to keep them busy and away from him (the abuser).[42]

Although conscientious victims will take assertive steps to protect their children, there are others that are solely focused on ways to survive one more day, and many times this is at the detriment of their children.

CASE STUDY #1 (A CHILD REBELS)

Kaylin, age twelve, disclosed that she had been repeatedly raped by her stepfather for over two years. Kaylin was fortunate to have avoided the stress of having to testify in a criminal trial because her stepfather pled guilty to the offense and was sentenced to three to five years in state prison. However, even though Kaylin participated in therapy to cope with her victimization that had happened, she was angry and blamed her mother for not protecting her. Kaylin became a disruptive teenager who got involved with alcohol and illegal drugs, and became promiscuous, engaging in sexual activity in her own home. Kaylin's mother was frustrated with her disruptive and deviant behavior and began using corporal punishment as a method in an attempt to control her daughter. After a couple months of implementing corporal punishment, Kaylin struck back and assaulted her mother. Kaylin was arrested and placed in a juvenile detention facility.

DOMESTIC VIOLENCE AND CHILD CUSTODY

When an abused intimate partner takes steps to put an end to the abusive relationship, the separation is tortuous as not only do they have to confront their intimate partner who may not want the separation, they also have to fight for custody of their children. This is especially troubling for the abused partner as the very reason they gather the strength to leave is due to their children being hurt. Many abusers will fight for custody as an extension of controlling their victims. They may demand custody for the sole purpose of staying involved in their victim's life, forcing the victim to make several court appearances as a tactic to prolong contact, using court mandated visitation or custody as an opportunity to commit physical violence against the victim. Intimidating the victim into joint custody during coercive mediation sessions or refusing to pay child support are just some examples of how the abuse can continue to occur as they drag their victim back into court.[43] In addition to controlling their victims through multiple court appearances, the abuser may seek joint custody, arguing that they want to be part of their child's life and manufacturing reasons such as school events, teachers/student meetings, or doctor's appointments as an additional tactic to force contact with their victim.[44]

Unfortunately, many victims are unprepared to deal with the realities of litigation in custody disputes as victims naïvely think that by reporting the child abuse their child will be believed and protected. Unfortunately, instead they find themselves the focus of attack.[45] To help alleviate some of the potential problems in court litigations, the abused partner should be prepared by keeping a diary about important incidents; saving letters, emails, and handwritten notes from the abuser; and keeping supplementary notes of the abuser's behavior as supportive evidence.[46]

The protective parent is not the only one to face stress and hardship of going through court proceedings. The children who have already witnessed violence or have been the direct recipient of violence now have to be concerned if they will have a place to live. The family court has broad discretionary power, which can be beneficial or in some cases detrimental to victims of abuse. The courts have to address both custody and visitation rights among the parents and act on what is in the best interest of the child. Unfortunately, that doctrine is not always followed as judges will sometimes base their decision on what is considered fair among the parents. This philosophy was derived from the U.S. Constitution as addressed in *Parham v. J.R.* (U.S. 584, 1979). This was not always the case as in the early 1900s custody issues involved in divorce proceeding usually applied the Tender Years Doctrine, where young children were primarily given to the mother. This is no longer the case as fathers are commonly granted joint custody; in other cases they may obtain sole custody.[47]

When judges attempt to address the custody of the child, they may appoint mental health professionals to help determine what is in the child's best interest. However, mental health evaluations can be subjective and not always in the best interest of the child. Additionally, each litigant should have a right to choose an expert. However, the laws vary among states as to when an expert witness can be introduced. Judges, while evaluating what they feel is in the best interest of the child, may make interim custodial and visitation decisions prior to the final divorce decree. This interim order sends a message to the child that the court will or will not help protect them from the violent parent whether the child is the direct victim or not.[48] For instance, many judges believe that there is no danger in allowing a violent spouse to have access to their child when there have been no substantiated reports of child abuse, despite the fact that there is significant literature that demonstrates that spousal abuse can lead to child abuse. It should be of paramount importance that courts should not dismiss the safety of a child only to focus on the rights of a parent.

Courts may unwittingly view the protective parent unfairly. The non-violent protective parent who is forced to fight for custody may be viewed in some circumstances as being unreasonable and angry about custody. The victim may come across not as the protector but instead as the root cause of the dispute. The courts may look at the accuser with skepticism, especially if there is no evidence of abuse through police or social worker investigations. It is important to note that the lack of intervention from either investigative entity does not mean that the abuse did not occur. This is a unique challenge for the victim who is usually the mother of the child and comes to family court in many circumstances without the same financial resources as that of the abuser. The abuser, who is more financially sound in many cases, is able to use child custody litigation as yet another avenue to control and intimidate the victim, and it is unwittingly sanctioned by the court.[49]

It should also be noted that one of the forms of domestic violence is through economic control limiting the partner to finances, including the opportunity to work outside the home. This history of abuse makes it more challenging for the abused partner to find the economic resources to defend their interest. A battered parent must rely on the wisdom of those making decisions for their safety and the safety of the children. Lawyers, judges, mental health workers, or others involved within the courts relating to child custody may not comprehend the dynamics of domestic violence at the detriment of those they are attempting to serve. Court officials acting in good faith make decisions on the safety of the child, and the child has no right to dispute where they will be placed. In fact, the accused's lawyer may convince the courts to find that the alleged abuser is the better parent, giving sole custody to the abuser. When the child is the recipient of these decisions, the child has no right to appeal, absent permission of the court, and cannot object to any ruling, even if the ruling has a direct effect on their well-being.[50] The irony in courts acting in good faith can force the abused spouse to reluctantly have to send their children to be with the abuser. If they fail to comply with the judge's ruling, they can be sanctioned by the court even if the children do not want to visit the abusing parent. It is not uncommon for some judges to express more outrage of a child not seeing their parent than they do to the impact of the abuse.[51] When custody issues are resolved, whether there were allegations of domestic violence or not, parents can circumvent joint custody orders through parental alienation.

PARENTAL ALIENATION

Parental alienation is when one parent (referred to as the alienating or favored parent) engages in behaviors that foster a child's unjustified rejection of and disaffection for the other parent. Baker and Fine, the authors of *Surviving Parental Alienation*, provide examples of the strategies parents employ against one another:

- Badmouthing/denigrating the other parent: speaks ill of the other parent in front of the children in a steady stream of negative messaging; emphasizes the negative aspects of the other parent's personality and choices; vilifies the other parent within the child's community.

- Limiting contact: interferes with the amount of time the children spend with the other parent, by picking them up early or dropping them off late; shows up during the other parent's parenting time and monopolizes the children's attention.
- Interfering with communication: blocks emails and text messages; does not share cell phone numbers; does not answer calls; does not deliver gifts and letters.
- Withholding love and approval from the children: parents become emotionally cold and distant when children show positive feelings and thoughts toward the targeted parent.
- Telling the children that the targeted parent does not love them: encourage the children to falsely believe that the targeted parent does not really care about them or value them.
- Allowing/forcing the children to choose between parents: By offering desirable alternatives to visitation and/or psychologically pressuring the children to forgo parenting time with the targeted parent.
- Creating the impression that the other parent is dangerous: The alienating parent does and says things in order to plant false memories of harm or misinterpreting events to falsely create the impression that the other parent will cause harm.
- Referring to the targeted parent by first name when speaking to the children and/or encouraging them to do the same: For example, instead of saying your father's on the phone, the alienating parent may say Fred is on the phone.
- Referring to a stepparent as Mom/Dad, and encouraging the children to do the same: The alienating parent may tell their children that they now have a new mommy or daddy.[52]

These are just some of the strategies of parents who manipulate their children in hopes of alienating their child's relationship with the other parent. The replacement parents are only too willing to accept these indoctrination tactics as they want to please their new mate and are gratified for being chosen and adored by the children.[53]

DIVORCE

Divorce can be a traumatic experience for any child as a divorce is considered a loss for all members of the family. Children who grew up witnessing abuse feel less initial sadness when their parents separate because they feel a sense of relief, but after some time, they start to struggle with the same type of grief that children from non-violent families face.[54] It is estimated that 40 to 55 percent of marriages end up in divorce. The rate of separation or divorce is as high in second marriages as well, causing the continuation of family disruption.[55] The security of a child's home is jeopardized. The child's physical living arrangements are altered as the parents continue to fight for custody, but the change in the family structure does not just solely refer to the fact that one of the parents is moving out. There is also an increase in stress with the dilemma as to who is moving in. It is not uncommon for someone who is married to seek another partner soon after the separation from their spouse, and on many occasions, this new person who moves in immediately takes on a pseudo-type parental role. This new individual in the child's life could have been one of the contributing factors that led to the divorce. In many of these cases, the natural parent may naïvely believe that their child will be accepting of the new adult in their life. Unfortunately, this can happen repeatedly as parents take on multiple new partners, expecting the child to always be accepting. The stressors from blended families can also precipitate future family violence. There are two myths about a child's view on their parents' divorce: the first is that they are relieved to see a bad marriage end, and second, as so many of their friend's parents are divorcing the trauma won't be as severe to the child.[56]

STALKING

In 1990, California became the first state to pass an anti-stalking law. Now, all fifty states, the District of Columbia, Puerto Rico, The Virgin Islands, and the federal government have passed similar laws making stalking illegal throughout the country.[57] Although stalking laws have been created in part to assist victims who are trying to leave an abusive relationship, the laws themselves don't always protect a victim from further harm. The fear of living in an abusive relationship is only enhanced when an abused victim tries to escape their abuser in an attempt to end the cycle of violence.[58] Stalking, which includes the following of an individual for the purpose of instilling fear or harassment, is often a prelude to violence. Other forms of stalking include making unwanted phone calls, showing up at places for no apparent reason, spreading rumors about the victim, or even vandalizing someone's property. Stalking may or may not involve threatened or actual violence.[59] However, the goal is to intimidate or create fear for the intended target. Data released by the National Center for Victims of Crime indicate that 81 percent of women who were stalked by a current or former husband or co-habiting partner were victims of physical assault, whereas 31 percent were sexually assaulted by that partner.[60] These acts of violence can occur in or out of the presence of the victim's children. The stalker can use the victim's children as a source of intimidation. For example, consider how frightening it would be to a victim to have a former boyfriend watch your child at their bus stop. Part of controlling a victim is through intimidation, which can be a powerful weapon especially if it is directed at children. Battered parents may be forced to enter a domestic violence shelter as the only recourse to ensure temporary safety.

DOMESTIC VIOLENCE SHELTERS

The first domestic violence shelter opened in England during the early 1970s. Since that time, shelters have become commonplace. The U.S. government took an active role in promoting the shelter movement in 1994 when it passed the first Violence Against Women Act.[61] Women have been using domestic violence shelters as a temporary residence when they attempt to escape from hostilities they are facing with their current intimate partner. Although these shelters are universally recognized as a place for women to stay, there is little discussion about what happens to the children of the domestic violence victims when the mother flees with her children. In one study of women entering domestic violence shelters between 2006 and 2015, it found that most women who arrive in a shelter enter with their children. Of those children who entered some type of shelter, 80 to 90 percent of these children reported that they witnessed their mother being abused and 59 percent of them who were placed in an emergency shelter with their mother were also direct victims of abuse.[62] Unfortunately, some women never take advantage of emergency shelters and can face the most severe price of not only their lives, but the lives of their children. Familicide, as discussed in chapter 6, involves killing one's intimate partner and their children. Familicide is the final ultimate act of domestic violence as the abuser feels like they have lost control of their family and, to their mind, murder is the only recourse they have.

Toy Eagle, a family advocate for the YWCA, explains how the services work for children who enter a shelter:

> As a Family Advocate in the YWCA Sadler House Program, I often see women come from an abusive relationship that have children. Our program is designed specifically with children in mind. We believe that children have the ability to stop the cycle of violence by educating them per their age bracket. Children that are exposed to violence via an intimate partner relationship that their parents/guardians are in are three times more likely to repeat the same behaviors in adulthood. With this information in mind, we have strict protocols to follow for when a family enters our emergency program. When a child is brought into our facility, within the first 24 hours we are required to complete a safety plan

Toy Eagle YWCA

with them. The safety plan is geared towards their age. This safety plan will be helpful if this family returns to the abusive relationship. Some of the areas that are discussed are code words between the mom and the children. This code word signals danger and the need for the individual to remove themselves from the situation and seek help if possible. There is a preplanned route for the child to take if they find themselves in a potentially violent situation. For example, which neighbor to go to for safety and/or who to call when they get there and places they can hide to avoid injury. All of this is critical information for a family that lives with domestic violence. A victim returns to their abuser approximately 8-10 times before leaving for good, if she is able to survive. So we recognize that children are pulled out and brought back to this type of environment so we have to make the time we have with them count. Within the first 72 hours of entering our doors we take pride in wrapping as many services around these families as possible. Within the 72 hours we will arrange for counseling to be set up, transportation accommodations made if applicable and provide documentation which would provide these families the appropriate information to begin receiving benefits such as: Supplemental Nutrition Assistance Program (SNAP), Temporary Assistance to Needy Families (TANF), Medicaid/Medicare, Child Care Assistance Vouchers and Fuel Assistance (Gas Cards). We work with them to establish an application for child support through The Division of Child Support Enforcement. If the family has entered during the school, we will analyze their situation and determine which route to take. A family that enters our program has two options: the first option is that they will continue going to their current school in the district that they live in. This is possible because of The Stewart B. McKinney Act. The McKinney Act was established under the homelessness clause which would allow the child to continue to go to the same school and the school would be responsible for providing appropriate transportation to and from their "home" school. The purpose of this is to prevent uprooting a child if at all possible. Children have to function as best they can under these circumstances. The second option for them is to attend the school that is in the district the emergency safe-house is located. This means they would transfer schools and be in classes as close to what they were previously attending as possible. Regardless of their choice, they qualify for free lunches as well as free school supplies. The hardship that children are forced to endure is difficult enough without factoring in what is going on at home. The idea behind this is to provide as much normalcy as possible.

Each domestic violence family is different, which means their needs may vary. If the family has decided to report the violence and there are pending court hearings we connect them with our Court Advocates that can assist them throughout the Criminal Justice Process. Some families will have civil cases only which means they have chosen to file a protective order. Throughout the protective order process we will arrange for child care so the child is not exposed to court and the court proceeding unless they have been summoned to be there as a witness. If the family has criminal charges pending then we will walk them through that process giving them information in order to prepare them for what to expect. The purpose of this is to assure these families that they are not alone and have someone with them at all times.

In addition to the services I have already mentioned we offer support groups for the adults as well as the children (twice) two times a week. These groups are designed to let (allow) both adults and children to decompress from what they are going through and offer some guidance and support. The topics of these groups vary but they are educational based. The children's group is structured so that each child completes a project, task or educational worksheet the first half and then the second half is to allow them to unwind by offering a craft or playtime. The purpose of the second half of the group time is to encourage these kids to be able to be kids. Research has stated that children exposed to domestic violence are aged prematurely by 7-10 years. We offer the children the ability to be "kids" since in situations like this they are made to become a protector or a caretaker. If a family successfully completes the program before all of their matters are completed we continue to work with them outside of the program to empower them to keep pushing forward. If a family returns to an abusive situation, we are required as mandated reporters to report to Child Protective Services that these children have returned to a volatile situation and will work with them in order to keep these children safe.[63]

TRACEY THURMAN

The case of *Tracey Thurman v. City of Torrington* brought to the forefront the dangers in domestic violence and the need for the criminal justice system to respond more effectively in cases of domestic violence. On June 10, 1983, Tracey Thurman was repeatedly kicked and stabbed in the presence of her child by her estranged husband Buck Thurman. It was reported that Tracey Thurman had repeatedly contacted the police with concerns for her safety and the police appeared dismissive of her complaints. On the day of the assault, police took over twenty minutes after receiving a call for help to arrive at her residence. Tracey Thurman was permanently disabled from the injuries inflicted upon her by her violent husband and was awarded over two million dollars from the City of Torrington for violating her rights by failing to protect her. This case brought sweeping changes to the criminal justice system when responding to domestic violence.

CRIMINAL JUSTICE
RESPONSE/LAWS OF ARREST/RESTRAINING LAWS

Whether an abused victim of domestic violence remains in their household, separates from their partner, or seeks a divorce, the criminal justice system can take steps on behalf of the victim. This was not always the case as the judicial system tended to view wife abuse as a family matter. It wasn't until the landmark case of *Self v. Self* (58 Cal. 2d 683) where the California Supreme Court ruled that a spouse can take legal action against their spouse for battering.[64] Since the case of Tracey Thurman achieved national attention, law enforcement and the criminal justice system have taken more aggressive steps to assist victims of domestic violence including mandatory arrest policies and warrantless arrests. States throughout the country have either adopted mandatory arrest policies or established policies to ensure the safety of those abused. Under mandatory arrest policies, the police officer will make an arrest of any abuser regardless of if the victim wishes to pursue charges. There are conflicting perspectives on mandatory arrest laws. States that have mandatory arrest policies require police to arrest the aggressor in a domestic violence situation if there is probable cause to do so. This gives police some leeway as they are the ones evaluating the situation to determine if probable cause has been established. This subjectivity of determining probable cause gives the officer the opportunity to avoid making an arrest if they choose to do so. However, the liability surrounding not making an arrest is significant, especially if the perpetrator brings further harm or even death to their partner. In addition to the liability the police officer faces for not apprehending the aggressor is their conscience, knowing that their failure to act was the cause of someone's injury. Those who support the law argue that it ensures the offender will seek justice and takes the burden off of the victim by not having to press charges. Those in opposition to this policy argue that the voice of the victim is being silenced by not giving them a say as to what happens. In addition to mandatory arrest policies sweeping the nation was the changing legal authority to make an arrest. During the early 1970s, only fourteen states allowed police to make an arrest on a misdemeanor that was not committed in their presence. These laws seriously infringed on domestic violence cases as any officer who arrived at a domestic violence scene and believed a misdemeanor crime was committed would have to return to the police station and seek out a complaint in order to obtain an arrest warrant. In the interim, the alleged perpetrator was free and could possibly harm the victim again. By 2008, all states authorized police officers to make warrantless misdemeanor arrests in domestic violence cases.[65] When a police officer makes an arrest it can be detrimental to the abused partner, especially if they have children. The child may not want their parents being victimized, but on the other hand, they also don't want to see the abusive parent go to jail. A trained officer will attempt to arrest the abuser outside the presence of the children if it is safe to do so. However, most children will still realize what has happened and may be resentful toward the other parent even if they didn't like the abuse that was taking place. A victim of abuse is not left without any avenues to pursue; they can also file for a restraining order, which prevents the abuser from having contact with their intimate partner and in some cases, implements restrictions on the access to their children. However, it should be noted that despite the issuance of restraining orders, judges can still issue visitation orders of the complainant's children while the restraining order is still in effect.[66]

CASE STUDY #2 (ABUSE OF PROTECTIVE ORDERS)

A woman filed a restraining order against her former boyfriend alleging violence to both herself and her children. Law enforcement served the restraining order on the alleged abuser with clear instructions for the accused abuser not to have any contact directly or indirectly with the accuser or her children. Within twenty-four hours of the restraining order being served, the woman called her boyfriend on the phone, crying saying that she was sorry for what had happened and asked him to meet her at a local Burger King parking lot. The women waited for her former boyfriend to arrive and when she saw him enter the parking lot, she immediately called the police in a feigned panic, stating how her boyfriend followed her into the Burger King parking lot and was in fear for her life. The police arrested the former boyfriend for violation of a protective order; he spent the night in jail, before making an appearance in court. The next day he was able to show through phone records that his former girlfriend initiated the call just prior to their meeting in that parking lot. The police dismissed the charges of violating a restraining order and the court rescinded the restraining order. It was never determined whether the woman set him up for an arrest due to the fact that she was concerned about him approaching her in the future or whether she ever felt that she was in danger and that the false allegations of abuse were orchestrated out of spite.

Children who are exposed to domestic violence during their childhood can yearn to escape a household of turmoil only to find themselves in another form of domestic violence, commonly referred to as dating violence. Research is still relatively rare in teenage dating violence compared to domestic violence involving adults. One of the obstacles is the challenges of interviewing children under the appropriate research guidelines. Many researchers choose the easier path to interview adults and have them express their opinions of what they experienced as a teenager, relying on the memory of an adult rather than first-hand information as the abuse is still happening or just recently occurred.[67]

TEEN DATING VIOLENCE

The National Institute of Justice conducted a national survey of students in grades nine through twelve in relation to their experience with dating violence. It found that over a period of twelve months, 10 percent of the students reported being a victim of physical violence in a romantic relationship.[68] Although teen violence is still considered misunderstood and underestimated, there have been significant strides in bringing the problem to the forefront. The One Love Foundation was founded in 2010 in honor of Yeardley Love, a college student who died as a result of domestic violence. The foundation works to prevent future acts of domestic violence by providing a curriculum to colleges, high schools, and community groups. There are currently 688 colleges, 435 high schools, and 385 community groups who participate in this program.[69] February is designated as the Teen Dating Violence Awareness and Prevention Month.

Why Does Teen Dating Violence Happen?

The Centers for Disease Control and Prevention reports the following indicators that put teenagers at risk for domestic violence:

- Belief that dating violence is acceptable
- Are depressed, anxious, or have other symptoms of trauma
- Display aggression toward peers or display other aggressive behaviors
- Use drugs or illegal substances
- Engage in early sexual activity and have multiple partners
- Have a teen friend in a violent dating relationship
- Have conflicts with their partner
- Witness or experience violence in the home.[70]

Teenagers who experience dating violence face at least four unique challenges compared with adults. The first being that their young age gives them limited experience, which can make it difficult for them to detect the early potential indicators of an abusive relationship. Second, teens are highly influenced by the norms of their age group and may feel peer pressure to stay in an abusive relationship; they may feel that there are negative social repercussions for ending a relationship. Third, technology is such a significant part of their life, but it places the child at risk as offenders can use technology to maintain control over their partners. Fourth, parents of teens in an abusive relationship struggle as to how to help their children have a happy and safe relationship. Loveisrespect.org reported in 2015 that 80 percent of parents did not believe that teen dating violence was an issue or that it was an issue that teens face. Although there is growing recognition of teen dating violence, clinical guidelines in addressing teen dating violence within a family counseling context is even more scarce.[71]

Although studies of dating violence are scare, there have been some conducted to give us some insight as to the magnitude of this problem. In one study, 730 college students aged eighteen to twenty-one were surveyed about their experiences with teen dating violence. Among both male and female respondents, dating violence was rarely reported as an isolated incident. They did convey that some types of dating violence occurred earlier than other forms of violence. Among females reporting dating violence, 44.7 percent stated that they first experienced controlling behavior when they were between the ages of thirteen to fifteen. The majority of females surveyed, 62.5 percent, had been pressured into engaging in sex with threats or physical force when they were between the ages of sixteen and seventeen. The males in this survey, aged thirteen to fifteen, reported that 60 percent were subjected to "put downs" or name calling. While most of the reporting teens experienced two to five occurrences of dating violence, approximately 15 percent of both males and females experienced over twenty different incidents of dating violence.[72]

In another study, thirty adolescents currently in high school, 60 percent of them female, were surveyed on their perception of teen dating violence, which was classified as adolescent dating violence. Adolescents identified risk factors associated with adolescent dating violence. Males referred to substance abuse, stress, and (lack of) anger management as the theme for male aggression. They discussed how dating violence is more likely to occur with alcohol consumption and that society tends to use alcohol as an excuse for their behavior Additionally, males agreed that there was is a negative stigma if boys expressed their emotions, and they lacked the appropriate coping skills to deal with their anger. In contrast, females identified family life, experiencing child abuse, and witnessing family violence as risk factors for dating violence. Females explained how abuse within their family created a model for abusive behaviors, making them susceptible to become adolescent dating violence victims or even a perpetrator. Females also expressed a concern that a teenager with a lack of friends or growing up alone creates attachment issues, and this makes them less likely to want to leave an abusive relationship.[73]

Emotional Abuse

Emotional abuse can take many forms in a teenage dating relationship. Autonomy and subservience is one form of emotional abuse as the abused partner may have to ask permission to spend time with their friends.[74]

Additional tactics of emotional abuse and control include:

- Calls constantly to check up on you
- Tells you how to dress
- Tells you how to spend your money
- Manipulates you into doing whatever they want
- Send harassing or threatening emails
- Physically or sexually abuses you
- Uses violence or intimidation to get their way
- Humiliates you or puts you down in public
- Spreads rumors about you
- Threatens suicide or self-harm.[75]

Sexual Abuse

Emotional abuse is often a precursor to sexual abuse. The abuser uses language to groom their target. The following are examples of emotional abuse that can be a precursor to eventual sexual abuse:

- Use of vulgar language in front of the target
- Making sexual noises and sounds
- Using specific sexual descriptions of what the abuser wants to do to the target
- Asking questions that are too personal or sexual in nature

The abuser uses graphic or offensive sexual language directed at their target for various reasons including to:

- Scare the target into participating in sexual acts
- Desensitize the target so that they become used to the language or eventually that type of sexual behavior
- Test the target's limits and boundaries
- Sexually arouse the target.[76]

Why is there such a desire to pressure girls into having sex? Can it be blamed on hormones, or are there sociological factors why boys try to dominate girls into sexual relations? Boys may believe their male friends won't respect them as real males unless they have sex with a girl, whether they are ready or not.[77] Whatever the reason that causes this behavior, this conduct should not be tolerated. Even when the act is consensual, there is a differing standard among teens when it comes to gender. A boy who is sexually active is considered popular, whereas a girl who is sexually active may have a reputation of "being loose" or is referred to as a slut. Sexual activity is common among teenagers in today's society as it has been reported that 39.9 percent of high school students have had sexual intercourse, whereas 9.7 percent of high school students have reported having sexual intercourse with multiple partners over their lifetime.[78] Some of these high school students feel that they have been pressured into engaging in sexual activity. However, victims who attempt to stand up against their abusive partner can still fall victim to sexual assault either through physical force, manipulation, or intimidation. The crime of sexual assault is a crime that certainly targets teenagers. Studies have shown that 40 percent of women who have experienced rape reported that it happened before their eighteenth birthday as indicated in the graph.[79]

Physical Abuse

Physical abuse can occur through various means that can include pushing, kicking, slapping, pulling of the hair, punching, or physical restraint. Whether the amount of force caused injury or not, or if it was just an expression of anger used to intimidate a partner, no one has the right to put their hands on anyone else without their permission. To do otherwise is a form of physical abuse that should warrant criminal sanctions.

Boundaries

There should be healthy restrictions in any and all relationships, dating or otherwise. The first being external boundaries, which relate to one's physical and sexual limitations. Physical boundaries protect your whole body; sexual boundaries protect not only your body but also your sexuality. Internal boundaries protect your thoughts and emotions. Your emotional boundaries protect your feelings, whereas your spiritual boundaries protect your sense of hope, trust, security, and sense of spirituality.[80]

Teen Stalking

The intimidation associated with stalking is enhanced with the unique opportunities that teenagers have through the use of technology. Most teenagers are rather savvy in their knowledge of technology. These skills can be used for nefarious purposes where they are easily involved in criminal activity unbeknownst to their parents. Teenagers can control their partners by reading their text messages without their permission, requiring dating partners to remove friends from their phone lists, using technology to spread rumors about their former partners, and demanding to know their passwords to their email accounts or internet accounts.[81] In addition to technology, a teenager's lifestyle is easy to follow, especially if you don't have access to a vehicle. Unlike most adult relationships, a teenager's romantic partner is almost always in close proximity as the teenagers who are in relationships usually attend the same school.

Homosexual Relationships

The social dynamics of teenage dating violence can be amplified with same sex relationships. Homosexual couples face the same challenges as heterosexual couples such as being victimized through emotional, physical, and sexual abuse. However, the stigma of homosexuality can keep some people in an abusive relationship in an attempt to avoid the public becoming aware of their sexual orientation. An abuser can control their partner through threats of exposure. This is significant as there are many teenagers who keep their sexual orientation secret from their parents. The threat of this exposure by an abusive partner can be a powerful tool to maintain control in a relationship. In a study of 117 adolescents who reported exclusively same sex romantic or sexual relationships, 25 percent disclosed some type of partner violence, with 10 percent reporting physical violence victimization. This study also revealed that males were a lot less likely to report their victimization.[82]

Criminal Justice Response to Teen Dating Violence:

In theory, the criminal justice system should provide the same protections to adolescent victims of domestic violence as any adult who sought protection through that same criminal justice system. Although the goals to protect children are the same as of adults, the ability to achieve these goals varies considerably. For instance, an adult can go into hiding, whether it's by entering a shelter, fleeing the area, or changing their name. In contrast, there are few shelters that will allow children access by themselves, and if the child decides to flee the area, the parents can report them as a runaway, where police will search for them and bring them back home, only to be targeted for future abuse. If the adolescent decides to rely on the police and courts for protection, they will soon be made aware that they don't experience the same protective rights of an adult. Not all states allow children to apply for protective order, and some of the states who do allow protective orders only distribute them with parental consent. Fortunately, an increasing number of states are granting protective orders without parental consent. There are also age restrictions on obtaining a protective order so a younger teenager may not have the authority to apply for an order of protection. To complicate the issue even further is the jurisdiction of a protective order once issued. If the offender is a juvenile, then there are the sanctions imposed through the juvenile justice system, which focuses on rehabilitation instead of punishment. In addition to the limited protection afforded to teens subjected to violence are the laws that impede sexual abuse. The legal remedies for sexual abuse of a child are becoming more obscure. Victims in teen dating violence are continually subjected to sexual abuse by older adolescents or younger adults. As discussed in chapter 3, legislatures around the country are implementing age of consent laws, making it easier for potentially abusive partners to legally engage in sexual activity with children. Finally, are teenage victims of domestic violence considered victims of child abuse? The Child Abuse Prevention and Treatment Act requires states to report child abuse for any physical or mental injury, sexual abuse, or negligent treatment of a child under the age of eighteen by a person who is responsible for the child's welfare. As victims of abuse in dating relationships are not "under the care and responsibility" of their intimate partner, there is no obligation to report. This puts professionals who are caring for teenagers in an ethical predicament. Do mental health providers, counselors, social workers, or teachers have an obligation to report dating violence to the parents of a teenage victim? Professionals in the field may want to encourage the teenagers to report the victimization to their parents.[83] If the parents are aware of the situation and fail to act, are they considered neglectful as they are the caretaker? Furthermore, should professionals who are listed as mandated reporters have an obligation to report the inactions of the parent?

CONCLUSION

Society has made significant strides in protecting adults from intimate partner violence. However, the indirect victimization that children face from witnessing domestic violence does not appear to garner the same level of attention. Research clearly indicates the long-term repercussions that children will encounter as a result of living in a hostile environment. Some children will learn to become abusers later on in life, whereas others learn to accept their victimization that results from domestic violence. For teenagers who do become victims of intimate partner violence, they soon discover that society does not provide them the same level of protection as that of an adult victim.

REVIEW QUESTIONS

1. How are teenagers not receiving the same level of protection in intimate partner violence in comparison to adult victims?

2. What are some of the circumstances surrounding stalking that does not involve actual violence?

3. How is parental alienation detrimental to a child?

4. Why was the Power and Control Wheel created?

5. How did the case of Tracey Thurman affect the role of law enforcement?

KEYWORDS

Domestic violence: Any criminal offense involving violence or physical harm committed by one family or household member against another.

Stalking: A course of conduct directed at a certain person that involves repeated following and/or harassing that would cause a reasonable person fear.

Dating violence: A pattern of abusive behaviors used to exert power and control over their dating partner.

Parental alienation: Behaviors which foster a child's unjustified rejection of and disaffection for the other parent.

NOTES

1. U.S. Department of Health and Human Services. "Child Information Gate Way. Definitions of Domestic Violence," 3. Accessed February 17, 2019. Available from https://www.childwelfare.gov/pubpdfs/defdomvio.pdf.

2. Stephen Meyer, *Child Abuse and Domestic Violence: Information Plus* (Farmington Hills, MI, 2017), 1.

3. Joyce Edward, *The Sibling Relationship: A Force for Growth and Conflict* (Lanham, MD: Rowman & Littlefield, 2011), 39.

4. Murray A. Straus, Richard J. Geles, and Suzanne K. Steinmetz, *Behind Closed Doors: Violence in the American Family* (Piscataway, NJ: Transaction Publishers, 2006, 52.

5. Elizabeth Quinn and Sara Brightman, *Crime Victimization: A Comprehensive Overview* (Durham, NC: Carolina Academic Press, 2015), 125.

6. Quinn and Brightman, *Crime Victimization*, 125.

7. Steven E. Barkan, *Criminology: A Sociological Understanding*, seventh edition (New York, NY: Pearson, 2018), 144.

8. Jeffrey L. Edleson, Narae Shin, and Katy K. Johnson Armendariz, "Measuring Children's Exposure to Domestic Violence: The Development and Testing of the Child Exposure to Domestic Violence (CEDV) Scale," *Children and Youth Services Review* 30, no. 5 (2007): 503.

9. Cindy L. Miller-Perrin, Robin D. Perrin, and Claire M. Renzetti, *Violence and Maltreatment in Intimate Relationships* (Thousand Oaks, CA: Sage, 2018), 131; Betsy McAlister Groves, *Children Who See Too Much: Lessons from Child Witness to Violence Project* (Boston, MA: Beacon Press, 2003), 37.

10. Straus, Geles, and Steinmetz, *Behind Closed Doors: Violence in the American Family*, 100–04.

11. Miller-Perrin, Perrin, and Renzeti, *Violence and Maltreatment in Intimate Relationships*, 237; Lundy Bancroft, *When Dad Hurts Mom: Helping Your Children Heal the Wound of Witnessing Abuse* (New York, NY: Berkeley, 2004), 120.

12. Nicole A. Maiocco and Mike Maiocco, *Family Violence: Beyond the Bruises* (Santa Ana, CA: Police & Fire Publishing, 2009), 66.

13. Tamara L. Taillieu and Douglas A. Brownridge, "Violence Against Pregnant Women: Prevalence, Patterns, Risk Factors, Theories, and Direction for Future Research," *Aggression and Violent Behavior* 15, no. 1 (2010): 24.

14. Beth A. Bailey, "Partner Violence during Pregnancy: Prevalence, Effect, Screening, and Management," *International Journal of Women's Health* 2, no. 1 (2009): 184–86; Jan L. Jasinski, "Pregnancy and Domestic Violence: A Review of the Literature," *Trauma Violence*

Abuse 5, no. 1 (2004): 55–56; Jeanne L. Alhusen, Ellen Ray, Phyllis Sharps, and Linda Bullock, "Intimate Partner Violence During Pregancy: Maternal and Neonatal Outcome," *Journal of Women's Health* 24, no. 1 (2015): 101.

15. World Health Organization, Intimate Partner Violence During Pregnancy. Accessed January 7, 2019. Available from http://apps.who.int/iris/bitstream/handle/10665/70764/WHO_RHR_11.35_eng.pdf;jsessionid=E10B685FD4A7B915A99AA6248D516DE9?sequence=1.

16. Straus, Geles, and Steinmetz, *Behind Closed Doors: Violence in the American Family*, 182.

17. Maiocco and Maiocco, *Family Violence: Beyond the Bruises*, 72.

18. Lisa Capretto, "One Mom's Life 11 Years After Her Husband Abused Her and Forced Their Son to Videotape It," *Huffington Post*, December 6, 2017. Accessed January 7, 2019. Available from https://www.huffingtonpost.com/2014/11/17/susan-still-abuse-update_n_6161258.html.

19. Monica L. McCoy and Stephanie M. Keen, *Child Abuse and Neglect*, second edition (New York, NY: Psychology Press, 2014), 103.

20. U.S. Department on Health and Human Services: Office on Women's Health, Effects of Domestic Violence on Children. Accessed January 7, 2019. Available from https://www.womenshealth.gov/relationships-and-safety/domestic-violence/effects-domestic-violence-children.

21. Christopher M. Adams, "The Consequences of Witnessing Family Violence on Children and Implications for Family Counselors," *The Family Journal* 14, no. 4 (2006): 335–38.

22. Robert J. Meadows, *Understanding Violence & Victimization*, seventh edition (New York,NY: Pearson, 2019), 26; Groves, *Children Who See Too Much*, 38.

23. Sherry Lewis Henry, *Trauma & Survivor Syndrome Effects on Children Who Witness Domestic Violence* (Houston, TX: Strategic Publishing, 2012), 28.

24. Henry, *Trauma & Survivor Syndrome Effects on Children Who Witness Domestic Violence*, 2–26.

25. Henry, *Trauma & Survivor Syndrome Effects on Children Who Witness Domestic Violence*, 26–27.

26. Meadows, *Understanding Violence & Victimization*, 58.

27. Mark S. Kiselica and Mandy Morrill-Richards, "Sibling Maltreatment: The Forgotten Abuse," *Journal of Counseling & Development* 85, no. 2 (20007): 149.

28. Straus, Geles, and Steinmetz, *Behind Closed Doors: Violence in the American Family*, 77–83.

29. Straus, Geles, and Steinmetz, *Behind Closed Doors: Violence in the American Family*, 83.

30. Edward, *The Sibling Relationship*, 92.

31. Vernon R. Wiehe, *What Parents Need to Know about Sibling Abuse: Breaking the Cycle of Violence* (Springfield, UT: Bonneville, 2002), 43–46.

32. Straus, Geles, and Steinmetz, *Behind Closed Doors: Violence in the American Family*, 84–92.

33. Wiehe, *What Parents Need to Know about Sibling Abuse*, 57.

34. Edward, *The Sibling Relationship* 93

35. Wiehe, *What Parents Need to Know about Sibling Abuse*, 62–63.

36. Kiselica and Morrill-Richards, "Sibling Maltreatment: The Forgotten Abuse," 150.

37. Edward, *The Sibling Relationship* 111-112

38. Wiehe, *What Parents Need to Know about Sibling Abuse*, 76–77.

39. Wiehe, *What Parents Need to Know about Sibling Abuse*, 106–12.

40. Straus, Geles, and Steinmetz, *Behind Closed Doors: Violence in the American Family*, 109–17; Wiehe, *What Parents Need to Know about Sibling Abuse*, 73.

41. Henry, *Trauma & Survivor Syndrome Effects on Children Who Witness Domestic Violence*, 40–41.

42. Bancroft, *When Dad Hurts Mom*, 180.

43. Emmaline Campbell, "How Domestic Violence Batterers Use Custody Proceedings in Family Courts to Abuse Victims and How Courts Can Put a Stop to It," *UCLA Women's Law Journal* 241, no. 1 (2017): 42.

44. Campbell, "How Domestic Violence Batterers Use Custody Proceedings in Family Courts to Abuse Victims and How Courts Can Put a Stop to It," 59.

45. Toby G. Kleinman and Daniel Pollack, *Domestic Abuse, Child Custody, and Visitation: Winning in Family Court* (New York, NY: Oxford, 2017), 120.

46. Bancroft, *When Dad Hurts Mom*, 232.

47. Bancroft, *When Dad Hurts Mom*, 240.

48. Kleinman and Pollack, *Domestic Abuse, Child Custody, and Visitation*, 3–4.

49. Kleinman and Pollack, *Domestic Abuse, Child Custody, and Visitation*, 13–49.

50. Kleinman and Pollack, *Domestic Abuse, Child Custody, and Visitation*, 65.

51. Kleinman and Pollack, *Domestic Abuse, Child Custody, and Visitation*, 52.

52. Amy J.L. Baker and Paul R. Fine, Surviving Parental Alienation: A Journey of Hope and Healing (Lanham, MD: Rowman & Littlefield, 2014), 8–11.

53. Baker and Fine, *Surviving Parental Alienation*, 89.

54. Bancroft, *When Dad Hurts Mom*, 208.

55. Edward, *The Sibling Relationship*, 40.

56. Marjorie J. Kostelnik, Anne K. Soderman, Alice Phipps Whiren, and Michelle L. Rupiper, *Guiding Children's Social Development & Learning: Theory and Skills*, ninth edition (Boston, MA: Cengage, 2018), 165.

57. Denise Kindschi Gosselin, *Heavy Hands: An Introduction to the Crimes of Family Violence*, fourth edition (Boston, MA: Pearson, 2010), 309.

58. William G. Doerner and Steven P. Lab, *Victimology*, seventh edition (Waltham, MA: Anderson Publishing, 2015), 208.

59. Ann Wolbert Burgess, Cheryl Regehr, and Albert R. Roberts, *Victimology: Theories and Applications*, second edition (Burlington, MA: Jones & Bartlett, 2013), 329.

60. Meadows, *Understanding Violence & Victimization*, 48.

61. Miller-Perrin, Perrin, and Renzeti, *Violence and Maltreatment in Intimate Relationships*, 17.

62. Liria Fernandez-Gonzalez, Esther Calvete, Izaskum Orve, and Alice Mauri, "Victims of Domestic Violence in Shelters: Impacts on Women and Children," *The Spanish Journal of Psychology* 21, no. e18 (2018): 6.

63. Toy Eagle, email message to author, January 4, 2019.

64. Meyer, *Child Abuse and Domestic Violence*, 163.

65. Meyer, *Child Abuse and Domestic Violence*, 160.

66. Kleinman and Pollack, *Domestic Abuse, Child Custody, and Visitation*, 4.

67. Susan M. Sanders, *Teen Dating Violence: The Invisible Peril* (New York, NY: Peter Lang Publishing, 2003), 4.

68. Office of Justice Programs: National Institute of Justice. Criminal Justice System Response to Teen Dating Violence. Accessed on January 15, 2019. Available from https://www.nij.gov/topics/crime/intimate-partner-violence/teen-dating-violence/Pages/system-response.aspx.

69. One Love Foundation. Accessed January 15, 2019. Available from https://www.joinonelove.org/.

70. Centers for Disease Control and Prevention. Teen Dating Violence. Accessed January 15, 2019. Available from https://www.cdc.gov/violenceprevention/intimatepartnerviolence/teen_dating_violence.html.

71. Christine E. Murray, Kelly King, and Allison Crowe, "Understanding and Addressing Teen Violence: Implications for Family Counselors," *The Family Journal* 24, no. 1 (2016): 53.

72. Amy E. Bonomi, Melissa L. Anderson, Julianna Nemeth, Suzanne Bartle-Haring, Cynthia Buettner, and Deborah Schipper, "Dating Violence Victimization across the Teen Years:

Abuse Frequency, Number of Abusive Partners, and Age of First Occurrence," *BMC Public Health* 12, no. 637 (2012): 6–8.

73. Sarah Taylor, Carrie A. Calkins, Ya Xia, and Rochelle L. Dalla, "Adolescent Perceptions of Dating Violence: A Qualitative Study," *Journal of Interpersonal Violence* 1, no. 21 (2017): 10–11.

74. Sanders, *Teen Dating Violence*, 80.

75. Kathleen M. McGee and Laura J. Buddenberg, *Unmasking Sexual Con Games: A Teen's Guide to Avoiding Emotional Grooming and Dating Violence*, third edition (Boys Town, NE: Boys Town Press, 2003), 42.

76. McGee and Buddenberg, *Unmasking Sexual Con Games*, 32–33.

77. Patricia Evans, *Teen Torment: Overcoming Verbal Abuse at Home and at School* (Avon, MA: Adams Media, 2003), 260.

78. Laura Kann, Tim McManus, William A. Harris, Shari L. Shanklin, Katherine H. Flint, Barbara Queen, Richard Lowry, David Chyen, Lisa Whittle, Jemekia Thornton, Connie Lim, Denise Bradford, Yoshimi Yamakawa, Michelle Leon, Nancy Brener, and Kathleen A. Ethier, "Youth Risk Behavior Surveillance-United States, 2017," *Surveillance Summaries* 67, no. 8 (2018): 1.

79. Matthew J. Breiding, Sharon G. Smith, Kathleen C. Basile, Mikel L. Waters, Jieru Chen, and Melissa T. Merrick, "Prevalence and Characteristics of Sexual Violence, Stalking, and Intimate Partner Violence Victimization—National Intimate Partner and Sexual Violence Survey, United States, 2011," *Surveillance Summaries* 63, no. 8 (2014): 4.

80. McGee and Buddenberg, *Unmasking Sexual Con Games*, 46.

81. Miller-Perrin, Perrin, and Renzeti, *Violence and Maltreatment in Intimate Relationships*, 194

82. Carolyn Tucker Halpern, Mary L. Young, Martha W. Waler, Sandra L. Matin, Lawrence L. Kupper, "Prevalence of Partner Violence in Same-Sex Romantic and Sexual Relationships in a National Sample of Adolescents," *Journal of Adolescent Health* 35, no. 2 (2004): 124.

83. Sanders, *Teen Dating Violence*, 46–48.

11

Child Abuse in School

◆ ◆ ◆

Before reading this chapter, it is important to note how the vast majority of teachers, administrators, and support staff have chosen a profession that involves children due to their commitment to help children in need and to assist every child in reaching their goals. School personnel are expected to create miracles from children who come from families that are in complete dysfunction whether through drug abuse, domestic violence, custody battles, or an evolving family structure. In fact, educators are consistently the primary reporters of child abuse. However, we would be remiss if we didn't identify the dangers that some children face within their school system. The Equal Protection Clause under the fourteenth amendment guarantees that every child has the same access to an education. However, the amendment doesn't ensure that each child be treated fairly and that they can safely pursue their education. We are placing our children in the trust and care of school officials, and most parents rely on that trust because they are unable to witness first-hand what takes place within a school setting. "Trust should be a slippery slope whenever public-sector workers conspire to lessen transparency. Public education contains voluminous information from which conclusions regarding quality of service can be ascertained, yet seldom does the education system undertake self-analysis where unwelcome findings are simplistically portrayed in the public arena."[1] This chapter is designed to take the secrecy of abuse out of our school systems and bring these issues to the forefront.

CHAPTER DESIGN

Dangers can arise from any adult caretaker who abuses children either through sexual, physical, or psychological abuse or neglect by failing to either provide an appropriate education or provide the expected safety when a child enters the facility. This chapter will address two primary factors relating to the victimization of children. The first segment will address how school personnel are directly responsible for the abuse of children whether through physical, psychological, or sexual means or neglecting to provide an appropriate education. The second segment of this chapter will address school violence and whether school administrators, teachers, and support staff are taking appropriate measures to protect children from harm. Before we can address either segment, we need to identify the significance of the problem. It can be a challenging endeavor whenever there is an attempt to measure the amount of abuse that takes place within a school system as the quantitative data may be insurmountable. However, there are resources available that address victimization in school.

MEASURING ABUSE

Schools are notoriously hesitant to allow researchers into their facilities for a variety of reasons including the fact that children are considered a protected population so conducting research that requires student participation faces increased scrutiny by institutional review boards. Schools who conduct their own research for internal school purposes may not need to obtain permission, but if they conducted research in partnership with a college or a university they would be subjected to additional guidelines.[2] The National Children's Advocacy Center reports on the sexual misconduct of teachers, administrators, coaches, counselors, tutors, and volunteers that work in school systems. They reported that in a five-year period 2,570 school personnel had their teaching credentials revoked, denied, surrendered, or sanctioned for sexual misconduct with a student. In 446 of these cases, the educator had multiple victims. Educational sexual misconduct can involve sexual innuendos; inappropriate touching; inappropriate texting, email, or other forms of social media; or soliciting sex from a student or sexual contact with a student.[3] However, these forms of abuse may have no official record of happening as schools are notorious for covering up misconduct handling the misconduct by "passing the trash."

PASSING THE TRASH

Title 9 of the educational amendments of 1972 requires schools to have procedures in place to protect students from sexual abuse from school personnel.[4] However, some school districts throughout the nation have the dubious reputation of protecting their fellow educators instead of the children they serve. Passing the trash refers to the practice of school officials allowing teachers suspected of sexual abuse to pursue another job at a different school district without revealing the tainted history of their former employee. The Prohibition of Aiding and Abetting Sexual Abuse, a provision in the U.S. Every Student Succeeds Act aims to eliminate the practice of passing the trash. Research has shown that only four states completely abide with the Every Student Succeeds Act, whereas several others are in the process of creating legislation or policy to address this issue. However, the vast majority of states have no plans or policies to be aligned with this provision.[5] Additionally, there is no central clearinghouse that tracks and reports cases of sexual misconduct of school personnel and the children they are supposed to protect.[6] The process that leads to passing the trash is that the offender forms an agreement with the school administration and the employees' union in which the offender voluntarily resigns from the school in exchange for:

- No reporting to the police
- No disciplinary action taken
- No indication of an allegation within their personnel file
- A positive letter of reference.[7]

In cases where teachers are reported and their teaching credentials revoked, many of these educators are able to seek employment at another school. The National Association of State Directors of Teacher Education and Certification is voluntary, and the association does not specify why a teacher's credentials were revoked.[8] In 2004, Charol Shakeshaft of Hofstra University submitted research to the Department of Education relating to sexual misconduct of educators and other school personnel. Through various studies and surveys, the most common offender of sexual abuse toward children were teachers, followed by coaches. Some of the other positons relating to sexual abuse of children within schools included substitute teachers, bus drivers, teacher's aides, security guards, principals, and counselors. The study also revealed that 57.2 percent of the offenders were male and 42.8 percent were female. The average age of the offender was twenty-eight, and same sex misconduct ranged from 18 to 28 percent of the offenses, depending on the study. Most of the victims in this study were female (56 percent) and most victims were Caucasian (51.5 percent), followed by children of African descent with 25.3 percent and Latino students representing 15.7 percent.[9] *USA Today* conducted their own research of educators who lost their teaching credentials for sexual misconduct and found that they were still able to find employment allowing them to work with children.

After locating one hundred teachers who lost their credentials, they discovered that:

- Twenty-two were working in public schools
- Twenty were working for higher education
- Eleven were working for religious groups
- Ten were working for youth sports
- Nine were in private schools
- Eight were providing private tutoring
- Six were classified as other
- Five were working in childcare facilities
- Five were working as private music teachers
- Four were working in charter schools.[10]

CASE STUDY #1 (SCHOOL CONCEALS TEACHER ACCUSED OF MASTURBATING)

Mr. Belcastro, a high school English teacher, was accused of kissing a student on the neck while she took a make-up exam after school. When the child told her parents, it was immediately reported to school officials who in turn told the family that they would investigate the matter. A year passed with no resolution, so the family reported the incident to the police, but the police told them that the statute of limitations had expired and they could no longer bring charges. Allegations against Mr. Belcastro continued just a few weeks later when another student reported that while taking her make-up exam alone after school she observed Mr. Belcastro masturbating behind his desk using his briefcase to cover his actions. The student, who was a senior, told the school officials that she can tell when a guy is "jerking off" and stated that she saw him cleaning himself off with a paper towel and then putting the towel in the trash. A few days later, a different student made the same allegation while she too was taking a make-up exam after school. It should be noted that none of the girls knew each other or were aware of the other allegations. The school district debated with their attorneys whether they needed to contact the police as there was no allegation of sexual contact. After a few days of conducting their own "investigation," the school officials contacted the police. The police were upset they were not notified immediately as they could have obtained DNA from both the briefcase and the paper towel that was discarded. Both girls wanted to pursue charges against Mr. Belcastro even though they were advised that the case would be difficult to prove, especially as school officials deliberately hindered the investigation. Mr. Belcastro was later found not guilty in court. The school offered him a lucrative buyout plan if he would leave the school. He was hired the following year by a different school district in a neighboring state and was arrested shortly after his employment for sexually assaulting two disabled female middle school students.

INAPPROPRIATE STUDENT/TEACHER RELATIONSHIPS

Each teacher has some type of relationship with their student whether it is an academic relationship in the classroom or through extracurricular activity such as coaching, mentoring, school dance supervision, or any school-related activity outside the traditional classroom. However, when a teacher establishes an interpersonal but not school-related activity with a student, it may be deemed inappropriate. However, not all relationships that form outside the school setting cross the line of professionalism. The use of technology has provided the opportunity for relationships to develop faster and this can occur twenty-four hours a day.[11] Social media outlets such as Facebook provide ample opportunities for teachers to form relationships readily with their students.

THE SEXUALLY ABUSIVE TEACHER

The abusing teacher may be a male or female, and their sexual attraction no matter how specific can be met with children kindergarten through twelfth grade. The pedophile that is sexually attracted to prepubescent children can easily find a pool of potential victims through their easy access to young people into their middle school years. Educators who have a primary attraction to early pubescent children (hebephilia) can often acquire children to meet their sexual desires in elementary or middle schools and the sexual attraction to older adolescents (ephebophilia) can be satisfied with those students in high schools. There is a legitimate concern with educators who are sexually attracted to children.

One can google teacher/child porn to see what appears to be an endless number of articles reporting those in the educational field being arrested for child pornography. Although there is the potential of child predators working within the school system who have a unique attraction to certain physical characteristics of children, according to Kurt Michael Brundage, most acts of sexual abuse are situational where the offender has a normal adult sexual relationship, and circumstance led them to a sexual encounter with a child, not due to the child's age but despite their age.[12] Sexual abuse can range from inappropriate contact to sexual intercourse or any other form of sexual exploitation. Sexual abuse may also take non-contact forms such as sexual harassment.

DOUBLE STANDARD

Females use the same techniques of gradualism, grooming, flirting, and targeting of male students as that of male teachers grooming female students. However, the motive for a male teacher to want sexual relations with a student may differ from that of a female teacher. Male teachers may engage in sexual abuse through sexual desires or midlife crises, whereas female teachers are looking for vulnerabilities, poor or missing family relationships, or sexual interests such as early stages of male puberty. Other motivations for female teachers may be the desire to care for a male child from a broken home, which then de-evolves into sex and a need to feel attractive and desired by a young male.[13] There are few studies on the perception of female perpetrators on male students. Is there a double standard when there is a female teacher who commits such a crime? Viewers can Google the "10 Hottest Female Sex Offender Teachers," or "The 18 Hottest Teachers Caught Having Sex With Their Students."[14] In one study analyzing over nine hundred online comments addressing female sex offenders, most commenters acknowledged that there is indeed a double standard when sentencing female offenders. Although the majority of respondents felt that females were treated more leniently then males, there were some comments that focused on the offender's body where 12.8 percent discussed how attractive they found her and how sexually desirable she appeared. Other commenters when addressing consent stated sex between a male student and a female teacher that is consensual is a valuable experience his future girlfriend or wife will appreciate. Other respondents blamed the victim, stating how they are ruining the teacher's life.

Only 10.3 percent of all commenters described the teacher-student sexual relationship as nonconsensual.[15]

BACKGROUND CHECKS

The Government Accountability Office reported that forty-six of the fifty states in the United States require background checks for applicants such as teachers or bus drivers seeking public school employment although the methods employed to conduct such background checks vary considerably. Some of the variations included matching date of birth to name. While some schools used fingerprints for backgrounds, only thirty-six states used both state and federal databases. Forty-two states established professional codes of conduct including stipulations that address boundaries between teachers and students. However, only eighteen of those of the forty-two states required the school district to provide the training to address these boundaries. Forty-six states have laws requiring school personnel to report sexual abuse, with forty-three of those states having penalties for not reporting.[16]

UNDERSTANDING THE TEACHER GROOMING PROCESS

The sexual grooming process for teachers is similar to that of any adult as the vast majority of sexual abuse occurs through manipulation. Like most groomers, teachers target a particular child and they attempt to "befriend" them to initiate the process, working toward sexual exploitation. Steps in the grooming process may include:

- Special attention to the targeted victim
- Special recognitions and awards, verbal praise, or gifts for the targeted victim
- Special privileges and opportunities for targeted victim
- Slowly increasing amounts of touching and sexual comments as to assess the student's response and likelihood of resisting or filing a complaint
- Progressive sexual behavior to desensitize the student to what is happening and further testing their resistance and the propensity to file a complaint
- Acts of sexual exploitation, which can occur in some instances for more than one grade
- Emphasis on the victim's mutual responsibility for the sexual activity and the need for secrecy.[17]

THE PHYSICALLY ABUSIVE TEACHER

Corporal punishment has been common in schools since the colonial period. In 1977, the U.S. Supreme Court ruled in *Ingraham v. Wright* that corporal punishment was constitutional and left it up to the states on whether they wanted to implement it. When parents place their children in private schools, school personnel act in loco parentis over the children. In public schools, however, discipline is not directly analogous to parental authority, but instead educators act through constitutional constraints.[18] Today, corporal punishment is legal in nineteen states where it is estimated that 160,000 students are subjected to physical discipline. Corporal punishment is being implemented in some states for what is considered serious behavioral issues that can involve a child's safety such as fighting, bullying, lighting off fireworks, etc. However, evidence shows that corporal punishment is also implemented for misbehaviors that do not rise to the same level of seriousness such as violating dress codes, running in hallways, not turning in homework, sleeping in class, etc. The argument for the use of physical means to discipline children has been accepted through the rationale that children need to have attention and obtain compliance with school rules.[19] The American Professional Society on the Abuse of Children calls for the elimination of all forms of corporal punishment as they believe it increases the risk for physical abuse and should not be used in the name of discipline. Other influential organizations such as the National Center on Child Abuse Prevention, the American Academy of Pediatrics, as well as the American Medical Association have advocated for banning physical punishment in schools. "As of May 2016, 49 countries worldwide had prohibited all corporal punishment of children, including in the home and at least 54 more countries had expressed a commitment to full prohibition."[20] (For the most current list, see http://www.endcorporalpunishment.org/.) In the United States, roughly half of the states have banned corporal punishment in their schools. Alabama has the dubious distinction of having the greatest number of students paddled.[21]

CASE STUDY #2 (TEACHER WHIPPING)

A woman came to the police station reporting that her son Joshua, age ten, sustained substantial injuries while attending a private Christian school. She explained that the pastor struck Joshua on his buttocks using his belt when he had not completed his homework. The woman acknowledged that she had signed a document allowing the school to use physical force to ensure discipline as a requirement of acceptance into this educational facility. She stated that the pastor did apologize, stating that he may have been too forceful in his discipline. These facts were brought to the attention of the local prosecutor who, although she was upset about the abuse, declined to prosecute.

THE EMOTIONALLY ABUSIVE TEACHER

Emotional abuse can be defined as,

> Any abusive behavior that isn't physical, which may include verbal aggression, intimidation, manipulation, and humiliation, which most often unfolds as a pattern of behavior over time **that aims to** diminish another person's sense of

identity, dignity and self-worth, and which often results in anxiety, depression, suicidal thoughts or behaviors, and post-traumatic stress disorder.[22]

The concept of emotional abuse is examined and delimited, and its prevalence is identified. Professionals such as teachers have a professional responsibility to reduce all forms of abuse, including emotional abuse, whether they are witnessing abuse by students or addressing their own behavior within the classroom.[23] The question is who sets the boundaries as to what is considered acceptable behavior among teachers. Emotional abuse may include not giving a child the opportunity to express their views by deliberately silencing them or making fun of their perspective and how they communicate their thoughts. Emotional abuse can also occur through inappropriate expectations of a child's developmental capability, as well as overprotection and limitation of exploration and learning or not allowing the student to participate in normal social interaction.[24] Additionally, teachers may simply ignore students as a form of emotional abuse. An educator can deliberately ignore a child who wishes to participate in a discussion, refuse to call on a student who raises their hand to answer a particular question, refuse to assist a child who is seeking guidance, or even ostracize the child.[25] The greatest risk of this form of child abuse is when the teacher does not have sufficient competence and self-control to maximize child learning within her educational setting. When an instructor loses her ability to achieve this goal, they may resort to emotional abuse in the name of discipline. Classroom discipline differs from emotional abuse but distinguishing between the two can be challenging at times.[26] Non-physical forms of punishment may include belittling, humiliating, demeaning, degrading, threatening, or scaring the child, which causes the child a great deal of stress. Educational institutions may have innovated tactics to humiliate children including:

- Deliberately humiliating a child in front of other students in class or during school assembly
- Pinning paper on the child's back with a derogatory label
- Tearing up notebooks/exam papers
- Making the child sit on the floor of the classroom
- Detention during break time and lunch
- Having the child stand outside the classroom
- Forcing students to read out loud in front of their peers regardless of their disabilities and speech impediments
- Ice-breaking games that force students to ask probing or personal questions of their peers
- Displaying a student's individual grades in front of the entire class.[27]

Depending on the school, this type of discipline may not be tolerated by the school administration, but a lot of individual disciplinary actions within a classroom never come to the attention of the administration or school board. However, in the day of social media, students are regularly recording events that occur within the classroom, making it more difficult for a teacher to deny an allegation of misbehavior. Other forms of emotional abuse may be achieved easily through passive-aggressive rejecting behaviors such as:

- Not calling on a student
- Failing to give a student a handout that the rest of the class received
- Never using the student's name despite recognizing the rest of the class by name
- Never choosing that student for special tasks
- Missing a student when something special is to happen (e.g., not sending a student for a special award they may have received or not calling out the student's name in front of the class when the student has done some exceptional academic work)
- Making sure that the student is always last, whether last in line for lunch, last to receive a grade, or last to use the bathroom.[28]

The emotionally abusive teacher can deliberately target a student by using the grading system as a weapon. However, the practice of grade manipulation is not easily accomplished in elementary school as papers are rather simple and answers are straightforward. The following are examples of how grading can be used to target a student that the teacher does not care for:

- Not assigning a grade to a well-done paper that would ordinarily be graded
- Marking answers wrong when they actually were correct
- Assigning grades based on excessively marking down items that were not related to the assignment
- Grading very low when there were few errors
- Assessing work that is usually not graded and assigning a low grade
- Not even reading the paper and simply assigning low grades
- Grading classroom activities low that have no basis for a grade.[29]

THE NEGLECTFUL TEACHER

Teachers are considered caretakers of our children where there is an understanding that they will provide the appropriate amount of care based on the child's age and ability. When educators do not meet this standard of care, they can be deemed neglectful. These four main categories address how educators do not meet the appropriate level of responsibility.

Educational Neglect

Most research on educational neglect focuses on the parent whether they fail to enroll their child in school, allow habitual truancy, or in some cases fail to advocate for their child who may need special educational assistance. However, it should be recognized that schools themselves can be guilty of educational neglect either by failing to provide an adequate education or failing to assess children appropriately. Compulsory education is the law in all fifty states. However, just because students are required to attend doesn't necessarily assure that they are receiving an adequate education. Every three years the Program for International Student Assessment will rank approximately sixty participating countries based on their performance in reading, math, and science. In 2015, the United States was ranked only average in science and reading and below average in math.[30] This may be due to the fact that the United States may not be properly assessing their students, which may be the direct result of manipulating a student's grade. For example, several schools manipulate the grades of their students where this practice is commonly referred to as "grade inflation," thus not accurately assessing their ability. Grade inflation refers to when teachers skew grades upward rather than in both directions. Teacher's bias toward inflation is based on their belief that the content was successfully taught, and they assume more from the student's answers than what should be credited. Students are put at a disadvantage from inflated scores as it provides them a false sense of security which comes to fruition when they struggle with SAT exams. High school educators may excuse this tendency to inflate grades by pointing out that grade inflation is rampant in universities as well. It has been determined by many schools that systematically bumping up grades made students more likely to obtain scholarships and entrance into universities. This practice generates few complaints as parents and students are unlikely going to appeal a higher grade. Cheating is another form of grade inflation that is frequently overlooked and often not even acknowledged.[31] "Teachers want parents and the public to trust unquestionably their assessments of student learning."[32]

Physical/Medical Neglect

Physical neglect and medical neglect are sometimes considered synonymous. However, there are unique differences when addressing a caretaker's responsibilities. For instance, although it is certainly the responsibility of parents to dress their child appropriately, school officials still play a role in appropriate attire. Younger children should not be allowed to attend outside functions, such as recess, unless the child is appropriately dressed for the current weather conditions. Additionally, school officials have a responsibility to care for any child that is injured or is ill while attending school. A teacher not allowing a child to see a school nurse when reporting feeling ill would be neglectful in their duty to properly care for the child.

Physical neglect can also involve bathroom use. Is using the bathroom a right or a privilege? One would be hard pressed to find people critical of a teacher who had to leave the classroom in order to use the bathroom, but it is challenging to comprehend why some teachers are not empathetic to the physical needs of students. There are documented cases where children have to bring notes from their physicians requesting that the student be able to use the bathroom when required.[33]

One aspect that is often overlooked when addressing medical issues relating to students is the child's mental health needs. School districts should be properly identifying each child's mental health and make sure they are receiving the appropriate care. Far too many times parents must fight the school districts for individual education plans as their child struggles in school, only to find out later that their child struggled due to a disability. The Centers for Disease Prevention and Control reports percentages of how many children suffer from some form of mental illness:

- 9.4 percent of children ages two to seventeen have been diagnosed with attention deficit hyperactivity disorder
- 7.4 percent of children ages three to seventeen have been diagnosed with a behavioral problem
- 7.1 percent of children ages three to seventeen have been diagnosed with anxiety
- 3.2 percent of children ages three to seventeen have been diagnosed with depression.[34]

Supervisory Neglect

School personnel, no matter how attentive, cannot prevent all injuries that occur within a school setting as children regularly engage in reckless activities that can result in some type of injury. However, the injuries can be minimized with proper supervision. For instance, when small children go out for recess, the teacher should be monitoring the children rather than conversing with a colleague. This lack of attentiveness can result in a preventable injury. The Centers for Disease Prevention and Control reports that more than twenty thousand children are treated each year for traumatic brain injury. About two-thirds of playground-related injuries occurred at school and places of recreation that include monkey bars, climbing equipment, or swings.[35]

Educators also have a responsibility to watch out for children who may be the victims of bullying. Research has shown that ignoring aggressive behavior creates a permissive atmosphere in which both the aggressor and their victim learn that aggression has its rewards.[36] It would be naïve to expect school employees to be everywhere to prevent every possible scenario where victimization can occur, but to simply ignore the potential dangers that children face is negligent.

Emotional Neglect

Emotional neglect is non-specific and can be very difficult to recognize, and therefore more unlikely to be reported, especially among co-workers. Children attending school are open in discussing what qualities they desire in their teacher. These students expect and deserve unconditional acceptance, genuineness, and kindness.[37] This should be a natural trait for most teachers as they enter the field of education not for financial rewards, but for their unwavering commitment to the care and education of children. Unfortunately, whether it is burnout or merely the demeanor of a teacher, some will fail to provide the necessary emotional support that so many students need and deserve.

CHILD IDENTITY THEFT

Although child abuse and neglect can take all forms in a school setting, identity theft is unique as children may not know that they are victims until their high school years or even after they graduate from school. Identity theft can occur in two circumstances: (1) school personnel who have direct access to children's personal information and use this opportunity to steal a child's identity for personal gain, and (2) school officials who do not take the appropriate safeguards to protect a child's identity leaving them vulnerable to potential perpetrators. Identity theft can occur in elementary school, middle school, and high school.

Elementary School

Almost every elementary classroom displays décor with the children's names. Additionally, some elementary schools post a child's birthday in the classroom for everyone to see, including the child's date of birth. Although this may seem like innocent fun, anyone who has access to that classroom now has the pertinent information to steal a child's identity.

Middle School

It is at this point of a child's educational life that students are most likely to engage with computers. Educators who fail to instruct on safety measures leave the children vulnerable to online victimization. It is also the age where teachers should be having more in-depth discussions of not only identity theft, but online predators as well.

High School

The high school environment presents the greatest challenge for protecting a student from identity theft as students have more independence from their teachers and less supervision. Teens are a big target for identity theft and are more likely to respond to ads, free downloads, and social media outlets.[38] For additional information on child identity theft, see appendix A.

THE ABUSIVE COACH

A coach may use their authority to abuse children through various means. The emotionally abusive coach may believe that verbal abuse toward their athlete is an appropriate form of teaching/methodology. The verbally abusive coach may not only believe that their style of coaching is okay but may also base their self-worth on leading a winning team. They believe this type of poor coaching is okay even as they disrespect people and perpetuate such abuse with impunity. Abusive coaching desensitizes students to the point that the tactic of name calling defines students as objects instead of people. It dehumanizes them as coaches assume that students who are involved in sports are immune to negative emotions or mental disorders that can lead to depressive thoughts or suicidal ideation.[39] The abusive coach, unlike the abuse inflicted in a classroom, has parents who condone such an abusive tone, or parents remain silent as they observe their child being subjected to harassment while engaging in sporting events. For some student athletes, they are not only subjected to harassment by their coaches, but by their parents as well. Some parents, maybe living vicariously through their own children, harass their children, exhibiting extreme levels of anger while watching from the sideline demanding that they compete more efficiently.[40]

Physical abuse can also occur with coaches who are obsessed with winning at all costs. Practices can be so physically intense that players obtain injuries or in some cases succumb to sudden cardiac death as a result from extreme practices.[41] When children enduring practice become injured, the coach whose priority is to win may tell the student to simply "shake it off," a term commonly used to suggest one ignores the pain and gets back to work.

Sexual abuse can also occur with athletes. In contrast to the emotionally abusive coach, the sexually abusive coach may appear to be extremely caring toward students and may go out of their way to help the child achieve their goals. They are willing to give certain students a great deal of individual time and are even willing to drive the child home from practice, which earns the child's parents' appreciation. Coaches who sexually abuse athletes may have hundreds of victims over the years as they are able to manipulate their victims into silence. Sexual abuse of young athletes not only occurs in traditional school settings but through specialized sporting camps where children are away from their parents at camps in an attempt to perfect their skills.

FALSE ALLEGATIONS

False allegations, as discussed in chapter 9, can be particularly devastating to teachers as a mere allegation can destroy one's life, especially the career of one working with children. Suspension of educators who have had an allegation made against them is problematic as an assessment has to be made as to the risk of having the accused remain in school while an investigation is conducted.[42] A false allegation can be attributed to a misunderstanding or it may be a malicious false statement meant to cause harm to a school employee. It would be naïve to ignore the fact that some students are savvy or malicious enough to create false accusations in order to cause harm to someone else. Even with questionable reliability of an allegation, school officials may suspend the accused as a precaution, despite that this very action will be seen by some as an indicator of their guilt. School administrators are in a quandary as they must protect the image of the school as they feel the pressure of moral panic from the school community. An allegation of a teacher accused of sexual misconduct but still having access to other children can cause mass hysteria.[43]

CULTURE OF ABUSE

Is there a belief among school personnel that it is okay to engage in sex with students because a great percentage of students are sexually active? According to the Centers for Disease Control and Prevention 2017 survey, 40 percent of students had sex with other students, whereas 10 percent of those students reported they have had multiple partners.[44] With so many students willfully engaging in sexual activity, do teachers believe they are not causing harm to a child when they engage in sexual acts with their students? Michael Brundage is a former high school teacher and convicted sex offender for his relationship with a high school student. Brundage is the author of *After 3 PM*, where he discusses the culture of abuse and works as an activist addressing the issue of unlawful teacher-student relationships. Brundage addresses the culture that leads to sexual misconduct. He states that it is not the evil person who abuses children, but it is the normal person who commits evil acts. It is the mindset and the blurred perspectives that lead teachers down that slippery slope. Teachers want to be liked by their students, and they can create that likability by engaging in non-curriculum conversations such as sports, music movies, etc. All of this can be innocent bonding with no ulterior motive. As teachers seek to be viewed by students as just regular people, the social discourse develops as students get to know their teacher on a more personal level; the slope grows more slippery by the second. When teachers start viewing students as peers instead of their work, the line between what is an appropriate teacher-student relationship becomes more blurred. Teachers may share their cell phone number, befriend the student on social media, or allow students to follow them on Twitter. At this point the student is no longer considered a subordinate, but instead considered a peer. The vast majority of principals, school administrators, and school districts turn a blind eye to this form of student-teacher relationships.[45] The acceptance of crossing these boundaries not only condones the inappropriate behavior, but it also may appear to encourage the continuance of the relationship.

SCHOOL VIOLENCE

The second segment of this chapter deals with school violence, which addresses how students victimize other students within a school setting. As discussed in chapter 6, children abusing other children are, from a legal perspective, not considered as committing child abuse as the abuser is not classified as a caretaker. This segment will address the various forms of victimization that occur among students and whether school districts are taking appropriate measures in response to this abuse. School victimization has come to the forefront of our concerns, as indicated in many victimology textbooks that commonly reserve an entire section devoted to school violence. However, it should be noted that there is little literature in victimology textbooks that addresses victimization of students that results from the inaction of school personnel.

Numerous children come from broken or violent homes, or they come to school with mental health disorders that are conducive to violent or disruptive behavior. It seems to be easier to blame school personnel for a culture of violence within our school systems as they are an easy scapegoat when addressing inappropriate child behavior. Educators certainly have a daunting task of maintaining discipline in a school setting while supplying an appropriate education. This does not mean that schools cannot do more to provide not only a safer environment but also a pleasurable environment for both students and school personnel. Before one can address the issue of school violence, it is necessary to recognize the scope of the problem.

MEASURING SCHOOL VIOLENCE

The Bureau of Justice Statistics reported in 2016 that the total rate of victimization varied between female and male students: the rate for female victimization was twenty per one thousand students and the rate of male victimization was thirty-eight per one thousand students. The students who reported being afraid of attack or harm decreased from 12 percent reported in 1995 to 3 percent in 2015.[46] The debilitating aspects of fear keep our youth from attending school and having the ability to concentrate on their studies.[47]

SCHOOL POLICIES

It's unimaginable that any school would have no policy on bullying, teacher-student relationships, or school violence. However, if the policies are written for the purpose of avoiding civil litigation, they are not worth the paper they are written on, as a policy to address student victimization has no merit if the objectives are neither achievable nor enforced. In an effort to address the inadequacy of simply having a policy in place, some states have created legislation mandating schools take action. For instance, in the State of Massachusetts, legislation was created in 2010 mandating that any teacher who witnesses bullying must report the incident to the school principal.[48] This chapter will address policies that are in place to address victimization and see if these measures are effective in reducing victimization.

BULLYING

National Bullying Prevention Month is October, and there is a nationwide campaign to raise awareness of the prevalence and consequences of bullying and highlight ways in which to prevent this harmful behavior.[49] The website stopbullying.gov defines bullying as the unwanted, aggressive behavior among school-aged children that involves a real or perceived power imbalance.[50] Bullying can occur in a school setting through three components: (1) the teacher bullying the student, which was addressed in the section "The Emotionally Abusive Teacher"; (2) children bullying teachers; and (3) students bullying one another in a school setting.[51] It is the latter that will be addressed in this segment. Bullying can occur through physical means, which may include pushing, hitting, tripping, spitting, etc. This type of bullying peaks during grades six to eight, and it is reported twice as often by boys than by girls. Verbal intimidation is another form of bullying that includes taunting, making threats, name calling, and other forms of derogatory comments. Social bullying involves rumors and behaviors aimed to deliberately exclude the targeted child. This type of bullying is more commonly reported by girls.[52] Most forms of bullying take place out of sight of a responsible adult, and due to a culture of a "code of silence" among the students, teachers and administrators may not be aware of the magnitude of the problem.[53] Bullying can happen anywhere within a school setting, whether it is in the classroom, hallways, bathrooms, locker rooms, athletic fields, playgrounds, or on the school bus. Students who are able to escape these venues may then find themselves being victimized through technology.

CYBER BULLYING

Cyber bullying involves using texting, emailing, or posting messages through social media and chat rooms to create a feeling of intimidation. Cyber bullies can either directly or indirectly target their victims. Direct attacks involve threats or nasty messages sent directly to the victim, whereas indirect targeting may involve malicious comments, pictures, or spreading rumors to others as a means of bullying the target.[54]

Cyber bullying is different from other forms of bullying as one has round-the-clock access to the target, and the perpetrator can continue the abuse even when the victim returns to the safety of their own home. The offender also has the opportunity to have a worldwide audience as anyone in the cyber community can witness the taunting. Additionally, the offender has the opportunity to have anonymity. Sites like Ask.FM and Yik Yak allow the offender to remain anonymous as they post disturbing information about their victim or they send troublesome messages directly to their target. Many sites like these do not verify the identity of their users, thus allowing offenders to use fake profiles. Finally, victims find themselves in an inescapable situation. Although a victim of bullying can walk away from a face-to-face encounter, it is significantly more difficult when the offender can continually track down someone online.[55] Cellphones are commonly used in classrooms with the teacher's discretion, under the guise of a viable instructional method. Some teachers tend to allow cellphone usage in class as they feel that they are unable to control it as so many students use their cellphones while in the classroom. The offender in cyber bullying can be aggressively harassing another student while appearing to engage in classroom activities.[56]

When teachers, administrators, or other school personnel hear about any form of bullying, they should take immediate steps to eliminate the problem and prevent future acts of maltreatment from occurring.

Some of the steps to eliminate cyber bullying include the following:

- Have a school culture that publicly addresses the facts surrounding cyber bullying with staff and students stating that there is a zero-tolerance policy.
- When a complaint is brought to the school's attention, group the suspected students in the same room with one another and discuss any disagreements. Have teachers, parents, and administrators present along with the school resource officer and record the event.

- Demand the behavior stop, both online and in person. Encourage all parties to remove themselves from social media platforms.
- Make sure all parties understand that if the behavior is reported again, the discipline system will be implemented.
- Make phone calls to parents of the students who were involved and describe what has happened immediately. Keep a record of any notification.
- Schedule follow-up conferences with parents and students immediately explaining what has come to their attention.
- If a parent refuses to cooperate or is in denial about their child's actions, leave a voice message and email reminding them of your duty as a teacher to protect all students.
- Contact law enforcement if there is a belief that the child's life is in danger.
- Encourage parents to file a restraining order against those who are guilty of bullying.
- Record every step for the record so it can be used for future reference.[57]

THE BULLY

There is conflicting evidence on which gender is more inclined to bully, so the sex of an individual may not be the best indicator for identifying an abuser. However, there seems to be a range of personality traits that are better predictors of who may be a bully, such as individuals with high rates of suspicion and jealousy, sudden and dramatic mood swings, poor self-control, a higher propensity for the approval of using violence, and higher levels of some type of personality disorder.[58]

Bystanders of Bullying

The level of bullying in a school setting can be a direct result of how bystanders who witness bullying react. Bystanders of bullying can fall under three categories:

- Hurtful bystanders: These bystanders may actually instigate the bullying by prodding someone to bully or laughing or cheering as the bullying takes place.
- Passive bystanders: They do nothing to encourage the bullying but unwittingly encourage the bullying by providing an audience for the abuser as the bully craves the attention of hurting another student.
- Helpful bystanders: These are students who come to the aid of bullying victims. This can be accomplished by directly defending the victims or seeking help of an adult to intervene. Helpful bystanders can also help through cyber bullying as they interject through online communication thus coming to the aid of the targeted victim.[59]

VICTIMS

Although any student is vulnerable to potential victimization within a school setting, certain characteristics of a victim such as a disability or a lifestyle can make them an attractive target for continued abuse.

Disabled Victims

When bullying is directed at a child because of a disability, it can be considered disability harassment, which falls under Section 504 of the Rehabilitation Act of 1973 and Title 11 of the Americans with Disabilities Act. One of the reasons children with disabilities are targeted is their lack of peer support. Schools can help reduce bullying of children with special needs by:

- Engaging students in developing high-risk activities in which everyone has a role in designing, executing, or participating in the activity
- Providing general upfront information to peers about the kinds of support children with special needs require, and have adults facilitate peer support
- Creating a buddy system for children with special needs
- Involving students in adaptive strategies in the classroom so that they participate in assisting and understanding the needs of others
- Conducting team-based learning activities and rotating student groupings
- Implementing social-emotional learning activities
- Rewarding positive, helpful, inclusive behavior.[60]

Although schools can take proactive steps to decrease bullying among disabled students, they still need to address the victimization of disabled students by faculty. It is certainly understood how students who are disabled, especially from a learning disability, should have special assistance whether it is through a teacher's aide or some other method of providing individual instruction. Not only is this an opportunity to subject a child to abuse without any witnesses, but the child themselves may have limited communication skills or comprehension as to the abuse that is taking place.

CASE STUDY #3 (SPECIAL EDUCATION TEACHER MOLESTS MIDDLE SCHOOL STUDENT)

Jamie, age thirteen, was a middle school student with a severe learning disability that required the school district to hire an assistant teacher's aide for the sole purpose of providing individual assistance to Jamie. The teacher's aide would help Jamie with her homework in a small room within the school where she was able to receive one-on-one instruction. One day Jamie came home crying to her parents reporting how her teacher put his hands down her pants and put his fingers inside her. The police conducted an interview with the assistance of a mental health worker where Jamie disclosed the abuse describing the digital penetration by her aide. The teacher's aide was charged with aggravated sexual assault On the day of the trial, the prosecutor asked what had happened and Jamie went into a fetal position while on the witness stand, apparently having a panic attack as she closed her eyes and pointed to the man who she previously stated assaulted her. Since Jamie was unable to verbally testify in court and substantiate the sexual abuse, the case was later dismissed.

Lesbian, Gay, Bisexual, Transgender, and Queer/Questioning Students

A hostile school environment perpetuates higher levels of truancy, absenteeism, and a higher dropout rate for the LGBTQ youth. Students are forced to decide between harassment and or facing sanctions through truancy.[61] According to data in the 2015 Youth Risk Behavior Survey of LGBTQ youth, it was reported that LGBTQ students are 140 percent more likely than heterosexual students to stay out of school for at least one day in a thirty-day period for safety concerns.

Specifically, students reported that:

- 10 percent were threatened or injured with a weapon on school property
- 34 percent were bullied on school property
- 28 percent were bullied electronically.[62]

Even though an increasing number of schools have antibullying policies, bullying remains a familiar behavior for LGBTQ youth. School polices are usually framed around how to respond to bullying once it occurs. LGBTQ students often use the term "equity" when they are spotlighting their concerns. Many schools that confront the problem of bullying equate having a safe school with implementing surveillance cameras, security guards, and mandatory identification badges for teachers and students. However, very few educational institutions frame safety around equity and inclusiveness.[63] By creating an atmosphere of inclusiveness, LGBTQ students can be accepted as part of the community and not be singled out for abuse. LGBTQ students consistently point out that there are not isolated incidents of harassment or bullying but realize that bullying is just an inevitable consequence of being queer in a culture or school that makes no space for it.[64] In fact, many LGBTQ students conceal their sexual orientation as they fear harassment, rejection, and further isolation. School teachers and administrators often use poor programs or intellectually insulting assemblies to help guide heterosexual students on how to accept LGBTQ students as being different from them when perhaps school officials should focus on the similarities they have, as similarities are more abundant.[65]

SCHOOL BUSES

Although the purpose of a school bus is to provide safe and convenient travel to and from school, the issue of safety frequently is a topic of concern for many parents. In one study, twenty-three mothers of children from a small rural school provided their perspectives on school bus safety. The study included ten mothers who had their children ride the bus and thirteen mothers who chose to drive their children to and from school, despite clear evidence that school buses are much safer than passenger cars. The study showed that of the thirteen mothers who drove their children to school, nine of the mothers were under the impression that passenger cars were safer than buses, and only one of the ten mothers whose children rode the bus believed buses were safer. The research demonstrated that the term "safety" had a broad definition as most parents were concerned about their child's safety from bullying and harassment from older students on the bus.[66] Due to financial restrictions in many rural communities, buses will carry children from all grade brackets, leaving younger children subjected to the negative influences and behaviors of older adolescents. Of course, safety concerns on school buses are not limited to rural travel. Larger populations that can afford separate transportation for elementary, middle, and high school students still face problems with victimization whether with verbal abuse, physical abuse, or in some cases, sexual assault. Abusive behavior can also be attributed to the size of the student's population on the bus. Research has shown that the more occupants, the more likely that not only will the bullying increase, but the severity of the bullying will intensify in relation to the fullness of a school bus.[67] Abusive behavior on school buses has either encouraged students to stay out of school or forced parents to transport their child out of concerns for their child's safety. To address these trepidations, some school districts have installed monitoring devices to discourage misbehavior or they have hired bus monitors in an attempt to ensure student safety.

EFFECTS OF BULLYING

Bullying can have lasting on a victim's mental health. Negative outcomes associated with bullying include depression, anxiety, and involvement in interpersonal or sexual violence, substance abuse, poor social functioning, poor academic performance, and poor attendance.[68] Additionally, victims of bullying have an increased risk for suicidal-related behavior. Students who report bullying others and being bullied themselves have the highest risk of suicidal-related behavior than any other group involving bullying. It should also be noted that youth that have observed but did not participate in bullying reported significantly more feelings of helplessness and a reduced sense of collectiveness and support from responsible adults when compared to youth that have not experienced bullying.[69] One of the significant contributors to bullying is the gangs that are forming in school districts throughout the nation.

GANGS

Schools can play a critical role in response to gang intervention, not only with academic remediation, but by working as collaborators in social services, recreational programs, and antigang curriculum. By having gang awareness, school staff and school personnel can provide an appropriate school environment to not only deter gang activity within the school, but can create programs that will discourage potential new gang members. Unfortunately, schools responding to youth violence tend to respond to gangs by providing better surveillance, security guards, and police, but these practices tend to form a climate of distrust between students and administrators that creates an incentive for students to affiliate with street gangs. It would benefit the educational institutions greatly to implement strategies that essentially simulate a healthy family environment that can provide at-risk youth a caring environment that will deter them from gangs. This can be accomplished by encouraging students to affiliate themselves with sports, classes, or elective classes that develop social skills, collaboration, teamwork, and enthusiasm about attending and participating in school.[70] If students are unable to engage in curriculum in lieu of gang activity and they perceive the school as being unsafe and disorderly, studies have shown these conditions will promote the likelihood of gang activity.[71] In addition to deterring gang membership, there is the need to focus on how gang activity affects those students who are non-gang members. Students who are not gang members express not only fear from bullying and the mere presence of gang members, but they also report annoyance of frequent class disruptions and recurrent fighting that takes place in the school. Although many students are either frightened by or annoyed by gang activity, some students have reported that they find the fighting that is gang related entertaining.[72] Unfortunately, many school districts may be in denial that gang activity even exists in their schools. Gang member attitudes and activities do not stop when entering the school building. Some administrators are immune to the community problem of gangs and fail to recognize the signs of gang activities. There are various reasons that school personnel will not acknowledge the existence of gang activity in their schools. First, they may not recognize the signs of gang activity. Second, public admission of gang activities within a school may be seen as the school's inability to properly control the environment. Third, school choice laws have been passed in many areas allowing parents to remove their children from a school with a reputation of gang activity, causing the school to possibly lose revenue from having lower enrollment numbers. Lastly, schools are sometimes hesitant to share information about children in fear of violating confidentiality laws.[73]

SHOOTINGS

The Gun-Free School Zone Act of 1990 prohibits any unauthorized person with a gun to be in a school zone, as defined by 18 USC 921. The Gun-Free School Act of 1994 mandated that any student who brought a firearm to school would face a minimum of a one-year expulsion. Although there are mandated penalties for violation of this statute, it has accomplished very little in protecting students from gun violence.

On April 20, 1999, Dylan Klebold, age seventeen, and Eric Harris, age eighteen, went on a killing spree at Columbine High School in Jefferson County, Colorado, where they killed thirteen people and wounded over twenty others before taking their own lives. Chilling footage was captured as these two students entered the high school and methodically shot their classmates and one teacher. This tragedy shocked the nation as parents, school personnel, and law enforcement brought to the forefront the need to protect school children. What was once an oddity in having school resource officers in high school was now about to become commonplace as local municipalities lined up for federal grants to hire school resource officers. The focus of the war on drugs in the 1980s in schools took a dramatic shift to addressing school violence as schools everywhere demanded security measures to ensure that the tragedy Columbine endured would not be repeated.

It didn't take long for school districts to realize that school shootings were not restricted to high schools. This was clearly evident in the case of Sandy Hook Elementary School in Newtown, Connecticut, where on December 14, 2012, twenty-year-old Adam Lanza fatally shot twenty-six people including twenty children between the ages of six and seven before taking his own life. This is now considered the deadliest school shooting in U.S. history. Tragedies of school shootings continued regularly across the nation where it has become so commonplace that it would be difficult for the average person in America to name the location of the last three school shootings. Even though the concern for children's safety has not diminished, the shock value of these acts has as citizens have seemingly become desensitized to the violence. It wasn't until February 14, 2018, when Nikolas Cruz, a former student of Marjory Stoneham Douglas High School in Parkland, Florida, opened fire in the school killing seventeen students and staff members and wounding several others before he was arrested. This case brought school shootings back to the forefront, not only for the magnitude of life that was lost that day, but the controversy about the school resource officer who did not immediately engage the shooter. Whether it is Columbine or any of the other numerous school shootings since then, there has been an ongoing debate on how to keep children safe from such violent acts. Many would argue that these acts are a matter of gun control and the shooters should not have access to firearms, whereas others advocate for arming teachers as a defense to protect students.

The most common error in discussing school shootings is the belief that all school shooters are a homogeneous group of people. Some school shooters have randomly selected their victims, whereas others have a specific target in mind. Some may be narcissist shooters who are seeking notoriety; others are desperate, depressed youths who are angry at the world; still others shoot their victims as a form of vengeance for real or perceived wrongs; some shooters believe their attacks are justified by political ideology or paranoid delusions.[74] Although schools throughout the country have established protocols such as lockdowns, secured buildings, school resource officers, or other security responses, these educational facilities need to address preventing school shootings through threat assessments. Many students make threats with no actual plans to carry them out, whereas there are those who have the desire, and means, and do indeed intend to act on their plan. The job of a threat assessment team is to distinguish real threats from false alarms. All school personnel should be trained to recognize warning signs of potential violence and report their observation to threat assessment teams.[75] This is significant as there is a repeated misperception that school shooters commit their crimes in retaliation to bullying. Studies involving school shooters show that 40 percent of them do indeed have a history of being harassed, but only one out of forty-eight perpetrators examined targeted a bully. In contrast, at least sixteen shooters targeted teachers or administrators, suggesting that many shooters were driven by rage in response to their failures at school and prior conflicts.[76] This does not lessen the fact that some shooters are the direct result of bullying and schools need to be proactive in addressing this behavior.

DRUGS/DRUG ABUSE RESISTANCE EDUCATION

Drug Abuse Resistance Education (DARE) is considered the largest drug prevention program in the United States. The DARE program was developed in 1983 from a local drug prevention program in Los Angeles, California. The program was designed to help elementary and middle school students resist the peer pressure of engaging in illegal drug activity. The program became so popular that there was even a presidential proclamation in 1988 signifying a National DARE Day. This program includes a course that is usually taught by a police officer with a core curriculum of seventeen lessons. Although there is great support for this program, literature reveals inconsistent research on its effectiveness. Studies have shown that the DARE program has shown less than even a small effect on drug use.[77] However, schools continue to provide this curriculum even though data through multiple studies question its efficiency. Additionally, DARE officers are unlikely to critique the value of their program as they may feel that they are actually making a difference. Today, schools throughout the country display signs that indicate that their school is a drug-free zone, which creates the illusion those schools are adequately controlling drug abuse among their students.

SEXUAL HARASSMENT IN SCHOOL

Bullying and sexual harassment are similar as they both function through imbalanced power relationships. However, they can be distinguished from one another as sexual harassment can be defined as mean-spirited behavior directed at a specific gender or sexual content that enforces the imbalance of power.[78] Although there is significant controversy when a school official either sexually assaults or sexually harasses students as described in the section "Passing the Trash," there is less controversy on how schools handle sexual assault allegations when the perpetrator is identified as another student. However, there are many cases of sexual harassment that largely go unreported or are unrecognized due to the lack of education and enforcement from both students and school staff. When it does occur in school whether in person or through cellphones, school personnel often believe it is too hard to prove or they dismiss it as typical student behavior. Failure to respond to sexual harassment only perpetuates its very existence.

Some forms of sexual harassment in school include, but are not limited to:

- Public displays of affection
- Grabbing peers by the waist
- Snapping bra straps
- Grabbing rear ends
- Bumping into one another so as to make contact with body parts
- Forcible hugging of students
- Making comments about the student's clothing in a sexual manner
- Making comments to other students about what they want to do to another sexually
- Daring one another to make physical contact with another student in a sexual manner.[79]

Although many people think of sexual harassment as an act committed solely by male students, female students can be guilty as well. Girls can engage in conversations of a sexual nature regarding body parts or sexual acts, also daring friends to engage in sexual acts with peers. Other methods of harassment can include forcing themselves on another for visual group attention or fully undressing in a locker room in front of unsuspecting peers with the purpose of making another student feel uncomfortable. It should be noted that students can sexually harass school staff as well through verbal comments toward a teacher or staff or deliberately leaving an anonymous note for a teacher to easily find.[80]

CONCLUSION

Schools throughout the nation consist of thousands of teachers, administrators, and supporting school staff dedicated to the care of children while providing an education. Children who attend schools may come from a variety of backgrounds that include family violence and other forms of dysfunction. Children in some cases look at school as a safe haven from what they face in their daily lives. Unfortunately, too many children enter school only to face victimization directly from the school personnel or they are placed in an environment where the school fails to protect them from their student peers. Forms of abuse directed at children include sexual abuse that schools are covering up such action or quietly dismissing the teacher in a process referred to as "passing the trash." Additionally, depending on the school district, teachers are allowed to use corporal punishment to maintain discipline in questionable behavioral situations. Furthermore, teachers are allowed to emotionally abuse children in their classrooms whether it is through deliberate humiliation or taking passive aggressive measures as a way to bully their students. School personnel are also responsible to ensure that each student has a safe and enjoyable environment while attending school. However, bullying and sexual harassment can be commonplace in a school setting, where school officials either fail to recognize the problem or casually keep a "blind eye" to the problem thus causing an atmosphere of tolerated aggressive behavior. Schools also need to address the problem of gangs within their districts and create programs to discourage gang activity. Unfortunately, some school districts will not acknowledge gang activity as they don't want the school to have a reputation that will discourage future enrollment.

REVIEW QUESTIONS

1. Why are school administrators so reluctant to identify gang activity within their schools?

2. Why are disabled students more likely to be victimized in school?

3. What does the term "passing the trash" refer to?

4. How are female teachers who sexually abuse children judged in comparison to male teachers?

5. Why is cyber bullying harder to avoid?

KEYWORDS

Bullying: The unwanted, aggressive behavior among school-aged children that involves a real or perceived power imbalance.

Pass the trash: Schools that have teachers suspected of sexual abuse allow those teachers to pursue another job at a different school without any record of sexual misconduct.

D.A. R. E.: Drug Abuse Resistance Education.

Emotional abuse: Any abusive behavior that isn't physical, which may include verbal aggression, intimidation, manipulation, and humiliation, which most often unfolds as a pattern of behavior over time **that aims to** diminish another person's sense of identity, dignity, and self-worth, and which often results in anxiety, depression, suicidal thoughts or behaviors, and posttraumatic stress disorder.

LGBTQ: Lesbian, gay, bisexual, transgender, and queer/questioning

NOTES

1. Jim Dueck, *Gender Fairness in Today's School: A Breach of Trust for Male Students* (Lanham, MD: Rowman & Littlefield Publishers, 2017), 2.

2. Sarah E. Daly, *Everyday School Violence: An Educator's Guide to Safer Schools* (Lanham, MD: Rowman & Littlefield, 2018), 24–25.

3. National Children's Advocacy Center. Educator Sexual Misconduct: Public Perception and Prevention. Accessed January 24, 2019. Available from https://mail.google.com/mail/u/0/#search/calio/FMfcgxwBVDCvxWNtQdKKXrVMDPqKJvbW.

4. Sierra Pace, *Sexual Abuse of Children: State and Federal Efforts Aimed at School Personnel and Child Care Facilities* (New York, NY: Nova Science Publishers, 2014), 2.

5. Billie-Jo Grant, Stephanie Wilkerson, and Molly Henschel, "Passing the Trash: Absence of State Laws Allows for Continued Sexual Abuse of K-12 Students by School Employees," *Journal of Child Sexual Abuse* 28, no. 1 (2018): 100.

6. Stephen Meyer, *Child Abuse and Domestic Violence: Information Plus.* (Farmington Hills, MI, 2017), 75.

7. Charles J. Hobson, *Passing the Trash: A Parent's Guide to Combat Sexual Abuse/Harassment of Their Children in School* (Charleston, SC: Create Space Independent Publishing, 2012), 32.

8. Lori Handrahan, *Epidemic: America's Trade in Child Rape* (Waterville, OR: Trine Day, 2018), 119.

9. Charol Shakeshaft, "Educator Sexual Misconduct: A Synthesis of Existing Literature," Hofstra University, June 2004, 24–29. Accessed February 1, 2019. Available from https://files.eric.ed.gov/fulltext/ED483143.pdf; Mark A. Winton and Barbara A. Mara, *When Teachers, Clergy, and Caretakers Sexually Abuse Children and Adolescents* (Durham, NC: Carolina Academic Press, 2013), 69.

10. Steve Reilly, "Teachers who Sexually Abuse Students Still Find Classroom Jobs: Despite Decades of Scandals, America's Schools Still Hide Actions of Dangerous Educators," *USA Today*, December 22, 2016. Accessed January 30, 2019. Available from https://www.usatoday.com/story/news/2016/12/22/teachers-who-sexually-abuse-students-still-find-classroom-jobs/95346790/.

11. Ernest J. Zarra, "Addressing Appropriate and Inappropriate Teacher-Student Relationships: A Secondary Education Professional Development Model," *CLEARvoz Journal* 3, no. 2 (2016): 16–17.

12. Kurt Michael Brundage, *After 3PM: Asking the Question: "Why Do Teachers Have Unlawful Relationships with Students?" . . . By a Teacher Who Did* (New York: Morgan James Publishing, 2018), 104.

13. Steve Albrecht, "Female Teachers as Sexual Predators: The Double Standard Remains," *Psychology Today* August 10, 2012. Accessed January 30, 2019. Available from https://www.psychologytoday.com/us/blog/the-act-violence/201208/female-teachers-sexual-predators.

14. eBaum's World, "10 Hottest Sex Offender Teachers." Accessed January 24, 2019. Available from http://www.ebaumsworld.com/pictures/10-hottest-female-sex-offender-teachers/84580681/.

15. Emma Zack, John T. Lang, and Danielle Dirks, "'It Must be Great to be a Female Pedophile!': The Nature of Public Perceptions about Female Sex Offenders," *Crime Media Culture: an International Journal* 14, no. 1 (2018): 69–72.

16. Pace, *Sexual Abuse of* Children, 5–15; Hobson, *Passing the Trash*, 18.

17. Hobson, *Passing the Trash*, 105–06.

18. Douglas E. Abrams, Susan Vivian Mangold, and Sarah H. Ramsey, *Children and the Law: In a Nutshell*, sixth edition (St. Paul, MN: West Academic, 2018), 125.

19. Richard Lawrence, *School Crime and Juvenile Justice*, second edition (New York, NY: Oxford, 2007), 180; Elizabeth T. Gerhoft and Sarah A. Font, "Corporal Punishment in U.S. Public Schools: Prevalence, Disparities in Use, and Status in State and Federal Policy," *Social Policy Report* 30, no. 1 (2016): 1.

20. American Professional Society on the Abuse of Children. APSAC Position Statement on Corporal Punishment of Children, 2. Accessed February 3, 2019. Available from https://apsac.memberclicks.net/assets/documents/Publications/apsac%20position%20statement%20on%20corporal%20punishment%20of%20children%20-%20final%20approved%207-26-16.pdf; Parminder Singh Bhullas, *Corporal Punishment in Schools* (New Delhi, India: Diamond Books, 2014), 38.

21. Bhullas, *Corporal Punishment in Schools*, 39.

22. One Love Foundation, What Emotional Abuse Really Means. Accessed February 6, 2019. Available from https://www.joinonelove.org/learn/emotional-abuse-really-means/.

23. Geoffrey Darnton, *Emotional Abuse in the Classroom: The Forgotten Dimension of Safeguarding, Child Protection, and Safer Recruitment*, second edition (Bournemouth, UK: Requirements Analytics, 2012), 1.

24. Darnton, *Emotional Abuse in the Classroom*, 13.

25. Darnton, *Emotional Abuse in the Classroom*, 18.

26. Darnton, *Emotional Abuse in the Classroom*, 33.

27. Bhullas, *Corporal Punishment in Schools*, 23–26; Sean M. Brooks, *Violence among Students and School Staff: Understanding and Preventing the Causes of School Violence* (Charleston, SC: Create Space, Independent Publishing, 2018), 20.

28. Dianne Prinz Callin, *The Last Bastion: Child Abuse and Child Neglect in the Brotherhood of America's Schools* (Middleton, DE: RFK Publishing, 2017), 142–43.

29. Callin, *The Last Bastion*, 165.

30. Callin, *The Last Bastion*, 61; PISA. Accessed January 30, 2019. Available from http://www.oecd.org/pisa/.

31. Dueck, *Gender Fairness in Today's School*, 39–48.

32. Dueck, *Gender Fairness in Today's School*, 51.

33. Irwin A. Hyman and Pamela A. Snook, *Dangerous Schools: What We Can Do About the Physical and Emotional Abuse of Our Children* (San Francisco, CA: Jossey-Bass Publishers, 1999), 34.

34. Centers for Disease Control and Prevention. Data and Statistics on Children's Mental Health. Accessed January 31, 2019. Available from https://www.cdc.gov/childrensmental-health/data.html.

35. Centers for Disease Control and Prevention. Protect the Ones You Love: Child Injuries are Preventable. Accessed January 30, 2019. Available from https://www.cdc.gov/safechild/playground/index.html.

36. Marjorie J. Kostelnik, Anne K. Sodeman, Alice Phipps Whiren, and Michelle L. Rupiper, *Guiding Children's Social Development & Learning: Theory and Skills* (Boston, MA: Cengage, 2018), 371.

37. Callin, *The Last Bastion*, 89.

38. Robert P. Chappell, *Child Identity Theft: What Every Parent Needs to Know* (Lanham, MD: Rowman & Littlefield, 2013), 55–56; Joe Mason, *Bankrupt at Birth: Why Child ID Theft is on the Rise and How It's Happening Under Parents' Noses* (Gaithersburg, MD: Nimble Cricket Press, 2012), 140.

39. Brooks, *Violence among Students and School Staff*, 47.

40. Patricia Evans, *Teen Torment: Overcoming Verbal Abuse at Home and at School* (Avon, MA: Adams Media Corp, 2003), 99–100.

41. Alan R. Kemp, *Abuse in Society: An Introduction* (Long Grove, IL: Waveland Press, 2017), 444.

42. Pat Sikes and Heather Piper, *Researching Sex and Lies in the Classroom: Allegations of Sexual Misconduct in Schools* (New York, NY: Routledge, 2010), 5.

43. Sikes and Piper, *Researching Sex and Lies in the Classroom*, 9.

44. Center for Disease Control and Prevention. CDC Releases 2017 Youth Risk Behavior Survey (YRBS) Results. Accessed January 27, 2019. Available from https://www.cdc.gov/nch-hstp/dear_colleague/2018/dcl-061418-YRBS.html.

45. Brundage, *After 3PM: Asking the Question*, 101–05.

46. Lauren Musu-Gillette, Anlan Zhang, Ke Wang, Jizhi Zhang, Jana Kemp, Melissa Diliberti, and Barbara A. Oudekerk, *Indicators of School Crime and Safety: 2017*. Available from https://www.bjs.gov/content/pub/pdf/iscs17.pdf.

47. William G. Doerner and Steven P. Lab, *Victimology*, seventh edition (Waltham, MA: Routledge, 2015), 425.

48. Doerner and Lab, *Victimology*, 432.

49. Office of Juvenile Justice Delinquency and Prevention. October is National Bullying Prevention Month. Accessed February 4, 2019. Available from https://www.ojjdp.gov/news-letter/252069/topstory.html.

50. Stop bullying.gov. What is bullying? Accessed January 30, 2019. Available from https://www.stopbullying.gov/what-is-bullying/index.html.

51. Darnton, *Emotional Abuse in the Classroom*, 6.

52. Ann Wolbert Burgess, Cheryle Regehr, and Albert R. Roberts, *Victimology: Theories and Applications*, second edition (Burlington, MA: Jones & Bartlett, 2013), 266.

53. Evans, *Teen Torment*, 123.

54. Juana Juvonen and Sandra Graham, "Bullying in School: The Power of Bullies and the Plight of Victims," *Annual Review of Psychology* 65 (2014): 169.

55. Josh Gunderson, *Cyber Bullying: Perpetrators, Bystanders & Victims* (Middleton, DE: Create Space, Independent Publishing, 2017), 7–9.

56. Brooks, *Violence among Students and School Staff*, 31.

57. Brooks, *Violence among Students and School Staff*, 38.

58. Darnton, *Emotional Abuse in the Classroom*, 21.

59. Gunderson, *Cyber Bullying:*, 21–22.

60. U.S. Department of Health and Human Services. Stop Bullying.gov. Bullying and Youth with Disabilities and Special Health Needs. Accessed January 28, 2019. Available from https://www.stopbullying.gov/at-risk/groups/special-needs/index.html.

61. Preston Mitchum and Aisha C. Moodie-Mills, Center for American Progress, Beyond Bullying: How Hostile School Climate Perpetuates the School to Prison Pipeline for LGBT Youth, February 2014. Accessed January 27, 2019. Available from https://www.american-progress.org/wp-content/uploads/2014/02/BeyondBullying.pdf.

62. Laura Kann, Emily O'Malley Olsen, Tim McManus, William A. Harris, Shari L. Shank-lin, Katherine H. Flint, Barbara Queen, Richard Lowry, David Chyen, Lisa Whittle, Jemekia Thornton, Connie Lim, Yoshimi Yamakawa, Nancy Brener, and Stephanie Zaza, "Sexual Iden-tity, Sex of Sexual Contacts, and Health Related Behaviors Among Students in Grades 9-12," *MMWR Surveill Summ* 65, no. SS-9 2(2016): 1–202.

63. Donn Short, *Am I Safe Here: LGBTQ Teens and Bullying in Schools* (Vancouver, BC: On Point Press, 2017), 12.

64. Short, *Am I Safe Here*, 47.

65. Brooks, *Violence among Students and School Staff*, 27.

66. Bruce B. Henderson, "The School Bus: A Neglected Children's Environment," *Journal of Rural Community Psychology* E12, no. 1: 7.

67. Juliana Raskauskas, "Bullying on the School Bus: A Video Analysis," *Journal of School Violence* 4, no. 3 (2005): 100–01.

68. Burgess, Regehr, and Roberts, *Victimology*, 268.

69. Centers for Disease Control and Prevention. CDC Releases 2017 Youth Risk Behavior Survey (YRBS) Results. Accessed January 27, 2019. Available from https://www.cdc.gov/nch-hstp/dear_colleague/2018/dcl-061418-YRBS.html.

70. Jill D. Sharkey, Zhanna Shekhtmeyster, Lizbeth Chavez-Lopez, Elizabeth Norris, and Laura Sass, "The Protective Influence of Gangs: Can Schools Compensate?" *Aggression and Violent Behavior* 16, no. 1 (2011): 50–51.

71. Michela Lenzi, Jill Sharkey Alessio, Ashley Mayworm, Danielle Dougherty, and Karen Nylund-Gibson, "Adolescent Gang Involvement: The Role of Individual, Family, Peer, and School Factors in a Multilevel Perspective," *Aggressive Behavior* 41, no. 4 (2015): 388.

72. Dena C. Carson and Finn-Aage Esbensen, "Gangs in School: Exploring the Experience of Gang-Involved Youth," *Youth Violence and Juvenile Justice* 17, no. 1 (2019): 14.

73. Michelle Arciaga, Wayne Sakamoto, and Erika Fearby Jones, Responding to Gangs in the School Setting, November 2010. Office of Juvenile Justice Delinquency and Prevention. Accessed February 4, 2019. Available from https://www.nationalgangcenter.gov/Content/Documents/Bulletin-5.pdf.

74. Peter Langman, *School Shooters: Understanding High School, College, and Adult Per-petrators* (Lanham, MD: Rowman & Littlefield, 2015), 1.

75. Langman, *School Shooters*, 183–84.

76. Langman, *School Shooters*, 163.

77. Wei Pan and Haiyan Bai, "A Multivariate Approach to a Meta-Analytical Review of the effectiveness of the D.A.R.E. Program," *International Journal of Environmental Research and Public Health* 6, no. 1 (2009): 268–74.

78. James Gruber and Susan Fineran, "Sexual Harassment, Bullying and School Outcomes for High School Girls and Boys," *Violence Against Women* 22, no. 1 (2016): 113. 9

79. Brooks, *Violence among Students and School Staff*, 69.

80. Brooks, *Violence among Students and School Staff*, 70.

12

Child Abuse
in Special Jurisdictions

◆ ◆ ◆

CHILD ABUSE IN THE MILITARY

CHILD ABUSE IS A WORLDWIDE problem where any child can be the target of abuse. Although all children are vulnerable, some children are more or less likely to be abused based on their family structure, culture, or jurisdiction. This chapter will focus on the unique dynamics of certain populations that may make specific children more susceptible to abuse.

Defining Child Abuse

The Department of Defense defines child abuse as

> The physical or sexual abuse, emotional abuse, or neglect of a child by a parent, guardian, foster parent, or by a caregiver, whether the caregiver is intrafamilial or extrafamilial, under circumstances indicating the child's welfare is harmed or threatened. Such acts by a sibling, other family member, or other person shall be deemed to be child abuse only when the individual is providing care under express or implied agreement with the parent, guardian or foster parent.[1]

It is important to note that child abuse and neglect typically fall under four categories, as follows:

Physical abuse: Acts that cause or had the potential to cause physical injury to a child, such as kicking the child or throwing objects at the child.
Sexual abuse: Any involvement of a child in a sexual activity to provide the offender with sexual gratification or financial benefit, such as forcing the child to engage in sexual acts or pose for child pornography.
Emotional abuse: Any act or omission that is not physical or sexual abuse that caused or had the potential to cause adverse effects on the child's psychological well-being, such as verbally abusive behavior or commit-

ting violent acts with the child as a witness (sometimes also called psychological abuse).

Neglect: Acts or omissions that negatively affect the welfare of a child, such as abandonment, educational neglect, medical neglect, and lack of supervision among other categories depending on local definitions.[2]

Although the definitions are similar, they still differ among civilian authorities who can have a direct effect on how an investigation is conducted and the actual data on child maltreatment.

Measuring Child Abuse

Military families have a much lower rate of child abuse and neglect when compared to civilian families, although children in military families may be subject to a higher level of abuse during times of deployment.[3] However, some researchers have noted a lower rate of child maltreatment among military families, which may be attributed to the rate of neglect complaints.[4] The vast majority of child maltreatment cases reported to the Department of Health and Human Services, which records child maltreatment within the civilian population, is neglect. The Department of Defense also reports that child neglect represents the largest percentage of child maltreatment incidents.[5] In fiscal year 2016, there were 13,916 reports of suspected child abuse and neglect to the Family Advocacy Program. The fiscal year 2016 rate of reported child abuse and neglect per one thousand children was 14.4, which is a 7 percent decrease in reports from fiscal year 2015 rates. There were 6,998 incidents of child abuse and neglect that met criteria in fiscal year 2016. The rate of incidents that met criteria per one thousand children remained consistent with fiscal year 2015 rates.[6] It should also be noted that the development of child abuse seems to be converging as the trend of civilian child abuse cases tends to be going down, whereas the rate of the military reports of abuse starting in 2010 appear to be increasing. There is still a significant gap in the rate of child abuse complaints within the military community: in one study it showed that in 2016 the rate of child abuse complaints was ten times higher with civilian authorities when comparing the amount of complaints based on the child population of civilian families versus military families.[7] Where you will see a significant difference in the rate of abuse is the number of cases that are founded. The Family Advocacy Program is much more likely to consider the allegation in a military family as founded.[8]

Although there are significant data on the rate of maltreatment within military families, there is controversy on whether the military has been forthright in disclosing child abuse within the military. This issue was highlighted in the case of Talia Williams, who was killed in 2005 by her father who had beaten her to death on a military base in Hawaii. Although there were multiple reports of abuse to military officers, it was kept within the military; child protective services was not notified of the abuse against Talia until it was too late. To further hinder the accuracy of child abuse in the military, the allegations of military abuse occurring within military families may, in some circumstances, not come to the attention of military authorities. Additionally, although it is stated in "Talia's Law" that the military is required to report child maltreatment to civilian authorities, there is not a reciprocal policy if the allegation of abuse comes directly to civilian authorities. There must be a memorandum of understanding in place between the military installation and the local child protective services.[9] "Pentagon officials have been asking states to enact laws or set policies that require local child protective agencies to work in conjunction with military authorities. Specifically, the military is requesting that civilian authorities immediately report any suspected abuse or neglect to the military. Fifteen states have enacted such laws or started to follow such policies that were already in place. Nine more states are considering similar bills this year."[10] Although the military has strived to improve its reporting law and work with civilian authorities, the secrecy of child abuse still exists. This is highlighted in the book *As You Were: Child Sex Abuse in the Military*. The author, Jerri L. Cook, writes about her childhood in the military where she was repeatedly sexually assaulted and beaten by her stepfather throughout her childhood, but the family maintained their pristine military family image as they transferred from military base to military base, alienating themselves from other family members and ensuring secrecy of abuse.[11]

The Military Family

Researchers who collect data on military families typically define military families as the spouses and dependent children of men or women that are active duty or are in the National Guard or Reserve.[12] It should be noted how family members of National Guard and Reserve military personnel are being called upon a great deal more to handle all family-related issues as reserve components are frequently activated into full-time service. In general, National Guard and Reserve members typically train one weekend a month and report for a two-week training session during the year. Military families represent a large segment of our population. In the past few decades, the number of service members has dropped by approximately 30 percent, but the use of the military overseas has tripled.[13] Since the creation of an all-volunteer force established in the 1970s, marriage, parenthood, and family life have become commonplace in military families with family members outnumbering service members.[14] A demographic report in 2015 listed that in the U.S. Armed Forces there were 1.7 million military children, composed of 297,809 Navy, 117,359 Marines, 431,851 Airforce, and 911,346 Army.[15] The military family population is fairly young when compared to civilian populations, although they are more likely to be married and have children at home. In fact, 90 percent of these children are raised by two parents.[16] The service member or the spouse of the service member has the potential to abuse their child; in some circumstances, both parents may be abusive. The children in these families can be subjected to the same types of abuse as those in a typical civilian family; like civilian children, military children have the same hopes and dreams and they rely on their parents to provide a safe and loving household.

Military Children

Despite child abuse being identified as a significant problem within the military, children in the military statistically are less likely to be abused. They are, however, still forced to be resilient as the lifestyle of a child in the military is unique with less stability than that of most children. Calling one place their home is not the reality for many military children. The instability of military life may result in children being forced to deal with their parent's deployment, with these family disruptions leading to depression and anxiety. Deployment of a parent can have an adverse effect on a child's academic performance and increase the likelihood of the child abusing alcohol and other drugs. Additionally, there has been greater gang activity reported in some teens with parents who have been deployed.[17] A child's reaction to parental deployment can vary with gender. In one study, it was more common for males to display anger and aggression, whereas females were more likely to have somatic complaints and internalized behaviors such as depression.[18] Finally, the child's age can be a factor when analyzing behavioral responses of parental deployment. Problem behaviors are lower between the ages of two and twelve years, but they increase during adolescence, reflecting that often older youth and behavioral issues are associated with decreased adult supervision.[19] In addition to the unique challenges military children face in response to deployment, military children can also be subjected to child maltreatment by the everyday stressors families face with military life. In an attempt to address the potential abuse within the military families, the Department of Defense has defined child abuse so that it can be properly identified and appropriately responded to. The abuse of children of military families may also occur outside of the military family.

Sex Offenders

There is a significant problem with sex offenders in the military. According to the *Associated Press*, who obtained their information from the Freedom of Information Act, 61 percent of inmates in U.S. military prisons were convicted of a sex crime and more than half of them involved children.[20] Although there is a protocol for punishing and recording sex offenders in the military, it was released from several news outlets in 2018 that the military was failing to protect military children who have been sexually assaulted by other military children. "Reports of assaults and rapes amongst kids on military bases often die on the desks of prosecutors, even when the attacker confesses. Other cases don't make it that far because criminal investigators shelve them, despite requirements they be pursued."[21] Further inquiry into the military handling of sexual abuse revealed that there were over six hundred reported cases of sexual assaults on children and teens on U.S. bases worldwide over a ten-year period.[22]

CHILD PORNOGRAPHY

Article 134 defines four unique criminal offenses related to child pornography:

1. Possessing, receiving, or viewing child pornography:
   a. That the accused knowingly and wrongfully possessed, received, or reviewed child pornography; and

   b. That, under the circumstances, the conduct of the accused was to the prejudice of good order and discipline in the armed forces or was of a nature to bring discredit upon the armed forces.
2. Possessing child pornography with the intention to distribute:
   a. That the accused knowingly and wrongfully possessed child pornography;
   b. That the possession was with the intent to distribute; and
   c. That under the circumstances, the conduct of the accused was to the prejudice of good order and discipline in the armed forces or was of a nature to bring discredit upon the armed forces.
3. Distributing child pornography:
   a. That the accused knowingly and wrongfully distributed child pornography to another; and
   b. That under the circumstances, the conduct of the accused was to prejudice of good order and discipline in the armed forces or was of a nature to bring discredit upon the armed forces.
4. Producing child pornography:
   a. That the accused knowingly and wrongfully produced child pornography; and
   b. That, under the circumstances, the conduct of the accused was to the prejudice of good order and discipline in the armed forces or was of a nature to bring discredit upon the armed forces.[23]

These laws clearly send the message that child pornography is not tolerated in the armed forces. However, the military has been negligent in gathering and making public comprehensive data on child pornography arrests. The military has the capacity to block child pornography from all military computers and conduct regular random searches of military electronics, including personal electronic devices for those with top security clearance, and should make it a priority to do so.[24] Although it can certainly be argued that the military can do more in fighting child pornography, they have taken aggressive steps in combating this crime. The Naval Criminal Investigative Service, Army Criminal Investigation Command, and other law enforcement agencies have ramped up their efforts as they target child porn offenders in their midst. In one such operation dubbed "Operation Flicker," initiated by Immigration and Customs Enforcement in 2006, they sought to dismantle sites that offered child pornography by subscription. Of the five thousand customers that were identified, 264 were identified as working for the Department of Defense including service members, civilians, and contractors. Of those, twenty-two had top secret security clearance and fifty-four had secret security clearance. This put the security of the United States at risk as enemies of the United States could blackmail those individuals to gain sensitive information.[25] However, the problem of child pornography continued as reported by journalist Bryan Bender of *The Boston Globe*, who reported in 2011 that up to fifty-two hundred Pentagon employees with top secret clearance were using Pentagon computers to access child pornography. Some of America's most elite military were committing this crime and yet were in a culture that appears to tolerate such behavior as there were almost no prosecutions. Yet again in the year 2012, the U.S. Missile Defense Agency issued a memo reminding staff not to download pornography at work.[26] In 2016, Daniel Payne, the Pentagon Defense Security Service Director, stated that the amount of child pornography on government computers is unbelievable. In Payne's statement, he reveals:

> At a time when the U.S. government is struggling to contain the problem of insider threats—employees who, for instance steal national secrets or unwittingly damage U.S. security with malicious software—pornographic images of children on government computers present a profound national security risk that if left unresolved could endanger American lives at home and abroad.[27]

Another more recent example of high-level military personnel involved in child pornography was the case of Army Colonel Robert Rice, who was arrested in 2013 and sentenced in 2016 to twelve years for child pornography. Rice, who had spent thirty-seven years in the military, had recently been assigned to the U.S. Army War College's Center for Strategic Leadership.[28] This is just one example of how even the most distinguished military leaders can engage in deviant behavior. Individuals in the military convicted for child pornography are categorized as sex offenders and will be subject to the sex offender registration.[29] Although the Department of Defense issues an annual report of sexual assaults on adults in the military, it does not address child sexual assaults or child pornography, which can be synonymous with one another.[30]

Sex Offender Registration

All fifty states are required to have sex offender registration in order to receive federal funding.[31] This requirement applies to military personnel as well. In 2015, the Sex Offender Registration and Notification Act was amended to "require the Department of Defense to submit information to the National Sex Offender Registry and the National Sex Offender Public Website about any person adjudged of a covered sex offense via court martial or released from a military correctional facility after being incarcerated for such an offense."[32] Service members convicted of a sex offense must register for between fifteen years to life depending on the severity of the offense.[33]

Military Jurisdiction

The military holds parents accountable through laws that differ from that of civilian legislation; these laws are known as the Uniform Code of Military Justice. In military families child maltreatment is handled by Family Advocacy Programs (FAPs) and local child protective services offices if the family is stationed in the United States.[34] In some circumstances, child protective services may receive a complaint of child abuse and may respond by classifying the allegation as a case that deserves an "alternative response," meaning the case should be handled within the military jurisdiction. For the FAP to be involved in reports of child abuse, alleged victims must be under the age of eighteen, incapable of self-support due to physical or mental incapacity, and in the legal care of a service member or military family member. The FAP will also intervene when a dependent military child is alleged to be the victim of abuse and neglect while in the care of a Department of Defense–sanctioned family childcare provider or installation facility such as a child development center, school, or youth program.[35] Service members who are accused of abusing their children can face imprisonment, court martial, or reduction in rank depending on the misconduct of the offender. Parents can also be charged within the civilian courts system depending on the location of the offense. For example, if a service member goes on leave (vacation) and commits a crime during that time frame, the military service member may be charged in the jurisdiction of the criminal offense. However, under no circumstances can the spouse of a service member be charged under the Uniform Code of Justice even if the offense takes place on a military base. In contrast, a service member in some circumstances can be prosecuted in both civilian and military courts, avoiding a procedural defense of double jeopardy.

Both service members and non-service members are subject to prosecution for child maltreatment even when they are stationed overseas. The particular legal jurisdiction where a service member is stationed overseas is dependent on the country they are deployed. Active duty U.S. military members and their accompanying non-active duty dependents must abide by the foreign countries' laws while residing overseas. The country where the U.S. military family is living may be considered their habitual residence in respect to certain legal issues. The NATO Status of Forces Agreement in place between the United States and North American Treaty Ogranization countries allows the host country to determine whether U.S. service members and their dependents are habitual residents making them subject to local laws and procedures.[36] In other words, it is the host country and not the military that decides who will prosecute any cases of child maltreatment. If a service member is convicted of a sex offense by a foreign court, the conviction must be obtained with sufficient safeguards and the accused must have received adequate due process. This does not mean that local jurisdictions must register service members who have been convicted in a foreign court. The Sex Offender Registration and Notification Act does not apply extraterritorially, or outside of the U.S. borders. It should also be noted that some overseas bases are located in countries that lack sex offender reporting requirements.[37]

CASE STUDY #1 (CAPTAIN IN TROUBLE)

A twenty-eight-year-old captain in the U.S. Army was on leave to attend his father's funeral. While staying at his mother's residence, a group of teenagers were racing up and down their street deliberately screeching their wheels and being loud. The Army captain, already overwhelmed with stress from his father's death, confronted the teenagers and demanded that they stop driving recklessly, explaining how he was visiting his mother and assisting with funeral arrangements. A verbal argument ensued where the teenagers, both age sixteen, started shouting vulgarities at the Army captain. Out of anger, the Army captain then pushed one of the teenagers in the chest. The teenagers began assaulting the Army captain to the extent that he required hospitalization for his extensive injuries. He was released from the hospital where he came to the police station stating he wanted to press charges. It was explained to the captain that the police could certainly file felony assault charges against the juveniles, but they could file misdemeanor charges against the captain if the teenager wanted to pursue charges. The captain explained to the police that the army would find out if he was charged and therefore didn't want to file charges against the teenager who was the more aggressive assailant. The captain decided not to pursue the matter further.

Causation

Individuals in the military can abuse children for the same reasons as any civilian family. However, the military can be unique as some of the causation of abuse may be the direct result of military life. The rate of child abuse can fluctuate depending on the stressors facing the military family. Stress can be enhanced as the result of frequent moves that take military parents away from their jobs and families, thus eliminating a potential support system.[38] Maltreating parents often feel they have very little support through their constant transitions. Some abusive parents feel they are isolated because their military family lifestyle requires them to move on a regular basis, thus lacking the opportunity to establish bonds that may be used as parental support. These stressors are accentuated during deployment.[39] Deployment is broken down into three distinct periods. **Predeployment** is the phase for the preparation for departure of the service member. The **deployment phase** is when the service member leaves their home and ends when they return home. The **postdeployment** phase begins on the day the service member returns home. Often these different phases of the deployment cycle cause an increase in stressors.[40] The stress of predeployment can be significant as tensions can rise between both parents as the service member does not wish to be deployed. Furthermore, the spouse's level of anxiety increases with the realization of additional parental responsibilities as the fact of being left alone becomes a reality. The stress of raising a child can certainly be amplified with the parents' attempt to prepare for such a drastic change in their life. The children remain a target of potential abuse as the family enters the deployment phase. The stressor associated with becoming a de facto single parent as one raises a child on their own has come to fruition. In some instances, deployed parents may seek the assistance of other relatives to care for their children until they are able to return. This familial help can provide the emotional support that is missing when one parent/spouse is not readily available. Children living with both biological parents have the lowest risk of child maltreatment. However, the frequency of maltreatment shows a dramatic increase when a child is raised by a single parent.[41] Maltreatment of children can continue as the family enters the final phase of postdeployment. Combat trauma, which may result in posttraumatic stress disorder, can have long-term impact on family function, specifically relating to the care of children. Posttraumatic stress disorder, which can be a direct result of deployment, is an anxiety disorder in response to experiencing extreme stress.[42] This disorder or any other mental health issue resulting from military deployment can have an adverse effect on the care of children. Posttraumatic stress disorder may present itself as expressions of anger toward both spouses and children.[43] Additionally, misuse of alcohol was a significant factor with soldiers returning from deployment.[44] Parents having substance abuse problems, such as with alcohol, can be more likely to abuse their children. Substance abuse hampers parents from properly parenting their children; they may physically, sexually, or emotionally abuse their children or fail to care for them.[45]

Anther stressor associated with military deployment is the potential of devastating injuries and/or death, causing one spouse to raise the children alone or have the burden of raising their children while caring for the injured spouse. These stressors are conducive to abuse or neglect of the children.

Let us not forget that there are still those risk factors that are not associated with deployment that also contribute to the likelihood of child abuse and neglect. Frequent moves and extended separations from family and support systems are common in military families, and these circumstances are contributing factors of abuse and neglect.[46] In conclusion, although there are several factors that can contribute to the abuse of children in military families, the family dynamic as a whole does not seem conducive to child maltreatment.

Sex Trade Involving Children: Meeting the Military Demand

There is a history of communities throughout the world building on the sex industry for those military personnel seeking prostitution while stationed overseas. It is clear that many children are engaged in prostitution to meet the high demands of these military personnel. Katheryn Farr did extensive research on sex trafficking and the global market for both women and children, specifically addressing the correlation between the military and childhood prostitution. The creation of military bases and installations has resulted in many instances of an overwhelming presence of prostitution or adult entertainment in areas adjacent to these facilities. Unfortunately, some of these "adult entertainment" businesses incorporate the sexual exploitation of children. For instance, in the Philippines, the United States negotiated an agreement with the Philippines known as The Visiting Forces agreement and The Status of Forces agreement, allowing military access to their facilities. The Philippines has had a long history of working with the U.S. military, which has furthered a substantial sex industry. Today there are at least four hundred thousand women working as registered prostitutes, with an unknown number of unregistered prostitutes. It is estimated that 25 percent of these prostitutes are children.[47] After the September 11 terrorist attacks in the United States, President George W. Bush declared the Philippines the "second front" in the war against terrorism and deployed several thousand troops to the islands. Most of these troops were stationed in the port of Zamboanga, where thousands of women and girls were relocated as prostitutes.[48] The sexual abuse of children is not confined just to the U.S. military or to the borders of the

Philippines, as the sex industry will meet the needs of military personnel wherever they are stationed.

CHILD ABUSE AND NATIVE AMERICANS

Native American Indian and Alaskan Native Groups

The tribal community consisting of Native American Indians and Alaskan Natives (AI/AN) in the United States are a diverse population of people. Diversity is reflected in the traditions within the community of culture, beliefs, and practices that are unique to these communities. There are nearly six hundred different AI/AN groups recognized in the United States.

Tribal communities have had a volatile history. This history has greatly influenced practices and culture today that still exists, some for the good and some not so good. Among the beliefs, the sacredness of children is apparent. In many tribal communities, there is a strong extended family network. Traditional ceremonies are celebrated for the children from birth through adolescence. These ceremonies help in the development of the child's sense of belonging, the ties to the family, and the history of their culture. This history or legacy is passed down through tribal language, dance, stories, and wisdom from the elders.

Despite the inherent strengths, the Native American population also face challenges. Community challenges include:

- High rate of unemployment
- Poverty
- Physical disparities
- Mental health disparities
- Violence
- Lower educational achievement.

Resulting from these community challenges, negative consequences ensue. To this end, there are higher rates of:[49]

- Suicide
- Substance abuse
- Mental health conditions
- Accidental deaths
- Violent victimization.

This section is going to cover some of the historical trauma that is passed down from generation to generation, evaluate child abuse in the AI/AN groups, and compare that to the child abuse statistics as a whole within the United States. This section will also discuss why the statistics for child abuse in the AI/AN population can be skewed. Finally, supreme court cases and laws that have affected the AI/AN population will be defined.

Definition

AI/AN are considered indigenous. The *Merriam-Webster Dictionary* defines indigenous as "having originated in and being produced, growing, living or occurring naturally in a particular region or environment."[50]

Multiple factors contribute to child abuse and neglect in the AI/AN communities. Due to tribal reporting guidelines and requirements as well as jurisdictional gaps in investigating abuse, the numbers are at best a rough guess. It is suspected that AI/AN children experience abuse and neglect at a rate of two times more than children of any other race in the United States. According to the website "Child Abuse and Death within Indian Country," tribal governments are not required to collect or share outcomes of children that are affected by the Indian Child Welfare Act.[51] AI/AN children are not only being abused, but they also are exposed to violence and trauma at a higher rate than any other race in the United States.[52] Domestic violence is high in the AI/AN community. According to the Advisory Committee Board, men who batter females are 49 to 70 percent more likely to abuse the children.

Historical Trauma

In order to understand the deep-rooted challenges that face the AI/AN population, it is necessary to delve into the historical trauma. As was stated in the introduction of this chapter, AI/AN communities have a rich legacy and tradition of historical storytelling that is passed from one generation to the other; this storytelling can lead to historical trauma.

Historical trauma is defined as a collective complex trauma that is inflicted on a group of people who share a specific group or affiliation. Affiliations can be ethnicity, nationality, or religion. The effects of this historical trauma being transmitted intergenerationally is that descendants continue sharing the pain of the ancestors.[53] Even though these events happened generations earlier, the impact is still relevant in AI/AN communities. Some examples of historical trauma that has impacted the native communities include:

- Warfare against the white man
- Divided communal tribal lands into individual allotments (General Allotment Act 1887)
- Boarding school era
- Outlaw of religious practices.

When first thinking of historical trauma, it does not make sense how this would be related to child abuse in the twenty-first century; but in fact, it does. Even though the trauma is far removed, it continues to impact the emotional life of the AI/AN communities. A study by Whitbeck in 2004[54] records the impact of historical trauma on elders and tribe members on two large reservations. A survey was completed which shows the following:

- One-fifth of the respondents still think daily about the loss of indigenous land.

- One-third of the respondents think daily of the loss of the indigenous language.
- More than one-third of the respondents think daily about the loss of culture.
- A total of 45.9 percent think about alcoholism and the community impact.

The elders at these two large reservations continue to express sadness, depression, anger, anxiety, and discomfort around the treatment of them by the white man. The elders express fear and distrust of the white man, which continues to lead to feelings of isolation and rage.[55]

In the 1950s, a movement began to move American Indians into urban areas. Now, approximately 78 percent of AI/AN are in cities rather than on reservations or tribal communities. Native Americans, whether in the city or tribe, are the most highly victimized group in the United States.

Boarding School Era

Whitbeck's study also attempted to put in perspective how historical trauma would affect the family unit. Many of the parents and/or grandparents were raised during the boarding school era. During this time, the children were removed from the parents and sent to boarding school against the child's and the family's wishes. The children were stripped from experiencing the traditional parental role model and placed in an institutional setting. Traditional practices, beliefs, and dress were outlawed and would be punished with no family to provide support. The children were also physically and sexually abused in the boarding schools.[56]

Alcohol and Drugs

Research points to how often members of AI/AN groups turn to alcohol to deal with trauma. Alcohol was and continues to be a way to numb the pain and to hide the feelings of rage. Alcohol continues to be a challenge in tribal communities and ultimately is linked to child abuse. High incidences of child physical and child sexual abuse in Indian Country revolves around drugs and alcohol abuse. Alcohol during pregnancy is higher among AI/AN women than the general population, leading to a higher percentage of birth defects along the fetal alcohol spectrum at 1.7 to 10.6 per one thousand births. This is a fivefold difference compared to the national rate.[57]

The mortality rate of the AI/AN population is four times higher than other races, with alcohol being a contributor of four of the ten leading causes of death. The alcohol mortality rate is 514 percent higher in the AI/AN population than the general population. The four of the top ten causes of death related to alcohol are as follows:[58]

- Accidents
- Chronic liver disease

- Suicide
- Homicide.

Wolf conducted research to try to identify why alcohol has affected the AI/AN population like it has. Based on his research, Wolf suggests that violence among the American Indians is related to alcohol blackout syndrome. Wolf describes this phenomenon as being related to damage to the medial thalamus, hypothalamus, and red nucleus. Destruction of the nuclei in these areas results in a loss of conscious control over emotions and ability to withhold aggression. Wolf suggests that this syndrome develops more rapidly in the Native Indian population.[59]

Marijuana has also been indicated as high usage within the AI/AN population. With alcohol and marijuana being problematic, additional drugs are being introduced. Methamphetamine is now overtaking alcohol and marijuana usage, causing a rise in child neglect and child abuse cases. In 2004, tribal service providers and law enforcement officers reported that parents were selling material items to obtain cash for drugs. The search for money to pay for drugs has continued to evolve, resulting in prostituting of children in order to receive money to buy drugs.[60]

As the old saying goes, children learn what they live; children in the AI/AN population learn from watching their elders. The children mimic the parents and begin to use drugs and alcohol at a young age. A total of 16 percent of AI/AN youth twelve years of age and older are reporting substance dependence or abuse.[61]

Suicide

Suicide is the second leading cause of death in the AI/AN population. Suicide rates are three times higher than the national average, and some reports suggest it can be as high as ten times the national average on the reservations. Suicide is so common in some native communities that it is becoming an acceptable solution in dealing with stress and burdens.[62]

Poverty

Poverty is also an issue that affects the AI/AN population at higher levels than the general population. Poverty can lead to increase in stress, which leads to alcohol and drug use. Alcohol and drug use are linked to child physical and sexual abuse. It is a vicious cycle and a difficult one to break. The Native Indian population accounts for approximately 1.5 percent of the total population; one-third of this population is below the age of eighteen. More than one-quarter of the Native Indian population is living in poverty.

Jurisdictional Gaps

When I (A. Rasmussen) first started researching AI/AN populations and thinking about reservations, I automatically thought the majority of the population on reservations is American Indians and/or Alaskan Natives. I was wrong. More than

75 percent of the residents on reservations are non-Indians; this number does not include those that work on the reservations that are non-Indians. A total of 50 percent of AI/AN women are married to non-Indians.[63] After all of the discussion on why the AI/AN population is at risk of abuse, research actually suggests that a large amount of abusers on the reservations are in fact non-Indians.

Having such a high population of non-Indians on a reservation is a challenge for the criminal justice system and the tribal government, which leads to jurisdictional gaps. The tribal governing body has specific crimes they can investigate, and these can only be related to the AI/AN population. Tribal governments do not have the authority to arrest and prosecute non-Indian offenders. The federal law says that only the federal government can prosecute, but most of the cases do not get prosecuted, leaving non-Indian residents on reservations to get away with multiple crimes, including crimes against children. In 2011, federal prosecutors rejected 61 percent of sexual abuse of children cases. Some reasons that the federal government may decline to prosecute a case are:

- Faraway locations
- Lack of evidence
- Lack of resources
- Investigative issues.

If the federal government does prosecute a case, the courthouse is usually far away from the reservation, with no Indian representative available. The AI/AN have become discouraged and believe that the cases will not be prosecuted, which has led to a high rate of underreporting.[64]

How Did We Get Here?

From 1778 to 1871, the United States' relations with individual American Indian nations indigenous to what is now the United States were defined and conducted largely through the treaty-making process. These "contracts among nations" recognized and established unique sets of rights, benefits, and conditions for the treaty-making tribes, who agreed to cede millions of acres of their homelands to the United States and accept its protection. Like other treaty obligations of the United States, Indian treaties are considered to be "the supreme law of the land," and they are the foundation upon which federal Indian law and the federal Indian trust relationship is based.[65] Tribes can establish and operate their own court systems. Multiple legal battles have resulted to determine jurisdiction and rights of the tribal community resulting in federal statutes and U.S. Supreme Court decisions. These decisions have determined concurrent and sometimes exclusive jurisdictional authority to federal or relevant state governments regarding certain crimes that occur on Indian lands. Four factors that have to be considered are:

1. Whether the crime was committed on Indian lands
2. Whether the victim is an Indian or non-Indian

3. Whether the perpetrator is an Indian or non-Indian
4. What type of crime was committed.[66]

In determining tribal sovereignty, three significant U.S. Supreme Court cases dictated how the tribes and reservations were viewed, guided, and directed.

Johnson v. M'Intosh

The federal government has the "preemptive right," or exclusive right, to extinguish an Indian title of occupancy (of land) either by purchase or conquer. Because Native Americans did not own lands they inhabited, the government ruled they lacked power to transfer position of land.[67] (Private citizens cannot purchase land from Native Americans.)

Cherokee Nation v. Georgia

Indian tribes are not considered foreign states but domestic-dependent nations. Indian tribes were described as being a ward to its guardian (the federal government). Indian tribes look to the federal government for protection, rely on its kindness and power, and appeal to the reliefs to their wants.[68]

Worcester v. Georgia

This case provided greater sovereignty to the Indian tribes. Indian nations have always been considered as distinct, independent political communities. The state government did not have authority to enact laws affecting tribal communities.[69]

Laws continue to get passed and amended to determine who governs the tribes and reservations and which authority rules on what crimes. Headway is still being made in 2019 in an attempt to decrease the jurisdictional gap that exists.

Laws Concerning American Indians and Alaskan Natives

Federal government has jurisdiction over many crimes in or on Indian land.

United States v. Lara

Lara was tried by the tribal government for assault on a police office. He was charged and sentenced to ninety days. The federal government then charged Lara for assaulting a police officer. Lara claimed that being charged for similar crimes is double jeopardy. The Supreme Court ruled that since the tribal nation was considered its own sovereign government, the federal government could also charge as a separate sovereign government and double jeopardy does not apply.[70] In addition, the Supreme Court granted Congress the broad general powers to legislate in respect to Indian tribes.

Congress passed two statutes in relation to the investigation of crimes involving Indian Country.

General Crimes Act

This was passed in 1817 and gave the federal government jurisdiction over all interracial crimes on tribal lands.

Major Crimes Act

This was passed in 1885. This gives the federal government jurisdiction over sixteen major crimes. The sixteen crimes include murder, manslaughter, rape, kidnapping, maiming, sexual abuse under Ch. 109-A, incest, assault with intent to commit murder, assault with a dangerous weapon, assault resulting in serious bodily injury, assault on a person younger than sixteen years old, felony child abuse, felony child neglect, arson, burglary, or theft under eighteen.[71]

In some situations, the state governing body is given jurisdiction over crimes in Indian county. There are three situations in which this may occur.

Situation #1: Public Law 280: Public Law 280 was enacted in 1953. The federal government gave federal jurisdictional authority over specific regions of Indian Country to a total of six states. In these six states, the federal government no longer has jurisdiction authority on the crimes committed under the General Crimes Act or Major Crimes Act. The six states are:

- Alaska
- California
- Minnesota
- Nebraska
- Oregon
- Wisconsin.

Also, under the PL 280, some states assumed some jurisdictional authority, but not full authority. These states are Nevada, South Dakota, Washington, Florida, Idaho, Montana, North Dakota, Arizona, Iowa, and Utah.

Situation #2: The state has been granted jurisdiction through grants, acts, or statewide enactments restoration acts, or land claim settlement act.[72]

Situation #3: The crime that was committed was a wholly non-Indian crime that occurred on Indian land.

Laws In Place to Protect Children in the American Indian/Alaska Native Community

Indian Child Welfare Act:

Before the Indian Child Welfare Act (ICWA) was established, Native American children were being removed from their homes at a rate of fifty to sixty times more than non-native American children. The welfare system was not as familiar with the parenting styles and customs of the AI/AN groups and was quick to remove and place children in foster care, mostly due to the difference in cultural misunderstanding. The purpose of the ICWA is to "protect the best interest of

Indian children and to promote stability and security of Indian tribes and families by the establishment of minimum Federal Standards for the removal of Indian children and placement of such children in homes which will reflect the unique values of Indian culture (25 U.S.C. 1902)."[73]

In order to enforce the ICWA, it is imperative to identify who is deemed an Indian child. This is addressed through §23.2, which states an Indian child is any unmarried person who is under the age of eighteen and either:

1. A member or citizen of an Indian tribe
2. Is eligible for membership or citizenship in an Indian tribe and is the biological child of a member or citizen of an Indian tribe.[74]

The ICWA acknowledges that abuse is similar to non-American Indians when it involves children.

Indian Religious Freedom Act of 1978

Prior to this act going into effect, AI/AN were prevented from celebrating traditional spiritual ceremonies and practices along with religious freedoms. The Indian Religious Freedom Act gave American Indians the right of freedom to believe, express, and exercise their traditional religions. The right included access to sites, use and possession of sacred objects, and freedom to worship through ceremonies and rites.[75]

Indian Child Protection and Family Violence Prevention Act 1990

The purpose of this act sets a minimum standard of character and suitability for federal and tribal employees who have regular contact with or control over Indian children. The Bureau of Indian Affairs was identified as the source to oversee these procedures.

Native American Child Safety Act of 2016

This act expanded the concept of the Indian Child Protection and Family Violence Prevention Act by recognizing that in addition to employees who serve children being cleared to act on children's behalf, the people with which the children are placed also needed to be screened. This act expanded background checks for all adults residing in a prospective foster home on all reservations. This act also calls for the Department of the Interior to consult tribes and issue guidance regarding procedures for criminal records checks. The establishment of standards for placement were introduced to be:

- Criminal records check
- Fingerprint-based check of the national criminal information databases
- Check of any abuse registries maintained by the tribes.[76]

Tribal Law and Order Act of 2010

The Tribal Law and Order Act was signed into law by President Obama on July 29, 2010. The purpose of this law is to help address crime in the tribal community and place strong emphasis on decreasing violence against AI/AN women. The law encourages the hiring of more law enforcement within the tribal community. It provides greater guidelines on handing sexual assault and domestic violence crimes. The law also encourages the development of more effective preventative programs to combat drug and alcohol abuse in the at-risk youth population.[77]

Ashlynne Mike AMBER Alert in Indian Country Act

Public Law 115-116, sponsored by Senator John McCain, was passed by the Senate and House of Representatives and went into effect for fiscal year 2019.[78] The Ashlynne Mike AMBER Alert amends the PROTECT Act to make Indian Tribes eligible for the AMBER Alert grant program for fiscal year 2019. The bill modifies the program by:

1. Adding, as a new purpose, the integration of the Tribal AMBER Alert systems into state AMBER Alert systems
2. Make Indian tribes eligible for AMBER Alert grants
3. Permit use of grant funds to integrate state or regional AMBER Alert communication plans with an Indian tribe
4. Allow the waiver of matching funds requirements for grants awarded to Indian tribes.[79]

LB 154

This is a legislative bill specific to Nebraska that was signed by the governor on March 7, 2019. This bill authorizes a study to improve reporting and investigation of Native American women and children. The bill authorizes the Nebraska State Patrol to work with the Commission on Indian Affairs, tribal, local law enforcement, and federally recognized tribes and urban indian organizations to conduct a study that is focused on:

- The scope of the problem
- Identifying barriers
- Creating partnerships to increase the reporting and investigating of missing Native American Women and Children.[80]

In studying the history of AI/AN groups, I have developed a deep respect for the perseverance of this race. The obstacles that have been overcome and the remaining challenges that are yet to be faced are substantial. As a nation, we have made strides but continue to have a long way to go to protect children in all cultures and jurisdictions.

CHILD ABUSE AND THE ILLEGAL IMMIGRANT

Trying to determine the rate of child abuse in the illegal immigrant community in the United States, like Native Americans, is a difficult task. Immigrants come to the United States from all over the world to try to escape the harsh realities of their own countries and to enjoy the freedoms of America. This escape comes with challenges. The rate of illegal immigrants entering the country is astounding. In 2017, it was approximated that the U.S. foreign-born population had risen to 44.5 million; this is 13.7 percent of the total population of the United States and the highest documented immigrant population since 1910. A total of 1.9 million of the illegal immigrants are under the age of eighteen.[81]

In 2015, approximately thirty thousand migrants, mostly mothers and children, were apprehended at the U.S. border. Many of these women and children were fleeing from the "northern triangle": Guatemala, El Salvador, and Honduras. With gang violence, human trafficking, and police corruption, these countries are some of the most dangerous countries in the world.[82] In addition, these countries face economic instability and poverty. There is also a rise at the southern border of unaccompanied children trying to get into the United States from these countries. These children are alone after having escaped the violence and left without a parent or have lost the parent along the journey. During the migration, it is not uncommon for the children to face imprisonment, rape, ethnic cleansing, physical violence, emotional distress, and torture both before arriving to the border and at the border.[83] The Tahirih Justice Center estimates that about 60 percent of the women and girls making the migration to the United States are raped along the journey. By the time the children arrive to the border, mental and physical health may need to be addressed.

When apprehended at the border, immigration authorities refer the unaccompanied children to the Office of Refugee and Resettlement, which is a division of U.S. Department of Health and Human Services. These children are placed in shelters, waiting to be claimed. In 2017, 40,810 children were referred to Office of Refugee and Resettlement, which was up from 13,625 in 2012.[84]

When families are able to migrate to the United States, many stressors continue. The stress of the journey and the violence imposed on the caregiver and/or family will greatly impact the emotional health of the caregiver and of the children. Any witnessed violence also will come into play. Studies conducted on undocumented children that have migrated to the United States have shown that they have a sense of not belonging. They are illegal immigrants so the family constantly has a fear of deportation. The child, even though they may spend most of their life in the United States, continues to have to try to bridge the feeling of belonging to the country from they fled and the country in which they now live. In addition to not feeling secure in the United States, there are limited resources that are available for undocumented persons, so the child can easily feel isolated.

Moving into a new country with language barriers and limited resources, many undocumented immigrants live in poverty. In fact, more than half of undocumented immigrants are living below the federal poverty level, even though many are working. The jobs in which undocumented immigrants are

working are low-paying jobs without benefits. One of the major health disparities is access to medical care. Medical care is a major barrier because undocumented immigrants are not eligible for federal government insurance such as
Medicaid. In 2010, the Patient Protection and Affordable Care Act was passed
and signed into law which provided insurance to millions of Americans; undocumented immigrants were excluded from having access to this insurance.[85]

When immigrants come to a country such as the United States, the immigrants bring with them their own parenting styles. Many times, that parenting
style is an authoritarian style in which the parent exhibits controlling behaviors
and lacks behaviors that respond to children's needs. Authoritarian parenting
styles, such as using corporal punishment, may conflict and cause issues with
the values of the United States. Many times, caregivers do not realize that the
parenting style they grew up with is not accepted in the United States and children may be removed because of it. By the same token, immigrant women and
children who are usually controlled by the dominant male may not realize that
they are being abused. Even if they are aware that abuse is occurring, the fear of
deportation or of losing their child may keep them from reporting the abuse.[86]
Undocumented immigrants are less likely to report any type of abuse other than
neglect.

The largest number of immigrants in the United States are Latino. Latino
children are the largest and fastest-growing ethnic minority in the United States.
In 2008, it was estimated that Latino children accounted for one-quarter of
the number of children in the United States; that number is expected to grow
to one-third by 2035. In the year 2000, 14.2 percent of children reported as
victims of child maltreatment in the United States were Latino. By 2008, that
number had risen to 20.8 percent. In 2008, reported child maltreatment in the
United States rated child physical abuse at 20.7 percent of the Latino children;
20.2 percent were sexually abused, 22.7 percent were neglected, and 33.8 percent of the cases were psychologically abused. Immigrant Latino children were
noted in this study to be abused at three times the rate compared to Latino
children born in the United States.[87] Part of the reason for such high numbers is,
as previously mentioned, the parenting style typically used by Latino caregivers,
which is an authoritarian style. This style of parenting is used to instill cultural
values and beliefs, parental obedience, family loyalty, and appropriate behaviors. The authoritarian style believes in the use of corporal punishment, which
is condemned by many social workers and is considered an excessive form of
discipline.

Special Immigrant Juvenile Status

Special Immigrant Juvenile Status (SIJS) is an immigration relief ruling that
allows undocumented children in the United States to obtain legal permanent
residence. SIJS is an amendment to the Immigration and Nationality Act that
went into effect in 1990 in response to the inability of unaccompanied children
to file for legal immigrant status. This was amended in 1997 and again in 2008.
The 1997 amendment clarified that SIJS was specific to abused, neglected, and/

or abandoned children. In 2008, it was amended by the William Wilberforce Trafficking Victims Protection Reauthorization Act, which provided protections for unaccompanied minors and expanded the definition of SIJS.[88]

SIJS provided immigration relief for undocumented children in the United States to obtain legal permanent status by federal statute (8.U.S.C.A. § 110 (a) (27) (J):

1. The child must be declared a dependent of the court, child must be placed in the custody of a state agency or department, or custody of child granted to an individual or entity because the child cannot be reunified with one or both parents.
2. Unable to reunify with one or both parents due to abuse, neglect, or abandonment.
3. Returning the child to the parent's country or nationality or the country of last habitual residence is not in the child's best interest.[89]

This requires an application process that must be followed. The state juvenile courts are responsible for entering specific findings so that children will qualify. If the findings are not entered appropriately, this will prevent the legal status from being granted and the child will have to face the possibility of deportation.

I (A. Rasmussen) have always lived in the United States, and for that I am thankful; I also realize how sheltered I am. I couldn't help but think, how is it that the children travel hundreds or thousands of miles with or without an adult? There are several ways these children end up in the United States:

1. The child comes with a parent as a young child. That child grows up and considers the United States their home.
2. The child travels to the United States with an adult relative or a family friend to reunite with family. Once they reach the United States, the family cannot be located.
3. The child begins the journey with the parent, but along the way something happens to the parent and the parent does not complete the trip.
4. The child is unaccompanied and has fled home to escape poverty, violence, or persecution.
5. The child has fled to escape the abuse of the parent, the child has been abandoned, or the child has been neglected
6. Sex and/or labor trafficking.

CONCLUSION

Children are abused as U.S. citizens; children are abused in the military; children withstand abuse no matter what country they are from or what their race is. With every special jurisdiction whether it is the military, AI/AN, or undocumented immigrants, children are at risk. Child abuse has to be recognized, people have to be educated, and society has to become more culturally competent. It is clear that the nation as a whole continues to face challenges in how to protect the children. Professionals working together need to continue to strive to make children the priority that they deserve to be, and keep our children safe.

REVIEW QUESTIONS

1. Why was it necessary to implement Talia's Law?

2. How can a service member's deployment affect the rate of abuse in a military family?

3. What can be done to increase trust between the reservations, the tribal communities, and the non-Indian communities?

4. How can the government and tribal communities work together to decrease the jurisdictional gap in investigating crimes in the tribal community?

5. What are some steps that can be done to become more culturally competent?

KEYWORDS

Uniform Code of Justice: A military justice system that lists criminal offenses under military law.

Family Advocacy Program: Program that works to stop domestic violence before it starts.

Indigenous: Having originated in and being produced, growing, living, or occurring naturally in a particular region or environment.

Immigrant: A person who lives in a country in which that person was not born.

NOTES

1. Department of Defense Family Advocacy Program, "Briefing the Defense Health Board April 23, 2018." Available from https://health.mil/Reference-Center/Presentations/2018/04/23/DoD-Family-Advocacy-Program.

2. Lynne M. Borden, Amy Gunty, Emily Jaeger, Zihui Lu, Mark Otto, Adeya Richmond, Rachel Roeske, Shelby Wilcox, and Rhiannon Williams, *Deployment and Child Abuse and Neglect: Understanding the Data*, 2. Available from https://reachmilitaryfamilies.umn.edu/sites/default/files/rdoc/Deployment_and_Child_Abuse_and_Neglect_DoD.pdf.

3. Sean C. Sheppard, Jennifer W. Malatras, and Allen C. Israel, "The Impact of Deployment on U.S. Military Families," *American Psychologist* 65, no. 6 (2010): 599–609.

4. James E. McCarroll, Robert J. Ursano, Zizhong Fan, and John H. Newby, "Comparison of U.S. Army and Civilian Substantiated Reports of Child Maltreatment," *Child Maltreatment* 9, no. 1 (2004): 103–10.

5. Stephen J. Cozza, Gloria L. Whaley, Joscelyn E. Fisher, Jing Zhou, Claudio D. Ortiz, James E. McCarroll, Carol S. Fullerton, and Robert J. Ursano, "Deployment Status and Child Neglect Types in the U.S. Army," *Child Maltreatment* 23, no. 1 (2018): 25–33.

6. Department of Defense, *Report on Child Abuse and Neglect and Domestic Abuse in the Military for Fiscal Year 2016*, May 2017, 2. Available from http://download.militaryonesource.mil/12038/MOS/Reports/FAP_FY16_DoD_Report.pdf.

7. Daniel Murphy, "Child Abuse in the Military," paper presented at the annual meeting for the Southern Criminal Justice Association," Pensacola, Florida, September 13, 2018.

8. Borden, Gunty, Jaeger, Lu, Otto, Richmond, Roeske, Wilcox, and Williams, *Deployment and Child Abuse and Neglect: Understanding the Data*, 6–8.

9. J.L. Cook, *As You Were: Child Sex Abuse in the Military* (Rib Lake, WI: Ice Age Press, 2016), 25.

10. Jen Fifield, "Why Child Abuse in Military Families May Go Unreported," PBS, 2017. Available from http://www.pewtrusts.org/en/research-and-analysis/blogs/stateline/2017/06/07/why-child-abuse-in-military-families-may-be-going-unreported.

11. Cook, *As You Were*, 1–125.

12. Stephen J. Cozza and Richard M. Lerner, "Military Children and Families: Introducing the Issue," *The Future of Children* 23, no. 2 (2013): 4.

13. T. Tanielian and L.H. Jaycox, *Invisible Wounds of War: Psychological and Cognitive Injuries, Their Consequences, and Services to Assist Recovery* (Santa Monica, CA: RAND Center for Military Health Policy Research, 2008).

14. Molly Clever and David R. Segal, "The Demographics of Military Children and Families," *The Future of Children* 23, no. 2 (2013): 13–17.

15. U.S. Department of Defense, "Month of the Military Child." Accessed August 18, 2018. Available from https://www.defense.gov/News/Special-Reports/0417_militarychild/.

16. Deborah A. Gibbs, Sandra L. Martin, Ruby E. Johnson, E. Danielle Rentz, Monique Clinton-Sherrod, and Jennifer Hardison, "Child Maltreatment and Substance Abuse Among U.S. Army Soldiers," *Child Maltreatment* 13, no. 3 (2008): 259–68.

17. Elizabeth M. Collins, "Experts Explain Mental State of Military Children," *Soldiers Magazine*, May 2015. Available from https://www.army.mil/article/147786/experts_explain_mental_state_of_military_children.

18. Anita Chandra, Laurie T. Martin, Stacey A. Hawkins, and Amy Richardson, "The Impact of Parental Deployment on Child Social and Emotional Functioning: Perspectives of School Staff," *Journal of Adolescent Health* 46, no. 3 (2010): 218–33.

19. Mona P. Ternus, "Support for Adolescents Who Experience Parental Military Deployment," *Journal of Adolescent Health* 46, no. 3 (2010): 203–06.

20. Richard Larrdner and Eileen Sullivan, "Child Sex Offenders Largest Group of Inmates in Military Prisons," *Associated Press*, November 18, 2015.

21. Justin Pritchard and Reese Dunklin, "U.S. Military Fails to Protect Children from Sexual Abuse on Bases," *Associated Press*, March 13, 2018.

22. Justin Pritchard and Reese Dunklin, "Military Seeks to Limit Congress Addressing Child Sexual Assaults on Bases," *Associated Press*, May 8, 2018.

23. Uniform Code of Military Justice, Article 134, 10.

24. Lori Handrahan, *Epidemic: America's Trade in Child Rape* (Walterville, OR: Trine Day LLC, 2018), 65.

25. Tim McGlone, "As Child Porn Acivity Grows, Efforts to Trap Offenders Do, Too," in Stefan Kiesbye (ed.), *Child Pornography: At Issue* (Farmington Hills, MI: Greenhaven Press, 2013), 22.

26. Handrahan, *Epidemic*, 59.

27. Aliya Sternstein, "Child Porn on Government Devices: A Hidden Security Threat," *Christian Science Monitor*, December 5, 2016.

28. Mark Scolforo, "Army Colonel Sentenced to 12 Years in Child Pornography Case," *Associated Press*, December 28, 2016.

29. Ryan D. Oakley, "A Lifetime of Consequences: Registering Convicted Military Sex Offenders," *The Reporter*, 2013, 4.

30. Terri Moon Cronk, "DOD Releases Latest Military Sexual Assualt Report," Department of Defense News, May 1, 2017.

31. Kimberly A. McCabe and Daniel G. Murphy, *Child Abuse: Today's Issues* (Boca Raton, FL: Taylor & Francis, 2016), 152.

32. Office of Justice Programs, SMART: Office of Sex Offender Sentencing, Monitoring, Apprehending, Registering and Tracking. Available from https://www.smart.gov/.

33. Oakley, "A Lifetime of Consequence," 4.

34. Monica L. McCoy and Stephanie M. Keen, *Child Abuse and Neglect*, second edition (New York, NY: Psychological Press, 2009), 37.

35. National Center on Domestic and Sexual Violence, Family Advocacy Program, 2018. Available from www.ncdsv.org/ncd_contacts.htm.

36. U.S. Department of State, U.S. Military Service Members Assigned Abroad: Information on Habitual Residence for Children and Spouses. Available from https://travel.state.gov/content/travel/en/International-Parental-Child-Abduction/for-providers/laws/us-military-serv-members-assign-abroad-info.html.

37. Oakley, "A Lifetime of Consequence," 3.

38. Jen Fifield, "Why Child Abuse in Military Families May Go Unreported," *PBS Newshour*, June 7, 2017. Available from https://www.pbs.org/newshour/nation/child-abuse-military-families-may-go-unreported; E.D. Rentz, S.W. Marshall, D. Loomis, C. Casteel, S.L. Martin, and D.A. Gibbs, "Effect of Deployment on the Occurrence of Child Maltreatment in Military and Nonmilitary Families," *American Journal of Epidemiology* 165, no. 10 (2007): 1199–206.

39. Rentz, Marshall, Loomis, Casteel, Martin, and Gibbs, "Effect of Deployment on the Occurrence of Child Maltreatment in Military and Nonmilitary Families," 1199–206; D.A. Gibbs, S.L. Martin, L.L. Kupper, and R. E. Johnson, "Child Maltreatment in Enlisted Soldiers' Families during Combat Related Deployments," *JAMA*, 298, no. 5 (2007): 528–35; C.J. Thomsen, M.M. Rabenhorst, R.J.McCarthy, J.S. Milner, W.J. Travis, R.E. Foster, and C.W. Copeland, "Child Maltreatment Before and After Combat-Related Deployment Among Active-Duty United States Air Force Maltreating Parents," *Psychology of Violence* 4, no. 2 (2014): 143–55; Clever and Segal, *The Demographics of Military Children and Families*, 29.

40. E.M. Flake, B.E. Davis, P.L. Johnson, and L.S. Middleton, "The Psychosocial Effects of Deployment on Military Children," *Journal of Developmental & Behavioral Pediatrics* 30, no. 4 (2009): 271–78; Denise Kindschi, *Heavy Hands: An Introduction to the Crimes of Family Violence*, fourth edition (Upper Saddle River, NJ: Pearson, 2010), 109.

41. A.J. Sedlak, J. Meteburg, M. Basena, I. McPherson, A. Greene, and S. Li, *Fourth National Incidence Study of Child Abuse and Neglect (NIS-4): Report to Congress* (Washington, DC: U.S. Department of Health and Human Services, Administration for Children and Families, 2010).

42. McCoy and Keen, *Child Abuse and Neglect*, 87.

43. T. Galovski and J. Lyns, "Psychological Sequelae of Combat Violence: A Review of the Impact of PTSD on Veteran's Family and Possible Interventions," *Aggression and Violent Behavior* 9, no. 5 (2004): 477–501.

44. Isabel G. Jacobson, Margaret A. Ryan, Tomoko I. Hooper, Tyler C. Smith, Paul J. Amoroso, Edward J. Boyko, Gary D. Gackstetter, Timothy S. Wells, and Nicole S. Bell, "Alcohol Use and Alcohol-Related Problems Before and After Military Combat Deployment," *JAMA* 300, no. 6 (2008): 663–75.

45. Cynthia Crosson-Tower, *Understanding Child Abuse and Neglect*, eighth edition (Boston, MA: Allyn & Bacon, 2010), 90.

46. W.R. Saltzman, P. Lester, W.R. Beardslee, C.M. Layne, K. Woodward, and W.P. Nash, "Mechanics of Risk and Resilience in Military Families: Theoretical and Empirical Basis of a Family-focused Resilience Enhancement Program," *Clinical Child and Family Psychology Review* 14, no. 3 (2011): 213–30.

47. Kathryn Farr, *Sex Trafficking: The Global Market in Women and Children* (New York, NY: Worth Publishers, 2005), 191.

48. Farr, *Sex Trafficking*, 193.

49. Michelle C. Sarche and Nancy R. Whitesell, "Child Development Research in North American Native American Communities—Looking Back and Moving Forward: Introduction," *Child Development Perspectives* 6, no. 1 (2012): 42–48.

50. *Merriam-Webster Dictionary*, "Indigenous." Accessed on March 17, 2019. Available from https://www.merriam-webster.com/dictionary/indigenous.

51. "Child Abuse and Death Within Indian Country." Accessed March 23, 2019. Available from https://dyinginindiancountry.com/2016/11/01/child-abuse-and-death-within-indian-country/.

52. Brittany Raia, "Protecting Vulnerable Children in Indian Country: Why and How Violence Against Women Reauthorizations Act of 2013 Should be Extended to Cover Child Abuse Committed on Indian Reservations," *American Criminal Law Review* 54, no. 1 (2017).

53. Teresa Evans-Campbell, "Historical Trauma in American Indian/Native Alaskan Communities: A Multilevel Framework for Exploring Impacts on Individuals, Families, and Communities," *Journal of Interpersonal Violence* 23, no. 3 (2008): 316–38.

54. Les Whitbeck, X. Chen, D. Hoyt, and G. Adams, "Discrimination, Historical Loss and Enculturation: Culturally Specific Risk and Resiliency Factors for Alcohol Abuse among American Indians," *Journal of Studies on Alcohol and Drugs* 65, no. 4 (2004): 409–18.

55. Evans-Campbell, "Historical Trauma in American Indian/Native Alaskan Communities," 316–38.

56. *Merriam-Webster Dictionary*, "Indigenous."

57. Michelle Sarche and Paul Spicer, "Poverty and Health Disparities for American Indian and Alaskan Native Children-Current Knowledge and Future Prospects," *Annals of the New York Academy of Sciences* 1136 (2008): 126–36.

58. Raia, "Protecting Vulnerable Children in Indian Country."

59. Michael L. Lobbs and Thomas D. Watts, *Native American Youth and Alcohol: An Annotated Bibliography* (Westport, CT: Greenwood Press, Inc., 1989), 21.

60. Raia, "Protecting Vulnerable Children in Indian Country."

61. Raia, "Protecting Vulnerable Children in Indian Country."

62. Raia, "Protecting Vulnerable Children in Indian Country."

63. Evans-Campbell, "Historical Trauma in American Indian/Native Alaskan Communities," 316–38.

64. Evans-Campbell, "Historical Trauma in American Indian/Native Alaskan Communities," 316–38.

65. Raia, "Protecting Vulnerable Children in Indian Country."

66. Evans-Campbell, "Historical Trauma in American Indian/Native Alaskan Communities," 316–38.

67. Evans-Campbell, "Historical Trauma in American Indian/Native Alaskan Communities," 316–38.

68. Evans-Campbell, "Historical Trauma in American Indian/Native Alaskan Communities," 316–38.

69. Evans-Campbell, "Historical Trauma in American Indian/Native Alaskan Communities," 316–38.

70. Sarche and Spicer, "Poverty and Health Disparities for American Indian and Alaskan Native Children," 126–36.

71. United States, *Petitioner v. Billy Jo Lara*, no. 03-107. Accessed on March 23, 2019. Available from https://www.law.cornell.edu/supct/html/03-107.ZO.html.

72. Evans-Campbell, "Historical Trauma in American Indian/Native Alaskan Communities," 316–38.

73. Indian Country Criminal Jurisdictional Chart. Accessed on March 23, 2019. Available at https://www.justice.gov/sites/default/files/usao-wdok/legacy/2014/03/25/Indian%20Country%20Criminal%20Jurisdiction%20ChartColor2010.pdf.

74. U.S. Department of the Interior Indian Affairs, Indian Child Welfare Act (ICWA). Accessed on March 23, 2019. Available from https://www.bia.gov/bia/ois/dhs/icwa.

75. *Merriam-Webster Dictionary*, "Indigenous."

76. U.S. Department of the Interior Indian Affairs, Indian Child Welfare Act (ICWA).

77. U.S. Senate Committee on Indian Affairs, *Safeguarding to the Seventh Generation: Protection and Justice for Indian Children and the Implementation of the Native American Children's Safety Act of 2016* (Washington, DC: U.S. Government Publishing Office, 2018).

78. "Tribal Law and Order Act signed into law July 29, 2010." Accessed on March 23, 2019. Available from https://www.justice.gov/tribal/tribal-law-and-order-act.

79. "An Act to Amend the PROTECT Act to Make Indian Tribes Eligible for AMBER Alert Grants to Begin in Fiscal Year 2019." Public Law 115-116. 115th Congress. Available from https://www.congress.gov/bill/115th-congress/senate-bill/772.

80. "An Act to Amend the PROTECT Act to Make Indian Tribes Eligible for AMBER Alert Grants to Begin in Fiscal Year 2019."

81. Nebraska Commission of Indian Affairs, LB 154. Accessed on March 23, 2019. Available from https://www.indianaffairs.state.ne.us.

82. Cindy D. Chang, "Social Determinants of Health and Health Disparities Among Immigrants and their Children," *Current Problems in Pediatric and Adolescent Health Care Journal* 49 (2018): 23–30.

83. Chang, "Social Determinants of Health and Health Disparities Among Immigrants and their Children," 23–30.

84. Chang, "Social Determinants of Health and Health Disparities Among Immigrants and their Children," 23–30.

85. Chang, "Social Determinants of Health and Health Disparities Among Immigrants and their Children," 23–30.

86. Tahirih Justice Center, "Profiting from Suffering: How the Inhumane Treatment of Refugee Women and Children Benefits Private Companies." Accessed on March 24, 2019. Available from https://www.tahirih.org/news/profiting-from-suffering-how-the-inhumane-treatment-of-refugee-women-and-children-benefits-private-companies/.

87. Michael G. Vaughn, C. Salas-Wright, J. Huang, L. Terzis, and J. Helton, "Adverse Childhood Experience Among Immigrants to the United States," *Journal of Interpersonal Violence* 32, no. 10 (2017): 1543–64.

88. Alan J. Dettlaff and Michelle A. Johnson, "Child Maltreatment Dynamics among Immigrant and U.S.-born Latino Children. Findings from the National Survey of Child and Adolescent Well-Being (NSCAW)," *Children and Youth Services Review* 33 (2011): 936–44.

89. Angie Junck, "Special Immigrants Juvenile Status: Relief for Neglected, Abused, and Abandoned Undocumented Children," *Juvenile & Family Court Journal* 63, no. 1 (2012): 48–62.

13

Child Abuse Around the World

◆ ◆ ◆

CHILDREN ARE BEING VICTIMIZED throughout the world by various forms of abuse and exploitation. This chapter will explore numerous types of abuse, including sex trafficking, labor trafficking, illegal adoptions, child brides, camel jockeying, child sex tourism, female genital mutilation (FGM), child victims of war, and the investigation of transnational crimes. Furthermore, we will identify the prevalence within varying regions and the cultural acceptance of what may be considered abuse, as well as the international response.

HUMAN TRAFFICKING

Defining Human Trafficking

In 1948, the United Nations General Assembly stated in Article 4 that no one shall be held in slavery or servitude and that slave trade shall be prohibited in all forms. In 1966, the United Nations under the Covenant on Civil and Political Rights reinforced the enslavement prohibition stating under Article 8 that "no one shall be held in slavery; slavery and the slavery-trade in all their forms shall be prohibited."[1] The United Nations in 2000 defined human trafficking as the "recruitment, transfer, harboring or receipt of persons by threat or use of force or other forms of coercion, of abduction, of fraud, of deception, of the abuse of power or of a position of vulnerability or of the giving or receiving of payments or benefits to achieve the consent of a person having control over another person, for the purpose of exploitation."[2] The United Nations enacted the protocol to prevent, suppress, and punish trafficking in persons, also known as the Palermo Protocol of 2000. This agreement was signed by more than 150 nations, requiring these governments to protect victims of trafficking by enacting national laws against trafficking which would shield victims from deportation and would prosecute traffickers with significant penalties.[3]

Magnitude of the Problem

Despite the history of the international community recognizing and condemning the crime of human trafficking, it is still a significant problem. In fact, today human trafficking, along with arms trafficking and drug trafficking, are considered the largest international crimes in the world.[4] However, unlike drug trafficking and in some cases arms trafficking, the crime of human trafficking is significantly lucrative as the product, the human body, can repeatedly be offered to prospective buyers. Human trafficking is a thirty to forty-five billion dollar industry.[5] Reasons for this thriving business include the fact that there are some countries that don't have the resources to track down and apprehend these traffickers and other countries where governments and law enforcement agencies are complicit in trafficking, and there are still additional nations that may not be adequately trained to recognize the signs and victims of trafficking.[6] According to the United Nations Office on Drugs and Crime, the most common form of human trafficking is sex trafficking based on the data of 155 countries. This data revealed that 79 percent of trafficking cases involve sex trafficking with victims being predominately female; almost 20 percent of trafficking victims are children. However, when looking at the data by region, as in some parts of Africa, children represent the majority of sex trafficked victims and in some regions make up almost 100 percent of the victims. Other research has shown that women and girls comprise up to 90 percent of sex trafficking victims. The second most common form of trafficking is labor, which makes up approximately 18 percent of trafficking victims, although this may be an underestimation as labor trafficking is more difficult to recognize and therefore less likely to be reported.[7] Overall, children make up approximately 27 percent of all human trafficking victims, and two of every three children trafficked are girls.[8]

The Tier System

The U.S. Department of State, through the Trafficking Victims Protection Act, established a tier system to evaluate and make public how countries are responding to human trafficking. The lists can change each year based on the respective government's response to human trafficking. For instance, the following countries changed their tier status in 2018. Thailand was listed under the Tier 2 watch list in 2017 but was upgraded to Tier 2 in 2018. Angola was downgraded to Tier 2 Watch List from Tier 2 in 2018. Armenia went from Tier 1 in 2017 to Tier 2 in 2018. Fortunately, Tier 3, which is considered the worst status to have in relation to combating human trafficking, contains the fewest number of countries.

> **Tier 1:** Countries whose governments fully meet the Trafficking Victims Protection Act minimum standards.
>
> **Tier 2:** Countries whose governments do not fully meet the Trafficking Victims Protection Act's minimum standards, but are making significant efforts to bring themselves into compliance with those standards.
>
> **Tier 2 Watch List:** Countries whose governments do not fully meet the Trafficking Victims Protection Act's minimum standards, but are making sig-

nificant efforts to bring themselves into compliance with those standards AND:

a) The absolute number of victims of severe forms of trafficking is very significant or is significantly increasing;

b) There is a failure to provide evidence of increasing efforts to combat severe forms of trafficking in persons from the previous year; or

c) The determination that a country is making significant efforts to bring itself into compliance with minimum standards was based on commitments by the country to take additional future steps over the next year.

Tier 3: Countries whose governments do not fully meet the minimum standards and are not making significant efforts to do so.

Tier 1 countries include Argentina, Aruba, Australia, Austria, The Bahamas, Bahrain, Belgium, Canada, Chile, Colombia, Cyprus, Czech Republic, Denmark, Estonia, Finland, France, Georgia, Germany, Guyana, Israel, Italy, Japan, Korea, South, Lithuania, Luxembourg, Netherlands, New Zealand, Norway, Philippines, Poland, Portugal, Slovakia, Slovenia, Spain, Sweden, Switzerland, Taiwan, United Kingdom, and the United States of America.

Tier 2 countries include Afghanistan, Albania, Antigua & Barbuda, Armenia, Azerbaijan, Barbados, Benin, Botswana, Brazil, Brunei, Bulgaria, Cambodia, Costa Rica, Cote d'Ivoire, Croatia, Curacao, Djibouti, Dominican Republic, Ecuador, Egypt, El Salvador, Ethiopia, Ghana, Greece, Honduras, Iceland, India, Indonesia, Ireland, Jamaica, Jordan, Kazakhstan, Kenya, Kosovo, Latvia, Lebanon, Lesotho, Macedonia, Malawi, Maldives, Malta, Marshall Islands, Mauritius, Mexico, Micronesia, Moldova, Morocco, Mozambique, Namibia, Nepal, Oman, Pakistan, Palau, Panama, Paraguay, Peru, Qatar, Romania, St. Lucia, St. Vincent & The Grenadines, Serbia, Seychelles, Singapore, Solomon Islands, Sri Lanka, Tanzania, Thailand, Timor-Leste, Togo, Tonga, Trinidad & Tobago, Tunisia, Turkey, Uganda, Ukraine, United Arab Emirates, Uruguay, Vietnam, and Zambia.

Tier 2 Watch List countries include Algeria, Angola, Bangladesh, Bhutan, Bosnia & Herzegovina, Central African Republic, Chad, Cuba, Eswatini, Fiji, The Gambia, Guatemala, Guinea, Guinea-Bissau, Haiti, Hong Kong, Hungary, Iraq, Kuwait, Kyrgyz Republic, Liberia, Macau, Madagascar, Malaysia, Maldives, Mali, Mongolia, Montenegro, Nicaragua, Niger, Nigeria, Saudi Arabia, Senegal, Seychelles, Sierra Leone, South Africa, Sudan, Senegal, South Africa, Sudan, Suriname, Tajikistan, Togo, Uzbekistan, and Zimbabwe.

Tier 3 countries include Belarus, Belize, Bolivia, Burundi, China (PRC), Comoros, Congo, Democratic Republic of Congo, Republic of Equatorial Guinea, Eritrea, Gabon, Iran, Korea, North, Laos, Mauritania, Papua New Guinea, Russia, South Sudan, Syria, Turkmenistan, and Venezuela.[9]

Trafficking of children can occur in any country and at every tier level. The following countries are examples of human trafficking from each tier, emphasizing the magnitude of the problem, the similarities, as well as the differences within each government.

United Kingdom (Tier 1)

Although the United Kingdom is considered a Tier 1 country as it meets the minimum standards set forth by the Trafficking Victims Protection Act, it would be naïve to believe that the United Kingdom or any other designated Tier 1 country does not struggle in combating human trafficking. The United Kingdom is considered a destination country where children around the world are lured into slavery under false pretenses. Slavery can include labor and prostitution. Although it is recognized that the United Kingdom faces significant challenges in fighting child trafficking, there are no reliable statistics describing the amount of trafficking within that country. The issue of trafficking of children came to prominence in the mid-1990s when an investigation focused on unaccompanied children arriving from West Africa who were thought to be in transit to other European countries.[10] Sexual exploitation is the most common form of human trafficking where children have been found in street prostitution who were from Albania, Bulgaria, China, Croatia, Lithuania, Latvia, Moldova, Nigeria, Pakistan, Romania, Russia, Somalia, Sri Lanka, Thailand, Turkey, and Vietnam. Labor exploitation of children is evident in the United Kingdom, but there is little evidence of serious organized use of illegal labor beyond that in service industries such as hotels and catering.[11] However, there are well-illustrated reports that West African children are being trafficked into the United Kingdom to clean houses and do chores without pay. The victims are mostly girls lured on the promise of a "Western education" despite not speaking the language, only to find themselves laboring for wealthy families. It is thought that up to ten thousand West African children enter the United Kingdom for private fostering, only to be forced into the underground world of domestic service slavery.[12] The United Kingdom's first domestic legislation to tackle human trafficking was through the Nationality Asylum and Immigration Act, which merely outlawed trafficking relating to prostitution. This was followed by the Sexual Offences Act, which expanded the sexual exploitation to offenses other than simply prostitution. This legislation explicitly criminalized child sexual exploitation, recognizing that trafficking can take place both domestically and internationally. Under this legislation, those convicted can face fourteen years in prison.[13] The Modern Slavery Act of 2015 was introduced to address the violations of human rights with a victim-centered approach.[14] In addition to legislative improvements in the response to human trafficking, law enforcement mandates that new police recruits and detectives complete training modules specifically dealing with human trafficking. In 2017, the United Kingdom provided an updated report on modern slavery within their country. The United Kingdom conveyed that in 2016, 3,804 potential victims were referred to the National Referral Mechanism Data, which indicated a 16 percent increase from 2015. Of those identified, 34 percent were children. The data collected represent England, Northern Ireland, Scotland, and Wales, with the vast majority of potential victims (92 percent) coming from England.[15]

India (Tier 2)

India has had a long history of slavery. An ancient practice promoting human bondage, called "Devadasi," is where young girls were dedicated at puberty to the goddess Yellamma. Ancient India was also known for the enslavement of defeated populations by various kings and their armies, with this dominance an acceptable practice until the seventeenth century. Rulers in India maintained large harems comprised of young women and boys who were kidnapped from various areas of the kingdom. Sexual exploitation was considered a right of aristocracy. Slave markets existed in major Indian cities and continued until the nineteenth century when European colonial powers were able to make profits from the slave trade.[16] India continues to struggle in its response to child trafficking as countless examples show how this crime permeates the country. It is believed that there are anywhere from thirty-five thousand to five hundred thousand children (as of 2007), mostly girls, engaged in some type of sexual exploitation.[17] The trend of human trafficking continued to rise: from 2009 to 2013, the rate of human trafficking increased by 38 percent.[18] Children were continually being exploited, and although most children in India who are sexually exploited are girls, many young boys fall prey to sex tourists from Europe and North America.[19] It is difficult to measure the number of actual crimes, as this is a crime of secrecy that doesn't come to the attention of the appropriate authorities. Additionally, some forms of sexual exploitation may be based on cultural interpretation; therefore, particular acts are not considered a form of victimization. For instance, some girls in Karnataka, India, choose work as devadasis, or religious sex workers, as part of their cultural heritage. These girls may not like what they do, but they still willingly participate as a sense of filial duty because doing dhandha (sex work) is incorporated into their models of female maturity.[20]

One of the unique challenges that India faces in the protection of their children is the large number of children in the country. India has the highest number of children in the world.[21] The vulnerability of so many children can occur through a vast array of circumstances. For example, some of these children are homeless, as their parents may be deceased and there are no other relatives to take care of them. In certain segments of India, families are too poor to keep their children at home, leaving these young ones vulnerable to exploitation.[22] The Dalit population, for instance, is considered one of the poorest, most disenfranchised groups and includes some of the most exploited people in India. The very term "Dalit" is rooted in the Sanskrit word "dal," which means suppressed, crushed, or oppressed.[23] There are two specific laws that criminalize human trafficking in India: the Immoral Trafficking Prevention Act of 1956 and the Child Marriage Restraint Act of 1929. The Indian constitution is in line with the United Nations Universal Declaration on Human Rights, which ensures dignity of the individual, a core value in its preamble. However, the actions of the government and the criminal justice response may present a different picture. For instance, although there are laws addressing trafficking in India, police in many cases seem insensitive to the crime and consider it a low priority. The police investigations are limited in their pursuit of these offenders and fail to coordinate with other agencies across state boundaries.[24]

South Africa (Tier 2 Watch List)

South Africa suffers from various forms of human trafficking, and the government has been unable to sufficiently address these crimes. In fact, the U.S. Department of State has moved South Africa from Tier 2 status to Tier 2 Watch status, indicating that the problem of human trafficking in South Africa has become more grave.[25] South Africa ratified the Palermo Protocol in 2005, and in compliance with international obligations passed the Prevention and Combatting of Trafficking of Persons Act which went into effect in 2015.[26] According to the U.S. Department of State, the government of South Africa has not demonstrated an increase in efforts from previous reporting years. It should be noted that the South African government last year convicted eight human traffickers; four of the offenders received a suspended sentence. Furthermore, South Africa, a country that is known for a progressive constitution, continues to struggle when addressing the rights of children. This is evident in their social services. Child protection agencies are not fully equipped to deal with victims of child trafficking despite legislation from the South African government mandating them to do so; thus victims' rights are violated once they leave their trafficking situation.[27]

Although the U.S. Department of State gives a rating of Tier 2, this rating is based on limited information as statistics are hard to acquire because the country is known for underreporting. In fact, human trafficking didn't seem to make any headlines until 2003. South Africa is considered a destination country as children are being trafficked to South Africa from Africa, Eastern Europe, and Southeast Asia.[28] For instance, South Africa made international news when it was discovered that boys were being trafficked into Cape Town, South Africa, from Kwa Zulu-Natal under the false premise that they would be entering a soccer club training school. Fortunately, this scam was uncovered and the boys were returned to their home country.[29] However, South Africa is also a source country as there is significant financial inequality; financial desperation makes families and children particularly vulnerable.[30] The overwhelming number of victims of trafficking are from South Africa, and these people are being utilized for labor. Other victims of trafficking were identified as originating from Thailand, Lesotho, Ethiopia, Mozambique, Ghana, Nigeria, Eswatini, Bulgaria, and Tanzania. Although a large number of victims have been identified as coming from other countries, the South African government has made little progress prosecuting traffickers from international syndicates.[31]

Russia (Tier 3)

Russia is considered a source, transit, and destination country for men, women, and children being trafficked. The surge in human trafficking in Russia originated from multiple factors including the dramatic fall of their economic system when the former Soviet Union dissolved. The reality of a postcommunist transition came hard and fast in the form of human trafficking.[32] Russia is known to use women and girls as a commodity, exporting them and trafficking them for sex, and they import victims to traffic for slave labor.

In December 2017, the United Nations Security Council, through resolution 2397, voted to limit North Korea from having fuel imports and limited other trade due to North Korea's defiance regarding missile testing. The Russian government, which is a permanent member of the United Nations Security Council, in response to this resolution, imported thousands of North Korean citizens to be used for slave labor. However, the official Russian governmental record of human trafficking does not reflect independent research on the actual magnitude of this offense. For instance, in 2017, the Russian government only identified twenty trafficking victims throughout their entire country, with ten of them being children. This was the result of nineteen investigations, with no reports of any of these cases being prosecuted.[33] These low numbers are consistent with the press reporting on human trafficking within the country. In the early 2000s there were several articles from numerous newspapers where journalists quoted experts, law enforcement officers, politicians, and international organizations on the problem of human trafficking in society. However, by 2014 there appeared to be silence on this topic as human trafficking seemed to be less observed. Although there was still some coverage about human trafficking, the discussion of migrant labor coming into Russia appeared to have been drowned out.[34] A question arises: "Is the lack of media coverage due to the fact that human trafficking is no longer a significant problem in Russian society, or is there now an unwillingness to acknowledge the problem of human trafficking within Russia?" Independent research suggests that the latter explanation may be more plausible.

Research indicates that trafficking through debt bondage is a significant problem in Russia. Russians who wish to leave their country find themselves trapped through inflated travel costs and special accommodations that make it difficult, if not impossible, to pay back. The activity of assisting Russian citizens out of the country is happening underground and is not easy to detect. Many of these victims leave Russia legally on tourist visas but upon arrival to their destination, their passports are confiscated and they find themselves unwillingly enslaved in prostitution, domestic labor, or some form of construction work. Women and girls are sold into brothels for sums ranging from five thousand dollars to more than twelve thousand dollars. If the captives resist, they are beaten or raped into submission. In other cases of children within Russia, there were reports of outright kidnappings where these children were either lured from the street, taken from orphanages, refugees, or even taken from their own home. Leonid Chekalin, head of the aid group Children Are Russia's Future, pointed out in 2004 that there were 190 child trafficking rings in the early 2000s.[35] These staggering numbers are in significant contrast to the twenty trafficking victims identified by the Russian government in 2017. Other accounts of child trafficking are identified through the correlation of the orphanages and forced labor as it was reported in one orphanage that 40 percent of the orphans had been trafficked in begging rings or labor of some kind. Lena Timofeeva, who worked as a therapist at a Moscow shelter, stated that the areas of Mitino are a high-risk region for trafficking victims; Timofeeva specifically named the streets Tverskaia and Arbat as a locations for child trafficking.[36] Trafficking of children may not be fully recognized in Russia, but the motivations are rather apparent.

REASONS FOR TRAFFICKING

Sex is considered the most common reason children are trafficked around the world, followed by labor. Other forms of child trafficking include providing child brides, illegal adoptions, child soldiering, and in some cases, organ trafficking. One of the challenges in identifying children who are being trafficked is the lack of an international system for tracking unaccompanied minors, making it easier for children to move from country to country without any restriction.[37] Fortunately, volunteer flight attendants through participating airlines are being trained to detect traffickers and victims. If they determine that a child is being trafficked they notify the pilot, who passes this information to authorities at the plane's destination, who will meet the suspected offender and child upon their arrival.[38]

SEX TRAFFICKING

Sex trafficking is considered the most common form of child trafficking. The illegal sex industry overall is the third-largest global criminal enterprise following drug and arms trafficking.[39] Not only are children trafficked marketed for prostitution, but many children are trafficked for pornography as well. There is a significant market for trafficking children as a child fills the desires of sexual offenders who may have a preference for pedophilia, hebephilia, and ephebophelia. Other offenders are willing to pay significant amounts of money to have the opportunity to engage in sex with a "virgin" as they think they will have a reduced risk of contracting sexually transmitted infections. This confidence is misplaced as children are more susceptible to contracting human immunodeficiency virus/acquired immune deficiency syndrome because they are at greater risk of injury through penetration, which leads to a higher likelihood of transmission of the virus when the offender engages in sexual intercourse.[40] Other physical repercussions through sex trafficking include sexually transmitted infections such as gonorrhea, syphilis, urinary tract infections, and pubic lice.[41]

Acquisition of Sex Slaves

The acquisition of children into sex trafficking primarily occurs in five ways.

- **Deceit:** A child is extended a false offer of employment, travel, or other economic incentive, creating the opportunity for sexual slavery. Children who are desperate due to the lack of economic opportunity are particularly vulnerable to deception, especially those who are displaced due to war or other civil strife. One of the most effective locations in the use of deceit is refugee camps where children may have been displaced due to genocide, civil war, environmental disaster, or some other type of crisis that caused displacement. It is estimated that tens of thousands of children migrate alone every year to escape war, persecution, or to find work or educational opportunities.[42]

- **Sale by family:** Some parents may make the heartbreaking decision to sell their child due to financial peril and possibly to save other children in their family. Some families may receive monthly remittances for the use of their child, whereas other parents sell their children outright.
- **Abduction:** Although abduction is a legitimate concern, it is not as common a tactic as deceit. A missing child can be a parent's worst nightmare, especially when the parent realizes the potential danger their child faces. The stranger/danger threat, although rare, continues to be the focal point of parents who are concerned about the safety of their children.
- **Seduction or romance:** Many victims find themselves involved in prostitution that originated through promises of love. Young, attractive, charismatic men prey on vulnerable girls offering "love" and expensive gifts, while convincing them to migrate to another country where they can build a life together. The perpetrator will usually send young women in advance by train or other form of transportation where a friend who is a slave trader or who owns a brothel waits for the victim's arrival.
- **Recruitment by former slaves:** Women who are former sex slaves themselves are dressed in the finest clothes, given a great deal of money, and promised a commission for each sex slave they can acquire. These recruiters solicit children with promises of a better life, but instead force them into a life of sexual slavery. It is not uncommon for women/girls to be more trusting of other females, making the female recruiter a valuable tool in exploiting girls.[43]

LABOR TRAFFICKING

Most international organizations and the national laws for individual countries have come to the realization that children may legally work in some capacity; however, some children are forced into labor with the consent of their government, whereas others are forced into labor through the secrecy of trafficking. An indicator of possible forced labor can be the appearance that the child is in the custody of a non-family member. However, in reality, the child's labor financially benefits someone outside the family and this child does not have the option to leave.[44] Traffickers use a variety of coercive methods to manipulate their victims and deprive them of free will. They render the victim subservient and dependent by destroying their sense of self and their connections to others by making their escape virtually impossible and destroying their physical and psychological defenses. The emotional and physical trauma, as well as the degradation associated with being subjected to humiliation and violence, and unrelenting abuse and fear keep the trafficker in control of their victim.[45] Additionally, victims may not be from their native countries, thus they may have a language barrier that hampers their ability to seek help. Other obstacles include being under constant surveillance and being held in isolation by their captors. Labor trafficking is much less likely than sex trafficking to be detected. It is especially difficult to discover victims in domestic servitude.[46] Other forms of control include debt bondage, which is considered the most prevalent kind of forced labor around the world.

DEBT BONDAGE

The United Nations Supplementary Convention on the Abolition of Slavery defines debt bondage as: "Debt bondage, that is to say, the status or condition arising from a pledge by a debtor of his personal services or of those of a person under his control as security for a debt, if the value of those services as reasonably assessed is not applied towards the liquidation of the debt or the length and nature of those services are not respectively limited and defined."[47] Currently, there are no accurate estimates of how many trafficking victims are being held under debt bondage. However, it is not considered a crime in many parts of the world as it is considered part of the culture and economy.[48] This debt can be through the funds the child owes for services the child receives or in some cases the child, with parental consent, is working to pay off the loans of their parents.[49] Unfortunately, in many cases, the cost that is placed on the laborer is designed in a way that the victim is never able to fully pay off their debt. Victims of labor trafficking may not realize that it is illegal for traffickers to dictate the terms of how their debt will be repaid.[50] Additionally, some traffickers may hold onto their debtor's identification and passports, preventing them from fleeing this debt.

Magnitude of Child Forced Labor

There are children throughout the world who are either working in deplorable conditions or are forced into labor that includes child trafficking. According to the International Labor Office, there are approximately 152 million children around the world working, which is approximately one out of ten children worldwide. Seventy-three million of these children work in hazardous conditions that directly affect their health, safety, and moral development. Children who are working around the world, both those in forced labor and those who experience permitted forms of legal employment, number around 218 million.[51] According to the global estimates on modern slavery, there are 4.3 million children in forced labor, representing 18 percent of the 24.8 million victims of forced labor worldwide. Of the 4.3 million children, one million are forced into sexual exploitation, three million are forced into labor exploitation, and three hundred thousand are victims of forced labor by state authorities.[52] Additionally, 70 percent of child labor has involved agriculture, although there has been little attention focused on child farm workers.[53] These workers can be relocated according to the seasonality of the produce, making it difficult to potentially identify a trafficking victim.[54]

ILLEGAL ADOPTIONS

Intercountry adoption began in North America in response to World War II, moving children from orphanages located in Europe to North America. Affluent areas had an increasing demand for babies, coupled with a marked decrease in the availability of domestic adoptions. It is believed that today there are approximately thirty thousand children being moved around from approximately one hundred countries. With the growth of intercountry adoption, the international community responded. The Hague Convention of 1993 set forth principles of adoption that were in the best interest of the child. These principles state that children must be protected against the risks of illegal, irregular, ill-prepared adoptions abroad. Unfortunately, most of the states where the children are being adopted from have either not accepted the Hague principles or are at the very early stages of implementation.[55] Carole Moore, author of *The Fight Against Human Trafficking*, tells of how most illegal adoptions take place in South and Central America where children have been abducted and sold on the "black market" through agencies that sell these children to adoptive parents in the United States without the prospective parents ever knowing that these children were abducted.[56] Other research has shown that the country of Greece is a prime destination for illegal adoptions. Greece has what is known as the 2447/96 law that permits private adoptions under certain circumstances. This law allows adoptive parents to be contacted directly by the birth mother. This practice is of concern as these private sales can lead to selling children for financial gain, thus having the potential for trafficking.[57]

CHILD BRIDES

The United Nations, since 2012, has designated October 11 as the International "Day of the Girl." This date highlights and addresses the needs of girls and the unique challenges they face in life. The United Nations recognizes that every girl should have the opportunity to recognize and sharpen their skills so that can empower themselves as their human right. Unfortunately, there are countries throughout the world that force girls under the age of eighteen into marriage. For instance, in India, almost all teenage girls are married to much older men. These marriages are protected by the Sharda Act, which allows a man to marry a child once they reach the age of fifteen.[58] A child marriage can disrupt a child's education and economic opportunities, increasing their chances of exposure to violence and abuse. Young girls who are married before they complete their education often drop out of school, ending their educational opportunities and limiting their economic prospects. With the lack of educational and economic openings available to them, the child's life of living in poverty becomes a reality. Child marriage is particularly prevalent in rural or poor populations of developing worlds, although child marriage still occurs in developed countries, especially among immigrant populations.[59] In 1962, the United Nations Convention on the Consent to Marry, Minimum Age for Marriage, and Registration of Marriages required that member countries establish a minimum age to marry, but did not specify what that minimum age should be.[60]

Magnitude of the Problem

The practice of child brides affects millions of girls, averaging thirty-nine thousand a day; nearly half of these children will marry before the age of fifteen. The World Health Organization estimates that there will be more than 140 million girls married between 2011 and 2020.[61] In Niger, 75 percent of the girls marry before the age of eighteen, and 36 percent marry before the age of fifteen. South Asia has the largest number of child brides where 40 percent of the women between the ages of twenty and twenty-four were married before the age of eighteen, and 18 percent of those women were married before the age of fifteen.[62] According to the U.S. Agency for International Development, some child brides are as young as eight or nine, and child brides under the age of fifteen are five times more likely to die from giving birth compared to a woman in her twenties.[63] Developed countries such as the United States still condone child marriages with parental consent. In one study of one thousand participants, 6.2 were married as children, with West Virginia, Hawaii, and North Dakota having higher rates of child marriage. The rate of children becoming child brides overall was significantly higher with Native American children and children of Chinese descent. The study also revealed that immigrant children were more likely to be married than children born in the United States.[64]

Causation for Child Brides

Economic factors such as poverty and the lack of education or employment opportunities are contributing factors toward child brides. Cultural factors and their social norms can contribute to child marriages. For instance, in some societies, a child has the option of staying in school or getting married. There is also preferential treatment in certain societies as to who will go to school as some may feel it is more important for a boy to be educated. Additionally, in many cultures, the parents may want their daughters to marry early as they don't want to risk the chance that they may engage in sexual activity outside of marriage. Furthermore, where families in certain countries face economic uncertainty, having a girl marry early means one less mouth to feed.[65] There can also be a financial incentive to have child brides. Marriage can bring a dowry to the bride's parents and in some cases, the younger the bride, the larger the dowry.[66]

CHILD CAMEL JOCKEYS

Over the past two decades, camel racing has become a popular sport in gulf countries. The trafficking and exploitation of children as camel jockeys has increased dramatically. Camel racing is a multi-million dollar industry where thousands of children as young as three or four are trafficked from Asia and Africa and sold into slavery as camel jockeys. The handler and trainers abuse with physical abuse and threats. These children are injured by the camels as well, adding to the dangers associated with this form of trafficking. Once a child reaches their teenage years due to size they are disposed of as they serve no other use for their masters.[67] Due to the outcry of the United Nations and individual countries, the use of children in camel jockeying is being replaced with robotic jockeys weighing no more than three kilos. In 2005, the United Arab Emirates banned anyone under the age of eighteen from camel jockeying in response to international pressure.[68]

CHILD SOLDIERS

Defining Child Soldier

Defining a child soldier can be challenging as their purpose in battles can vary considerably. For instance, whereas some children may be used in the military as fighters, others who are considered soldiers may have different functions and may be acquired for the sole purpose of being a suicide bomber; they may be used in a fighting unit as a porter, or to meet the sexual desires of military service members. The definition of a child soldier can be deduced only indirectly from the international community because of varying treaties and national legislation. The definition of a child itself is addressed through the Convention on the Rights of a Child in that a child is described as a human being younger than the age of eighteen, unless the law applicable to the child states that their majority status is attained earlier. The definition of a child soldier used by the United Nations Children's Fund states that a child soldier is any person younger than eighteen years of age who is part of any kind of regular or irregular armed forces in any capacity such as cook, porter, or messenger. The United Nations Children's Fund also includes in their definition of a child soldier girls that are recruited for sexual purposes and forced marriages.[69]

Magnitude of Child Soldiering

In 2005, the United Nations adopted Resolution 1612 condemning the recruitment and use of child soldiers by parties to armed conflict. "The council also reaffirmed its intention to consider imposing country specific resolutions such as ban on the export and supply of small arms and other military equipment against parties to armed conflicts on the agenda of the Council and in violation of applicable international law relating to the rights and protection of children in armed conflict."[70] There are child solders being used throughout the world. Certain organizations claim that the number of children being used as soldiers is about three hundred thousand, with the majority of active child soldiers in Africa and to a lesser extent in the Middle East.[71] Child soldiers are frequently recruited from poorer nations, but child soldiering is still part of several industrialized countries, and not all child soldiers are recruited from non-state armed groups. Of the nineteen North American Treaty Organization members, thirteen of them recruit children younger than the age of eighteen. Of the five permanent members of the United Nations Security Council, only Russia does not recruit children below the age of eighteen. The United States accepts volunteers from the age of seventeen with parental permission, though they cannot be deployed in combat. The United Kingdom recruits from the age of sixteen with parental permission, though they cannot be deployed in combat. There are currently between six thousand and seven thousand soldiers younger than the age of eighteen fighting in the British armed forces.[72] It should be noted, however, that the majority of child soldiers are members of irregular armed groups.[73] This is especially significant in countries facing substantial poverty, political turmoil, or currently involved in conflicts, which are primary factors in the recruitment of child soldiers. Some of these areas that recruit children are state sponsored, whereas others use children to fight against their government. Currently, the Democratic Republic of the Congo is among those countries that have the largest number of child soldiers.[74]

Mode of Recruitment

Although some children are forced into child soldiering through abduction, others are subjected to death threats either toward the children or the child's family. There are those, however, who join voluntarily as they may be living where there is currently an armed conflict; joining the conflict gives the child an opportunity for employment, as well as providing an escape from an oppressive family situation. Hunger and poverty are considered epidemic in conflict zones. Poverty itself is the single most identifiable characteristic of child soldiers. Some children are faced with family disruption as their parents have been killed, and they are forced to fend for themselves and assume the additional responsibility of being the head of the household.[75]

Female Child Soldiers

It has been estimated that there are 120,000 girl soldiers.[76] Since the 1990s, it has been reported that girls have participated in armed conflicts in fifty-eight countries with up to 30 to 40 percent in African conflicts. For instance, during the armed conflict in Sierra Leone girls not only fought, but they also cooked, cleaned, and performed sexual services. Many of these girls were also given as wives to men or boys in bush marriages as a reward for effective fighting, although the Sierra Leonne special court ruled that forced marriages were considered a crime against humanity.[77]

Children as Suicide Bombers

Children can easily be convinced to volunteer to kill themselves in the name of religion as they lay down their lives to defend their communities or redress inequalities or discrimination. However, religious leaders will not brainwash small children into sacrificing their lives by carrying out suicide attacks as it may be considered a waste of potential good candidates for future use. The recruiters prefer to postpone this indoctrination until the child is older and can cause more damage. Adolescent males will be targeted as they find the act as a way to prove their masculinity. Adolescents may strive for Istishhad, which is the Arabic word for heroic death.[78] For example, the Palestinian educational system indoctrinates children to hate Israel and in many instances they desire martyrdom. These children are less likely to disobey or try to flee as such actions can lead to punishment for failing to comply. Terrorist organizations will use children to recruit their peers to blow themselves up. Children used specifically as suicide bombers will wear or drive a vehicle full of explosives into a particular area and detonate themselves upon arrival.[79] In addition to the use of children as suicide bombers, children are also deliberately placed in harm's way for the purpose of propaganda. For instance, in the Palestinian-Israeli conflict, boys who may want to be seen as heroes will throw Molotov cocktails at Israelis. These events are organized as they are pressured to throw something at Israeli soldiers. The organizers who incite them to attack Israeli soldiers want the soldiers to shoot at them as they then can use their deaths as media propaganda.[80]

Consequences for Child Soldiers

Under children's right laws, child soldiers are predominantly considered victims when recruited under the legally accepted age. Child soldiers may be treated as perpetrators depending on the country if they have reached the minimum age for criminal responsibility. Voluntary recruitment may be determined by the context and the circumstances that question whether their entry was indeed voluntary. Children's right laws fail to strike a balance between victimhood and perpetratorhood. However, as international children's rights prohibit any criminal accountability younger than the age of eighteen, it would be difficult to have child soldiers face criminal sanctions. Other forms of child accountability could be considered to confront the child soldier for their actions, but also to help them reintegrate into their communities.[81] Still, severe criminal sanctions are still employed against child soldiers. For instance, since the year 2000, the government of the Democratic Republic of Congo has executed one fourteen-year-old child soldier for war crimes and has sentenced twenty others to death.[82] The U.S. response was to, on December 23, 2008, sign into law the Child Soldiers Prevention Act (CSPA), which took effect on June 21, 2009. The CSPA requires publication annually in the Trafficking in Persons Report, listing foreign governments that have been identified in the previous year as having either governmental armed forces or government supported armed groups that recruit and use child soldiers. In 2017, the CSPA was amended to include police and other security forces in addition to governmental armed forces. The CSPA reported that in 2015/2016 the recruitment of children in armed conflicts continued as children engaged in fighting roles, support roles, and sexual slavery. Countries that continue to engage in the use of child soldiers include:

- Afghanistan
- South Sudan
- Sudan
- Burma
- Democratic Republic of Congo

- Iraq
- Nigeria
- Rwanda
- Syria
- Somalia
- Yemen.[83]

CHILD SEX TOURISM

Child sex tourism involves people who leave their own country for the purpose of engaging in a sexual act with a child. At least thirty-two countries have extra-territorial laws that allow for the prosecution of citizens who travel abroad for child sex tourism. In 2003 the United States strengthened their laws for combating child sex tourism by passing the Prosecutorial Remedies and Other Tools to End the Exploitation of Children Today Act and the Trafficking Victims Protection Reauthorization Act where the penalties were increased to a maximum of thirty years for engaging in child sex tourism.[84] Since its implementation, this new legislation has led to the arrest of over sixty Americans leaving their own country to engage in sex with children abroad.[85] Other laws to address the exploitation of children include the Mann Act, also known as the White Slave Traffic Act, which was signed into law by President Taft in 1910 and prevents the transportation of women and girls for the purpose of immoral acts.[86] Although the United States and other countries around the world have a history of combating child sex tourism, the child sex trade is still flourishing in many parts of the world. Countries in Asia, Africa, and Central and South America are considered primary hosts for child sex tourism, whereas North Americans are considered the primary consumer.[87] One of the reasons that may contribute to so many Americans seeking child sexual encounters is that virginity is relatively rare among adults, and these sex tourists are looking for the opportunity to have sex with a virgin.[88] Child sex tourists primarily choose Eastern countries as it has been postulated that the rates of child sex tourism is higher in Eastern countries compared to Western countries.[89] It has also been hypothesized that perpetrators seek foreign victims because the social distance makes the encounter seem less like a crime.[90] According to the United Nations Human Rights Office, child sex tourism is a twenty billion dollar annual business. Although it is recognized as a lucrative business, the number of child victims is unclear due to the secrecy of the crime itself. There are no mandatory reporting laws for child sexual abuse even though the U.S. Immigration and Customs Enforcement agency strongly encourages reporting such abuse. Furthermore, the age of consent can vary among countries, making the sexual act with children legal under some circumstances.[91] Although child sex tourism can be found throughout the world, there are certain countries that have a dubious reputation for being a primary destination for the child sex industry. There are a variety of ways tourists can gain access to children. Abusers may seek out children on the street, at hotels, or at brothels. In countries where child marriage is allowed, families may allow their children to marry a tourist for the length of their visit. Other avenues to access children are through the illegal adoption of children for the purpose of sexual exploitation.[92]

Child Sexual Tourism Distribution Center

Providing child sex tourism can be a secretive but lucrative business. Companies that participate in this illegal enterprise may use coded terms such as exotic holidays for men, virginity regained, innocent pleasures, or select your companion on arrival. These coded phrases that may be recognized by the child offender are also used as an attempt to avoid law enforcement detection. Rackets can be through hotels, travel companies, or through the use of corrupt law enforcement officials. In this unofficial enterprise, tour guides, front office staff, housekeeping workers, and drivers become the nexus between the tourist and the custodian of the child. These professions are easy for tourists to find, and so these workers can learn easily what the tourist is looking for and provide guidance on how to access children.[93] The internet has been a valuable tool for child predators where they can learn where they can participate in child sex tourism; abusers access these services using highly sophisticated encryption, making it virtually impossible for law enforcement to decode. Furthermore, the use of public telephone or prepaid calling cards provides a degree of anonymity when arranging a child sexual encounter. For mobile communication, a prepaid SIM card not requiring registration can be used to avoid tracking by law enforcement.[94] Sex trafficking and sex tourism are not the only avenues for children to be sexually abused. Unlike most victims of sex trafficking or sex tourism, there are some cultures who use boys as sex slaves where children are forced to first entice their adult perpetrators and then become victims of sexual abuse.

Bacha Bazi

Bacha bazi, which means boy play, is the practice of using boys as sex slaves by men of power. Although sexual slavery is condemned throughout the world, it is still a common practice in Afghanistan. Bacha bazi boys are routinely required to dress like girls and dance before their abusers or they may be rented out for all-male parties and then sexually exploited. The boys can then be sold or shared among wealthy Afghan men.[95] Bacha bazi is not considered homosexual in Afghanistan. Instead, bacha bazi, which has boys dressed up as pretty women, symbolizes power and primacy. The perpetrators are referred to as bacha baz as they believe women are for children and boys are for pleasure. However, this is considered against Islamic law and was forbidden under Taliban rule from 1993 to 2001.[96] The United Nations General Assembly through the Human Rights Council submitted a written statement condemning the practice of bacha bazi, reporting how boys between the ages of nine and eighteen are sold to warlords, businessmen, and former military commanders to dance seductively for them; the boys were beaten if they refused to dance. These injuries often result in internal/anal hemorrhaging, rectal prolapse, protrusion of intestines, displaced pelvis bones, internal bleeding, rectal wall tearing, and non-sexual-related injuries including broken fingers, fractures, broken teeth, and strangulation. The act, although common, is considered illegal in Afghanistan. For the first time in 2018, Afghan President Ashraf Ghani laid out stringent penalties against bacha bazi, but the government has given no time frame when it will be enforced.[97]

INVESTIGATING TRANSNATIONAL CRIME

Although the United Nations has condemned the concept of human trafficking and has vowed to take a united stance in fighting against this form of slavery, the implementation of this united front can be challenging. Child exploitation through trafficking is rampant throughout the world, but law enforcement must face the challenges of varying legal systems such as common law, civil law, socialist law, sacred law, and hybrid law. In order for law enforcement to be successful in the fight against transnational child exploitation, they must have letters rogatory, mutual legal assistance treaties, and extradition treaties.[98] A letter rogatory refers to a formal request to the court of a foreign government within a specific jurisdiction to obtain information or evidence from a specific person. A mutual legal assistance treaty is an agreement between two or more countries to gather and exchange information with the common goal of combating crime. Some of the requests through mutual legal assistance treaties can include:

- Taking the testimony and statement of persons
- Providing documents, records, and evidence
- Executing requests for searches and seizures; transferring persons in custody for testimonial purposes
- Locating persons
- Initiating proceedings upon request
- Freezing and confiscating proceeds and instrumentalities of crime.[99]

Although countries may cooperate in the investigative phase of human trafficking, there can be a dispute as to which jurisdiction is in charge of the investigation. As each country wants to prosecute those who traffic children, which jurisdiction prevails in the prosecution of offenders can be a challenge. Extradition refers to the act of delivery of a person who has been accused of a crime from one jurisdiction to face criminal charges within another jurisdiction. An extradition requires a legal mechanism between two counties (usually a bilateral treaty) as well as a finding that the crime that is alleged is an extraditable offense.[100] Countries may be reluctant to extradite any offender, especially if the requesting country allows capital punishment and the suspect currently resides in a jurisdiction where the death penalty is not observed. Other considerations for prosecution include that the offender be prosecuted in multiple jurisdictions if the act is a transnational crime. Although there has been significant progress in fighting child exploitation, cooperation among national and local law enforcement agencies continues to be more ad hoc than systematic as the willingness to share information needs to be improved and the information systems currently in place are still frequently incompatible. Also, the trust and respect among governments need to be improved in order to remove any potential derisiveness.[101]

Although there are obstacles throughout the world hampering law enforcement's battle against human trafficking, there are still agencies in various jurisdictions that have an impact in addressing this crime. The Trafficking Victims Protection Reauthorization Act of 2003 requires foreign governments provide the U..S Department of State data on trafficking investigations, prosecutions, convictions, and sentences in order to meet the minimum standards for the elimination of trafficking (Tier 1). In 2015, the Department of State reported that there were 18,930 prosecutions, with 6,609 convictions. These data support a significant increase from data collected in 2008 where there were only 5,212 prosecutions, with 2,983 convictions.[102] These statistics support the initiative of law enforcement combating human trafficking. However, the data also can be a solemn reminder that the number of trafficking victims has increased threefold.

FEMALE GENITAL MUTILATION

The World Health Organization divides FGM into four categories:

- **Clitoridectomy:** Removal to whatever extent of the clitoris which is an elongated, sensitive, and erectile organ; only a small sensitive part in the front is visible. It is almost impossible to remove the entire clitoris
- **Excision:** Removal of at least some of the clitoris and also the labia minora (the inside lips that surround the vagina) and, in some cases, the removal of the labia majora (the outside lips)
- **Infibulation:** When the labia, whether or not otherwise cut or scraped away, are sealed (often sewn, with pins, thread, or thorns) so that only a small hole remains for the excretion of urine and menstrual blood. The clitoris is often excised before the infibulation, and the girl's legs may be bound together for some weeks to ensure the seal is effectively formed.
- **Other:** This may include piercing, scraping, cauterizing (burning), pricking, lengthening, or pulling the labia or otherwise harming the female genitalia.[103]

The practice of FGM has existed for thousands of years. The Romans, for example, would fasten a clasp or fibula through the women's labia majora to prevent sexual intercourse among slaves: females who did not bear children would bring a higher price on the slave market.[104] Although the methods and rationale have varied over time, the following are some of the more common reasons why FGM is still practiced today:

- Reduces sexual desire among young women to control their sexuality, which is believed would otherwise be rampant
- Increases modesty and purity (required by various religions and belief sets) and keeps the girl clean
- Increases bride price or dowry for the family and the likelihood of a good marriage
- Is an important element of maintaining traditions and customs.[105]

Egypt, Mali, and Sudan have a high national approval rate among their citizens for support of FGM, but there are disparities in the attitudes between urban and rural dwellers as more rural women compared to urban women approve of the practice.[106] Despite the rationality that some cultures have in support of FGM, it only inflicts harm and in some cases results in death. It is estimated that in some areas where FGM is practiced, 10 percent of the girls die from this procedure, which is sometimes explained away as fate or bad spirits instead of acknowledging the cutting itself has caused the girl's death. In addition to the tragic deaths associated with FGM, many young girls face physical wounds from this procedure:

- Hemorrhage
- Tetanus
- Shock
- Infections
- Damaged organs
- Urinary infections
- Human immunodeficiency virus
- Infertility
- Bladder incontinence
- Dysmenorrhea.[107]

Instruments used to perform FGM include special knives, scissors, razors, or a piece of glass; on rare occasions the use of a sharp stone is employed.[108] The traditional circumciser is usually an elderly woman who executes the procedure that can take up to twenty minutes as the girl struggles and is held down. In some circumstances a male barber who has specialized scissors will perform the practice. FGM is most commonly performed on girls between the ages of four and twelve, although some parents may want it done earlier to reduce the trauma for the child and avoid any resistance from an older child.[109] In some communities, FGM is performed in the first few weeks of life.[110] Although this practice is usually done individually, it can be performed on groups of girls or women.[111] In urban areas and some rural areas, affluent families are able to utilize health professionals to perform the circumcision, although it may still be performed without anesthetics and antiseptics. This procedure by health professionals is nevertheless condemned by the international medical community.[112] Since 2003, there has been an annual International Day of Zero Tolerance for Female Genital Mutilation, which is observed on February 6. This date was declared by Stella Obansanjo, who was the first lady of Nigeria, while attending a conference by the Inter-African Committee of Traditional Practices Affecting the Health of Women and Children, and is now observed by the United Nations.[113]

Magnitude of the Problem

The practice of FGM has persisted in Africa due to strong sociocultural beliefs that ensure that it is secretly performed and underreported.[114] The World Health

Organization states that most girls who have experienced FGM live in twenty-eight African countries, parts of Western Asia, and in the Middle East. It is estimated that there are over two hundred million women and girls alive today that have undergone FGM.[115] In one study of the prevalence of genital mutilation in a comparison of twenty-two countries, it was discovered that the majority of women who experienced FGM had flesh removed from their genitals either through partial or total removal of their clitoris and labia. Infibulation is still practiced throughout much of sub-Saharan Africa, although the use of this procedure has declined in most of these countries. However, in Chad, Mali, and Sierra Leone, the rate of FGM has increased from 2 to 8 percentage points over the last thirty years. The symbolic nicking of the genitalia is relatively rare but is becoming more common in Burkina Faso, Chad, Guinea, and Mali.[116] The World Health Organization estimates that 90 percent of cases of FGM involve clitoridectomy, excision, or scraping, whereas the remaining 10 percent include infibulation, which is considered the most serious form of FGM.[117]

Female Genital Mutilation in the United States

Girls and women throughout the world where FGM is practiced have immigrated to the United States. With this influx of new immigrants come varying cultures, including cultures that still support FGM. FGM is illegal in the United States under Federal Law 18 U.S. Code 116, but there are twenty-four states with no legislation addressing this procedure. In April 2017, a Michigan doctor was charged for performing FGM, along with two others. Although this is the first case that has resulted in criminal charges, it is not believed to be the first instance of this act occurring in the United States.[118] This procedure is also performed on American girls who are taken out of the country in order to have this procedure. Some immigrants have attempted to maintain the practice of FGM by returning to their countries of origin for the purpose of having them cut. This practice is commonly referred to as "vacation cutting." In response to this tactic, Congress in 2013 passed the Transport for Female Genital Mutilation Act, making it a crime to knowingly transport a girl out of the United States for the purpose of FGM.[119]

VICTIMS OF WAR

In the past twenty years, armed conflicts have occurred in 37 percent of countries.[120] There has been a long history of children being victimized during times of war; however, this gruesome reality has only increased with the use of more explosive weapons and advanced technologies. During the last two years, thousands of children have been killed or maimed in at least forty-one different countries in conflict. An estimated 2,685 children were killed or maimed by explosive weapons in 898 incidents where the child's age was identified. Nearly 84 percent of recorded child casualties occurred in populated areas where an average of 103 children were recorded injured or killed each month.[121] Although accurate mortality and morbidity statistics on the effect of war on children can be challenging, it is estimated that over one billion children younger than the age of eighteen live in countries affected by armed conflict.[122] The United Nations Children's Fund declared 2014 as one of the most devastating years for children.

It is estimated that there are 230 million children around the world living in countries and areas affected by armed conflicts.[123] In certain war zones, children may be killed or injured by mines and unexploded armaments, which may detonate years after the conflict has ended.[124] Illness is another direct result of war as a child's health can deteriorate in war. Nutrition, water safety, sanitation, and access to health services are affected by hostilities. Refugee children are particularity vulnerable to malnutrition and infectious illness. Along with the physical injuries sustained in war are the psychological consequences. Severe losses and disruptions in the lives of these children can lead to high rates of depression and anxiety.[125] The violence associated with war can have long-term consequences such as posttraumatic stress disorder, which can haunt people well into their adulthood.

CONCLUSION

This chapter has addressed the various forms of child victimization throughout the world. This segment of child exploitation revealed that come forms of child abuse are unique to certain cultures, whereas some forms of child maltreatment appear to be universal.

Human trafficking occurs throughout the world and the U.S. Department of State rates the severity of human trafficking and how the individual governments are responding to this unique form of victimization. The Trafficking Victims Protection Act evaluates individual countries through a tier system (1 to 3), with a 3 rating considered the worst.

Human trafficking takes on all forms, but sexual slavery is considered the most common. Other forms of trafficking can include labor trafficking where some children are lured into a different jurisdiction under false pretenses and are forced to work for little or no pay. Other forms of child trafficking include illegal adoptions and child brides. These forms of abuse can occur with or without the parent's knowledge.

Child camel jockeying does not receive the same attention as other forms of trafficking, but the dangers children face are significant. Fortunately, there is a trend now in some countries where children are being replaced with robotic jockeys.

Child soldiering is another form of child trafficking, but like camel jockeying, this type of trafficking is occurring in only certain segments of the world. Child soldiers can be used for combat, whereas others are used for supportive roles such cooking for the soldiers. Child soldiers are primarily boys, but when girls are recruited they are used for sex or wives for the male soldiers. Child soldiering is not the only form of child trafficking primarily targeting boys.

The practice of bacha bazi exclusively targets boys where boys are forced to dress up like girls and dance before men, which in many circumstances leads to sexual victimization. Not all forms of child victimization result from human trafficking.

FGM involves the cutting of the clitoris so that young girls are discouraged from engaging in sexual intercourse. FGM occurs in four ways, ranging from scraping of the clitoris to full removal; in some cases, a child's vaginal lips are sewn only leaving enough room for the girl to urinate or for menstrual discharge.

The United Nations has condemned the various forms of child maltreatment, but outside of verbal condemnation, the international community is limited in their response. There are unique challenges in investigating transnational crimes that only hamper the opportunity to rescue any child in need. Finally, child victims of war face unique challenges including but not limited to abandonment, physical harm, and the psychological repercussions from exposure to violence.

REVIEW QUESTIONS

1. Why is FGM an accepted practice in some cultures?

2. What are some of the reasons child soldiers are used besides combat?

3. What is a transnational crime and what are some of the jurisdictional challenges with investigating this type of offense?

4. Why do trafficking victims find it so difficult to escape from debt bondage?

5. How do social norms contribute to child marriage?

KEYWORDS

Human trafficking: Recruitment, transfer, harboring, or receipt of persons by threat or use of force or other forms of coercion, abduction, fraud, deception, the abuse of power, a position of vulnerability, or the giving or receiving of payments or benefits to achieve the consent of a person having control over another person, for the purpose of exploitation.

Debt bondage: The status or condition arising from a pledge by a debtor of their personal services or of those of a person under their control as security for a debt, if the value of those services as reasonably assessed is not applied toward the liquidation of the debt or the length and nature of those services are not respectively limited and defined.

Bacha bazi: The practice of using boys for sex.

Transnational crimes: Crimes involving two or more countries.

Female genital mutilation: The practice of partially or totally removing the genitalia of girls for non-medical reasons.

Child sex tourism: Tourism involving people who leave their own country to enter another country for the purpose of engaging in a sexual act with a child.

Child soldier: Any person younger than eighteen years of age who is part of any kind of regular or irregular armed forces in any capacity such as cooks, porters, messengers, etc.

Vacation cutting: The practice of using a school vacation to travel to a country of origin for the purpose of having the procedure of FGM performed.

NOTES

1. United Nations, Universal Declaration of Human Rights. Accessed October 22, 2018. Available from http://www.un.org/en/universal-declaration-human-rights/.

2. Kathryn Farr, *Sex Trafficking: The Global Market in Women and Children* (New York, NY: Worth Publishers, 2005), 220; Kimberly A. McCabe, *The Trafficking of Persons: National and International Responses* (New York, NY: Peter Lang Publishing, 2008), 4.

3. Alison Marie Behnke, *Up for Sale: Human Trafficking and Modern Slavery* (Minneapolis, MN: Lerner Publishing, 2015), 55–55.

4. Daniel Sheinis, "The Links Between Human Trafficking, Orgainized Crime, and Terrorism," *American Intelligence Journal* 30, no. 1 (2012): 68–77.

5. Behnke, *Up for Sale*, 8.

6. Behnke, *Up for Sale*, 56.

7. United Nations Office on Drugs and Crime, UNODC Report on Human Trafficking Exposes Modern Form of Slavery, February 12, 2009. Available from https://www.unodc.org/unodc/en/frontpage/unodc-report-on-human-trafficking-exposes-modern-form-of-slavery-.html; Roslyn Muraskin, *Women and Justice: It's a Crime*, fifth edition (Boston, MA: Pearson, 2012), 210.

8. Behnke, *Up for Sale*, 8.

9. U.S. Department of State. Tier Placements. Accessed October 26, 2018. Available from https://www.state.gov/j/tip/rls/tiprpt/2017/271117.htm.

10. William Hughes, "The Nature and Extent of Trafficking Women and Children in the United Kingdom," in Obi N.I. Ebbe and Dilip K. Das (eds.), *Criminal Abuse of Women and Children: An International Perspective* (Boca Raton, FL: CRC Press, 2010), 113.

11. Hughes, "The Nature and Extent of Trafficking Women and Children in the United Kingdom," 114–15; Alinka Gearon, "Child Trafficking: Young People's Experiences of Front-Line Services in England," *British Journal of Criminology* 59, no. 2 (2018): 7; Theresa May. Draft: Modern Day Slavery Bill. Accessed December 28, 2018. Available from https://assets.publishing.service.gov.uk/government/uploads/system/uploads/attachment_data/file/266165/Draft_Modern_Slavery_Bill.pdf.

12. Julia O'Connell Davidson, *Children in the Global Sex Trade* (Malden, MA: Polity Press, 2005), 74; Gabby Hinsliff, "Children Forced into UK Slavery," *Observer*, May 18, 2003.

13. Margaret Melrose, "Mercenary Territory: A UK Perspective on Human Trafficking," in Kimberly A. McCabe and Sabita Manian (eds.), *Sex Trafficking: A Global Perspective* (Lanham, MD: Rowman & Littlefield, 2010), 63–64.

14. Gearon, "Child Trafficking: Young People's Experiences of Front-Line Services in England," 2.

15. Amber Rudd, 2017 UK Annual Report on Modern Slavery, 8–9. Accessed December 28, 2018. Available from https://assets.publishing.service.gov.uk/government/uploads/system/uploads/attachment_data/file/652366/2017_uk_annual_report_on_modern_slavery.pdf.

16. Arvind Verma, "Trafficking in India," in Kimberly A. McCabe and Sabita Manian (eds.), *Sex Trafficking: A Global Perspective* (Lanham, MD: Rowman & Littlefield, 2010), 102.

17. Emily K. Harlan, "It Happens in the Dark: Examining Current Obstacles to Identifying and Rehabilitating Child Sex Trafficking Victims in India and the United States," *University of Colorado Law Review* 83 (2007): 1127–29.

18. Sajoy Roy and Chandan Chaman, "Human Rights and Trafficking in Women and Children in India," *Journal of Historical Archaeology & Anthropological Sciences* 1, no. 5 (2017): 164.

19. Verma, "Trafficking in India," 101.

20. Treena Rae Orchard, "Girl, Woman, Lover, Mother: Towards a New Understanding of Child Prostitution Among Young Devadasis in Rural Karnataka, India," *Social Science and Medicine* 64, no. 12 (2007): 2388; John Wall, *Children's Rights: Today's Global Challenge* (Lanham, MD: Rowman & Littlefield, 2017), 117; Yateendra Singhjafa, "Criminal Exploitation of Women and Children in India: Its Control," in Obi N.I. Ebbe and Dilip K. Das (eds.), *Criminal Abuse of Women and Children: An International Perspective* (Boca Raton, FL: CRC Press, 2010), 224.

21. Wall, *Children's Rights*, 76.

22. Obi N.I. Ebbe, "The Scope and Causes of Criminal Abuse of Children," in Obi N.I. Ebbe and Dilip K. Das (eds.), *Criminal Abuse of Women and Children: An International Perspective* (Boca Raton, FL: CRC Press, 2010), 47–62.

23. Siddharth Kara, *Sex Trafficking: Inside the Business of Modern Slavery* (New York, NY: Columbia University Press, 2009), 271.

24. Verma, "Trafficking in India," 104.

25. U.S. Department of State, Trafficking in Persons Report: 2018. Accessed December 31, 2018. Available from https://www.state.gov/j/tip/rls/tiprpt/2018/.

26. Ajwang Warria, "Challenges in Assistance Provisions to Child Victims of Transnational Trafficking in South Africa," *European Journal of Social Work* 21, no. 5 (2018): 713.

27. Warria, "Challenges in Assistance Provisions to Child Victims of Transnational Trafficking in South Africa," 714.

28. Lindiwe Mtimkulu, "Criminal Exploitation of Women and Children: A South African Perspective," in Obi N.I. Ebbe and Dilip K. Das (eds.), *Criminal Abuse of Women and Children: An International Perspective* (Boca Raton, FL: CRC Press, 2010), 166.

29. "South Africa: Western Cape Social Development Warns of Child Trafficking Soccer Scam." Press release. January 14, 2016. London: Albawaba. Available from https.www.arrivealive.co.zo.

30. William J. Mathias and Kimberley A. McCabe, "Sex Trafficking in the Countries of South Africa, Mozambique, and Zimbabwe," in Kimberly A. McCabe and Sabita Manian (eds.), *Sex Trafficking: A Global Perspective* (Lanham, MD: Rowman & Littlefield, 2010), 26.

31. Department of State, "Trafficking in Persons Report: 2018, 388–90. Accessed December 31, 2018. Available from https://www.state.gov/j/tip/rls/tiprpt/2018/.

32. Yuliya Tverdova, "Human Trafficking in Russia and Other Post-Soviet States," *Human Rights Review* 12, no. 3 (2011): 329.

33. Department of State, "Trafficking in Persons Report: 2018," 388–90.

34. Mary Buckley, *The Politics of Unfree Labour in Russia: Human Trafficking and Labour Migration* (New York, NY: Cambridge University Press, 2018), 94.

35. Buckley, *The Politics of Unfree Labour in Russia*, 58.

36. Buckley, *The Politics of Unfree Labour in Russia*, 175.

37. Kimberly A. McCabe and Daniel G. Murphy, *Child Abuse: Today's Issues* (Boca Raton, FL: CRC Press, 2017), 117.

38. Carole Moore, "The Fight Against Human Trafficking," *Law Enforcement Technology* 44, no. 7 (2017): 38.

39. April Rieger, "Missing the Mark: Why the Trafficking Victims Protection Act Fails to Protect Sex Trafficking Victims in the United States," *Harvard Journal of Law and Gender* 30, no. 1 (2007): 231–32.

40. Harvey Wallace and Cliff Roberson, *Victimology: Legal, Psychological, and Social Perspectives*, fourth edition (Boston, MA: Pearson, 2015), 82.

41. Neha A. Deshpande and Nawal M. Nour, "Sex Trafficking of Women and Girls," *Review in Obstetrics & Gynecology* 6, no. 1 (2013): e25.

42. Wall, *Children's Rights*, 13.

43. Kara, *Sex Trafficking*, 7–9.

44. Robert J. Meadows, *Understanding Violence & Victimization*, seventh edition (New York, NY: Pearson, 2019), 198.

45. Yvonne Rafferty, "Children for Sale: Child Trafficking in Southeast Asia," *Child Abuse Review* 16, no. 6 (2007): 410.

46. McCabe, *The Trafficking of Persons*, 44.

47. Ann Jordan, "Slavery, Forced Labor, Debt Bondage, and Human Trafficking: from Conceptual Confusion to Targeted Solutions," *Center for Human Rights & Humanitarian Law* no. 2 (2011): 6.

48. Jordan, "Slavery, Forced Labor, Debt Bondage, and Human Trafficking from Conceptual Confusion to Targeted Solutions," 6.

49. Wall, *Children's Rights*, 100

50. McCabe, *The Trafficking of Persons*, 46.

51. International Labour Office, Global Estimates of Child Labour: Results and Trends, 2012-2016, 11. Accessed October 25, 2018. Available from https://www.ilo.org/wcmsp5/groups/public/---dgreports/---dcomm/documents/publication/wcms_575499.pdf.

52. International Labour Office, Global Estimates of Child Labour: Results and Trends, 2012-2016, 13.

53. Erica G. Polakoff, "Globalization and Child Labor: Review of the Issues," *Journal of Developing Societies* 23, no. 1-2 (2007): 266.

54. McCabe, *The Trafficking of Persons:* 44

55. Mary Mather, "Intercountry Adoption," *Archives of Disease in Childhood* 92, no. 6 (2007): 480.

56. Carole Moore, "The Fight against Human Trafficking," *Law Enforcement Technology* 44, no. 7 (2017): 38.

57. Katerina Nanou, "The Social Acceptance of Illegal Practices in the Greek Domestic Adoption System," *Adoption and Fostering* 35, no. 3 (2011): 61.

58. Kara, *Sex Trafficking*, 271.

59. Gayle Tzemach Lemmon and Lynn S. Elharake, "High Stakes for Young Lives: Examining Strategies to Stop Child Marriage," The Council on Foreign Relations, 2014.

60. United Nations Human Rights, Convention on Consent to Marriage, Minimum Age for Marriage, and Registration of Marriages. Accessed October 30, 2018. Available from https://www.ohchr.org/en/professionalinterest/pages/minimumageformarriage.aspx.

61. World Health Organization, Child Marriages: 39,000 Every Day. Accessed October 30, 2018. Available from http://www.who.int/mediacentre/news/releases/2013/child_marriage_20130307/en/.

62. Rachel Vogelstein, "Ending Child Marriage: How Elevating the Status of Girls Advances U.S. Foreign Policy Objectives," Council on Foreign Relations, May 2013, 3–5.

63. U.S. Agency for International Development, Preventing and Responding to Child, Early and Forced Marriage. Accessed October 30, 2018. Available from www.usaid.gov/what-we-do/gender-equality-and-womens-empowerment/child-marriage.

64. Allisa Koski and Jody Heymann, "Child Marriage in the United States: How Common is the Practice, and Which Children are at Greatest Risk," *Perspectives on Sexual and Reproductive Health* 50, no. 2 (2018): 59; Gayle Tzemach Lemmon "Fragile States, Fragile Lives: Child Marriage Amid Disaster and Conflict," Council on Foreign Relations, June 2014, 37.

65. Quentin Wodon, Chata Male, Ada Nayihouba, Adenike Onagoruwa, Aboudrahyme Savadogo, Ali Yedan, Jeff Edmeades, Aslihan Kes, Neetu John, Lydia Murithi, Mara Steinhaus, and Suzanne Petroni, "Economic Impacts of Child Marriage: Global Synthesis Report," June 2017, 23. Accessed October 30, 2018. Available from http://documents.worldbank.org/curated/en/530891498511398503/pdf/116829-WP-P151842-PUBLIC-EICM-Global-Conference-Edition-June-27.pdf.

66. Santosh K. Mahato, "Causes and Consequences of Child Marriage: A Perspective," *International Journal of Scientific & Engineering Resources* 7, no. 7 (2016): 700, 2

67. Wallace and Roberson, *Victimology: Legal, Psychological, and Social Perspectives*, 286; McCabe and Murphy, *Child Abuse: Today's Issues* (Boca Raton, FL:CRC Press, 2016), 117;

Dennie Caine, "Child Camel Jockeys: A Present Day Tragedy Involving Children and Sport," *Clinical Journal of Sport Medicine* 15, no. 5 (2005): 287.

68. Unifeed, United Arab Emiates/Camel Jockeys. Accessed November 12, 2018. Available from https://www.unmultimedia.org/tv/unifeed/asset/U070/U070102b/.

69. U.C. Jha, *Child Soldiers: Practice, Law and Remedies* (New Delhi, Vij Books, 2018), 5–6.

70. United Nations, Security Council Establishes Monitoring, Reporting Mechanism on Use of Child Soldiers, Unanimously Adopting Resolution 1612, 2005. Accessed October 20, 2018. Available from https://www.un.org/press/en/2005/sc8458.doc.htm.

71. Alexandre J. Vautravers, "Why Child Soldiers are Such a Complex Issue," *Refugee Survey Quarterly* 27, no. 4 (2008): 96.

72. Jha, *Child Soldiers*, 24; Vautravers, "Why Child Soldiers are Such a Complex Issue," 106.

73. Vautravers, "Why Child Soldiers are Such a Complex Issue," 107; Wall, *Children's Rights*, 112.

74. Jha, *Child Soldiers*, 47.

75. Jha, *Child Soldiers*, 13.

76. Amy J. Stevens, "The Invisible Soldiers: Understanding How the Life Experiences of Girl Child Soldiers Impact Their Health and Rehabilitation," *Archives of Disease in Childhood* 99, no. 5 (2014): 458–62.

77. Jha, *Child Soldiers*, 18; Jina Moore, "In Africa, Justice for Bush Wives," *The Christian Science Monitor*, June 10, 2008.

78. Anat Berko, *The Smarter Bomb: Women and Children as Suicide Bombers* (Lanham, MD: Rowman & Littlefield, 2012), 76.

79. Jha, *Child Soldiers*, 92–93.

80. Berko, *The Smarter Bomb*, 60–63.

81. Ilse Derluyn, Wouler Vandenhole, Stepen Parmentier, and Cindy Mels, "Victims and/or Perpetrators? Towards an Interdisciplinary Dialogue on Child Soldiers," *International Health and Human Rights* 15, no. 28 (2015): 8.

82. Wall, *Children's Rights*, 113.

83. Meadows, *Understanding Violence & Victimization*, 199; Congress.gov. H.R. 1191: Child Soldiers Prevention Act of 2017 (2017), 2–3. Accessed October 22, 2018. Available from https://www.congress.gov/115/bills/hr1191/BILLS-115hr1191ih.pdf.

84. U.S. Department of State, The Facts About Child Sex Tourism. Accessed November 9, 2018. Available from https://2001-2009.state.gov/g/tip/rls/fs/2005/51351.htm.

85. William J. Newman, Ben W. Holt, John S. Rabun, Gary Phillips, and Charles L. Scott, "Child Sex Tourism: Extending the Borders of Sexual Offender Legislation," *International Journal of Law and Psychiatry* 34, no. 2 (2011): 119.

86. Newman, Holt, Rabun, Phillips, and Scott, "Child Sex Tourism," 117.

87. Thomas R. Panko and Babu P. George, "Child Sex Tourism: Exploring the Issues," *Criminal Justice Studies* 25, no. 1 (2012): 67.

88. Babu P. George and Thomas R. Panko, "Child Sex Tourism: Facilitating Conditions, Legal Remedies, and Other Inventions," *Vulnerable Children and Youth Studies* 6, no. 2 (2011): 135–36.

89. Mahathi D. Kosuri and Elizabeth L. Jeglic, "Child Sex Tourism: American Perception of Foreign Victims," *Journal of Sexual Aggression* 23, no. 2 (2017): 208.

90. Kosuri and Jeglic, "Child Sex Tourism," 209.

91. Newman, Holt, Rabun, Phillips, and Scott, "Child Sex Tourism," 119.

92. United Nations Human Rights, Combatting Child Sex Tourism. Accessed November 9, 2018. Available from https://www.ohchr.org/en/newsevents/pages/childsextourism.aspx.

93. Panko and George, "Child Sex Tourism," 71.

94. Panko and George, "Child Sex Tourism," 76–77; Babu P. George and Thomas R. Panko, "Child Sex Tourism," 140–41.

95. Samuel V. Jones, "Ending Bacha Bazi: Boy Sex Slavery and the Responsibility to Protect Doctrine," *Indiana International & Comparative Law Review* 25, no. 1 (2014): 67.

96. Elif Erdogdu, Sienna McNett, Daniel Winstead, and Raymond Friend, "Breaking the Stigma against Child Sex Trafficking and Bacha Bazi in Afghanistan," (2016): 4.

97. Yakobcuk Viacheslav, "Stolen Boys: Life after Sexual Slavery in Afghanistan," *journal. ie*. Accessed November 15, 2018. Available from http://jrnl.ie/3464413; United Nations General Assembly, Human Rights Council, Thirty-first session, Agenda Item 5: Written statement submitted by European Centre for Law and Justice, The Centre European pour le droit, les Justice et les droits de l'homme, a non-governmental organization in special consultative status.

98. Virginia M. Kendall and T. Markus Funk, *Child Exploitation and Trafficking: Examining the Global Challenges and U.S. Responses* (New York, NY: Rowman & Littlefield, 2012), 203.

99. Kendall and Funk, *Child Exploitation and Trafficking*, 212.

100. Kendall and Funk, *Child Exploitation and Trafficking*, 220.

101. Kendall and Funk, *Child Exploitation and Trafficking*, 233.

102. Department of State, Trafficking in Persons Report (2016), 40. Accessed October 18, 2018. Available from https://www.state.gov/documents/organization/258876.pdf.

103. Hilary Burrage, *Female Mutilation: The Truth Behind the Horrifying Global Practice of Genital Mutilation* (London: New Holland Publishers, 2016), 16; Wall, *Children's Rights*, 12.

104. Rosemarie Skaine, *Female Genital Mutilation: Legal, Cultural and Medical Issues* (Jefferson, NC: McFarland, 2005), 9; Akin-Tunde A. Odukogbe, Bosede B. Afolabi, Oluwasomidoyin O. Bello, and Ayodeji S. Adeyanju, "Female Genital Mutilation/Cutting in Africa," *Translational Andrology and Urology* 6, no. 2 (2017): 139. 1

105. Burrage, *Female Mutilation*, 17.

106. Skaine, *Female Genital Mutilation*, 45.

107. Skaine, *Female Genital Mutilation*, 23.

108. Odukogbe, Afolabi, Bello, and Adeyanju, "Female Genital Mutilation/Cutting in Africa," 141.

109. Skaine, *Female Genital Mutilation*, 14. Odukogbe, Afolabi, Bello, and Adeyanju, "Female Genital Mutilation/Cutting in Africa," 141.

110. Burrage, *Female Mutilation*, 11.

111. Odukogbe, Afolabi, Bello, and Adeyanju, "Female Genital Mutilation/Cutting in Africa," 139.

112. Skaine, *Female Genital Mutilation*, 12–15.

113. Burrage, *Female Mutilation*, 19.

114. Odukogbe, Afolabi, Bello, and Adeyanju, "Female Genital Mutilation/Cutting in Africa," 139.

115. Skaine, *Female Genital Mutilation*, 35; World Health Organization, Female Genital Mutilation (FGM). Accessed November 13, 2018. Available from http://www.who.int/reproductivehealth/topics/fgm/prevalence/en/.

116. Alissa Koski and Jody Heymann, "Thirty-year Trends in the Prevalence and Severity of Female Genital Mutilation: A Comparison of 22 Countries," *Journal of Clinical Pathology* 2, no. 4 (2017): 1.

117. World Health Organization, Female Genital Mutilation (FGM).

118. De Elizabeth, "The First Female Genital Mutilation Prosecution in America is a Chilling Reminder It Happens Here Too," *Bustle*, May 21, 2018. Available from https://www.bustle.com/p/the-first-female-genital-mutilation-prosecution-in-america-is-a-chilling-reminder-it-happens-here-too-8058419.

119. Howard Goldberg, Paul Stupp, Ekwutosi Okoroh, Ghenet Besera, David Goodmab, and Isabella Danel, "Female Genital Mutilation/Cutting in the United States: Updated Estimates of Women and Girls at Risk, 2012," *Public Health Reports* 131, no. 2 (2016): 341.

120. Delan Devakumar, Marion Burch, David Osrin, Egbert Sondorp, and Jonathan C.K. Wells, "The Intergenerational Effect of War on the Health of Children," *BMC Medicine* 12, no. 1 (2014): 1.

121. Jha, *Child Soldiers*, 105.

122. Zulfiqar A. Bhutta, William J. Keenan, and Susan Bennett, "Children of War: Urgent Action is Needed to Save a Generation," *The Lancet* 388, no. 10051 (2016): 1275.

123. United Nations Children's Fund, With 15 Million Children Caught up in Major Conflicts, UNICEF Declares 2014 a Devastating Year for Children, December 2014. Accessed November 14, 2018. Available from https://www.unicef.org/mena/press-releases/unicef-declares-2014-devastating-year-for-children.

124. Judith A. Myers-Walls, "Children as Victims of War and Terrorism," in Janet L. Mullings, James W. Marquart, and Deborah J. Hartley (eds.), *The Victimization of Children: Emerging Issues* (Binghamton, NY: Haworth Press, 2003), 43.

125. Joanna Santa Barbara, "Impact of War on Children and Imperative to End War," *Croatian Medical Journal* 47, no. 6 (2006): 892; Bhutta, Keenan, and Bennett, "Children of War," 1275.

14

The Judicial Response

◆ ◆ ◆

WE BEGAN BY DISCUSSING in detail how child maltreatment has been chronicled from antiquity through recent history. Throughout this book, we have provided examples of how and where child abuse occurs and the devastating effects of this form of victimization. It is only in recent history we can see a willingness to combat child maltreatment through investigatory, judicial, and community responses. In this final chapter, we will address the official criminal/civil justice response, which will include key legislation, criminal and civil court, and highlight some of the key professionals who come to the aid of children. It wasn't until the case of Mary Ellen Wilson that the wheels of justice began to significantly turn on behalf of child abuse victims.

MARY ELLEN WILSON

This child was born in 1864 and became the poster child for unveiling the secrecy of child abuse. It was reported that Mary Ellen was severely beaten, lacked adequate food, and wasn't supplied with sufficient clothing. Surprisingly, it was the American Society for Prevention of Cruelty to Animals who sought to bring charges against the caretakers of this maltreated young girl. Mary Ellen's compelling testimony told of her victimization, and finally a human face was put on child abuse. This case was so inspirational that it led to the creation of the New York Society for the Prevention of Cruelty to Children, which was established in December 1874 and was believed to the first agency in the world devoted to protecting children.[1]

With the issue of child abuse finally coming to the forefront, the criminal justice system was slowly beginning to address the needs of children and the necessity for legislative sustenance. This assistance was highlighted in the case of *Prince v. Massachusetts* where the Supreme Court ruled that parents do not have the absolute ultimate authority over their children and that states can act as *parens patriae* for the well-being of children, and that the state's interest is not only strong, but can trump the way a parent wishes to raise their child.[2] The concept of child abuse being just a family matter was no longer the case. In fact, the federal government created its first comprehensive legislation to address the needs of children who have been victims of abuse.

THE CHILD ABUSE PREVENTION AND TREATMENT ACT

In 1974, Congress passed the Child Abuse Prevention and Treatment Act (CAPTA), which created federal programs to research the causes of child abuse and neglect, and provided funding to support state child welfare programs. States wishing to receive federal funding had to comply with numerous conditions. CAPTA had certain requirements of states: mandatory reporting systems and the creation of a system to differentiate valid from invalid reports of abuse, which included measures that would be taken if it were discovered that a child was a victim of abuse. Furthermore, CAPTA required specific remedies in court cases involving child abuse. Specifically, CAPTA required that courts appoint a guardian ad litem (GAL) to represent every child during a judicial welfare proceeding and make recommendations as to what was in the best interest of the child.[3] The initiative to continue with additional legislation beyond CAPTA was addressed in the creation of the Protect Act of 2003.

THE PROTECT ACT OF 2003

The Prosecutorial Remedies and Other Tools to End the Exploitation of Children Today (Protect) Act strengthens law enforcement's ability to prevent, investigate, and prosecute crimes against children, and also established enhanced penalties for Americans engaging in sex tourism with children. This law not only enhanced the Amber Alert System by informing the public of abducted children, but added subsequent legislation addressing missing persons with the creation of Suzanne's Law. Under this statute local authorities are required to notify the National Crime Information Center if anyone between the ages of eighteen to twenty-one goes missing.

The Protect Act also:

- Establishes criminal liability for attempting to remove a child from the United States with intent to obstruct the lawful exercise of parental rights.
- Provides for mandatory life imprisonment of a person convicted of a federal sex offense against a minor if the perpetrator has a prior sex conviction in which a minor was the victim, unless a death sentence is imposed.
- Bars pretrial release of persons charged with specified offenses against or involving children.
- Requires the designated authority for a public building to establish procedures for locating a child who is missing in the building.
- Prohibits: (1) making a visual depiction that is a digital image, computer image, or computer-generated image of, or that is indistinguishable from an image of, a minor engaging in specified sexually explicit conduct; (2)

knowingly advertising, promoting, presenting, distributing, or soliciting through the mails or in commerce, including by computer, any material that is or contains an obscene visual depiction of a minor engaging in sexually explicit conduct or a visual depiction of an actual minor engaging in such conduct; (3) knowingly distributing, offering, sending, or providing to a minor any such visual depiction using the mail or commerce, including by computer, for purposes of inducing or persuading a minor to participate in an illegal act; and (4) knowingly producing, distributing, receiving, or possessing with intent to distribute a visual depiction of any kind, including a drawing, cartoon, sculpture, or painting, that, under specified circumstances, depicts a minor engaging in sexually explicit conduct and is obscene, or depicts an image that is or appears to be of a minor engaging in such conduct and such depiction lacks serious literary, artistic, political, or scientific value.[4] CAPTA and The Protect Act highlight some of the key legislation that has been created in response to child maltreatment.

MANDATED REPORTERS

The first mandatory reporting law of any kind was the result of the work by Colorado pediatrician C. Henry Kempe and his medical colleagues in identifying cases of severe child physical abuse and conceptualizing this as "the battered-child syndrome." Due to their understanding and empathy to this abuse, they realized that doctors were encountering these types of cases and, although recognizing the severity of the maltreatment, were failing to take any further action to protect these victims. After treating these children, physicians would allow offending parents to take their children home with the potential to suffer additional abuse, and in some cases eventual death.[5] Individual states began to implement mandatory reporting laws in the 1960s, but the focus of these laws was on how to address the physical abuse of children, rather than the prevention of the maltreatment. The purpose of these laws was to target professional doctors who were in an occupation that was more likely to see any physical injuries. The philosophy of mandatory reporting laws began to evolve and started to focus on non-physical injuries, thus expanding the role of mandated reporter to those outside of the medical community.[6] All fifty states of the United States are currently abiding by the mandatory reporting laws as required by CAPTA. However, the mandating laws themselves still vary from state to state. For example, "approximately 48 States, the District of Columbia, American Samoa, Guam, the Northern Mariana Islands, Puerto Rico, and the Virgin Islands designate professions whose members are mandated by law to report child maltreatment."[7] The occupations required as mandated reporters can also vary from state to state. Social workers, law enforcement officers, mental health workers, medical workers, school officials, and childcare workers are commonly listed as professionals mandated to report. Eleven states have added jobs such as faculty, administrators, athletics staff, and volunteers who work for institutions for higher learning.[8] Some states differ considerably when classifying clergy as mandatory reporters. For instance, Washington and Virginia stand out as states that categorize clergy as those who are not counted as mandated reporters. As of this writing, Virginia has proposed legislation requiring that clergy be added as mandated reporters. If this legislation passes, it will leave Washington as the sole state that does not mandate clergy to report abuse under any circumstances.[9]

School officials are consistently the most frequent reporters of child abuse. Schools usually have a designated reporter (in many cases the school nurse) who will act as the school liaison for reporting cases of suspected abuse. Not all states require that only professionals report suspected abuse. In several states, reporting laws list the mandated reporting professionals and add a clause at the very end of their statute that asserts "or any other person," thus making every responsible adult liable to report.[10] Clergy, for example, who are not specified as "professional" mandated reporters would be required to report suspected child abuse under the stipulation of the "any other person" statute.

The bar is set rather low when determining whether to report abuse: Mandated reporters are not required to prove that abuse has occurred, as they only need to suspect child maltreatment in order to call the appropriate authorities. The caller, if acting in good faith, is immune from liability should their suspicions not be warranted. In contrast, in some states mandatory reporters who fail to report suspected abuse can be held criminally liable. The process for reporting is rather simple as several states have universal tollfree phone numbers to child protective services in an attempt to make it simpler for the potential caller. Callers also have the option of reporting abuse anonymously, although it may be difficult to reveal specific details of an allegation without identifying one's self. Anonymous callers may face a higher risk of having their calls screened out, thus allowing for the potential of a legitimate case of child maltreatment slipping through the cracks. Potential reporters have the additional option of contacting law enforcement, especially if they believe the child is in imminent danger as many child protective workers are often available exclusively Monday through Friday. If law enforcement is contacted, they can immediately intervene and report their findings to social services.[11]

STATUTE OF LIMITATIONS

These laws require that criminal prosecution commence within a designated time period from when the alleged criminal act occurred. Individuals accused of committing crimes that are beyond a certain time limit are shielded from prosecution through these statutes. The statute of limitations is an affirmative defense where the prosecution must establish that the time to formally charge a defendant has not elapsed. The statute of limitations is different from that of the right to a speedy trial. The timeline for a defendant's constitutional right to a speedy trial does not commence until formal charges have been initiated.[12] States have recognized that there are times when victims refrain from immediately reporting attacks to law enforcement, especially in cases involving sexual assault. States began extending the time when a victim can report a crime in an effort to increase the prosecution of sex offenders.[13] These laws are essential as some victims of sexual abuse may not be willing to come forward until after years of receiving therapeutic assistance.

CASE STUDY #1

Teresa, in her late sixties, went to her local law enforcement agency to report that her husband had been having sexual intercourse with each of her three daughters when each child was about twelve years of age (her daughters were now fully grown women). Teresa stated that she had always been aware of the sexual abuse her daughters endured, including sexual intercourse and other forms of sexual contact throughout the girls' childhood. Teresa further revealed that the reason she did not bring the abuse allegations to the attention of the authorities was that she had been trying to put an end to the abuse through continuous prayer. Teresa was advised by law enforcement that they could not intervene at the time of her report as the statute of limitations had expired.

SEX OFFENDER REGISTRATION

The Sex Offender Registration and Notification Act (SORNA) is federal legislation that requires that states maintain a system for monitoring and tracking sex offenders who are either working or residing within their jurisdiction. All fifty states have developed a registry with a notification policy of some form, which can vary from state to state. However, most states have implemented websites that provide information on convicted sex offenders, which can include the offender's name, address, picture, and place of employment. Additionally, some states may give details of the sexual offense, including the exact charge the offender was convicted of, whether or not the offender is considered violent, and/or if the conviction involved sexual abuse of a minor. Registered sex offenders are also required to stay away from certain areas dictated by residency requirements. Localities nationwide have passed residency laws that require sex offenders to abstain from living within a specific distance from schools, daycare centers, and churches.[14] Some jurisdictions have added specific legislation mandating that convicted sex offenders must keep their front lights off when children are trick or treating.

There have been two cases centered on the constitutionality of sex offender registries that were both decided in the year 2003. The first case was *Smith v. Doe* (2003), which dealt with Alaska's registration law that required any sex offender to register with the correctional system or local law enforcement within one day of entering the state. The two unnamed sex offenders affected by this law argued that they were both convicted of their sex crimes prior to the implementation of the Alaskan registration law and further argued the law was punitive and violated their constitutional rights. The Supreme Court ruled that the registration was a civil proceeding and thus served as regulatory, public safety purpose and was not a violation of their constitutional rights. In the second case of *Connecticut Public Safety v. Doe* (also in 2003), the defendant argued that required pictures of sex offenders and their personal information violated their constitutional rights, noting the due process clause of the Fourteenth Amendment did not allow him to establish his low-risk status as a sex offender. The Supreme Court ruled again that it was not a violation of one's constitutional rights as the registration process was a civil proceeding and was used in the best interests of the public.[15] Although the Supreme Court has ruled on the constitutionality of sex offender registration, they refused to hear a case of residency restrictions. In the year 2005, the Eighth Circuit ruled in *Doe v. Miller* (2005) that the Constitution of the United States does not prevent the state of Iowa from regulating residency of sex offenders.[16] Research examining the impact of SORNA and how it affects re-offense rates has been inconclusive, whereas other studies have found little to no effect on sexual recidivism.[17]

Romeo and Juliet Laws

States are allowed to waive sex offender registration for those who are convicted of statutory rape under specific circumstances occurring under laws commonly known as Romeo and Juliet Laws. Under these provisions a person convicted of statutory rape whose age falls within a certain range may avoid the requirement of being placed on the sexual offender registry. In fact, in some states sexual intercourse with a minor may not be considered a sexual offense if the offender and victim are within a certain number of years of one another, but the act may be classified under a different form of child maltreatment, thus sex offender registration will not apply.

Registration/Notification

There is a distinction between sexual offender registration laws and sex offender notification laws. Registration laws require convicted sex offenders to provide information about themselves to a segment of the government (such as the local police) and their information is kept confidential. Registration requirements were intended solely to aid law enforcement in monitoring offenders and responding to the possibility of sexual crime recidivism. In contrast, notification laws require sex offenders information be disseminated to the public.[18] The process of registration eventually led to public notification originated with the Jacob Wetterling Act.

Jacob Wetterling Crimes Against Children and Sexually Violent Offender Registration Act

The Jacob Wetterling Act was created as part of the Federal Violent Crime Control and Law Enforcement Act of 1994. This legislation requires each state to have a sex offender registration database where law enforcement agencies can keep track of sex offenders in their communities. This act was created in honor of Jacob Wetterling of Long Prairie, Minnesota, who at the age of eleven was abducted by a stranger in 1989. Jacob's death was not confirmed until 2016, when the suspect in his abduction (Danny James Heinrich) led authorities to Jacob's remains.

Megan's Law

In 1994, Megan Kanka of Hamilton Township, New Jersey, at age seven was raped and murdered by her neighbor Jesse Timmendequas, who lured Megan into his house under the guise of seeing his puppies. When this crime came to light, the community was outraged for two reasons. The first being the heinous crime itself, and secondly how someone so incredibly dangerous could be living among them without their knowledge. It was revealed that Timmendequas had two prior sexual assault convictions. In response to this tragedy, New Jersey legislators on October 31, 1994, signed into law a sexual offender registry that required community notification.[19] This crime garnered such national attention that Congress in 1996 passed a federal version of Megan's Law, thus amending the Jacob Wetterling Act, which required states' law enforcement agencies to not only keep track of sex offenders, but to also provide public notification of their whereabouts. Additionally, an international Megan's Law was created that requires registered sex offenders who are traveling abroad give law enforcement twenty-one days' notice of their impending trip. Further registration laws were created to track sex offenders including the Pam Lychner Sexual Offender Tracking and Identification Act.

Pam Lychner Sexual Offender Tracking and Identification Act

This act, which amends the Jacob Wetterling Act, was established in late 1996 and authorized the Federal Bureau of Investigation to establish a law enforcement–only national database to track the whereabouts of sex offenders across state lines. This registry allows authorities to obtain all information on sex offenders from every state on a continuous basis and act as a more proficient registry until all states implemented their own registries that met federal government standards.[20] This act, however, did not allow for a universal notification system of sex offenders. In response to this gap, on July 27, 2006, President George W. Bush signed into law the Adam Walsh Child Protection and Safety Act. This act included Dru's Law, which, among other things, changed the name of the National Sex Offender Public Registry to the Dru Sjodin National Sex Offender Public Website, which provides information to the public on the whereabouts of registered sex offenders despite state boundaries. This website was created in honor of Dru Sjodin who at age twenty-two was murdered by a convicted sex offender.

The Adam Walsh Child Protection and Safety Act of 2006

The Adam Walsh Child Protection and Safety Act categorizes registered sex offenders into three tiers, with the third tier being the most serious. Convicted offenders under this new tier system must update their whereabouts based on which tier level they are classified under. Tier 3 offenders are mandated to update their whereabouts every three months for the remainder of their life. Tier 2 offenders need to update their whereabouts every six months for a period of twenty-five years, and Tier 1 offenders must update their whereabouts every year for a period of fifteen years. Sex offenders must provide a DNA sample, fingerprints, social security number, home and work addresses, vehicle details, as well as additional information. Juvenile sex offenders who meet certain criteria also fall under this purview.[21] The Adam Walsh Act also has a provision for civil commitment should an offender still be deemed sexually dangerous despite having served their sentence. The Adam Walsh Act was named after Adam, who was abducted from a Sears department store; his severed head was found approximately two weeks later.

Registration of Juvenile Perpetrators

The Adam Walsh Child Protection and Safety Act also addressed the registration of juvenile sex offenders as indicated in Title 1.

> SORNA requires the registration of juveniles who 1) were 14 years of age or older at the time of the offense, and 2) were adjudicated delinquent of an offense equivalent to or more severe than aggravated sexual abuse (as described in 18 U.S.C. § 2241). Because of the severity of these offenses, these juveniles are categorized as tier III offenders under SORNA and are subject to applicable duration and in-person verification requirements. However, SORNA does not require lifetime registration without qualification, allowing registration to be terminated after 25 years for those offenders who have maintained a clean record.[22]

AGE OF CONSENT

Prior to the 1890s, states addressed age of consent by adopting English common law regarding statutory rape. Statutory rape was considered a strict liability offense that only addressed the sexual exploitation of young girls between the ages of ten to twelve, and were only enforced in instances of violation of white girls.[23] In chapter 11, we discussed how prevalent sexual activity is among high school students where surveys show that around 40 percent of students engage in sexual activity, with some of these adolescents' actions falling under the current age of consent statutes. Additional research has shown that many adolescents engage in sexual activity with older partners who, in some circumstances, are legal adults. Studies have demonstrated that there are several personal and interpersonal reasons why adolescents are sexually involved with an older person including sexual attraction, sexual experience, and emotional maturity, but the most consistent factor attracting adolescent to older sexual partners was their emotional support.[24] In response to the immense number of adolescents engaging in sexual activity with older individuals, jurisdictions around the country have changed their focus from targeting the older individual with criminal sanctions to altering the laws allowing the sexual act to be deemed legal. These laws are referred to as the age of consent laws and they can vary depending on the state. These statutes often include exceptions, most notably marital exceptions, and age gap exceptions at times referred to as the Romeo and Juliet clauses, as discussed earlier in this chapter, which permits adolescents to engage in sexual activity with other parties within a certain specified range of their own age, usually two to five years. In many jurisdictions, there are special provisions for a "person of authority," preventing certain individuals, such as teachers, law enforcement officers, etc., no matter what their age, from legally engaging in sex with a minor.[25]

LAWS AND TECHNOLOGY

With evolving technology come new tactics on how to exploit children. Legislatures are constantly attempting to create laws that respond to the ever-fluctuating forms of online victimization.

The Protection of Children from Sexual Predators Act

This act

> Amends the Federal criminal code to prohibit, and set penalties for using the mail or any facility or means of interstate or foreign commerce to knowingly initiate the transmission of the name, address, telephone number, social security number, or electronic mail address of a person under age 16 with intent to entice, encourage, offer, or solicit any person to engage in illegal sexual activity.[26]

The Keeping the Internet Devoid of Predators Act

This legislation requires that sex offenders must register "any electronic mail address, instant message address, or other similar Internet identifier the sex offender used or will use to communicate over the Internet."[27] Although this legislation can help monitor sex offenders, the legislation itself is an insufficient deterrent when combating child abuse whether the abuse occurs through technology or through personal contact. When perpetrators ignore the laws designed to protect the most vulnerable segment of the population, the judicial system is called upon to ensure offenders are held accountable.

THE COURTS

Although there are several examples of legislation that address child abuse and exploitation, anyone accused of an offense that falls under this category has the presumption of innocence. The courts are used as an arbitrator to pursue justice, whether that is through consequences for those found guilty or providing the means to exonerate those who are falsely accused. The courts are also there to protect the constitutional rights of the accused. One of the steps in the court process that may be used in the pursuit of justice is the right to challenge the accuser through a taint hearing.

Taint Hearings

The practice of taint hearings started in New Jersey and continued through various states, although it appears that states with legislation supporting taint hearings are in the minority. Taint hearings are also used in federal and military courts.[28] Taint hearings are a form of pretrial hearings to determine whether the statements of the alleged child abuse victim should be excluded. The argument in these cases is that the child's testimony is corrupted as a result of improper interviewing techniques (whether it is by law enforcement members or any other interviewer) and that these improper "forensic" interviews significantly affected the child's testimony. Given the training that modern forensic interviewers receive, fewer taint hearing cases are being requested. Taint hearings, however, are more likely to occur because of prejudice and influence exerted on a child witness by their family members. The threshold for defense attorneys to request a taint hearing is high as they must provide evidence and not mere speculation that a child's memory has been improperly and unduly influenced.[29] In addition to taint hearings being used to determine the child's reliability, a child may be evaluated on their competency.

Competency Hearing

Competency hearings are formal hearings outside the presence of a jury to determine whether a child is competent to testify. Children must be able to distinguish between a truth and a lie and know the difference between real and pretend. The federal rules of evidence abolish all age-bound assumptions that a child is not competent to testify. This has been a long-standing principle that was established in 1895 in *Wheeler v. United States* (159 U.S. 523) where the court ruled that there is no precise age that determines the child's competency.[30] In order to testify in court, every witness must be deemed competent. However, each state has its own statute as to what defines competence, but generally the statutes say that they can perceive, remember, communicate, and that they are legally and morally obligated to tell the truth.[31] In many states, however, sexual abuse victims of any age are competent as a matter of law to testify about their abuse. In fact, children as young as three years of age have been allowed to testify.[32] The defendant has the right under the constitution to be present at all hearings including competency hearings, which can be an intimidating experience for any child. Some jurisdictions have addressed this issue by allowing competency and other hearings to be conducted via closed circuit camera.[33] If it is determined that a child is indeed competent to testify and that their testimony will be considered reliable, the defendant then must decide whether they prefer to challenge the accusation and demand a trial, or try to negotiate a disposition through a plea agreement.

Plea Bargain

In the American criminal justice system, approximately 90 percent of criminal cases are resolved through plea bargains. A plea bargain is an agreement between the prosecuting attorney and defense counsel on what the parties involved consider to be a reasonable or at least a palatable disposition for the person accused of the criminal act. If the two opposing attorneys with the defendant's approval agree with one another, they present this deal to the judge presiding over the case to see if they are in agreement. The judge may ask the victim or caretaker, in the case of young child abuse victims, whether they agree with the proposal. Most states either have statutory provisions that authorize or require prosecutor's consultation with crime victims regarding plea negotiations or plea agreements.[34]

The general public does not usually comprehend the unique dynamics of how plea bargains are reached, and citizens may express their support but mostly they share their dismay at the end result. The media certainly can fuel the emotions of a plea bargain by highlighting the sentence of the accused. For example, John Doe only receives one year in jail for the rape of a six-year-old child. Based on the prima facie information, the public will be outraged asking why someone was allowed to get away with such a horrific act, and the judge who imposed this sentence is vilified in the court of public opinion. This is not to say that judges can't be too lenient in some sexual assault cases, but in many instances the challenges of convicting a sexual predator are particularly difficult to overcome. The judge in these scenarios reluctantly accepts the agreement that was formed between the opposing counsels. For instance, if a prosecutor believes that the victim/witness will function poorly on the witness stand, they are left with the decision whether to take that chance, and if the child does poorly, the result may be a finding of not guilty. The prosecutor's only option may be to try and negotiate with the defense counsel for an agreement that is tolerable for everyone involved. The prosecutor is only afforded one attempt to prove their case. If the defendant is declared "not guilty," the prosecutor cannot retry the very same case as this would be considered "double jeopardy," which is a violation of the Fifth Amendment. In contrast, defense counsel is allowed to appeal a conviction, potentially forcing the child to relive the traumatic events through a subsequent trial. Plea bargains that appear to be excessively lenient can be the direct result of lack of cooperation from the victim's family. The prosecution will find it challenging to go to trial if the child is petrified about testifying or if the caretakers of the child do not want their loved one to be subjected to additional trauma. Victim advocates are used to assist in the apprehensiveness of any victim or their families, which can help reduce the number of any unwarranted plea bargains.

Victim Advocate

Although the premise of the court system is to stand up for the victim and see that the perpetrator is held accountable for their acts, the court system, through its very design, can revictimize the child in their pursuit of justice. Victim advocates are called upon to help children deal with the pain of victimization as they guide them through the judicial process. The victim advocate works to make the victim/witness as comfortable as possible, seeing that the child may feel victimized once again as they are forced to maneuver through the judicial process and share embarrassing graphic details of a very traumatic time in their lives. These memories, with all their details and the emotions, must be relived in front of loved ones, total strangers, and the accused, all in an awkward environment. A victim advocate can initiate something as simple as an extending a hand to grasp as a signal that they will stand by them no matter what is to come. Working as a victim advocate can be a rewarding but stressful career. Dealing with such raw emotions on a continual basis leads to strain, which can lend these vital components in the judicial process prone to secondary traumatic stress disorder (STS). STS is the natural consequent behaviors and emotions resulting from being aware of an event experienced by another and the stress associated with trying to support that suffering person.[35] Currently, there is little known regarding the experiences of victim advocates as STS victims. However, a study was conducted on the prevalence of STS among victim advocates. This particular study revealed that there was a higher rate of STS in victim advocates when dealing with adult sexual assault victims as compared to when assisting child sexual assault victims.[36] Elizabeth Wilson, a victim advocate, explains what is involved when a child proceeds through the criminal justice system.

> As a Victim Witness Advocate, we see various cases of criminal victimization, including the victimization of children. When a child has been identified as a victim of abuse, the assigned advocate will immediately make contact with the child's parent(s) or guardian(s). In special circumstances we may be asked to assist law enforcement at the crime scene or local emergency department. Wrapping services around a victim as well as their family is important for many reasons; however, it is crucial to establish a good rapport with the victim and their family. The criminal justice process can be complex and lengthy so having a rapport will allow them to reach out for information as needed. Considering the trauma that the victim and their family have endured, we do our best to make them feel as comfortable and knowledgeable as possible throughout each step. Because the criminal justice system has many facets, it will require us to set up multiple meetings in order to prepare for the necessary steps. The victim and their family will be introduced to the prosecutor as well as the advocate on the case. Age appropriate children may be asked to testify, and in those cases we will familiarize the child with the courtroom as well as the Judge; this can reduce the victim's fear of the unknown. During the meetings we strive to provide as much insight on what is expected or what could happen as possible. Every case is different so we address them based on the needs of the victim as well as the prosecutor. As an advocate we will walk children through the entire criminal justice process from beginning to end. We will also give them some direction on the victim impact statement if that is of interest to them. The victim witness advocate will keep the child's family up to date on the status of the case such as bond hearings and when the case is set to be tried. The advocate will also help accompany the child and their parent(s) or guardian(s) with obtaining a protective order against the defendant.
>
> Cases vary however, but many cases qualify for a Victims Fund which is designed to help with medical related expenses as well as transportation costs, prescription reimbursement, and reimbursement for moving expenses if applicable. This is a service that our office assists victims and their families with as a courtesy. We have a vast number of community partners that we work with that allows us to make referrals as necessary to assist the victim as much as possible. The victim witness advocates have a working relationship with counselors, local

Elizabeth (Liz) Wilson Victim Advocate

domestic violence shelters, and sexual violence affiliates. We can even include case workers to provide supplemental services if needed.

Once the case has been set for trial, the victim advocate assigned to the case will reach out to the child's parent(s) or guardian(s) and set up a meeting. At this meeting the advocate and prosecutor will meet with the child and the family to go over how the proceeding will take place and answer any questions they may have. We then like to meet with the child without their parent(s) or guardian(s) present to get the child to tell us about the crime that happened to them. Our office does this because we find that sometimes the child will feel more comfortable disclosing some information without the presence of their family. Depending on the type of crime and the age of the child, two-way closed circuit television may be an option for the child when it comes time for him/her to testify. Two-way closed circuit television allows for the child to testify just in front of the prosecutor, defense attorney, and the judge without having to see the defendant. The defendant will have a monitor at counsel table that will allow he/she to be able to see and hear what the child testifies to while the child is in a separate room with just the judge, prosecutor, and defense attorney. However, in order for the child to qualify for two-way closed circuit testimony, the child must be 14 years of age or under at the time of the offense and 16 years of age or under at the time of trial. Another provision for two-way closed circuit television is for any child age 14 or under at the time of trial. The court may also order two-way closed circuit television if the court finds through expert opinion testimony, that the child will suffer severe emotional trauma if the child was to testify in open court.

The day of trial, the child will meet the victim witness advocate and prosecutor at the Commonwealth's Attorney's Office to see if there are any last minute questions and also to try and make the child feel as comfortable as possible. The victim witness advocate will put the child in a separate room and get the child when it is his/her time to testify. After the child has finished his/her testimony, the child will be assisted back to the room until the case is concluded and the defendant and his/her family/friends have left the courtroom. The prosecutor and advocate will meet with the child and his/her parent(s) or guardian(s) to once again answer any questions or concerns. If the defendant was found guilty the advocate will keep in touch with the child's parent(s) or guardian(s) about when the sentencing date is set. The child will also be strongly encouraged to complete a Victim Impact Statement. The purpose of the Victim Impact Statement is to allow the child to express to the judge and defendant exactly how the crime that was committed against him/her has affected them. This may include physical, psychological, or financial damage to the child. The child has the option to do a written Victim Impact Statement and/or an oral Victim Impact Statement. Our office as a whole strives to be as transparent as possible while being committed to seeking justice where justice is deserved.[37]

MENTAL HEALTH WORKERS

The mental health professional is an essential component in both identifying and caring for child abuse victims. In many circumstances, mental health workers may be the first contact a child victim encounters. Parents and other caretakers may send their child for "counseling" due to inappropriate behavior, only to discover this behavior was the direct result of being abused. It is in this therapeutic setting that children may make their disclosure of abuse, thus automatically initiating the official criminal justice response.[38] Mental health workers continue to provide invaluable assistance as they work with children well after their initial disclosure. They can be beneficial with their insight in both criminal and civil proceedings. The disclosure of abuse may have been initially revealed to a therapist. However, in many cases, the child is referred to mental health services after disclosing abuse to another responsible adult or official.

Children are sent to therapists for clinical evaluations to discover if their victimization has manifested into any psychological disorders and, if so, formulate a plan for treatment. The primary focus of a clinical evaluation is to assist the mental health therapist in identifying a child's needs and carrying out an appropriate treatment plan. The therapist, while evaluating a child, may need to effect change in the child's behavior, whether it is their emotions and/or cognitions in order to assist the child to deal with their victimization.[39] Although the benefits of appropriate therapy are innumerable, defense attorneys can use successful therapy to their advantage during the judicial process, as discussed in Case Study #2.

CASE STUDY #2

Jacqueline, aged fourteen, the repeated victim of rape at the hands of her biological father, finally had the courage to disclose her abuse to authorities. She was interviewed by law enforcement where she divulged how she was subjected to sexual intercourse with her father on a regular basis for a period of approximately two years. During the interview, Jacqueline was visibly shaking, crying, and on many occasions pausing as she was unable to speak. Jacqueline's father was subsequently arrested for rape, but the trial was delayed on several occasions. It finally went to trial, over a year after the date of the original disclosure. In the interim until the eventual trial, Jacqueline was receiving extensive therapy to deal with emotions regarding her victimization. After more than a year of intensive therapy, and now at the age of sixteen, Jacqueline testified in an unemotional, clear, detailed, and decisive manner. However, the defense attorney used this to his advantage as he addressed the jury asking, "Does this girl look like someone who is traumatized from the allegations she is claiming?" The jury deliberated for less than two hours before rendering a verdict of "not guilty." It should also be noted that Jacqueline's father had previously been investigated for masturbating outside an elementary school, fondling a teenage girl as she was being transported by ambulance, and deliberately raising his kilt while wearing no underwear during a parade. None of these prior investigations were admissible as they were deemed to be prejudicial to the jury.

CRIMINAL COURT

The stages of the criminal court process are initiated as soon as an arrest is made by law enforcement. However, not all criminal proceedings start from the physical arrest by a police officer. In some cases, the police officer may elect to have the courts decide whether probable cause exists in order to bring charges against the accused. This is done through a grand jury where prosecutors provide evidence to a group of jurors and they render a decision of whether probable cause exists, thus either "dropping the charges" or issuing an arrest warrant. Grand juries are also utilized to confirm that probable cause exists when a police officer has previously made an arrest. In either case, the jury may indict the offender, which in turn initiates formal charges. It should be noted that this applies only to felony cases, and some child abuse cases, although few, will fall into the classification of misdemeanor, which initiates an entirely different judicial process.

When the court process proceeds, it is the accused that is afforded all the federal constitutional rights no matter how heinous the alleged act may be. There are still no federal constitutional rights given to victims, even if they are children.[40] The defendant can use these afforded rights to the detriment of the child/accuser. One constitutional right afforded the offender is addressed in the Sixth Amendment, which guarantees the right of the accused to a speedy trial. An attorney can file a motion to dismiss all charges if the prosecutor does not bring charges in a timely manner. In theory, the criminal justice system is designed to advocate for the victim and bring an abuser to justice in a timely fashion, and fulfilling this timely form of justice can be a daunting task. While the wheels of justice are turning and prosecution is working to find a resolution, a defense attorney can file several motions of continuance for a variety of reasons, which in many cases can affect a child's willingness and ability to testify. Although constitutional rights seem to provide protections exclusively for the accused, there has been at least some case law that has assisted victims in their testimony that does not conflict with the accused's rights under the Sixth Amendment to face their accuser. This was addressed in *Maryland v. Craig*.

Maryland v. Craig (1990)

Sandra Craig was charged with sexually assaulting a six-year-old child in a daycare she operated. The judge in this case ruled that the child could testify via one-way closed circuit television after hearing from an expert that it would be too emotionally traumatic for the child to testify in person. The child was allowed to testify in a separate room while in the presence of the prosecuting and defense attorneys. The defendant, judge, and jury could watch the child's testimony within the courtroom via the closed circuit television. Craig was found guilty and appealed her conviction on the basis of her Sixth Amendment right to face her accuser. The Maryland Court of Appeals reversed the decision of the trial court, but this decision was reversed again by the U.S. Supreme Court upholding the original conviction. The U.S. Supreme Court stated in a five-to-four ruling that the confrontation clause does not guarantee a face-to-face encounter; therefore, the defendant's constitutional rights were not violated.[41] Although the child is able to avoid a face-to-face encounter with their abuser, the child can't escape the skilled and sometimes manipulative tactics of a defense attorney. These attorneys are able to confuse a child and imply to the jury that the child is not credible.

Criminal Court Continued

Once all the evidence is presented, a jury will go into deliberations to discuss the facts of the case in order to determine guilt or innocence. In many cases, it is difficult to prove a case as jury members may not want to believe that anyone could be capable of committing such a vile act and the lack of physical evidence may only support their naïve views. If a defendant is found not guilty then they cannot be tried again, even if new evidence was introduced as it would be a violation of their constitutional rights under double jeopardy of the Fifth Amendment. In some cases, the jury will not be in agreement of what the verdict should be. In this case, the judge is forced to declare a mistrial where the prosecution will have the option to pursue charges once again. This outcome is to the defendant's advantage as the child and their family may not wish to go through another traumatic trial. Additionally, the prosecution may not want to pursue the charges a second time as they suspect a similar verdict may be reached. A potentially guilty sexual predator is then set free, allowing them the opportunity to possibly target another child. In cases where the defendant is found guilty, they face possible incarceration and in some circumstances are held in captivity well after completely serving their criminal sanction. This process is implemented when it is believed that offenders are still dangerous. The accused may face additional sanctions through civil detention.

Civil Detention

The issue of double jeopardy involving civil detention was addressed in *Kansas v. Hendricks* (1997). In this case, a convicted sex offender who received a ten-year prison sentence was nearing release when the State of Kansas argued that he was still a threat to society and he should be sent to a mental institution as a dangerous sexual predator. Hendricks admitted that he quit the therapy program offered while he was incarcerated, noting that he had no control over his sexual urges toward children. He was ordered to be held on a civil detention order as he was still considered dangerous. Hendricks appealed this detention, arguing that it violated his constitutional right as penalizing him twice was a violation of his constitutional rights under the Fifth Amendment (double jeopardy). The U.S. Supreme Court in a five-to-four decision ruled that Kansas had distanced the civil proceeding from that of the criminal proceedings, and therefore the statute was not considered punitive. This topic of civil detention came up again in *United States v. Comstock* (2010) whether the federal government had the authority to commit a federal prisoner after completing his term for a federal sex crime. Defense counsel for Comstock argued that civil commitment statutes that detain unsecured sexual predators surpass the powers contained in the Constitution. The U.S. Supreme Court rejected this argument with a seven-to-two margin.[42]

THE ROLE OF POLICE IN COMPARISON WITH CHILD PROTECTIVE SERVICES

In chapter 7, we discussed how the investigative role of police and child protection workers (social services) investigated child abuse complaints. The role of law enforcement and social services does not end once a determination of abuse has occurred, but their roles from that point on are dramatically different. The law enforcement officer will work in conjunction with the prosecuting attorney to continue investigating the case, even though the defendant has already been arrested. For a law enforcement officer to make an arrest, all that is needed is probable cause. They need to build on that probable cause as it goes through the criminal courts where the burden of proof has now shifted from probable cause to that of proof "beyond a reasonable doubt." In contrast, when social services brings charges of child maltreatment, it is considered a civil proceeding and the burden of proof is lowered to "a preponderance of evidence." Although the role of law enforcement usually concludes at the end of a judicial hearing, the role of child protective services continues whether or not there was ever court intervention.

CHILD PROTECTIVE SERVICES

Child protective services' role goes well beyond the investigative stage of determining whether child abuse has occurred. Their organization now proceeds into the next stage of providing services to ensure the abuse will no longer occur and that they establish a plan to strengthen the family unit. One of the primary tasks is to determine the risk assessment for that child. Despite the enormous amount of literature that details risk factors for child maltreatment, the actual identification of the threat may be difficult to determine.[43] The National Association of Public Welfare Administrators outlines various levels of services based on the risk present in a family.

High-Risk Families

This category presents the highest risk to children (serious physical injury, sexual abuse, and neglect) that can require court intervention, intensive family preservation, child removal, and foster care. Due to the level of harm to a child, this level of category may require the assistance of law enforcement and criminal prosecution.

Moderate-Risk Families

In these families, child abuse and neglect may be the result of excessive or inappropriate discipline, inadequate medical care, and inadequate supervision. Intervention can include safety plans or family or community support as the focus is on the child's safety.

Low-Risk Families

Although the level of risk is low, there is a risk that may require child protective services to intervene. Risk factors such as family stress, emotional stress, and economic stress are factors for potential abuse where strategies of early intervention programs such as family support, parental education, housing assistance, and community and neighborhood advocacy may be implemented.[44]

CIVIL COURT

As stated earlier, a criminal trial involving child maltreatment will begin once the defendant is formally charged with a crime. In contrast, a civil child abuse case is usually heard in juvenile court or family court and commences once a petition is filed. Depending on the jurisdiction, there are statutory requirements as to the maximum number of days allowed between hearings once a petition is filed. A petition does not charge anyone with an offense, but instead contains allegations of child maltreatment and the need for the state to intervene. The first such hearing after a petition is filed is referred to in some jurisdictions as the preliminary or initial hearing. The second hearing in this process is called the adjudicatory hearing, which is similar to a criminal trial as witnesses are called up to testify to support the allegations of maltreatment. Although similar to a criminal trial, there are unique differences such as the burden of proof is limited to a preponderance of evidence and that in these cases the proceedings are not open to the public. Furthermore, the verdict in these cases is rendered by the judge as this type of civil case is not allotted a jury. If there is a finding of child maltreatment, the court will schedule a dispositional hearing to determine what services are needed for the child and have an appropriate safety plan to avoid potential future abuse. It should be noted that a judge can order services and a safety plan at any stage of the judicial process. To ensure that the appropriate services and protection are in place, a judge can order a review hearing in order to determine the current status of a child. During any phase of this process, the judge may want to rely on professionals responsible for the best interest of the child for their insight and recommendations. These individuals may be ordered to submit a formal report to the court so that the judge can use their findings as a guide to render the appropriate decision.

COURT-APPOINTED SPECIAL ADVOCATE

The court-appointed special advocate (CASA) is an essential part of a multi-disciplinary approach to child abuse. They are also unique as most of individuals who work as CASAs are trained volunteers who are appointed by the court in cases of child abuse and neglect and make recommendations on what they believe is in the best interest of the child.[45] The CASA movement began in 1977 where a Seattle juvenile court judge who was concerned about making drastic decisions on the welfare of a child with insufficient information conceived the idea of volunteers speaking up and addressing what is in the best interest of children. The program of having volunteers speak on behalf of children flourished across the nation. In 2017, it was reported that there were more than eighty-five thousand CASA volunteers who have helped more than 260,000 children in forty-nine states and the District of Columbia.[46] A study was conducted to evaluate the effectiveness of CASAs where judges were asked to rate the helpfulness of CASA reports. The studies' findings suggest that when a CASA is assigned to a child abuse and neglect case, it will expand the depth and breadth of information to the court. CASA reports were deemed to be more helpful than those of child protective services and the GAL. This particular study revealed that judges were more likely to get complete information on relative topics as CASA volunteers are more likely to visit children in their homes and were more likely to investigate whether there are appropriate alternative services for the child and their family.[47]

GUARDIAN AD LITEM

A GAL is a court-appointed attorney who is assigned to a child in cases of child abuse and neglect. GAL are also utilized in custody disputes between parents as parents can employ dubious tactics that are not always in the best interest of the child. Their role, whether being at a child abuse hearing or a custody dispute, is to make recommendations to the court on what they believe is in the best interest of the child. This can be a daunting task at times, as their recommendations are not always in line with what the primary caretakers believe should happen. Attorney J. Michael Sharman, a GAL and an educator for aspiring attorneys wanting to work with children, explains the role of a GAL and provides examples of cases where they are called in to assist a child in need.

> Adults can either speak for themselves in court or hire an attorney to do so, but a child can't, so the judge will appoint a Guardian ad Litem to investigate the situation, advocate for the child's best interests and make a recommendation to the court.
>
> The Guardian ad Litem (commonly called the GAL) is an attorney <u>for</u> the child, but is not the child's attorney. The relationship of the GAL and child is different from the relationship of attorney and client.
>
> An attorney working for a client is bound by legal ethics to obey his client's directives (as long as they are legal, of course) even if the attorney knows the client's plan is unwise or even counter-productive.
>
> Unlike other attorneys, a Guardian ad Litem does not have a "client," the GAL has a "ward" that he or she is duty-bound to protect. The Guardian ad litem vigorously represents the child, but does so with the goal of fully protecting the child's <u>best</u> interest and welfare.
>
> As GALs, we are to faithfully represent the interests of the child we were appointed to serve, even if the child doesn't like or agree with what we are doing for them. The 11-year-old pregnant girl doesn't want to tell the father's name, the 14-year-old boy doesn't ever want to go to school again, but the Guardian ad Litem has to find out the "why" behind those silences and then advocate for what appears to be, in the Guardian ad Litem's judgment, a result that would be in the child's best interest.

The Guardian ad Litem has the same powers as other attorneys to file pleadings, subpoena witnesses and documents but the law grants them much more access to schools, counselors and health care records. With this increased power comes greater need for the Guardian ad Litem to be neutral and not biased for one person or against another, but the GAL should always be seeking the process and result that will be in the child's best interest.

The Guardian ad Litem should do a thorough investigation, including a home visit, interviews with the parents and other relatives, talks with the teachers, counselors and sometimes neighbors too. The Guardian ad Litem will get records from the school, health care providers, law enforcement and all prior court filings. If indicated, the Guardian ad Litem can request the parents (and even the child) be drug tested or have a psychological evaluation.

At the end of a hearing involving a child, the judge will ask the other attorneys for their closing arguments, but he will ask the Guardian ad Litem to make a recommendation to the court of what the court should do. Perhaps it is that distinction that best sums up the critical role of the Guardian ad litem. Everything the GAL has done in the case since being appointed for the child has been preparation for that crucial moment when the Guardian ad litem provides the judge with that recommendation of what is in the child's best interest.

Sometimes the GAL's responsibility for the child ends at the end of that particular hearing, but if an appeal is filed by the GAL or another party, or if later there are other court cases involving the child, the GAL will continue to act on the child's behalf. Unfortunately, that means that all too often, because the parents, family members, teachers, counselors, probation officers and social workers come and go in the child's life, the Guardian ad litem is the only adult that remains consistently involved with the child until they reach adulthood. Their legal role as a GAL ends there, but many times the now-adult child will continue to reach out to them for support as the only real cheerleader, mentor or lifeline they know. Here are some examples of the cases that a GAL will assist in:

- At the local hospital a baby is born addicted to drugs.
- The ER doctors report a toddler was brought in with symptoms of Shaken Baby Syndrome but both parents deny doing anything that could have caused the injury.
- A 6th grade teacher reports an 11-year-old student is pregnant but the child won't tell Social Services the father's name.
- A 12-year-old boy is charged with threatening his mother with a knife but he says he did it to keep her from leaving the apartment to go get more heroin.
- A 14-year-old boy has missed the last month of school but won't explain why, except to say he hates school and won't go anymore.
- A developmentally disabled teen is caught hiding a bag under a tree on school grounds. The bag has an antique pistol in it.
- A mother has filed and then dropped three Protective Orders against her live-in companion who is the father of her middle child. He then files for custody of all three children.
- A grandparent is seeking full custody of her deceased son's child because of the mother's current abusive relationship and recent overdose.
- A high-income couple is divorcing and it looks like the litigation over property, alimony and child support could get intense.[48]

FOSTER CARE

The U.S. federal government defines foster care as twenty-four-hour substitute care for children placed away from their parents or guardians and for whom the Title IV-E agency has placement and care responsibility.[49] The Department of Health and Human Services through the Adoption and Foster Care Analysis and Reporting System (AFCARS) reports that as of September 30, 2017, there were 442,995 children in foster care. These numbers reflect a continuous increase in foster children each year starting in 2013, when there were 400,394 children in foster care. Data from 2017 reveal that 52 percent of the children in foster care are males. AFCARS reports that most children who are in foster care are placed in a foster home with non-relatives. Children placed with family members who are deemed foster homes represented 32 percent of the children where the remaining children would be given other placement options. Circumstances associated with a child's removal from home include:

- Neglect
- Drug abuse (parent)
- Caretaker inability to cope
- Physical abuse
- Housing
- Child behavior problem
- Parent incarceration
- Alcohol abuse (parent)
- Abandonment
- Sexual abuse
- Drug abuse (child)
- Child disability
- Parent death.[50]

Relative Foster Care

Relative foster care, also referred to as kinship care, is a licensed or unlicensed home of the child's relative regarded by Title IV-E agency as a foster care living arrangement for children. Kinship care are homes where the child is related though blood, marriage, adoption, tribal or clan, or other relationship bond with the child.

Non-relative Family Foster Care

Non-relative family foster care is defined as a family foster home licensed by the Title IV-E agency that is used as a foster care living arrangement. This form of placement is usually used because kinship care is not a viable option. This is disheartening as more children are placed in non-relative family foster care in comparison to relative foster care.

The goal of foster care is to keep children safe by providing temporary care when necessary until the child can be safely returned to their home or permanently placed with a relative or adoptive family. With the passage of the 1980 Adoption Assistance and Child Welfare Act, states are required to make reasonable efforts to try to keep children with their families. This legislation was created in response to the growing number of children in long-term foster care.[51] Even with the changing legislation, there is still a significant need for foster care, as shortages for children who need this temporary assistance continue to grow. Fortunately, in response to this plight, there are a substantial number of adoptions each year from what was formally temporary foster care. This was not always an easy process. At one point in time, public and private child placement agencies were often requiring prospective foster parents, as a condition of receiving temporary custody, to sign a document that they would not seek to adopt the child. This requirement was pursued because foster agencies wanted to discourage the emotional bonding between foster parents and the child as they sought to reunify the child with the biological family.[52] Unfortunately, in some cases, the child is never returned to their biological parents as the parents' actions can never justify such a reunion.

PARENTAL TERMINATION

The Supreme Court has been sympathetic to parents' arguments in termination hearings and may carry greater due process protections compared to other civil proceedings. If termination is ordered, the parents become a legal stranger as the child has no right to support or any type of inheritance, and the parent has no legal right to see the child or even know the child's whereabouts.[53] These hearings can be contentious as the parent's rights versus the child's best interest are not always in sync. Other cases of parental termination are less debatable. For instance, a parent may be sentenced to a lengthy term in prison for a criminal act against their child and/or the convicted parent may not wish to contest their rights. Furthermore, in some cases, the sentence may be so long that the earliest day of parole or completion of their sentence may be after their child reaches adulthood, making parental rights a moot issue.

CONCLUSION

It is only in recent history that the criminal justice system began to address the needs of children suffering from child maltreatment. CAPTA was the first comprehensive and significant legislation to focus on the problem of child abuse. Other laws specifically addressing child abuse in this chapter include mandatory reporting laws, statute of limitation laws, and age of consent laws. In addition to key legislation addressing child maltreatment, this chapter explains how both the criminal court system and the civil court system are used in these cases, specifically noting how the criminal court requires proof beyond a reasonable doubt in order to hold the accused accountable, whereas the civil court system merely mandates a preponderance of evidence. Furthermore, this chapter elaborates on some of the key figures working within the criminal justice system who respond to child maltreatment. Although their roles may differ, they all have the same objective of acting in the child's best interest.

REVIEW QUESTIONS

1. Why is a victim advocate susceptible to secondary traumatic stress?

2. How does criminal court differ from civil court proceedings when handling child abuse complaints?

3. Why did the case of Megan Khanka affect the Jacob Wetterling Act?

4. Why have civil detention orders been ruled constitutional?

5. What is the purpose of a taint hearing?

KEYWORDS

Preponderance of evidence: The burden of proof that shows that it is more likely than not of their guilt.

Proof beyond a reasonable doubt: Not absolute certainty of someone's guilt, but rather that they are probably guilty without any reasonable explanation for doubt.

Foster care: Twenty-four-hour substitute care for children placed away from their parents or guardians.

Competency hearing: A hearing to determine the competency of a potential witness.

Taint hearing: A hearing designed to determine if a child's testimony has been coerced.

Sex offender registration: Legislation that requires that states maintain a system for monitoring and tracking sex offenders who are either working or residing within a community.

Statute of limitations: The statute of limitations requires that criminal prosecution commence within a specific amount of time from when the criminal act took place.

NOTES

1. Howard Markel, "Case Shined First Light on Abuse of Children," *New York Times*, December 14, 2009. Accessed February 10, 2019. Available from https://www.nytimes.com/2009/12/15/health/15abus.html.

2. Joshua B. Kay, "Legal Responses to Child Abuse and Neglect," in J. Bart Klika and Jon R. Conte (eds.), *The APSAC Handbook on Child Maltreatment*, fourth edition (Thousand Oaks, CA: Sage, 2018), 183; Douglas E. Abrams, Susan Vivian Mangold, and Sarah H. Ramsey, *Children and the Law: In a Nutshell*, sixth edition (St. Paul, MN: West Academic, 2018), 18.

3. Kay, "Legal Responses to Child Abuse and Neglect," 186–87.

4. Congress.gov, S.151-Protect Act. Accessed February 26, 2019. Available from https://www.congress.gov/bill/108th-congress/senate-bill/151.

5. Ben Mathews, "Mandatory Reporting Laws: Their Origin, Nature, and Development Over Time," in Ben Mathews and Donald C. Bross (eds.), *Mandatory Reporting Laws and the Identification of Severe Child Abuse and Neglect* (New York, NY: Springer, 2015), 4.

6. Monica L. McCoy and Stephanie M. Keen, *Child Abuse and Neglect*, second edition (New York, NY: Psychology Press, 2014), 43.

7. Child Welfare Information Gateway, Children's Bureau, Mandatory Reporters of Child Abuse and Neglect, 2. Accessed February 10, 2019. Available from https://www.childwelfare.gov/pubpdfs/manda.pdf.

8. Child Welfare Information Gateway, Children's Bureau, Mandatory Reporters of Child Abuse and Neglect, 2.

9. Child Welfare Information Gateway, Children's Bureau, Mandatory Reporters of Child Abuse and Neglect, 3.

10. Kimberly A. McCabe and Daniel G. Murphy, *Child Abuse: Today's Issues* (Boca Raton, FL: CRC Press, 2017), 156.

11. McCabe and Murphy, *Child Abuse: Today's Issues*, 168–69.

12. Cliff Roberson and Harvey Wallace, *Principle of Criminal Law*, sixth edition (Upper Saddle River, NJ: Pearson, 2016), 97.

13. Christina Mancini, *Sex Crime Offenders & Society* (Durham, NC: Carolina Press, 2014), 244.

14. Kelly K. Bonnar-Kidd, "Sexual Offender Laws and Prevention of Sexual Violence or Recidivism," *American Journal of Public Health* 100, no. 3 (2010): 415.

15. Mancini, *Sex Crime Offenders & Society*, 241.

16. S. Maddan and L. Pazzani, *Sex Offenders: Crimes and Processing in the Criminal Justice System* (Frederick, MD: Wolters Kluwer, 2017), 238.

17. Michelle A. Cubellis, Scott M. Walfield, and Andrew J. Harris, "Collateral Consequences and Effectiveness of Sex Offender Registration and Notification: Law Enforcement Perspectives," *International Journal of Offender Therapy and Comparative Criminology* 62, no. 4 (2018): 1081.

18. J.J. Prescott and Jonah E. Rockoff, "Do Sex Offender Registration and Notification Laws Affect Criminal Behavior?" *Journal of Law and Economics* 54, no. 1 (2008): 163.

19. The State of New Jersey, Office of the Attorney General, Megan's Law. Accessed February 13, 2019. Available from https://www.nj.gov/njsp/spoff/megans_law.html.

20. Congress.gov, Pam Lychner, Sexual Offender Tracking and Identification Act of 1996. Accessed March 23, 2019. Available from https://www.congress.gov/bill/104th-congress/senate-bill/1675.

21. William Doerner and Steven P. Lab, *Victimology*, seventh edition (Waltham, MA: Anderson Publishing, 2015), 342.

22. Office of Justice Programs, Office of Sex Offender Sentencing, Monitoring, Apprehending, Registering, and Tracking, Juvenile Registration and Notification Requirements Under SORNA. Accessed February 13, 2019. Available from https://www.smart.gov/juvenile_offenders.htm.

23. Joseph J. Fischel, *Sex and Harm in the Age of Consent* (Minneapolis, MN: University of Minnesota Press, 2016), 88.

24. Dafna Tener, "Perspectives on Adolescent Sexual Relations with Older Persons: A Systematic Review of the Literature," *Trauma, Violence, & Abuse* 20, no. 10 (2018): 9.

25. Stacy L. Mallicoat and Connie Estrada Ireland, *Women and Crime: The Essentials* (Thousand Oaks, CA: Sage, 2014), 84.

26. Congress.gov, Protection of Children From Sexual Predators Act of 1998. Accessed March 5, 2019. Available from https://www.congress.gov/bill/105th-congress/house-bill/3494.

27. Govtrack, Keeping the Internet Devoid of Sexual Predators Act of 2008. Accessed March 5, 2019. Available from https://www.govtrack.us/congress/bills/110/s431/text.

28. Kenneth E. Blackstone, "The Fallibility of Forensic Interviewing: Understanding the Michaels Decision and the Taint Hearing," *Forensic Examiner* 18, no. 4 (2009): 53.

29. Kresta Daly, "The Purpose of the Forensic Interview: A Lawyer's Perspective," in William T. O'Donohue and Matthew Fanetti (eds.), *Forensic Interviews Regarding Child Sexual Abuse: A Guide to Evidence-Based Practice* (New York, NY: Springer, 2016), 35–37.

30. Lucy S. McGough, "Asking the Right Questions: Reviewing the Voir Dire for Child Witnesses," *George State University Law Review* 5, no. 2 (1989): 570; Stephen Meyer, *Child Abuse and Domestic Violence: Information Plus* (Farmington Hills, MI: Cengage, 2017), 86.

31. Kresta Daly, "The Purpose of the Forensic Interview: A Lawyer's Perspective," in William T. O'Donohue and Matthew Fanetti (eds.), *Forensic Interviews Regarding Child Sexual Abuse: A Guide to Evidence-Based Practice* (New York, NY: Springer, 2016), 23–27.

32. Abrams, Mangold, and Ramsey, *Children and the Law: In a Nutshell*, 229.

33. Daly, "The Purpose of the Forensic Interview," 23–27.

34. Peggy M. Tobolowsky, Mario T. Gaboury, Arrick L. Jackson, and Ashley G. Blackburn, *Crime Victim Rights and Remedies*, second edition (Durham, NC: Carolina Press, 2010), 78.

35. Charles R. Figley, *Compassion Fatigue: Coping with Secondary Traumatic Stress Disorder in Those Who Treat the Traumatized* (London: Routledge, 1995).

36. Lorraine T. Benuto, Rory Newlands, Allison Ruork, Sierra Hooft, and Andrew Ahrendt, "Secondary Traumatic Stress among Victim Advocates: Prevalence and Correlates," *Journal of Evidence-Informed Social Work* 15, no. 5 (2018): 504.

37. Elizabeth Wilson, email message to author, January 29, 2019.

38. McCabe and Murphy, *Child Abuse: Today's Issues*, 164.

39. Kathryn Kuehnle and Mary Connel, "Child Sexual Abuse Suspicion: Treatment Considerations during Investigation," *Journal of Child Sexual Abuse* 19, no. 5 (2010): 560–61.

40. Tobolowsky, Gaboury, Jackson, and Blackburn, *Crime Victim Rights and Remedies*, 12.

41. Wikipedia, *Maryland v. Craig*. Accessed February 24, 2019. Available from https://en.wikipedia.org/wiki/Maryland_v._Craig.

42. Doerner and Lab, *Victimology*, 346.

43. Stephanie Cuccaro-Alamin, Regan Foust, Rhema Vaithianathan, and Emily Putnam-Hornstein, "Risk Assessment and Decision Making in Child Protection Services: Predictive Risk Modeling in Context," *Children and Youth Services Review* 79 (2017): 291.

44. McCoy and Keen, *Child Abuse and Neglect*, 323.

45. McCabe and Murphy, *Child Abuse: Today's Issues*, 169.

46. CASA. Accessed February 17, 2019. Available from http://www.casaforchildren.org/site/c.mtJSJ7MPIsE/b.5301295/k.BE9A/Home.htm.

47. Victoria Weisz and Nghi Thai, "The Court-Appointed Special Advocate (CASA) Program: Bringing Information to Child Abuse & Neglect," *Child Maltreatment* 8, no. 3 (2003): 208.

48. J. Michael Sharman, email message to author, February 15, 2019.

49. Code of Federal Regulations. Accessed March 31, 2019. Available from https://www.childwelfare.gov/search/?addsearch=foster+care.

50. U.S. Department of Health and Human Services, Children's Bureau, The AFCARS Report. Accessed February 13, 2019. Available from https://www.acf.hhs.gov/sites/default/files/cb/afcarsreport25.pdf.

51. Lisa Schelbe, Jennifer M. Geiger, Shamra Boel-Studt, and Francie J. Julien-Chinn, "Foster Care," in J. Bart Klika and Jon R. Conte (eds.), *The APSAC Handbook on Child Maltreatment*, fourth edition (Thousand Oaks, CA: Sage, 2018), 216–17.

52. Abrams, Mangold, and Ramsey, *Children and the Law: In a Nutshell*, 283.

53. Abrams, Mangold, and Ramsey, *Children and the Law: In a Nutshell*, 141.

Appendix A
Financial Exploitation of Children

◆ ◆ ◆

A FORM OF CHILD ABUSE that is unique and rarely discussed is the financial exploitation of children. What is so unique about this form of child maltreatment compared to all other forms of child abuse is the fact that the child doesn't know that they have been exploited until well into their adolescent years, if not their young adulthood. Financial exploitation of a child comes in the form of child identity theft, which is a lucrative business for those who are willing to target children. Children can be the target of identity theft soon after their birth but don't realize they have been a victim until later on in their lives when they may apply for some form of credit, job application, or financial aid when applying for college. It is only at this point in their lives that they discover they are in debt for thousands of dollars, hindering their ability to access financial credit.

MEASURING IDENTITY THEFT

Measuring identity theft can be challenging as the "dark figure of crime" is significant. Many victims may try to resolve the issue by contacting their credit card company or, in the case where the victim's identity was stolen by their parents, they may be reluctant to report it as they don't want to see their parents face any legal repercussions. Financial institutions are in a better position to report identity theft. However, by these institutions releasing data on identity theft, it may cause significant embarrassment and unwanted regulatory attention.[1] Financial institutions, along with some individual victims, are reluctant to report identity theft, which makes measuring this type of crime a daunting task. Additionally, the difficulty of measuring child identity theft is even more difficult as so many children are unaware of their victimization until later on in their life.

THE OFFENDERS

It is relatively easy to use a child's identity in order to open new lines of credit. Contrary to popular belief, companies that issue credit do not have a system in place that can determine the applicant's age. Additionally, identity thieves can also use a child's information such as their social security number to obtain a driver's license, medical insurance, or employment. Other thieves may use a child's identity to disguise themselves as they use that identity in the commission of a crime. These are just some examples of why professional thieves or anyone can steal a child's identity. However, not all identity thieves are professional crime thieves or opportunists who have access to your child's information; in many cases, it is the parent who steals their own child's identity. In these scenarios, the parents may find themselves in some difficult financial times and justify their actions as a temporary solution in order to get out of a financial jam. What started off as an illegal but necessary task can turn into a primary tactic for financial gain. Some parents may soon discover that by using their children's identity, they not only are able to avoid potential financial crises but find that by using their child's identity, it can become a lucrative business as it opens the door for continuous financial opportunities.[2]

WHO ARE THE VICTIMS?

Any child has the potential to have their identity stolen, but some classifications of children are more vulnerable than others. Hispanic children have a higher rate of identity theft victimization compared to most children in the United States due to their proximity to other countries with high Hispanic populations. Undocumented aliens from south of the American border will steal American identification of children with Hispanic descent as they enter the country illegally and use the child's identity as a means to apply for employment and access American services.[3] Additionally, military children are extremely susceptible to identity theft as they endure a life of continuously being in transit, where their documentation is constantly transferred to different facilities, opening the door for unlawful access. Military families also face the additional risk of identity theft when a parent is deployed overseas. There is a relatively new scam where someone who represents themselves as a member of the American Red Cross calls a military spouse and advises them that their deployed spouse is seriously injured and is being flown to Germany for treatment. Treatment in Germany requires notification of the spouse, as well as verbal verification of dates of birth of the spouse and their children.[4]

SOCIAL SECURITY NUMBER

The social security program started in 1935 as part of the New Deal social program with the primary purpose of tracking individuals for social security benefits. Up until the mid-1980s most young people never thought about getting a social security number until their teenage years when they were applying for their first job. It was also during this era that the Internal Revenue Service declared there was widespread fraud where taxpayers were claiming children that didn't exist or children that they were not supporting as their legal dependents. In response to this fraud, Congress passed the Tax Reform Act of 1986, which required that for the first time, any dependent over the age of five would have their own Social Security number. The following year, the Internal Revenue Service reported that there were approximately seven million fewer claimed dependents. In 1990, Congress lowered the threshold to one year old. Parents need to have a social security number for their child if they want to claim them as a dependent.[5] Today, the Social Security Administration states that "getting a Social Security number for your newborn is voluntary, but getting a number when your child is born is a good idea."[6] The Social Security Administration states that the easiest time to get a child's social security number is when the mother is still at the hospital as they will be provided with the appropriate application forms.[7]

The Tax Reform Act may have reduced fraud with false claims of dependents, but it simultaneously opened the door to a new pool of identity theft victims as children are now targeted for their social security number soon after it is assigned. Identity thieves are able to either steal a child's social security number or fraudulently apply for a social security number after a child's death. Beginning in 1962, the Social Security Administration created the Social Security Death Index, which is a database for recording people's deaths. It should be noted, however, that the Social Security Administration only records the death of people who have been issued a social security number. Children who died very young may not have been issued a social security number, allowing a savvy thief to use that child's information to create another identity that can't be cross-referenced. Stealing a newborn's information can be as easy as going to the cemetery and stealing the child's identity from the gravestone or from reading a child's obituary.

If your child doesn't have a social security number, all an identity thief needs to do is either steal or forge a child's birth certificate or other documents such as an adoption decree; doctor, clinical, or hospital records; school records; or school identification card and use this information to apply for a social security number.[8] Additionally, some thieves are able to determine what a child's social security number might be. Social security numbers can be determined with anyone with some statistical knowledge by analyzing "publicly available records in the SSA Death Master File (DMF) to detect statistical patterns in the SSN assignment for individuals whose deaths have been reported to the SSA; thereafter, by interpolating an alive person's state and date of birth with the patterns detected across deceased individuals' SSNs, to predict a range of values likely to include his or her SSN."[9]

Parents can protect their children from identity theft by either monitoring their child's credit reports or by placing a credit freeze on their child's credit files where permissible. When monitoring your young child's credit report, you should expect the credit agency to respond by stating that there is no record. It should be noted that although larger creditors report to all three credit bureaus, regional retailers and chains may only report to a single bureau. In addition, most credit reporting agencies do not receive records of cellphone accounts being established, apartments being rented, or utility accounts being started.[10] Parents should also question the necessity of releasing their child's social security number. For instance, is it pertinent for a coach to have the social security number of their athletes? Social security numbers are a convenient way to use a specific identifier of children when other methods are available without placing the child's identity in jeopardy.

SOLVING IDENTITY THEFT

The clearance rate for solving identity theft is considered very low because this crime is considered extremely complex compared to other types of theft crimes. Additionally, jurisdictional problems make this crime unusually difficult, especially if this crime occurred over the internet. Offenders and victims can be from different cities, states, or even countries, which can make it difficult for the victim just to file a complaint with law enforcement.[11] Although the crime of identity theft may be difficult to solve, the repercussion from this form of victimization can be minimized through early detection.

SIGNS OF IDENTITY THEFT

There are multiple signs that should warn a parent that their child's identity may have been stolen. Some of the signs include, but are not limited to:

- Child receiving mail for credit card offers
- Receiving legal notices
- Phone calls from debt collectors
- Law enforcement inquiries.[12]

NOTES

1. Chris Jay Hoofnagle, "Identity Theft: Making the Known Unknowns Known," *Harvard Journal of Law & Technology* 21, no. 1 (2007): 99.

2. Robert P. Chappell Jr., *Child Identity Theft: What Every Parent Needs to Know* (Lanham, MD: Rowman & Littlefield, 2013), 2–3.

3. Chappell, *Child Identity Theft*, 19.

4. Chappell, *Child Identity Theft*, 66.

5. Joe Mason, *Bankrupt at Birth: Why Child ID Theft is on the Rise and How It's Happening Under Parent's Noses* (Gaithersburg, MD: Nimble Cricket Press, 2012), 42.

6. Social Security Administration, Social Security Numbers for Children. Accessed March 8, 2019. Available from https://www.ssa.gov/pubs/EN-05-10023.pdf.

7. Social Security Administration, Social Security Numbers for Children.

8. Chappell, *Child Identity Theft*, 10.

9. Alessandro Acquisti and Ralph Gross, "Predicting Social Security Numbers from Public Data," *Proceedings of the National Academy of Science of the United States of America* 106, no. 27 (2009): 10975.

10. Mason, *Bankrupt at Birth*, 148–60.

11. Stuart F.H. Allison, Amie M. Schuck, and Kim Michelle Lersch, "Exploring the Crimes of Identity Theft: Prevalence, Clearance Rates, and Victim/Offender Characteristics," *Journal of Criminal Justice* 33, no. 1 (2005): 21.

12. Chappell, *Child Identity Theft*, 78.

Appendix B
Indian Child Welfare Quarterly and Annual Report

◆ ◆ ◆

Directions: Tribes must only fill out the section(s) (Part A and/or Part B) below that pertains to their tribal program(s).

PART A: INDIAN CHILD WELFARE ACT (ICWA) DATA

ICWA Contract/Grant No. _____

Name of Program _____

    1. Do you have any Tribal/State Agreements, i.e., Title IV-E Agreements, etc., involving child welfare/assistance? ___ Yes or ___ No *(Check One)*

Please explain: _____
_____

2. ICWA Notifications	Q1	Q2	Q3	Q4	TOTAL
Total Number New Received					
Total Number Acted On					
Participated in State Court Hearing					
Participated in Case Planning					
Transferred to Tribal Court					
Placement with Relative					
Placement in Indian Foster Home					
Placement in non-Indian Foster Home					
Total Number New Acted On (Non-Tribal)					
3. Placement Funding Source	**Q1**	**Q2**	**Q3**	**Q4**	**TOTAL**
Title IV-E					
BIA Child Assistance					
Other, Please specify					

PART B: TRIBAL CHILD ABUSE AND NEGLECT DATA

(Only those Tribes/Grantees that operate a child protection program should complete Part B. If the Tribe's child protection program is carried out by the State, then Part B of this form is not required.)

Tribal Child Abuse and Neglect Data	Q1	Q2	Q3	Q4	TOTAL
Total Reports/Referrals Received					
Substantiated					
Unsubstantiated					
Sexual Abuse					
Physical Abuse					
Neglect					
Alcohol Involved					
Drugs and/or Inhalants					
Recurring Cases					
Cases of Siblings Involved					
Placements Out of Home					
Petition to Tribal Court					
Referral to Tribal Social Services					
Domestic Violence Involved					
Total Number of Child Protection Workers					

Name of Tribe:

Fiscal Year: Date:

Preparer's Signature and Title:

Preparer's Name (Please Print):

INSTRUCTIONS

Indian Child Welfare Quarterly and Annual Report

The Tribe/Grantee should complete the Indian Child Welfare Quarterly and Annual Report on a quarterly basis, in accordance with the following schedule:

Reporting by Fiscal Year	
For Reporting Period:	**Please Submit Your Report By:**
Q1: First Quarter (October 1–December 31)	Thirty days after the end of Q1
Q2: Second Quarter (January 1–March 31)	Thirty days after the end of Q2
Q3: Third Quarter (April 1–June 30)	Thirty days after the end of Q3
Q4: Fourth Quarter (July 1–September 30)	Forty-five days after the end of Q4
End of the Year Total	

Reporting Requirements

There are two parts to the Indian Child Welfare Quarterly and Annual Report: Part A: Indian Child Welfare Act (ICWA) Data, and Part B: Child Abuse and Neglect Data.

Part A: *All* Tribes/Grantees should complete Part A.

Part B: Only those Tribes/Grantees that operate a child protection program should complete Part B. If the Tribe's child protection program is carried out by the State, then Part B of this form is not required.

Explanation of Reporting Indicators

Note: All quarterly entries should be "new" for each quarter. Do not "carryover" quarterly entries. The End of Year (EOY) total should be the sum of all four quarters.

For example: For Q1, there were two *new* children placed in foster homes;

In Q2, there were no *new* children placed;

In Q3, there was one *new* child placed;

In Q4, there were no *new* children placed.

The total for EOY = 3 children placed in foster homes during the fiscal year.

PART A: INDIAN CHILD WELFARE ACT (ICWA) DATA

Identify the ICWA Contract/Grant No. and the Name of the Program.

1. Do you have any Tribal/State Agreements regarding child welfare/assistance?

    Please indicate whether the Tribe has a Tribal/State Agreement regarding child welfare/assistance by checking the appropriate response ("yes" or "no").

    Next, please explain the different types of agreements your Tribe has in place with the State (if any). *For example*: Title IV-E agreements, Title IV-E contracts, Joint Power Agreements, and so forth. If your Tribe has no Agreements in place, please write "none."

2. ICWA Notifications

    A. Total Number Received: Enter the number of new ICWA notifications your Tribe received during the quarter.

    B. Total Number Acted On: Enter the number of new ICWA notifications the Tribe acted on during the quarter. "Acted on" means action taken by the Tribe after receiving and processing the ICWA notification.

      1. Participated in State Hearing: Enter the number of new ICWA cases in which your Tribe participated in a state court hearing.

      2. Participated in Case Planning: Enter the number of new ICWA cases in which your Tribe participated in case planning.

      3. Transferred to Tribal Court: Enter the number of new ICWA cases transferred from a State Court to Tribal Court.

4. Placement with Relative: Enter the number of new children placed with the Indian child's relative as of the end of the quarter.
5. Placement in Indian Foster Home: Enter the number of new children placed in Indian/Tribal foster homes as of the end of the quarter.
6. Placement in non-Indian Foster Home: Enter the number of new children placed in non-Indian/non-Tribal foster homes as of the end of the quarter.

C. Total Acted On (Non-Tribal): Enter the number of new ICWA notifications regarding non-tribal members the Tribe acted on during the quarter. "Acted on" means action taken by the Tribe after receiving and processing the ICWA notification. "Non-tribal" means a case when the child or parents are not members of a Federally recognized tribe.

3. Placement Funding Source
   A. Title IV-E: Enter the number of new child placements for the quarter that are paid through Title IV-E funds under the Child Welfare and Adoption Assistance Act of 1980 (P.L. 96-272).
   B. BIA Child Assistance: Enter the number of new child placements for the quarters that were paid through BIA Child Care Assistance.
   C. Other, Please specify: Enter the number of new child placements for each quarter that are paid through sources *other than* IV-E or BIA Child Care Assistance. Please explain/provide examples of the other sources in each applicable quarter.

PART B: TRIBAL CHILD ABUSE AND NEGLECT DATA

1. Tribal Child Abuse and Neglect Data
   A. Total Reports/Referrals Received: Enter the number of child abuse and neglect reports your Tribe received during the quarter.
      1. Substantiated: Enter the number of child abuse and neglect reports substantiated during the quarter.
      2. Unsubstantiated: Enter the number of child abuse and neglect reports unsubstantiated during the quarter.
      3. Sexual Abuse: Enter the number of child abuse and neglect reports involving sexual abuse.
      4. Physical Abuse: Enter the number of child abuse and neglect reports involving physical abuse.
      5. Neglect: Enter the number of child abuse and neglect reports involving neglect.
      6. Alcohol Involved: Enter the number of child abuse and neglect reports involving alcohol.
      7. Drugs and/or Inhalants Involved: Enter the number of child abuse and neglect reports involving drugs and/or inhalants.

8. Recurring Cases: Enter the number of child abuse and neglect reports in which the child and/family has had previous reports made.

9. Cases of Siblings Involved: Enter the number of child abuse and neglect reports involving siblings.

10. Placements Out of Home: Enter the number of child abuse and neglect reports resulting in the child's placement out of the home.

11. Petition to Tribal Court: Enter the number of child abuse and neglect reports that result in a petition to tribal court.

12. Referral to Tribal Social Services: Enter the number of child abuse and neglect reports referred to Tribal Social Services.

13. Domestic Violence Involved: Enter the number of child abuse and neglect reports involving domestic violence.

14. Total No. Of Child Protection Workers: Enter the number of child protection workers in the tribe's child protection system. Fractions can be entered. For example, if the tribe has one worker who spends 20 hours during a work week doing child protection, ½ or .5 may be entered. For this category, no yearly total is applicable.

The preparer (i.e., Tribe/Grantee) must sign and date the form, and send it to their appropriate BIA Regional ICWA contact by the due dates listed on the first page (after each quarter). The ICWA contact must make a copy of the report for their files, and forward the original to the following Central Office contact:

Evangeline Campbell, Division of Human Services Chief
Department of Interior – BIA, Office of Indian Services
1849 C Street, NW (MS-4513-MIB)
Washington, DC 20240

Please direct any questions on this form to the Bureau of Indian Affairs (BIA) ICWA Coordinator for the appropriate BIA Region.

PAPERWORK REDUCTION ACT STATEMENT

This information is being collected for management, planning, and budgetary purposes and to provide BIA with baseline data for setting and measuring performance goals. Response to this request is required to obtain a benefit in accordance with 25 CFR 23. You are not required to respond to this collection of information unless it displays a currently valid OMB control number. Public reporting burden for this form is estimated to average 15 minutes per response per section (Part A and Part B), including the time for reviewing instructions, gathering and maintaining data, and completing and reviewing the form. Direct comments regarding the burden estimate or any other aspect of this form to: Information Collection Clearance Officer – Indian Affairs, 1849 C Street, NW, MS-3642, Washington, DC 20240

Index

◆ ◆ ◆

About the Authors

◆ ◆ ◆

Daniel Murphy, MJA, is assistant professor of criminology at the University of Lynchburg in Lynchburg, Virginia. Professor Murphy has been teaching at colleges and universities for over fourteen years. His areas of specialization are police policy and procedures, child abuse, juvenile justice and victims. Professor Murphy created and teaches a course on child abuse which has been recognized as an academic resource through the American Professional Society on the Abuse of Children (APSAC). He has written other books and articles on the subject of child abuse and exploitation, including *Child Abuse: Today's Issues* (2016, with Kimberly McCabe). Professor Murphy has lectured nationally on topics including but not limited to "Child Abuse in the Military" and "How to Measure Emotional Abuse." Professor Murphy recently completed research on evaluating the child abuse mandatory reporting laws and will be presenting his findings at the Southern Criminal Justice Conference. Prior to teaching, he served as a police officer in New England for twenty-one years where he specialized in the investigations of child exploitation, and he received the "Officer of the Year" award twice during his tenure in law enforcement.

April Goin Rasmussen is a registered nurse with the Commonwealth of Virginia and Forensic Nurse Examiner. Rasmussen is also an adjunct professor of health at Central Virginia Community College as well as for criminal forensics at the University of Lynchburg. She has lectured nationally on the subject of children's advocacy and child sexual exploitation.